W9-BTZ-421

Ninth Edition

The Little, Brown
Compact
Handbook

Jane E. Aaron

PEARSON

Boston   Columbus   Hoboken   Indianapolis   New York   San Francisco
Amsterdam   Cape Town   Dubai   London   Madrid   Milan
Munich   Paris   Montréal   Toronto   Delhi   Mexico City   São Paulo
Sydney   Hong Kong   Seoul   Singapore   Taipei   Tokyo

Vice President and Editor in Chief:
  Joseph Opiela
Program Manager: Eric Jorgensen
Senior Development Editor: Anne
  Brunell Ehrenworth
Executive Field Marketing Manager:
  Joyce Nilsen
Product Marketing Manager: Ali Arnold
Executive Digital Producer: Stefanie
  A. Snajder
Content Specialist: Erin Jenkins
Project Manager: Shannon Kobran
Project Coordination, Text Design,
  and Electronic Page Makeup:
  Cenveo® Publisher Services

Design Lead: Heather Scott
Cover Illustration/Photo: *Left*:
  Stack of reading material (Jocic/
  Shutterstock); *Right*: Laptop
  (Boule/Shutterstock)
Photo Research: QBS Learning
Senior Manufacturing Buyer:
  Roy L. Pickering, Jr.
Printer/Binder: R.R. Donnelley/
  Crawfordsville
Cover Printer: Lehigh-Phoenix Color/
  Hagerstown

Acknowledgments of third-party content appear on page 569, which constitutes an extension of this copyright page.

PEARSON, ALWAYS LEARNING, and MYWRITINGLAB are exclusive trademarks, in the United States and/or other countries, of Pearson Education, Inc., or its affiliates.

Unless otherwise indicated herein, any third-party trademarks that may appear in this work are the property of their respective owners and any references to third-party trademarks, logos, or other trade dress are for demonstrative or descriptive purposes only. Such references are not intended to imply any sponsorship, endorsement, authorization, or promotion of Pearson's products by the owners of such marks, or any relationship between the owner and Pearson Education, Inc., or its affiliates, authors, licensees, or distributors.

Library of Congress Cataloging-in-Publication Data

Aaron, Jane E.
  The Little, Brown compact handbook / Jane E. Aaron. – Ninth edition.
    pages cm
  Includes index.
  ISBN 978-0-321-98650-4
1. English language–Grammar–Handbooks, manuals, etc. 2. English language–Rhetoric–Handbooks, manuals, etc. I. Title. II. Title: Compact handbook.
  PE1112.A23 2014
  808'.042–dc23
                          2014041652

10 9 8 7 6 5 4 3 2 1—DOC—17 16 15 14

Student
ISBN-10: 0-321-98650-4
ISBN-13: 978-0-321-98650-4
A la Carte
ISBN-10: 0-134-04802-9
ISBN-13: 978-0-134-04802-5

PEARSON   www.pearsonhighered.com

Preface for Students

The Little, Brown Compact Handbook contains the basic information you'll need for writing in and out of school. Here you can find how to get ideas, use commas, craft an argument, find sources for research projects, cite sources, and write a résumé—all in a convenient, accessible package.

This book is mainly a reference for you to dip into as needs arise. You probably won't read the book all the way through, nor will you use everything it contains: you already know much of the content anyway, whether consciously or not. The trick is to figure out what you *don't* know—taking cues from your own writing experiences and the comments of others—and then to find the answers to your questions in these pages.

Using this book will not by itself make you a good writer; for that, you need to care about your work at every level, from finding a subject to spelling words. But learning how to use the handbook and its information can give you the means to write *what* you want in the *way* you want.

Reference aids

You have many ways to find what you need in the handbook:

- **Use a directory.** The brief contents inside the front cover displays all the book's parts and chapters. The more detailed contents inside the back cover provides each chapter's subheadings as well.
- **Use a tabbed divider.** At each tab, a detailed outline directs you to the material covered in that part of the book.
- **Use a glossary.** "Glossary of Usage" (**Gl** pp. 545–57) clarifies more than 275 words that are commonly confused and misused. "Glossary of Terms" (**Gl** pp. 558–68) defines every grammar term used in the handbook.
- **Use the index.** At the end of the book, the extensive index includes every term, concept, and problem word or expression mentioned in the book.
- **Use a list.** Two helpful aids fall inside the book's back cover: First, the "Culture Language Guide" (just before "Contents") pulls together all the book's material for students who are using standard American English as a second language or a second dialect. And "Editing Symbols" (back cover flap) explains abbreviations often used to comment on papers.
- **Use the elements of the page.** As shown in the illustration on the next page, the handbook constantly tells you where you are and what you can find there.

The handbook's page elements

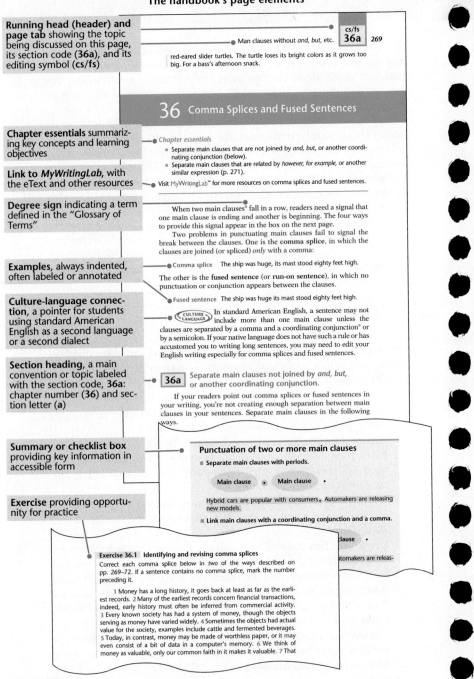

Running head (header) and page tab showing the topic being discussed on this page, its section code (**36a**), and its editing symbol (**cs/fs**)

cs/fs
36a   269

Man clauses without *and, but*, etc.

red-eared slider turtles. The turtle loses its bright colors as it grows too big. For a bass's afternoon snack.

36   Comma Splices and Fused Sentences

Chapter essentials summarizing key concepts and learning objectives

Chapter essentials
  ■ Separate main clauses that are not joined by *and, but*, or another coordinating conjunction (below).
  ■ Separate main clauses that are related by *however, for example*, or another similar expression (p. 271).

Link to *MyWritingLab*, with the eText and other resources

Visit MyWritingLab™ for more resources on comma splices and fused sentences.

Degree sign indicating a term defined in the "Glossary of Terms"

When two main clauses° fall in a row, readers need a signal that one main clause is ending and another is beginning. The four ways to provide this signal appear in the box on the next page.

Two problems in punctuating main clauses fail to signal the break between the clauses. One is the **comma splice**, in which the clauses are joined (or spliced) *only* with a comma:

Examples, always indented, often labeled or annotated

Comma splice   The ship was huge, its mast stood eighty feet high.

The other is the **fused sentence** (or **run-on sentence**), in which no punctuation or conjunction appears between the clauses.

Fused sentence   The ship was huge its mast stood eighty feet high.

Culture-language connection, a pointer for students using standard American English as a second language or a second dialect

CULTURE LANGUAGE   In standard American English, a sentence may not include more than one main clause unless the clauses are separated by a comma and a coordinating conjunction° or by a semicolon. If your native language does not have such a rule or has accustomed you to writing long sentences, you may need to edit your English writing especially for comma splices and fused sentences.

Section heading, a main convention or topic labeled with the section code, 36a: chapter number (**36**) and section letter (**a**)

36a   Separate main clauses not joined by *and, but*, or another coordinating conjunction.

If your readers point out comma splices or fused sentences in your writing, you're not creating enough separation between main clauses in your sentences. Separate main clauses in the following ways.

Summary or checklist box providing key information in accessible form

Punctuation of two or more main clauses

  ■ **Separate main clauses with periods.**

  Main clause   .   Main clause   .

  Hybrid cars are popular with consumers. Automakers are releasing new models.

  ■ **Link main clauses with a coordinating conjunction and a comma.**

  ...clause   .

Exercise providing opportunity for practice

...tomakers are releas-

Exercise 36.1   Identifying and revising comma splices

Correct each comma splice below in *two* of the ways described on pp. 269–72. If a sentence contains no comma splice, mark the number preceding it.

1 Money has a long history, it goes back at least as far as the earliest records. 2 Many of the earliest records concern financial transactions, indeed, early history must often be inferred from commercial activity. 3 Every known society has had a system of money, though the objects serving as money have varied widely. 4 Sometimes the objects had actual value for the society, examples include cattle and fermented beverages. 5 Today, in contrast, money may be made of worthless paper, or it may even consist of a bit of data in a computer's memory. 6 We think of money as valuable, only our common faith in it makes it valuable. 7 That

Preface for Instructors

The Little, Brown Compact Handbook provides writers with an accessible reference, one that helps them find what they need and then use what they find. Combining the authority of its parent, *The Little, Brown Handbook,* with a brief and more convenient format, the *Compact Handbook* addresses writers of varying experience, in varying fields, answering common questions about the writing process, grammar and style, research writing, and more.

This new edition improves on the handbook's strengths as a clear, concise, and accessible reference, while keeping pace with rapid changes in writing and its teaching. In the context of the handbook's many reference functions, the following pages highlight as New the most significant additions and changes.

A reference for academic writing

The handbook gives students a solid foundation in the goals and requirements of college writing.

- New The chapter on academic writing, now at the start of Part 2, includes a greatly expanded overview of common academic genres, such as responses, critical analyses, arguments, informative and personal writing, and research papers and reports. The discussion highlights key features of each genre and points students to examples in the handbook.

- New Eleven examples of academic writing in varied genres appear throughout the handbook, among them a new informative essay and a new social-science research report documented in APA style.

- New Emphasizing critical analysis and writing, the expanded chapter on critical reading and writing includes a student's analysis of a Web advertisement and a revised discussion of writing critically about texts and visuals.

- New Pulling together key material on academic integrity, Chapter 9 on academic writing and Chapter 53 on plagiarism discuss developing one's own perspective on a topic, using and managing sources, and avoiding plagiarism. Other chapters throughout the handbook reinforce these important topics.

- Synthesis receives special emphasis wherever students might need help balancing their own and others' views, such as in responding to texts.

- Parts 7 and 8 give students a solid foundation in research writing and writing in the disciplines (literature, other humanities, social sciences, natural and applied sciences), along with extensive coverage of documentation in MLA, Chicago, APA, and CSE styles.

A reference for research writing and documentation

With detailed advice, the handbook always attends closely to research writing and source citation. The discussion stresses using the library Web site as the gateway to finding sources, managing information, evaluating and synthesizing sources, integrating source material, and avoiding plagiarism.

- ▪ **New** Coverage of developing a working bibliography groups sources by type, reflecting a streamlined approach to source material throughout the handbook.
- ▪ **New** The discussion of libraries' Web sites covers various ways that students may search for sources—catalog, databases, and research guides.
- ▪ **New** A revised discussion of keywords and subject headings helps students develop and refine their search terms.
- ▪ **New** A streamlined discussion of gathering information from sources stresses keeping accurate records of source material, marking borrowed words and ideas clearly, and using synthesis.
- ▪ **New** A chapter on documenting sources explains key features of source documentation, defines the relationship between in-text citations and a bibliography, and presents the pros and cons of bibliography software.
- ▪ The discussion of evaluating sources—library, Web, and social media—helps students discern purposes and distinguish between reliable and unreliable sources. Case studies show the application of critical criteria to sample articles and Web documents.
- ▪ The extensive chapter on avoiding plagiarism discusses deliberate and careless plagiarism, shows examples of plagiarized and revised sentences, and gives updated advice about avoiding plagiarism with online sources.
- ▪ A research paper-in-progress on green consumerism follows a student through the research process and culminates in an annotated paper documented in MLA style.

An updated guide to documentation

The extensive coverage of four documentation styles—MLA, Chicago, APA, and CSE—reflects each style's latest version.

- ▪ **New** To help students match their sources with appropriate citation formats, a succinct guide accompanies the index to the models in each style.
- ▪ **New** Reorganized chapters for all four styles group sources by type, thus simplifying the process of finding appropriate models and clarifying differences among print, database, Web, and other sources.
- ▪ **New** Updated, annotated samples of key source types illustrate MLA and APA documentation, showing students how to find the bibliographical information needed to cite each type and

highlighting the similarities and differences between print and database sources.

■ New A complete social-science research report shows APA style in the context of student writing.

■ New The discussion of CSE documentation reflects the new eighth edition of *Scientific Style and Format: The CSE Manual for Authors, Editors, and Publishers*.

■ For all styles, color highlighting makes authors, titles, dates, and other citation elements easy to grasp.

A reference for writing as a process

The handbook takes a practical approach to assessing the writing situation, generating ideas, developing the thesis statement, revising, and other elements of the writing process.

■ New An expanded discussion of thesis covers using the thesis statement to preview organization.

■ New A reorganized presentation of drafting, revising, and editing distinguishes revising more clearly as a step separate from editing.

■ New A revised discussion of preparing a writing portfolio gives an overview of common formats and requirements.

■ New Chapter 7 on paragraphs offers new, relevant examples illustrating paragraph development.

■ New A revised and streamlined chapter on presenting writing focuses on essential information related to document design, visuals and other media, and writing for online environments.

A reference on usage, grammar, and punctuation

The handbook's core reference material reliably and concisely explains basic concepts and common errors, provides hundreds of annotated examples from across the curriculum, and offers frequent exercises in connected discourse.

■ New Dozens of new and revised examples and exercises clarify and test important concepts.

■ New Two common trouble spots—sentence fragments and passive voice—are discussed in greater detail and illustrated with new and more examples.

■ New Added examples in Chapter 18 on appropriate language show common shortcuts of texting and other electronic communication and how to revise them for academic writing.

■ Summary and checklist boxes provide quick-reference help with color highlighting to distinguish sentence elements.

A guide to visual and media literacy

The handbook helps students process nonverbal information and use it effectively in their writing.

- New A student's analysis of a Web advertisement illustrates critical thinking about a visual.
- New Updated and detailed help with preparing or finding illustrations appears in Chapter 8 on presenting writing and Chapter 51 on finding sources.
- Thorough discussions of critically reading advertisements, graphs, and other visuals appear in Chapter 10 on critical reading, Chapter 11 on argument, and Chapter 52 on working with sources.

A guide for culturally and linguistically diverse writers

At notes and sections labeled ⟨CULTURE LANGUAGE⟩, the handbook provides extensive rhetorical and grammatical help, illustrated with examples, for writers whose first language or dialect is not standard American English.

- Fully integrated coverage, instead of a separate section, means that students can find what they need without having to know which problems they do and don't share with native SAE speakers.
- "⟨CULTURE LANGUAGE⟩ Guide," on pp. 618–20, orients students with advice on mastering SAE and pulls all the integrated coverage together in one place.

A guide for writing beyond the classroom

A chapter on public writing extends the handbook's usefulness beyond academic writing.

- New Discussions of writing for social media encourage students to consider their potential audience now and in the future, whether they are writing to express themselves or to represent an organization.
- New Updated coverage of writing a job application discusses cover letters, résumés, and professional online profiles.

An accessible reference guide

The handbook is an open book for students, with a convenient lay-flat binding, tabbed dividers, and many internal features that help students navigate and use the content.

- New The approach to terminology facilitates reference and reading: headings in the text and menus avoid or explain terms, necessary new terms are defined in the text, and recurrent terms, marked °, are defined in a new "Glossary of Terms" (**Gl** pp. 558–68).
- A clean, uncluttered page design uses color and type clearly to distinguish parts of the book and elements of the pages.
- A brief table of contents inside the front cover provides an at-a-

glance overview of the book, while a detailed table of contents appears inside the back cover.

- Color highlighting in boxes and on documentation models distinguishes important elements.
- An unusually accessible organization groups related problems so that students can easily find what they need.
- Cross-references give divider numbers in addition to page numbers, sending students directly to the appropriate tabbed section—for instance, "See **3** pp. 156–58."
- Annotations on both visual and verbal examples connect principles and illustrations.
- Dictionary-style headers in the index make it easy to find entries.
- A preface just for students details reference aids and explains the page layout.

Writing resources and supplements

Pearson offers a variety of support materials for teachers and students. The following resources are geared specifically to *The Little, Brown Compact Handbook*. For more information on these and scores of additional supplements, visit *pearsonhighered.com* or contact your local Pearson sales representative.

- MyWritingLab This tutorial, homework, and assessment program provides engaging experiences for teaching and learning. Flexible and easy to customize, *MyWritingLab* helps students improve their writing through context-based learning. Whether through self-study or instructor-led learning, *MyWritingLab* supports and complements course work.

  Writing at the center: In new composing and "Review Plan" spaces, *MyWritingLab* brings together student writing, instructor feedback, and remediation via rich multimedia activities, allowing students to learn through their own writing.

  Student success: *MyWritingLab* identifies the skills needed for success in composition classes and provides personalized remediation for students who need it.

  Assessment tools: *MyWritingLab* generates powerful gradebook reports whose visual analytics give insight into student achievement at individual, section, and program levels.

- The answer key to *The Little, Brown Compact Handbook* includes answers to all of the book's exercises.
- *Developmental Exercises to Accompany The Little, Brown Compact Handbook* provides activities in a workbook for developmental writers. An answer key is available.
- *Diagnostic and Editing Tests and Exercises* are cross-referenced to *The Little, Brown Compact Handbook* and are available online.

Acknowledgments

The Little, Brown Compact Handbook remains relevant and fresh because instructors give feedback: they talk with Pearson's sales representatives and editors, answer questionnaires, write detailed reviews, and send us personal notes. For the ninth edition, I wish to thank the following instructors who communicated with me directly or through reviews. Their experiences and their insights into the handbook led to the improvements in this new edition: Monique Leslie Akassi, Bowie State University; Joshua Austin, Cumberland County College; Ken Bishop, Itawamba Community College; LaToya W. Bogard, Mississippi State University; Cheryl Borman, Hillsborough Community College, Ybor City Campus; Sonia Bush, North Lake College; Helen Ceraldi, North Lake College; Michael Dittman, Butler County Community College; Jesse Doiron, Lamar University–Beaumont; Genesis Downey, Owens Community College; Anthony Edgington, University of Toledo; Guy Steven Epley, Samford University; Marilyn Y. Ford, East Mississippi Community College; Jacquelyn Gaiters-Jordan, Pikes Peak Community College; Patricia Gallo, Delaware Technical Community College; Jennifer Hazel, Owens Community College; Sue Henderson, East Central College; Debra Johanyak, University of Akron, Wayne College; Cheryl Johnson, Lamar University; Melisa Jones, Texarkana College; Erin Kramer, Owens Community College; Elizabeth Kuechenmeister, Lindenwood University; Isera Tyson Miller, State College of Florida; Steve Moore, Arizona Western College; Ann C. Spurlock, Mississippi State University; Ishmael Matthew Stabosz, Delaware Technical Community College; Greg Stone, Tulsa Community College, Metro Campus; Alex Tavares, Hillsborough Community College; John Valliere, Saint Petersburg College; Joy Walsh, Butler Community College; Natasha Whitton, Southeastern Louisiana University; Debbie Williams, Abilene Christian University; L. Ureka Williams, Tulsa Community College, Metro Campus; Sara Yaklin, University of Toledo.

In responding to the ideas of these thoughtful critics, I had the help of several creative people. Valerie Vlahakis, John Wood Community College, prompted me to rethink and reorganize the documentation chapters, and she graciously allowed me to adapt her guide to finding appropriate models. Sigrid Anderson Cordell, University of Michigan, guided me through the ever-changing contemporary academic library. Sylvan Barnet continued to lend his expertise in the chapter "Reading and Writing about Literature," which is adapted from his *Short Guide to Writing about Literature* (with William E. Cain) and *Introduction to Literature* (with William Burto and William E. Cain). Ellen Kuhl provided creative, meticulous, and invaluable help with the material on research writing. And Carol Hollar-Zwick, sine qua non, served brilliantly as originator, sounding board, critic, coordinator, researcher, producer, and friend.

PART 1

The Writing Process

The Writing Process

2

1 The Writing Situation

Chapter essentials

- Assess the writing situation (below).
- Choose a subject appropriate to the assignment (p. 5).
- Define your purpose (p. 6).
- Consider your audience (p. 7).
- Understand the genre (p. 8).

Visit MyWritingLab™ for more resources on the writing situation.

Like most writers (even very experienced ones), you may find writing sometimes easy but more often challenging, sometimes smooth but more often halting. Writing involves creation, and creation requires freedom, experimentation, and even missteps. Instead of proceeding in a straight line on a clear path, you might start writing without knowing what you have to say, circle back to explore a new idea, or keep going even though you're sure you'll have to rewrite later.

As uncertain as the writing process may be, you can bring some control to it by assessing your writing situation, particularly your subject, purpose, audience, and genre.

1a Assessing the writing situation

Any writing you do for others occurs in a context that both limits and clarifies your choices. You are communicating something about a particular subject to a particular audience of readers for a specific reason. You may be required to write in a particular genre. You may need to conduct research. You'll probably be up against a length requirement and a deadline. And you may be expected to present your work in a certain format and medium.

These are the elements of the **writing situation**, and analyzing them at the very start of a project can tell you much about how to proceed.

Context

- **What is your writing for?** A course in school? Work? Something else? What do you know of the requirements for writing in this context?
- **What are the basic requirements of the writing task?** Consider length, deadline, subject, purpose, audience, and genre. What leeway do you have?
- **What medium will you use to present your writing?** Will you deliver it on paper, online, or orally? What does the presentation

3

method require in preparation time, special skills, and use of technology?

Subject (pp. 5–6)

- **What does your writing assignment require you to write about?** If you don't have a specific assignment, what subjects might be appropriate for this situation?
- **What interests you about the subject?** What do you already know about it? What questions do you have about it?
  What does the assignment require you to do with the subject?

Purpose (pp. 6–7)

- **What aim does your assignment specify?** For instance, does it ask you to explain something or argue a position?
- **Why are you writing?**
- **What do you want your work to accomplish?** What effect do you intend it to have on readers?
- **How can you best achieve your purpose?**

Audience (pp. 7–8)

- **Who will read your writing?** Why will your readers be interested (or not) in your writing? How can you make your writing interesting to them?
- **What do your readers already know and think about your subject?** Do they have any characteristics—such as educational background, experience in your field, or political views—that could influence their reception of your writing?
- **How should you project yourself in your writing?** What role should you play in relation to readers, and what information should you give? How informal or formal should your writing be?
- **What do you want readers to do or think after they read your writing?**

Genre (pp. 8–9)

- **What genre, or type of writing, does the assignment call for?** Are you to write an analysis, a report, a proposal, or some other type? Or are you free to choose the genre in which to write?
- **What are the conventions of the genre you are using?** For example, readers might expect a claim supported by evidence, a solution to a defined problem, clear description, or easy-to-find information.

Research (7 pp. 347–409)

- **What kinds of evidence will best suit your subject, purpose, audience, and genre?** What combination of facts, examples, and expert opinions will support your ideas?
- **Does your assignment require research?** Will you need to consult sources of information or conduct other research, such as interviews, surveys, or experiments?

- **Even if research is not required, what additional information do you need to develop your subject?** How will you obtain it?
- **What style should you use to cite your sources?** (See **7** pp. 408–09 on source documentation in the academic disciplines.)

Deadline and length

- **When is the assignment due?** How will you apportion the work you have to do in the available time?
- **How long should your writing be?** If no length is assigned, what seems appropriate for your subject, purpose, and audience?

Presentation

What format or method of presentation does the assignment specify or imply? For guidance in presenting academic writing, see pp. 55–56. See also **2** pp. 121–25 on oral presentations and pp. 126–36 on format in public writing.

- **How might you use headings, lists, illustrations, video, and other elements to achieve your purpose?** (See pp. 55–62.)

1b Finding your subject

A subject for writing has several basic requirements:

- **It should be suitable for the assignment.**
- **It should be neither too general nor too limited for the assigned deadline and paper length.**
- **It should be something that interests you and that you are willing to learn more about.**

When you receive an assignment, study its wording and its implications about your writing situation to guide your choice of subject:

- **What's wanted from you?** Many writing assignments contain words such as *discuss, describe, analyze, report, interpret, explain, define, argue,* or *evaluate.* These words specify your approach to your subject, the kind of thinking expected, your general purpose, and even the form your writing should take. (See pp. 6–7.)
- **For whom are you writing?** Many assignments will specify or imply your readers, but sometimes you will have to figure out for yourself who your audience is and what it expects of you. (For more on analyzing your audience, see pp. 7–8.)
- **What kind of research is required?** An assignment may specify the kinds of sources you are expected to consult, and you can use such information to choose your subject. (If you are unsure whether research is required, check with your instructor.)
- **Does the subject need to be narrowed?** To do the subject justice in the length and time required, you'll often need to limit it. (See the next page.)

Answering questions about your assignment will help set some boundaries for your choice of subject. Then you can explore your own interests and experiences to narrow the subject so that you can cover it adequately within the space and time assigned. Federal aid to college students could be the subject of a book; the kinds of aid available or why the government should increase aid would be a more appropriate subject for a four-page paper due in a week. Here are some guidelines for narrowing broad subjects:

- **Break your broad subject into as many specific subjects as you can think of.** Make a list.
- **For each specific subject that interests you and fits the assignment, roughly sketch out the main ideas.** Consider how many paragraphs or pages of specific facts, examples, and other details you would need to pin those ideas down. This thinking should give you at least a vague idea of how much work you'd have to do and how long the resulting paper might be.
- **Break a too-broad subject down further,** repeating the previous steps.

1c   Defining your purpose

Your **purpose** in writing is your chief reason for communicating something about your subject to a particular audience of readers. It is your answer to a potential reader's question, "So what?"

Most writing you do will have one of four main purposes:

- **To entertain readers.**
- **To express your feelings or ideas.**
- **To inform or to explain something to readers (exposition).**
- **To persuade readers to accept or act on your opinion (argument).**

These purposes often overlap in a single essay, but usually one predominates. And the dominant purpose will influence your slant on your subject, the details you choose, and even the words you use.

Many writing assignments narrow the purpose by using a signal word, such as the following:

- **Report:** Survey, organize, and objectively present the available evidence on the subject.
- **Summarize:** Concisely state the main points in a text, argument, theory, or other work.
- **Discuss:** Examine the main points, competing views, or implications of the subject.
- **Compare and contrast:** Explain the similarities and differences between two subjects. (See also pp. 49–50.)
- **Define:** Specify the meaning of a term or a concept—distinctive characteristics, boundaries, and so on. (See also pp. 48–49.)

- **Analyze:** Identify the elements of the subject, and discuss how they work together. (See also p. 49 and **2** pp. 87–88.)
- **Interpret:** Infer the subject's meaning or implications.
- **Evaluate:** Judge the quality or significance of the subject, considering pros and cons. (See also **2** p. 89.)
- **Argue:** Take a position on the subject, and support your position with evidence. (See also **2** pp. 100–08.)

You can conceive of your purpose more specifically, too, in a way that incorporates your particular subject and the outcome you intend:

To explain the methods of an engineering study so that readers understand and accept your conclusions

To explain the steps in a new office procedure so that staffers will be able to follow it without difficulty

To analyze how Annie Dillard's "Total Eclipse" builds to its climax so that readers appreciate the author's skill

To argue against additional regulation of guns so that readers will perceive the disadvantages for themselves

To argue that gun deaths would be reduced through a new program of background checks

1d Considering your audience

The readers likely to see your work—your **audience**—may influence your choice of subject and your definition of purpose. Your audience will certainly influence what you say about your subject and how you say it—for instance, how much background information you provide and whether you adopt a serious or a friendly tone.

For much academic and public writing, readers have specific needs and expectations. You still have many choices to make based on audience, but the options are somewhat defined. (See **2** pp. 69–80 on academic writing and **2** pp. 126–36 on public writing.) In other writing situations, the conventions are vaguer and the choices are more open. The following box contains questions that can help you define and make these choices.

Questions about audience

Identity and expectations

- **Who *are* my readers?**
- **What are my readers' expectations for the genre of my writing?**
  Do they expect features such as a particular organization and format, distinctive kinds of evidence, or a certain style of documenting sources?
- **What do I want readers to know or do after reading my work?**
  How should I make that clear to them?

(continued)

Questions about audience

(continued)

■ **How should I project myself to my readers?** How formal or informal will they expect me to be? What role and tone should I assume?

Characteristics, knowledge, and attitudes

■ **What characteristics of readers are relevant for my subject and purpose?** For instance:

Age and sex
Occupation: students, professional colleagues, etc.
Social or economic role: subject-matter experts, voters, car buyers, potential employers, etc.
Economic or educational background
Ethnic background
Political, religious, or moral beliefs and values
Hobbies or activities

■ **How will the characteristics of readers influence their attitudes toward my subject?**

■ **What do readers already know and *not* know about my subject?** How much do I have to tell them? What aspects of my subject will be interesting and relevant to them?

■ **How should I handle any specialized terms?** Will readers know them? If not, should I define them?

■ **What ideas, arguments, or information might surprise, excite, or offend readers?** How should I handle these points?

■ **What misconceptions might readers have of my subject and/or my approach to it?** How can I dispel these misconceptions?

Uses and format

■ **What will readers do with my writing?** Should I expect them to read every word from the top, to scan for information, or to look for conclusions? Can I help readers by providing a summary, headings, illustrations, or other aids? (See pp. 54–66 on presenting writing.)

1e Understanding genres

Writers use familiar **genres,** or types of writing, to express their ideas. You can recognize many genres: the poems and novels of literature, the résumé in business writing, the news article about a sports event. In college you will be asked to write in a wide range of genres, such as analyses, lab reports, reviews, proposals, oral presentations, even blog posts.

Most simply, a genre is the conventional form that writing takes in a certain context. In academic writing, genre conventions help to further the aims of the disciplines; for instance, the features of a lab report emphasize the procedures, results, and conclusions that are important in scientific investigation. The conventions also help to improve communication because the writer knows what readers expect and readers can predict what they will encounter in the writing.

When you receive a writing assignment, be sure to understand any requirements relating to genre:

- **Is a particular genre being assigned?** An assignment that asks you to write, say, an analysis, an argument, or a report has specified the genre for you to use.
- **What are the conventions of the genre?** Your instructor and/or your textbook will probably outline the requirements for you. You can also learn about a genre by reading samples of it. Consult **2** pp. 70–73 for more on genre and descriptions of the sample documents in this handbook.
- **What flexibility do you have?** Within their conventions, most genres still allow plenty of room for your own approach and voice. Again, reading samples will show you much about your options.

2 Invention

Chapter essentials
- Keep a journal (next page).
- Observe your surroundings (p. 11).
- Freewrite or brainstorm (pp. 11 and 12).
- Draw your ideas (p. 12).
- Ask questions (p. 13).

Visit MyWritingLab™ for more resources on invention.

Writers use a host of techniques to help invent or discover ideas and information about their subjects. **Whichever of the following techniques you use, do your work in writing, not just in your head.** Your ideas will then be retrievable, and the very act of writing will lead you to fresh insights.

CULTURE LANGUAGE The discovery process encouraged here rewards rapid writing without a lot of thinking beforehand about what you will write or how. If your first language is not standard American English, you may find it helpful initially to do this exploratory writing in your native language or dialect and then to translate the worthwhile material for use in your drafts. This process can be productive, but it is extra work. You may want to try it at first and gradually move to composing in standard American English.

2a   Keeping a journal

A **journal** is a diary of ideas kept on paper or on a computer. It gives you a place to record your responses, thoughts, and observations about what you read, see, hear, or experience. It can also provide ideas for writing. Because you write for yourself, you can work out your ideas without the pressure of an audience "out there" who will evaluate logic or organization or correctness. If you write every day, even just for a few minutes, the routine will loosen your writing muscles and improve your confidence.

You can use a journal for varied purposes: perhaps to confide your feelings, explore your responses to movies and other media, practice certain kinds of writing (such as poems or news stories), pursue ideas from your course, or think critically about what you read. One student, Katy Moreno, used her journal for the last purpose. Her composition instructor had distributed "It's a Flat World, after All," an essay by Thomas L. Friedman about globalization and the job market, and gave the following assignment, calling for a response to reading.

Instructor's assignment

In "It's a Flat World, after All," Thomas L. Friedman describes today's global job market, focusing not on manufacturing jobs that have been "outsourced" to overseas workers but on jobs that require a college degree and are no longer immune to outsourcing. Friedman argues that keeping jobs in the United States requires that US students, parents, and educators improve math and science education. As a college student, how do you respond to this analysis of the global market for jobs? What do you think today's college students should be learning?

On first reading the essay, Moreno had found it convincing because Friedman's description of the job market matched her family's experience: her mother had lost her job when it was outsourced to India. After rereading the essay, however, Moreno was not persuaded that more math and science would necessarily improve students' opportunities and preserve their future jobs. She compared Friedman's advice with details she recalled from her mother's experience, and she began to develop her own angle on the topic in her journal.

Student's journal entry

Friedman is certainly right that more jobs than we realize are going overseas—that's what happened to Mom's job and we were shocked! But he gives only one way for students like me to compete—take more math and science. At first I thought he's totally right. But then I thought that what he said didn't really explain what happened to Mom—she had lots of math + science + tons of experience, but it was her salary, not better training, that caused her job to be outsourced. An overseas worker would do her job for less money. So she lost her job because of money + because she wasn't a manager. Caught in the middle. I want to major in computer science, but I don't think it's smart to try for the kind of job Mom had—at least not as long as it's so much cheaper for companies to hire workers overseas.

(Further examples of Moreno's writing appear in the next three chapters.)

CULTURE LANGUAGE A journal can be especially helpful if your first language is not standard American English. You can practice writing to improve your fluency, try out sentence patterns, and experiment with vocabulary words. Equally important, you can experiment with applying what you know from experience to what you read and observe.

2b Observing your surroundings

Sometimes you can find a good subject or good ideas by looking around you, not in the half-conscious way most of us move from place to place in our daily lives but deliberately, all senses alert. On a bus, for instance, are there certain types of passengers? What seems to be on the driver's mind? To get the most from observation, you should have a notepad and pen or a device available for taking notes and making sketches. Back at your desk, study your notes and sketches for oddities or patterns that you'd like to explore further.

2c Freewriting

Writing into a subject

Many writers find subjects or discover ideas by **freewriting**: writing without stopping for a certain amount of time (say, ten minutes) or to a certain length (say, one page). The goal of freewriting is to generate ideas and information from *within* yourself by going around the part of your mind that doesn't want to write or can't think of anything to write. You let words themselves suggest other words. *What* you write is not important; that you *keep* writing is. Don't stop, even if that means repeating the same words until new words come. Don't go back to reread, don't censor ideas that seem off-track or repetitious, and above all don't stop to edit: grammar, punctuation, spelling, and the like are irrelevant at this stage.

If you can dim or turn off your computer monitor, you can try **invisible writing** to keep moving forward while freewriting. As you type to a dark screen, the computer will record what you type but keep it from you and thus prevent you from tinkering with your prose. Invisible writing may feel uncomfortable at first, but it can free the mind for very creative results.

CULTURE LANGUAGE Invisible writing can be especially helpful if you are uneasy writing in standard English and you tend to worry about errors while writing. The blank computer screen leaves you no choice but to explore ideas without regard for their expression. If you choose to write with the monitor on, concentrate on *what* you want to say, not *how* you're saying it.

Focused freewriting

Focused freewriting is more concentrated: you start with your subject and write about it without stopping for, say, fifteen minutes or one full page. As in all freewriting, you push to bypass mental blocks and self-consciousness, not debating what to say or editing what you've written. With focused freewriting, though, you let the physical act of writing take you into and around your subject.

An example of focused freewriting can be found in Katy Moreno's journal response to Thomas L. Friedman's "It's a Flat World, after All" on pp. 10–11. Since she already had an idea about Friedman's essay, Moreno was able to start there and expand on the idea.

2d Brainstorming

A method similar to freewriting is **brainstorming**—focusing intently on a subject for a fixed period (say, fifteen minutes), pushing yourself to list every idea and detail that comes to mind. Like freewriting, brainstorming requires turning off your internal editor so that you keep moving ahead. (The technique of invisible writing, described on the previous page, can help you move forward.)

Here is an example of brainstorming by a student, Johanna Abrams, on what a summer job can teach:

summer work teaches—
    how to look busy while doing nothing
    how to avoid the sun in summer
    seriously: discipline, budgeting money, value of money
which job? Burger King cashier? baby sitter? mail-room clerk?
mail room: how to sort mail into boxes: this is learning??
how to survive getting fired—humiliation, outrage
Mrs. King! the mail-room queen as learning experience
the shock of getting fired: what to tell parents, friends?
Mrs. K was so rigid—dumb procedures
initials instead of names on the mail boxes—confusion!
Mrs. K's anger, resentment: the disadvantages of being smarter than your boss
The odd thing about an office: a world with its own rules for how to act
what Mr. D said about the pecking order—big chick (Mrs. K) pecks on little
    chick (me)
a job can beat you down—make you be mean to other people

2e Drawing

Like freewriting and brainstorming, the technique of **clustering**, or **idea mapping**, uses free association to produce rapid, unedited work. But it emphasizes the relations between ideas by combining writing and nonlinear drawing. Start with your topic at a center point and then radiate outward with ideas. Pursue related ideas in a branching structure until they seem exhausted. Then do the same with other ideas, continuously branching out or drawing arrows to show connections.

The example below shows how a student used clustering for ten minutes to expand on a subject he arrived at through freewriting: money in college football.

Clustering or idea mapping

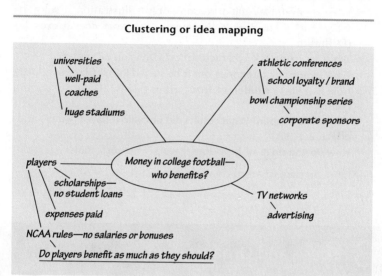

2f Asking questions

Asking yourself a set of questions about your subject—and writing out the answers—can help you look at the subject objectively and see fresh possibilities in it.

1 Journalist's questions

A journalist with a story to report poses a set of questions:

- **Who was involved?**
- **What happened, and what were the results?**
- **When did it happen?**
- **Where did it happen?**
- **Why did it happen?**
- **How did it happen?**

These questions can also be useful in probing an essay subject, especially when you are examining causes and effects or telling a story.

2 Questions about patterns

We understand a vast range of subjects through patterns such as narration, classification, and comparison and contrast. Asking questions based on the patterns can help you view your subject from many angles. Sometimes you may want to develop an entire essay using just one pattern.

- **How did it happen?** (Narration)
- **How does it look, sound, feel, smell, taste?** (Description)
- **What are examples of it or reasons for it?** (Illustration or support)
- **What is it? What does it encompass, and what does it exclude?** (Definition)
- **What are its parts or characteristics?** (Division or analysis)
- **What groups or categories can it be sorted into?** (Classification)
- **How is it like, or different from, other things?** (Comparison and contrast)
- **Why did it happen? What results did or could it have?** (Cause-and-effect analysis)
- **How do you do it, or how does it work?** (Process analysis)

For more on these patterns, with examples, see pp. 47–51.

3 Thesis and Organization

Chapter essentials
- Develop a thesis statement (below).
- Organize your ideas (p. 18).

Visit MyWritingLab™ for more resources on thesis and organization.

Finding your main idea gives you focus and direction. Organizing your raw material helps you clear away unneeded ideas, spot possible gaps, and energize your subject.

3a Conceiving a thesis statement

Your readers will expect your essay to be focused on and controlled by a main idea, or **thesis**. The thesis is the intellectual position you are taking on your topic. Often you will express the thesis in a one- or two-sentence **thesis statement** toward the beginning of your paper.

As an expression of the thesis, the thesis statement serves three crucial functions and one optional one:

Functions of the thesis statement

- **The thesis statement narrows your subject to a single, central idea** that you want readers to gain from your essay.
- **It claims something specific and significant about your subject,** a claim that requires support.
- **It conveys your purpose**—often explanatory or argumentative in college writing.
- **It often concisely previews the arrangement of ideas,** in which case it can also help you organize your essay.

---

1 Formulating a thesis question

A thesis statement probably will not leap fully formed into your head. You can start on it by posing a **thesis question** to help you figure out your position, organize your ideas, start drafting, and stay on track.

Consider again Katy Moreno's assignment on p. 10:

> . . . As a college student, how do you respond to [Friedman's] analysis of the global market for jobs? What do you think today's college students should be learning?

To respond to the assignment, Moreno reread Friedman's essay and her journal entry (pp. 10–11). Then she wrote a question that could guide her thinking by connecting Friedman's essay and her experience of her mother's job loss:

> How does my mother's job loss contradict Friedman's argument about technical training as key to success in the global job market?

2 Drafting a thesis statement

Drafting a thesis statement can occur at almost any time in the process of writing. Some instructors suggest that students develop a thesis statement when they have a good stock of ideas, to give a definite sense of direction. Other instructors suggest that students work with their thesis question at least through drafting, to keep their options open. And no matter when it's drafted, a thesis statement can change during the writing process, as the writer discovers ideas and expresses them in sentences.

Katy Moreno chose to try writing her thesis statement before drafting. Working from her thesis question (above), she wrote a sentence that named a topic and made a claim about it:

> The outsourcing of my mother's job proves that Thomas L. Friedman's advice to improve students' technical training is too narrow.

Moreno later revised her thesis statement (see opposite), but this draft statement gave her direction for the first draft of her paper.

Following are more examples of thesis questions and answering thesis statements. Each statement consists of a topic and a claim. Notice how each statement also expresses purpose. Statements 1–2 are **explanatory**: the writers mainly want to explain something to readers. Statements 3–4 are **argumentative**: the authors mainly want to convince readers of something. Most of the thesis statements you write in college papers will be either explanatory or argumentative.

Thesis question	Explanatory thesis statement
1. Why did Abraham Lincoln delay in emancipating the slaves?	Lincoln delayed emancipating any slaves until 1863 because his primary goal was to restore and preserve the Union, with or without slavery. [**Topic:** Lincoln's delay. **Claim:** was caused by his goal of preserving the Union.]
2. What steps can prevent juvenile crime?	Juveniles can be diverted from crime by active learning programs, full-time sports, frequent contact with positive role models, and intervention by consistent mentors. [**Topic:** juvenile crime. **Claim:** can be prevented in four ways.]

Thesis question	Argumentative thesis statement
3. Why should drivers' use of cell phones be banned?	Drivers' use of cell phones should be outlawed because people who talk and drive at the same time cause accidents. [**Topic:** drivers' use of cell phones. **Claim:** should be outlawed because it causes accidents.]
4. Which college students should be entitled to federal aid?	As an investment in its own economy, the federal government should provide a tuition grant to any college student who qualifies academically. [**Topic:** federal aid. **Claim:** should be provided to any college student who qualifies academically.]

Note that statement 2 previews the organization of the essay. Readers often appreciate such a preview, and students often prefer it because it helps them organize their main points during drafting.

Thesis statement

Juveniles can be diverted from crime by active learning programs, full-time sports, frequent contact with positive role models, and intervention by consistent mentors.

Organization of essay

Discussion one by one of four ways to reduce juvenile crime.

CULTURE LANGUAGE In some cultures it is considered rude or unnecessary for a writer to state his or her main idea outright. When writing in standard American English for school or work, you can assume that readers expect a clear and early idea of what you think.

3 Revising the thesis statement

You may have to write and rewrite a thesis statement before you come to a conclusion about your position. Katy Moreno used her draft thesis statement (p. 15) in the first draft of her paper, but she saw that it put too little emphasis on her actual topic (*technical training*) and overstated her disagreement with Friedman (*proves . . . is too narrow*). After several revisions, her final thesis statement clarified the claim and said why the subject was significant:

> My mother's experience of having her job outsourced taught a lesson that Friedman overlooks: technical training by itself can be too narrow to produce the communicators and problem solvers needed by contemporary businesses.

As you draft and revise your thesis statement, ask the following questions:

Checklist for revising the thesis statement

- **How well does the subject of your statement capture the subject of your writing?**
- **What claim does your statement make about your subject?**
- **What is the significance of the claim?** How does it answer "So what?" and convey your purpose?
- **How can the claim be limited or made more specific?** Does it state a single idea and clarify the boundaries of the idea?
- **How unified is the statement?** How does each word and phrase contribute to a single idea?
- **How well does the statement preview the organization of your writing?**

Here are examples of thesis statements revised to meet these requirements:

Original	Revised
This new product brought in over $300,000 last year. [A statement of fact, not a claim about the product: what is significant about the product's success?]	This new product succeeded because of its innovative marketing campaign, including widespread press coverage, in-store entertainment, and a consumer newsletter.
People should not go on fad diets. [A vague statement that needs limiting with one or more reasons: what's wrong with fad diets?]	Fad diets can be dangerous when they deprive the body of essential nutrients or rely excessively on potentially harmful foods.

Original	Revised
Televised sports are different from live sports. [A general statement that needs to be made more specific: how are they different, and why is the difference significant?]	Although television cannot transmit all the excitement of a live game, its close-ups and slow-motion replays reveal much about the players and the strategy of the game.
Cell phones can be convenient, but they can also be dangerous. [Not unified: how do the two parts of the sentence relate to each other?]	The convenience of cell phones does not justify the risks of driving while talking or texting.

Exercise 3.1 Evaluating thesis statements

Evaluate the thesis statements below considering whether each is limited, specific, and unified. Rewrite the items as needed to meet these goals.

1 Aggression usually leads to violence, injury, and even death, and we should use it constructively.
2 The religion of Islam is widely misunderstood in the United States.
3 One evening of a radio talk show amply illustrates both the appeal of such shows and their silliness.
4 Good manners make our society work.
5 The poem is about motherhood.
6 Television is useful for children and a mindless escape for adults who do not want to think about their problems.
7 I disliked American history in high school, but I like it in college.
8 Drunken drivers, whose perception and coordination are impaired, should receive mandatory suspensions of their licenses.
9 Business is a good major for many students.
10 The state's lenient divorce laws undermine the institution of marriage, which is fundamental to our culture, and they should certainly be made stricter for couples who have children.

3b Organizing your ideas

Most essays share a basic pattern of introduction (states the subject), body (develops the subject), and conclusion (pulls the essay's ideas together). Introductions and conclusions are discussed on pp. 51–54. Within the body, every paragraph develops some aspect of the essay's main idea, or thesis. See pp. 38–39 for Katy Moreno's essay, with annotations highlighting the body's pattern of support for the thesis statement.

CULTURE LANGUAGE If you are not used to reading and writing American academic prose, its pattern of introduction-body-conclusion and the organization schemes discussed on the next page may seem unfamiliar. For instance, instead of introductions that focus quickly on the topic and thesis, you may be used to openings that establish personal connections with readers. And instead of body paragraphs that stress general points and support those points with evidence, you may be used to general statements without support (because writers can assume that readers will supply the evidence themselves) or to evidence without explanation (because writers can assume that readers will infer the general points). When writing American academic prose, you need to take into account readers' expectations for directness and for the statement and support of general points.

1 The general and the specific

To organize material for an essay, you need to distinguish general and specific ideas and see the relations between ideas. General and specific refer to the number of instances or objects included in a group signified by a word. The following "ladder" illustrates a general-to-specific hierarchy:

Most general

↑ life form
  plant
  rose
↓ Uncle Dan's prize-winning American Beauty rose

Most specific

As you arrange your material, pick out the general ideas and then the specific points that support them. Set aside points that seem irrelevant to your key ideas. On a computer you can easily experiment with various arrangements of general ideas and supporting information: save your master list of ideas to a new file, and then move material around.

2 Schemes for organizing essays

An essay's body paragraphs may be arranged in many ways that are familiar to readers. The choice depends on your subject, purpose, and audience.

- **Spatial:** In describing a person, place, or thing, move through space systematically from a starting point to other features—for instance, top to bottom, near to far, left to right.
- **Chronological:** In recounting a sequence of events, arrange the events as they actually occurred in time, first to last.
- **General to specific:** Begin with an overall discussion of the subject; then fill in details, facts, examples, and other support.
- **Specific to general:** First provide the support; then draw a conclusion from it.
- **Climactic:** Arrange ideas in order of increasing importance to your thesis or increasing interest to the reader.
- **Problem-solution:** First outline a problem that needs solving; then propose a solution.

3 Outlines

It's not essential to craft a detailed outline before you begin drafting an essay; in fact, too detailed a plan could prevent you from discovering ideas while you draft. Still, even a rough scheme can show you patterns of general and specific, suggest proportions, and highlight gaps or overlaps in coverage.

There are several kinds of outlines, some more flexible than others.

Scratch or informal outline

A scratch or informal outline includes key general points in the order they will be covered. It may also list evidence for the points.

Here is Katy Moreno's scratch outline for her essay on the global job market:

Thesis statement

My mother's experience of having her job outsourced taught a lesson that Friedman overlooks: technical training by itself can be too narrow to produce the communicators and problem solvers needed by contemporary businesses.

Scratch outline

Mom's outsourcing experience
    Excellent tech skills
    Salary too high compared to overseas tech workers
    Lack of planning + communication skills, unlike managers who kept jobs
Well-rounded education to protect vs. outsourcing
    Tech training, as Friedman says
    Also, communication, problem solving, other management skills

Tree diagram

In a tree diagram, ideas and details branch out in increasing specificity. Unlike more linear outlines, this diagram can be supplemented and extended indefinitely, so it is easy to alter. From her brainstorming about a summer job (p. 12), Johanna Abrams created the tree diagram on the facing page to develop this thesis statement:

Thesis statement

Two months working in a large agency taught me that an office's pecking order should be respected.

Formal outline

A formal outline not only lays out main ideas and their support but also shows the relative importance of all the essay's elements. On the basis of her scratch outline above, Katy Moreno prepared the formal outline on the next page for her essay on the global job market.

Thesis statement

My mother's experience of having her job outsourced taught a lesson that Friedman overlooks: technical training by itself can be too narrow to produce the communicators and problem solvers needed by contemporary businesses.

Tree diagram

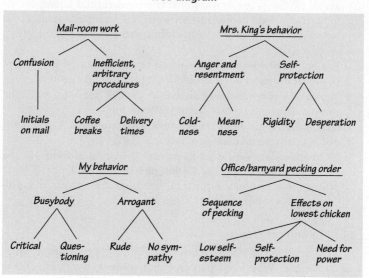

Formal outline

I. Summary of Friedman's article
   A. Reasons for outsourcing
      1. Improved technology and access
      2. Well-educated workers
      3. Productive workers
      4. Lower wages
   B. Need for improved technical training in US
II. Experience of my mother
   A. Outsourcing of job
      1. Mother's education, experience, performance
      2. Employer's cost savings
   B. Retention of managers' jobs
      1. Planning skills
      2. Communication skills
III. Conclusions about ideal education
   A. Needs of US businesses
      1. Technical skills
      2. Management skills
         a. Communication
         b. Problem solving
         c. Versatility
   B. Consideration of personal goals
      1. Technical training
      2. English and history courses for management skills

This example illustrates several principles of outlining that can ensure completeness, balance, and clear relationships:

- **All parts are systematically indented and labeled:** Roman numerals (I, II) for primary divisions; indented capital letters (A, B) for secondary divisions; further indented Arabic numerals (1, 2) for supporting examples; and still further indented small letters (a, b) for details.
- **The outline divides the material into several groups.** A long list of points at the same level should be broken up into groups.
- **Topics of equal generality appear in parallel headings,** with the same indention and numbering or lettering.
- **All subdivided headings break into at least two parts.** A topic cannot logically be divided into only one part.
- **All headings are expressed in parallel grammatical form**—in the example, as phrases using a noun plus modifiers. This is a topic outline; in a sentence outline all headings are expressed as full sentences (see **8** p. 481).

4 Unity and coherence

Two qualities of effective writing relate to organization: unity and coherence. When you perceive that someone's writing "flows well," you are probably appreciating these qualities.

To check an outline or draft for **unity,** ask these questions:

- **Is each section relevant to the main idea (thesis) of the essay?**
- **Within main sections, does each example or detail support the principal idea of that section?**

To check your outline or draft for **coherence,** ask the following questions:

- **Do the ideas follow a clear sequence?**
- **Are the parts of the essay logically connected?**
- **Are the connections clear and smooth?**

The following informative essay illustrates some ways of achieving unity and coherence (highlighted in the annotations).

Who Benefits from the Money in College Football?

Anyone who follows Division 1-A college football cannot fail to

Introduction establishing subject of essay

notice the money that pours into every aspect of the sport—the lavish stadiums, corporate sponsorships, televised games, and long post-season bowl series. The influx of money may seem to benefit the players, but in reality the institutions that promote college football, not the players,

Thesis statement

have gotten rich. College football is a multimillion-dollar industry not for the players but for the colleges and universities, conferences, and television networks.

Paragraph idea, linked to thesis statement

Colleges and universities are major players in the for-profit football industry. A vibrant football program attracts not only skilled coaches and talented players but also wealthy, sports-minded donors who give money for state-of-the art stadiums and facilities. These great facilities in turn attract fans, some of whom are willing to pay high ticket prices to watch games in luxurious sky boxes and thus generate more profits for the schools' athletic departments.

Paragraph developed with evidence supporting its idea

The athletic conferences to which the schools belong—such as the Big Ten, the Atlantic Coast Conference, and the Pac-12—reap financial rewards from college football. Each conference maintains a Web site to post schedules and scores, sell tickets and merchandise, and promote interest in its teams. However, the proceeds from ticket and merchandise sales surely pale in comparison to the money generated by the annual Bowl Championship Series—the three-week-long post-season football extravaganza. Each game is not only televised but also carries the name of a corporate sponsor that pays for the privilege of having its name attached to a bowl game.

Paragraph idea, linked to thesis statement

Paragraph developed with evidence supporting its idea

Like the schools and athletic conferences, the television networks profit from football. Networks sell advertising slots to the highest bidders for every televised game during the regular season and the Bowl Championship Series, and they work to sustain fans' interest in football by cultivating viewers on the Web. For instance, one network generates interest in up-and-coming high school players through *Scout.com*, a Web site that posts profiles of boys being recruited by colleges and universities and that is supported, at least in part, through advertising and paid subscriptions.

Paragraph idea, linked to thesis statement

Paragraph developed with evidence supporting its idea

Amid these money-making players are the actual football players, the young men who are bound by NCAA rules to play as amateurs and to receive no direct compensation for their hours of practice and field time. They may receive scholarships that cover tuition, room and board, uniforms, medical care, and travel. Yet these payments are a small fraction of the millions of dollars spent on and earned from football.

Transition and new paragraph idea, linked to thesis statement

Paragraph developed with evidence supporting its idea

Many critics have pointed out the disparity between players' rewards and the industry's profits. Recent efforts to unionize the players and file lawsuits on their behalf have caused schools, conferences, and the NCAA to make some concessions in scholarship packages and rules. However, these changes do not fundamentally alter a system in which the big benefits go to everyone but the players.

Conclusion echoing thesis statement and summarizing

—Terrence MacDonald (student)

See also pp. 42–47 on unity and coherence in paragraphs.

Exercise 3.2 Organizing ideas

The following list of ideas was extracted by a student from freewriting he did for a brief paper on soccer in the United States. Using his thesis statement as a guide, pick out the general ideas and arrange the relevant specific points under them. In some cases you may have to infer general ideas to cover specific points in the list.

Thesis statement

Although its growth in the United States has been slow and halting, professional soccer may finally be poised to become a major American sport.

List of ideas

In countries of South and Latin America, soccer is the favorite sport.

In the United States the success of a sport depends largely on its ability to attract huge TV audiences.

Soccer was not often presented on US television.

In 2010 and 2014 the World Cup final was broadcast on ABC and on Spanish-language Univision.

In the past, professional soccer could not get a foothold in the United States because of poor TV coverage and lack of financial backing.

The growing Hispanic population in the United States could help soccer grow as well.

Investors have poured hundreds of millions of dollars into the top US professional league.

Potential fans did not have a chance to see soccer games.

Failures of early start-up leagues made potential backers wary of new ventures.

Recently, the outlook for professional soccer has changed dramatically.

The US television audience for the 2014 US–Ghana match was larger than the average US television audience for baseball's World Series.

4 Drafting

Chapter essentials

- To begin a draft, just start writing (below).
- To complete a draft, maintain momentum (facing page).

Visit MyWritingLab™ for more resources on drafting.

Drafting is an occasion for exploration. Don't expect to transcribe solid thoughts into polished prose: solidity and polish will come with revision and editing. Instead, while drafting let the very act of writing help you find and form your meaning.

4a   Starting to draft

Beginning a draft sometimes takes courage, even for professionals. Procrastination may actually help if you let ideas for writing simmer at the same time. At some point, though, you'll have to face the blank paper or screen. The following techniques can help you begin:

- **Read over what you've already written**—notes, outlines, and so on. Immediately start your draft with whatever comes to mind.
- **Freewrite** (see p. 11).
- **Skip the opening and start in the middle.** Or write the conclusion.
- **Write a paragraph.** Explain what you think your essay will be about when you finish it.
- **Start writing the part that you understand best.** Using your outline, divide your work into chunks—say, one for the introduction, another for the first point, and so on. One of these chunks may call out to be written.

4b Maintaining momentum

Drafting requires momentum: the forward movement opens you to fresh ideas and connections. To keep moving while drafting, try one or more of these techniques:

- **Set aside enough time.** For a brief essay, a first draft is likely to take at least an hour or two.
- **Work in a quiet place.**
- **If you must stop working, write down what you plan to do next.** Then you can pick up where you stopped with minimal disruption.
- **Be as fluid as possible.** Spontaneity will allow your attitudes toward your subject to surface naturally in your sentences.
- **Keep going.** Skip over sticky spots; leave a blank if you can't find the right word; put alternative ideas or phrasings in brackets so that you can consider them later. If an idea pops out of nowhere but doesn't seem to fit in, quickly jot it down, or write it into the draft and bracket or boldface it for later attention.
- **Resist self-criticism.** Don't worry about your grammar, spelling, and the like. Don't worry about what your readers will think. These are very important matters, but save them for revision.
- **Use your thesis statement and outline.** They can remind you of your planned purpose, organization, and content. However, if your writing leads you in a more interesting direction, follow.

If you write on a computer, frequently save the text you're drafting—at least every five or ten minutes and every time you leave the computer.

4c Examining a sample first draft

Katy Moreno's first-draft response to Thomas L. Friedman's "It's a Flat World, after All" appears on the next two pages. (The first two paragraphs include the page numbers in Friedman's article that Moreno summarized material from.) As part of her assignment, Moreno showed the draft to four classmates whose suggestions for revision appear in the margin. They used the Comment function of *Microsoft Word*, which allows users to add comments without inserting words into the text of the document. (Notice that the classmates ignore mistakes in grammar and punctuation, concentrating instead on larger issues such as the thesis, the clarity of ideas, and overall unity.)

Title?

In "It's a Flat World, after All," Thomas L. Friedman argues that, most US students are not preparing themselves as well as they should to compete in today's economy. Not like students in India, China, and other countries are (34-37). The outsourcing of my mother's job proves that Thomas L. Friedman's advice to improve students' technical training is too narrow.

> **Comment [Jared]:** Your mother's job being outsourced is interesting, but your introduction seems rushed.

> **Comment [Rabia]:** The end of your thesis statement is a little unclear—too narrow for what?

Friedman describes a "flat" world where technology like the Internet and wireless communication makes it possible for college graduates all over the globe, in particular in India and China, to get jobs that once were gotten by graduates of US colleges and universities (37). He argues that US students need more math and science in order to compete (37).

> **Comment [Erin]:** Can you include the reasons Friedman gives for overseas students' success?

I came to college with first-hand knowledge of globalization and outsourcing. My mother, who worked for sixteen years in the field of information technology (IT), was laid off six months ago when the company she worked for decided to outsource much of its IT work to a company based in India. My mother majored in computer science, had sixteen years of experience, and her bosses always gave her good reviews. She never expected to be laid off and was surprised when she was. She wasn't laid off because of her background and performance. In fact, my mother had a very strong background in math and science and years of training and job experience. The reason was because her salary and benefits cost the company more than outsourcing her job did. Which hurt my family financially, as you can imagine.

> **Comment [Nathaniel]:** Tighten this paragraph to avoid repetition? Also, how does your mother's experience relate to Friedman and your thesis?

A number of well-paid people in the IT department where my mother worked, namely IT managers, were not laid off. As my mother explained at the time, they kept their jobs because they were better at planning and they communicated better, they were better writers and speakers than my mother.

> **Comment [Erin]:** What were the managers better at planning for?

Like my mother, I am more comfortable in front of a
computer than I am in front of a group of people. I planned
to major in computer science. Since my mother lost her job,
though, I have decided to take courses in English and history
too, where the classes will require me to do different kinds of
work. When I enter the job market, my well-rounded education will make me a more attractive job candidate, and, will
help me to be a versatile, productive employee.

We know from our history that Americans have been innovative, hard-working people. We students have educational
opportunities to compete in the global economy, but we must
use our time in college wisely. As Thomas L. Friedman says,
my classmates and I need to be ready for a rapidly changing
future. We will have to work hard each day, which means being prepared for class, getting the best grades we can, and
making the most of each class. Our futures depend on the decisions we make today.

Comment [Nathaniel]: Can you be more specific about the kinds of work you'll need to do?

Comment [Rabia]: Can you work this point into your thesis?

Comment [Jared]: Conclusion seems to go off in a new direction. Friedman mentions hard work, but it hasn't been your focus before.

Comment [Rabia]: Don't forget your works cited.

5 Revising

Chapter essentials
- Read your work critically (next page).
- Use a revision checklist (p. 29).
- Collaborate on revisions (p. 28).

Visit MyWritingLab™ for more resources on revising.

Revising is an essential task in creating an effective piece of writing. During revision—literally, "re-seeing"—you shift your focus outward from yourself and your subject toward your readers, concentrating on what will help them respond as you want. Many writers revise in two stages: first they view the work as a whole, evaluating and improving its overall meaning and structure (this chapter); then they edit sentences for wording, grammar, punctuation, spelling, and so on (next chapter).

In revising your writing, you may work alone or you may receive input from your instructor and/or other students in a collaborative group. Whether you are responding to your own evaluation or that of readers, you may need to rethink your thesis, move or delete whole paragraphs, clarify how ideas relate to the thesis, or support ideas with details or further research. Knowing that you will edit later gives you the freedom to look beyond the confines of the page or screen to see the paper as a whole.

5a Reading your work critically

To revise your writing, you have to read it critically, and that means you have to create some distance between your draft and yourself. These techniques may help you to see your work objectively:

- **Take a break after finishing the draft.** A few hours may be enough; a whole night or day is preferable.
- **Ask someone to respond to your draft.** A roommate, family member, or tutor in the writing center can call attention to what needs revising.
- **Read your draft in a new medium.** Typing a handwritten draft or printing out a word-processed draft can reveal weaknesses that you didn't see in the original.
- **Outline your draft.** Highlight the main points supporting the thesis, and convert these sentences to outline form. Then examine the outline you've made for logical order, gaps, and digressions. A formal outline can be especially illuminating because of its careful structure (see pp. 20–22).
- **Listen to your draft.** Read the draft out loud to yourself or to a friend or classmate, record and listen to it, or have someone read the draft to you.
- **Use a revision checklist.** Don't try to re-see everything in your draft at once. Use the checklist on the facing page, making a separate pass through the draft for each item.

5b Revising collaboratively

In many writing courses students work together, often commenting on each other's writing to help with revision. This collaborative writing provides experience in reading written work critically and in reaching others through writing. The collaboration may occur face to face in small groups, on paper via drafts and comments, or online, either through a course-management system such as *Blackboard* or *Canvas* or through a class blog, e-mail list, or wiki.

Whatever the medium of collaboration, following a few guidelines will help you gain more from others' comments and become a more constructive reader yourself.

Benefiting from comments on your writing

- **Think of your readers as counselors or coaches.** They can help you see the virtues and flaws in your work and sharpen your awareness of readers' needs.

Checklist for revision

Assignment

How have you responded to the assignment for this writing? Verify that your subject, purpose, and genre are appropriate for the requirements of the assignment.

Purpose

What is the purpose of your writing? Does it conform to the assignment? Is it consistent throughout the paper? (See pp. 6–7.)

Audience

How does the writing address the intended audience? How does it meet readers' likely expectations for your subject? Where might readers need more information?

Genre

How does your writing conform to the conventions of the genre you're writing in—features such as organization, kinds of evidence, language, and format?

Thesis

What is the thesis of your writing? Where does it become clear? How well do thesis and paper match: Does any part of the paper stray from the thesis? Does the paper fulfill the commitment of the thesis? (See pp. 14–17.)

Organization

What are the main points of the paper? (List them.) How well does each support the thesis? How effective is their arrangement for the paper's purpose? (See pp. 18–22.)

Development

How well do details, examples, and other evidence support each main point? Where, if at all, might readers find support skimpy or have trouble understanding the content? (See pp. 5–6, 47–51.)

Unity

What does each sentence and paragraph contribute to the thesis? Where, if at all, do digressions occur? Should they be cut, or can they be rewritten to support the thesis? (See pp. 22, 42.)

Coherence

How clearly and smoothly does the paper flow? Where does it seem rough or awkward? Can any transitions be improved? (See pp. 22, 43–47.)

Title, introduction, conclusion

How accurately and interestingly does the title reflect the essay's content? (See pp. 31–32.) How well does the introduction engage and focus readers' attention? (See pp. 51–53.) How effective is the conclusion in providing a sense of completion? (See pp. 53–54.)

Using a word processor to manage drafts

When you revise on a computer, take a few precautions to avoid losing your work and to keep track of your drafts:

- **Save your work every five to ten minutes.**
- **After doing any major work on a project, create a backup version of the file.**
- **Work on a copy of your latest draft.** Then the original will remain intact until you're truly finished with it. On the copy you can use your word processor's Track Changes function, which shows changes alongside the original text and allows you to accept or reject alterations later.
- **Save each draft under its own file name.** You may need to consult previous drafts for ideas or phrasings.

- **Read or listen to comments closely.**
- **Know what the critic is saying.** If you need more information, ask for it, or consult the appropriate section of this handbook.
- **Don't become defensive.** Letting comments offend you will only erect a barrier to improvement in your writing. As one writing teacher advises, "Leave your ego at the door."
- **Revise your work in response to appropriate comments.** You will learn more from the act of revision than from just thinking about changes.
- **Remember that you are the final authority on your work.** You should be open to suggestions, but you are free to decline advice when you think it is inappropriate.
- **Keep track of both the strengths and the weaknesses others identify.** Then in later assignments you can build on your successes and give special attention to problem areas.

Commenting on others' writing

- **Be sure you know what the writer is saying.** If necessary, summarize the paper to understand its content. (See **2** pp. 85–87.)
- **Address only your most significant concerns with the work.** Focus on the deep issues in other writers' drafts, especially early drafts: thesis, purpose, audience, organization, and support for the thesis. Use the revision checklist on p. 29 as a guide to what is significant. Unless you have other instructions, ignore mistakes in grammar, punctuation, spelling, and the like. (The temptation to focus on such errors may be especially strong if the writer is less experienced than you are with standard American English.) Emphasizing mistakes will contribute little to the writer's revision.
- **Remember that you are the reader, not the writer.** Don't edit sen-

tences, add details, or otherwise assume responsibility for the paper.

■ **Phrase your comments carefully.** Avoid misunderstandings by making sure comments are both clear and respectful. If you are responding on paper or online, not face to face with the writer, remember that the writer has nothing but your written words to go on. He or she can't ask you for immediate clarification and can't infer your attitudes from gestures, facial expressions, and tone of voice.

■ **Be specific.** If something confuses you, say *why*. If you disagree with a conclusion, say *why*.

■ **Be supportive as well as honest.** Tell the writer what you like about the paper. Phrase your comments positively: instead of *This paragraph doesn't interest me*, say *You have an interesting detail here that I almost missed.* Question the writer in a way that emphasizes the effect of the work on you, the reader: *This paragraph confuses me because. . . .* And avoid measuring the work against a set of external standards: *This essay is poorly organized. Your thesis statement is inadequate.*

■ **While reading, make your comments in writing.** Even if you will be delivering your comments in person later on, the written record will help you recall what you thought.

■ **Link comments to specific parts of a paper.** Especially if you are reading the paper on a computer, be clear about what in the paper each comment relates to. You can use a word processor's Comment function, which annotates documents.

(**CULTURE LANGUAGE**) In some cultures writers do not expect criticism from readers, or readers do not expect to think and speak critically about what they read. If critical responses are uncommon in your native culture, collaboration may at first be uncomfortable for you. As a writer, think of a draft or even a final paper as more an exploration of ideas than the last word on your subject; then you may be more receptive to readers' suggestions. As a reader, know that your tactful questions and suggestions about focus, content, and organization will usually be considered appropriate.

5c Writing a title

The revision stage is a good time to consider a title because summing up your essay in a phrase focuses your attention sharply on your topic, purpose, and audience. The title should tell the reader what your paper is about, but it should not restate the assignment or the thesis statement. Most titles fall into one of these categories:

■ **A *descriptive title* announces the subject clearly and accurately.** Such a title is almost always appropriate, and it is usually expected for academic writing. Katy Moreno's final title—"Can We Compete? College Education for the Global Economy"—is an example.

■ A *suggestive title* hints at the subject to arouse curiosity. Such a title is common in popular magazines and may be appropriate for writing that is somewhat informal. Moreno might have chosen a suggestive title such as "Training for the New World" or "Education for a Flat World" (echoing Thomas L. Friedman's title).

For more information on essay titles, see **MLA** p. 479 (MLA format), **APA** p. 513 (APA format), and **6** p. 336 (capitalizing words in a title).

5d   Examining a sample revision

Katy Moreno was satisfied with her first draft: she had her ideas down, and the arrangement seemed logical. Still, from the revision checklist she knew the draft needed work, and her classmates' comments (pp. 26–27) highlighted what she needed to focus on. Following is the first half of her revised draft, with marginal annotations highlighting the changes. Moreno used the Track Changes function on her word processor, so that deletions are crossed out and additions are in blue.

Descriptive title names topic and forecasts approach.	Can We Compete? College Education for the Global Economy ~~Title?~~
Expanded introduction draws readers into Moreno's topic, clarifies her point of agreement with Friedman, and states her revised thesis.	Today's students cannot miss news stories about globalization of the economy and outsourcing of jobs, but are students aware of how these trends are affecting the job market? In "It's a Flat World, after All," Thomas L. Friedman argues that most US students are not preparing themselves as well as ~~they should to compete in today's economy. Not like~~ students in India, China, and other countries ~~are~~ to compete in today's economy, which requires hard-working, productive scientists and engineers (34-37). Friedman's argument speaks to me because my mother recently lost her job when it was outsourced to India. But her experience taught a lesson that Friedman overlooks: technical training by itself can be too narrow to produce the communicators and problem solvers needed by contemporary businesses. ~~The outsourcing of my mother's job proves that Thomas L. Friedman's advice to improve students'.technical training is too narrow.~~
Expanded summary of Friedman's article specifies qualities of overseas workers.	Friedman describes a "flat" world where recent technology like the Internet and wireless communication makes it possible for college graduates all over the globe~~, in particular~~ to compete for high paying jobs that once belonged to graduates of US colleges and universities (34). He focuses on workers in India and China~~,~~ who graduate from college with ex-

cellent educations in math and science, who are eager for new opportunities, and who are willing to work exceptionally hard, often harder than their American counterparts and, for less money ~~to get jobs that once were gotten by graduates of US colleges and universities~~ (37). ~~He~~ Friedman argues that US students must be better prepared academically, especially in ~~need more~~ math and science, so that they can get and keep jobs that will otherwise go overseas ~~in order to compete~~ (37).

~~I came to college with first hand knowledge of globalization and outsourcing. My mother, who worked for sixteen years in the field of information technology (IT), was laid off six months ago when the company she worked for decided to outsource much of its IT work to a company based in India. My mother~~ At first glance, my mother's experience of losing her job might seem to support the argument of Friedman that better training in math and science is the key to competing in the global job market. Her experience, however, adds dimensions to the globalization story, which Friedman misses. First my mother had the kind of strong background in math and science that Friedman says, today's workers need. She majored in computer science, rose within the information technology (IT) department of a large company, ~~had sixteen years of experience,~~ and her bosses always gave her good performance reviews. Still, when her employer decided to outsource most of its IT work, my mother lost her job. ~~She never expected to be laid off and was surprised when she was. She wasn't laid off because of her background and performance. In fact, my mother had a very strong background in math and science and years of training and job experience.~~ The reason wasn't because her technical skills were inadequate. Instead, her salary and benefits cost the company more than outsourcing her job did. Until wages rise around the globe, jobs like my mother's will be vulnerable. No matter how well you are trained. ~~Which hurt my family financially, as you can imagine.~~

New opening sentences connect to introduction and thesis statement, restating points of agreement and disagreement with Friedman.

Revisions condense long example of mother's experience.

Paragraph's concluding sentences reinforce the point and connect to thesis statement.

6 Editing, Formatting, and Proofreading

Chapter essentials

- Edit the revised draft (next page).
- Use an editing checklist (p. 35).
- Format and proofread the final draft (p. 37).

Visit MyWritingLab™ for more resources on editing, formatting, and proofreading.

After you have revised your essay so that you are satisfied with the content, turn to the work of editing your sentences to correct them and clarify your ideas.

6a Editing the revised draft

In your editing, work first for clear and effective sentences that flow smoothly from one to the next. Then check your sentences for correctness. Use the questions in the checklist on the next page to guide your editing.

1 Discovering what needs editing

Try these approaches to gain distance from your work:

- **Take a break.** Even fifteen minutes can clear your head.
- **Read the draft slowly, and read what you actually see.** Otherwise, you're likely to read what you intended to write but didn't. (If you have trouble slowing down, try reading your draft from back to front, sentence by sentence.)
- **Read as if you are encountering the draft for the first time.** Put yourself in the reader's place.
- **Have a classmate, friend, or relative read your work.** Make sure you understand and consider the reader's suggestions, even if eventually you decide not to take them.
- **Read the draft aloud or, even better, record it.** Listen for awkward rhythms, repetitive sentence patterns, and missing or clumsy transitions.
- **Learn from your own experience.** Keep a record of the problems that others have pointed out in your writing. When editing, check your work against this record.

2 A sample edited paragraph

The third paragraph of Katy Moreno's edited draft appears below and on p. 36. Among other changes, she tightened wording, improved parallelism (with *consistently received*), corrected several comma errors, and repaired the final sentence fragment.

> At first glance, my mother's experience of losing her job might seem to support ~~the~~ Friedman's argument ~~of Friedman~~ that better training in math and science is the key to competing in the global job market. However, ~~H~~her experience~~, however,~~ adds dimensions to the globalization story~~, which~~ that Friedman misses. First, my mother had the kind of strong background in math and science that Friedman says~~,~~ today's workers need. She majored in computer science, rose within the information technology (IT) department of a large company, and consistently received ~~her bosses always gave her~~ good performance reviews. Still, when her employer

Checklist for editing

Are my sentences clear?

Do my words and sentences mean what I Intend them to mean? Is anything confusing? Check especially for these:

Exact language (**3** pp. 163–72)
Parallelism (**3** pp. 148–50)
Clear modifiers (**4** pp. 258–63)
Clear reference of pronouns (**4** pp. 244–47)
Complete sentences (**4** pp. 264–67)
Sentences separated correctly (**4** pp. 269–72)

Are my sentences effective?

How well do words and sentences engage and hold readers' attention? Where does the writing seem wordy, choppy, or dull? Check especially for these:

Emphasis of main ideas (**3** pp. 139–46)
Smooth and informative transitions (pp. 45–46)
Variety in sentence length and structure (**3** pp. 152–54)
Appropriate language (**3** pp. 156–62)
Concise sentences (**3** pp. 174–78)

Do my sentences contain errors?

Where do surface errors interfere with the clarity and effectiveness of my sentences? Check especially for these:

- **Spelling errors (6** pp. 325–30)
- **Sentence fragments (4** pp. 264–67)
- **Comma splices (4** pp. 269–72)
- **Verb errors**
  Verb forms, especially -*s* and -*ed* endings, correct forms of irregular verbs, and appropriate helping verbs (**4** pp. 204–16)
  Verb tenses, especially consistency (**4** pp. 216–22)
  Agreement between subjects and verbs, especially when words come between them or the subject is *each, everyone,* or a similar word (**4** pp. 227–32)

- **Pronoun errors**
  Pronoun forms, especially subjective (*he, she, they, who*) vs. objective (*him, her, them, whom*) (**4** pp. 234–39)
  Agreement between pronouns and antecedents, especially when the antecedent contains *or* or the antecedent is *each, everyone, person,* or a similar word (**4** pp. 240–43)

- **Punctuation errors**
  Commas, especially with comma splices (**4** pp. 269–72) and with *and* or *but*, with introductory elements, with nonessential elements, and with series (**5** pp. 282–91)
  Apostrophes in possessives but not plural nouns (*Dave's/witches*) and in contractions but not possessive personal pronouns (*it's/its*) (**5** pp. 304–09)

decided to outsource most of its IT work, my mother lost her job. The reason wasn't ~~because~~ that her technical skills were inadequate. Instead, her salary and benefits cost the company more than outsourcing her job did. Until wages rise around the globe, jobs like my mother's will be vulnerable,~~.~~ ~~N~~no matter how well ~~you are~~ a person is trained.

3 | Working with spelling and grammar/style checkers

A spelling checker and grammar/style checker can be helpful *if* you work within their limitations. The programs miss many problems and may even flag items that are actually correct. Further, they know nothing of your purpose and your audience, so they cannot make important decisions about your writing. Always use these tools critically:

- **Read your work yourself to ensure that it's clear and error-free.**
- **Consider a checker's suggestions carefully against your intentions.** If you aren't sure whether to accept a checker's suggestion, consult a dictionary, writing handbook, or other source. Your version may be fine.

Using a spelling checker

Your word processor's spelling checker can be a great ally: it will flag words that are spelled incorrectly and will usually suggest alternative spellings that resemble what you've typed. However, this ally can also undermine you because of its limitations:

- **The checker may flag a word that you've spelled correctly** just because the word does not appear in its dictionary.
- **The checker may suggest incorrect alternatives.** In providing a list of alternative spellings for your word, the checker may highlight the one it considers most likely to be correct. For example, if you misspell *definitely* by typing *definately*, your checker may highlight *defiantly* as the correct option. You need to verify that the alternative suggested by the checker is actually what you intend before selecting it. Consult an online or printed dictionary when you aren't sure about the checker's recommendations.
- **Most important, a spelling checker will not flag words that appear in its dictionary but you have misused.** The paragraph in the screen shot on the facing page contains eleven errors that a spelling checker overlooked. Can you spot them?

Using a grammar/style checker

Grammar/style checkers can flag incorrect grammar or punctuation and wordy or awkward sentences. However, these programs can call your attention only to passages that *may* be faulty. They miss many errors because they are not yet capable of analyzing language in all its complexity. (For instance, they can't accurately distinguish

Spelling checker

The whether effects all of us, though it's affects are different for different people. Some people love a fare day with warm temperatures and sunshine. They revel in spending a hole day outside. Other people enjoy dark, rainy daze. They like to slow down and here they're inner thoughts. Most people agree, however, that to much of one kind of weather makes them board.

A spelling checker failed to catch any of the eleven errors in this paragraph.

a word's part of speech when there are different possibilities, as *light* can be a noun, a verb, or an adjective.) And they often question passages that don't need editing, such as an appropriate passive verb or a deliberate and emphatic use of repetition.

You can customize a grammar/style checker to suit your needs and habits as a writer. Most checkers allow you to specify whether to check grammar only or grammar and style. Some style checkers can be set to the level of writing you intend, such as formal, standard, and informal. (For academic writing choose formal.) You can also instruct the checker to flag specific grammar and style problems that tend to occur in your writing, such as mismatched subjects and verbs, overused passive voice, or a confusion between *its* and *it's*.

6b Formatting and proofreading the final draft

After editing your essay, format and proofread it before you submit it to your instructor. Follow any required format for your paper, such as MLA (**MLA** pp. 478–80) and APA (**APA** pp. 512–15). See also pp. 54–66 for help with designing papers.

Be sure to proofread the final essay several times to spot and correct errors. To increase the accuracy of your proofreading, you may need to experiment with ways to keep yourself from relaxing into the rhythm and the content of your prose. Here are a few tricks, including some used by professional proofreaders:

- ▪ **Read printed copy,** even if you will eventually submit the paper electronically. Most people proofread more accurately when reading type on paper than when reading it on a computer screen. (At the same time, don't view the printed copy as error-free just because it's clean. Clean-looking copy may still harbor errors.)
- ▪ **Read the paper aloud,** very slowly, and distinctly pronounce exactly what you see.
- ▪ **Place a ruler under each line as you read it.**
- ▪ **Read "against copy,"** comparing your final draft one sentence at a time against the edited draft.

- **Ignore content.** To keep the content of your writing from distracting you, read the essay backward sentence by sentence. Or use your word processor to isolate each paragraph from its context by printing it on a separate page. (Of course, reassemble the paragraphs before submitting the paper.)

6c | Examining a sample final draft

Katy Moreno's final essay appears on these pages, presented in MLA format except for page numbers. Comments in the margins point out key features of the essay's content.

Katy Moreno

Professor Lacourse

English 110

14 February 2014

Can We Compete?

College Education for the Global Economy

Descriptive title	
Introduction	Today's students cannot miss news stories about globalization of the economy and outsourcing of jobs, but are students aware of how
Summaries of Friedman cited with parenthetical page numbers using MLA style (MLA p. 436)	these trends are affecting the job market? In "It's a Flat World, after All," Thomas L. Friedman argues that most US students are not preparing themselves as well as students in India, China, and other countries to compete in today's economy, which requires hard-working, productive scientists and engineers (34-37). Friedman's argument speaks to me because my
Thesis statement: basic disagreement with Friedman	mother lost her job when it was outsourced to India. But her experience taught a lesson that Friedman overlooks: technical training by itself can be too narrow to produce the communicators and problem solvers needed by contemporary businesses.
Summary of Friedman's article	Friedman describes a "flat" world where technology like the Internet and wireless communication makes it possible for college graduates all over the globe to compete for high-paying jobs that once belonged to graduates of US colleges and universities (34). He focuses on workers in India and China who graduate from college with excellent educations in math and science, who are eager for new opportunities, and who are willing to work exceptionally hard, often harder than their American counterparts, and for less money (37). Friedman argues that US students must be better prepared academically, especially in math and science, so that they can get and keep jobs that will otherwise go overseas (37).
Transition to disagreements with Friedman	At first glance, my mother's experience of losing her job might seem to support Friedman's argument that better training in math and science

is the key to competing in the global job market. However, her experience adds dimensions to the globalization story that Friedman misses. First, my mother had the kind of strong background in math and science that Friedman says today's workers need. She majored in computer science, rose within the information technology (IT) department of a large company, and consistently received good performance reviews. Still, when her employer decided to outsource most of its IT work, my mother lost her job. The reason wasn't that her technical skills were inadequate; instead, her salary and benefits cost the company more than outsourcing her job did. Until wages rise around the globe, jobs like my mother's will be vulnerable, no matter how well a person is trained.

First disagreement with Friedman

Examples to support first disagreement

Clarification of first disagreement

The second dimension that Friedman misses is that a number of well-paid people in my mother's IT department, namely IT managers, were not laid off. As my mother explained at the time, they kept their jobs because they were experienced at figuring out the company's IT needs, planning for changes, researching and proposing solutions, and communicating in writing and speech—skills that her more narrow training and experience had missed. Friedman misses these skills by focusing only on technical training. Without the ability to solve problems creatively and to communicate, people with technical expertise alone may not have enough to save their jobs, as my mother learned.

Second disagreement with Friedman

Explanation of second disagreement

Conclusion summarizing both disagreements with Friedman

Like my mother, I am more comfortable in front of a computer than I am in front of a group of people, and I had planned to major in computer science. Since my mother lost her job, however, I have decided to take courses in English and history as well. Classes in these subjects will require me to read broadly, think critically, research, and communicate ideas in writing—in short, to develop skills that make managers. When I enter the job market, my well-rounded education will make me a more attractive job candidate and will help me to become the kind of forward-thinking manager that US companies will always need to employ here in the United States.

Final point: business needs and author's personal goals

Explanation of final point

Many jobs that require a college degree are indeed going overseas, as Thomas L. Friedman says, and my classmates and I need to be ready for a rapidly changing future. But rather than focus only on math and science, we need to broaden our academic experiences so that the skills we develop make us not only employable but also indispensable.

Conclusion recapping points of agreement and disagreement with Friedman and summarizing essay

[New page.]

Work Cited

Friedman, Thomas L. "It's a Flat World, after All." *New York Times Magazine* 3 Apr. 2005: 32–37. Print.

*Work cited in MLA style (see **MLA** p. 445)*

6d Preparing a writing portfolio

Your instructor may ask you to assemble samples of your writing into a portfolio once or more during the course. A portfolio gives you a chance to consider all your writing over a period and to choose the work that best represents you as a writer.

The purposes and requirements for portfolios vary. As you consider what work to include in your portfolio, answer the following questions:

- **What is the purpose of the portfolio?** A portfolio may be intended to showcase your best work, demonstrate progress you have made, or provide examples of your versatility as a writer.
- **What are the requirements of the portfolio?** You may be asked to submit final drafts of your best work; journal entries, notes, early drafts, and a final draft of one or more essays; or projects representing different types of writing—say, one narrative, one critical analysis, one argument, and so on.
- **Is a reflective essay or letter required as part of the portfolio?** Many teachers require an opening essay or letter in which you discuss the portfolio selections, explain why you chose each one, and perhaps evaluate your development as a writer. If a reflective essay is required, be sure you understand its purpose and scope.
- **Should the portfolio be print or electronic, or can you choose the medium?** If you plan to submit your portfolio electronically, be sure you know how to upload your files before the deadline.
- **How will the portfolio be evaluated?** Will it be read by peers, your instructor, or a committee of teachers? Will it be graded?

Unless the guidelines specify otherwise, provide error-free copies of your final drafts and label all your samples with your name before you place them in a folder or upload them as files.

7 Paragraphs

Chapter essentials
- Relate each paragraph to the essay as a whole (next page).
- Unify each paragraph around a central idea (p. 42).
- Make each paragraph coherent (p. 43).
- Develop the central idea of each paragraph (p. 47).
- Create introductory and concluding paragraphs that set up and finish your writing (p. 51).

Visit MyWritingLab™ for more resources on paragraphs.

Paragraphs generally develop the main ideas that support the central idea, or thesis, of a piece of writing, and they break these supporting ideas into manageable chunks. For readers, paragraphs signal the movement between ideas and provide breathers from long stretches of text.

CULTURE LANGUAGE Not all cultures share the paragraphing conventions of American academic writing. In some other languages, writing moves differently on the page from English—not left to right, but right to left or down rows from top to bottom. Even in languages that move as English does on the page, writers may not use paragraphs at all, or they may use paragraphs but not state their central ideas. If your native language is not English and you have difficulty writing paragraphs, don't worry about paragraphing during drafting. Instead, during a separate step of revision, divide your text into parts that develop your main points and mark those parts with indentions.

Checklist for revising paragraphs

- **Does each paragraph contribute to the essay as a whole?** Does each paragraph support the essay's central idea, or thesis? Does it relate to the paragraphs that come before and after it? (See below.)
- **Is each paragraph unified?** Does it adhere to one general idea that is either stated in a topic sentence or otherwise apparent? (See the next page.)
- **Is each paragraph coherent?** Do the sentences follow a clear sequence? Are the sentences linked as needed by parallelism, repetition or restatement, pronouns, consistency, and transitional expressions? (See p. 43.)
- **Is each paragraph developed?** Is the general idea of the paragraph well supported with specific evidence such as details, facts, examples, and reasons? (See p. 47.)

7a Relating paragraphs in the essay

Paragraphs do not stand alone: they are key units of a larger piece of writing. Even if you draft a paragraph separately, it needs to connect to your central idea, or thesis—explaining it and deepening it. Together, paragraphs need to flow from one to the other so that readers easily grasp the points you are making and how each point contributes to the whole essay.

To see how effective body paragraphs work to help both writer and reader, look at the fourth paragraph of Katy Moreno's essay "Can We Compete?" from the previous chapter. Responding to an article by Thomas L. Friedman, Moreno is supporting her thesis that Friedman overlooks the need for technical employees to be good communicators and problem solvers.

The second dimension that Friedman misses is that a number of well-paid people in my mother's IT department, namely IT managers, were not laid off. As my mother explained at the time, they kept their jobs because they were experienced at figuring out the company's IT needs, planning for changes, researching and proposing solutions, and communicating in writing and speech—skills that her more narrow training and experience had missed. Friedman misses these skills by focusing only on technical training. Without the ability to solve problems creatively and to communicate, people with technical expertise alone may not have enough to save their jobs, as my mother learned.

New main point linking to previous paragraph and to thesis

Details to support new point

Concluding sentence summing up paragraph and linking to previous paragraph and to thesis

7b   Maintaining paragraph unity

Just as readers expect paragraphs to relate clearly to an essay's thesis, they also generally expect each paragraph to be **unified**—that is, to develop a single idea. Often this idea is expressed in a **topic sentence**. For an example, look again at the paragraph above by Katy Moreno: the opening statement conveys Moreno's promise that she will explain something lacking in Friedman's argument, and the following sentences keep the promise. But what if Moreno had written the following paragraph instead?

The second dimension that Friedman misses is that a number of well-paid people in my mother's IT department, namely IT managers, were not laid off. As my mother explained at the time, they kept their jobs because they were experienced at figuring out the company's IT needs, planning for changes, researching and proposing solutions, and communicating in writing. Like my mother, these managers had families to support, so they were lucky to keep their jobs. Our family still struggles with the financial and emotional effects of my mother's unemployment.

Topic sentence

Details supporting sentence

Digression

By wandering from the topic of why some managers kept their jobs, this paragraph fails to deliver on the commitment of its topic sentence. The paragraph is not unified.

A topic sentence need not always come first in the paragraph. For instance, it may come last, presenting your idea only after you have provided the evidence for it. Or it may not be stated at all, especially in narrative or descriptive writing in which the point becomes clear in the details. But always the idea should govern the paragraph's content as if it were standing guard at the opening.

7c Achieving paragraph coherence

When a paragraph is **coherent**, readers can see how it holds together: the sentences seem to flow logically and smoothly into one another. Exactly the opposite happens with this paragraph:

> The ancient Egyptians were masters of preserving dead people's bodies by making mummies of them. Mummies several thousand years old have been discovered nearly intact. The skin, hair, teeth, finger- and toenails, and facial features of the mummies were evident. One can diagnose the diseases they suffered in life, such as smallpox, arthritis, and nutritional deficiencies. The process was remarkably effective. Sometimes apparent were the fatal afflictions of the dead people: a middle-aged king died from a blow on the head, and polio killed a child king. Mummification consisted of removing the internal organs, applying natural preservatives inside and out, and then wrapping the body in layers of bandages.

The paragraph is hard to read. The sentences lurch instead of gliding from point to point.

The paragraph as it was actually written appears below. It is much clearer because the writer arranged information differently and also built links into his sentences so that they would flow smoothly:

- After stating the central idea in a topic sentence, the writer moves to two more specific explanations and illustrates the second with four sentences of examples.
- Words in green repeat or restate key terms or concepts.
- Words in orange link sentences and clarify relationships.
- Underlined phrases are in parallel grammatical form to reflect their parallel content.

> The ancient Egyptians were masters of preserving dead people's bodies by making mummies of them. — Topic sentence
>
> Basically, mummification consisted of removing the internal organs, applying natural preservatives inside and out, and then wrapping the body in layers of bandages. And the process was remarkably effective. Indeed, mummies several thousand years old have been discovered nearly intact. — Explanation
>
> Their skin, hair, teeth, finger- and toenails, and facial features are still evident. Their diseases in life, such as smallpox, arthritis, and nutritional deficiencies, are still diagnosable. Even their fatal afflictions are still apparent: a middle-aged king died from a blow on the head; a child king died from polio. — Specific examples
>
> —Mitchell Rosenbaum (student),
> "Lost Arts of the Egyptians"

1 Paragraph organization

A coherent paragraph organizes information so that readers can easily follow along. These are common paragraph schemes:

- **General to specific:** Sentences downshift from more general statements to more specific ones. (See the paragraph by Rosenbaum on the previous page.)
- **Climactic:** Sentences increase in drama or interest, ending in a climax. (See the paragraph beginning below about sleep.)
- **Spatial:** Sentences scan a person, place, or object from top to bottom or in some other way that approximates the way people look at things. (See the paragraph by Woolf on p. 48.)
- **Chronological:** Sentences present events as they occurred in time, earlier to later. (See the paragraph about the common cold beginning on the facing page.)

2 Parallelism

One way to achieve paragraph coherence is through parallelism,° the use of similar grammatical structures for similar elements of meaning within or among sentences. In the next paragraph the underlined parallel structures link all sentences after the first one, and parallelism also appears within many of the sentences (as in *He served . . . , survived . . . , and earned* in sentence 8). The paragraph comes from a student's profile of President Ronald Reagan.

> Ronald Reagan holds a particularly interesting place in American history, combining successful careers in show business and in politics. After graduating from college in 1932, he worked as a radio sports announcer with an affinity for describing game details. He then launched a successful film career, starring in dozens of movies. After a stint in the US Army, he assumed the role of host for *General Electric Theater*, a weekly TV program that ran from 1953 to 1962. He first entered politics by supporting candidates and making speeches in the 1950s and early 1960s. He became governor of California in 1966 and served for eight years. He ran unsuccessfully for the US presidency in 1976 and then won the job in 1980, when he became the fortieth President. He served two terms, survived an assassination attempt, and earned a popularity that most politicians can only envy.
>
> —William Brooks (student), "Ronald Reagan, the Actor President"

3 Repetition and restatement

Repeating or restating key words helps make a paragraph coherent and also reminds readers what the topic is. In the following paragraph note the underlined repetition of *sleep* and the restatement of *adults*.

> Perhaps the simplest fact about sleep is that individual needs for it vary widely. Most adults sleep between seven and nine hours, but occasionally people turn up who need twelve hours or so, while some rare

types can get by on three or four. Rarest of all are those <u>legendary types</u> who require almost no <u>sleep</u> at all; respected researchers have recently studied three <u>such people</u>. One of them—a healthy, happy woman in her seventies—<u>sleeps</u> about an hour every two or three days. The other two are men in early middle age, who get by on a few minutes a night. One of them complains about the daily fifteen minutes or so he's forced to "waste" in <u>sleeping</u>.
—Lawrence A. Mayer, "The Confounding Enemy of Sleep"

4 Pronouns

Pronouns° such as *she, he, it, they,* and *who* refer to and function as nouns. Thus pronouns naturally help relate sentences to each other. In the paragraph on the facing page by William Brooks, *he* works just this way by substituting for *Ronald Reagan*.

5 Consistency

Consistency (or the lack of it) occurs primarily in the person° and number° of nouns and pronouns and in the tense° of verbs. Any inconsistencies not required by meaning will interfere with a reader's ability to follow the development of ideas.

Note the underlined inconsistencies in the next paragraphs:

Shifts in tense

In the Hopi religion, water <u>is</u> the driving force. Since the Hopi <u>lived</u> in the Arizona desert, they <u>needed</u> water urgently for drinking, cooking, and irrigating crops. Their complex beliefs <u>are</u> focused in part on gaining the assistance of supernatural forces in obtaining water. Many of the Hopi kachinas, or spirit essences, <u>were</u> directly concerned with clouds, rain, and snow.

Shifts in number

<u>Kachinas</u> represent the things and events of the real world, such as clouds, mischief, cornmeal, and even death. A <u>kachina</u> is not worshiped as a god but regarded as an interested friend. <u>They</u> visit the Hopi from December through July in the form of men who dress in kachina costumes and perform dances and other rituals.

Shifts in person

Unlike the man, the Hopi <u>woman</u> does not keep contact with kachinas through costumes and dancing. Instead, <u>one</u> receives a small likeness of a kachina, called a *tihu,* from the man impersonating the kachina. <u>You</u> are more likely to receive a tihu as a girl approaching marriage, though a child or older woman may receive one, too.

6 Transitional expressions

Transitional expressions such as *therefore, in contrast,* and *meanwhile* can forge specific connections between sentences, as do the underlined expressions in this paragraph:

Medical science has <u>thus</u> succeeded in identifying the hundreds of viruses that can cause the common cold. It has <u>also</u> discovered the most

°See "Glossary of Terms," **GI** p. 558.

effective means of prevention. One person transmits the cold viruses to another most often by hand. For instance, an infected person covers his mouth to cough. He then picks up the telephone. Half an hour later, his daughter picks up the same telephone. Immediately afterward, she rubs her eyes. Within a few days, she, too, has a cold. And thus it spreads. To avoid colds, therefore, people should wash their hands often and keep their hands away from their faces.

—Kathleen LaFrank (student), "Colds: Myth and Science"

Note that you can use transitional expressions to link paragraphs as well as sentences. In the first sentence of LaFrank's paragraph, the word *thus* signals that the sentence refers to an effect discussed in the preceding paragraph.

The following box lists many transitional expressions by the functions they perform.

Transitional expressions

To add or show sequence
again, also, and, and then, besides, equally important, finally, first, further, furthermore, in addition, in the first place, last, moreover, next, second, still, too

To compare
also, in the same way, likewise, similarly

To contrast
although, and yet, but, but at the same time, despite, even so, even though, for all that, however, in contrast, in spite of, nevertheless, notwithstanding, on the contrary, on the other hand, regardless, still, though, yet

To give examples or intensify
after all, an illustration of, even, for example, for instance, indeed, in fact, it is true, of course, specifically, that is, to illustrate, truly

To indicate place
above, adjacent to, below, elsewhere, farther on, here, near, nearby, on the other side, opposite to, there, to the east, to the left

To indicate time
after a while, afterward, as long as, as soon as, at last, at length, at that time, before, earlier, eventually, formerly, immediately, in the meantime, in the past, later, meanwhile, now, shortly, simultaneously, since, so far, soon, subsequently, suddenly, then, thereafter, until, until now, when

To repeat, summarize, or conclude
all in all, altogether, as has been said, in brief, in conclusion, in other words, in particular, in short, in simpler terms, in summary, on the whole, that is, therefore, to put it differently, to summarize

To show cause or effect
accordingly, as a result, because, consequently, for this purpose, hence, otherwise, since, then, therefore, thereupon, thus, to this end

Note Draw carefully on the list of transitional expressions because the ones in each group are not interchangeable. For instance, *besides, finally,* and *second* may all be used to add information, but each has its own distinct meaning.

(CULTURE LANGUAGE) If transitional expressions are not common in your native language, you may be tempted to compensate when writing in English by adding them to the beginnings of most sentences. But such explicit transitions aren't needed everywhere, and in fact too many can be intrusive and awkward. When inserting transitional expressions, consider the reader's need for a signal: often the connection from sentence to sentence is already clear from the context or can be made clear by relating the content of sentences more closely (see **3** pp. 141–42). When you do need transitional expressions, try varying their positions in your sentences, as illustrated in the sample paragraph by LaFrank on pp. 45–46.

7d Developing paragraphs

An effective, well-developed paragraph always provides the specific information that readers need and expect in order to understand you and to stay interested in what you say. Paragraph length can be a rough gauge of development: anything much shorter than 100 to 150 words may leave readers with a sense of incompleteness.

To develop or shape an idea in a paragraph, one or more of the following patterns may help. (These patterns may also be used to develop entire essays. See p. 14.)

1 Narration

Narration retells a significant sequence of events, usually in the order of their occurrence (that is, chronologically). A narrator is concerned not just with the sequence of events but also with their consequence, their importance to the whole.

> Jill's story is typical for "recruits" to religious cults. She was very lonely in college and appreciated the attention of the nice young men and women who lived in a house near campus. They persuaded her to share their meals and then to move in with them. Between intense bombardments of "love," they deprived her of sleep and sometimes threatened to throw her out. Jill became increasingly confused and dependent, losing touch with any reality besides the one in the group. She dropped out of school and refused to see or communicate with her family. Before long she, too, was preying on lonely college students.
> —Hillary Begas (student), "The Love Bombers"

2 Description

Description details the sensory qualities of a person, scene, thing, or feeling, using concrete and specific words to convey a dominant mood, illustrate an idea, or achieve some other purpose.

The sun struck straight upon the house, making the white walls glare between the dark windows. Their panes, woven thickly with green branches, held circles of impenetrable darkness. Sharp-edged wedges of light lay upon the window-sill and showed inside the room plates with blue rings, cups with curved handles, the bulge of a great bowl, the criss-cross pattern in the rug, and the formidable corners and lines of cabinets and bookcases. Behind their conglomeration hung a zone of shadow in which might be a further shape to be disencumbered of shadow or still denser depths of darkness.   —Virginia Woolf, *The Waves*

3 Illustration or support

An idea may be developed with several specific examples, like those used by William Brooks on p. 44, or with a single extended example, as in the next paragraph:

Teaching teenagers to drive is a nerve-racking job. During his first lesson, one particularly inept student refused to drive faster than ten miles per hour, forcing impatient drivers behind the car to pass on a residential street with a speed limit of twenty-five and cyclists in the bike lanes. Making a left turn at a four-way stop, the student didn't await his turn and nearly collided with an oncoming car. A few moments later, he jumped the curb when turning right and had to slam on the brakes to avoid hitting a concrete barrier. For a driving instructor, every day is an exercise in keeping one's fear and temper in check.

—Jasmine Greer (student)

Sometimes you can develop a paragraph by providing your reasons for stating a general idea. For instance:

There are three reasons, quite apart from scientific considerations, that mankind needs to travel in space. The first reason is the need for garbage disposal: we need to transfer industrial processes into space, so that the earth may remain a green and pleasant place for our grandchildren to live in. The second reason is the need to escape material impoverishment: the resources of this planet are finite, and we shall not forgo forever the abundant solar energy and minerals and living space that are spread out all around us. The third reason is our spiritual need for an open frontier: the ultimate purpose of space travel is to bring to humanity not only scientific discoveries and an occasional spectacular show on television but a real expansion of our spirit.

—Freeman Dyson, "Disturbing the Universe"

4 Definition

Defining a complicated, abstract, or controversial term often requires extended explanation. The following definition of the professional middle class comes from a book about changes in the American middle class:

Before this story [of changes in America's middle class] can be told, I must first introduce its central character, the professional middle class. This class can be defined, somewhat abstractly, as all those people whose economic and social status is based on education, rather than on ownership of capital or property. Most professionals are included, and so are white-collar managers, whose positions require at least a college degree, and increasingly also a graduate degree. Not all white-collar people are included, though; some of these are entrepreneurs who are better classified as "workers." But the professional middle class is still extremely broad, and includes such diverse types as schoolteachers, anchorpersons, engineers, professors, government bureaucrats, corporate executives (at least up through the middle levels of management), scientists, advertising people, therapists, financial managers, architects, and, I should add, myself.

—Barbara Ehrenreich, *Fear of Falling: The Inner Life of the Middle Class*

5 Division or analysis

With division or analysis, you separate something into its elements—for instance, you might divide a newspaper into its sections. You may also approach the elements critically, interpreting their meaning and significance (see **2** pp. 87–88):

Reality TV shows are anything but "real." Participants are selected from thousands of applicants, and they have auditioned to prove themselves to be competent in front of a camera. The settings for the action are often environments created especially for the shows. Scenes that seem unscripted are often planned to capture entertaining footage. The wardrobes of the participants may be designed to enhance participants' "characters" and to improve their looks on camera. And footage is clearly edited to create scenes that seem authentic and tell compelling stories.   —Darrell Carter (student), "(Un)Reality TV"

6 Classification

When you classify items, you sort them into groups. The classification allows you to see and explain the relations among the items. The following paragraph identifies three groups, or classes, of parents:

In my experience, the parents who hire daytime sitters for their school-age children tend to fall into one of three groups. The first group includes parents who work and want someone to be at home when the children return from school. These parents are looking for an extension of themselves, someone who will give the care they would give if they were at home. The second group includes parents who may be home all day themselves but are too disorganized or too frazzled by their children's demands to handle child care alone. They are looking for an organizer and helpmate. The third and final group includes parents who do not want to be bothered by their children, whether they are home all day or not. Unlike the parents in the first two groups, who care for their children however they can, these parents seek a permanent substitute for themselves.   —Nancy Whittle (student), "Modern Parenting"

7 Comparison and contrast

Comparison and contrast may be used separately or together to develop an idea. The following paragraph illustrates one of two common ways of organizing a comparison and contrast: **subject by subject**, first one subject and then the other.

> Consider the differences also in the behavior of rock and classical music audiences. At a rock concert, the audience members yell, whistle, sing along, and stamp their feet. They may even stand during the entire performance. The better the music, the more active they'll be. At a classical concert, in contrast, the better the performance, the more *still* the audience is. Members of the classical audience are so highly disciplined that they refrain from even clearing their throats or coughing. No matter what effect the powerful music has on their intellects and feelings, they sit on their hands.
> —Tony Nahm (student), "Rock and Roll Is Here to Stay"

The next paragraph illustrates the other common organization: **point by point**, with the two subjects discussed side by side and matched feature for feature.

> Arguing is often equated with fighting, but there are key differences between the two. Participants in an argument approach the subject to find common ground, or points on which both sides agree, while people engaged in a fight usually approach the subject with an "us-versus-them" attitude. Participants in an argument are careful to use respectful, polite language, in contrast to the insults and worse that people in a fight use to get the better of their opponents. Finally, participants in an argument commonly have the goal of reaching a new understanding or larger truth about the subject they're debating, while those in a fight have winning as their only goal.
> —Erica Ito (student),"Is an Argument Always a Fight?"

8 Cause-and-effect analysis

When you use analysis to explain why something happened or what did or may happen, then you are determining causes or effects. In the following paragraph the author looks at the cause of an effect— Japanese collectivism:

> The *shinkansen* or "bullet train" speeds across the rural areas of Japan giving a quick view of cluster after cluster of farmhouses surrounded by rice paddies. This particular pattern did not develop purely by chance, but as a consequence of the technology peculiar to the growing of rice, the staple of the Japanese diet. The growing of rice requires the construction and maintenance of an irrigation system, something that takes many hands to build. More importantly, the planting and the harvesting of rice can only be done efficiently with the cooperation of twenty or more people. The "bottom line" is that a single family working alone cannot produce enough rice to survive, but a dozen families working together can produce a surplus. Thus the Japanese have had to develop the capacity to work together in harmony, no matter what the forces of disagreement or social disintegration, in order to survive.
> —William Ouchi, *Theory Z*

9 Process analysis

When you analyze how to do something or how something works, you explain a process. The following example identifies a process, describes the equipment needed, and details the steps in the process:

> As a car owner, you waste money when you pay a mechanic to change the engine oil. The job is not difficult, even if you know little about cars. All you need is a wrench to remove the drain plug, a large, flat pan to collect the draining oil, plastic bottles to dispose of the used oil, and fresh oil. First, warm up the car's engine so that the oil will flow more easily. When the engine is warm, shut it off and remove its oil-filler cap (the owner's manual shows where this cap is). Then locate the drain plug under the engine (again consulting the owner's manual for its location) and place the flat pan under the plug. Remove the plug with the wrench, letting the oil flow into the pan. When the oil stops flowing, replace the plug and, at the engine's filler hole, add the amount and kind of fresh oil specified by the owner's manual. Pour the used oil into the plastic bottles and take it to a waste-oil collector, which any garage mechanic can recommend.
> —Anthony Andreas (student), "Do-It-Yourself Car Care"

7e Writing introductory and concluding paragraphs

1 Introductions

An introduction draws readers from their world into yours.

- It focuses readers' attention on the topic and arouses curiosity about what you have to say.
- It specifies your subject and implies your attitude.
- Often it includes your thesis statement.
- It is concise and sincere.

The box below gives options for focusing readers' attention.

Some strategies for introductions

- Ask a question.
- Relate an incident.
- Use a vivid quotation.
- Create a visual image that represents your subject.
- Offer a surprising statistic or other fact.
- Provide background.
- State an opinion related to your thesis.
- Outline the argument your thesis refutes.
- Make a historical comparison or contrast.
- Outline a problem or dilemma.
- Define a word central to your subject.
- In some business or technical writing, simply state your main idea.

CULTURE LANGUAGE These options for an introduction may not be what you are used to if your native language is not English. In other cultures readers may seek familiarity or reassurance from an author's introduction, or they may prefer an indirect approach to the subject. In academic and business English, however, writers and readers prefer concise, direct expression.

Effective openings

A very common introduction opens with a statement of the essay's general subject, clarifies or limits the subject in one or more sentences, and then asserts the point of the essay in the thesis statement (underlined in the following examples):

> Watching television wastes time, destroys brain cells, contributes to obesity, and can even turn viewers violent. These attitudes are supported by serious research as well as popular belief. However, television watching can actually benefit some people. It provides replacement voices that can ease the loneliness of viewers, spark their healthful laughter, and even teach young children.
>
> —Craig Holbrook, "TV Can Be Good for You"

> The Declaration of Independence is so widely regarded as a statement of American ideals that its origins in practical politics tend to be forgotten. Thomas Jefferson's draft was intensely debated and then revised in the Continental Congress. Jefferson was disappointed with the result. However, a close reading of both the historical context and the revisions themselves indicates that the Congress improved the document for its intended purpose.
>
> —Ann Weiss (student), "The Editing of the Declaration of Independence"

In much public writing, it's more important to tell readers immediately what your point is than to try to engage them. This introduction to a brief memo quickly outlines a problem and (in the thesis statement) suggests a way to solve it:

> Starting next month, the holiday rush and staff vacations will leave our department short-handed. We need to hire two or perhaps three temporary keyboarders to maintain our schedules for the month.

Additional effective introductions appear in sample papers in this book: pp. 23 and 38, **2** pp. 98 and 113, **8** p. 420, and **MLA** p. 482.

Openings to avoid

When writing and revising your introduction, avoid approaches that are likely to bore or confuse readers:

- **A vague generality or truth.** Don't extend your reach too wide with a line such as *Throughout human history . . .* or *In today's world. . . .* You may have needed a warm-up paragraph to start drafting, but your readers can do without it.

- **A flat announcement.** Don't start with *The purpose of this essay is . . .*, *In this essay I will . . .*, or any similar presentation of your intention or topic.
- **A reference to the essay's title.** Don't refer to the title of the essay in the first sentence—for example, *This is a big problem* or *This book is about the history of the guitar.*
- **According to Webster. . . .** Don't start by citing a dictionary definition. A definition can be an effective springboard to an essay, but this kind of lead-in has become dull with overuse.
- **An apology.** Don't fault your opinion or your knowledge with *I'm not sure if I'm right, but I think . . . , I don't know much about this, but . . .*, or a similar line.

2 Conclusions

Your conclusion finishes off your essay and tells readers where you think you have brought them. It answers the question "So what?"

Effective conclusions

Usually set off in its own paragraph, the conclusion may consist of a single sentence or a group of sentences. It may take one or more of the approaches listed in the following box.

Some strategies for conclusions

- Recommend a course of action.
- Summarize the paper.
- Echo the approach of the introduction.
- Restate your thesis and reflect on its implications.
- Strike a note of hope or despair.
- Give a symbolic or powerful fact or other detail.
- Give an especially compelling example.
- Create an image that represents your subject.
- Use a quotation.

The following paragraph concludes the essay on the Declaration of Independence whose introduction appears on the previous page. The writer both summarizes her essay and echoes her introduction.

> The Declaration of Independence has come to be a statement of this nation's political philosophy, but that was not its purpose in 1776. Jefferson's passionate expression had to bow to the goals of the Congress as a whole to forge unity among the colonies and to win the support of foreign nations.
>
> —Ann Weiss (student), "The Editing of the Declaration of Independence"

In the next paragraph the author concludes an essay on environmental protection with a call for action:

> Until we get the answers, I think we had better keep on building power plants and growing food with the help of fertilizers and such

insect-controlling chemicals as we now have. The risks are well known, thanks to the environmentalists. If they had not created a widespread public awareness of the ecological crisis, we wouldn't stand a chance. But such awareness by itself is not enough. Flaming manifestos and prophecies of doom are no longer much help, and a search for scapegoats can only make matters worse. The time for sensations and manifestos is about over. Now we need rigorous analysis, united effort and very hard work.

—Peter F. Drucker, "How Best to Protect the Environment"

Conclusions to avoid

Several kinds of conclusions rarely work well:

- **A repeat of the introduction.** Don't simply replay your introduction. The conclusion should capture what the paragraphs of the body have added to the introduction.
- **A new direction.** Don't introduce a subject that is different from the one your essay has been about.
- **A sweeping generalization.** Don't conclude more than you reasonably can from your evidence. If your essay is about your frustrating experience trying to clear a parking ticket, you cannot reasonably conclude that *all* local police forces are too tied up in red tape to be of service to the people.
- **An apology.** Don't cast doubt on your essay. Don't say, *Even though I'm no expert* or *This may not be convincing, but I believe it's true* or anything similar. Rather, to win your readers' confidence, display confidence.

8 Presenting Writing

Chapter essentials

- Follow the document format of the discipline you are writing in (facing page).
- Use visuals and other media appropriately in multimodal writing (p. 57).
- Consider design when writing for the Web (p. 62).

Visit MyWritingLab™ for more resources on presenting writing.

Presenting your writing gives you an opportunity to display your hard work in the best possible light. Most of the time, presenting writing also involves challenges: to fulfill the requirements of the assignment, the conventions of the genre, and the expectations of your audience.

8a | Formatting academic writing

Many of the assignments you receive in college will require you to submit a written text either on paper or electronically—for instance, attached to an e-mail or uploaded to a course Web site. For most print papers and files of papers, the example below shows a basic format that will help make your writing attractive and readable.

Many academic style guides recommend specific formats. This book details two such formats:

- **MLA style,** used in English, foreign languages, and some other humanities (**MLA** pp. 478–80).
- **APA style,** used in the social sciences (**APA** pp. 512–15).

Sample paper in MLA format

Torres 1

Mia Torres
Mr. O'Donnell
English 131
14 March 2014

Creating the Next Generation of Smokers

    Parents warn their children not to smoke. Schools teach kids and teens about the dangers of smoking. States across the country have enacted smoking bans, making it illegal for adults to smoke in restaurants, bars, workplaces, and public buildings. Yet despite these efforts, smoking among teens and young adults continues, and it does so in part because the film industry creates movies that promote smoking.

    According to the organization Smoke Free Movies, a group based in the School of Medicine at the University of California, San Francisco, tobacco companies and filmmakers collaborate to promote smoking: tobacco companies pay filmmakers to feature their products, and filmmakers show celebrity actors smoking in movies and portray smoking as glamorous and socially acceptable (4-5). Stopping young people's exposure to images of smoking in movies requires stopping each of these activities.

    Despite proof that showing smoking in movies encourages young people to start smoking, more than half of movies feature well-known stars smoking (Fox). As fig. 1 shows, cigarettes often figure prominently, with the cigarette held close to the celebrity's head so that it is an integral part of the shot.

Fig. 1. The actress Scarlett Johansson in *Black Dahlia*, one of many movies released each year in which characters smoke. From *Daily Mail*; Associated Newspapers, 2006; Web; 9 Mar. 2014.

Annotations:
- Writer's last name and page number.
- Identification: writer's name, instructor's name, course title, date.
- Title centered.
- Double-spaced throughout.
- 1" margins on top, bottom, and sides.
- Indentions marking paragraph breaks.
- Source citation in MLA style (see **MLA** p. 436).
- Photograph introduced to indicate its meaning and purpose.
- Caption allowing photograph to be read independently from the text.

Considering readers with vision loss

If your audience may include readers who have low vision, problems with color perception, or difficulties processing visual information, adapt your design to meet these readers' needs:

- **Use large type fonts.** Most guidelines call for 14 points or larger.
- **Use standard type fonts.** Many people with low vision find it easier to read sans serif fonts such as Arial than serif fonts. Avoid decorative fonts with unusual flourishes, even in headings.
- **Avoid words in all-capital letters.**
- **Avoid relying on color alone to distinguish elements.** Label elements, and distinguish them by position or size.
- **Use red and green selectively.** To readers who are red-green colorblind, these colors will appear in shades of gray, yellow, or blue.
- **Use contrasting colors.** To make colors distinct, choose them from opposite sides of the color spectrum—violet and yellow, for instance, or orange and blue.
- **Use only light colors for tints behind type.** Make the type itself black or a very dark color.

Although they do vary, most academic formats share preferences for the design of standard elements:

- **Margins:** minimum one inch on all sides.
- **Line spacing:** double-spaced throughout.
- **Type fonts and sizes:** standard 10- or 12-point fonts such as Times New Roman and Cambria (serif fonts, with small lines finishing the letters) or Arial and Calibri (sans serif fonts, lacking the small lines). Serif fonts are generally easier to read on paper, while sans serif fonts are easier to read on a screen.
- **Highlighting:** underlining, *italics*, or **boldface** to mark headings and emphasize text elements such as terms being defined.
- **Headings:** one or two levels as needed to direct readers' attention to significant ideas and transitions. Word headings consistently —for instance, all questions (*What Is Sustainability?*) or all phrases with -*ing* words (*Understanding Sustainability*). Indicate the relative importance of headings with highlighting and position—perhaps bold for first-level headings and lightface italic for second-level headings. (Document format in psychology and some other social sciences requires a particular treatment of headings. See **APA** pp. 514–15.)
- **Lists:** numbered or bulleted (as in the list you're reading), to show the relationship of like items, such as the elements of a document or the steps in a process or proposal.
- **Color:** mainly for illustrations, occasionally for headings, bullets, and other elements. Always use black for the text of a paper, and make sure that any other colors are dark enough to be legible.

8b Using visuals and other media in multimodal writing

Academic writing is often **multimodal**—that is, it includes more than one medium, whether text, charts, photographs, video, or audio. A simple multimodal paper involves just two media—mainly text with some illustrations embedded in the text. A paper submitted online might add links to audio or video files as well. This section provides tips for selecting and using such media in your writing. The next section treats media in Web compositions, blogs, and wikis.

Caution **Any visual or media file you include or link to in your writing requires the same detailed citation as a written source.** See **7** pp. 400–05 for more on acknowledging sources.

1 Selecting visuals and other media

Depending on your writing situation, you might use anything from a table to a bar chart to a video to support your writing. The following pages describe and illustrate the options.

Note The Web is an excellent resource for images, audio, and video (see **7** pp. 370–72). Your computer may include a program for creating illustrations, or you can work with specialized software such as *Excel* (for graphs and charts) or *Adobe Illustrator* (for diagrams, maps, and the like). Use *PowerPoint, Prezi,* or a similar program for visuals in oral presentations (see **2** pp. 123–25).

Selecting visuals

Visuals can be placed in print or electronic documents. They include tables, pie charts, bar charts, line graphs, infographics, diagrams, flowcharts, and images such as photographs, maps, fine art, advertisements, and cartoons. (See the box on the next two pages.)

Selecting video and audio

You can use video or audio files to emphasize or support points in digital writing, such as Web pages or blogs, and in oral presentations. For example, you might explain a process with a video of how something works, support an interpretation of a play with a video of a scene from a performance, or illustrate a profile of a person by linking to a podcast interview. The screen shot on p. 60 shows a passage of text from an online paper that links to video of the poet Rita Dove reading her poem "American Smooth."

2 Using visuals and other media effectively

An image or a video clip can attract readers' attention, but if it does no more it will amount to mere decoration or, worse, it will detract from the substance of your writing. Before using any type of media, consider whether it meets the requirements of your assignment, serves a purpose, and is appropriate for your audience.

(continued on p. 60)

Selecting visuals

Tables

Tables present raw data to show how variables relate to one another or how two or more groups contrast. Place a descriptive title above the table, and use headings to label rows and columns.

Table 1

Public- and private-school enrollment of US students, 2013

	Number of students (in thousands)	Percentage in public school	Percentage in private school
All students	74,603	85	15
Kindergarten through grade 8	39,179	88	12
Grades 9-12	16,332	92	8

Source: Data from *Digest of Education Statistics: 2013*; Natl. Center for Educ. Statistics, Apr. 2014; Web; 10 May 2014; table 2.

Diagrams and flowcharts

Diagrams show concepts visually, such as the structure of an organization or the way something works or looks.

Fig. 4. *MyPlate,* a graphic representation of daily food portions recommended for a healthy diet. From *ChooseMyPlate.gov;* US Dept. of Agriculture, 2011; Web; 8 July 2014.

Images

Photographs, maps, paintings, advertisements, and cartoons can be the focus of critical analysis or can support points you make.

Fig. 5. View of Saturn from the *Cassini* spacecraft, showing the planet and its rings. From *Cassini-Huygens: Mission to Saturn and Titan;* US Natl. Atmospheric and Space Administration, Jet Propulsion Laboratory, 24 Feb. 2005; Web; 26 June 2014.

Pie charts

Pie charts show the relations among the parts of a whole, adding up to 100%. Use a pie chart to show shares of data. Label each pie slice, and make it proportional to its share of the whole.

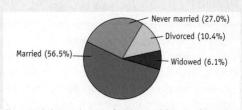

Fig. 1. Marital status in 2013 of adults age eighteen and over. Data from *2013 Statistical Abstract*; US Census Bureau, Jan. 2014; Web; 26 Feb. 2014.

Bar charts

Bar charts compare groups or time periods. Use a bar chart when relative size is important. On the vertical scale, start with a zero point in the lower left and label the values being measured. On the horizontal scale, label the groups being compared.

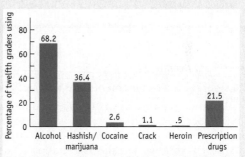

Fig. 2. Lifetime prevalence of use of alcohol, compared with other drugs, among twelfth graders in 2013. Data from *Monitoring the Future: A Continuing Study of American Youth*; U of Michigan, 3 Feb. 2013; Web; 16 Mar. 2014.

Line graphs

Line graphs compare many points of data to show change over time. On the vertical scale, start with a zero point in the lower left and label the values being measured. On the horizontal scale, label the range of dates. Label the data lines, and distinguish them with color, dots, or dashes.

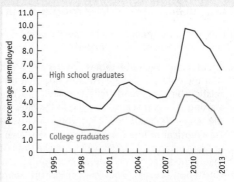

Fig. 3. Unemployment rates of high school graduates and college graduates, 1995-2013. Data from *Economics News Release*; US Dept. of Labor, Bureau of Labor Statistics, 7 Oct. 2013; Web; 6 June 2014.

Link to video file

Often a reading by the poet reinforces both the sound and the meaning of the poem. In Rita Dove's "American Smooth," two people move self-consciously through an intricate dance, smiling and holding their bodies just so, when suddenly they experience a moment of perfection: they nearly float. When Dove reads the poem aloud, she builds to that moment, allowing listeners to feel the same magic (http://www.poetryfoundation.org/features/video/267).

(continued from p. 57)

Considering the requirements and limits of your writing situation

What do the type of writing you're doing and its format allow? Look through examples of similar writing to gauge the kinds of media, if any, that your readers will expect. It matters, too, how you will present your work: a short animation sequence might be terrific in a *PowerPoint* presentation or on the Web, but a printed document requires photographs, drawings, and other static means of explanation.

Using visuals and other media responsibly

Visuals and other media require special care to avoid distortion and to ensure honest use of others' material.

- **Create and evaluate tables, charts, and graphs carefully.** Verify that the data you use are accurate and that the highlighted changes, relationships, or trends reflect reality. In a line graph, for instance, starting the vertical axis at zero puts the lines in context (see the sample on p. 59). See **2** pp. 111–13 on misrepresentations in visuals.
- **Be skeptical of images you find on the Web.** Altered photographs are posted and circulated widely on the Web. If a photograph seems inauthentic, check into its source or don't use it.
- **Cite your sources.** You must credit the source whenever you use someone else's data to create a visual, embed someone else's visual in your document, or link to someone else's media file. See the examples on page 62.
- **Obtain permission if it is required.** For projects that will reside on the Web, you may need to clear permission from the copyright holder of a visual or a media file. See **7** p. 407 for a discussion of copyright and permission.

Making visuals and other media support your writing

Ensure that any visual you use relates directly to a point in your writing, adds to that point, and gives your audience something to think about. In an evaluation of an advertisement, the ad itself would support the claim you make about it. In a paper arguing for earthquake preparedness, a photograph could show earthquake damage and a chart could show levels of current preparedness.

The two images below supported a paper with this thesis: *By the mid-1960s, depictions of women in advertising reflected changing attitudes toward the traditional role of homemaker.*

Visuals as support

| Visual examples support the thesis about changing attitudes toward women as homemakers. | Caption explains the visuals, tying them to the text of the paper and providing source information. |

Fig. 1. An advertisement from 1945 (left) and a brochure from 1965 (right) showing a change in the relationship between homemaking women and their appliances. Left: Hoover advertisement; 1945; print. Right: *Electric Ranges by Frigidaire*; 1965; print.

Integrating visuals and other media into your writing

Readers should understand why you are including visuals or other media in your writing and how they relate to the overall project:

- **In projects with embedded visuals, connect the visuals to your text.** Refer to the visuals at the point(s) where readers will benefit from consulting them—for instance, "See fig. 2" or "See table 1." Number figures and tables separately (Fig. 1, Fig. 2, and so on; Table 1, Table 2, and so on). And always include a title above a table and a caption under a visual (see the next page).

- **In online projects using audio or video, work the files or links into your text.** Your audience should know what you intend the media to show, whether you link to a photograph from a mainly text document or you integrate text, sound, still images, and video into a complex Web project.

Writing captions and source notes

For a figure such as a chart, graph, or diagram, always provide a caption that performs two functions: it ties a visual to your text so that readers don't have to puzzle out your intention; and it cites the source of the data or the entire visual. For examples in MLA style, see the captions below and with the appliance ads on the previous page. Other styles use slightly different formats for captions and source information.

Figure caption (MLA style)

Fig. 1. Marital status in 2013 of adults age eighteen and over. Data from *2014 Statistical Abstract*; US Census Bureau, Jan. 2014; Web; 26 Sept. 2014.

For a table, provide a title on top that tells readers what the content shows, and then give a note at the bottom that cites the source.

Table title (MLA style)

Table 1
Public- and private-school enrollment of US students, 2013

Table source note (MLA style)

Source: Data from *Digest of Education Statistics: 2013*; Natl. Center for Educ. Statistics, Apr. 2014; Web; 10 Oct. 2014; table 2.

8c Presenting writing on the Web

Many creators of Web-based projects upload files into existing forms that make design fairly easy. Even if you choose to use such software, you will still have to make choices about elements such as fonts, colors, layout, headings, and so on. The design guidelines for academic writing on pp. 55–56 can help you with such decisions, as can the following discussion of academic Web compositions such as a Web site or a multimodal project posted on a blog or wiki.

1 Conceiving a Web composition

Whether you are developing a Web site or preparing a digital composition to be posted on the Web, the following general guidelines will help you plan your project:

- **Consider how design can reflect your purpose and your sense of audience.** Type fonts and sizes, headings, visuals and other media, background colors, and other design elements can connect with readers and further the purpose of your writing.
- **Anticipate how readers will move within your composition.** A digital document with links to other pages, posts, Web sites, and

media can disorient readers as they scroll up and down and pursue various links. Page length, links, menus, and other cues should work to keep readers oriented.

- **Imagine what readers may see on their screens.** Each reader's screen frames and organizes the experience of reading online. Screen space is limited, and it varies widely. Text and visual elements should be managed for maximum clarity and effectiveness on a variety of screens.
- **Integrate visuals, audio, and video into the text.** Web compositions will likely include visuals such as charts and photographs as well as video (such as animation or film clips) and audio (such as music or excerpts from interviews). Any visual or sound element should add essential information that can't be provided otherwise, and it should be well integrated with the rest of your composition. See pp. 57–62 for tips on using media effectively.
- **Acknowledge your sources.** It's easy to incorporate text, visuals, audio, and video from other sources into a Web composition, but you have the same obligation to cite your sources as you do in a printed document. (See **7** pp. 400–05 on citing sources.) Your Web composition is a form of publication, like a magazine or a book. Unless the material you are using explicitly allows copying without permission, you may need to seek the copyright holder's permission, just as print publishers do. (See **7** p. 407 for more on copyright.)

Note If you anticipate that some of your readers may have visual, hearing, or reading disabilities, you'll need to consider their needs while designing writing that will appear on a screen. Some of these considerations are covered on p. 56, and others are fundamental to any effective Web-based design, as discussed in this section. In addition, avoid any content that relies exclusively on visuals or sound, instead supplementing such elements with text descriptions. At the same time, try to provide key concepts in words as well as in visuals and sound. For more on Web design for readers with disabilities, visit the World Wide Web Consortium at *www.w3.org/WAI.*

2 Creating a Web site

Traditional printed documents are intended to be read page by page in sequence. In contrast, Web sites are intended to be examined in whatever order readers choose as they follow links to pages within a site and to other sites. The diagram on the next page shows a schematic Web site, with pages at different levels (orange and then blue squares) interconnecting with the home page and with one another.

While reading Web sites, readers generally alternate between skimming pages for highlights and focusing intently on one section of text. To facilitate this kind of reading, you'll want to consider the

Web site organization

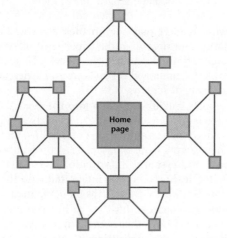

guidelines on the previous two pages and also the site's structure and content, flow, and ease of navigation.

Structure and content

Organize a Web site so that it efficiently arranges your content and also orients readers:

- **Sketch possible site plans before getting started.** A diagram like the one above can help you develop the major components of your project and create a logical space for each component.
- **Consider how menus can provide overviews of the organization as well as direct access to the linked content.** The Web site shown on the next page includes a menu near the top of the page.
- **Treat the first few sentences of any page as a get-acquainted space for you and your readers.** In the sample Web site on the next page, the text hooks readers with questions and orients them with general information.
- **Distill your text so that it includes only essential information.** Concise prose is essential in any writing situation, of course, but readers of Web sites expect to scan text quickly.

Flow

Take advantage of the Web's visual nature by thinking about how information will flow on each page:

- **Standardize elements of your design to create expectations in readers and to fulfill those expectations.** For instance, develop a uniform style for the main headings of pages, for headings within pages, and for menus.

Web site home page

This week's tutoring schedule

Extended drop-in hours

This month's featured book

Annual Awards Dinner: May 23

Meet our new tutors

Tutor and student of the month

ReadingWorks

Springfield VA Hospital

HOME   ABOUT US   PROJECTS   PUBLICATIONS   MEDIA   PARTNERS   LINKS   CONTACT US

Welcome to ReadingWorks!

Do you know a veteran who needs help with reading and writing?

Do you need to improve your reading and writing skills to get a job?

ReadingWorks of Springfield VA Hospital can make a difference. Volunteer tutors help military veterans achieve literacy and prepare them for lifelong learning.

Search box allowing users to search site.

Banner identifying sponsoring organization.

Menu providing overview of the site's organization and content.

Introductory text appealing to readers' interests.

Menu linking to information that changes regularly.

■ **Make scanning easy for readers.** Focus readers on crucial text by adding space around it. Add headings to break up text and to highlight content. Use lists to reinforce the parallel importance of items. (See p. 56 for more on design elements.)

Navigation

Provide a menu so that readers can navigate your Web site. Like the table of contents in a book, a menu lists the features of a site, giving its plan at a glance.

You can embed a menu at the top, side, or bottom of a page— or use more than one position. Menus at the top or side allow readers to move around the site without having to read the full home page. Menus at the bottom prevent readers from dead-ending—that is, reaching a point where they can't easily move forward or backward.

In designing a menu, keep it simple: many different type fonts and colors will overwhelm readers instead of orienting them. And make your menus look the same from one page to the next so that readers recognize them easily.

3 Posting to a blog or a wiki

Blogs and wikis are Web sites that allow users to post text and media such as images and video. Unlike other Web sites, which are generally designed to provide information, blogs and wikis encourage interaction: readers can comment on blog posts or, on a wiki, contribute to posts and collaborate on documents. The illustration below shows a student's post (a personal essay) on his class blog.

You may create a blog or a wiki as an academic assignment, in which case you will need to make decisions about the appearance of the site as a whole. For most academic blog or wiki writing, however, you will post drafts of your papers and comment on your classmates' work. You can compose and edit your text in your word processor and paste the text into the blog or wiki. At that point, you'll have the opportunity to write a descriptive title for your post, upload images and other media, and add links to other Web sites. You can also preview the post before making it public.

Literacy narrative posted to a blog

FRIDAY, FEBRUARY 21, 2014
Literacy narrative draft

Comics: Telling Stories in Words and Art

For my seventh birthday, I received a Calvin and Hobbes comic book. I devoured the book, reading it cover to cover countless times, and was instantly attracted to how drawings and words worked together to tell very funny stories about the characters. I didn't always understand the vocabulary, the jokes, and references to the 1980s, but I laughed at what I did get: the funny arguments, crazy games, and hilarious schemes.

The summer after my birthday I began drawing my own comics. I created two characters modeled on Calvin and Hobbes—a boy named Timmy and his dog Snuffy. Over the next five years, I drew hundreds of comics about Timmy, Snuffy, and Timmy's family and friends. I drew the strip shown here, about one of Timmy's many mishaps, when I was ten. I have this strip and some of my other favorites posted on my personal blog: johnsdoodles @blogger.com.

Descriptive title providing context for the post.

Standard font for readability.

Embedded link to another Web site.

Illustration supporting a point in the post.

Timmy experienced much of what I did over the next several years. He went on vacation to places I visited with my family, like New York and San Francisco. He visited aunts, uncles, and grandparents. He exasperated his parents, annoyed his sister, learned to play an instrument, and dreamed of being a pilot. He also did things I had not experienced: he once trained for the school marathon and came in third, dreamed of going to the prom like his sister, and slid down what seemed like a mile-long hill on a sled. Through Timmy, I used language and drawing to explore ideas, dreams, experiences, and feelings, all the time trying to make them funny.

Although I still draw and write, I left Timmy behind the summer I turned twelve. However, occasionally I look back at my Timmy comics and find it interesting to see how I used words and images to develop and display my sense of place in the world.

Posted by John Heywood at 4:23 PM.

Writing in and out of College

Writing in and out of College

9 Academic Writing

Chapter essentials

- Analyze the purpose and audience in each writing situation (below).
- Use an appropriate academic genre (next page).
- Choose appropriate structure and content (p. 73).
- Use sources with integrity (p. 74).
- Use academic language (p. 76).
- Communicate effectively with instructors and classmates (p. 79).

Visit MyWritingLab™ for more resources on academic writing.

When you take college courses, you enter a community of teachers and students whose basic goal is to share and build knowledge about a subject, whether it is English, history, engineering, or something else. You participate in this community by studying each subject, by asking questions, and by communicating your answers in writing. This chapter gives you ways to approach academic-writing situations and make a contribution to knowledge building.

9a Determining purpose and audience

Like any writing, academic writing occurs in a particular situation created by your assignment and by your subject, purpose, audience, and genre. The assignment and subject will be different for each project, but some generalizations can be made about the other elements. (If you haven't already done so, read **1** pp. 3–9 on writing situations and their elements.)

1 Purpose

For most academic writing, your general purpose will be mainly explanatory or mainly argumentative. That is, you will aim to clarify your subject by analyzing, describing, or reporting on it so that readers understand it as you do; or you will aim to gain readers' agreement with a debatable idea about the subject. (See **1** pp. 6–7 for more on general purposes and pp. 104–13 for more on argument.)

Your specific purpose—including your subject and how you hope readers will respond—depends on the genre, the kind of writing that you're doing. (See the next page.) For instance, in a literature review for a biology class, you want readers to understand the research area you're covering, the recent contributions made by researchers, the issues needing further research, and the sources you consulted. Not coincidentally, these topics correspond to the major sections of a literature review. In following the standard format, you both help to define your purpose and begin to meet the discipline's (and thus your instructor's) expectations.

Your specific purpose will be more complex as well. You take a course to learn about a subject and the ways experts think about it. Your writing, in return, contributes to the discipline through the knowledge you uncover and the lens of your perspective. At the same time, as a student you want to demonstrate your competence with research, evidence, format, and other requirements of the discipline.

2 Audience

Many academic writing assignments will specify or assume an educated audience or an academic audience. Such readers look for writing that is clear, balanced, well organized, and well reasoned. Other assignments will specify or assume an audience of experts on your subject, readers who look in addition for writing that meets the subject's requirements for claims and evidence, organization, language, format, and other qualities.

Much of your academic writing will have only one reader besides you: the instructor of the course for which you are writing. Instructors fill two main roles as readers:

- **They represent the audience you are addressing.** They may actually be members of the audience, as when you address academic readers or subject experts. Or they may imagine themselves as members of your audience—reading, for instance, as if they sat on the city council. In either case, they're interested in how effectively you write for the audience.
- **They serve as coaches,** guiding you toward achieving the goals of the course and, more broadly, toward the academic aims of building and communicating knowledge.

Like everyone else, instructors have preferences and peeves, but you'll waste time and energy trying to anticipate them. Do attend to written and spoken directions for assignments, of course. But otherwise view your instructors as representatives of the community you are writing for. Their responses will be guided by the community's aims and expectations and by a desire to teach you about them.

9b Using an academic genre

Many academic writing assignments will suggest the genre in which you are to write—the kind of writing and/or the format. Sometimes the genre is prescribed, such as the literature review mentioned earlier, with its standard content and format. Other assignments imply the genre, such as those that ask you to analyze, explain, compare, and argue. In these cases your responses would most likely be conventional academic essays—introduction, thesis statement, supporting paragraphs, conclusion—that analyze and compare in order to explain or argue.

Whether genre is specified or implied in your assignment, you are being asked to demonstrate your ability to write competently in that genre. The descriptions below and on the following pages discuss genres commonly assigned in college courses and point out examples that appear elsewhere in this book. In addition, Chapter 12 explains the special requirements of essay exams, and Chapter 14 contains examples of genres used in public writing: application letter and résumé, memo, report, proposal, social-media post, and newsletter.

1 Responses to texts or visuals

Responses to texts or visuals involve close reading, summary, and analysis. For more on analyzing and responding to texts and visuals, see Chapter 10.

- **Personal response to a reading:** Use your own experiences, observations, and opinions to explain how and why you agree or disagree (or both) with the author's argument. A personal-response essay usually includes a thesis statement that conveys the essence of your response, a brief summary of the author's main points, and your own main points of agreement or disagreement. (See **1** pp. 38–39 for a response to a reading.)
- **Critical analysis (critique) of a text or a visual:** Closely examine a text or visual, identifying and describing important elements of the work and analyzing how the elements contribute to the whole. Often a critical analysis, or critique, also includes evaluation of the quality and significance of the work. The genre contains an arguable thesis stating your interpretation, a brief summary or description of the work, and examples from the text or visual as support for your thesis and main points. (See pp. 97–99 for a critique of an essay.)
- **Literary analysis:** Argue for an interpretation of a work based on careful reading, giving particular attention to the work's language, structure, meaning, and themes. In a literary analysis, you state your interpretation in a thesis and then support your thesis with examples from the work. Some literary analyses draw on others' views and information, such as a scholar's interpretation of the work or facts about the author's life. (See **8** pp. 420–22 for a literary analysis that draws on such secondary sources.)

2 Arguments

Argument seeks to persuade readers, moving them to action or convincing them to think as you do. Written arguments contain an arguable thesis statement—a claim reasonable people can disagree over—usually with support for its main points and acknowledgment of opposing views. Arguments often involve research, but not always. For a detailed discussion of writing arguments, see Chapter 11.

- **Proposal argument:** Define a problem, give a solution, explain how the solution can be implemented, and respond to possible objections to the solution. (See pp. 113–16 and **7** pp. 482–90 for two proposal arguments that involve research.)
- **Position argument:** Seek to convince readers to agree with your position on a debatable issue such as lowering the drinking age or requiring military service. A position argument introduces the issue, conveys your position in a thesis statement, makes claims and gives evidence to support your position, and responds to views opposed to your own. Depending on the assignment, evidence may be personal or gathered from research or both. (A type of position argument is literary analysis, described on the previous page, in which you make a case for your interpretation of a work of literature. See **8** pp. 420–22 for an example.)
- **Evaluation argument:** Judge whether something is good or effective. A common type of evaluation argument is a critical analysis of a text or visual, described on the previous page. (See pp. 97–99 for an evaluation of a text.) Reviews of books, movies, exhibits, and so on are also evaluation arguments.

3 | Informative writing

Informative writing seeks to teach readers about a subject. When you write to inform, you explore a subject in depth and provide information that readers may not know. Informative writing often, but not always, involves research. In the social, natural, and applied sciences, informative writing can include summaries and case studies in addition to research-based writing.

- **Informative essay:** Explain a subject such as a situation or a process. Typically, an informative essay begins with an introduction and a thesis statement that previews your major points. Then the body paragraphs support the thesis with evidence. Depending on the assignment, an informative essay may focus on a nonpersonal subject (see the essay in **1** pp. 22–23 on money in college football), or it may arise from personal experience and thus overlap the personal essay (see below).
- **Informative research paper or report:** Draw on research to explain a subject, answer a question, or describe the results of a survey or an experiment. This genre includes research papers, research reports, and laboratory reports, all described on the facing page. (See **8** pp. 516–20 for a sample research report.)

4 | Personal writing

A personal essay often narrates the writer's experience or describes a person or place, usually in vivid detail. What makes a personal essay interesting is the insight the writer provides, showing why the subject is significant to the writer and to readers.

A literacy narrative is a particular kind of personal story: your experience with learning to read and/or write. (See **1** p. 66 for a student's literacy narrative.)

5 Research papers and reports

Most research projects involve reporting information or results, interpreting a range of views on a topic, or analyzing a problem and arguing for a solution.

- **Research paper:** Develop an informative or argumentative thesis statement, draw on and cite multiple sources to support the thesis, and emphasize synthesis of your sources' views and data from your own perspective. (See **7** pp. 482–90 for a sample research paper.)
- **Research report:** Explain your own original research or your attempt to replicate someone else's research. A research report generally includes an abstract (or summary), an introduction describing your research and reviewing prior research on the subject, a description of methods, the results, discussion of the results, and a list of any sources you have cited. (See **8** pp. 516–20 for a research report.)

9c Choosing structure and content

Academic writing assignments vary widely, of course, but they tend to share the following key goals. Each goal is discussed in more detail on the pages cited.

- **Develop a main point in your writing.** Most academic papers center on a main point, or thesis, and support that thesis with evidence. Depending on the genre you are writing in, the main point may be an opinion, a summary of findings, or a conclusion based on primary research you have conducted, such as an experiment or a survey. (For more on thesis statements, see **1** pp. 14–17.)
- **Support the main point with evidence, drawn usually from your reading, personal experience, or primary research.** The kinds of evidence you use will depend on the discipline you're writing in and the type of paper you're doing. For more on evidence, see p. 102 (argument) and **8** pp. 418 (literature) and 423, 425, and 428 (other disciplines).
- **Synthesize your own and others' ideas.** College writing often involves researching and interacting with the works of other writers—being open to their ideas, responding to them, questioning them, comparing them, and using them to answer

questions. Such interaction requires you to read critically (the subject of the next chapter) and to synthesize, or integrate, others' ideas into your own. For more on synthesis in academic writing, see pp. 96–97 and **7** pp. 387–89.

- **Use academic language.** Unless your instructor specifies otherwise, choose formal, standard English. (For more on academic language, see pp. 76–78 and also **3** pp. 156–62.)
- **Acknowledge sources fully, including online sources.** Academic writers build on the work of others by citing borrowed ideas and information. Always record the publication information for your sources, put other writers' words in quotation marks, and cite the source of every quotation, paraphrase, and summary. *Not* acknowledging sources is plagiarism. See the following section and **7** (Chapters 52–54) for more on using and acknowledging sources.
- **Organize clearly within the framework of the type of writing you're doing.** Develop your ideas as simply and directly as your purpose and content allow. Relate sentences, paragraphs, and sections clearly so that readers always know where they are in the paper's development.

CULTURE LANGUAGE These features of academic writing are not universal. In some cultures academic writing may be indirect, may assume that readers will discover the thesis, or may be based only on well-known sources whose ideas are closely adhered to. In US colleges and universities, students are expected to look for relevant and reliable sources, well known or not, and to use sources mainly to support their own ideas.

9d Using sources with integrity

Academic integrity is the foundation of academic knowledge building. Trusting in one another's honesty allows students and scholars to examine and extend the work of other scholars, and it allows teachers to guide and assess the progress of their students.

You can build your integrity as a writer by working to develop your own ideas and by handling sources responsibly. The following tips can help. See also **7** (Chapters 51–54) for extensive discussions of researching and citing sources.

1 Avoiding plagiarism

Many writing assignments will require you to consult sources such as journal articles, Web sites, and books. These works belong to their creators; you are free to borrow from them *if* you do so with integrity. That means representing the sources accurately—not misinterpreting or distorting what they say. It also means crediting the sources—not plagiarizing, or presenting sources' ideas and information as if they were your own. On most campuses, plagiarism is a punishable offense.

Plagiarism can be deliberate or careless:

- **Deliberate plagiarism** is outright cheating: copying another writer's sentence or idea and passing it off as your own, buying a paper from the Web, or getting someone else to write a paper for you.
- **Careless plagiarism** is more common among students, often arising from inattentive or inexperienced handling of sources. For instance, you might cut and paste source information into your own ideas without clarifying who said what, or you might present a summary of a source without recognizing that parts of it are actually quoted. In these cases the plagiarism is unintentional, but it is still plagiarism.

See Chapter 53 for more on plagiarism.

2 Developing perspective on a subject

Consider your own knowledge and perspective on a subject before you start to research. This forethought will make it easier for you to recognize other authors' perspectives and to treat them fairly in your writing—whether or not you agree with them.

- **Before you consult sources, gauge what you already know and think about your subject.** Give yourself time to know your own mind before looking to others for information. Then you'll be able to reflect on how the sources reinforce, contradict, or expand what you already know.
- **Evaluate sources carefully.** Authors generally write from particular perspectives, and some are more overt about their biases than others. You needn't reject a source because it is biased; indeed, often you'll want to consider multiple perspectives. But you do need to recognize and weigh the writer's position. See **7** pp. 375–87 for a discussion of evaluating sources.
- **Treat sources fairly.** Represent an author's ideas and perspectives as they were originally presented, without misunderstanding or distortion. Be careful in paraphrasing and summarizing not to misrepresent the author's meaning. Be careful in editing quotations not to omit essential words.

3 Managing sources

You can avoid plagiarism by keeping track of the sources you consult, the ideas that influence your thinking, and the words and sentences you borrow—and by carefully citing the sources in your writing. If these habits are unfamiliar to you, keep the following list handy.

- **Keep track of source information as you read.** Get in the habit of always recording publication information (the author, title, date, and so on) of any source you read as well as any ideas you glean from it. See the box in **7** p. 354 for a list of what to record.

- **Be careful with quotations.** If you cut and paste a portion of an article, Web site, or other source into your document, put quotation marks around it so that you don't mix your words and the source's words accidentally. Check any quotation that you use in your own writing against the original source. For a more detailed discussion of how to quote sources, see **7** pp. 393–94.

- **Use your own words in paraphrases and summaries.** A paraphrase or summary presents the ideas of a source but not in the exact words of the original and not in quotation marks. You will be less likely to use the source author's words (and thus plagiarize) if you look away from the source while you write down what you remember from it. Note, though, that you must still cite the source of a summary or paraphrase, just as you do with a quotation. For a more detailed discussion of how to summarize and paraphrase sources, see **7** pp. 391–92.

- **Cite your sources.** As you draft, be conscious of when you're using source information and be conscientious about clearly marking where the borrowed material came from. In your final draft you'll use a particular style of citation within your text to refer to a detailed list of sources at the end. This book presents four such styles: MLA style for English and some other humanities (**MLA** pp. 435–77); APA style for the social sciences (**APA** pp. 494–512); Chicago style for history, philosophy, and some other humanities (**Chic** pp. 524–35); and CSE style for the natural and applied sciences (**CSE** pp. 536–41).

9e Using academic language

American academic writing relies on a dialect called standard American English. The dialect is also used in business, the professions, government, the media, and other sites of social and economic power where people of diverse backgrounds must communicate with one another. It is "standard" not because it is better than other forms of English, but because it is accepted as the common language, much as the dollar bill is accepted as the common currency.

In writing, standard American English varies a great deal, from the formality of an academic research report to the more relaxed language of this handbook to informal e-mails between coworkers in a company. Even in academic writing, standard English allows much room for the writer's own tone and voice, as these passages on the same topic show:

More formal

Responsibility for the widespread problem of obesity among Americans depends on the person or group describing the problem and proposing a solution. Some people believe the cause lies with individuals who make poor eating choices for themselves and parents who feed unhealthy foods to their children. Others take strong issue with the food industry, citing food manufacturers and fast-food chains that create and advertise food that is high in sugar, fat, and sodium. Still others place responsibility on American society as a whole for preferring a sedentary lifestyle centered on screen-based activities such as watching television and using computers for video games and social interaction.

> Drawn-out phrasing, such as *widespread problem of obesity among Americans.*
>
> More complicated sentence structures, such as *take strong issue with the food industry, citing food manufacturers and fast-food chains that create and advertise. . . .*
>
> More formal vocabulary: *responsibility, children, television.*

Less formal

Who or what is to blame for the obesity epidemic depends on who is talking and what they want to do about the problem. Some people blame eaters for making bad choices and parents for feeding their kids unhealthy foods. Others demonize food manufacturers and fast-food chains for creating and advertising sugary, fatty, and sodium-loaded food. Still others point to Americans generally for spending too much time in front of screens watching TV, playing video games, or going on *Facebook.*

> More informal phrasing, such as *obesity epidemic.*
>
> Less complicated sentence structures, such as *demonize food manufacturers and fast-food chains for creating and advertising. . . .*
>
> More informal vocabulary: *blame, kids, TV.*

As different as they are, both examples illustrate several common features of academic language:

- **It follows the conventions of standard American English for grammar and usage.** These conventions are described in guides to the dialect, such as this handbook.
- **It uses a standard vocabulary,** not one that only some groups understand, such as slang, an ethnic dialect, or another language. (See **3** pp. 156–59 for more on specialized vocabularies.)
- **It does *not* use the informalities of everyday speech, texting, and instant messaging,** including incomplete sentences, slang, no capital letters, and shortened spellings (*u* for *you, b4* for *before, thru* for *through,* and so on). (See **3** p. 157–58 for more on these forms.)
- **It generally uses the third person** *(he, she, it, they).* The first person *I* is sometimes appropriate to express personal opinions, but academic writers tend to avoid it and make conclusions speak for themselves. The first-person *we* can connect with readers

and invite them to think along, but, again, many academic writers avoid it. The second-person *you* is appropriate only in addressing readers directly (as in this handbook), and even then it may seem condescending or too chummy. Definitely avoid using or implying *you* in conversational expressions such as *You know what I mean* and *Don't take this the wrong way.*

■ **It is authoritative and neutral.** In the examples on the previous page, the writers express themselves confidently, not timidly as in *Explaining the causes of obesity requires the reader's patience because.* . . . The writers also refrain from hostility (*The food industry's callous attitude toward health* . . .) and enthusiasm (*The food industry's clever and appealing advertisements* . . .).

At first, the diverse demands of academic writing may leave you groping for an appropriate voice. In an effort to sound fresh and confident, you may write too casually, as if speaking to friends or family:

Too casual
Getting the truth about the obesity epidemic in the US requires some heavy lifting. It turns out that everyone else is to blame for the problem—big eaters, reckless corporations, and all those Americans who think it's OK to be a couch potato.

In an effort to sound "academic," you may produce wordy and awkward sentences:

Wordy and awkward
The responsibility for the problem of widespread obesity among Americans depends on the manner of defining the problem and the proposals for its solution. In some discussions, the cause of obesity is thought to be individuals who are unable or unwilling to make healthy choices in their own diets and parents who similarly make unhealthy choices for their children. [The passive voice in this example—*cause . . . is thought to be* instead of *people blame*—adds to its wordiness and indirection. See **4** pp. 224–26 for more on verb voice.]

A cure for writing too informally or too stiffly is to read academic writing so that the language and style become familiar and to edit your writing (see **1** pp. 34–36).

⟨CULTURE / LANGUAGE⟩ If your first language or dialect is not standard American English, learning to write standard English in no way requires you to abandon your first language. Like most multilingual people, you are probably already adept at switching between languages as the situation demands—speaking one way with your relatives, say, and another way with an employer. As you practice academic writing, you'll develop the same flexibility with it.

Exercise 9.1 Using academic language
Revise the following paragraph to make the language more academic while keeping the factual information the same.

If you buy into the stereotype of girls chatting away on their cell phones, you should think again. One of the major wireless companies surveyed 1021 cell phone owners for a period of five years and—surprise!—reported that guys talk on cell phones more than girls do. In fact, guys were way ahead of girls, using an average of 571 minutes a month compared to 424 for girls. That's 35% more time on the phone! The survey also asked about conversations on land lines, and while girls still beat the field, the guys are catching up.

9f | Communicating in an academic setting

As a member of an academic community, you will not only write papers and projects but also write directly to instructors, classmates, and other people at your school via e-mail, course-management systems such as *Blackboard* and *Canvas,* and other electronic media. Your written communication with instructors and classmates will rarely be as formal as assigned writing, but it will also rarely be as informal as a text to a friend, a tweet, or a comment on *Facebook.*

Even in a short e-mail, your message will receive a better hearing if you present yourself well and show respect for your reader(s). The following message illustrates an appropriate mix of formality and informality when addressing an instructor.

E-mail message

To: cmwhite@cms.edu

Subject: Research paper planning conference

Dear Professor White:

I am in your 8:10 English 111 class, and I'm writing to schedule a planning conference to discuss possible subjects for my research paper. I recently read an article about smoking in movies, and I'm interested in pursuing the topic for my research paper. However, I know I'll have to narrow the topic, and I'm not sure how to do that. Would you be available to meet sometime between 11:00 and 1:00 next Tuesday or Thursday?

Sincerely,

Rachel Rogers
292-8954

- Uses subject line to describe the content of the message.
- Addresses instructor formally with title and last name.
- Provides context for request.
- Uses complete sentences and words.
- Signs with full name and phone number.

Here are guidelines for such communication.

- **Use the medium your instructor prefers.** Don't text, tweet, or use a social-networking site unless you're invited to do so.
- **Use names.** In the body of your message, address your reader(s) by name if possible. Unless your teachers instruct otherwise, always address them formally, using *Professor, Dr., Ms.,* or *Mr.,*

as appropriate, followed by the last name. Sign off with your own name and information on how to contact you.

- **Pay attention to tone.** Don't use all capital letters, which SHOUT. And use irony or sarcasm only cautiously: in the absence of facial expressions, either one can lead to misunderstanding.
- **Pay attention to correctness.** Especially when you write to instructors, avoid the shortcuts of texting and tweeting, such as incomplete sentences and abbreviations (*u* for *you*, *r* for *are*, and so on). (See also pp. 76–78.) Proofread for errors in grammar, punctuation, and spelling.
- **Send messages only to the people who need them.** As a general rule, avoid sending messages to many recipients at once—all the students in a course, say—unless what you have to say applies to all of them. Before you hit Reply All in response to a message, ensure that "all" want to see the response.
- **Guard your own and others' privacy.** Online tools allow us to broadcast hurtful information about others—and allow others to do the same to us. Before you post a message about yourself or someone else, consider whether it's worthwhile and who will see it, not only now but in the future. When forwarding messages, make sure not to pass on previous private messages by mistake.
- **Don't write anything that you wouldn't say face to face or wouldn't write in a printed letter.** Electronic messages can be saved and forwarded and can be retrieved in disputes over grades and other matters.

10 Critical Reading and Writing

Chapter essentials
- Use techniques of critical reading (next page).
- Summarize (p. 85).
- Form a critical response through analysis, interpretation, synthesis, and sometimes evaluation (p. 87).
- View visuals critically (p. 90).
- Write critical analyses of texts and visuals (p. 95).
- Learn from a sample critical analysis (p. 97).

Visit MyWritingLab™ for more resources on critical reading and writing.

___

Throughout college and beyond, you will be expected to think, read, and write critically. **Critical** here does not mean "negative" but "skeptical," "exacting," "creative," "curious." You already operate critically every day as you figure out why things happen to you or what your experiences mean. This chapter introduces more formal methods for reading and writing critically.

10a Using techniques of critical reading

In college much of your critical thinking will focus on written texts (a short story, a journal article, a blog) or on visual or multimedia texts (a photograph, an advertisement, a film). Like all subjects worthy of critical consideration, such works operate on at least three levels:

1. **What the creator actually says or shows.**
2. **What the creator does not say or show but builds into the work, intentionally or not.**
3. **What you think in response.**

Discovering each level of the work involves a number of reading techniques that are discussed in this chapter.

CULTURE LANGUAGE The idea of reading critically may require you to make some adjustments if readers in your native culture tend to seek understanding or agreement more than engagement from what they read. Readers of English use texts for all kinds of reasons, including pleasure, reinforcement, and information. But they also read questioningly, to uncover the author's motives (*What are this author's biases?*), test their own ideas (*Can I support my point of view as well as this author supports hers?*), and arrive at new knowledge (*Why is the author's evidence so persuasive?*).

1 Previewing the material

When you're reading a work of literature, such as a short story or a poem, it's often best just to plunge right in. But for critical reading of other works, it's worthwhile to skim before reading word for word, forming expectations and even some preliminary questions. The preview will make your reading more informed and fruitful.

- **Gauge length and level.** Is the material brief and straightforward so that you can read it in one sitting, or will it require more time?
- **Check the facts of publication.** Does the date of publication suggest currency or datedness? Does the publisher or publication specialize in scholarly articles, popular books, or something else? For a Web publication, who or what sponsors the site— an individual? a nonprofit organization? a government body? a college or university?
- **Look for content cues.** What do the title, introduction, headings, illustrations, conclusion, and other features tell you about the topic, the author's approach, and the main ideas?
- **Learn about the author.** Does a biography tell you about the

author's publications, interests, biases, and reputation in the field? If there is no biography, what can you gather about the author from his or her words? Use a Web search to trace unfamiliar authors.

■ **Consider your preliminary response.** What do you already know about the topic? What questions do you have about either the topic or the author's approach to it? What biases of your own—for instance, curiosity, boredom, or an outlook similar or opposed to the author's—might influence your reading of the work?

Following is an essay by Thomas Sowell, an economist who writes on economics, politics, and education. The essay was first published in the 1990s, but the debate over student loans has hardly subsided. Since Sowell wrote, the number of college graduates with loan debt has increased by a third and the average amount they owe has almost tripled. Preview the essay using the guidelines in the preceding list, and then read it until you think you understand what the author is saying. Note your questions and reactions in writing.

Student Loans

The first lesson of economics is scarcity: There is never enough of 1 anything to fully satisfy all those who want it.

The first lesson of politics is to disregard the first lesson of econom- 2 ics. When politicians discover some group that is being vocal about not having as much as they want, the "solution" is to give them more. Where do politicians get this "more"? They rob Peter to pay Paul.

After a while, of course, they discover that Peter doesn't have 3 enough. Bursting with compassion, politicians rush to the rescue. Needless to say, they do not admit that robbing Peter to pay Paul was a dumb idea in the first place. On the contrary, they now rob Tom, Dick, and Harry to help Peter.

The latest chapter in this long-running saga is that politicians have 4 now suddenly discovered that many college students graduate heavily in debt. To politicians it follows, as the night follows the day, that the government should come to their rescue with the taxpayers' money.

How big is this crushing burden of college students' debt that we 5 hear so much about from politicians and media deep thinkers? For those students who graduate from public colleges owing money, the debt averages a little under $7000. For those who graduate from private colleges owing money, the average debt is a little under $9000.

Buying a very modestly priced automobile involves more debt than 6 that. And a car loan has to be paid off faster than the ten years that college graduates get to repay their student loans. Moreover, you have to keep buying cars every several years, while one college education lasts a lifetime.

College graduates of course earn higher incomes than other peo- 7 ple. Why, then, should we panic at the thought that they have to repay loans for the education which gave them their opportunities? Even graduates with relatively modest incomes pay less than 10 percent of their annual salary on the first loan the first year—with declining percentages in future years, as their pay increases.

Political hysteria and media hype may focus on the low-income 8 student with a huge debt. That is where you get your heart-rending stories—even if they are not all that typical. In reality, the soaring student loans of the past decade have resulted from allowing high-income people to borrow under government programs.

Before 1978, college loans were available through government 9 programs only to students whose family income was below some cut-off level. That cut-off level was about double the national average income, but at least it kept out the Rockefellers and the Vanderbilts. But, in an era of "compassion," Congress took off even those limits.

That opened the floodgates. No matter how rich you were, it still 10 paid to borrow money through the government at low interest rates. The money you had set aside for your children's education could be invested somewhere else, at higher interest rates. Then, when the student loan became due, parents could pay it off with the money they had set aside—pocketing the difference in interest rates.

To politicians and the media, however, the rapidly growing loans 11 showed what a great "need" there was. The fact that many students welshed when time came to repay their loans showed how "crushing" their burden of debt must be. In reality, those who welsh typically have smaller loans, but have dropped out of college before finishing. People who are irresponsible in one way are often irresponsible in other ways.

No small amount of the deterioration of college standards has been 12 due to the increasingly easy availability of college to people who are not very serious about getting an education. College is not a bad place to hang out for a few years, if you have nothing better to do, and if someone else is paying for it. Its costs are staggering, but the taxpayers carry much of that burden, not only for state universities and city colleges, but also to an increasing extent even for "private" institutions.

Numerous government subsidies and loan programs make it pos- 13 sible for many people to use vast amounts of society's resources at low cost to themselves. Whether in money terms or in real terms, federal aid to higher education has increased several hundred percent since 1970. That has enabled colleges to raise their tuition by leaps and bounds and enabled professors to be paid more and more for doing less and less teaching.

Naturally all these beneficiaries are going to create hype and hyste- 14 ria to keep more of the taxpayers' money coming in. But we would be fools to keep on writing blank checks for them.

When you weigh the cost of things, in economics that's called 15 "trade-offs." In politics, it's called "mean-spirited." Apparently, if we just took a different attitude, scarcity would go away.

—Thomas Sowell

2 Reading

Reading is itself more than a one-step process. You want to understand the first level on which the text operates—what the author actually says—and begin to form your impressions.

First reading

The first time through new material, read as steadily and smoothly as possible, trying to get the gist of what the author is saying.

- **Read in a place where you can concentrate.** Choose a quiet environment away from distractions such as music or talking.
- **Give yourself time.** Rushing yourself or worrying about something else you have to do will prevent you from grasping what you read.
- **Try to enjoy the work.** Seek connections between it and what you already know. Appreciate new information, interesting relationships, forceful writing, humor, good examples.
- **Make notes sparingly during this first reading.** Mark major stumbling blocks—such as a paragraph you don't understand—so that you can try to resolve them before rereading.

(CULTURE LANGUAGE) If English is not your first language and you come across unfamiliar words, don't stop and look up every one. You will be distracted from an overall understanding of the text. Instead, try to guess the meanings of the unfamiliar words by using context clues, such as examples and synonyms of the words. Be sure to circle the words and look them up later. You may want to keep a vocabulary log of the words, their definitions, and the sentences in which they appeared.

Rereading and annotating

After the first reading, plan on at least one other. This time read *slowly*. Your main concern should be to grasp the content and how it is constructed. That means rereading a paragraph if you didn't get the point or using a dictionary to look up words you don't know.

Use the tips below to highlight and annotate a text:

- **Distinguish main ideas from supporting ideas.** Mark the central idea (the thesis), the main idea of each paragraph or section, and the evidence supporting ideas.
- **Note key terms.** Understand both their meanings and their applications.
- **Identify the connections among ideas.** Be sure you see why the author moves from point A to point B to point C and how those points relate to support the central idea. It often helps to outline the text or to summarize it (see opposite).
- **Distinguish between facts and opinions.** Especially when reading an argument, mark the author's opinions as well as the facts on which the opinions are based. (See pp. 101–02 for more on facts and opinions.)
- **Add your own comments.** In the margins or separately, note links to other readings or to class discussions, questions to explore

further, possible topics for your writing, points you find especially strong or weak.

An example of critical reading

The following sample shows how a student, Charlene Robinson,
approached "Student Loans." After her first reading, Robinson went
through Sowell's text more slowly, adding comments and questions
in the margin and writing about the essay in her journal. Following
are samples of her annotations:

> The first lesson of economics is scarcity: There is never
> enough of anything to fully satisfy all those who want it.   *fact*
>
> The first lesson of politics is to disregard the first les-   *related opinion—*
> son of economics. When politicians discover some group   *basic contradiction*
> that is being vocal about not having as much as they   *between economics*
> want, the "solution" is to give them more. Where do poli-   *and politics*
> ticians get this "more"? They rob Peter to pay Paul.   ← *biblical reference?*
>
> After a while, of course, they discover that Peter
> doesn't have enough. Bursting with compassion, politi-   *ironic and*
> cians rush to the rescue. Needless to say, they do not   *dismissive*
> admit that robbing Peter to pay Paul was a dumb idea in   *language*
> the first place. On the contrary, they now rob Tom, Dick,
> and Harry to help Peter.   *politicians =*
>   *fools? or*
> The latest chapter in this long-running saga is that   *irresponsible?*
> politicians have now suddenly discovered that many
> college students graduate heavily in debt. To politicians   *example supporting*
> it follows, as the night follows the day, that the govern-   *opinion about*
> ment should come to their rescue with the taxpayers'   *economics &*
> money.   *politics*

10b Summarizing

A good way to master the content of a text and to see its strengths
and weaknesses is to **summarize** it—that is, distill it to its main
points, in your own words. The following box gives a method of
summarizing:

Writing a summary

- **Understand the meaning.** Look up words or concepts you don't
  know so that you understand the author's sentences and how they
  relate to one another.
- **Understand the organization.** Work through the text to identify its
  sections—single paragraphs or groups of paragraphs focused on a
  single topic. To understand how parts of a work relate to one another,
  try drawing a tree diagram or creating an outline (1 pp. 19–22).
- **Distill each section.** Write a one- or two-sentence summary of each

(continued)

Writing a summary
(continued)

section you identify. Focus on the main point of the section, omitting examples, facts, and other supporting evidence.

■ **State the main idea.** Write a sentence or two capturing the author's central idea.

■ **Support the main idea.** Write a full paragraph (or more, if needed) that begins with the central idea and supports it with the sentences that summarize sections of the work. The paragraph should concisely and accurately state the thrust of the entire work.

■ ***Use your own words.*** By writing, you re-create the meaning of the work in a way that makes sense for you. You also avoid plagiarism.

■ ***Cite the source.*** If you use a summary in writing that you do for others, always acknowledge the source.

Summarizing even a passage of text can be tricky. Here we'll look at attempts to summarize the following material from an introductory biology textbook.

Original text

As astronomers study newly discovered planets orbiting distant stars, they hope to find evidence of water on these far-off celestial bodies, for water is the substance that makes possible life as we know it here on Earth. All organisms familiar to us are made mostly of water and live in an environment dominated by water. They require water more than any other substance. Human beings, for example, can survive for quite a few weeks without food, but only a week or so without water. Molecules of water participate in many chemical reactions necessary to sustain life. Most cells are surrounded by water, and cells themselves are about 70–95% water. Three-quarters of Earth's surface is submerged in water. Although most of this water is in liquid form, water is also present on Earth as ice and vapor. Water is the only common substance to exist in the natural environment in all three physical states of matter: solid, liquid, and gas.

—Neil A. Campbell and Jane B. Reece, *Biology*

The first attempt to summarize the passage accurately restates ideas in the original, but it does not pare the passage to its essence:

Draft summary

Astronomers look for water in outer space because life depends on it. It is the most common substance on Earth and in living cells, and it can be a liquid, a solid (ice), or a gas (vapor).

The work of astronomers and the three physical states of water add color and texture to the original, but they are asides to the key concept that water sustains life because of its role in life. The following revision narrows the summary to this concept:

Revised summary

Water is the most essential support for life, the dominant substance on Earth and in living cells and a component of life-sustaining chemical processes.

When Charlene Robinson summarized Thomas Sowell's "Student Loans," she first drafted this sentence about paragraphs 1–4:

Draft summary

As much as politicians would like to satisfy voters by giving them everything they ask for, the government cannot afford a student loan program.

Reading the sentence and Sowell's paragraphs, Robinson saw that this draft misread the text by asserting that the government cannot afford student loans. She realized that Sowell's point is more complicated than that and rewrote her summary:

Revised summary

As their support of the government's student loan program illustrates, politicians ignore the economic reality that using resources to benefit one group (students in debt) involves taking the resources from another group (taxpayers).

Caution Using your own words when writing a summary not only helps you understand the meaning but also constitutes the first step in avoiding plagiarism. The second step is to cite the source when you use the summary in something written for others. See 7 pp. 403–05.

Note Do not count on the AutoSummarize function on your word processor for summarizing texts that you may have copied and pasted into a file. The summaries are rarely accurate, and you will not gain the experience of interacting with the texts on your own.

10c Developing a critical response

Once you've grasped the content of what you're reading—what the author says—then you can turn to understanding what the author does not say outright but suggests or implies or even lets slip. At this stage you are concerned with the purpose or intention of the author and with how he or she carries it out.

Critical thinking and reading consist of four overlapping operations: analyzing, interpreting, synthesizing, and (often) evaluating.

1 Analyzing

Analysis is the separation of something into its parts or elements, the better to understand it. To see these elements in what you are reading, begin with a question that reflects your purpose in analyzing the text: why you're curious about it or what you're trying to make out of it. This question will serve as a kind of lens that highlights some features and not others.

Analyzing Thomas Sowell's "Student Loans" (pp. 82–83), you might ask one of these questions:

Questions for analysis	Elements
What is Sowell's attitude toward politicians?	References to politicians: content, words, tone
How does Sowell support his assertions about the loan program's costs?	Support: evidence, such as statistics and examples

2 Interpreting

Identifying the elements of something is only a start: you also need to interpret the meaning or significance of the elements and of the whole. Interpretation usually requires you to infer the author's **assumptions**—opinions or beliefs about what is or what could or should be. (*Infer* means to draw a conclusion based on evidence.)

Assumptions are pervasive: we all adhere to certain values, beliefs, and opinions. But assumptions are not always stated outright. Speakers and writers may judge that their audience already understands and accepts their assumptions; they may not even be aware of their assumptions; or they may deliberately refrain from stating their assumptions for fear that the audience will disagree. That is why your job as a critical thinker is to interpret what the assumptions are.

Thomas Sowell's "Student Loans" is based on certain assumptions, some obvious, some not. Analyzing Sowell's attitude toward politicians requires focusing on the statements about them. They "disregard the first lesson of economics" (paragraph 2), which implies that they ignore important principles (knowing that Sowell is an economist himself makes this a reasonable assumption). Politicians also "rob Peter to pay Paul," are "[b]ursting with compassion," "do not admit . . . a dumb idea," are characters in a "long-running saga," and arrive at the solution of spending taxes "as the night follows the day"—that is, inevitably (paragraphs 2–4). From these statements and others, we can infer the following:

> Sowell assumes that politicians become compassionate when a cause is loud and popular, not necessarily just, and they act irresponsibly by trying to solve the problem with other people's (taxpayers') money.

3 Synthesizing

If you stopped at analysis and interpretation, critical thinking and reading might leave you with a pile of elements and possible meanings but no vision of the whole. With **synthesis** you make connections among the parts of the text *or* between the text and other texts. You consider the text through the lens of your knowledge and beliefs, drawing conclusions about how the text works as a whole.

A key component of academic reading and writing, synthesis receives attention in the next chapter (pp. 96–97) and then in the context of research writing (see **7** pp. 387–89). Sometimes you'll respond directly to a text, as in the following statement about Thomas Sowell's essay "Student Loans," which connects Sowell's assumptions about politicians to a larger idea also implied by the essay:

> Sowell's view that politicians are irresponsible with taxpayers' money reflects his overall opinion that the laws of economics, not politics, should drive government.

Often synthesis will take you outside the text to its surroundings. The following questions can help you investigate the context of a work:

- **How does the work compare with similar works?** For instance, how have other writers responded to Sowell's views on student loans?
- **How does the work fit into the context of other works by the same author or group?** How do Sowell's views on student loans typify, or not, the author's other writing on politics and economics?
- **What cultural, economic, or political forces influence the work?** What other examples might Sowell have given to illustrate his view that economics, not politics, should determine government spending?
- **What historical forces influence the work?** How has the indebtedness of college students changed over the past four decades?

4 Evaluating

Critical reading and writing often end at synthesis: you form and explain your understanding of what the work says and doesn't say. If you are also expected to **evaluate** the work, however, you will go further to judge its quality and significance:

- **Collect and test your judgments.** Determine that they are significant and that they apply to the whole work.
- **Turn the judgments into assertions**—for instance, *The poet creates fresh, intensely vivid images* or *The author does not summon the evidence to support his case.*
- **Support these statements with evidence from the text**—mainly quotations and paraphrases.

Evaluation takes a certain amount of confidence. You may think that you lack the expertise to cast judgment on another's work, especially if the work is difficult or the author well known. True, the more informed you are, the better a critical reader you are. But conscientious reading and analysis will give you the internal authority to judge a work *as it stands* and *as it seems to you,* against your own unique bundle of experiences, observations, and attitudes.

10d Viewing visuals critically

Every day we are bombarded with visuals—pictures on billboards, pop-up ads on our devices, graphs in textbooks, and charts on Web sites, to name just a few examples. Most visuals slide by without our noticing them, or so we think. But visuals, sometimes even more than text, can influence us covertly. Their creators have purposes, some worthy, some not, and understanding those purposes requires critical reading. The method parallels that in the previous section for reading text critically: preview, read for comprehension, analyze, interpret, synthesize, and (often) evaluate.

1 Previewing a visual

Your first step in exploring a visual is to form initial impressions of its origin and purpose and to note its distinctive features. This previewing process is like the one for previewing a text (pp. 81–82):

- **What do you see?** What is most striking about the visual? What is its subject? What is the gist of any text or symbols? What is the overall effect of the visual?
- **What are the facts of publication?** Where did you first see the visual? Was it created especially for that location or for others as well? What can you tell about when the visual was created?
- **What do you know about the person or group that created the visual?** For instance, was the creator an artist, scholar, news organization, or corporation? What seems to have been the creator's purpose?
- **What is your preliminary response?** What about the visual interests, confuses, pleases, or disturbs you? Are the form, style, and subject familiar or unfamiliar? How might your knowledge, experiences, and values influence your reception of the visual?

If possible, print a copy of the visual or scan it into your reading journal, and write comments in the visual's margins or separately.

2 Reading a visual

Reading a visual requires the same level of concentration as reading a text. Try to answer the following questions about the visual. If some answers aren't clear at this point, skip the question until later.

- **What is the purpose?** Is the visual mainly explanatory, conveying information, or is it argumentative, trying to convince readers of something or to persuade them to act? What information or point of view does it seem intended to get across?

- **Who is the intended audience?** What does the source of the visual, including its publication facts, tell about the expectations of its creator for readers' knowledge, interests, and attitudes? What do the features of the visual itself add to your impression?
- **What do any words or symbols add?** Whether located on the visual or outside it (such as in a caption), do words or symbols add information, focus your attention, or alter your impression?
- **What action, change, people, places, or things are shown?** Does the visual tell a story? Do its characters or other features tap into your knowledge, or are they unfamiliar?
- **What is the form of the visual?** Is it a photograph, advertisement, painting, graph, diagram, cartoon, or something else? How do its content and apparent purpose and audience relate to its form?

The illustration below shows the notes that a student, Richard Oliva, made on an advertisement for *Teach.org*.

Annotation of an advertisement

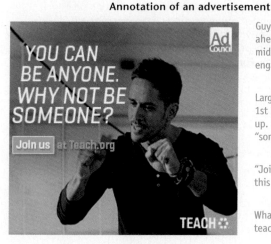

Guy in photo: Eyes focused ahead (on students?). Caught in mid-speech. Clenched hands = intense, engaged, passionate.

Large, white type highlights message. 1st sentence: what kids hear growing up. 2nd sentence: a challenge to be "someone" important, like a celebrity.

"Join us": direct invitation to be like this guy.

What is Teach.org? Recruits new teachers?

Advertisement for *Teach.org*

3 Analyzing a visual

Elements for analysis

As when analyzing a written work, you analyze a visual by identifying its elements. The visual elements you might consider appear in the box on the next page. Few visuals include all the elements, and you can narrow the list further by posing a question about the visual you are reading, as discussed after the box.

Elements of visuals

- **Emphasis:** Most visuals pull your eyes to certain features: a graph line moving sharply upward, a provocative figure, bright color, thick lines, and so on.
- **Narration:** Most visuals tell stories, whether in a sequence (a TV commercial or a graph showing changes over time) or at a single moment (a photograph, a painting, or a pie chart). Sometimes dialog or a title or caption contributes to the story.
- **Point of view:** The creator of the visual influences responses by taking account of both the viewer's physical relation to the subject—for instance, whether it is seen head-on or from above—and the viewer's assumed attitude toward the subject.
- **Arrangement:** Pattern, foreground versus background, and separation can contribute to the visual's meaning and effect.
- **Color:** Color can direct the viewer's attention, convey the creator's attitude, and suggest a mood.
- **Characterization:** The qualities of figures and objects—sympathetic or not, desirable or not—reflect their roles in the visual's story.
- **Context:** The source of a visual affects its meaning, whether it is a graph from a scholarly journal or a car ad on the Web.
- **Tension:** Visuals often communicate a problem or seize attention with features that seem wrong, such as misspelled or misaligned words, distorted figures, or controversial relations between characters.
- **Allusions:** An **allusion** is a reference to something the audience is likely to recognize and respond to. Examples include a cultural symbol such as a dollar sign, a mythological figure such as a unicorn, or a familiar movie character such as Darth Vader from *Star Wars*.

Question for analysis

You can focus your analysis of elements by framing your main interest in the visual as a question. Richard Oliva concentrated his analysis of the *Teach.org* ad by asking the question *Does the ad move viewers to imagine themselves as teachers?* The question led Oliva to focus on some elements of the ad and ignore others:

Elements of the ad	Responses
Emphasis	The photo grabs the viewer, placing emphasis on the teacher. Then the lines of white text draw the eye away from the photo to the message.
Narration	In just a few words, the ad tells a story about what viewers could become. It appeals to their

	wish to be known in some way, like a celebrity, but doing important, interesting work, like the guy in the photo. The orange "Join us" then invites viewers to take a step toward that dream.
Point of view	The guy is looking down, probably at his students in front of him, not at the viewer. This might be off-putting, but the man is so engaged in speaking that it's not. Instead, the viewer catches his intensity.
Characterization	The guy's intensity about what he's doing is appealing. He seems to have independence and authority—he's not at a desk and is wearing a casual shirt and bracelets, not a suit. He makes teaching look interesting, rewarding, even cool.

Sample Web pages for analysis

The screen shots on the next page are from *AIDS Clock*, an interactive Web site sponsored by the United Nations Population Fund (*www.unfpa.org/aids_clock*). The top image is the home page, displaying a traditional world map. The bottom image appears when viewers click on "Resize the map": now each country's size reflects the number of its people who live with HIV, the virus that causes AIDS. (For example, South Africa grows while the United States shrinks.) The large blue number at the top changes every twelve seconds to give the total number of people living with HIV in the world. Try to answer the questions in the annotations above the screen shots.

4 Interpreting a visual

The strategies for interpreting a visual parallel those for interpreting a written text (p. 88). In this process you look more deeply at the elements, considering them in relation to the likely assumptions and intentions of the visual's creator. You aim to draw reasonable inferences about *why* the visual looks as it does, such as this inference about the *Teach.org* advertisement on p. 91:

> The creators of the *Teach.org* ad assume that viewers want careers that make them feel important.

This inference is supported by the second sentence of the ad: "Why not be someone?"

5 Synthesizing ideas about a visual

As discussed on pp. 88–89, with synthesis you take analysis and interpretation a step further to consider how a work's elements and underlying assumptions relate and what the overall message is. You

Elements of Web pages

Emphasis and color: What elements on these pages draw your attention? How does color distinguish and emphasize elements?

Narration: What story do the two Web pages tell? What does each map contribute to the story? What does the blue number contribute? (Notice that the number changes from the first screen to the second.)

Arrangement: What does the arrangement of elements on the pages contribute to the story being told?

Tension: How do you respond to the distorted map in the second image? What does the distortion contribute to your view of the Web site's effectiveness?

Context: How does knowing the Web site's sponsoring organization, the United Nations Population Fund, affect your response to these images?

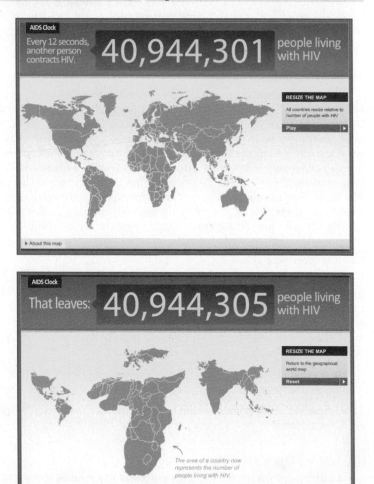

AIDS Clock Web pages, 2014

may also want to view the visual in the larger context of similar works of history and culture.

Placing a visual in its context often requires research. For instance, to learn more about the assumptions underlying the *Teach.org* advertisement and the goals of the larger ad campaign, Richard Oliva visited the *Teach.org* Web site. The following entry from his reading journal synthesizes his research and his own ideas about the ad:

> The *Teach.org* ad is part of a larger campaign designed to attract young people to careers in teaching. Viewers who go to the *Teach.org* Web site can find information about going to college to become a teacher, getting scholarships for college, and preparing for a job search. They can also watch videos of young teachers talking about what inspired them to choose teaching. The ad with the man talking that popped up on my screen is one of several in the campaign, and the elements of the ad are designed to attract viewers by making teaching look exciting and important.

6 | Evaluating a visual

If your critical reading moves on to evaluation, you'll form judgments about the quality and significance of the visual: Is the message of the visual accurate and fair, or is it distorted and biased? Can you support, refute, or extend the message? Does the visual achieve its apparent purpose, and is the purpose worthwhile? How does the visual affect you?

10e | Writing critically

Many academic writing assignments ask for **critical analysis**, or **critique**, in which you write critically about texts or visuals. As you form a response to a work, you integrate its ideas and information with yours to come to your own conclusions (see pp. 89–90). As you write your response, you support your ideas about the work by citing evidence from it.

Note Critical writing is *not* summarizing. You might summarize to clarify a text or a visual for yourself, and you might briefly summarize a work in your larger piece of writing. But in critical writing you go further to bring your own perspective to the work.

1 | Deciding how to respond

When an assignment asks you to respond directly to a text or a visual, you might take one of the following approaches to decide on your position.

- Agree with and extend the ideas expressed in the work, exploring related ideas and providing additional examples.
- Agree with some of the ideas but disagree with others.
- Disagree with one or more ideas.

■ **Explain how the work achieves a particular effect,** such as balancing opposing views or conveying a mood.

■ **Analyze the overall effectiveness of the work**—for example, how well a writer supports a thesis with convincing evidence or whether an advertisement succeeds in its unstated purpose.

2 Shaping a critical analysis

You will likely have an immediate response to at least some of the texts and visuals you analyze: you may agree or disagree strongly with what the author says or shows. But for some other responses, you may need to use the process of critical reading described on pp. 81–90 to take notes on the text, summarize it, and develop a view of it. Then, as you write, you can use the tips in the following box to convey your response to readers.

Responding to a text

■ **Make sure your writing has a point**—a central idea, or thesis, that focuses your response. (For more on developing a thesis, see **1** pp. 14–17.)

■ **Include a very brief summary if readers may be unfamiliar with your subject.** But remember that your job is not just to report what the text says or what a visual shows; it is to *respond* to the work from your own critical perspective. (For more on summary, see pp. 85–87.)

■ **Center each paragraph on an idea of your own that supports your thesis.** Generally, state the idea outright, in your own voice.

■ **Support the paragraph idea with evidence from the text**—quotations, paraphrases, details, and examples.

■ **Conclude each paragraph with your interpretation of the evidence.** As a general rule, avoid ending paragraphs with source evidence; instead, end with at least a sentence that explains what the evidence shows.

---

3 Emphasizing synthesis in your response

Following the suggestions in the preceding box will lead you to show readers the synthesis you achieved as you developed a critical response to the text or visual. That is, you integrate your perspective on the work with that of the author or creator in order to support a conclusion of your own.

A key to synthesis is deciding how to present evidence from your critical reading or viewing. Especially when you are writing about a relatively unfamiliar subject, you may be tempted to let a text or other source do the talking for you through extensive summary or quotations. However, readers of your academic writing will expect to see you managing ideas and information to make your points.

A typical paragraph of text-based writing should open with your own idea, give evidence from the text, and conclude with your interpretation of the evidence. You can see this pattern in the following paragraph from an essay that appears later in this chapter.

> The most fundamental and most debatable assumption underlying Sowell's essay is that higher education is a kind of commodity that not everyone is entitled to. In order to diminish the importance of graduates' average debt from education loans, Sowell claims that a car loan will probably be higher (131). This comparison between education and an automobile implies that the two are somehow equal as products and that an affordable higher education is no more a right than a new car is. Sowell also condemns the "irresponsible" students who drop out of school and "the increasingly easy availability of college to people who are not very serious about getting an education" (132). But he overlooks the value of encouraging education, including the education of those who don't finish college or who aren't scholars. For many in the United States, education has a greater value than that of a mere commodity like a car. And even from an economic perspective such as Sowell's, the cost to society of an uneducated public needs to be taken into account. By failing to give education its due, Sowell undermines his argument at its core.

[margin labels: Writer's idea; Evidence; Interpretation; Evidence; Interpretation; Writer's conclusion]

Note Effective synthesis requires careful handling of evidence from the text (quotations and paraphrases) so that it meshes smoothly into your sentences yet is clearly distinct from your own ideas. See **7** pp. 395–99 on integrating borrowed material.

10f A sample critical analysis

The following essay illustrates a common academic assignment, a critical analysis, or critique, of a text. In the essay, Charlene Robinson responds to Thomas Sowell's essay "Student Loans" (pp. 82–83). Robinson arrived at her response, an argument, through the process of critical reading outlined in this chapter and then by gathering and organizing her ideas, developing a thesis about Sowell's text that synthesized his ideas and hers, and supporting her thesis with evidence from her own experience and from Sowell's text.

Robinson did not assume that her readers would see the same things in Sowell's essay or share her views, so her essay offers evidence of Sowell's ideas in the form of direct quotations, summaries, and paraphrases (restatements in her own words). Robinson documents these borrowings from Sowell using the style of the Modern Language Association (MLA): the numbers in parentheses are page numbers in the book containing Sowell's essay, listed at the end as a work cited. (See **MLA** pp. 436–77 for more on MLA style.)

Weighing the Costs

Introduction   In the essay "Student Loans," the economist Thomas Sowell challenges the US government's student-loan program for three main reasons:

Summary of
Sowell's essay   a scarce resource (taxpayers' money) goes to many undeserving students,
a high number of recipients fail to repay their loans, and the easy availability of money has led to both lower academic standards and higher
college tuitions. Sowell wants his readers to "weigh the costs of things"
(133) in order to see, as he does, that the loan program should not
receive so much government funding. Sowell wrote his essay in the 1990s,
but the argument he makes is still heard frequently today and is worth

Robinson's
critical question   examining. Does Sowell provide the evidence of cost and other problems
to lead the reader to agree with his argument? The answer is no, because

Thesis
statement   hard evidence is less common than debatable and unsupported assumptions about students, scarcity, and the value of education.

First main point   Sowell's portrait of student-loan recipients is questionable. It is
based on averages, some statistical and some not, but averages are of-

Evidence for
first point:
paraphrases
and quotations
from Sowell's
text   ten deceptive. For example, Sowell cites college graduates' low average
debt of $7,000 to $9,000 (131) without giving the full range of statistics
or acknowledging that when he was writing many students' debt was much
higher. (Today the average debt itself is much higher.) Similarly, Sowell
dismisses "heart-rending stories" of "the low-income student with a huge
debt" as "not at all typical" (132), yet he invents his own exaggerated
version of the typical loan recipient: an affluent slacker ("Rockefellers"
and "Vanderbilts") for whom college is a "place to hang out for a few
years" sponging off the government, while his or her parents clear a

Evidence for
first point:
Sowell's
omissions   profit from making use of the loan program (132). Although such students
(and parents) may well exist, are they really typical? Sowell does not offer
any data one way or the other—for instance, how many loan recipients
come from each income group, what percentage of loan funds go to
each group, how many loan recipients receive significant help from their

Conclusion
of first point:
Robinson's
interpretation   parents, and how many receive none. Together, Sowell's statements and
omissions cast doubt on the argument that students don't need or deserve
the loans.

Transition to
second main
point   Another set of assumptions in the essay has to do with "scarcity":

Second main
point   "There is never enough of anything to fully satisfy all those who want it,"
Sowell says (131). This statement appeals to readers' common sense, but
the "lesson" of scarcity does not necessarily apply to the student-loan

Evidence for
second point:
Sowell's omis-
sions   program. Sowell omits many important figures needed to prove that the
nation's resources are too scarce to support the program, such as the total
cost of the program, its percentage of the total education budget and the

total federal budget, and its cost compared to the cost of defense, Medicare, and other expensive programs. Moreover, Sowell does not mention the interest paid by loan recipients, even though the interest must offset some of the costs of running the program and covering unpaid loans. Thus his argument that there isn't enough money to run the student loan program is unconvincing.

Conclusion of second point: Robinson's interpretation

The most fundamental and most debatable assumption underlying Sowell's essay is that higher education is a kind of commodity that not everyone is entitled to. In order to diminish the importance of gradu-ates' average debt from education loans, Sowell claims that a car loan will probably be higher (131). This comparison between education and an automobile implies that the two are somehow equal as products and that an affordable higher education is no more a right than a new car is. Sowell also condemns the "irresponsible" students who drop out of school and "the increasingly easy availability of college to people who are not very serious about getting an education" (132). But he overlooks the value of encouraging education, including the education of those who don't finish college or who aren't scholars. For many in the United States, education has a greater value than that of a mere commodity like a car. And even from an economic perspective such as Sowell's, the cost to society of an uneducated public needs to be taken into account. By failing to give education its due, Sowell undermines his argument at its core.

Third main point

Evidence for third point: paraphrases and quotations from Sowell's text

Evidence for third point: Sowell's omissions

Conclusion of third point: Robinson's interpretation

Sowell writes with conviction, and his concerns are valid: high taxes, waste, unfairness, declining educational standards, obtrusive government. However, the essay's flaws make it unlikely that Sowell could convince readers who do not already agree with him. He does not support his portrait of the typical loan recipient, he fails to demonstrate a lack of resources for the loan program, and he neglects the special nature of education compared to other services and products. Sowell may have the evidence to back up his assumptions, but by omitting it he himself does not truly weigh the costs of the loan program.

Conclusion

Acknowledg-ment of Sowell's concerns

Summary of three main points

Return to theme of introduction: weighing costs

[New page.]

Work Cited

Sowell, Thomas. "Student Loans." *Is Reality Optional? and Other Essays.* Stanford: Hoover, 1993. 131-33. Print.

—Charlene Robinson (student)

*Work cited in MLA style (**MLA** p. 445)*

11 Argument

Chapter essentials

- Use the elements of argument: subject, claims, evidence, and assumptions (below).
- Write reasonably, with logical thinking, appropriate appeals, acknowledgment of opposing views, and no fallacies (p. 103).
- Organize effectively (p. 108).
- Consider using visual arguments (p. 109).
- Learn from a sample argument (p. 113).

Visit MyWritingLab™ for more resources on argument.

Argument is writing that attempts to solve a problem, open readers' minds to an opinion, change readers' opinions, or move readers to action. Using various techniques, you engage readers to find common ground and narrow the distance between your views and theirs. (**CULTURE·LANGUAGE**) Argument as described here may be initially uncomfortable to you if your native culture approaches such writing differently. In some cultures, for example, a writer is expected to avoid asserting his or her opinion outright, to rely for evidence on appeals to tradition, or to establish a compromise rather than argue a position. In American academic and business settings, writers aim for a well-articulated opinion, evidence gathered from many sources, and a direct and concise argument for the opinion.

11a Understanding and using the elements of argument

An argument has four main elements: subject, claims, evidence, and assumptions. (The last three are adapted from the work of the British philosopher Stephen Toulmin.)

1 The subject

An argument starts with a subject and often with a view of the subject as well—that is, an idea that makes you want to write about the subject. (If you don't have a subject or you aren't sure what you think, see 1 pp. 10–14 for some invention techniques.) Your subject should meet several requirements:

- **It can be disputed:** reasonable people can disagree over it.
- **It *will* be disputed:** it is controversial.
- **It is narrow enough to research and argue in the space and time available.**

On the flip side of these requirements are several kinds of subjects that will not work as the starting place of argument: indisputable facts, such as the functions of the human liver; personal preferences or beliefs, such as a moral commitment to vegetarianism; and ideas that few would disagree with, such as the virtues of a secure home.

Exercise 11.1 Testing argument subjects

Analyze each subject below to determine whether it is appropriate for argument. Explain your reasoning in each case.

1 Granting of athletic scholarships
2 Care of automobile tires
3 Censoring the Web sites of hate groups
4 History of the town park
5 Housing for the homeless
6 Billboards in urban residential areas or in rural areas
7 Animal testing for cosmetics research
8 Cats versus dogs as pets
9 Ten steps in recycling wastepaper
10 Benefits of being a parent

2 Claims

Claims are statements that require support. In an argument you develop your subject into a central claim or thesis, asserted outright in a thesis statement (see **1** pp. 14–17). This central claim is what the argument is about.

A thesis statement is always an **opinion**—that is, a judgment based on facts and arguable on the basis of facts. It may be one of the following:

■ **A claim about past or present reality:**

In both its space and its equipment, the college's chemistry lab is outdated.

Academic cheating increases with students' economic insecurity.

■ **A claim of value:**

The new room fees are unjustified given the condition of the dormitories.

Computer music pirates undermine the system that encourages the very creation of music.

■ **A recommendation for a course of action,** often a solution to a perceived problem:

The college's outdated chemistry lab should be replaced incrementally over the next five years.

Schools and businesses can help to resolve the region's traffic congestion by implementing car pools and rewarding participants.

The backbone of an argument consists of specific claims that support the thesis statement. These may also be statements of opinion, or they may fall into one of two other categories:

■ **Statements of *fact,*** including facts that are generally known or are verifiable (such as the cost of tuition at your school) and those that can be inferred from verifiable facts (such as the monetary value of a college education).

■ **Statements of *belief,*** or convictions based on personal faith or values, such as *The primary goal of government should be to provide equality of opportunity for all.* Although seemingly arguable, a statement of belief is not based on facts and so cannot be contested on the basis of facts.

3 Evidence

Evidence demonstrates the validity of your claims. The evidence to support the claim that the school needs a new chemistry lab might include the present lab's age, an inventory of facilities and equipment, and the testimony of chemistry professors.

There are several kinds of evidence:

■ **Facts,** statements whose truth can be verified or inferred: *Poland is slightly smaller than New Mexico.*

■ **Statistics,** facts expressed as numbers: *Of those polled, 22% prefer a flat tax.*

■ **Examples,** specific instances of the point being made: *Many groups, such as the elderly and people with disabilities, would benefit from this policy.*

■ **Expert opinions,** the judgments formed by authorities on the basis of their own examination of the facts: *Affirmative action is necessary to right past injustices, a point argued by Howard Glickstein, a past director of the US Commission on Civil Rights.*

■ **Appeals to readers' beliefs or needs,** statements that ask readers to accept a claim in part because it states something they already accept as true without evidence: *The shabby, antiquated chemistry lab shames the school, making it seem a second-rate institution.*

Evidence must be reliable to be convincing. Ask these questions about your evidence:

■ **Is it accurate**—trustworthy, exact, and undistorted?

■ **Is it relevant**—authoritative, pertinent, and current?

■ **Is it representative**—true to its context, neither under- nor over-representing any element of the sample it's drawn from?

■ **Is it adequate**—plentiful and specific?

4 Assumptions

An **assumption** is an opinion, a principle, or a belief that ties evidence to claims: the assumption explains why a particular piece of evidence is relevant to a particular claim. For instance:

Claim: The college needs a new chemistry laboratory.
Evidence (in part): The testimony of chemistry professors.
Assumption: Chemistry professors are the most capable of evaluating the present lab's quality.

Assumptions are not flaws in arguments but necessities: we all acquire beliefs and opinions that shape our views of the world. Interpreting a work's assumptions is a significant part of critical reading and viewing (see pp. 88 and 93), and recognizing your own assumptions is a significant part of argument. If your readers do not share your assumptions or if they perceive that you are not forthright about your biases, they will be less receptive to your argument.

11b Writing reasonably

Reasonableness is essential if an argument is to establish common ground between you and your readers. Readers expect logical thinking, appropriate appeals, fairness toward the opposition, and, combining all of these, writing that is free of fallacies.

1 Logical thinking

The thesis of your argument is a conclusion you reach by reasoning about evidence. Two processes of reasoning, induction and deduction, are familiar to you even if you don't know their names.

Induction

When you're about to buy a used car, you consult friends, relatives, and consumer guides before deciding what kind of car to buy. Using **induction**, or **inductive reasoning**, you make specific observations about cars (your evidence) and you induce, or infer, a **generalization** that Car X is most reliable. The generalization is a claim supported by your observations.

You might also use inductive reasoning in a term paper on print advertising:

Evidence: Advertisements in newspapers and magazines.
Evidence: Comments by advertisers and publishers.
Evidence: Data on the effectiveness of advertising.
Generalization or claim: Print is the most cost-effective medium for advertising.

Reasoning inductively, you connect your evidence to your generalization by assuming that what is true in one set of circumstances (the evidence you examine) is also true in a similar set of circumstances (evidence you do not examine). With induction you create new knowledge out of old.

The more evidence you accumulate, the more probable it is that your generalization is true. Note, however, that absolute certainty is not possible. At some point you must *assume* that your evidence justifies your generalization, for yourself and your readers. Most errors in inductive reasoning involve oversimplifying either the evidence or the generalization. See pp. 105–07 on fallacies.

Deduction

You use **deduction,** or **deductive reasoning,** when you proceed from your generalization that Car X is the most reliable used car to your own specific circumstances (you want to buy a used car) to the conclusion that you should buy Car X. In deduction your assumption is a generalization, principle, or belief that you think is true. It links the evidence (new information) to the claim (the conclusion you draw). With deduction you apply old information to new.

Say that you want the school administration to postpone new room fees for one dormitory. You can base your argument on a deductive **syllogism:**

> **Premise:** The administration should not raise fees on dorm rooms in poor condition. [A generalization or belief that you assume to be true.]
> **Premise:** The rooms in Polk Hall are in poor condition. [New information: a specific case of the first premise.]
> **Conclusion:** The administration should not raise fees on the rooms in Polk Hall. [Your claim.]

As long as the premises of a syllogism are true, the conclusion derives logically and certainly from them. Errors in constructing syllogisms lie behind many of the fallacies discussed on pp. 106–07.

2 | Rational, emotional, and ethical appeals

In most arguments you will combine **rational appeals** to readers' capacities for logical reasoning with **emotional appeals** to readers' beliefs and feelings. The following example illustrates both: the second sentence makes a rational appeal (to the logic of financial gain), and the third sentence makes an emotional appeal (to the sense of fairness and open-mindedness).

> Advertising should show more people who are physically challenged. The millions of Americans with disabilities have considerable buying power, yet so far advertisers have made no attempt to tap that power. Further, by keeping people with disabilities out of the mainstream depicted in ads, advertisers encourage widespread prejudice against disability, prejudice that frightens and demeans those who hold it.

For an emotional appeal to be successful, it must be appropriate for the audience and the argument:

- **It must not misjudge readers' actual feelings.**
- **It must not raise emotional issues that are irrelevant to the claims and the evidence.** See p. 106 on specific inappropriate appeals, such as bandwagon and ad hominem.

A third kind of approach to readers, the **ethical appeal,** is the sense you give of being a competent, fair person who is worth heeding. A rational appeal and an appropriate emotional appeal contribute to your ethical appeal, and so does your acknowledging opposing views (see below). An argument that is concisely written and correct in grammar, spelling, and other matters will underscore your competence. In addition, a sincere and even tone will assure readers that you are a balanced person who wants to reason with them.

A sincere and even tone need not exclude language with emotional appeal—words such as *frightens* and *demeans* at the end of the example above about advertising. But avoid certain forms of expression that will mark you as unfair:

- **Insulting words,** such as *idiotic* or *fascist*.
- **Biased language,** such as *fags* or *broads* (see **3** pp. 159–62).
- **Sarcasm,** such as the phrase *What a brilliant idea* to indicate contempt for the idea and its originator.
- **Exclamation points!** They'll make you sound shrill!

3 Acknowledgment of opposing views

A good test of your fairness in argument is how you handle possible objections. Assuming your thesis is indeed arguable, then others can marshal their own evidence to support a different view or views. By dealing squarely with those opposing views, you show yourself to be honest and fair. You strengthen your ethical appeal and thus your entire argument.

Before or while you draft your essay, list for yourself all the opposing views you can think of. You'll find them in your research, by talking to friends and classmates, and by critically thinking about your own ideas. You can also look for a range of views in an online discussion that deals with your subject.

A common way to handle opposing views is to state them, refute those you can, grant the validity of others, and demonstrate why, despite their validity, the opposing views are less compelling than your own. A somewhat different approach, developed by the psychologist Carl Rogers, emphasizes the search for common ground. In a **Rogerian argument** you start by showing that you understand readers' views and by establishing points on which you and readers agree and disagree. Creating a connection in this way can be especially helpful when you expect readers to resist your argument, because the connection encourages them to hear you out as you develop your claims. For more on how to organize a Rogerian argument, see p. 108.

4 Fallacies

Fallacies—errors in argument—either evade the issue of the argument or treat the argument as if it were much simpler than it is.

Evasions

An effective argument squarely faces the central issue or question it addresses. An ineffective argument may dodge the issue in one of the following ways:

- **Begging the question:** treating an opinion that is open to question as if it were already proved or disproved.

  The college library's expenses should be reduced by cutting subscriptions to useless periodicals. [Begged questions: Are some of the library's periodicals useless? Useless to whom?]

- **Non sequitur** (Latin: "It does not follow"): linking two or more ideas that in fact have no logical connection. Usually the problem is an unstated assumption that supposedly links the ideas but is false.

  She uses a wheelchair, so she must be unhappy. [Unstated assumption: People who use wheelchairs are unhappy.]

- **Red herring:** introducing an irrelevant issue intended to distract readers from the relevant issues.

  A campus speech code is essential to protect students, who already have enough problems coping with rising tuition. [Tuition costs and speech codes are different subjects. What protections do students need that a speech code will provide?]

- **Appeal to readers' fear or pity:** substituting emotions for reasoning.

  She should not have to pay taxes because she is an aged widow with no friends or relatives. [Appeals to people's pity. Should age and loneliness, rather than income, determine a person's tax obligation?]

- **Bandwagon:** inviting readers to accept a claim because everyone else does.

  As everyone knows, marijuana use leads to heroin addiction. [What is the evidence?]

- **Ad hominem** (Latin: "to the man"): attacking the qualities of the people holding an opposing view rather than the substance of the view itself.

  One of the scientists has been treated for emotional problems, so his pessimism about nuclear waste merits no attention. [Do the scientist's previous emotional problems invalidate his current views?]

Oversimplifications

In a vain attempt to create something neatly convincing, an ineffective argument may conceal or ignore complexities in one of the following ways:

■ **Hasty generalization:** making a claim on the basis of inadequate evidence.

It is disturbing that several of the youths who shot up schools were users of violent video games. Obviously, these games can breed violence, and they should be banned. [A few cases do not establish the relation between the games and violent behavior. Most youths who play violent video games do not behave violently.]

■ **Sweeping generalization:** making an insupportable statement. Many sweeping generalizations are **absolute statements** involving words such as *all, always, never,* and *no one* that allow no exceptions. Others are **stereotypes**, conventional and oversimplified characterizations of a group of people:

People who live in cities are unfriendly.
Californians are fad-crazy.
Women are emotional.
Men can't express their feelings.

(See also **3** pp. 159–62 on sexist and other biased language.)

■ **Reductive fallacy:** oversimplifying (reducing) the relation between causes and effects.

Poverty causes crime. [If so, then why do people who are not poor commit crimes? And why aren't all poor people criminals?]

■ **Post hoc fallacy** (from Latin, *post hoc, ergo propter hoc:* "after this, therefore because of this"): assuming that because *A* preceded *B*, then *A* must have caused *B*.

The town council erred in permitting the adult book store to open, for shortly afterward two women were assaulted. [It cannot be assumed without evidence that the women's assailants visited or were influenced by the bookstore.]

■ **Either/or fallacy:** assuming that a complicated question has only two answers, one good and one bad, both good, or both bad.

Either we permit mandatory drug testing in the workplace or productivity will continue to decline. [Productivity is not necessarily dependent on drug testing.]

Exercise 11.2 Identifying and revising fallacies

Fallacies tend to appear together, as each of the following sentences illustrates. Identify at least one fallacy in each sentence. Then revise the sentences to make them more reasonable.

1 The American government can sell nuclear technology to non-nuclear nations, so why can't individuals, who after all have a God-given right to earn a living as they see fit?

2 A successful marriage demands a maturity that no one under twenty-five possesses.
3 Students' persistent complaints about the grading system prove that it is unfair.
4 People watch television because they are too lazy to talk or read or because they want mindless escape from their lives.
5 Racial tension is bound to occur when people with different backgrounds are forced to live side by side.

11c   Organizing an argument

All arguments include the same parts:

■ **The *introduction* establishes the significance of the subject and provides background.** The introduction may run a paragraph or two, and it generally includes the thesis statement. However, if you think your readers may have difficulty accepting your thesis statement before they see at least some support for it, then it may come later in the paper. (See 1 pp. 51–53 for more on introductions.)

■ **The *body* states and develops the claims supporting the thesis.** In one or more paragraphs, the body develops each claim with clearly relevant evidence. See below for more on organizing the body.

■ **The *response to opposing views* details and addresses those views,** either demonstrating your argument's greater strengths or conceding the opponents' points. See below on organizing this response.

■ **The *conclusion* completes the argument,** restating the thesis, summarizing the supporting claims, and making a final appeal to readers. (See 1 pp. 53–54 for more on conclusions.)

The structure of the body and the response to opposing views depends on your subject, purpose, audience, and form of reasoning. Here are several possible arrangements:

A common scheme	The Rogerian scheme
Claim 1 and evidence	Common ground and concession
Claim 2 and evidence	to opposing views
Claim X and evidence	Claim 1 and evidence
Response to opposing views	Claim 2 and evidence
	Claim X and evidence
A variation	
Claim 1 and evidence	The problem-solution scheme
Response to opposing views	The problem: claims and evidence
Claim 2 and evidence	The solution: claims and evidence
Response to opposing views	Response to opposing views
Claim X and evidence	
Response to opposing views	

11d Using visual arguments

Arguments can be visual as well as verbal. Advertisements often provide the most vivid and memorable examples of visual arguments, but writers in almost every field—from medicine to music, from physics to physical education—support their claims with images. The main elements of written arguments discussed on pp. 100–03—claims, evidence, and assumptions—appear also in visual arguments.

Caution Any visual you include in a paper requires the same detailed citation as a written source. If you plan to publish your argument online, you will also need to seek permission from the author. See **7** pp. 400–07 on citing sources and obtaining permission.

1 Claims

The claims in a visual may be made by composition as well as by content, with or without accompanying words. For instance:

Visual   A photograph framing hundreds of chickens crammed into small cages, resembling familiar images of World War II concentration camps.

Claim   Commercial poultry-raising practices are cruel and unethical.

Visual   A chart with dramatically contrasting bars that represent the optimism, stress, and heart disease reported by people before and after they participated in a program of daily walking.

Claim   Daily exercise leads to a healthier and happier life.

The advertisement on the next page is one in the "Army Strong" series that the United States Army runs for recruitment. As noted in the annotations, the ad makes several claims both in the photograph and in the text.

2 Evidence

The kinds of evidence offered by visuals parallel those found in written arguments:

- **Facts:** You might provide facts in the form of data, as in a graph showing a five-year rise in oil prices or in the text of the US Army advertisement on the next page promising "one of over 150 career opportunities." Or you might draw an inference from data, as the army ad does by stating that the army provides "money for college."
- **Examples:** Most often, you'll use examples to focus on an instance of your argument's claims. In the army ad, the soldier using technical equipment is an example supporting the claim that the army gives soldiers technical training.

Claims in a visual

Visual claim: Serving in the US Army requires technical knowledge and skill.

Visual claim: The US Army provides soldiers with technical knowledge and skill.

Text claim: Service in the US Army can give soldiers technical expertise that they may have thought was beyond them.

BELIEVING IN YOURSELF IS STRONG. ACHIEVING WHAT YOU NEVER BELIEVED POSSIBLE IS ARMY STRONG.

There's strong. And then there's Army Strong. There is no limit to the things you can learn from one of over 150 career opportunities available to you in the Army. You can also receive money for college. Find out more at goarmy.com/strong.

U.S.ARMY

ARMY STRONG.

Advertisement by the United States Army

- **Expert opinions:** You might present a chart from an expert showing a trend in unemployment among high school graduates.
- **Appeals to beliefs or needs:** You might depict how things clearly ought to be (an anti-drug brochure featuring a teenager who is confidently refusing peer pressure) or, in contrast, show how things clearly should not be (a Web site for an anti-hunger campaign featuring images of emaciated children).

To make a visual work hard as evidence, be sure it relates directly to a point in your argument and that it accurately represents the subject. The first graph on the facing page seems to provide good visual evidence for this claim: *The rising birthrate of US teens is an issue that must be addressed.* The data come from the Centers for Disease Control and Prevention (CDC), a US agency and a reputable source. But the data are incomplete, so the claim is inaccurate and the graph is misleading.

Incomplete and unreliable evidence in a visual

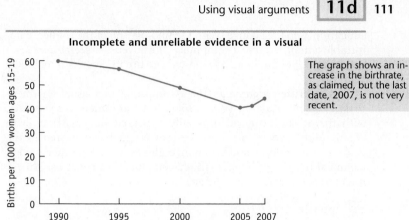

The graph shows an increase in the birthrate, as claimed, but the last date, 2007, is not very recent.

In fact, later data show that the birthrate resumed its downward trend in 2008. The graph below uses more recent data to support a modified claim: *Although the birthrate of US teens has fallen almost every year since 1990, teen pregnancy remains an issue that must be addressed.*

Complete and reliable evidence in a visual

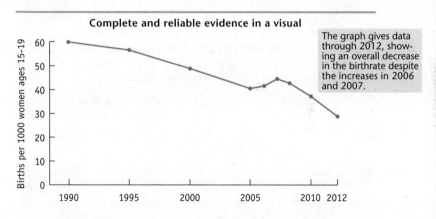

The graph gives data through 2012, showing an overall decrease in the birthrate despite the increases in 2006 and 2007.

For more on using visuals and other media in your writing, see 1 pp. 57–62.

3 Assumptions

Like a written argument, a visual argument is based on assumptions—your ideas about the relation between evidence and claims (pp. 102–03). Look again at the US Army ad opposite. The advertiser seems to have assumed that a strictly factual claim about the benefits of joining the army would not attract as many recruits as a photograph and text that together claim opportunities for training, education, and life change. With the photograph of the soldier, comfortable among technical equipment, the advertiser seems also to be appealing to young men and women who are interested in technical training.

As in written arguments, the assumptions in a visual argument must be appropriate for your readers if the argument is to succeed with them. The army ad originally appeared in magazines with young adult readers, an audience that might be interested in the possibility of training and life change. But to readers uninterested in technical training, the photograph's emphasis on using equipment might actually undermine the ad's effectiveness.

4 Appeals

Visuals can help to strengthen the rational, emotional, and ethical appeals of your written argument (pp. 104–05):

- **Visuals can contribute evidence,** as long as they come from reliable sources, present information accurately and fairly, and relate clearly to the argument's claims.
- **Visuals can appeal to a host of ideas and emotions,** including patriotism, curiosity, moral values, sympathy, and anger. Any such appeal should correctly gauge readers' beliefs and feelings, and it should be clearly relevant to the argument.
- **Visuals can show that you are a competent, fair, and trustworthy source of information,** largely through their relevance, reliability, and sensitivity to readers' needs and feelings.

To see how appeals can work in visuals, look at the billboard below from the Ad Council. The visual illustrates this claim: *Public-*

Appeals in a visual

Rational appeal: Backs up the writer's claim with text that uses slang to address young drivers and a photograph that shows the results of drunk driving.

Emotional appeal: Dramatically illustrates the attempt to discourage young drivers from drinking.

Ethical appeal: Conveys the writer's competence through the appropriateness of the visual for the point being made.

service advertisers try to discourage young drivers from drinking by addressing them directly and depicting the risks.

5 Recognizing fallacies

When making a visual argument, you'll need to guard against all the fallacies discussed on pp. 106–07. Here we'll focus on specific visual examples. The first, which appears in the army ad on p. 110, is snob appeal: inviting readers to be like someone they admire. The soldier is clearly comfortable and competent with the equipment, and the ad appeals to the reader's wish to be someone who is equally as capable and fulfilled. If you join the US Army, the ad says subtly, you too may become strong. The ad does have some substance in its specific and verifiable claim of "over 150 career opportunities" and "money for college," but the soldier in quiet command of his equipment makes a stronger claim.

Another example of a visual fallacy is the hasty generalization, a claim that is based on too little evidence or that misrepresents the facts. The first graph on p. 111 illustrates this fallacy: in omitting recent data that undercut the writer's claim, the graph misrepresents the facts.

11e Examining a sample argument

The following essay by Aimee Lee is a proposal argument that illustrates the principles discussed in this chapter. As you read the essay, notice especially the structure, the relation of claims and supporting evidence (including illustrations), the kinds of appeals Lee makes, and the ways she addresses opposing views.

Awareness, Prevention, Support:

A Proposal to Reduce Cyberbullying

My roommate and I sat in front of her computer staring at the vicious message under her picture. She quickly removed the tag that identified her, but the comments already posted on the photo proved that the damage was done. While she slept, my roommate had become the victim of a cyberbully. She had joined an increasing number of college students who are targeted in texts, e-mails, social-networking sites, and other Web sites that broadcast photographs, videos, and comments. My roommate's experience alerted me that our campus needs a program aimed at awareness and prevention of cyberbullying and support for its victims.

> Introduction: identification of the problem

> Thesis statement: proposal for a solution to the problem

Although schoolyard bullying typically ends with high school graduation, cyberbullying continues in college. According to data gathered by

Evidence of the problem: pub-lished research

researchers at the Massachusetts Aggression Reduction Center (MARC) of Bridgewater State College, cyberbullying behavior decreases when students enter college, but it does not cease. Examining the experiences of first-year students, the researchers found that 8% of college freshmen had been cyberbullied at college and 3% admitted to having cyberbullied another student (Englander, Mills, and McCoy 217-18). In a survey of fifty-two freshmen, I found further evidence of cyberbullying on this campus. I asked two questions: (1) Have you been involved in cyberbullying as a victim, a bully, or both? (2) If you answered "no" to the first question, do you know anyone who has been involved in cyberbullying as a victim, a bully, or both? While a large majority of the students I surveyed (74%) have not been touched by cyberbullying, more than one-fourth (26%) have been involved personally or know someone who has, as shown in fig. 1. Taken together, the evidence demonstrates that cyberbullying is significant in colleges and specifically on our campus.

Evidence of the problem: student's own research

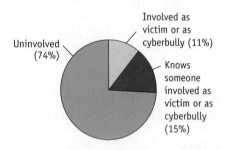

Pie chart showing results of student's research

Fig. 1. Involvement in cyberbullying among fifty-two first-year students.

Explanation of proposed solu-tion: goals of the program

The proposed "Stop Cyberbullying" program aims to reduce the behavior through a month-long campaign of awareness, prevention, and support modeled on the college's "Alcohol Awareness Month" program. The program can raise awareness of cyberbullying by explaining what cyberbul-lying is and by informing students about the college's code of conduct, which prohibits cyberbullying behavior but which few people read. The program can work to prevent cyberbullying by appealing to students to treat those around them respectfully. And, with the participation of the counseling department, the program can provide support for victims, their friends, and others involved in the behavior.

Explanation of proposed solu-tion: specific actions

If adopted, the program can use online and print media to get the message out to the entire college community. For instance, an extensive brochure distributed to first-year students and available through the coun-seling center can describe cyberbullying and how it violates the college's code of conduct, give strategies for avoiding it, and provide resources for help. During the month-long campaign, flyers posted on campus (see fig. 2) can also raise awareness of the problem, and brief postings to the college's Web site, *Facebook* page, and *Twitter* feed can reach students who take online and hybrid classes as well as those in traditional classes.

Have YOU been a victim of cyberbullying? Have you read something about yourself that made you feel embarrassed, intimidated, or just bad?

Are YOU a cyberbully? Have you sent a message or posted something that you knew would make someone feel embarrassed, intimidated, or just bad?

Do YOU know someone who is being cyberbullied or who is bullying someone else?

Together WE can BREAK the cycle:
- **Wait before you post!** Think about who may read it and how they might respond.
- **Be informed about our campus code of conduct** and what it says about cyberbullying.
- **Get help if you need it.** The counseling office is available to help you cope with or stop cyberbullying.

You can help stop cyberbullying STOP
www.mrcc.edu/cyberbullying

Visual evidence of program publicity

Fig. 2. Sample flyer for proposed "Stop Cyberbullying" program.

Because this college already has a code of conduct in place and because the state has recently enacted anti-bullying legislation that includes cyberbullying, some students and administrators may contend that enough is being done to deal with the problem. To the administration's credit, the code of conduct contains specific language about online behavior, but promises of punishment for proven allegations do not address several aspects of the problem.

Anticipation of objection: code of conduct does enough

First, cyberbullies are sometimes anonymous. To accuse another student of cyberbullying, the victim needs to know the identity of the bully. While postings on *Facebook* are attached to real names, most college gossip sites are anonymous. On such sites, a cyberbully can post photographs, videos, and aggressive messages under the cover of anonymity.

Response to objection: anonymity of cyberbullies

Second, even when the identities of cyberbullies are known, the bullying is often invisible to those in a position to take action against it. According to Ikuko Aoyama and Tony L. Talbert at Baylor University, cyberbullying occurs frequently in groups of people who know each other

Response to objection: invisibility of the problem

and who attack and retaliate: students are rarely "pure bullies" or "pure victims" but instead are often part of a "bully-victim group" (qtd. in Laster). Moreover, even if students want to separate from bullying groups, Englander, Mills, and McCoy found that they probably will not report cyberbullying incidents to authorities because students generally believe that administrators are unlikely to do anything about cyberbullying (221). Thus counselors and administrators who may be interested in helping students to cope are often unaware of the problem.

Response to objection: conduct codes ineffective

Third, conduct codes rarely affect cyberbullying. While some cyberbullying has resulted in tragedy, many aggressive incidents do not rise to the level of punishable offenses ("Cyberbullying"). More often they consist of a humiliating photograph or a mean message—hurtful, to be sure, but not necessarily in violation of the law or the code of conduct. Indeed, the hurdles to getting recourse through official channels are fairly high.

Conclusion

Given its hidden nature and the inability of punitive measures to stop it, cyberbullying needs another approach—namely, a program that teaches students to recognize and regulate their own behavior and provides help when they find themselves in a difficult situation. This program will not heal the wound suffered by my roommate, nor will it prevent all cyberbullying. But if adopted, the program will demonstrate to the college community that the administration is aware of the problem, eager to prevent it, and willing to commit resources to support students who are affected by it. [New page.]

Works cited in MLA style (MLA p. 445)

Works Cited

"Cyberbullying Goes to College." *Bostonia*. Boston U, Spring 2009. Web. 18 Feb. 2014.

Englander, Elizabeth, Elizabeth Mills, and Meghan McCoy. "Cyberbullying and Information Exposure: User-Generated Content in Post-Secondary Education." *Violence and Society in the Twenty-First Century*. Spec. issue of *International Journal of Contemporary Sociology* 46.2 (2009): 213-30. Web. 21 Feb. 2014.

Laster, Jill. "Two Scholars Examine Cyberbullying among College Students." *Chronicle of Higher Education*. Chronicle of Higher Education, June 2010. Web. 18 Feb. 2014.

—Aimee Lee (student)

12 Essay Exams

Chapter essentials

- Prepare in advance for an essay exam (below).
- Take a few minutes to plan your answer before you start to write (below).
- Open an essay exam with a direct response to the question (p. 119).
- Develop your response (p. 119).
- Reread the essay before you turn it in (p. 120).

Visit MyWritingLab™ for more resources on essay exams.

In writing an essay for an examination, you summarize or analyze a topic, usually in several paragraphs or more and usually within a time limit. An essay question not only tests your knowledge of a subject (as short-answer and objective questions do) but also tests your ability to think critically about what you have learned. If you have not already done so, read Chapter 10 on critical reading and writing.

12a Preparing for an essay examination

To do well on an essay exam, you will need to understand the course content, not only the facts but also the interpretation of them and the relations between them.

- **Take careful lecture notes.**
- **Thoughtfully, critically read the assigned texts or articles.**
- **Review regularly.** Give the material time to sink in and stimulate your thinking.
- **Create summaries.** Recast others' ideas in your own words, and extract the meaning from notes and texts. (See pp. 85–87 for instructions on summarizing.)
- **Prepare notes or outlines to reorganize the course material around key topics or issues.** One technique is to create and answer likely essay questions. For instance, in a business course you might focus on the advantages and disadvantages of several approaches to management. In a short-story course you might locate a theme running through all the stories you have read by a certain author or from a certain period. In a psychology course you might outline various theorists' views of what causes a disorder such as schizophrenia.

12b Planning your time and your answer

When you first receive an examination, take a few minutes to get your bearings and plan an approach. The time will not be wasted.

- **Read the exam all the way through at least once.** Don't start answering any questions until you've seen them all.
- **Weigh the questions.** Determine which questions seem most important, which ones are going to be most difficult for you, and approximately how much time you'll need for each question. (Your instructor may help by assigning a point value to each question as a guide to its importance or by suggesting an amount of time for you to spend on each question.)

Planning continues when you turn to an individual essay question. Resist the temptation to rush right into an answer without some planning: a few minutes can save you time later and help you produce a stronger essay.

- **Read the question at least twice.** You will be more likely to stick to the question and answer it fully.
- **Examine the words in the question and consider their implications.** Look especially for words such as *describe, define, explain, summarize, analyze, evaluate,* and *interpret,* each of which requires a different kind of response. Here, for example, is an essay question whose key term is *explain*:

Question
Given humans' natural and historical curiosity about themselves, why did a scientific discipline of anthropology not arise until the 20th century? Explain, citing specific details.

See **1** pp. 47–51 for discussions of many of the terms likely to appear in essay questions.

- **Make a brief outline of the main ideas you want to cover.** Use the back of the exam sheet or booklet for scratch paper. In the brief outline below, a student planned her answer to the anthropology question above.

Outline
1. Unscientific motivations behind 19th-c anthro.

   Imperialist/colonialist govts.
   Practical goals
   Nonobjective and unscientific (Herodotus, Cushing)
2. 19th-c ethnocentricity (vs. cultural relativism)
3. 19th-c anthro. = object collecting

   20th-c shift from museum to univ.
   Anthro. becomes acad. disc. and professional (Boas, Malinowski)

- **Write a thesis statement for your essay that responds directly to the question and represents your view of the topic.** (If you are unsure of how to write a thesis statement, see **1** pp. 14–17.) Include key phrases that you can expand with supporting evidence for your view. The thesis statement of the student whose outline appears above concisely previews a three-part answer to the sample question:

Thesis statement
Anthropology did not emerge as a scientific discipline until the 20th century because of the practical and political motivations behind 19th-century ethnographic studies, the ethnocentric bias of Western researchers, and a conception of culture that was strictly material.

12c Starting the essay

An essay exam does not require a smooth and inviting opening. Instead, begin by stating your thesis immediately and giving an overview of the rest of your essay. Such a capsule version of your answer tells your reader (and grader) generally how much command you have and also how you plan to develop your answer. It also gets you off to a good start.

12d Developing the essay

Develop your essay as you would develop any piece of sound academic writing:

- **Observe the methods, terms, or other special requirements of the discipline in which you are writing.**
- **Support your thesis statement with solid generalizations,** each one perhaps the topic sentence of a paragraph.
- **Support each generalization with specific, relevant evidence.**

If you observe a few *don't*s as well, your essay will have more substance:

- **Avoid filling out the essay by repeating yourself.**
- **Avoid other kinds of wordiness that pad and confuse,** whether intentionally or not. (See **3** pp. 174–78.)
- **Avoid resorting to purely subjective feelings.** Keep focused on analysis, or whatever is asked of you. (It may help to abolish the word *I* from the essay.)

The following essay illustrates a successful answer to the sample essay question on the facing page about anthropology. It was written in the allotted time of forty minutes. Marginal comments on the essay highlight its effective elements.

Essay exam response

Anthropology did not emerge as a scientific discipline until the 20th century because of the practical and political motivations behind 19th-century ethnographic studies, the ethnocentric bias of Western researchers, and a conception of culture that was strictly material.

Introduction stating thesis

Direct answer to question and preview of three-part response

Before the 20th century, ethnographic studies were almost always used for practical goals. The study of human culture can

First main point: practical aims

Example

be traced back at least as far as Herodotus's investigations of the Mediterranean peoples. Herodotus was like many pre-20th-century "anthropologists" in that he was employed by a government that needed information about its neighbors, just as the colonial nations in the 19th century needed information about their newly conquered subjects. The early politically motivated ethnographic studies that the colonial nations sponsored tended to be isolated projects, and they aimed less to advance general knowledge than to solve a specific problem. Frank Hamilton

Example

Cushing, who was employed by the American government to study the Zuni tribe of New Mexico, and who is considered one of the pioneers of anthropology, didn't even publish his findings. The political and practical aims of anthropologists and the nature of their research prevented their work from being a scholarly discipline in its own right.

Second main point: ethnocentricity

Anthropologists of the 19th century also fell short of the standards of objectivity needed for truly scientific study. This partly had to do with anthropologists' close connection to imperialist governments. But even independent researchers were hampered by the prevailing assumption that Western cultures were inherently superior. While the modern anthropologist believes that a culture must be studied in terms of its own values, early ethnographers were ethnocentric: they judged "primitive" cultures by their own "civilized" values. "Primitive" peoples were seen as uninteresting in their own right. The reasons to study them, ultimately, were to satisfy curiosity, to exploit them, or to prove their inferiority. There was even some debate as to whether so-called savage peoples were human.

Third main point (with transition *Finally*): focus on objects

Finally, the 19th century tended to conceive of culture in narrow, material terms, often reducing it to a collection of artifacts. When not working for a government, early ethnographers usually worked for a museum. The enormous collections of exotica still found in many museums today are the legacy of this 19th-century object-oriented conception of anthropology, which ignored the myths, symbols, and rituals the objects related to. It was only when the museum tradition was broadened to include all aspects of a culture that anthropology could come into existence as a scien-

Examples

tific discipline. When anthropologists like Franz Boas and Bronislaw Malinowski began to publish their findings for others to read and criticize and began to move from the museum to the university, the discipline gained stature and momentum.

Conclusion, restating thesis supported by essay

In brief, anthropology required a whole series of ideological shifts to become modern. Once it broke free of its purely practical bent, the cultural prejudices of its practitioners, and the narrow conception that limited it to a collection of objects, anthropology could grow into a science.

12e Rereading the essay

The time limit on an essay examination does not allow for the careful rethinking and revision you would give an essay or research paper. You need to write clearly and concisely the first time. But try to leave yourself a few minutes after finishing the entire exam for rereading the essay (or essays) and doing touch-ups.

- **Correct mistakes:** illegible passages, misspellings, grammatical errors, and accidental omissions.
- **Verify that your thesis is accurate**—that it is, in fact, what you ended up writing about.
- **Ensure that you have supported all your generalizations.** Cross out irrelevant ideas and details, and add any information that now seems important. (Write on another page, if necessary, keying the addition to the page on which it belongs.)

13 Oral Presentations

Chapter essentials

- Prepare and organize an oral presentation (below).
- Plan the delivery of a presentation, including any visual aids (p. 122).
- Practice in advance (p. 124).

Visit MyWritingLab™ for more resources on oral presentations.

Speaking to a group can produce anxiety, even for those who are experienced at it. This chapter shows how to use organization, voice, and other techniques to present your writing to a listening audience.

13a Organizing the presentation

Give your oral presentation a recognizable shape so that listeners can see how ideas and details relate to each other.

The introduction

The beginning of an oral presentation should try to accomplish three goals:

- **Gain the audience's attention and interest.** Begin with a question, an unusual example or statistic, or a short, relevant story.
- **Put yourself in the speech.** Demonstrate your expertise, experience, or concern to gain the interest and trust of your audience.
- **Introduce and preview your topic and purpose.** By the time your introduction is over, listeners should know what your subject is and the direction you'll take to develop your ideas.

Your introduction should prepare your audience for your main points but not give them away. Think of it as a sneak preview of your speech, not the place for an apology such as *I wish I'd had more time to prepare . . .* or a dull statement such as *My speech is about. . . .*

Supporting material

Just as you do when writing, you should use facts, statistics, examples, and expert opinions to support the main points of your oral presentation. In addition, you can make your points more memorable with vivid description, well-chosen quotations, true or fictional stories, and analogies.

The conclusion

You want your conclusion to be clear, of course, but you also want it to be memorable. Remind listeners of how your topic and main idea connect to their needs and interests. If your speech was motivational, tap an emotion that matches your message. If your speech was informational, give some tips on how to remember important details.

13b Delivering the presentation

Methods of delivery

You can deliver an oral presentation in several ways:

- **Impromptu, without preparation:** Make a presentation without planning what you will say. Impromptu speaking requires confidence and excellent general preparation.
- **Extemporaneously:** Prepare notes to glance at but not read from. This method allows you to look and sound natural while ensuring that you don't forget anything.
- **Speaking from a text:** Read aloud from a written presentation. You won't lose your way, but you may lose your audience. Avoid reading for an entire presentation.
- **Speaking from memory:** Deliver a prepared presentation without notes. You can look at your audience every minute, but the stress of retrieving the next words may make you seem tense and unresponsive.

Vocal delivery

The sound of your voice will influence how listeners receive you. Rehearse your presentation several times until you are confident that you are speaking loudly, slowly, and clearly enough for your audience to understand you.

Physical delivery

You are more than your spoken words when you make an oral presentation. If you are able, stand up to deliver your presentation, turning your body toward one side of the room and then the other, stepping out from behind any lectern or desk, and gesturing as appropriate. Above all, make eye contact with your audience as you speak. Looking directly in your listeners' eyes conveys your honesty, your confidence, and your control of the material.

(CULTURE LANGUAGE) Eye contact is customary in the United States, both in conversation and in oral presentation. Listeners expect it and may perceive a speaker who doesn't make eye contact as evasive or insincere.

Visual aids

You can supplement an oral presentation with visual aids such as posters, models, slides, or videos.

- **Use visual aids to underscore your points.** Short lists of key ideas, illustrations such as graphs or photographs, and objects such as models can make your presentation more interesting and memorable. But use visual aids judiciously: a constant flow of illustrations or objects will bury your message.
- **Match visual aids and setting.** An audience of five people may be able to see a photograph and share a chart; a classroom or an audience of a hundred will need projected images.
- **Coordinate visual aids with your message.** Time each visual to reinforce a point you're making. Tell listeners what they're looking at. Give them enough viewing time so that they don't mind turning their attention back to you.
- **Show visual aids only while they're needed.** To regain your audience's attention, remove or turn off any aid as soon as you have finished with it.

Many speakers use *PowerPoint*, *Prezi*, or other software to project main points, key images, video, or other elements. To use such software effectively, follow the guidelines with the samples on the next page and also these tips:

- **Don't put your whole presentation on screen.** Select key points and distill them to as few words as possible. Use slides as quick, easy-to-remember summaries or ways to present examples. For a twenty-minute presentation, plan to use approximately ten slides.
- **Use a simple design.** Avoid turning your presentation into a show about the software's many capabilities and special effects.
- **Make text readable.** The type should be easy to see for viewers in the back of the room, whether the lights are on or not.
- **Use a consistent design.** For optimal flow through the presentation, each slide should be formatted similarly.
- **Add relevant images and media.** Presentation software allows you to play images, audio, and video as part of your speech. Before you add them, however, be sure each has a point so that

Presentation slides

First slide, introducing the project and presentation.

Making a Difference?

A Service-Learning Project at ReadingWorks

Springfield Veterans Administration Hospital

Jessica Cho
Nathan Hall
Alex Ramirez
Spring 2014

Simple, consistent slide design focusing viewers' attention on information, not software features.

Second slide, including a title and brief, bulleted points to be explained by the speaker.

Semester goals

• Research adult literacy.
• Tutor military veterans.
• Keep a journal.
• Collaborate on documents for ReadingWorks.
• Report experiences and findings.

Later slide, expanding on earlier "Semester goals" slide.

Link to video about the project's activities.

Photograph reinforcing the project's activities.

Tutor veterans

Participate in tutor training.
http://www.youtube.com/watch?v=526phLMJg

Get matched with a student.

Tutor two hours each week at ReadingWorks.

you don't overload the presentation. See **1** pp. 57–61 on choosing and using visuals and other media.

■ **Review all your slides before the presentation.** Go through the slides to be sure they are complete, consistent, and easy to read. Proofread each slide.

- **Don't talk to the computer or the projection during the presentation.** Move away from both and face the audience.
- **Pace your presentation and your slides.** If a section of your presentation doesn't have a slide keyed to it, insert a blank slide to project during that section.

Practice

Take time to rehearse your presentation out loud, with the notes you will be using. Gauge your performance by making an audio- or videotape of yourself or by practicing in front of a mirror. Practicing out loud will also tell you if your presentation is running too long or too short.

If you plan to use visual aids, you'll need to practice with them, too. Your goal is to eliminate hitches (slides in the wrong order, missing charts) and to weave the visuals seamlessly into your presentation.

Stage fright

Many people report that speaking in front of an audience is their number-one fear. Even many experienced and polished speakers have some anxiety about delivering an oral presentation, but they use this nervous energy to their advantage, letting it propel them into working hard on each presentation. Several techniques can help you reduce anxiety:

- **Use simple relaxation exercises.** Deep breathing or tensing and relaxing your stomach muscles can ease some of the physical symptoms of speech anxiety—stomachache, rapid heartbeat, and shaky hands, legs, and voice.
- **Think positively.** Instead of worrying about the mistakes you might make, concentrate on how well you've prepared and practiced your presentation and how significant your ideas are.
- **Don't avoid opportunities to speak in public.** Practice and experience build speaking skills and offer the best insurance for success.

14 Public Writing

At some point in your life, you're likely to write for a public audience—readers beyond your instructor, classmates, family, and friends. The conventions of public writing depend on the purpose of the writing, who will read it, and its genre. This chapter discusses several common public-writing situations.

CULTURE LANGUAGE Public writing in the United States, especially in business, favors efficiency and may seem abrupt or impolite compared with such writing in your native culture. For instance, a business letter elsewhere may be expected to begin with polite questions about the addressee or with compliments for the addressee's company, whereas US business letters are expected to get right to the point.

14a Writing on social media

Public writing on social media varies tremendously. It may be thoughtful and carefully crafted, or it may be quick and artless, as in a comment on a Web news story dashed off in frustration or anger. As you make your own writing public—and make yourself public, too—consider these questions:

- **How are you presenting yourself?** How do you want to be viewed by readers—as knowledgable, reasonable, witty, heartfelt, emotional, ranting, or something else? Consider whether your message comes across in the way you intend.
- **Who might read your post?** Once posted, your words may have a very large audience consisting of people whom you do not know and who do not necessarily see things as you do.
- **Are you protecting your own and others' privacy?** Comments, tweets, and photographs that reveal personal information can be hurtful or embarrassing to you and others. Consider who may see your message or photo.
- **How will you feel about the post in the future?** Some online posts, such as comments on news stories, are never fully erased. Think

how the message or photo will reflect on you months or years from now.
- **Would you say face to face what you've written?** Imagine saying what you've written to the person your message is about or is addressed to. If you wouldn't say it, don't post it.

14b Writing business letters

When you write for business, you are addressing busy people who want to see quickly why you are writing and how they should respond to you. Follow these general guidelines:

- **State your purpose right at the start.**
- **Be straightforward, clear, concise, objective, and courteous.**
- **Observe conventions of grammar and usage,** which make your writing clear and impress your reader with your care.

1 Business letter format

Business letters sent on paper or by e-mail have similar formats, with differences for the different media.

Letters on paper

Use either unlined white paper measuring 8½" × 11" or letterhead stationery with your address preprinted at the top of the sheet. Print the letter single-spaced (with double spacing between elements) on one side of a sheet. The sample on the next page shows a common format.

- **The *return-address heading* gives your address and the date.** Do not include your name. If you are using letterhead, add only the date.
- **The *inside address* shows the name, title, and complete address of the person you are writing to.**
- **The *salutation* greets the addressee.** Whenever possible, address your letter to a specific person. (Contact the company or department to ask whom to address.) If you can't find a person's name, then use a job title (*Dear Human Resources Manager, Dear Customer Service Manager*) or use a general salutation (*Dear Smythe Shoes*). Use *Ms.* as the title for a woman.
- **The *body* contains the substance.** Instead of indenting the first line of each paragraph, double-space between paragraphs.
- **The *close* should reflect the level of formality in the salutation:** *Respectfully, Cordially, Yours truly,* and *Sincerely* are more formal closes; *Regards* and *Best wishes* are less formal.
- **The *signature* has two parts:** your name typed four lines below the close, and your handwritten signature in the space between.

Business letter (cover letter)

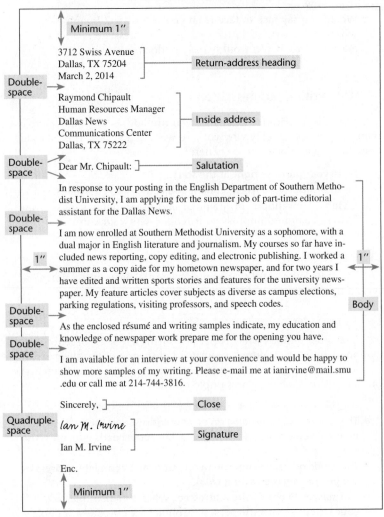

Minimum 1″

3712 Swiss Avenue
Dallas, TX 75204 ⎤——— Return-address heading
March 2, 2014 ⎦

Double-space →

Raymond Chipault
Human Resources Manager
Dallas News ⎤——— Inside address
Communications Center
Dallas, TX 75222 ⎦

Double-space

Dear Mr. Chipault: ⎤——— Salutation

In response to your posting in the English Department of Southern Metho-dist University, I am applying for the summer job of part-time editorial assistant for the Dallas News.

Double-space →

I am now enrolled at Southern Methodist University as a sophomore, with a dual major in English literature and journalism. My courses so far have in-cluded news reporting, copy editing, and electronic publishing. I worked a summer as a copy aide for my hometown newspaper, and for two years I have edited and written sports stories and features for the university news-paper. My feature articles cover subjects as diverse as campus elections, parking regulations, visiting professors, and speech codes.

1″ ⟷   1″ ⟷   Body

Double-space

As the enclosed résumé and writing samples indicate, my education and knowledge of newspaper work prepare me for the opening you have.

Double-space

I am available for an interview at your convenience and would be happy to show more samples of my writing. Please e-mail me at ianirvine@mail.smu .edu or call me at 214-744-3816.

Sincerely, ⎤——— Close

Quadruple-space

Ian M. Irvine ⎤——— Signature
Ian M. Irvine ⎦

Enc.

Minimum 1″

Enclose a printed business letter in an envelope that will accom-modate the letter once it is folded horizontally in thirds. The enve-lope should show your name and address in the upper left corner and the addressee's name, title, and address in the center.

Letters by e-mail

An e-mailed business letter lacks some parts of a paper letter: the return-address heading, handwritten signature, and envelope. Your mailing address falls at the end of the letter rather than the top. Otherwise, it has the same parts listed above: salutation, body, close, and typed signature. And it has two features that paper letters do not:

- **Your e-mail address:** Use a businesslike address that is a variation on your name, such as *john.doe, johndoe,* or *jdoe.* Do not use an address with an anonymous username.
- **The subject line:** Make it short and accurate, reflecting the message of your letter: for instance, *Subscription problem* or *Copy aide position.*

14c Writing a job application

In applying for a job or requesting a job interview, you will submit both a résumé and a cover letter, probably in electronic form. You may also create a social-media profile that prospective employers can consult when they are considering your application.

1 Cover letter

The sample on the preceding page illustrates the key features of a cover letter:

- **Interpret your résumé for the particular job.** Don't detail your entire résumé, reciting your job history. Instead, tailor your letter to the job description, highlighting how your qualifications and experience match the job you are applying for.
- **Announce at the outset what job you seek and how you heard about it.**
- **Include any special reason you have for applying,** such as a specific career goal.
- **Summarize your qualifications for this particular job,** including relevant facts about education and employment history and emphasizing notable accomplishments. Mention that additional information appears in an accompanying résumé.
- **Describe your availability.** At the end of the letter, mention that you are free for an interview at the convenience of the addressee, or specify when you will be available (for instance, when your current job or classes leave you free).

2 Résumé

Your résumé should provide information in table format that allows a potential employer to evaluate your qualifications. The résumé should include your name and address, the position you seek, your education and employment history, any special skills or awards, and how to obtain your references. Fit all the information on one uncrowded page unless your education and experience are extensive.

Most job seekers prepare two versions of their résumé: a formatted version to print and take to in-person interviews (sample below) and a plainer version to submit online (sample on the facing page). Employers may add the electronic version to a computerized database of applicants, so the format and language are important to ensure that your résumé is retrievable.

Résumé (print)

Name and contact information	**Ian M. Irvine**	3712 Swiss Avenue Dallas, TX 75204 214-744-3816 ianirvine@mail.smu.edu
Desired position stated simply and clearly	**Position desired**	Part-time editorial assistant.
Education before work experience for most college students	**Education**	*Southern Methodist University*, 2012 to present. Current standing: sophomore. Major: English literature and journalism. Journalism courses: news reporting, copy editing, electronic publishing, communication arts, broadcast journalism. *Abilene (Texas) Senior High School*, 2008-12. Graduated with academic, college-preparatory degree.
Headings marking sections, set off with space and highlighting	**Employment history**	2012 to present. Reporter, *Daily Campus*, student newspaper of Southern Methodist University. Write regular coverage of baseball, track, and soccer teams. Write feature stories on campus policies and events. Edit sports news, campus listings, features.
Conventional use of capital letters: yes for proper nouns and after periods; no for job titles, course names, department names, and so on		Summer 2013. Copy aide, *Abilene Reporter-News*. Assisted reporters with copy routing and research. Summer 2012. Painter, Longhorn Painters, Abilene. Prepared and painted exteriors and interiors of houses.
	Special skills	Fluent in Spanish. Proficient in Internet research and word processing.
Standard, consistent type font	**References**	Available on request: Placement Office Southern Methodist University Dallas, TX 75275

■ **Keep the design simple for accurate scanning or electronic transmittal.** Avoid images, bullets, boldface, italics, underlining, unusual fonts, more than one column, centered headings, and vertical or horizontal lines.

■ **Use concise, specific words to describe your skills and experience.** The employer's computer may use keywords (often nouns) to identify the résumés of suitable job candidates, and you want to ensure that your résumé includes keywords that match the

Résumé (scannable or electronic)

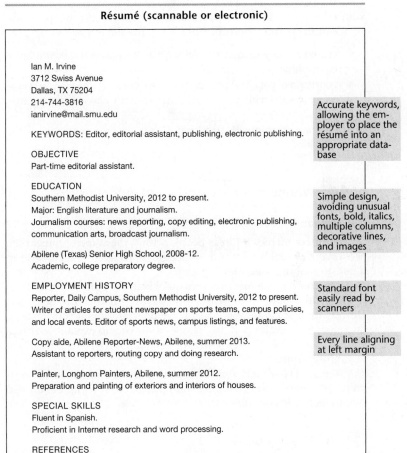

Ian M. Irvine
3712 Swiss Avenue
Dallas, TX 75204
214-744-3816
ianirvine@mail.smu.edu

KEYWORDS: Editor, editorial assistant, publishing, electronic publishing.

OBJECTIVE
Part-time editorial assistant.

EDUCATION
Southern Methodist University, 2012 to present.
Major: English literature and journalism.
Journalism courses: news reporting, copy editing, electronic publishing, communication arts, broadcast journalism.

Abilene (Texas) Senior High School, 2008-12.
Academic, college preparatory degree.

EMPLOYMENT HISTORY
Reporter, Daily Campus, Southern Methodist University, 2012 to present.
Writer of articles for student newspaper on sports teams, campus policies, and local events. Editor of sports news, campus listings, and features.

Copy aide, Abilene Reporter-News, Abilene, summer 2013.
Assistant to reporters, routing copy and doing research.

Painter, Longhorn Painters, Abilene, summer 2012.
Preparation and painting of exteriors and interiors of houses.

SPECIAL SKILLS
Fluent in Spanish.
Proficient in Internet research and word processing.

REFERENCES
Available on request:
Placement Office
Southern Methodist University
Dallas, TX 75275

Accurate keywords, allowing the employer to place the résumé into an appropriate database

Simple design, avoiding unusual fonts, bold, italics, multiple columns, decorative lines, and images

Standard font easily read by scanners

Every line aligning at left margin

field and the job description. Look for likely keywords in the employer's description of the job you seek, and name your specific skills. Write concretely with words like *manager* (not *person with responsibility for*) and *reporter* (not *staff member who reports*).

3 Creating an online profile

Many job seekers use social-networking sites such as *LinkedIn* to create online profiles. Like a résumé, an online profile should state the position you seek and use keywords to accurately describe your education, skills, and previous work and volunteer experience. In addition, an online profile often contains the following:

- **A summary of your qualifications, goals, and experience,** similar to the opening paragraphs of a cover letter.
- **A portfolio of your best projects that are relevant to the job you seek—** for instance, writing that you completed for classes, internships, or jobs.
- **A current, high-quality headshot of you,** dressed as you would be for a job.

14d Writing memos, reports, and proposals

1 Memos

Business memos address people within the same organization. Most memos deal briefly with a specific topic, such as an answer to a question or an evaluation.

The content of a memo comes quickly to the point and discusses it efficiently. State your reason for writing in the first sentence. Devote the first paragraph to a concise presentation of your answer, conclusion, or evaluation. In the rest of the memo explain your reasoning or evidence. Use headings or lists as appropriate to highlight key information.

Memos are usually sent by e-mail. See the sample on the next page and consult the guidelines on pp. 79–80 for using e-mail and other electronic communication.

2 Reports and proposals

Reports and proposals are text-heavy documents, sometimes lengthy, that convey information such as the results of research, a plan for action, or a recommendation for change.

Reports and proposals usually divide into sections. The sections vary depending on the purpose of the document, but usually they

Memo

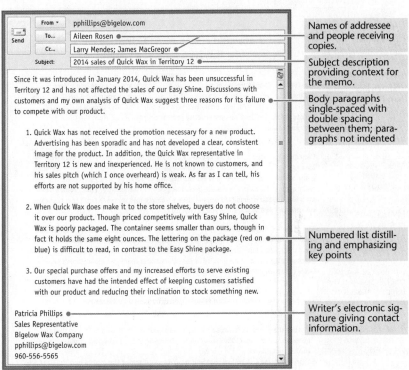

From ▾	pphillips@bigelow.com
To...	Aileen Rosen ●
Cc...	Larry Mendes; James MacGregor ●
Subject:	2014 sales of Quick Wax in Territory 12 ●

Since it was introduced in January 2014, Quick Wax has been unsuccessful in Territory 12 and has not affected the sales of our Easy Shine. Discussions with customers and my own analysis of Quick Wax suggest three reasons for its failure ● to compete with our product.

1. Quick Wax has not received the promotion necessary for a new product. Advertising has been sporadic and has not developed a clear, consistent image for the product. In addition, the Quick Wax representative in Territory 12 is new and inexperienced. He is not known to customers, and his sales pitch (which I once overheard) is weak. As far as I can tell, his efforts are not supported by his home office.

2. When Quick Wax does make it to the store shelves, buyers do not choose it over our product. Though priced competitively with Easy Shine, Quick Wax is poorly packaged. The container seems smaller than ours, though in fact it holds the same eight ounces. The lettering on the package (red on ● blue) is difficult to read, in contrast to the Easy Shine package.

3. Our special purchase offers and my increased efforts to serve existing customers have had the intended effect of keeping customers satisfied with our product and reducing their inclination to stock something new.

Patricia Phillips ●
Sales Representative
Bigelow Wax Company
pphillips@bigelow.com
960-556-5565

Names of addressee and people receiving copies.

Subject description providing context for the memo.

Body paragraphs single-spaced with double spacing between them; paragraphs not indented

Numbered list distilling and emphasizing key points

Writer's electronic signature giving contact information.

include an overview or summary, which tells the reader what the document is about; a statement of the problem or need, which justifies the report or proposal; a statement of the plan or solution, which responds to the need or problem; and a recommendation or evaluation. See the sample report on the next page and consider the following guidelines as you prepare a report or proposal:

- **Do your research.** To write a successful report or proposal, you must be well informed. Be alert to where you have enough information or where you don't.
- **Focus on the purpose of each section.** Stick to the point of each section, saying only what you need to say, even if you have additional information. Each section should accomplish its purpose and contribute to the whole.
- **Follow an appropriate format.** In many businesses, reports and proposals have specific formatting requirements. If you are unsure about the requirements, ask your supervisor.

Report

Descriptive title conveying report's contents

Standard format: summary, statement of the problem, solutions, and (not shown) recommendations

Major sections delineated by headings

Formal tone, appropriate to a business-writing situation

Single spacing with double spacing between paragraphs and around the list

Bulleted list emphasizing alternative solutions

Canada Geese at ABC Institute: An Environmental Problem

Summary

The flock of Canada geese on and around ABC Institute's grounds has grown dramatically in recent years to become a nuisance and an environmental problem. This report reviews the problem, considers possible solutions, and proposes that ABC Institute and the US Fish and Wildlife Service cooperate to reduce the flock by humane means.

The Problem

Canada geese began living at Taylor Lake next to ABC Institute when they were relocated there in 1995 by the state game department. As a nonmigratory flock, the geese are present year-round, with the highest population each year occurring in early spring. In recent years the flock has grown dramatically. The Audubon Society's annual Christmas bird census shows a thirty-fold increase from the 37 geese counted in 1996 to the 1125 counted in 2013.

The principal environmental problem caused by the geese is pollution of grass and water by defecation. Geese droppings cover the ABC Institute's grounds as well as the park's picnicking areas. The runoff from these droppings into Taylor Lake has substantially affected the quality of the lake's water, so that local authorities have twice (2012 and 2013) issued warnings against swimming.

Possible Solutions

The goose overpopulation and resulting environmental problems have several possible solutions:

- Harass the geese with dogs and audiovisual effects (light and noise) so that the geese choose to leave. This solution is inhumane to the geese and unpleasant for human neighbors.
- Feed the geese a chemical that will weaken the shells of their eggs and thus reduce growth of the flock. This solution is inhumane to the geese and also impractical, because geese are long-lived.
- Kill adult geese. This solution is, obviously, inhumane to the geese.
- Thin the goose population by trapping and removing many geese (perhaps 600) to areas less populated by humans, such as wildlife preserves.

Though costly (see figures below), the last solution is the most humane. It would be harmless to the geese, provided that sizable netted enclosures are used for traps. [Discussion of solution and "Recommendations" section follow.]

14e Writing for community work

At some point in your life, you're likely to volunteer for a community organization such as a soup kitchen, a daycare center, or a literacy program. Many college courses involve service learning, in which you do such volunteer work, write about the experience for your course, and write *for* the organization you're helping.

The writing you do for a community group may include creating or maintaining the group's Web site, updating its presence on social media such as *Facebook* and *Twitter,* or producing more formal newsletters, flyers, and brochures. The following tips and the samples below and on the next page can help you with such writing:

- **Craft your writing for its purpose and audience.** You are trying to achieve a specific aim with your readers, and the approach and tone you use will influence their responses. For example, if you were writing letters to local businesses to raise funds for a homeless shelter, you would address the readers formally and focus on the shelter's benefits to them and the community. If you were recruiting volunteers through the shelter's *Facebook* page, you would be more conversational and enthusiastic, emphasizing the rewards of helping out.
- **Remember that your writing represents the organization.** Social media in particular encourage informal written communication, but while representing the organization you are obligated to be professional. If you respond to a negative comment on your organization's blog, for example, avoid sounding angry.
- **Expect to work with others.** Much public writing is the work of more than one person. Even if you draft the document on your own, others will review the content, tone, and design. Such collaboration is rewarding, but it sometimes requires patience and goodwill. See **1** pp. 28–31 for advice on collaborating.

Social-media post

Congratulations to ReadingWorks tutors and students, who last year logged more tutoring hours and passed more levels of proficiency than in any prior year. We are proud of you! We will celebrate your accomplishments at the Annual Awards Dinner on May 23. Please mark your calendars and watch for details— at ReadingWorks.

Online post written in a conversational style

Photograph illustrating information in the post

Like • Comment • Share   📖 12

Newsletter

Multicolumn format allowing room for headings, articles, and other elements on a single page

Two-column heading emphasizing the main article

Elements helping readers skim for highlights: spacing, varied font sizes, lines, and a bulleted list

Color focusing readers' attention on banner, headlines, and table of contents

Lively but uncluttered overall appearance

Box in the first column highlighting table of contents

ReadingWorks

ReadingWorks

Springfield Veterans Administration Hospital　　　SUMMER 2014

From the director

Can you help? With more and more learners in the ReadingWorks program, we need more and more tutors. You may know people who would be interested in participating in the program, if only they knew about it.

Those of you who have been tutoring VA patients in reading and writing know both the great need you fulfill and the great benefits you bring to the students. New tutors need no special skills—we'll provide the training—only patience and an interest in helping others.

We've scheduled an orientation meeting for Friday, September 12, at 6:30 PM. Please come and bring a friend who is willing to contribute a couple of hours a week to our work.

Thanks,
Kate Goodman

FIRST ANNUAL AWARDS DINNER

A festive night for students and tutors

The first annual ReadingWorks Awards Dinner on May 23 was a great success. Springfield's own Golden Fork provided tasty food and Amber Allen supplied lively music. The students decorated Suite 42 on the theme of books and reading. In all, 127 people attended.

The highlight of the night was the awards ceremony. Nine students, recommended by their tutors, received certificates recognizing their efforts and special accomplishments in learning to read and write:

Ramon Berva
Edward Byar
David Dunbar
Tony Garnier
Chris Guigni
Akili Haynes
Josh Livingston
Alex Obeld
B. J. Resnansky

In addition, nine tutors received certificates commemorating five years of service to ReadingWorks:

Anita Crumpton
Felix Cruz-Rivera
Bette Elgen
Kayleah Bortoluzzi
Harriotte Henderson
Ben Obiso
Meggie Puente
Max Smith
Sara Villante

Congratulations to all!

PTSD: New Guidelines

Most of us are working with veterans who have been diagnosed with post-traumatic stress disorder. Because this disorder is often complicated by alcoholism, depression, anxiety, and other problems, the National Center for PTSD has issued some guidelines for helping PTSD patients in ways that reduce their stress.

- The hospital must know your tutoring schedule, and you need to sign in and out before and after each tutoring session.

- To protect patients' privacy, meet them only in designated visiting and tutoring areas, never in their rooms.

- Treat patients with dignity and respect, even when (as sometimes happens) they grow frustrated and angry. Seek help from a nurse or orderly if you need it.

PART 3

Clarity and Style

Clarity and Style

15 Emphasis

When you speak, your tone of voice, facial expressions, and even hand gestures work with your words and sentences to convey your meaning. When you write, your words and sentences must alone do the work of emphasizing your main ideas. In addition to the techniques of emphasis discussed in this chapter, see also Chapter 20 on writing concisely.

15a Using subjects and verbs effectively

The heart of every sentence is its subject,° which usually names the actor, and its predicate verb,° which usually specifies the subject's action: *Children* [subject] *grow* [verb]. When these elements do not identify the key actor and action in the sentence, readers must find that information elsewhere and the sentence may be wordy and unemphatic.

In the following sentences, the subjects and verbs are underlined.

> Unemphatic The intention of the company was to expand its workforce. A proposal was also made to diversify the backgrounds and abilities of employees.

These sentences are unemphatic because their key ideas do not appear in their subjects and verbs. In the revision below, the sentences are not only clearer but more concise.

> Revised The company intended to expand its workforce. It also proposed to diversify the backgrounds and abilities of employees.

The following constructions usually drain meaning from a sentence's subject and verb.

Nouns made from verbs

Nouns° made from verbs can obscure the key actions of sentences and add words. These nouns include *intention* (from *intend*), *proposal* (from *propose*), *decision* (from *decide*), *expectation* (from *expect*), and *inclusion* (from *include*).

°See "Glossary of Terms," GI p. 558.

139

Unemphatic	After the company made a <u>decision</u> to hire more workers with disabilities, its next <u>step</u> was the <u>construction</u> of wheelchair ramps and other facilities.
Revised	After the company <u>decided</u> to hire more workers with disabilities, it next <u>constructed</u> wheelchair ramps and other facilities.

Weak verbs

Weak verbs, such as *made* and *was* in the unemphatic sentence above, tend to stall sentences just where they should be moving and often bury key actions:

Unemphatic	The company <u>is</u> now the leader among businesses in complying with the 1990 disabilities act. Its officers <u>make</u> frequent speeches on the act to business groups.
Revised	The company now <u>leads</u> other businesses in complying with the 1990 disabilities act. Its officers frequently <u>speak</u> on the act to business groups.

Forms of *be, have,* and *make* are often weak, but don't try to eliminate every use of them: *be* and *have* are essential as helping verbs° (*is going, has written*); *be* links subjects and words describing them (*Planes are noisy*); and *have* and *make* have independent meanings (among them "possess" and "force," respectively). But do consider replacing a form of *be, have,* or *make* when a word after it could be made into a strong verb itself, as in the following examples.

Unemphatic	Emphatic
<u>was</u> influential	influenced
<u>have</u> a preference	prefer
<u>had</u> the appearance	appeared, seemed
<u>made</u> a claim	claimed

Passive voice

Verbs in the passive voice° state actions received by, not performed by, their subjects. Thus the passive de-emphasizes the true actor of the sentence, sometimes omitting it entirely. Generally, prefer the active voice,° in which the subject performs the action. (See also **4** pp. 225–26 for help with editing the passive voice.)

Unemphatic	The 1990 law <u>is seen</u> by most businesses as fair, but the costs of complying <u>have</u> sometimes <u>been objected to</u>.
Revised	Most businesses <u>see</u> the 1990 law as fair, but <u>some have objected to</u> the costs of complying.

Exercise 15.1 Revising: Emphasis of subjects and verbs

Rewrite the sentences in the following paragraph so that their subjects and verbs identify the key actors and actions.

---

1 Many heroes were helpful in the emancipation of the slaves. 2 However, the work of Harriet Tubman, an escaped slave herself, stands above the rest. 3 Tubman's accomplishments included the guidance of hundreds of slaves to freedom on the Underground Railroad. 4 A return to slavery was risked by Tubman or possibly death. 5 During the Civil War she was also a carrier of information from the South to the North. 6 After the war Tubman was instrumental in helping to raise money for former slaves who were in need of support.

15b Using sentence beginnings and endings

Readers automatically seek a writer's principal meaning in the main clause° of a sentence—that is, in the subject° that names the actor and in the verb° that usually specifies the action (see p. 139). Thus you can help readers understand the meaning you intend by controlling the information in your subjects and the relation of the main clause to any modifiers attached to it.

Old and new information

Generally, readers expect the beginning of a sentence to contain information that they already know or that you have already introduced. They then look to the sentence ending for new information. In the unemphatic passage below, the second and third sentences both begin with new topics, while the old topics appear at the ends of the sentences. The pattern of the passage is A→B. C→B. D→A.

Unemphatic Education often means controversy these days, with rising
                    A   B
costs and constant complaints about its inadequacies.
                                           C
But the value of schooling should not be obscured by the
                 B   D
controversy. The single best means of economic advance-
                                              A
ment, despite its shortcomings, remains education.

In the more emphatic revision, the old information begins each sentence and new information ends the sentence. The passage follows the pattern A→B. B→C. A→D.

Revised   Education often means controversy these days, with rising
                   A   B
costs and constant complaints about its inadequacies.
                         B   C
But the controversy should not obscure the value of
                    A
schooling. Education remains, despite its shortcomings,
                              D
the single best means of economic advancement.

°See "Glossary of Terms," **GI** p. 558.

Cumulative and periodic sentences

You can call attention to information by placing it first or last in a sentence, reserving the middle for incidentals:

Unemphatic	Education remains the single best means of economic advancement, despite its shortcomings. [Emphasizes shortcomings.]
Revised	Despite its shortcomings, education remains the single best means of economic advancement. [Emphasizes advancement more than shortcomings.]
Revised	Education remains, despite its shortcomings, the single best means of economic advancement. [De-emphasizes shortcomings.]

A sentence that adds modifiers° to the main clause is called **cumulative** because it accumulates information as it proceeds:

| Cumulative | Education has no equal in opening minds, instilling values, and creating opportunities. |
| Cumulative | Most of the Great American Desert is made up of bare rock, rugged cliffs, mesas, canyons, mountains, separated from one another by broad flat basins covered with sun-baked mud and alkali, supporting a sparse and measured growth of sagebrush or creosote or saltbush, depending on location and elevation.   —Edward Abbey |

The opposite kind of sentence, called **periodic**, saves the main clause until just before the end (the period) of the sentence. Everything before the main clause points toward it:

| Periodic | In opening minds, instilling values, and creating opportunities, education has no equal. |
| Periodic | With people from all over the world—Korean doctors, Jamaican cricket players, Vietnamese engineers, Haitian cabdrivers, Chinese grocers, Indian restaurant owners—the American mosaic is continually changing. |

The periodic sentence creates suspense by reserving important information for the end. But readers should already have an idea of the sentence's subject—because it was mentioned in the preceding sentence—so that they know what the opening modifiers describe.

Exercise 15.2 Sentence combining: Beginnings and endings

Locate the main idea in each numbered group of sentences. Then combine each group into a single sentence that emphasizes that idea by placing it at the beginning or the end. For sentences 2–5, determine the position of the main idea by considering its relation to the previous sentences: if the main idea picks up a topic that's already been introduced, place it at the beginning; if it adds new information, place it at the end.

°See "Glossary of Terms," **GI** p. 558.

Example:

The storm blew roofs off buildings. It caused extensive damage. It knocked down many trees.

Main idea at beginning: The storm caused extensive damage, blowing roofs off buildings and knocking down many trees.

Main idea at end: Blowing roofs off buildings and knocking down many trees, the storm caused extensive damage.

1 Pat Taylor strode into the room. The room was packed. He greeted students called "Taylor's Kids." He nodded to their parents and teachers.
2 This was a wealthy Louisiana oilman. He had promised his "Kids" free college educations. He was determined to make higher education available to all qualified but disadvantaged students.
3 The students welcomed Taylor. Their voices joined in singing. They sang "You Are the Wind beneath My Wings." Their faces beamed with hope. Their eyes flashed with self-confidence.
4 The students had thought a college education was beyond their dreams. It seemed too costly. It seemed too demanding.
5 Taylor had to ease the costs and the demands of getting to college. He created a bold plan. The plan consisted of scholarships, tutoring, and counseling.

15c Using coordination

Use **coordination** to show that two or more elements in a sentence are equally important in meaning and thus to clarify the relationship between them:

Ways to coordinate information in sentences

- **Link main clauses° with a comma and a coordinating conjunction°:** *and, but, or, nor, for, so, yet.*

  Independence Hall in Philadelphia is faithfully restored, but many years ago it was in bad shape.

- **Relate main clauses with a semicolon alone or a semicolon and a conjunctive adverb°:** *however, indeed, therefore, thus,* etc.

  The building was standing; however, it suffered from neglect.

- **Within clauses, link words and phrases° with a coordinating conjunction:** *and, but, or, nor.*

  The people and officials of the nation were indifferent to Independence Hall or took it for granted.

- **Link main clauses, words, or phrases with a correlative conjunction°:** *both . . . and, not only . . . but also,* etc.

  People not only took the building for granted but also neglected it.

°See "Glossary of Terms," **Gl** p. 558.

coord

1 Coordinating to relate equal ideas

Coordination shows the equality between elements, as illustrated by the examples in the preceding box. At the same time that it clarifies meaning, it can also help smooth choppy sentences:

Choppy sentences | We should not rely so heavily on oil. Coal and natural gas are also overused. We have a substantial energy resource in the moving waters of our rivers. Smaller streams add to the total volume of water. The resource renews itself. Oil and coal are irreplaceable. Gas is also irreplaceable. The cost of water does not increase much over time. The costs of coal, oil, and gas fluctuate dramatically.

The following revision groups coal, oil, and uranium and clearly opposes them to water (the connecting words are underlined):

Ideas coordinated | We should not rely so heavily on oil, coal, and natural gas, for we have a substantial energy resource in the moving waters of our rivers and streams. Oil, coal, and gas are irreplaceable and thus subject to dramatic cost fluctuations; water, however, is self-renewing and more stable in cost.

2 Coordinating effectively

Use coordination only to express the *equality* of ideas or details. A string of coordinated elements—especially main clauses—implies that all points are equally important:

Excessive coordination | The weeks leading up to the resignation of President Nixon were eventful, and the Supreme Court and the Congress closed in on him, and the Senate Judiciary Committee voted to begin impeachment proceedings, and finally the President resigned on August 9, 1974.

Such a passage needs editing to stress the important points (underlined below) and to de-emphasize the less important information:

Revised | The weeks leading up to the resignation of President Nixon were eventful, as the Supreme Court and the Congress closed in on him and the Senate Judiciary Committee voted to begin impeachment proceedings. Finally, the President resigned on August 9, 1974.

Even within a single sentence, coordination should express a logical equality between ideas:

Faulty | John Stuart Mill was a nineteenth-century utilitarian, and he believed that actions should be judged by their usefulness or by the happiness they cause. [The two clauses are not separate and equal: the second expands on the first by explaining what a utilitarian such as Mill believed.]

Revised | John Stuart Mill, a nineteenth-century utilitarian, believed that actions should be judged by their usefulness or by the happiness they cause.

Exercise 15.3 Sentence combining: Coordination

Combine sentences in the following passages to coordinate related ideas in the ways that seem most effective to you. You will have to supply coordinating conjunctions or conjunctive adverbs and the appropriate punctuation.

1 Many chronic misspellers do not have the time to master spelling rules. They may not have the motivation. They may rely on spelling checkers and dictionaries to catch misspellings. Most dictionaries list words under their correct spellings. One kind of dictionary is designed for chronic misspellers. It lists each word under its common *mis*spellings. It then provides the correct spelling. It also provides the definition.

2 Henry Hudson was an English explorer. He captained ships for the Dutch East India Company. On a voyage in 1610 he passed by Greenland. He sailed into a great bay in today's northern Canada. He thought he and his sailors could winter there. The cold was terrible. Food ran out. The sailors mutinied. The sailors cast Hudson adrift in a small boat. Eight others were also in the boat. Hudson and his companions perished.

15d | Using subordination

Use **subordination** to indicate that some elements in a sentence are less important than others for your meaning. Usually, the main idea appears in the main clause,° and supporting details appear in subordinate structures:

Ways to subordinate information in sentences

- Use a subordinate clause° beginning with a subordinating word: *who (whom), that, which, although, because, however, if, therefore, unless, whereas,* etc.

  Although some citizens had tried to rescue Independence Hall, they had not gained substantial public support.

  The first strong step was taken by the federal government, which made the building a national monument.

- Use a phrase.°

  Like most national monuments, Independence Hall is protected by the National Park Service.

  Protecting many popular tourist sites, the service is a highly visible government agency.

- Use a short modifier.°

  At the red brick Independence Hall, park rangers give guided tours, answer visitors' questions and protect the irreplaceable building from vandalism.

°See "Glossary of Terms," **Gl** p. 558.

1 Subordinating to emphasize main ideas

A string of main clauses can make everything in a passage seem equally important:

String of main clauses	Computer prices have dropped, and production costs have dropped more slowly, and computer manufacturers have had to struggle, for their profits have been shrinking.

Emphasis comes from keeping the truly important information in the main clause (underlined) and subordinating the less important details:

Revised	Because production costs have dropped more slowly than prices, <u>computer manufacturers have had to struggle with shrinking profits.</u>

2 Subordinating effectively

Use subordination only for the less important information in a sentence.

Faulty	Ms. Angelo was in her first year of teaching, although she was a better instructor than others with many years of experience.

The preceding sentence suggests that Angelo's inexperience is the main idea, whereas the writer intended to stress her skill *despite* her inexperience. Reducing the inexperience to a subordinate clause and elevating the skill to the main clause (underlined) gives appropriate emphasis:

Revised	Although Ms. Angelo was in her first year of teaching, <u>she was a better instructor than others with many years of experience.</u>

Subordination loses its power to emphasize when too much loosely related detail crowds into one long, meandering sentence:

Overloaded	The boats that were moored at the dock when the hurricane, which was one of the worst in three decades, struck were ripped from their moorings, because the owners had not been adequately prepared, since the weather service had predicted that the storm would blow out to sea, which they do at this time of year.

The revision stresses important information in the main clauses (underlined):

Revised	Struck by one of the worst hurricanes in three decades, <u>the boats at the dock were ripped from their moorings.</u> <u>The owners were unprepared</u> because the weather service had said that hurricanes at this time of year blow out to sea.

Exercise 15.4 Sentence combining: Subordination

Combine each of the following pairs of sentences twice, each time using one of the subordinate structures in parentheses to make a single sentence. You will have to add, delete, change, and rearrange words.

Example:

During the late eighteenth century, workers carried beverages in brightly colored bottles. The bottles had cork stoppers. (*Clause beginning that. Phrase beginning with.*)

During the late eighteenth century, workers carried beverages in brightly colored bottles that had cork stoppers.

During the late eighteenth century, workers carried beverages in brightly colored bottles with cork stoppers.

1 The bombardier beetle sees an enemy. It shoots out a jet of chemicals to protect itself from the predator. (*Clause beginning when. Phrase beginning seeing.*)

2 The beetle's spray consists of hot and irritating chemicals. It is often fatal to other insects. (*Clause beginning because. Phrase beginning consisting.*)

3 The spray's two chemicals are stored separately in the beetle's body and mixed in the spraying gland. The chemicals resemble a nerve-gas weapon. (*Phrase beginning stored. Clause beginning which.*)

4 The tip of the beetle's abdomen sprays the chemicals. The tip revolves like a turret on a World War II bomber. (*Phrase beginning revolving. Phrase beginning spraying.*)

5 The beetle defeats most of its enemies. It is still eaten by spiders and birds. (*Clause beginning although. Phrase beginning except.*)

Exercise 15.5 Revising: Effective subordination

Revise the following paragraph to eliminate faulty or excessive subordination and thus to emphasize the main ideas. Correct faulty subordination by reversing main and subordinate structures. Correct excessive subordination by coordinating equal ideas or by making separate sentences.

1 Genaro González is a successful writer, which means that his stories and novels have been published to critical acclaim. 2 In interviews, he talks about his love of writing, even though he has also earned a doctorate in psychology because he enjoys teaching. 3 González's first story, which reflects his growing consciousness of his Aztec heritage and place in the world, is titled "Un Hijo del Sol." 4 He wrote the first version of "Un Hijo del Sol" while he was a sophomore at the University of Texas–Pan American, which is in the Rio Grande valley of southern Texas, which González called "el Valle" in the story, and where he now teaches psychology. 5 González's latest book, which is about a teenager and is titled *A So-Called Vacation,* is a novel about how the teen and his family live for a summer as migrant fruit pickers, which was the experience his father had when he first immigrated to the United States from Mexico.

Exercise 15.6 Revising: Coordination and subordination

The following paragraph consists entirely of simple sentences. Use coordination and subordination to combine sentences in the ways you think most effective to emphasize main ideas.

Sir Walter Raleigh personified the Elizabethan Age. That was the period of Elizabeth I's rule of England. The period occurred in the last half of the sixteenth century. Raleigh was a courtier and poet. He was also an explorer and entrepreneur. Supposedly, he gained Queen Elizabeth's favor. He did this by throwing his cloak beneath her feet at the right moment. She was just about to step over a puddle. There is no evidence for this story. It does illustrate Raleigh's dramatic and dynamic personality. His energy drew others to him. He was one of Elizabeth's favorites. She supported him. She also dispensed favors to him. However, he lost his queen's goodwill. Without her permission he seduced one of her maids of honor. He eventually married the maid of honor. Elizabeth died. Then her successor imprisoned Raleigh in the Tower of London. Her successor was James I. The king falsely charged Raleigh with treason. Raleigh was released after thirteen years. He was arrested again two years later on the old treason charges. At the age of sixty-six he was beheaded.

16 Parallelism

Chapter essentials

- Use parallelism with *and, but, or, nor,* and *yet* (facing page).
- Use parallelism with *both . . . and, not . . . but,* or another correlative conjunction (facing page).
- Use parallelism in comparisons, lists, headings, and outlines (p. 150).

Visit MyWritingLab™ for more resources on parallelism.

Parallelism gives similar grammatical form to sentence elements that have similar function and importance.

The air is dirtied by factories belching smoke
                        and
                        cars spewing exhaust.

In the preceding example the two underlined phrases° have the same function and importance (both specify sources of air pollution), so

°See "Glossary of Terms," **Gl** p. 558.

they also have the same grammatical construction. Parallelism makes form follow meaning.

16a Using parallelism with *and, but, or, nor, yet*

The coordinating conjunctions° *and, but, or, nor,* and *yet* always signal a need for parallelism.

The industrial base was <u>shifting</u> and <u>shrinking</u>. [Parallel words.]

Politicians rarely <u>acknowledged the problem</u> or <u>proposed alternatives</u>. [Parallel phrases.]

Industrial workers were understandably disturbed <u>that they were losing their jobs</u> but <u>that no one seemed to care</u>. [Parallel clauses.]

When sentence elements linked by coordinating conjunctions are not parallel in structure, the sentence is awkward and distracting:

Nonparallel	The reasons steel companies kept losing money were that <u>their plants were inefficient</u>, <u>high labor costs</u>, and <u>foreign competition was increasing</u>.
Revised	The reasons steel companies kept losing money were <u>inefficient plants</u>, <u>high labor costs</u>, and <u>increasing foreign competition</u>.
Nonparallel	Success was difficult even for efficient companies because of the shift away from <u>all manufacturing in the United States</u> and <u>the fact that steel production was shifting toward emerging nations</u>.
Revised	Success was difficult even for efficient companies because of the shift away from <u>all manufacturing in the United States</u> and <u>toward steel production in emerging nations</u>.

All the words required by idiom or grammar must be stated in compound constructions° (see also p. 173):

Faulty	Given training, workers can acquire the <u>skills</u> and <u>interest</u> in other jobs. [Idiom dictates different prepositions with *skills* and *interest*.]
Revised	Given training, workers can acquire the skills <u>for</u> and interest <u>in</u> other jobs.

16b Using parallelism with *both . . . and, not . . . but,* or another correlative conjunction

Correlative conjunctions° stress equality and balance between elements. Parallelism confirms the equality.

It is not <u>a tax bill</u> but <u>a tax relief bill</u>, providing relief not <u>for the needy</u> but <u>for the greedy</u>.
　　　　　　　　　　　　　　　　　　　—Franklin Delano Roosevelt

°See "Glossary of Terms," **GI** p. 558.

With correlative conjunctions, the element after the second connector must match the element after the first connector:

Nonparallel	Huck Finn learns not only that human beings have an enormous capacity for folly but also enormous dignity. [The first element includes *that human beings have*; the second element does not.]
Revised	Huck Finn learns that human beings have not only an enormous capacity for folly but also enormous dignity. [Repositioning *that human beings have* makes the two elements parallel.]

16c | Using parallelism in comparisons

Parallelism confirms the likeness or difference between two elements being compared using *than* or *as*:

Nonparallel	Huck Finn proves less a bad boy than to be an independent spirit. In the end he is every bit as determined in rejecting help as he is to leave for "the territory."
Revised	Huck Finn proves less a bad boy than an independent spirit. In the end he is every bit as determined to reject help as he is to leave for "the territory."

(See also **4** pp. 250–51 on making comparisons logical.)

16d | Using parallelism with lists, headings, and outlines

The items in a list or outline are coordinate and should be parallel. Parallelism is essential in a formal topic outline and in the headings that divide a paper into sections. (See **1** pp. 21–22 and 56 for more on outlines and headings.)

Nonparallel	Revised
Changes in Renaissance England	Changes in Renaissance England
1. Extension of trade routes	1. Extension of trade routes
2. Merchant class became more powerful	2. Increased power of the merchant class
3. The death of feudalism	3. Death of feudalism
4. Upsurging of the arts	4. Upsurge of the arts
5. Religious quarrels began	5. Rise of religious quarrels

Exercise 16.1 Revising: Parallelism

Revise the following paragraph as needed to create parallelism for grammar and coherence. Add or delete words or rephrase as necessary.

1 The ancient Greeks celebrated four athletic contests: the Olympic Games at Olympia, the Isthmian games were held near Corinth, at Delphi the Pythian Games, and the Nemean Games were sponsored by the people of Cleone. 2 Each day the games consisted of either athletic events or holding ceremonies and sacrifices to the gods. 3 Competitors participated in running sprints, spectacular chariot and horse races, and running long distances while wearing full armor. 4 The purpose of such events was to develop physical strength, demonstrating skill and endurance, and sharpening the skills needed for war. 5 The athletes competed less to achieve great wealth than for gaining honor both for themselves and their cities. 6 Of course, exceptional athletes received financial support from patrons, poems and statues by admiring artists, and they even got lavish living quarters from their sponsoring cities. 7 With the medal counts and flag ceremonies, today's Olympians sometimes seem to be proving their countries' superiority more than to demonstrate individual talent.

Exercise 16.2 Sentence combining: Parallelism

Combine each group of sentences below into one concise sentence in which parallel elements appear in parallel structures. You will have to add, delete, change, and rearrange words. Each item has more than one possible answer.

Example:

The new process works smoothly. It is efficient, too.
The new process works smoothly and <u>efficiently</u>.

1 People can develop post-traumatic stress disorder (PTSD). They develop it after experiencing a dangerous situation. They will also have felt fear for their survival.
2 The disorder can be triggered by a wide variety of events. Combat is a typical cause. Similarly, natural disasters can result in PTSD. Some people experience PTSD after a hostage situation.
3 PTSD can occur immediately after the stressful incident. Or it may not appear until many years later.
4 Sometimes people with PTSD will act irrationally. Moreover, they often become angry.
5 Other symptoms include dreaming that one is reliving the experience. They include hallucinating that one is back in the terrifying place. In another symptom one imagines that strangers are actually one's former torturers.

17 Variety and Details

Chapter essentials
- Vary sentence length (below).
- Vary sentence structure with subordination, sentence combining, and sentence beginnings (below).
- Add relevant and informative details (p. 155).

Visit MyWritingLab™ for more resources on variety and details.

Writing that's interesting as well as clear has at least two features: the sentences vary in length and structure, and they are well textured with details.

17a Varying sentence length

Sentences generally vary from about ten to about forty words. When sentences are all at one extreme or the other, readers may have difficulty focusing on main ideas and seeing the relations among them.

- **Long sentences.** If most of your sentences contain thirty-five words or more, your main ideas may not stand out from the details that support them. Break some of the long sentences into shorter, simpler ones.
- **Short sentences.** If most of your sentences contain fewer than ten or fifteen words, all your ideas may seem equally important and the links between them may not be clear. Try combining sentences with coordination (p. 143) and subordination (p. 145) to show relationships and stress main ideas over supporting information.

17b Varying sentence structure

A passage will be monotonous if all its sentences follow the same pattern, like soldiers marching in a parade. Try the following techniques for varying structure.

1 Subordination

A string of main clauses° can make all ideas seem equally important and be especially plodding.

°See "Glossary of Terms," **GI** p. 558.

| Monotonous | The moon is now drifting away from the earth. It moves away at the rate of about one inch a year. This movement is lengthening our days. They increase a thousandth of a second every century. Forty-seven of our present days will someday make up a month. We might eventually lose the moon altogether. Such great planetary movement rightly concerns astronomers, but it need not worry us. It will take 50 million years. |

Enliven such writing—and make the main ideas stand out—by expressing the less important information in subordinate clauses° and phrases.° In the revision below, underlining indicates subordinate structures that used to be main clauses:

| Revised | The moon is now drifting away from the earth about one inch a year. At a thousandth of a second every century, this movement is lengthening our days. Forty-seven of our present days will someday make up a month, if we don't eventually lose the moon altogether. Such great planetary movement rightly concerns astronomers, but it need not worry us. It will take 50 million years. |

2 Sentence combining

As the preceding example shows, subordinating to achieve variety often involves combining short, choppy sentences into longer units that link related information and stress main ideas. Here is another unvaried passage:

| Monotonous | Astronomy may seem a remote science. It may seem to have little to do with people's daily lives. However, many astronomers find otherwise. They see their science as soothing. It gives perspective to everyday routines and problems. |

Combining five sentences into one, the following revision is both clearer and easier to read. Underlining highlights the changes.

| Revised | Astronomy may seem a remote science having little to do with people's daily lives, but many astronomers find their science soothing because it gives perspective to everyday routines and problems. |

3 Varied sentence beginnings

An English sentence often begins with its subject,° which generally captures old information from a preceding sentence (see p. 141):

The defendant's lawyer was determined to break the prosecution's witness. He relentlessly cross-examined the stubborn witness for more than a week.

°See "Glossary of Terms," **Gl** p. 558.

However, an unbroken sequence of sentences beginning with the subject quickly becomes monotonous:

> **Monotonous** The defendant's lawyer was determined to break the prosecution's witness. He relentlessly cross-examined the witness for more than a week. The witness had expected to be dismissed within an hour and was visibly irritated. She did not cooperate. She was reprimanded by the judge.

Beginning some of these sentences with other expressions improves readability and clarity:

> **Revised** The defendant's lawyer was determined to break the prosecution's witness. For more than a week he relentlessly cross-examined the witness. Expecting to be dismissed within an hour, the witness was visibly irritated. She did not cooperate. Indeed, she was reprimanded by the judge.

The underlined expressions represent the most common choices for varying sentence beginnings:

- **Adverb modifiers,°** such as *For a week* (modifies the verb *cross-examined*).
- **Adjective modifiers,°** such as *Expecting to be dismissed within an hour* (modifies *witness*).
- **Transitional expressions,°** such as *Indeed*. (See **1** p. 46 for a list.)

CULTURE LANGUAGE In standard American English, placing some negative adverb modifiers at the beginning of a sentence requires you to use the word order of a question, in which the verb or a part of it precedes the subject. These modifiers include *never, rarely, seldom,* and adverb phrases beginning in *no, not since,* and *not until.*

>   verb
>   adverb   subject phrase
> **Faulty** Seldom a witness has held the stand so long.

>   helping   main
>   adverb verb subject verb
> **Revised** Seldom has a witness held the stand so long.

4 | Varied word order

Occasionally you can vary a sentence and emphasize it at the same time by inverting the usual order of parts:

> A dozen witnesses testified for the prosecution, and the defense attorney barely questioned eleven of them. The twelfth, however, he grilled. [Normal word order: *He grilled the twelfth, however.*]

Inverted sentences used without need are artificial. Use them only when emphasis demands.

17c Adding details

Relevant details such as facts and examples create the texture and life that keep readers awake and help them grasp your meaning. For instance:

Flat   Constructed after World War II, Levittown, New York, consisted of thousands of houses in two basic styles. Over the decades, residents have altered the houses so dramatically that the original styles are often unrecognizable.

Detailed   Constructed on potato fields after World War II, Levittown, New York, consisted of more than seventeen thousand houses in Cape Cod and ranch styles. Over the decades, residents have added expansive front porches, punched dormer windows through roofs, converted garages to sun porches, and otherwise altered the houses so dramatically that the original styles are often unrecognizable.

Note The details in the revised passage are effective because they relate to the writer's point and make that point clearer. Details that don't support and clarify your point will likely distract or annoy readers.

Exercise 17.1 Revising: Variety

The following paragraph consists entirely of simple sentences that begin with their subjects. Use the techniques discussed in this chapter to vary the sentences. Delete, add, change, and rearrange words to make the paragraph more readable and to make important ideas stand out clearly.

The Italian volcano Vesuvius had been dormant for many years. It then exploded on August 24 in the year AD 79. The ash, pumice, and mud from the volcano buried two busy towns. Herculaneum is one. The more famous is Pompeii. Both towns lay undiscovered for many centuries. Herculaneum and Pompeii were discovered in 1709 and 1748, respectively. The excavation of Pompeii was the more systematic. It was the occasion for initiating modern methods of conservation and restoration. Herculaneum was simply looted of its more valuable finds. It was then left to disintegrate. Pompeii appears much as it did before the eruption. A luxurious house opens onto a lush central garden. An election poster decorates a wall. A dining table is set for breakfast.

18 Appropriate and Exact Language

Chapter essentials

- Choose words that are appropriate for your writing situation (below).
- Avoid sexist and biased language (p. 159).
- Choose words that express your meaning exactly (p. 163).

Visit MyWritingLab™ for more resources on appropriate and exact language.

To write clearly and effectively, choose words that fit both the context in which you are writing and the meaning that you are trying to convey.

18a Choosing appropriate language

Appropriate language suits your writing situation—your subject, purpose, and audience. In most college and career writing you should rely on what's called **standard American English**, the dialect of English normally expected and used in school, business, the professions, government, and the communications media. (For more on its role in academic writing, see **2** pp. 76–78.)

The vocabulary of written standard English is huge, allowing you to express an infinite range of ideas and feelings. However, it does exclude words that are too imprecise for writing and that only some groups of people use, understand, or find inoffensive. The types of excluded words are discussed in this section. Whenever you doubt a word's status, consult a dictionary (see pp. 163–64). A label such as *nonstandard, slang,* or *colloquial* tells you that the word is not generally appropriate in academic or business writing.

1 Dialects other than standard English

Like many countries, the United States includes scores of regional, social, and ethnic groups with their own distinct **dialects**, or versions of English. Standard American English is one of those dialects, and so are African American Vernacular English, Appalachian English, Creole, and the English of coastal Maine. All the dialects of English share many features, but each also has its own vocabulary, pronunciation, and grammar.

If you speak a dialect other than standard English, you are probably already adept at moving between your dialect and standard English in speech and writing. Dialects are not wrong in themselves, but forms imported from one dialect into another may still be perceived as unclear or incorrect. When standard English is expected, such as in academic and public writing, edit your work to revise expressions that you know (or have been told) differ from standard English. These expressions may include *theirselves, hisn, them books,* and others labeled *nonstandard* by a dictionary. They may also include certain verb forms, as discussed in **4** pp. 204–12. For help identifying and editing nonstandard language, see the "🔲 Guide" just before the back endpapers of this book.

Your participation in the community of standard English does not require you to abandon your own dialect. You may want to use it in writing you do for yourself, such as journals, notes, and drafts, which should be composed as freely as possible. You may want to quote it in an academic paper, as when analyzing or reporting conversation in dialect. And, of course, you will want to use it with others who speak it.

2 | **Shortcuts of texting and other electronic communication**

Rapid communication by e-mail and text or instant messaging encourages some informalities that are inappropriate for academic writing. If you use these media frequently, you may need to proofread your academic papers especially to identify and revise errors such as the following:

- **Sentence fragments.** Make sure every sentence has a subject and a predicate. (See **4** pp. 264–66.)

  Not   Observed the results.
  But   Researchers observed the results.

- **Missing punctuation.** Between and within sentences, use standard punctuation marks. Check especially for missing commas within sentences and missing apostrophes in possessives and contractions. (See **5** pp. 282–94 and 304–07.)

  Not   The dogs bony ribs visible through its fur were evidence of neglect.
  But   The dog's bony ribs, visible through its fur, were evidence of neglect.

- **Missing capital letters.** Use capital letters at the beginnings of sentences, for proper nouns and adjectives, and in titles. (See **6** pp. 333–36.)

  Not   scholars have written about abraham lincoln more than any other american.
  But   Scholars have written about Abraham Lincoln more than any other American.

- **Nonstandard abbreviations and spellings.** Write out most words, avoiding forms such as *2* for *to* or *too, b4* for *before, bc* for *because, ur* for *you are* or *you're,* and + or & for *and.* (See **6** pp. 340–42 and 327–30.)

Not	Students + tutors need to meet b4 the third week of the semester.
But	Students and tutors need to meet before the third week of the semester.

3 Slang

Slang is the language used by a group, such as musicians or computer programmers, to reflect common experiences and to make technical references efficient. The following example is from an essay on the slang of "skaters" (skateboarders):

> Curtis slashed ultra-punk crunchers on his longboard, while the Rube-man flailed his usual Gumbyness on tweaked frontsides and lofty fakie ollies.
> —Miles Orkin, "Mucho Slingage by the Pool"

Among those who understand it, slang may be vivid and forceful. It often occurs in dialog, and an occasional slang expression can enliven an informal essay. But most slang is too flippant and imprecise for effective communication, and it is generally inappropriate for college or business writing:

Slang	Many students start out pretty together but then get weird.
Revised	Many students start out with clear goals but then lose their direction.

4 Colloquial language

Colloquial language is the everyday spoken language, including expressions such as *chill out, go nuts,* and *get off on.*

When you write informally, colloquial language may be appropriate to achieve the casual, relaxed effect of conversation. But colloquial language generally is not precise enough for college, public, and professional writing. In these more formal writing situations, avoid any words and expressions labeled *informal* or *colloquial* in your dictionary.

Colloquial	According to a Native American myth, the Great Creator had a dog hanging around with him when he created the earth.
Revised	According to a Native American myth, the Great Creator was accompanied by a dog when he created the earth.

Note See also 2 pp. 76–78 for a discussion of formal and informal language in academic writing.

5 Technical words

All disciplines and professions rely on specialized language that allows the members to communicate precisely and efficiently with each other. Chemists, for instance, have their *phosphatides,* and literary critics have their *motifs* and *subtexts.* Without explanation, technical words are meaningless to nonspecialists. When you are writing for nonspecialists, avoid unnecessary technical terms and carefully define terms you must use.

For revising the overly complicated language that is also sometimes called jargon, see p. 178.

6 | Indirect and pretentious writing

In most writing, small, plain, and direct words are preferable to evasive or showy words.

- **Euphemisms** are presumably inoffensive words that substitute for words deemed potentially offensive or too direct, such as *passed away* for "died." Euphemisms can soften the truth, but they are appropriate only when blunt, truthful words would needlessly hurt or offend your audience.
- **Double talk** (also called *doublespeak* or *weasel words*) is language intended to confuse or be misunderstood. It is unfortunately common in politics and advertising—the *revenue enhancement* that is really a tax, for example. Double talk has no place in honest writing.
- **Pretentious writing** is excessively showy. Such writing is more fancy than its subject requires. Choose your words for their exactness and economy. The big, ornate word may be tempting, but pass it up. Your readers will be grateful.

Pretentious	Hardly a day goes by without a new revelation about the devastation of the natural world, and to a significant extent our dependence on the internal combustion engine is the culprit. Respected scientific minds coalesce around the argument that carbon dioxide emissions, such as those from automobiles imbibing gasoline, are responsible for a gradual escalation in temperatures on the planet earth.
Revised	Much of the frequent bad news about the environment can be blamed on the internal combustion engine. Respected scientists argue that carbon dioxide emissions, such as those from gas-powered cars, are warming the earth.

7 | Sexist and other biased language

Even when we do not mean it to, our language can reflect and perpetuate hurtful prejudices toward groups of people. Such biased language can be obvious—words such as *nigger, honky, mick, kike, fag, dyke,* and *broad.* But it can also be subtle, generalizing about groups in ways that may be familiar but that are also inaccurate or unfair.

Biased language reflects poorly on the user, not on the person or persons whom it mischaracterizes or insults. Unbiased language does not submit to false generalizations. It treats people respectfully as individuals and labels groups as they wish to be labeled.

Stereotypes of race, ethnicity, religion, age, and other characteristics

A **stereotype** is a generalization based on poor evidence, a kind of formula for understanding and judging people simply because of their membership in a group:

> Men are uncommunicative.
> Women are emotional.
> Liberals want to raise taxes.
> Conservatives are affluent.

At best, stereotypes betray a noncritical writer, one who is not thinking beyond notions received from others. In your writing, be alert for statements that characterize whole groups of people:

Stereotype   Elderly drivers should have their licenses limited to daytime driving only. [Asserts that all elderly people are poor night drivers.]

Revised   Drivers with impaired night vision should have their licenses limited to daytime driving only.

Some stereotypes have become part of the language, but they are still potentially offensive:

Stereotype   The administrators are too blind to see the need for a new gymnasium. [Equates vision loss and lack of understanding.]

Revised   The administrators do not understand the need for a new gymnasium.

Sexist language

Among the most subtle and persistent biased language is that expressing narrow ideas about men's and women's roles, position, and value in society. Like other stereotypes, this **sexist language** can wound or irritate readers, and it indicates the writer's thoughtlessness or unfairness. The following box suggests some ways of eliminating sexist language.

Eliminating sexist language

■ **Avoid demeaning and patronizing language:**

Sexist   Dr. Keith Kim and Lydia Hawkins coauthored the article.

Revised   Dr. Keith Kim and Dr. Lydia Hawkins coauthored the article.

Revised   Keith Kim and Lydia Hawkins coauthored the article.

Sexist   Ladies are entering almost every occupation formerly filled by men.

Revised   Women are entering almost every occupation formerly filled by men.

■ **Avoid occupational or social stereotypes:**

Sexist   The considerate doctor commends a nurse when she provides his patients with good care.

Revised The considerate doctor commends a nurse who provides good care for patients.

Sexist   The grocery shopper should save her coupons.

Revised Grocery shoppers should save their coupons.

■ **Avoid referring needlessly to gender:**

Sexist   Marie Curie, a woman chemist, discovered radium.

Revised Marie Curie, a chemist, discovered radium.

Sexist   The patients were tended by a male nurse.

Revised The patients were tended by a nurse.

However, don't overcorrect by avoiding appropriate references to gender: *Pregnant women* [not *people*] *should avoid drinking alcohol.*

■ **Avoid using *man* or words containing *man* to refer to all human beings.** Here are a few alternatives:

businessman	businessperson
chairman	chair, chairperson
congressman	congressperson, legislator
craftsman	craftsperson, artisan
layman	layperson
mailman	letter carrier, mail carrier
mankind	humankind, humanity, human beings, humans
manmade	handmade, manufactured, synthetic, artificial
manpower	personnel, human resources
policeman	police officer
salesman	salesperson

Sexist   Man has not reached the limits of social justice.

Revised Humankind [or Humanity] has not reached the limits of social justice.

Sexist   The furniture consists of manmade materials.

Revised The furniture consists of synthetic materials.

■ **Avoid the generic *he*,** the male pronoun used to refer to both genders. (See also **4** pp. 241–42.)

Sexist   The newborn child explores his world.

Revised Newborn children explore their world. [Use the plural for the pronoun and the word it refers to.]

Revised The newborn child explores the world. [Avoid the pronoun altogether.]

Revised The newborn child explores his or her world. [Substitute male and female pronouns.]

Use the last option sparingly—only once in a group of sentences and only to stress the singular individual.

CULTURE LANGUAGE   Forms of address vary widely from culture to culture. In some cultures, for instance, one shows respect by referring to all older women as if they were married, using the equivalent of *Mrs.* Usage in the United States is changing toward making no assumptions about marital status, rank, or other characteristics—for instance, addressing a woman as *Ms.* unless she is known to prefer *Mrs.* or *Miss.*

Appropriate labels

We often need to label groups: *swimmers, politicians, mothers, Christians, Westerners, students.* But labels can be shorthand stereotypes, slighting the person labeled and ignoring the preferences of the group members themselves. Although sometimes dismissed as "political correctness," showing sensitivity about labels hurts no one and helps gain your readers' trust and respect.

- **Avoid labels that (intentionally or not) insult the person or group you refer to.** A person with emotional problems is not a *mental patient.* A person with cancer is not a *cancer victim.* A person using a wheelchair is not *wheelchair-bound.*
- **Use names for racial, ethnic, and other groups that reflect the preferences of each group's members,** or at least many of them. Examples of current preferences include *African American* or *black* and *people with disabilities* (rather than *the disabled* or *the handicapped*). But labels change often. To learn how a group's members wish to be labeled, ask them directly, attend to usage in reputable periodicals, or check a recent dictionary.
- **Identify a person's group only when it is relevant to the point you're making.** Consider the context of the label: Is it a necessary piece of information? If not, don't use it.

Exercise 18.1 Revising: Appropriate words

Rewrite the following paragraphs as needed for standard American English, focusing on inappropriate slang, technical or pretentious language, and biased language. Consult a dictionary to determine whether particular words are appropriate and to find suitable substitutes.

1 Acquired immune deficiency syndrome (AIDS) is a major deal all over the world, and those who think the disease is limited to homos, mainliners, and foreigners are quite mistaken. 2 Indeed, stats suggest that in the United States one in every five hundred American college kids carries the HIV virus that causes AIDS. 3 If such numbers are to be believed, then doctors and public health officials will continue to have a whole lot of HIV and AIDS victims on their hands in the years to come. 4 A person with HIV or a full-blown AIDS sufferer deserves to be treated with respect, like someone with any other disease. 5 He should not be dissed or subjected to exclusionary behavior on the part of his

fellow citizens. 6 Instead, each victim has the necessity for all the medical care and financial assistance due those who are in the extremity of illness. 7 Many professionals in the medical and social-service communities are committed to helping HIV and AIDS patients. 8 For example, a doctor may help his patients by obtaining social services for them as well as by providing medical care. 9 A social worker may visit an HIV or AIDS victim and determine whether he qualifies for public assistance, since many patients don't have the bucks for insurance or drugs. 10 Patients who are very ill may require the ministrations of a home-care nurse. 11 She can administer medications and make the sick person as comfy as possible.

Exercise 18.2 Revising: Sexist language

Revise the following paragraph to eliminate sexist language. If you change a singular noun or pronoun to plural, be sure to make any needed changes in verbs or other pronouns.

1 When a student applies for a job, he should prepare the best possible résumé because the businessman who is scanning a stack of résumés will read them all quickly. 2 The person who wants his résumé to stand out will make sure it highlights his best points. 3 A person applying for a job as a mailman should emphasize his honesty and responsibility. 4 A girl applying for a position as a home-care nurse should also emphasize her honesty and responsibility as well as her background of capable nursing. 5 Someone seeking work as a computer programmer will highlight his experience with computers. 6 Students without extensive job experience should highlight their volunteer work. 7 For instance, a student may have been chairman of a campus organization or secretary of her church's youth group. 8 If the applicant writing a résumé considers what the man who will read it is looking for, he will know better what he should include and how he should format that information.

18b Choosing exact language

To write clearly and effectively, you will want to find the words that fit your meaning exactly and convey your attitude precisely.

1 Word meanings and synonyms

For writing exactly, a dictionary is essential and a thesaurus can be helpful.

Dictionaries

A dictionary defines words and provides pronunciation, grammatical functions, etymology (word history), and other information. The following sample is from the print version of *Merriam-Webster's Collegiate Dictionary*.

Print dictionary entry

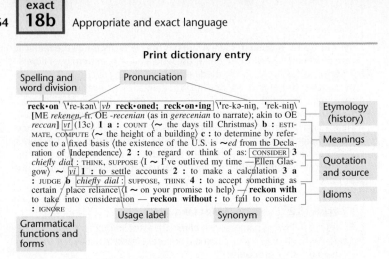

Spelling and word division · Pronunciation · Etymology (history) · Meanings · Quotation and source · Idioms · Grammatical functions and forms · Usage label · Synonym

Besides *Merriam-Webster,* other good print dictionaries include *American Heritage College Dictionary, Random House Webster's College Dictionary,* and *Webster's New World College Dictionary.*

Most dictionary publishers offer online dictionaries that give the same information in less abbreviated form and also allow you to hear how a word is pronounced. Here is part of the entry for *reckon* from *Merriam-Webster Online:*

Partial online dictionary entry

reck·on ◄) *verb* \'re-kən\

reck·oned | **reck·on·ing** ◄)

Definition of RECKON

transitive verb

1 a : COUNT *<reckon* the days till Christmas>

   b : ESTIMATE, COMPUTE *<reckon* the height of a building>

   c : to determine by reference to a fixed basis <the existence of the United States is *reckoned* from the Declaration of Independence>

2 : to regard or think of as : CONSIDER

3 *chiefly dialect :* THINK, SUPPOSE <I *reckon* I've outlived my time — Ellen Glasgow>

Other useful online resources are *Dictionary.com* and *The Free Dictionary,* which provide entries from several dictionaries at once.

CULTURE LANGUAGE If English is not your native language, you probably should have a dictionary prepared especially for students using English as a second language (ESL). Such a dictionary contains special information on prepositions, count versus noncount nouns, and many other matters. The following are reliable print ESL dictionaries, each with an online version: *Longman Dictionary of Contemporary English, Oxford Advanced Learner's Dictionary, Merriam-Webster Advanced Learner's English Dictionary.*

Thesauruses

To find a word with the exact shade of meaning you intend, you may want to consult a thesaurus, or collection of **synonyms**—words with approximately the same meaning. A print or online thesaurus lists most imaginable synonyms for thousands of words. For instance, on the site *Thesaurus.com*, the word *reckon* has nearly fifty synonyms, including *account, evaluate,* and *judge.*

Because a thesaurus aims to open up possibilities, its lists of synonyms include approximate as well as precise matches. The thesaurus does not define synonyms or distinguish among them, however, so you need a dictionary to discover exact meanings. In general, don't use a word from a thesaurus—even one you like the sound of—until you are sure of its appropriateness for your meaning.

Exercise 18.3 Using a dictionary

Look up five of the following words in a dictionary. For each word, write down (*a*) the division into syllables, (*b*) the pronunciation, (*c*) the grammatical functions and forms, (*d*) the etymology, (*e*) each meaning, and (*f*) any special uses indicated by labels. Finally, use the word in two sentences of your own.

1 depreciation	5 assassin	8 steal
2 secretary	6 astrology	9 plain (*adjective*)
3 grammar	7 toxic	10 ceremony
4 manifest		

---

2 The right word for your meaning

All words have one or more basic meanings, called **denotations**—the meanings listed in the dictionary, without reference to emotional associations. If readers are to understand you, you must use words according to their established meanings.

- **Consult a dictionary whenever you are unsure of a word's meaning.**
- **Distinguish between similar-sounding words that have widely different denotations:**

Inexact   Older people often suffer infirmaries [places for the sick].

Exact   Older people often suffer infirmities [disabilities].

Some words, called **homonyms**, sound exactly alike but differ in meaning: for example, *principal/principle* and *rain/reign/rein.* (See **6** pp. 325–26 for a list of commonly confused homonyms.)

■ **Distinguish between words with related but distinct meanings:**

Inexact   Television commercials continuously [unceasingly] interrupt programming.

Exact   Television commercials continually [regularly] interrupt programming.

In addition to their emotion-free meanings, many words carry related meanings that evoke specific feelings. These **connotations** can shape readers' responses and are thus a powerful tool for writers. The following word pairs have related denotations but very different connotations:

pride: sense of self-worth
vanity: excessive regard for oneself

firm: steady, unchanging, unyielding
stubborn: unreasonable, bullheaded

enthusiasm: excitement
mania: excessive interest or desire

A dictionary can help you track down words with the exact connotations you want. Besides providing meanings, your dictionary may also list and distinguish synonyms to guide your choices. A thesaurus can also help if you use it carefully, as discussed on the previous page.

Exercise 18.4   Revising: Denotation

Revise any underlined word below that is used incorrectly. Consult a dictionary if you are uncertain of a word's precise meaning.

1 The acclaimed writer Maxine Hong Kingston sites her mother's stories about ancestors and ancient Chinese customs as the sources of her first two books, *The Woman Warrior* and *China Men*. 2 One of her mother's tales, about a pregnant aunt who was ostracized by villagers, had a great affect on the young Kingston. 3 The aunt gained avengeance by drowning herself in the village water supply. 4 Kingston made the aunt infamous by giving her immortality in *The Woman Warrior*. 5 Two of Kingston's progeny, her great-grandfathers, are the focal points of *China Men*. 6 Both men led rebellions against suppressive employers: a sugarcane farmer and a railroad-construction engineer. 7 Kingston's innovative writing infers her opposition to racism and sexism both in the China of the past and in the United States of the present. 8 She was rewarded many prizes for these distinguished books.

Exercise 18.5   Considering the connotations of words

Fill in the blank in each sentence below with the most appropriate word from the list in parentheses. Consult a dictionary to be sure of your choices.

1 Infection with the AIDS virus, HIV, is a serious health _____.
(*problem, worry, difficulty, plight*)

2 Once the virus has entered the blood system, it _____ T-cells. (*murders, destroys, slaughters, executes*)

3 The _____ of T-cells is to combat infections. (*ambition, function, aim, goal*)

4 Without enough T-cells, the body is nearly _____ against infections. (*defenseless, hopeless, desperate*)

5 To prevent exposure to the virus, one should be especially _____ in sexual relationships. (*chary, circumspect, cautious, calculating*)

3 | Concrete and specific words

Clear, exact writing balances abstract and general words, which outline ideas and objects, with concrete and specific words, which sharpen and solidify.

- **Abstract words** name ideas: *beauty, inflation, management, culture, liberal.* **Concrete words** name qualities and things we can know by our five senses of sight, hearing, touch, taste, and smell: *sleek, humming, rough, salty, musty.*

- **General words** name classes or groups of things, such as *birds, weather,* and *buildings,* and include all the varieties of the class. **Specific words** limit a general class, such as *buildings,* by naming a variety, such as *skyscraper, Victorian courthouse,* or *hut.*

Abstract and general words are useful in the broad statements that set the course for your writing.

> The wild horse in America has a <u>romantic</u> history.

> Relations between the sexes today are more <u>relaxed</u> than they were in the past.

But such statements need development with concrete and specific detail. Detail can turn a vague sentence into an exact one:

> **Vague** The size of his hands made his smallness real. [How big were his hands? How small was he?]

> **Exact** Not until I saw his delicate, doll-like hands did I realize that he stood a full head shorter than most other men.

Note You can use your computer's Find function to help you find and revise abstract and general words that you tend to overuse. Examples of such words include *nice, interesting, things, very, good, a lot, a little,* and *some.*

Exercise 18.6 Revising: Concrete and specific words

Make the following paragraph vivid by expanding the sentences with appropriate details of your own choosing. Replace the abstract and general words that are underlined with specific and concrete alternatives.

1 I remember <u>clearly</u> how <u>awful</u> I felt the first time I <u>attended</u> Mrs. Murphy's second-grade class. 2 I <u>had recently</u> moved from a <u>small</u> town

in Missouri to a crowded suburb of Chicago. 3 My new school looked big from the outside and seemed dark inside as I walked down the long corridor toward the classroom. 4 The class was noisy as I neared the door; but when I entered, everyone became quiet and looked at me. 5 I felt uncomfortable and wanted a place to hide. 6 However, in a loud voice Mrs. Murphy directed me to the front of the room to introduce myself.

Exercise 18.7 Using concrete and specific words

For each abstract or general word below, give at least two other words or phrases that are increasingly specific or concrete. Consult a dictionary as needed. Use the most specific or concrete word from each group in a sentence of your own.

Example:
awake, watchful, vigilant
Vigilant guards patrol the buildings.

1 fabric	6 green	11 teacher
2 delicious	7 walk (*verb*)	12 nice
3 car	8 flower	13 virtue
4 narrow-minded	9 serious	14 angry
5 reach (*verb*)	10 pretty	15 crime

4 Idioms

Idioms are expressions in any language that do not fit the rules for meaning or grammar—for instance, *put up with, plug away at, make off with.*

Idioms that involve prepositions° can be especially confusing for both native and nonnative speakers of English. Some idioms with prepositions are listed in the following box. (More appear in **4** pp. 215–16.)

Idioms with prepositions

abide by a rule	angry with
in a place or state	aware of
according to	based on
accords with	belong in or on a place
accuse of a crime	to a group
accustomed to	capable of
adapt from a source	certain of
to a situation	charge for a purchase
afraid of	with a crime
agree on a plan as a group	concur in an opinion
to someone else's plan	with a person
with a person	

°See "Glossary of Terms," **GI** p. 558.

contend for a principle
     with a person
	occupied by a person
	     in study
	     with a thing

dependent on	opposed to

differ about or over a question
    from in some quality
    with a person
	part from a person
	    with a possession

disappointed by or in a person in or with a thing	prior to
	proud of
familiar with	related to

identical with or to	rewarded by the judge
	    for something done
	    with a gift

impatient for a raise with a person	
independent of	similar to
infer from	sorry about an error for a person
inferior to	superior to

involved in a task
    with a person
	wait at, beside, by, under a place or thing
	    for a train, a person

oblivious of or to surroundings
    of something forgotten
	in a room
	    on a customer

CULTURE LANGUAGE If you are learning standard American English, you may find its prepositions difficult; their meanings can shift depending on context, and they have many idiomatic uses. In mastering the prepositions of standard English, you probably can't avoid memorization. But you can help yourself by memorizing related groups, such as *at/in/on* and *for/since.*

At, in, or *on* in expressions of time

- Use *at* before actual clock time: *at 8:30.*
- Use *in* before a month, year, century, or period: *in April, in 2012, in the twenty-first century, in the next month.*
- Use *on* before a day or date: *on Tuesday, on August 3, on Labor Day.*

At, in, or *on* in expressions of place

- Use *at* before a specific place or address: *at the school, at 511 Iris Street.*
- Use *in* before a place with limits or before a city, state, country, or continent: *in the house, in a box, in Oklahoma City, in Ohio, in China, in Asia.*
- Use *on* to mean "supported by" or "touching the surface of": *on the table, on Iris Street, on page 150.*

For or *since* in expressions of time

■ Use *for* before a period of time: *for an hour, for two years.*

■ Use *since* before a specific point in time: *since 1999, since Friday.*

A dictionary of English as a second language is the best source for the meanings of prepositions; see the suggestions on p. 165.

Exercise 18.8 Using prepositions in idioms

In the following paragraph insert the preposition that correctly completes each idiom. Consult the box on the previous two pages or a dictionary as needed.

1 Children are waiting longer to become independent __of__ their parents. 2 According __in__ US Census data for young adults ages eighteen to twenty-four, 57% of men and 47% of women live full-time with their parents. 3 Some of these adult children are dependent _____ their parents financially. 4 In other cases, the parents charge their children _____ housing, food, and other living expenses. 5 Many adult children are financially capable _____ living independently but prefer to save money rather than contend _____ high housing costs.

Exercise 18.9 Using prepositions in idioms (CULTURE · LANGUAGE)

Complete the following paragraph by filling in the blanks with the appropriate prepositions.

1 The Eighteenth Amendment _____ the US Constitution was ratified _____ 1919. 2 It prohibited the "manufacture, sale, or transportation _____ intoxicating liquors." 3 Temperance groups __in__ the United States wanted to prevent drinking, but the more striking effect of Prohibition was the boost it gave to organized crime. 4 According _____ legend, the most smuggling and bootlegging occurred _____ Chicago. 5 There, _____ February 14, 1929, Al Capone gained control _____ the Chicago underworld by ordering the execution _____ his rival Bugsy Moran and his men _____ a city parking garage. 6 Though Moran escaped unharmed, Capone ruled Chicago _____ two bloody years before he was convicted of tax evasion _____ 1931.

5 Figurative language

Figurative language (or a **figure of speech**) departs from the literal meanings of words, usually by comparing very different ideas or objects:

Literal   As I try to write, I can think of nothing to say.

Figurative   As I try to write, my mind is a slab of black slate.

Imaginatively and carefully used, figurative language can capture meaning more precisely and emotionally than literal language. Here is a figure of speech at work in technical writing (paraphrasing the physicist Edward Andrade):

The molecules in a liquid move continuously like couples on an over-crowded dance floor, jostling each other.

The two most common figures of speech are the simile and the metaphor. Both compare two things of different classes, often one abstract and the other concrete.

- A *simile* makes the comparison explicit and usually begins with *like* or *as*:

  Whenever we grow, we tend to feel it, <u>as</u> a young seed must feel the weight and inertia of the earth when it <u>seeks</u> to break out of its shell on its way to becoming a plant. —Alice Walker

- A *metaphor* claims that the two things are identical, omitting such words as *like* and *as*:

  A school is a hopper into which children are heaved while they are young and tender; therein they are pressed into certain standard shapes and covered from head to heels with official rubber stamps.
  —H. L. Mencken

To be successful, figurative language must be not only fresh but unstrained, calling attention not to itself but to the writer's meaning. Be especially wary of mixed metaphors, which combine two or more incompatible figures:

Mixed	Various thorny problems that we try to sweep under the rug continue to bob up all the same.
Improved	Various thorny problems that we try to weed out continue to thrive all the same.

Exercise 18.10 Using figurative language

Invent appropriate similes or metaphors of your own to describe each scene or quality below, and use the figure in a sentence.

Example:
The attraction of a lake on a hot day
The small waves like fingers beckoned us irresistibly.

1 The sound of a kindergarten classroom
2 People waiting in line to buy tickets to a rock concert
3 The politeness of strangers meeting for the first time
4 A streetlight seen through dense fog
5 The effect of watching television for ten hours straight

6 Trite expressions

Trite expressions, or **clichés**, are phrases so old and so often repeated that they have become stale. They include the following:

acid test	better late than never
add insult to injury	cold, hard facts

crushing blow	pride and joy
easier said than done	ripe old age
face the music	rude awakening
few and far between	shoulder the burden
flat as a pancake	shoulder to cry on
green with envy	sneaking suspicion
hard as a rock	sober as a judge
heavy as lead	stand in awe
hit the nail on the head	strong as an ox
hour of need	thin as a rail
ladder of success	tired but happy
moving experience	tried and true
needle in a haystack	untimely death
point with pride	wise as an owl

To edit clichés, listen to your writing for any expressions that you have heard or used before. You can also supplement your efforts with a style checker, which may include a cliché detector. When you find a cliché, substitute fresh words of your own or restate the idea in plain language.

Exercise 18.11 Revising: Trite expressions
Revise the following paragraph to eliminate trite expressions.

1 The disastrous consequences of the war have shaken the small nation to its roots. 2 Prices for food have shot sky high, and citizens have sneaking suspicions that others are making a killing on the black market. 3 Medical supplies are so few and far between that even civilians who are sick as dogs cannot get treatment. 4 With most men fighting or injured or killed, women have had to bite the bullet and shoulder the burden in farming and manufacturing. 5 Last but not least, the war's heavy drain on the nation's pocketbook has left the economy in shambles.

19 Completeness

Chapter essentials
- Write complete compounds (next page).
- Add words needed for clarity (next page).

Visit MyWritingLab™ for more resources on completeness.

The most serious kind of incomplete sentence is the grammatical fragment (see **4** pp. 264–66). But sentences are also incomplete when they omit one or more words needed for clarity.

19a | Writing complete compounds

You may omit words from a compound construction° when the omission will not confuse readers, as in the following examples.

> Environmentalists have hopes for alternative fuels and [for] public transportation.
> Some cars will run on electricity and some [will run] on hydrogen.

Such omissions are possible only when the words omitted are common to all the parts of a compound construction.° When the parts differ in any way, all words must be included in all parts.

> One new car gets eighty miles per gallon; some old cars get as little as five miles per gallon. [One verb is singular, the other plural.]
> Environmentalists believe in and work for fuel conservation. [Idiom requires different prepositions with *believe* and *work*.]

19b | Adding needed words

In haste or carelessness, do not omit small words that are needed for clarity:

Incomplete   Regular payroll deductions are a type painless savings. You hardly notice missing amounts, and after period of years the contributions can add a large total.

Revised   Regular payroll deductions are a type of painless savings. You hardly notice the missing amounts, and after a period of years the contributions can add up to a large total.

Attentive proofreading is the only insurance against this kind of omission. *Proofread all your papers carefully.* See **1** pp. 37–38 for tips.

(CULTURE LANGUAGE) If your native language or dialect is not standard American English, you may have difficulty knowing when to use the English articles *a, an,* and *the.* For guidelines see **4** pp. 254–56.

Exercise 19.1   Revising: Completeness

Add words to the following paragraph so that the sentences are complete and clear.

1 The first ice cream, eaten China in about 2000 BC, was lumpier than modern ice cream. 2 The Chinese made their ice cream of milk, spices, and overcooked rice and packed in snow to solidify. 3 Ice milk and fruit ices became popular among wealthy in fourteenth-century Italy. 4 At her wedding in 1533 to king of France, Catherine de Médicis offered several flavors of fruit ices. 5 Modern sherbets resemble her ices; modern ice cream her soft dessert of thick, sweetened cream.

°See "Glossary of Terms," **Gl** p. 558.

20 Conciseness

Chapter essentials

- Focus on the subject and verb (below).
- Cut empty words and unneeded repetition (opposite and p. 176).
- Tighten modifiers (p. 177).
- Revise *there is* and *it is* constructions (p. 177).
- Combine sentences (p. 177).
- Rewrite jargon (p. 178).

Visit MyWritingLab™ for more resources on conciseness.

Concise writing makes every word count. Conciseness is not the same as mere brevity: detail and originality should not be cut with needless words. Rather, the length of an expression should be appropriate to the thought.

You may find yourself writing wordily when you are unsure of your subject or when your thoughts are tangled. It's fine, even necessary, to grope while drafting. But you should straighten out your ideas and eliminate wordiness during revision and editing.

(CULTURE LANGUAGE) Wordiness is not a problem of incorrect grammar. A sentence may be perfectly grammatical but still contain unneeded words that make it unclear or awkward.

20a Focusing on the subject and verb

Using the subjects° and verbs° of your sentences for the key actors and actions will reduce words and emphasize important ideas. (See pp. 139–40 for more on this topic.)

Wordy	The reason why most of the country shifts to daylight time is that summer days are much longer than winter days.
Concise	Most of the country shifts to daylight time because summer days are much longer than winter days.

Focusing on subjects and verbs will also help you avoid several other causes of wordiness discussed further on pp. 139–40:

Nouns° made from verbs

Wordy	The occurrence of the shortest day of the year is about December 22.
Concise	The shortest day of the year occurs about December 22.

Weak verbs

Wordy	The earth's axis has a tilt as the planet is in orbit around the sun so that the northern and southern hemispheres are alternately in alignment toward the sun.

°See "Glossary of Terms," **Gl** p. 558.

Ways to achieve conciseness

Wordy (87 words)

The highly pressured nature of critical-care nursing is due to the fact that the patients	Focus on subject and verb, and cut or shorten empty words and phrases.
have life-threatening illnesses. Critical-care nurses must have possession of steady nerves	Avoid nouns made from verbs.
to care for patients who are critically ill and	Cut unneeded repetition.
very sick. The nurses must also have posses-sion of interpersonal skills. They must also	Combine sentences.
have medical skills. It is considered by most	Change passive voice to active voice.
health-care professionals that these nurses are essential if there is to be improvement of	Revise *there is* con-structions.
patients who are now in critical care from that status to the status of intermediate care.	Cut unneeded repeti-tion, and tighten modi-fiers.

Concise (37 words)

Critical-care nursing is highly pressured because the patients have life-threatening illnesses. Critical-care nurses must possess steady nerves and interpersonal and medical skills. Most health-care professionals consider these nurses essential if patients are to improve to intermediate care.

Concise The earth's axis tilts as the planet orbits the sun so that the northern and southern hemispheres alternately align toward the sun.

Passive voice°

Wordy During its winter the northern hemisphere is tilted farthest away from the sun, so the nights are made longer and the days are made shorter.

Concise During its winter the northern hemisphere tilts away from the sun, which makes the nights longer and the days shorter.

See also **4** pp. 225–26 on changing the passive voice to the active voice,° as in the example above.

20b Cutting empty words

Empty words walk in place, gaining little or nothing in meaning. Many can be cut entirely. The following are just a few examples:

all things considered	in a manner of speaking
as far as I'm concerned	in my opinion
for all intents and purposes	last but not least
for the most part	more or less

°See "Glossary of Terms," **Gl** p. 558.

Other empty words can also be cut, usually along with some of the words around them.

area	element	kind	situation
aspect	factor	manner	thing
case	field	nature	type

Still others can be reduced from several words to a single word:

For	Substitute
at all times	always
at the present time	now, yet
because of the fact that	because
due to the fact that	because
for the purpose of	for
in the event that	if
in the final analysis	finally

Cutting or reducing such words and phrases will make your writing move faster and work harder:

> Wordy   In my opinion, the council's proposal to improve the nature of the city center is inadequate for the reason that it ignores pedestrians.

> Concise   The council's proposal to improve the city center is inadequate because it ignores pedestrians.

20c | Cutting unneeded repetition

Unnecessary repetition weakens sentences:

> Wordy   Many unskilled workers without training in a particular job are unemployed and do not have any work.

> Concise   Many unskilled workers are unemployed.

Be especially alert to phrases that say the same thing twice. In the examples below, the unneeded words are underlined:

circle around	important [basic] essentials
consensus of opinion	puzzling in nature
cooperate together	repeat again
final completion	return again
frank and honest exchange	square [round] in shape
the future to come	surrounding circumstances

CULTURE LANGUAGE   The preceding phrases are redundant because the main word already implies the underlined word or words. A dictionary will tell you what meanings a word implies. *Assassinate,* for instance, means "murder someone well known," so the following sentence is redundant: *Julius Caesar was assassinated and killed.*

20d | Tightening modifiers

Modifiers° can be expanded or contracted depending on the emphasis you want to achieve. When editing your sentences, consider whether any modifiers can be tightened without loss of emphasis or clarity.

Wordy   The weight-loss industry faces new competition from lipolysis, which is a cosmetic procedure that is relatively noninvasive.

Concise   The weight-loss industry faces new competition from lipolysis, a relatively noninvasive cosmetic procedure.

20e | Revising *there is* and *it is*

You can postpone the sentence subject with the words *there* and *it*: *There are three points made in the text. It was not fair that only seniors could vote.* These **expletive constructions** can be useful to emphasize the subject (as when introducing it for the first time) or to indicate a change in direction. But often they just add words and weaken sentences:

Wordy   There is a completely noninvasive laser treatment that makes people thinner by rupturing fat cells and releasing the fat into the spaces between cells. It is the expectation of some doctors that the procedure will replace liposuction.

Concise   A completely noninvasive laser treatment makes people thinner by rupturing fat cells and releasing the fat into the spaces between cells. Some doctors expect that the procedure will replace liposuction.

CULTURE / LANGUAGE   When you must use an expletive construction, be careful to include *there* or *it*. Only commands and some questions can begin with verbs.

20f | Combining sentences

Often the information in two or more sentences can be combined into one tight sentence.

Wordy   People who receive fat-releasing laser treatments can lose inches from their waists. They can also lose inches from their hips and thighs. They do not lose weight. The released fat remains in their bodies.

Concise   People who receive fat-releasing laser treatment can lose inches from their waists, hips, and thighs; but they do not lose weight because the released fat remains in their bodies.

°See "Glossary of Terms," **GI** p. 558.

20g Rewriting jargon

Jargon can refer to the special vocabulary of any discipline or profession (see pp. 158–59). But it has also come to describe vague, inflated language that is overcomplicated, even incomprehensible. When it comes from government or business, we call it **bureaucratese.**

Jargon
: The necessity for individuals to become separate entities in their own right may impel children to engage in open rebelliousness against parental authority or against sibling influence, with resultant bewilderment of those being rebelled against.

Translation
: Children's natural desire to become themselves may make them rebel against bewildered parents or siblings.

Exercise 20.1   Revising: Writing concisely

Make the following paragraph more concise. Combine sentences when doing so reduces wordiness.

If sore muscles after exercising are a problem for you, there are some measures that can be taken by you to ease the discomfort. It is advisable to avoid heat for the first day of soreness. The application of heat within the first twenty-four hours can cause an increase in muscle soreness and stiffness. In contrast, the immediate application of cold will help to reduce inflammation. Blood vessels are constricted by cold. Blood is kept away from the injured muscles. There are two ways the application of cold can be made: you can take a cold shower or use an ice pack. Inflammation of muscles can also be reduced with aspirin, ibuprofen, or another anti-inflammatory medication. When healing is occurring, you need to take it easy. A day or two after overdoing exercise, it is advisable for you to get some light exercise and gentle massage.

Exercise 20.2   Revising: Conciseness

Make the following paragraph as concise as possible. Be merciless.

At the end of a lengthy line of reasoning, he came to the conclusion that the situation with carcinogens [cancer-causing substances] should be regarded as similar to the situation with the automobile. Instead of giving in to an irrational fear of cancer, we should consider all aspects of the problem in a balanced and dispassionate frame of mind, making a total of the benefits received from potential carcinogens (plastics, pesticides, and other similar products) and measuring said total against the damage done by such products. This is the nature of most discussions about the automobile. Instead of responding irrationally to the visual, aural, and air pollution caused by automobiles, we have decided to live with them (while simultaneously working to improve on them) for the benefits brought to society as a whole.

PART 4

Sentence Parts and Patterns

Sentence Parts and Patterns

181

Basic Grammar

Grammar describes how language works, and understanding it can help you create clear and accurate sentences. This section explains the kinds of words in sentences (Chapter 21) and how to build basic sentences (22), expand them (23), and classify them (24).

21 Parts of Speech

Chapter essentials

- Recognize nouns and pronouns (below and opposite).
- Recognize verbs (opposite).
- Recognize adjectives and adverbs (p. 185).
- Recognize prepositions, conjunctions, and interjections (pp. 186, 189).

Visit MyWritingLab™ for more resources on parts of speech.

All English words fall into eight groups, or **parts of speech**, such as nouns, verbs, adjectives, and adverbs. A word's part of speech determines its form and its position in a sentence. The same word may even serve as different parts of speech in different sentences, as these examples show:

The government sent <u>aid</u> to the city. [*Aid* is a noun.]
Governments <u>aid</u> citizens. [*Aid* is a verb.]

The *function* of a word in a sentence always determines its part of speech in that sentence.

21a Recognizing nouns

Nouns name. They may name a person (*Helen Mirren, Barack Obama, astronaut*), a thing (*chair, book, Mt. Rainier*), a quality (*pain, mystery, simplicity*), a place (*city, Washington, ocean, Red Sea*), or an idea (*reality, peace, success*).

The forms of nouns depend partly on where they fit in certain groups. As the following examples indicate, the same noun may appear in more than one group.

- **A *common noun* names a general class of things and does not begin with a capital letter:** *earthquake, citizen, earth, fortitude, army.*
- **A *proper noun* names a specific person, place, or thing and begins with a capital letter:** *Angelina Jolie, Washington Monument, El Paso, US Congress.*

- A *count noun* names a thing considered countable in English. Most count nouns add *-s* or *-es* to distinguish between singular (one) and plural (more than one): *citizen, citizens; city, cities*. Some count nouns form irregular plurals: *woman, women; child, children*.
- A *noncount noun* names things or qualities that aren't considered countable in English: *earth, sugar, chaos, fortitude*. Noncount nouns do not form plurals.
- A *collective noun* is singular in form but names a group: *army, family, herd, US Congress*.

In addition, most nouns form the **possessive** by adding *-'s* to show ownership (*Nadia's books, citizen's rights*), source (*Auden's poems*), and some other relationships.

21b Recognizing pronouns

Most **pronouns** substitute for nouns and function in sentences as nouns do: *Susanne Ling enlisted in the Air Force when she graduated.*
Pronouns fall into groups depending on their form or function:

- A *personal pronoun* refers to a specific individual or to individuals: *I, you, he, she, it, we,* and *they.*
- An *indefinite pronoun* does not refer to a specific noun: *anyone, everything, no one, somebody,* and so on. *No one came. Nothing moves. Everybody speaks.*
- A *relative pronoun* relates a group of words to a noun or another pronoun: *who, whoever, which, that. Everyone who attended received a prize. The book that won is a novel.*
- An *interrogative pronoun* introduces a question: *who, whom, whose, which, what. What song is that? Who will contribute?*
- A *demonstrative pronoun* identifies or points to a noun: *this, these, that, those,* and so on. *Those berries are ripe. This is the site.*
- An *intensive pronoun* emphasizes a noun or another pronoun: *myself, himself, itself, themselves,* and so on. *I myself asked that question. The price itself is in doubt.*
- A *reflexive pronoun* indicates that the sentence subject also receives the action of the verb: *myself, himself, itself, themselves,* and so on. *He perjured himself. They injured themselves.*

The personal pronouns *I, he, she, we,* and *they* and the relative pronouns *who* and *whoever* change form depending on their function in the sentence. (See Chapter 30.)

21c Recognizing verbs

Verbs express an action (*bring, change, grow, consider*), an occurrence (*become, happen, occur*), or a state of being (*be, seem, remain*).

1 Forms of verbs

Verbs have five distinctive forms. If a word's form can change as described here, the word is a verb:

■ **The *plain form* is the dictionary form of the verb.** When the subject is a plural noun or the pronoun *I, we, you,* or *they,* the plain form indicates action that occurs in the present, occurs habitually, or is generally true.

A few artists live in town today.
They hold classes downtown.

■ **The *-s form* ends in *-s* or *-es*.** When the subject is a singular noun, a pronoun such as *everyone,* or the personal pronoun *he, she,* or *it,* the *-s* form indicates action that occurs in the present, occurs habitually, or is generally true.

The artist lives in town today.
She holds classes downtown.

■ **The *past-tense form* indicates that the action of the verb occurred before now.** It usually adds *-d* or *-ed* to the plain form, although most irregular verbs create it in different ways (see pp. 204–06).

Many artists lived in town before this year.
They held classes downtown. [Irregular verb.]

■ **The *past participle* is usually the same as the past-tense form, except in most irregular verbs.** It combines with forms of *have* or *be* (*has climbed, was created*), or by itself it modifies nouns and pronouns (*the sliced apples*).

Artists have lived in town for decades.
They have held classes downtown. [Irregular verb.]

■ **The *present participle* adds *-ing* to the verb's plain form.** It combines with forms of *be* (*is buying*), modifies nouns and pronouns (*the boiling water*), or functions as a noun (*Running exhausts me*).

A few artists are living in town today.
They are holding classes downtown.

The verb *be* has eight forms rather than the five forms of most other verbs:

Plain form	be		
Present participle	being		
Past participle	been		
	I	*he, she, it*	*we, you, they*
Present tense	am	is	are
Past tense	was	was	were

2 | Helping verbs

Some verb forms combine with **helping verbs** to indicate time, possibility, obligation, necessity, and other kinds of meaning: _can run, was sleeping, had been working_. In these **verb phrases** _run, sleeping,_ and _working_ are **main verbs**—they carry the principal meaning.

Verb phrase

Helping   Main

Artists can train others to draw.
The techniques have changed little.

The most common helping verbs are listed in the box below. See pp. 209–12 for more on helping verbs.

Common helping verbs

Forms of _be_: be, am, is, are, was, were, been, being

Forms of _have_: have, has, had, having

Forms of _do_: do, does, did

be able to	could	may	ought to	used to
be supposed to	had better	might	shall	will
can	have to	must	should	would

Exercise 21.1 Identifying nouns, pronouns, and verbs
Identify the words that function as nouns (N), pronouns (P), and verbs (V) in the following paragraph.

Example:

  N   N   V   N
Ancestors of the gingko tree lived 175 to 200 million years ago.

1 The ginko tree, which is one of the world's oldest trees, is large and picturesque. 2 Gingko trees may grow to over a hundred feet in height. 3 Their leaves look like fans and are about three inches wide. 4 The leaves turn yellow in the fall. 5 Because it tolerates smoke, low temperatures, and low rainfall, the gingko appears in many cities. 6 A shortcoming, however, is the foul odor of its fruit. 7 Inside the fruit is a large white seed, which some people value as food. 8 The fruit often does not appear until the tree is mature. 9 The tree's name means "apricot" in the Japanese language. 10 Originally, the gingko grew only in China, but it has now spread throughout the world.

21d | Recognizing adjectives and adverbs

Adjectives describe or modify nouns and pronouns. They specify which one, what quality, or how many.

     old   city   generous   one   two   pears
  adjective noun   adjective pronoun   adjective noun

Adverbs describe or modify verbs, adjectives, other adverbs, and whole groups of words. They specify when, where, how, and to what extent.

An -*ly* ending often signals an adverb, but not always: *friendly* is an adjective; *never* and *not* are adverbs. The only way to tell whether a word is an adjective or an adverb is to determine what it modifies.

Adjectives and adverbs appear in three forms: **positive** (*green, angrily*), **comparative** (*greener, more angrily*), and **superlative** (*greenest, most angrily*).

See Chapter 33 for more on adjectives and adverbs.

Exercise 21.2 Identifying adjectives and adverbs

Identify the adjectives (ADJ) and adverbs (ADV) in the following paragraph. Mark *a, an,* and *the* as adjectives.

> *Example:*
>   ADV
> Stress can hit people when they least expect it.

1 You can reduce stress by making a few simple changes. 2 Get up fifteen minutes earlier than you ordinarily do. 3 Eat a healthy breakfast, and eat it slowly so that you enjoy it. 4 Do your more unpleasant tasks early in the day. 5 Carry something to read when you know you'll have to wait in line somewhere. 6 Make promises sparingly and keep them faithfully. 7 Plan ahead to prevent the most stressful situations—for example, carrying spare keys so you won't be locked out of your car or house. 8 See a doctor and dentist regularly. 9 And every day, do at least one thing you really enjoy.

21e Recognizing connecting words: Prepositions and conjunctions

Connecting words are mostly small words that link parts of sentences. They never change form.

1 Prepositions

Prepositions form nouns or pronouns (plus any modifiers) into word groups called **prepositional phrases:** *about love,* down *the stairs.* These phrases usually serve as modifiers° in sentences, as in *The plants trailed down the stairs.* (See p. 195.)

CULTURE LANGUAGE The meanings and uses of English prepositions can be difficult to master. See 3 pp. 168–70 for a discussion of prepositions in idioms, such as *proud of* and *angry with.* See pp. 215–16 for two-word verbs that include prepositions, such as *look after* and *look up.*

°See "Glossary of Terms," **Gl** p. 558.

Common prepositions

about	before	except for	of	throughout
above	behind	excepting	off	till
according to	below	for	on	to
across	beneath	from	onto	toward
after	beside	in	on top of	under
against	between	in addition to	out	underneath
along	beyond	inside	out of	unlike
along with	by	inside of	outside	until
among	concerning	in spite of	over	up
around	despite	instead of	past	upon
as	down	into	regarding	up to
aside from	due to	like	round	with
at	during	near	since	within
because of	except	next to	through	without

2 | Subordinating conjunctions

Subordinating conjunctions form sentences into word groups called **subordinate clauses**, such as *when the meeting ended* or *that she knew*. These clauses serve as parts of sentences: *Everyone was relieved when the meeting ended*. *She said that she knew*. (See pp. 200–01.)

Common subordinating conjunctions

after	even if	rather than	until
although	even though	since	when
as	if	so that	whenever
as if	if only	than	where
as long as	in order that	that	whereas
as though	now that	though	wherever
because	once	till	whether
before	provided	unless	while

CULTURE LANGUAGE Learning the meanings of subordinating conjunctions can help you to express your ideas clearly. Note that each one conveys its meaning on its own. It does not need help from another function word, such as the coordinating conjunction *and, but, for,* or *so:*

Faulty Even though the parents cannot read, <u>but</u> their children may read well. [*Even though* and *but* have the same meaning, so both are not needed.]

Revised Even though the parents cannot read, their children may read well.

3 | Coordinating and correlative conjunctions

Coordinating and correlative conjunctions connect words or word groups of the same kind, such as nouns or sentences.

Coordinating conjunctions consist of a single word:

Coordinating conjunctions

and	nor	for	yet
but	or	so	

Dieting or exercise alone is not enough for most people to maintain a healthy weight.

Dieting takes discipline, but exercise takes discipline and time.

Correlative conjunctions are combinations of coordinating conjunctions and other words:

Common correlative conjunctions

both . . . and	neither . . . nor
not only . . . but also	whether . . . or
not . . . but	as . . . as
either . . . or	

Both a balanced diet and regular exercise are necessary to maintain a healthy weight.

Neither diet nor exercise alone will substantially improve a person's health.

Exercise 21.3 Adding connecting words

Fill each blank in the following paragraph with the appropriate connecting word: a preposition, a subordinating conjunction, or a coordinating conjunction. Consult the lists on p. 187 and above if you need help.

> *Example:*
> A Trojan priest warned, "Beware _____ Greeks bearing gifts."
> (*preposition*)
> A Trojan priest warned, "Beware of Greeks bearing gifts."

　　1 Just about everyone has heard the story _____ the Trojan Horse. (*preposition*) 2 This incident happened at the city of Troy _____ was planned by the Greeks. (*coordinating conjunction*) 3 The Greeks built a huge wooden horse _____ a hollow space big enough to hold many men. (*preposition*) 4 At night, they rolled the horse to the gate of Troy _____ left it there filled with soldiers. (*coordinating conjunction*) 5 _____ the morning, the Trojans were surprised to see the enormous horse. (*preposition*) 6 They were amazed _____ they saw that the Greeks were gone. (*subordinating conjunction*) 7 _____ they were curious to examine this gift from the Greeks, they dragged the horse into the city and left it outside the temple. (*subordinating conjunction*) 8 In the middle of the night, the hidden Greeks emerged _____ the horse and began setting fires all over town. (*preposition*) 9 _____ the Trojan soldiers awoke and came out of their houses, the Greeks killed them one by one. (*subordinating conjunction*) 10 By the next morning, the Trojan

men were dead _____ the women were slaves to the Greeks. (*coordinating conjunction*)

21f Recognizing interjections

Interjections express feeling or command attention. They are rarely used in academic or business writing.

<u>Oh</u>, the meeting went fine.
They won seven thousand dollars! <u>Wow</u>!

22 The Sentence

Chapter essentials

- Recognize subjects and predicates (below).
- Recognize the basic predicate patterns (p. 191).

Visit MyWritingLab™ for more resources on the sentence.

The **sentence** is the basic unit of expression, forming a complete thought. Its subject and predicate usually name an actor and an action.

22a Recognizing subjects and predicates

Most sentences make statements. First the **subject** names something; then the **predicate** makes an assertion about the subject or describes an action by the subject.

Subject	Predicate
Art	thrives.

The **simple subject** consists of one or more nouns° or pronouns,° whereas the **complete subject** also includes any modifiers.° The **simple predicate** consists of one or more verbs,° whereas the **complete predicate** adds any words needed to complete the meaning of the verb plus any modifiers.

Sometimes, as in the short example *Art thrives*, the simple and complete subject and predicate are the same. More often, they are different:

Subject	Predicate
┌────── complete ──────┐	┌──── complete ────┐
┌ simple	simple ┐
Some contemporary art	stirs controversy.

°See "Glossary of Terms," **Gl** p. 558.

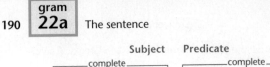

Subject   Predicate

┌———complete———┐ ┌———complete———┐

◄—simple—►   ◄—simple—►

<u>Congress</u> and the <u>media</u>   <u>discuss</u> and <u>dispute</u> its value.

In the example above, the simple subject and simple predicate are both **compound**: in each, two words joined by a coordinating conjunction (*and*) serve the same function.

Tests to find subjects and predicates

The tests below use the following example:

Art that makes it into museums has often survived controversy.

Identify the subject.

- Ask *who* or *what* **is acting or being described in the sentence.**

  Complete subject   art that makes it into museums

- **Isolate the simple subject by deleting modifiers**—words or word groups that don't name the actor of the sentence but give information about it. In the example, the word group *that makes it into museums* does not name the actor but modifies it.

  Simple subject   art

Identify the predicate.

- Ask what the sentence asserts about the subject: what is its action, or what state is it in? In the example, the assertion about *art* is that it *has often survived controversy.*

  Complete predicate   has often survived controversy

- **Isolate the verb, the simple predicate, by changing the time of the subject's action.** The simple predicate is the word or words that change as a result.

Example	Art . . . has often survived controversy.
Present	Art . . . often survives controversy.
Future	Art . . . will often survive controversy.
Simple predicate	has survived

Note If a sentence contains a word group such as *that makes it into museums* or *because viewers agree about its quality,* you may be tempted to mark the subject and verb in the word group as the subject and verb of the sentence. But these word groups are subordinate clauses, made into modifiers by the words they begin with: *that* and *because.* See pp. 200–01 for more on subordinate clauses.

CULTURE LANGUAGE The subject of a sentence in standard American English may be a noun (*art*) or a pronoun that refers to the noun (*it*), but not both. (See pp. 275–76.)

Faulty	Art it can stir controversy.
Revised	Art can stir controversy.
Revised	It can stir controversy.

When identifying the subject and the predicate of a sentence, be aware that some English words can serve as both nouns and verbs. For example, *visits* below functions as a verb and as a noun:

She visits the museum every Saturday. [Verb.]
Her visits are enjoyable. [Noun.]

Exercise 22.1 Identifying subjects and predicates

In the following sentences, label the subject and the predicate and insert a slash between them. Then use each sentence as a model to create a sentence of your own.

> *Example:*
> subject   predicate
> An important scientist / spoke at commencement.
> *Sample imitation:* The hungry family ate at the diner.

1 The leaves fell.
2 October ends soon.
3 The orchard owners made apple cider.
4 They examined each apple carefully for quality.
5 Over a hundred people will buy cider at the roadside stand.

Exercise 22.2 Identifying subjects and predicates

In the following sentences, insert a slash between the complete subject and the complete predicate. Underline each simple subject once and each simple predicate twice.

> *Example:*
> The pony, the light horse, and the draft horse / are the three main types of domestic horses.

1 The horse has a long history of service to humanity but today is mainly a show and sport animal. 2 A member of the genus *Equus*, the domestic horse shares its lineage with the ass and the zebra. 3 The domestic horse and its relatives are all plains-dwelling herd animals. 4 The modern horse evolved in North America. 5 It migrated to other parts of the world and then became extinct in the Americas. 6 The Spaniards reintroduced the domestic horse to the Americas. 7 North American wild horses are actually descended from escaped domestic horses. 8 According to records, North Americans hunted and domesticated horses as early as four to five thousand years ago. 9 The earliest ancestor of the modern horse may have been eohippus, approximately 55 million years ago.

22b Recognizing predicate patterns

All English sentences are based on five patterns, each differing in the complete predicate (the verb and any words following it).

The five basic sentence patterns

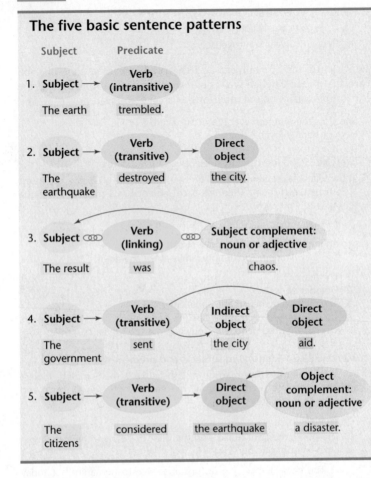

Subject   Predicate

1. **Subject** → **Verb (intransitive)**

   The earth   trembled.

2. **Subject** → **Verb (transitive)** → **Direct object**

   The earthquake   destroyed   the city.

3. **Subject** — **Verb (linking)** — **Subject complement: noun or adjective**

   The result   was   chaos.

4. **Subject** → **Verb (transitive)** **Indirect object** **Direct object**

   The government   sent   the city   aid.

5. **Subject** → **Verb (transitive)** → **Direct object** **Object complement: noun or adjective**

   The citizens   considered   the earthquake   a disaster.

CULTURE LANGUAGE Word order in English sentences may not correspond to word order in the sentences of your native language or dialect. For instance, some other languages prefer the verb first in the sentence, whereas English strongly prefers the subject first.

Pattern 1: The earth trembled.

In the simplest pattern the predicate consists only of an **intransitive verb**, a verb that does not require a following word to complete its meaning.

Subject   Predicate
          Intransitive verb

The earth   trembled.
The hospital   may close.

Pattern 2: The earthquake destroyed the city.

In pattern 2 the verb is followed by a **direct object**, a noun° or pronoun° that identifies who or what receives the action of the verb. A verb that requires a direct object to complete its meaning is called **transitive**.

Subject	Predicate	
	Transitive verb	Direct object
The earthquake	destroyed	the city.
Education	opens	doors.

(CULTURE LANGUAGE) Only transitive verbs may be used in the passive voice°: *The city was destroyed by the earthquake.* Your dictionary says whether a verb is transitive or intransitive, often with an abbreviation such as *tr.* or *intr.* Some verbs (*begin, learn, read, write,* and others) can be either transitive or intransitive.

Pattern 3: The result was chaos.

In pattern 3 the verb is followed by a **subject complement**, a word that renames or describes the subject. A verb in this pattern is called a **linking verb** because it links its subject to the description following. The linking verbs include *be, seem, appear, become, grow, remain, stay, prove, feel, look, smell, sound,* and *taste.* Subject complements are usually nouns or adjectives.

Subject	Predicate	
	Linking verb	Subject complement
The result	was	chaos. [Noun.]
The man	became	an accountant. [Noun.]
The car	seems	expensive. [Adjective.]

Pattern 4: The government sent the city aid.

In pattern 4 the verb is followed by a direct object and an **indirect object**, a word identifying to or for whom the action of the verb is performed. The direct object and indirect object refer to different things, people, or places.

Subject	Predicate		
	Transitive verb	Indirect object	Direct object
The government	sent	the city	aid.
One company	offered	its employees	bonuses.

A number of verbs can take indirect objects, including *send* and *offer* (preceding examples) and *allow, bring, buy, deny, find, get, give, leave, make, pay, read, sell, show, teach,* and *write.*

(CULTURE LANGUAGE) With some verbs that express action done to or for someone, the indirect object must be turned into a

°See "Glossary of Terms," **GI** p. 558.

phrase° beginning with *to* or *for*. In addition, the phrase must come after the direct object. The verbs that require these changes include *admit, announce, demonstrate, explain, introduce, mention, prove, recommend, say,* and *suggest*.

	indirect object	direct object
Faulty	The manual explains workers the new procedure.	

	direct object	*to* phrase
Revised	The manual explains the new procedure to workers.	

Pattern 5: The citizens considered the earthquake a disaster.

In pattern 5 the verb is followed by a direct object and an **object complement**, a word that renames or describes the direct object. Object complements may be nouns or adjectives.

Subject	Predicate		
	Transitive verb	*Direct object*	*Object complement*
The citizens	considered	the earthquake	a disaster.
Success	makes	some people	nervous.

Exercise 22.3 Identifying sentence parts

In the following sentences identify the subject (S) and verb (V) as well as any direct object (DO), indirect object (IO), subject complement (SC), or object complement (OC).

Example:

```
      S       V    V     DO
Crime statistics can cause surprise.
```

1 The number of serious crimes in the United States decreased.
2 A decline in serious crimes occurred each year.
3 The Crime Index measures serious crime.
4 The FBI invented the index.
5 The four serious violent crimes are murder, robbery, forcible rape, and aggravated assault.
6 The Crime Index calls auto theft, burglary, arson, and larceny-theft the four serious crimes against property.
7 The Crime Index gives the FBI a measure of crime.
8 The index shows trends in crimes and the people who commit them.
9 The nation's largest cities showed the largest decline in crime.
10 However, crime actually increased in smaller cities, proving that the decline in crime is unrepresentative of the nation.

Exercise 22.4 Identifying sentence patterns

In the following sentences, identify each verb as intransitive, transitive, or linking. Then identify each direct object (DO), indirect object (IO), subject complement (SC), and object complement (OC).

Example:

```
       transitive
         verb          IO           DO            DO
Children give their parents both headaches and pleasures.
```

°See "Glossary of Terms," **GI** p. 558.

1 Many people find New York City exciting.
2 Tourists flock to New York each year.
3 Often they visit Times Square first.
4 The square's lights are astounding.
5 The flashing signs sell visitors everything from TVs to underwear.

23 Phrases and Subordinate Clauses

Chapter essentials

- Recognize phrases: prepositional, verbal, absolute, appositive (below).
- Recognize subordinate clauses (p. 200).

Visit MyWritingLab™ for more resources on phrases and subordinate clauses.

Most sentences contain word groups that serve as adjectives, adverbs, or nouns and thus cannot stand alone as sentences.

- A *phrase* lacks either a subject° or a predicate° or both: *fearing an accident*; *in a panic*.
- A *subordinate clause* contains a subject and a predicate but begins with a subordinating word: *when prices rise*; *whoever laughs*.

23a Recognizing phrases

1 Prepositional phrases

A **prepositional phrase** consists of a preposition° plus a noun,° a pronoun,° or a word group serving as a noun, called the **object° of the preposition**. A list of prepositions appears on p. 187.

Preposition	Object
of	spaghetti
on	the surface
with	great satisfaction
upon	entering the room
from	where you are standing

Prepositional phrases usually function as adjectives° or adverbs.°

Life on a raft was an opportunity for adventure.
 adjective phrase   adjective phrase

Huck Finn rode the raft by choice.
              adverb phrase

With his companion, Jim, Huck met many types of people.
 adverb phrase   adjective phrase

°See "Glossary of Terms," **GI** p. 558.

Exercise 23.1 Identifying prepositional phrases

Identify the prepositional phrases in the following passage, and underline the word that each phrase modifies.

Example:

After an hour I finally arrived at the home of my professor.

1 On July 3, 1863, at Gettysburg, Pennsylvania, General Robert E. Lee gambled unsuccessfully for a Confederate victory in the American Civil War. 2 The battle of Pickett's Charge was one of the most disastrous conflicts of the war. 3 Confederate and Union forces faced each other on parallel ridges separated by almost a mile of open fields. 4 After an artillery bombardment of the Union position, nearly 12,000 Confederate infantry marched toward the Union ridge. 5 The Union guns had been silent but suddenly roared against the approaching Confederates. 6 Within an hour, perhaps half of the Confederate soldiers lay wounded or dead.

Exercise 23.2 Sentence combining: Prepositional phrases

To practice writing sentences with prepositional phrases, combine each group of sentences below into one sentence that includes one or two prepositional phrases. You will have to add, delete, and rearrange words. Some items have more than one possible answer.

Example:
I will start working. The new job will pay the minimum wage.
I will start working at a new job for the minimum wage.

1 The slow loris protects itself well. Its habitat is Southeast Asia. It possesses a poisonous chemical.
2 The loris frightens predators when it exudes this chemical. The chemical comes from a gland. The gland is on the loris's upper arm.
3 The loris's chemical is highly toxic. The chemical is not like a skunk's spray. Even small quantities of the chemical are toxic.
4 A tiny dose can affect a human. The dose would get in the mouth. The human would be sent into shock.
5 Predators probably can sense the toxin. They detect it at a distance. They use their nasal organs.

2 Verbal phrases

Certain forms of verbs°, called **verbals**, can serve as modifiers° or nouns. Often these verbals appear with their own modifiers and objects in **verbal phrases**.

Note A verbal is not a verb: it cannot serve as the complete verb of a sentence. *The sun rises over the dump* is a sentence; *The sun rising over the dump* is a sentence fragment. (See p. 265.)

Participial phrases

Present participles end in *-ing*: *living, walking*. **Past participles** usually end in *-d* or *-ed*: *lived, walked*. **Participial phrases** are made from participles plus modifiers and objects. Participles and participial phrases usually serve as adjectives.

°See "Glossary of Terms," **GI** p. 558.

Strolling shoppers fill the malls.
Participle

They make selections determined by personal taste.
Participial phrase

Note With irregular verbs, the past participle may have a different ending—for instance, *hidden funds.* (See pp. 205–06.)

CULTURE LANGUAGE The present and past participles of verbs that express feelings have different meanings. The present participle modifies the thing that causes the feeling: *It was a boring lecture.* The past participle modifies the thing that experiences the feeling: *The bored students slept.* See p. 253.

Gerund phrases

A **gerund** is the *-ing* form of a verb when it serves as a noun. Gerunds and gerund phrases can do whatever nouns can do.

sentence
subject
Shopping satisfies personal needs.
noun

object of preposition
Malls are good at creating such needs.
noun phrase

Infinitive phrases

An **infinitive** is the plain form° of a verb plus *to*: *to hide.* Infinitives and infinitive phrases serve as adjectives, adverbs, or nouns.

sentence
subject   subject complement
To design a mall is to create an artificial environment.
noun phrase   noun phrase

Malls are designed to make shoppers feel safe.
adverb phrase

The environment supports the impulse to shop.
adjective

CULTURE LANGUAGE Infinitives and gerunds may follow some verbs and not others and may differ in meaning after a verb: *The cowboy stopped to sing* (he stopped to do the activity). *The cowboy stopped singing* (he finished the activity). (See pp. 213–15.)

Exercise 23.3 Identifying verbals and verbal phrases

The following sentences contain participles, gerunds, and infinitives as well as participial, gerund, and infinitive phrases. Identify each verbal or verbal phrase.

Example:

Laughing, the talk-show host prodded her guest to talk.

1 Written in 1850 by Nathaniel Hawthorne, *The Scarlet Letter* tells the story of Hester Prynne. 2 Shunned by the community because of her

°See "Glossary of Terms," **Gl** p. 558.

adultery, Hester endures loneliness. 3 She is humble enough to withstand her Puritan neighbors' cutting remarks. 4 Enduring the cruel treatment, the determined young woman refuses to leave her home. 5 By living a life of patience and unselfishness, Hester eventually becomes the community's angel.

Exercise 23.4 Sentence combining: Verbals and verbal phrases

To practice writing sentences with verbals and verbal phrases, combine each of the following pairs of sentences into one sentence. You will have to add, delete, change, and rearrange words. Each item has more than one possible answer.

Example:
My father played mean pranks. For instance, he hid the neighbor's cat.
My father played mean pranks such as hiding the neighbor's cat.

1 Air pollution is a health problem. It affects millions of Americans.
2 The air has been polluted mainly by industries and automobiles. It contains toxic chemicals.
3 Environmentalists pressure politicians. They think politicians should pass stricter laws.
4 Many politicians waver. They often favor environmentalism.
5 The problems are too complex. They cannot be solved easily.

3 Absolute phrases

An **absolute phrase** consists of a noun or pronoun and a participle, plus any modifiers. It modifies the entire rest of the sentence it appears in.

```
_____ absolute phrase _____
```
Their own place established, many ethnic groups are making way for new arrivals.

Unlike a participial phrase (p. 196), an absolute phrase always contains a noun that serves as a subject.

```
participial
___ phrase ___
```
Learning English, many immigrants discover American culture.

```
_____ absolute phrase _____
```
Immigrants having learned English, their opportunities widen.

Exercise 23.5 Sentence combining: Absolute phrases

To practice writing sentences with absolute phrases, combine each pair of sentences below into one sentence that contains an absolute phrase. You will have to add, delete, change, and rearrange words.

Example:
The flower's petals wilted. It looked pathetic.
Its petals wilted, the flower looked pathetic.

1 Geraldine Ferraro's face beamed. She enjoyed the crowd's cheers after her nomination for Vice President.

2 A vacancy had occurred. Sandra Day O'Connor was appointed the first female Supreme Court justice.
3 The vote was complete. Madeleine Albright was confirmed as the first female secretary of state.
4 Her appointment was confirmed. Condoleezza Rice became the first female national security adviser.
5 The election was over. Nancy Pelosi became the first female speaker of the House of Representatives.

4 | Appositive phrases

An **appositive** is usually a noun that renames another noun. An appositive phrase includes modifiers as well.

> ⤹———appositive phrase———⌐
> Bizen ware, a dark stoneware, is produced in Japan.

Appositives and appositive phrases sometimes begin with *that is, such as, for example,* or *in other words.*

> ⤹————————appositive phrase——————
> Bizen ware is used in the Japanese tea ceremony, that is, the Zen Buddhist
>
> observance that links meditation and art.

Exercise 23.6   Sentence combining: Appositive phrases

Combine each pair of sentences into one sentence that contains an appositive phrase. You will have to delete and rearrange words. Some items have more than one possible answer.

Example:

The largest land animal is the elephant. The elephant is also one of the most intelligent animals.

The largest land animal, the elephant, is also one of the most intelligent animals.

1 Some people perform amazing feats when they are very young. These people are geniuses from birth.
2 John Stuart Mill was a British philosopher. He had written a history of Rome by age seven.
3 Two great artists began their work at age four. They were Paul Klee and Gustav Mahler.
4 Mahler was a Bohemian composer of intensely emotional works. He was also the child of a brutal father.
5 Paul Klee was a Swiss painter. As a child he was frightened by his own drawings of devils.

Exercise 23.7   Identifying phrases

In the paragraphs below, identify every verbal and appositive and every verbal, appositive, prepositional, and absolute phrase. (All the sentences include at least two such words and phrases.)

1 With its many synonyms, or words with similar meanings, English can make choosing the right word a difficult task. 2 Borrowing words from early Germanic languages and from Latin, English acquired an unusual number of synonyms. 3 With so many choices, how does a writer

decide between *motherly* and *maternal* or among *womanly, feminine,* and *female*?

4 Some people prefer longer and more ornate words to avoid the flatness of short words. **5** Indeed, during the Renaissance a heated debate occurred between the Latinists, favoring Latin words, and the Saxonists, preferring Anglo-Saxon words derived from Germanic roots. **6** Today, students in writing classes are often told to choose the shorter word, usually an Anglo-Saxon derivative. **7** Better advice, wrote William Hazlitt, is the principle of choosing "the best word in common use." **8** Keeping this principle in mind, a writer would choose either *womanly*, the Anglo-Saxon word, or *feminine*, a French derivative, according to meaning and situation. **9** Of course, synonyms rarely have exactly the same meaning, usage having created subtle but real differences over time. **10** To take another example, *handbook*, an old English word, has a slightly different meaning from *manual*, a French derivative.

23b Recognizing subordinate clauses

A **clause** is any group of words that contains both a subject° and a predicate.° There are two kinds of clauses, and the distinction between them is important.

- A *main clause* makes a complete statement and can stand alone as a sentence: *The sky darkened.*
- A *subordinate clause* is just like a main clause *except* that it begins with a subordinating word: *when the sky darkened; whoever calls.* The subordinating word reduces the clause from a complete statement to a single part of speech: an adjective,° adverb,° or noun.° Use subordinate clauses to support the ideas in main clauses, as described in **3** pp. 145–46.

Note A subordinate clause punctuated as a sentence is a sentence fragment. (See p. 266.)

Adjective clauses

An **adjective clause** modifies a noun or pronoun.° It usually begins with the relative pronoun° *who, whom, whose, which,* or *that.* The relative pronoun is the subject or object° of the clause it begins. The clause ordinarily falls immediately after the word it modifies.

⌐ adjective clause ⌐
Parents who cannot read may have bad memories of school.

⌐ adjective clause ⌐
One school, which is open year-round, helps parents learn to read.

Adverb clauses

An **adverb clause** modifies a verb, an adjective, another adverb, or a whole word group. It always begins with a subordinating conjunction,° such as *although, because, if,* or *when* (see p. 187 for a list).

°See "Glossary of Terms," **Gl** p. 558.

_____ adverb clause _____

The school began teaching parents when adult illiteracy gained national attention.

_____ adverb clause _____ ——main clause ——

Because it was directed at people who could not read, advertising had to be inventive.

Noun clauses

A **noun clause** replaces a noun in a sentence and serves as a subject, object, or complement.° It begins with *that, what, whatever, who, whom, whoever, whomever, when, where, whether, why,* or *how.*

_____ sentence subject _____

Whether the program would succeed depended on door-to-door advertising.
noun clause

_____ object of verb _____

Teachers explained in person how the program would work.
noun clause

Exercise 23.8 Identifying clauses

Underline the subordinate clauses in the following paragraph and identify each one as adjective (ADJ), adverb (ADV), or noun (N) by determining how it functions in its sentence.

1 The Prophet Muhammad, who was the founder of Islam, was born about 570 CE in the city of Mecca. 2 He grew up in the care of his grandfather and an uncle because both of his parents had died when he was very young. 3 His extended family was part of a powerful Arab tribe that lived in western Arabia. 4 When Muhammad was about forty years old, he had a vision while he was in a cave outside Mecca. 5 He believed that God had selected him to be the prophet of a true religion for the Arab people. 6 Viewed as God's messenger, Muhammad attracted many followers before he lost the support of the clans of Mecca. 7 He and his followers moved to Medina, where they established an organized Muslim community that sometimes clashed with the Meccans and with Jewish clans. 8 Throughout his life Muhammad continued as the religious, political, and military leader of Islam as it spread in Asia and Africa. 9 He continued to have revelations, which are recorded in the sacred book of Muslims, the Koran.

Exercise 23.9 Sentence combining: Subordinate clauses

To practice writing sentences with subordinate clauses, combine each pair of main clauses into one sentence. Use either subordinating conjunctions or relative pronouns as appropriate, referring to the lists on pp. 183 and 187 if necessary. You will have to add, delete, and rearrange words. Each item has more than one possible answer.

Example:

She did not have her tire irons with her. She could not change her bicycle tire.

Because she did not have her tire irons with her, she could not change her bicycle tire.

°See "Glossary of Terms," **Gl** p. 558.

1 Moviegoers expect something. Movie sequels should be as exciting as the original films.
2 A few sequels are good films. Most sequels are poor imitations of the originals.
3 A sequel to a blockbuster film arrives in the theater. Crowds quickly line up to see it.
4 Viewers pay to see the same villains and heroes. They remember these characters fondly.
5 Afterward, viewers often grumble about filmmakers. The filmmakers rehash tired plots and characters.

24 Sentence Types

Chapter essentials

- Recognize simple sentences (below).
- Recognize compound sentences (below).
- Recognize complex sentences (opposite).
- Recognize compound-complex sentences (opposite).

Visit MyWritingLab™ for more resources on sentence types.

The four basic sentence structures vary in the number of main clauses° and subordinate clauses.° Each structure gives different emphasis to the main and supporting information in a sentence.

24a Recognizing simple sentences

A **simple sentence** consists of a single main clause and no subordinate clause.

┌─────── main clause ───────┐
Last summer was unusually hot.

┌──────────────────── main clause ────────────────────┐
The summer made many farmers leave the area for good or reduced them
to bare existence.

24b Recognizing compound sentences

A **compound sentence** consists of two or more main clauses and no subordinate clause.

┌── main clause ──┐ ┌── main clause ──┐
Last July was hot, but August was even hotter.

┌──────── main clause ────────┐ ┌──────── main clause ────────┐
The hot sun scorched the earth, and the lack of rain killed many crops.

°See "Glossary of Terms," **GI** p. 558.

24c Recognizing complex sentences

A **complex sentence** consists of one main clause and one or more subordinate clauses.

┌── main clause ──┐ ┌───────── subordinate clause ──────────┐
Rain finally came, although many had left the area by then.

┌───────────── main clause ─────────────┐ ┌── subordinate clause ──
Those who remained were able to start anew because the government
    └ subordinate clause ┘

───────────┐
came to their aid.

24d Recognizing compound-complex sentences

A **compound-complex sentence** has the characteristics of both the compound sentence (two or more main clauses) and the complex sentence (at least one subordinate clause).

┌──────── subordinate clause ────────┐ ┌───────── main clause ─────────
When government aid finally came, many people had already been reduced

─────────┐ ┌──────── main clause ────────┐
to poverty and others had been forced to move.

Exercise 24.1 Identifying sentence structures

Mark the main clauses and subordinate clauses in the following paragraphs. Then identify each sentence as simple, compound, complex, or compound-complex.

Example:

┌─────────── main clause ───────────┐ ┌── subordinate clause ──
The human voice is produced in the larynx, which has two bands

──────────┐
called vocal cords. [Complex.]

1 Our world has many sounds, but they all have one thing in common. 2 They are all produced by vibrations. 3 Vibrations make the air move in waves, and these sound waves travel to the ear. 4 When the waves enter the ear, the auditory nerves convey them to the brain, and the brain interprets them. 5 Some sounds are pleasant, and others, which we call noise, are not. 6 Pleasant sounds, such as music, are produced by regular vibrations at regular intervals. 7 Most noises are produced by irregular vibrations at irregular intervals; an example is the barking of a dog.

8 Sounds, both pleasant and unpleasant, have frequency and pitch. 9 When an object vibrates rapidly, it produces high-frequency, high-pitched sounds. 10 People can hear sounds over a wide range of frequencies, but dogs, cats, and many other animals can hear high frequencies that humans cannot.

Verbs

Verbs express actions, conditions, and states of being. The following chapters explain and solve the most common problems with verbs' forms (Chapter 25), tenses (26), mood (27), and voice (28) and show how to make verbs match their subjects (29).

25 Verb Forms

Chapter essentials

- Use the correct forms of *sing/sang/sung* and other irregular verbs (below).
- Distinguish between *sit* and *set, lie* and *lay,* and *rise* and *raise* (p. 207).
- Use the *-s* and *-ed* forms of the verb when they are required (p. 208).
- Use helping verbs with main verbs appropriately (p. 209).
- Use a gerund or an infinitive after a verb as appropriate (p. 213).
- Use the appropriate particles with two-word verbs (p. 217).

Visit MyWritingLab™ for more resources on verb forms.

The five basic forms of verbs are outlined on p. 184. This chapter focuses on the forms that most often cause difficulty.

25a	Use the correct forms of *sing/sang/sung* and other irregular verbs.

Most verbs are **regular**: they form their past tense° and past participle° by adding *-d* or *-ed* to the plain form.

Plain form	Past tense	Past participle
live	lived	lived
act	acted	acted

About two hundred English verbs are **irregular**: they form their past tense and past participle in some irregular way. A dictionary lists the forms of irregular verbs: plain form,° past tense, and past participle in that order (*go, went, gone*). If the dictionary gives only two forms (as in *think, thought*), then the past tense and the past participle are the same.

Common irregular verbs

Plain form	Past tense	Past participle
be	was, were	been
become	became	become

°See "Glossary of Terms," **GI** p. 558.

Plain form	Past tense	Past participle
begin	began	begun
bid	bid	bid
bite	bit	bitten, bit
blow	blew	blown
break	broke	broken
bring	brought	brought
burst	burst	burst
buy	bought	bought
catch	caught	caught
choose	chose	chosen
come	came	come
cut	cut	cut
dive	dived, dove	dived
do	did	done
dream	dreamed, dreamt	dreamed, dreamt
drink	drank	drunk
drive	drove	driven
eat	ate	eaten
fall	fell	fallen
find	found	found
flee	fled	fled
fly	flew	flown
forget	forgot	forgotten, forgot
freeze	froze	frozen
get	got	got, gotten
give	gave	given
go	went	gone
grow	grew	grown
hang (suspend)	hung	hung
have	had	had
hear	heard	heard
hide	hid	hidden
hold	held	held
keep	kept	kept
know	knew	known
lead	led	led
leave	left	left
lend	lent	lent
let	let	let
lose	lost	lost
pay	paid	paid
ride	rode	ridden
ring	rang	rung
run	ran	run
say	said	said
see	saw	seen
shake	shook	shaken
sing	sang, sung	sung
sink	sank, sunk	sunk

(continued)

Common irregular verbs

(continued)

Plain form	Past tense	Past participle
sleep	slept	slept
slide	slid	slid
speak	spoke	spoken
spring	sprang, sprung	sprung
stand	stood	stood
steal	stole	stolen
swim	swam	swum
swing	swung	swung
take	took	taken
tear	tore	torn
throw	threw	thrown
wear	wore	worn
write	wrote	written

CULTURE LANGUAGE Some English dialects use verb forms that differ from those of standard American English: for instance, *drug* for *dragged*, *growed* for *grew*, *come* for *came*, or *went* for *gone*. In situations requiring standard English, use the forms in the preceding list or in a dictionary.

Faulty They have <u>went</u> to the movies.
Revised They have <u>gone</u> to the movies.

Exercise 25.1 Using irregular verbs

For each irregular verb in brackets, supply either the past tense or the past participle, as appropriate, and identify the form you used.

1 The world population had [grow] by two-thirds of a billion people in less than a decade. 2 Recently it [break] the 7 billion mark. 3 Population experts have [draw] pictures of a crowded future, predicting that the world population may have [slide] up to as many 9.5 billion by the year 2050. 4 The supply of food, clean water, and land is of particular concern. 5 Even though the food supply [rise] in the last decade, the share to each person [fall]. 6 At the same time the water supply, which had actually [become] healthier in the twentieth century, [sink] in size and quality. 7 Changes in land use [run] nomads and subsistence farmers off their fields, while the overall number of species on earth [shrink] by 20%.

8 Yet not all the news is bad. 9 Recently some countries have [begin] to heed these and other problems and to explore how technology can be [drive] to help the earth and all its populations. 10 Population control has [find] adherents all over the world. 11 Crop management has [take] some pressure off lands with poor soil, allowing their owners to produce food, while genetic engineering promises to replenish food supplies that have [shrink]. 12 Some new techniques for waste processing have [prove] effective. 13 Land conservation programs have [give] endangered species room to reproduce and thrive.

25b Distinguish between *sit* and *set*, *lie* and *lay*, and *rise* and *raise*.

The forms of *sit* and *set*, *lie* and *lay*, and *rise* and *raise* are easy to confuse.

Plain form	Past tense	Past participle
sit	sat	sat
set	set	set
lie	lay	lain
lay	laid	laid
rise	rose	risen
raise	raised	raised

In each of these confusing pairs, one verb is intransitive (it does not take an object°) and one is transitive (it does take an object). (See pp. 192–93 for more on this distinction.)

Intransitive

The patients lie in their beds. [*Lie* means "recline" and takes no object.]

Visitors sit with them. [*Sit* means "be seated" or "be located" and takes no object.]

Patients' temperatures rise. [*Rise* means "increase" or "get up" and takes no object.]

Transitive

Nursing aides lay the dinner trays on tables. [*Lay* means "place" and takes an object, here *trays*.]

The aides set the trays down. [*Set* means "place" and takes an object, here *trays*.]

The aides raise the shades. [*Raise* means "lift" or "bring up" and takes an object, here *shades*.]

Note The verb *lie* meaning "to tell an untruth" is a regular verb. Its past tense and past participle forms are *lied*: *Nikki lied to us. She has lied to us for many years.*

Exercise 25.2 Distinguishing between *sit/set, lie/lay, rise/raise*

Choose the correct verb from the pair given in brackets. Then supply the past tense or past participle, as appropriate.

Example:

I [lie, lay] down my books, and then I [sit, set] the table.
I laid down my books, and then I set the table.

1 Yesterday afternoon the child [lie, lay] down for a nap. *lay*
2 The child has been [rise, raise] by her grandparents. *raised*
3 Most days her grandfather has [sit, set] with her, reading her stories. *sat*
4 She has [rise, raise] at dawn most mornings. *risen*
5 Her toys were [lie, lay] on the floor. *laid*

| **25c** | Use the *-s* and *-ed* forms of the verb when they are required. | |

Speakers of some English dialects and nonnative speakers of English sometimes omit the *-s* and *-ed* verb endings when they are required in standard American English.

Note If you tend to omit these endings in writing, practice pronouncing them when speaking or when reading correct verbs aloud, such as those in the examples here. The spoken practice can help you remember the endings in writing.

1 Required *-s* ending

Use the *-s* form of a verb when *both* of these situations hold:

■ **The subject° is a singular noun° (*woman*), an indefinite pronoun° (*everyone*), or *he, she,* or *it*.** These subjects are **third person,** used when someone or something is being spoken about.

■ **The verb's action occurs in the present.**

> The letter asks [not ask] for a quick response.
> Delay costs [not cost] money.
> It wastes [not waste] time.
> Everyone hopes [not hope] for a good outcome.

Be especially careful with the *-s* forms of *be* (*is*), *have* (*has*), and *do* (*does, doesn't*). These forms should always be used to indicate present time with third-person singular subjects.

> The company is [not be] late in responding.
> It has [not have] problems.
> It doesn't [not don't] have the needed data.
> The contract does [not do] depend on the response.

In addition, *be* has the *-s* form *was* in the past tense° with *I* and third-person singular subjects:

> The company was [not were] in trouble before.

Except for the past tense *I was,* the pronouns *I* and *you* and all plural subjects do *not* take the *-s* form of verbs:

> I am [not is] a student.
> You are [not is] also a student.
> They are [not is] students, too.

2 Required *-ed* or *-d* ending

The *-ed* or *-d* verb form is required in *any* of these situations:

■ **The verb's action occurred in the past.**

> The company asked [not ask] for more time.

■ **The verb form functions as a modifier.°**

°See "Glossary of Terms," **Gl** p. 558.

The data concerned [not concern] should be retrievable.

■ **The verb form combines with a form of *be* or *have*.**

The company is supposed [not suppose] to be the best.
It has developed [not develop] an excellent reputation.

Watch especially for a needed *-ed* or *-d* ending when it isn't pronounced clearly in speech, as in *asked, discussed, mixed, supposed, walked,* and *used.*

Exercise 25.3 Using *-s* and *-ed* verb endings CULTURE LANGUAGE
Supply the correct form of each verb in brackets. Be careful to include *-s* and *-ed* (or *-d*) endings where they are needed for standard English.

Example:
Unfortunately, the roof on our new house already [leak].
Unfortunately, the roof on our new house already leaks.

1 A teacher sometimes [ask] too much of a student. 2 In high school I was once [punish] for being sick. 3 I had [miss] a week of school because of a serious case of the flu. 4 I [realize] that I would fail a test unless I had a chance to make up the class work, so I [discuss] the problem with the teacher. 5 He said I was [suppose] to make up the work while I was sick. 6 At that I [walk] out of the class. 7 I [receive] a failing grade then, but it did not change my attitude. 8 I [work] harder in the courses that have more understanding teachers. 9 Today I still balk when a teacher [make] unreasonable demands or [expect] miracles.

25d **Use helping verbs with main verbs appropriately.** CULTURE LANGUAGE

Helping verbs° combine with main verbs° in verb phrases°: *The line should have been cut. Who was calling?*

1 Required helping verbs

Standard American English requires helping verbs in certain situations:

■ **The main verb ends in *-ing.***

Researchers are conducting fieldwork all over the world. [Not Researchers conducting. . . .]

■ **The main verb is *been* or *be.***

Many have been fortunate in their discoveries. [Not Many been. . . .]
Some could be real-life Indiana Joneses. [Not Some be. . . .]

■ **The main verb is a past participle,°** such as *talked, thrown,* or *begun.*

Their discoveries were covered in newspapers and magazines. [Not Their discoveries covered. . . .]

°See "Glossary of Terms," **GI** p. 558.

The researchers <u>have</u> given interviews on TV. [Not The researchers given. . . .]

The omission of a helping verb may create an incomplete sentence, or sentence fragment,° because a present participle° (*conducting*), an irregular past participle (*been*), or the plain form° *be* cannot stand alone as the only verb in a sentence. To work as sentence verbs, these verb forms need helping verbs.

2 Combination of helping verb + main verb

Helping verbs and main verbs combine into verb phrases in specific ways.

Note The main verb in a verb phrase (the one carrying the main meaning) does not change to show a change in subject or time: *she has <u>sung</u>, you had <u>sung</u>*. Only the helping verb may change.

Form of *be* + present participle

The **progressive tenses** indicate action in progress. Create them with *be, am, is, are, was, were,* or *been* followed by the main verb's present participle, the *-ing* form:

She <u>is working</u> on a new book.

Be and *been* always require additional helping verbs to form progressive tenses:

can	might	should ⎫		have ⎫	
could	must	will	<u>be working</u>	has	<u>been working</u>
may	shall	would ⎭		had ⎭	

When forming the progressive tenses, be sure to use the *-ing* form of the main verb.

Faulty   Her ideas are <u>grow</u> more complex. She is <u>developed</u> a new approach to ethics.

Revised Her ideas are <u>growing</u> more complex. She is <u>developing</u> a new approach to ethics.

Form of *be* + past participle

The **passive voice** of the verb indicates that the subject *receives* the action of the verb. Create the passive voice with a form of *be* (*be, am, is, are, was, were, being,* or *been*) followed by the main verb's past participle.

Her latest book <u>was completed</u> in four months.

Be, being, and *been* always require additional helping verbs to form the passive voice.

°See "Glossary of Terms," **Gl** p. 558.

have ⎫		am	was ⎫	
has ⎬ been completed		is	were ⎬ being completed	
had ⎭		are		

will <u>be</u> completed

Always use the main verb's past participle for the passive voice:

Faulty   Her next book will be <u>publish</u> soon.

Revised   Her next book will be <u>published</u> soon.

Note Only transitive verbs° may form the passive voice:

Faulty   A philosophy conference <u>will be occurred</u> in the same week.
            [*Occur* is not a transitive verb.]

Revised   A philosophy conference <u>will occur</u> in the same week.

See pp. 224–26 for advice on when to use and when to avoid the passive voice.

Forms of *have*

Four forms of *have* serve as helping verbs: *have, has, had, having.* One of these forms plus the main verb's past participle creates one of the **perfect tenses**, those expressing action completed before another specific time or action:

Some students <u>have complained</u> about the laboratory.
Others <u>had complained</u> before.

Will and other helping verbs sometimes accompany forms of *have* in the perfect tenses:

Several more students <u>will have complained</u> by the end of the week.

Forms of *do*

Do, does, and *did* have three uses as helping verbs, always with the plain form of the main verb:

- **To pose a question:** *How <u>did</u> the trial <u>end</u>?*
- **To emphasize the main verb:** *It <u>did end</u> eventually.*
- **To negate the main verb, along with *not* or *never*:** *The judge <u>did not withdraw</u>.*

Be sure to use the main verb's plain form with any form of *do*:

Faulty   The judge did <u>remained</u> in court.

Revised   The judge did <u>remain</u> in court.

Modals

The modal helping verbs include *can, may, should, would,* and several two- and three-word combinations, such as *have to* and *be able to.* Use the plain form of the main verb with a modal unless the modal combines with another helping verb (usually *have*).

°See "Glossary of Terms," **Gl** p. 558

Faulty	The equipment can detects small vibrations. It should have detect the change.
Revised	The equipment can detect small vibrations. It should have detected the change.

Modals convey various meanings, with these being most common:

■ **Ability:** *can, could, be able to*

The equipment can detect small vibrations. [Present.]

The equipment could detect small vibrations. [Past.]

The equipment is able to detect small vibrations. [Present. Past: *was able to.* Future: *will be able to.*]

■ **Possibility:** *could, may, might; could/may/might have* + past participle

The equipment could fail. [Present.]
The equipment may fail. [Present or future.]
The equipment might fail. [Present or future.]
The equipment may have failed. [Past.]

■ **Necessity or obligation:** *must, have to, be supposed to*

The lab must purchase a backup. [Present or future.]
The lab has to purchase a backup. [Present or future. Past: *had to.*]
The lab will have to purchase a backup. [Future.]
The lab is supposed to purchase a backup. [Present. Past: *was supposed to.*]

■ **Permission:** *may, can, could*

The lab may spend the money. [Present or future.]
The lab can spend the money. [Present or future.]
The lab could spend the money. [Present or future, more tentative.]
The lab could have spent the money. [Past.]

■ **Intention:** *will, shall, would*

The lab will spend the money. [Future.]

Shall we offer advice? [Future. Use *shall* for questions requesting opinion or consent.]

We would have offered advice. [Past.]

■ **Request:** *could, can, would*

Could [or Can or Would] you please obtain a bid? [Present or future.]

■ **Advisability:** *should, had better, ought to; should have* + past participle

You should obtain three bids. [Present or future.]
You had better obtain three bids. [Present or future.]
You ought to obtain three bids. [Present or future.]
You should have obtained three bids. [Past.]

■ **Past habit:** *would, used to*

In years past we <u>would obtain</u> five bids.
We <u>used to obtain</u> five bids.

Exercise 25.4 Using helping verbs ⟨CULTURE LANGUAGE⟩

Add helping verbs to the following paragraph where they are needed for standard American English. If a sentence is correct as given, mark the number preceding it.

1 For as long as I can remember, I been writing stories. 2 While I living with my grandparents one summer, I wrote mystery stories. 3 Nearly every afternoon I sat at the computer and wrote about two brothers who solved mysteries while their mother be working. 4 By the end of the summer, I written four stories. 5 When I returned to school in the fall, I was very happy when one of my stories published in the school newspaper.

Exercise 25.5 Revising: Helping verbs plus main verbs ⟨CULTURE LANGUAGE⟩

Revise the paragraph below to use helping verbs and main verbs correctly. If a sentence is correct as given, mark the number preceding it.

1 A report from the Bureau of the Census has confirm a widening gap between rich and poor. 2 As suspected, the percentage of people below the poverty level did increased over the last decade. 3 The richest 1% of the population is make 24% of all the income. 4 These people will keeping an average of $1.3 million after taxes. 5 The other 99% all together will average about $300,000.

25e Use a gerund or an infinitive after a verb as appropriate. ⟨CULTURE LANGUAGE⟩

A **gerund** is the *-ing* form of a verb used as a noun: *Smoking is unhealthful.* An **infinitive** is the plain form° of a verb preceded by *to*: *Try not to smoke.* Gerunds and infinitives may follow certain verbs but not others. Sometimes the use of a gerund or an infinitive with the same verb changes the meaning.

1 Either gerund or infinitive

A gerund or an infinitive may come after the following verbs with no significant difference in meaning.

begin	continue	intend	prefer
can't bear	hate	like	start
can't stand	hesitate	love	

The pump began <u>working</u>.
The pump began <u>to work</u>.

2 Meaning change with gerund or infinitive

With four verbs, a gerund has quite a different meaning from an infinitive.

°See "Glossary of Terms," **GI** p. 558.

forget	stop
remember	try

The man stopped eating. [He no longer ate.]
The man stopped to eat. [He stopped in order to eat.]

3 Gerund, not infinitive

Do not use an infinitive after these verbs:

admit	discuss	mind	recollect
adore	dislike	miss	resent
appreciate	enjoy	postpone	resist
avoid	escape	practice	risk
consider	finish	put off	suggest
deny	imagine	quit	tolerate
detest	keep	recall	understand

Faulty   He finished to eat lunch.
Revised He finished eating lunch.

4 Infinitive, not gerund

Do not use a gerund after these verbs:

agree	claim	manage	promise
appear	consent	mean	refuse
arrange	decide	offer	say
ask	expect	plan	wait
assent	have	prepare	want
beg	hope	pretend	wish

Faulty   He decided checking the meter.
Revised He decided to check the meter.

5 Noun or pronoun + infinitive

Some verbs may be followed by an infinitive alone or by a noun or pronoun and an infinitive. The presence of a noun° or pronoun° changes the meaning.

ask	dare	need	wish
beg	expect	promise	would like
choose	help	want	

He expected to wait.
He expected his friends to wait.

Some verbs *must* be followed by a noun or pronoun before an infinitive:

advise	command	force	oblige
allow	convince	hire	order
cause	encourage	instruct	permit
challenge	forbid	invite	persuade

°See "Glossary of Terms," **GI** p. 558.

remind	require	tell	urge
request	teach	train	warn

He told <u>his friends</u> <u>to wait.</u>

Do not use *to* before the infinitive when it follows one of these verbs and a noun or pronoun:

feel	hear	make ("force")	watch
have	let	see	

He watched his friends <u>leave</u> without him.

Exercise 25.6 Revising: Verbs plus gerunds or infinitives *CULTURE LANGUAGE*

Revise the following paragraph so that gerunds or infinitives are used correctly with verbs. Mark the number preceding any sentence that is correct as given.

1 A program called *Boostup.org* aims to improve students' school attendance. 2 People and organizations supporting this program hope that more students will to graduate. 3 Parents can choose tracking their child's attendance. 4 The program persuades parents signing up via its Web site, *Facebook* page, and *Twitter* feed. 5 Because of *Boostup.org*, many students who might have dropped out now plan going to college.

25f Use the appropriate particles with two-word verbs. *CULTURE LANGUAGE*

Standard American English includes some verbs that consist of two words: the verb itself and a **particle**, a preposition° or adverb° that affects the meaning of the verb.

<u>Look up</u> the answer. [Research the answer.]
<u>Look over</u> the answer. [Examine the answer.]

The meanings of these two-word verbs are often quite different from the meanings of the individual words that make them up. A dictionary of English as a second language will define two-word verbs and say whether the verbs may be separated in a sentence, as explained below. (See **3** pp. 164–65 for a list of ESL dictionaries.)

Note Many two-word verbs are more common in speech than in academic or business writing. For formal writing, consider using *research* instead of *look up*, *examine* instead of *look over*.

1 Inseparable two-word verbs

Verbs and particles that may not be separated by any other words include the ones below and on the next page:

catch on	get along	go over	keep on
come across	give in	grow up	look into

°See "Glossary of Terms," **GI** p. 558.

| play around | run out of | stay away | take care of |
| run into | speak up | stay up | turn up at |

Faulty   Children <u>grow</u> quickly <u>up</u>.
Revised Children <u>grow up</u> quickly.

2 Separable two-word verbs

Most two-word verbs that take direct objects° may be separated by the object.

Parents <u>help out</u> their children.
Parents <u>help</u> their children <u>out</u>.

If the direct object is a pronoun,° the pronoun *must* separate the verb from the particle.

Faulty   Parents <u>help out</u> them.
Revised Parents <u>help</u> them <u>out</u>.

The separable two-word verbs include the following:

call off	give away	look over	take out
call up	give back	look up	take over
drop off	hand in	make up	try out
fill out	hand out	point out	turn on
fill up	help out	put off	wrap up

Exercise 25.7 Revising: Verbs plus particles (CULTURE LANGUAGE)

The two- and three-word verbs in the paragraph below are underlined. Some are correct as given, and some are not because they should or should not be separated by other words. Revise the verbs and other words that are incorrect. Consult the lists on these pages or an ESL dictionary if necessary to determine which verbs are separable.

1 American movies treat everything from <u>going out with</u> someone to <u>making up</u> an ethnic identity. 2 Some filmmakers like to address current topics, such as <u>getting</u> in today's world <u>along</u>. 3 Others, however, <u>stay</u> from serious topics <u>away</u> and choose lighter themes. 4 Whatever the topic, viewers fill theaters <u>up</u> when a movie is controversial. 5 It seems that filmmakers will <u>keep</u> creating controversy <u>on</u>. 6 They are always eager to make money and <u>point</u> their influence <u>out</u> to the public.

26 Verb Tenses

Chapter essentials

- Observe the special uses of the present tense (*sing*) (p. 218).
- Observe the uses of the perfect tenses (*have/had/will have sung*) (p. 218).

°See "Glossary of Terms," **GI** p. 558.

- Observe the uses of the progressive tenses (*is/was/will be singing*) (p. 219).
- Keep tenses consistent (p. 219).
- Use the appropriate sequence of verb tenses (p. 220).

Visit MyWritingLab™ for more resources on verb tenses.

Tense shows the time of a verb's action. The box below illustrates the tense forms for a regular verb. (Irregular verbs have different forms. See pp. 204–06.)

Tenses of a regular verb (active voice)

Present Action that is occurring now, occurs habitually, or is generally true

Simple present Plain form or -*s* form

I walk.
You/we/they walk.
He/she/it walks.

Present progressive *Am, is,* or *are* plus -*ing* form

I am walking.
You/we/they are walking.
He/she/it is walking.

Past Action that occurred before now

Simple past Past-tense form (-*d* or -*ed*)

I/he/she/it walked.
You/we/they walked.

Past progressive *Was* or *were* plus -*ing* form

I/he/she/it was walking.
You/we/they were walking.

Future Action that will occur in the future

Simple future *Will* plus plain form

I/you/he/she/it/we/they will walk.

Future progressive *Will be* plus -*ing* form

I/you/he/she/it/we/they will be walking.

Present perfect Action that began in the past and is linked to the present

Present perfect *Have* or *has* plus past participle (-*d* or -*ed*)

I/you/we/they have walked.
He/she/it has walked.

Present perfect progressive *Have been* or *has been* plus -*ing* form

I/you/we/they have been walking.
He/she/it has been walking.

Past perfect Action that was completed before another past action

Past perfect *Had* plus past participle (-*d* or -*ed*)

I/you/he/she/it/we/they had walked.

Past perfect progressive *Had been* plus -*ing* form

I/you/he/she/it/we/they had been walking.

Future perfect Action that will be completed before another future action

Future perfect *Will have* plus past participle (-*d* or -*ed*)

I/you/he/she/it/we/they will have walked.

Future perfect progressive *Will have been* plus -*ing* form

I/you/he/she/it/we/they will have been walking.

CULTURE LANGUAGE In standard American English, a verb conveys time through its form. In some other languages and English dialects, various markers besides verb form may indicate the time of a verb. For instance, in African American Vernacular English, *I be attending class on Tuesday* means that the speaker attends class every Tuesday. But to someone who doesn't know the dialect, the sentence could mean last Tuesday, this Tuesday, or every Tuesday. In standard English, the intended meaning is indicated by verb tense:

> I attended class on Tuesday. [Past tense indicates *last* Tuesday.]
>
> I will attend class on Tuesday. [Future tense indicates *next* Tuesday.]
>
> I attend class on Tuesday. [Present tense indicates habitual action, *every* Tuesday.]

26a Observe the special uses of the present tense (*sing*).

The present tense has several distinctive uses.

Action occurring now
She understands the problem.
We define the problem differently.

Habitual or recurring action
Banks regularly undergo audits.
The audits monitor the banks' activities.

A general truth
The mills of the gods grind slowly.
The earth is round.

Discussion of literature, film, and so on
Huckleberry Finn has adventures we all envy.
In that article the author examines several causes of crime.

Future time
Next week we draft a new budget.
Funding ends in less than a year.

(The present tense shows future time with expressions like those in the examples above: *next week, in less than a year.*)

26b Observe the uses of the perfect tenses (*have/had/will have sung*).

The **perfect tenses** consist of a form of *have* plus the verb's past participle° (*closed, hidden*). They indicate an action completed before another specific time or action. The present perfect tense also indicates action begun in the past and continued into the present.

> present perfect
> The dancer has performed here only once. [The action is completed at the time of the statement.]

°See "Glossary of Terms," **GI** p. 558.

present perfect
Critics <u>have written</u> about the performance ever since. [The action began in the past and continues now.]

past perfect
The dancer <u>had trained</u> in Asia before his performance. [The action was completed before another past action.]

future perfect
He <u>will have danced</u> here again by the end of the year. [The action begins now or in the future and will be completed by a specific time in the future.]

 With the present perfect tense, the words *since* and *for* are followed by different information. After *since*, give a specific point in time: *The play has run <u>since 1989</u>.* After *for*, give a span of time: *It has run <u>for decades</u>.*

26c Observe the uses of the progressive tenses (*is/was/will be singing*).

The **progressive tenses** indicate continuing (therefore progressive) action. In standard American English the progressive tenses consist of a form of *be* plus the verb's *-ing* form. (The words *be* and *been* must be combined with other helping verbs. See pp. 210–11.)

present progressive
The team <u>is improving</u>.

past progressive
Last year the team <u>was losing</u>.

future progressive
The owners <u>will be watching</u> for signs of improvement.

present perfect progressive
Sports writers <u>have been expecting</u> an upturn.

past perfect progressive
New players <u>had been performing</u> well.

future perfect progressive
If the season goes badly, fans <u>will have been watching</u> their team lose for ten straight years.

Note Verbs that express unchanging conditions (especially mental states) rather than physical actions do not usually appear in the progressive tenses. These verbs include *adore, appear, believe, belong, care, hate, have, hear, know, like, love, mean, need, own, prefer, remember, see, sound, taste, think, understand,* and *want.*

Faulty   She <u>is wanting</u> to study ethics.
Revised   She <u>wants</u> to study ethics.

26d Keep tenses consistent.

Within a sentence, the tenses of verbs and verb forms need not be identical as long as they reflect actual changes in time: *Ramon*

will graduate from college thirty years after his father arrived in America.
But needless shifts in tense will confuse or distract readers:

Inconsistent tense	Immediately after Booth shot Lincoln, Major Rathbone threw himself upon the assassin. But Booth pulls a knife and plunges it into the major's arm.
Revised	Immediately after Booth shot Lincoln, Major Rathbone threw himself upon the assassin. But Booth pulled a knife and plunged it into the major's arm.
Inconsistent tense	The main character in the novel suffers psychologically because he has a clubfoot, but he eventually triumphed over his disability.
Revised	The main character in the novel suffers psychologically because he has a clubfoot, but he eventually triumphs over his disability. [Use the present tense to discuss the content of literature, film, and so on.]

Exercise 26.1 Revising: Consistent past tense

In the paragraph below, change the tenses of the verbs as needed to maintain consistent simple past tense. If a sentence is correct as given, mark the number preceding it.

1 The 1960 presidential race between Richard Nixon and John F. Kennedy was the first to feature a televised debate. 2 Despite his extensive political experience, Nixon perspires heavily and looks haggard and uneasy in front of the camera. 3 By contrast, Kennedy was projecting cool poise and providing crisp answers that made him seem fit for the office of President. 4 The public responded positively to Kennedy's image. 5 His poll ratings shoot up immediately, while Nixon's take a corresponding drop. 6 The popular vote was close, but Kennedy won the election.

Exercise 26.2 Revising: Consistent present tense

In the paragraph below, change the tenses of the verbs as needed to maintain consistent simple present tense. If a sentence is correct as given, mark the number preceding it.

1 E. B. White's famous children's novel *Charlotte's Web* is a wonderful story of friendship and loyalty. 2 Charlotte, the wise and motherly spider, decided to save her friend Wilbur, the young and childlike pig, from being butchered by his owner. 3 She made a plan to weave words into her web that described Wilbur. 4 She first weaves "Some Pig" and later presented "Terrific," "Radiant," and "Humble." 5 Her plan succeeded beautifully. 6 She fools the humans into believing that Wilbur was a pig unlike any other, and Wilbur lived.

26e Use the appropriate sequence of verb tenses.

The **sequence of tenses** is the relation between the verb tense in a main clause° and the verb tense in a subordinate clause.° The

°See "Glossary of Terms," **Gl** p. 558.

tenses should change when necessary to reflect changes in actual or relative time.

1 Past or past perfect tense in main clause

When the verb in the main clause is in the past or past perfect tense, the verb in the subordinate clause must also be past or past perfect:

| main clause: | subordinate clause: |
| past | past |

The researchers <u>discovered</u> that people <u>varied</u> widely in their knowledge of public events.

| main clause: | subordinate clause: |
| past | past perfect |

The variation <u>occurred</u> because respondents <u>had been born</u> in different decades.

| main clause: | subordinate clause: |
| past perfect | past |

None of them <u>had been born</u> when Dwight Eisenhower <u>was</u> President.

Exception Always use the present tense for a general truth, such as *The earth is round*:

| main clause: | subordinate clause: |
| past | present |

Most <u>understood</u> that popular Presidents <u>are</u> not necessarily good Presidents.

2 Conditional sentences

A **conditional sentence** states a factual relation between cause and effect, makes a prediction, or speculates about what might happen. Such a sentence usually contains a subordinate clause beginning with *if, when,* or *unless* and a main clause stating the result. The three kinds of conditional sentences use distinctive verbs.

Factual relation

Statements linking factual causes and effects use matched tenses in the subordinate and main clauses:

| subordinate clause: | main clause: |
| present | present |

When a voter <u>casts</u> a ballot, he or she <u>has</u> complete privacy.

| subordinate clause: | main clause: |
| past | past |

When voters <u>registered</u> in some states, they <u>had</u> to pay a poll tax.

Prediction

Predictions generally use the present tense in the subordinate clause and the future tense in the main clause:

| subordinate clause: | main clause: |
| present | future |

Unless citizens <u>regain</u> faith in politics, they <u>will</u> not <u>vote</u>.

Sometimes the verb in the main clause consists of *may, can, should,* or *might* plus the verb's plain form°: *If citizens <u>regain</u> faith, they <u>may vote</u>.*

°See "Glossary of Terms," **Gl** p. 558.

Speculation

The verbs in speculations depend on whether the linked events are possible or impossible. For possible events in the present, use the past tense in the subordinate clause and *would, could,* or *might* plus the verb's plain form in the main clause:

subordinate clause:	main clause:
past	*would* + verb

If voters <u>had</u> more confidence, they <u>would vote</u> more often.

Use *were* instead of *was* in the subordinate clause, even when the subject is *I, he, she, it,* or a singular noun. (See the next page for more on this distinctive verb form.)

subordinate clause:	main clause:
past	*would* + verb

If the voter <u>were</u> more confident, he or she <u>would vote</u> more often.

For impossible events in the present—events that are contrary to fact—use the same forms as above (including the distinctive *were* when applicable):

subordinate clause:	main clause:
past	*might* + verb

If Lincoln <u>were</u> alive, he <u>might inspire</u> confidence.

For impossible events in the past, use the past perfect tense in the subordinate clause and *would, could,* or *might* plus the present perfect tense in the main clause:

subordinate clause:	main clause:
past perfect	*might* + present perfect

If Lincoln <u>had lived</u> past the Civil War, he <u>might have helped</u> stabilize the country.

Exercise 26.3 Using correct tense sequence

In the following paragraph, change the tense of each bracketed verb so that it is in correct sequence with other verbs.

1 Diaries that Adolf Hitler [<u>be</u>] supposed to have written surfaced in Germany. 2 Many people believed that the diaries [<u>be</u>] authentic because a well-known historian [<u>have</u>] declared them so. 3 However, the historian's evaluation was questioned by other authorities, who [<u>call</u>] the diaries forgeries. 4 They claimed, among other things, that the paper [<u>be</u>] not old enough to have been used by Hitler. 5 Eventually, the doubters won the debate because they [<u>have</u>] the best evidence.

Exercise 26.4 Revising: Tense sequence with conditional sentences

In the following paragraph, use the forms of *be* that create correct tense sequence for all verbs.

1 If you think you [<u>be</u>] exposed to the flu, you should get a flu shot. 2 You may avoid the illness altogether, and if you contract it your illness [<u>be</u>] milder. 3 Avoid the vaccine only if you [<u>be</u>] allergic to eggs. 4 If every person [<u>be</u>] willing and able to get the shot, there [<u>be</u>] very little serious flu each year. 5 But nearly universal vaccination [<u>be</u>] possible only if public outreach [<u>be</u>] improved and vaccine supplies [<u>be</u>] adequate.

Chapter essentials
- Use the subjunctive verb forms appropriately, as in *I wish I were* (below).
- Keep mood consistent (next page).

Visit MyWritingLab™ for more resources on verb mood.

Mood in grammar is a verb form that indicates the writer's attitude:

- The *indicative mood* states a fact or opinion or asks a question: *The theater needs support.*
- The *imperative mood* expresses a command or gives direction: *Support the theater.*
- The *subjunctive mood* expresses wishes, suggestions, requirements, and other attitudes, using *he were* and other distinctive verb forms described below.

27a Use the subjunctive verb forms appropriately, as in *I wish I were*.

The subjunctive mood expresses a wish or desire, a suggestion, a requirement, or a request, or it states a condition that is contrary to fact (that is, imaginary or hypothetical).

- Verbs such as *ask, insist, urge, require, recommend,* and *suggest* indicate request or requirement. They often precede a subordinate clause° beginning with *that* and containing the substance of the request or requirement. For all subjects,° the verb in the *that* clause is the plain form°:

  plain form
  Rules require that every donation be mailed.

- Contrary-to-fact clauses state imaginary or hypothetical conditions. They usually begin with *if* or *unless,* or they follow *wish.* For present contrary-to-fact clauses, use the verb's past-tense form° (for *be,* use the past-tense form *were* for all subjects):

       past   past
  If the theater were in better shape and had more money, its future would be assured.

      past
  I wish I were able to donate money.

  For past contrary-to-fact clauses, use *had* plus the verb's past participle°:

             past perfect
  The theater would be better funded if it had been better managed.

°See "Glossary of Terms," **GI** p. 558.

Note Do not use the helping verb° *would* or *could* in a contrary-to-fact clause beginning with *if*:

Not Many people would have helped if they would have known.

But Many people would have helped if they had known.

See also p. 222 on verb tenses in sentences like these.

27b | Keep mood consistent.

Shifts in mood within a sentence or among related sentences can be confusing. Such shifts occur most frequently in directions.

Inconsistent mood	Cook the mixture slowly, and you should stir it until the sugar is dissolved. [Mood shifts from imperative to indicative.]
Revised	Cook the mixture slowly, and stir it until the sugar is dissolved. [Consistently imperative.]

Exercise 27.1 Revising: Subjunctive mood

Revise the following paragraph with appropriate subjunctive verb forms. If a sentence is correct as given, mark the number preceding it.

1 If John Hawkins would have known of all the dangerous side effects of smoking tobacco, would he have introduced the plant to England in 1565? 2 In promoting tobacco, Hawkins noted that if a Florida Indian man was to travel for several days, he would have smoked tobacco to satisfy his hunger and thirst. 3 Early tobacco growers in the United States feared that their product would not gain acceptance unless it was perceived as healthful, so they spread Hawkins's story. 4 But local governments, more concerned about public safety and morality than health, passed laws requiring that colonists smoked tobacco only if they were five miles from any town. 5 To prevent decadence, in 1647 Connecticut passed a law mandating that one's smoking of tobacco was limited to once a day in one's own home.

28 Verb Voice

Chapter essentials

- Prefer the active voice (opposite).
- Use the passive voice when the actor is unknown or unimportant (p. 226).
- Keep voice consistent (p. 226).

Visit MyWritingLab™ for more resources on verb voice.

The voice of a verb tells whether the subject of the sentence performs the action (active) or is acted upon (passive).

°See "Glossary of Terms," **GI** p. 558.

Active voice

She wrote the book. [The subject performs the action.]
subject verb

Passive voice

The book was written by her. [The subject receives the action.]
subject   verb

CULTURE LANGUAGE A passive verb always consists of a form of *be* plus the past participle° of the main verb: *Rents are controlled. People were inspired.* Other helping verbs° must also be used with the words *be, being,* and *been*: *Rents will be controlled. Rents are being controlled. Rents have been controlled. People would have been inspired.* Only a transitive verb° (one that takes an object) may be used in the passive voice. (See p. 193.)

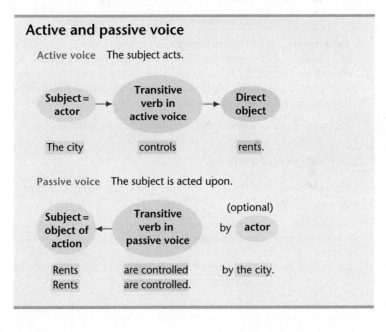

Active and passive voice

Active voice The subject acts.

| Subject = actor | → | Transitive verb in active voice | → | Direct object |

| The city | controls | rents. |

Passive voice The subject is acted upon.

| Subject = object of action | ← | Transitive verb in passive voice | by | (optional) actor |

| Rents | are controlled | by the city. |
| Rents | are controlled. | |

28a Generally, prefer the active voice.

The active voice is usually clearer, more concise, and more forthright than the passive voice.

Weak passive The library is used by both students and teachers, and the plan to expand it has been praised by many.

Strong active Both students and teachers use the library, and many have praised the plan to expand it.

°See "Glossary of Terms," **Gl** p. 558.

28b Use the passive voice when the actor is unknown or unimportant or when naming the actor might be offensive.

The passive voice can be useful when naming the actor is not possible or desirable.

- **The actor is unknown, unimportant, or less important than the object of the action.** In the following sentences, the writer wishes to stress the Internet rather than the actors.

  The Internet <u>was established</u> in 1969 by the US Department of Defense. The network <u>has been extended</u> internationally to governments, universities, corporations, and private individuals.

  In the next example the person who performed the experiment, perhaps the writer, is less important than the procedure. Passive sentences are common in scientific writing.

  After the solution <u>had been cooled</u> to 10°C, the acid <u>was added</u>.

- **The actor should be neutral background to the action.** Particularly in sensitive correspondence, this use of the passive can avoid offending readers. In the next example, not naming the person who turned away the shelter residents focuses on the action without accusing anyone specifically.

  The residents of the shelter <u>were turned away</u> from your coffee shop.

28c Keep voice consistent.

Shifts in voice that involve shifts in subject are usually unnecessary and confusing.

Inconsistent subject and voice	Blogs <u>cover</u> an enormous range of topics. Opportunities for people to discuss their interests <u>are provided</u> on these sites.
Revised	Blogs <u>cover</u> an enormous range of topics <u>and provide</u> opportunities for people to discuss their interests.

A shift in voice is appropriate when it helps focus the reader's attention on a single subject, as in *The <u>candidate</u> <u>campaigned</u> vigorously and <u>was nominated</u> on the first ballot.*

Exercise 28.1 Converting between active and passive voices

Convert the verbs in the following sentences from active to passive or from passive to active. (In converting from passive to active, you may need to add a subject.) Which version of the sentence seems more effective and why?

Example:
The actor was discovered in a nightclub.
A talent <u>scout</u> <u>discovered</u> the actor in a nightclub.

1 When the Eiffel Tower was built in 1889, it was thought by the French to be ugly.
2 At the time, many people still resisted industrial technology.
3 The tower's naked steel construction typified this technology.
4 Beautiful ornament was expected to grace fine buildings.
5 Further, a structure without solid walls could not even be called a building.

Exercise 28.2   Revising: Using the active voice

In the following paragraph, rewrite passive sentences into the active voice, adding new sentence subjects as needed.

1 Water quality is determined by many factors. 2 Suspended and dissolved substances are contained in all natural waters. 3 The amounts of the substances are controlled by the environment. 4 Some dissolved substances are produced by pesticides. 5 Other substances, such as sediment, are deposited in water by fields, livestock feedlots, and other sources. 6 The bottom life of streams and lakes is affected by sediment. 7 Light penetration is reduced by sediment, and bottom-dwelling organisms may be smothered. 8 The quality of water in city systems is measured frequently. 9 Some contaminants can be removed by treatment plants. 10 If the legal levels are exceeded by pollutants, the citizens must be notified by city officials.

29 Agreement of Subject and Verb

Chapter essentials

- Make the subject and verb agree even when other words come between them (p. 229).
- Make the verb agree with a subject joined by *and, or,* or *nor* (p. 229).
- Make the verb agree when the subject is *everyone* or another indefinite pronoun (p. 230).
- Make the verb agree when the subject is *team* or another collective noun (p. 230).
- Make the verb agree with the antecedent of *who, which,* or *that* (p. 231).
- Use a singular verb for *news* and other singular nouns ending in *-s* (p. 231).
- Make the verb and subject agree even when the verb comes first (p. 232).
- Make *is, are,* and other linking verbs agree with their subjects (p. 232).
- Use a singular verb with titles and words being defined (p. 232).

Visit MyWritingLab™ for more resources on agreement of subject and verb.

A subject and its verb should agree in number and person:

Daniel Inouye was the first Japanese American in Congress.
 subject   verb

More Japanese Americans live in Hawaii and California than elsewhere.
<u>subject</u>   <u>verb</u>

Person	Number *Singular*	*Plural*
First	I eat.	We eat.
Second	You eat.	You eat.
Third	He/she/it eats.	They eat.
	The bird eats.	Birds eat.

Most problems of subject-verb agreement arise when endings are omitted from subjects or verbs or when the relation between sentence parts is uncertain.

29a	The *-s* and *-es* endings work differently for nouns and verbs.

An *-s* or *-es* ending does opposite things to nouns and verbs: it usually makes a noun *plural,* but it always makes a present-tense° verb *singular.* Thus a singular-noun subject will not end in *-s,* but its verb will. A plural-noun subject will end in *-s,* but its verb will not. Between them, subject and verb use only one *-s* ending.

Singular subject	Plural subject
The boy plays.	The boys play.
The bird soars.	The birds soar.

The only exception involves the nouns that form irregular plurals, such as *child/children, woman/women.* The irregular plural still requires a plural verb: *The children play. The women sing.*

<u>CULTURE LANGUAGE</u> If your first language or dialect is not standard American English, subject-verb agreement may be difficult, especially for the following reasons:

■ **Some English dialects omit the *-s* ending for singular verbs or use the *-s* ending for plural verbs.**

Nonstandard	The voter resist change.
Standard	The voter resists change.
Standard	The voters resist change.

The verb *be* changes spelling for singular and plural in both present and past tense.° (See also p. 185.)

Nonstandard	Taxes is high. They was raised just last year.
Standard	Taxes are high. They were raised just last year.

Have also has a distinctive *-s* form, *has:*

Nonstandard	The new tax have little chance of passing.
Standard	The new tax has little chance of passing.

°See "Glossary of Terms," GI p. 558.

■ **Some other languages change all parts of verb phrases° to match their subjects.** In English verb phrases, however, only the helping verbs° *be*, *have*, and *do* change for different subjects. The modal° helping verbs—*can*, *may*, *should*, *will*, and others—do not change:

Nonstandard   The tax <u>mays</u> pass next year.
Standard   The tax <u>may</u> pass next year.

The main verb° in a verb phrase also does not change for different subjects:

Nonstandard   The tax may <u>passes</u> next year.
Standard   The tax may <u>pass</u> next year.

29b Subject and verb should agree even when other words come between them.

The survival of hibernating frogs in freezing temperatures <u>is</u> [not <u>are</u>] fascinating.

A chemical reaction inside the cells of the frogs <u>stops</u> [not <u>stop</u>] the formation of ice crystals.

Note Phrases beginning with *as well as, together with, along with,* and *in addition to* do not change a singular subject to plural:

The president, together with the deans, <u>has</u> [not <u>have</u>] agreed.

29c Subjects joined by *and* usually take plural verbs.

Frost and Roethke <u>were</u> contemporaries.

Exceptions When the parts of the subject form a single idea or refer to a single person or thing, they take a singular verb:

Avocado and bean sprouts <u>is</u> a California sandwich.

When a compound subject is preceded by the adjective *each* or *every,* the verb is usually singular:

Each man, woman, and child <u>has</u> a right to be heard.

29d When parts of a subject are joined by *or* or *nor,* the verb agrees with the nearer part.

Either the painter or the carpenter <u>knows</u> the cost.

°See "Glossary of Terms," **Gl** p. 558.

The cabinets or the bookcases are too costly.

When one part of the subject is singular and the other plural, avoid awkwardness by placing the plural part closer to the verb so that the verb is plural:

Awkward   Neither the owners nor the contractor agrees.

Revised   Neither the contractor nor the owners agree.

29e With *everyone* and other indefinite pronouns, use a singular or plural verb as appropriate.

Indefinite pronouns° include *anyone, anybody, each, everyone, everybody, nobody, no one, nothing,* and *someone.* Most indefinite pronouns are singular in meaning (they refer to a single unspecified person or thing), and they take a singular verb:

Something smells.   Neither is right.

Four indefinite pronouns are always plural in meaning: *both, few, many, several.*

Both are correct.   Several were invited.

Six indefinite pronouns may be either singular or plural in meaning: *all, any, more, most, none, some.* The verb with one of these pronouns depends on what the pronoun refers to:

All of the money is reserved for emergencies. [*All* refers to *money.*]

All of the funds are reserved for emergencies. [*All* refers to *funds.*]

None may be singular even when referring to a plural word, especially to emphasize the meaning "not one": *None* [*Not one*] *of the animals has a home.*

CULTURE
LANGUAGE   See p. 257 for the distinction between *few* ("not many") and *a few* ("some").

29f Collective nouns such as *team* take singular or plural verbs depending on meaning.

A collective noun° has singular form and names a group of persons or things: *army, audience, committee, crowd, family, group, team.* Use a singular verb with a collective noun when the group acts as a unit.

The team has won five of the last six meets.

But when the group's members act separately, not together, use a plural verb.

°See "Glossary of Terms," **GI** p. 558.

The old team have gone to various colleges.

If a combination such as *team have* seems awkward, reword the sentence: *The members of the old team have gone to various colleges.*

The collective noun *number* may be singular or plural. Preceded by *a*, it is plural; preceded by *the*, it is singular:

A number of people are in debt.

The number of people in debt is very large.

 Some noncount nouns° (nouns that don't form plurals) are collective nouns because they name groups: for instance, *furniture, clothing, mail, machinery, equipment, military, police*. These noncount nouns usually take singular verbs: *Mail arrives daily.* But some of these nouns take plural verbs, including *clergy, military, people, police*, and any collective noun that comes from an adjective, such as *the poor, the rich, the young, the elderly.* If you mean one representative of the group, use a singular noun such as *police officer* or *poor person.*

29g *Who, which,* and *that* take verbs that agree with their antecedents.

When used as subjects, *who, which,* and *that* refer to another word in the sentence, called the **antecedent**. The verb agrees with the antecedent:

Mayor Garber ought to listen to the people who work for her.

Bardini is the only aide who has her ear.

Agreement problems often occur with *who* and *that* when the sentence includes *one of the* or *the only one of the*:

Bardini is one of the aides who work unpaid. [Of the aides who work unpaid, Bardini is one.]

Bardini is the only one of the aides who knows the community. [Of the aides, only one, Bardini, knows the community.]

In phrases beginning with *one of the*, be sure the noun is plural: *Bardini is one of the aides* [not *aide*] *who work unpaid.*

29h *News* and other singular nouns ending in *-s* take singular verbs.

Singular nouns ending in *-s* include *athletics, economics, mathematics, measles, mumps, news, physics, politics,* and *statistics*, as well as place names such as *Athens, Wales,* and *United States.*

°See "Glossary of Terms," **GI** p. 558.

After so long a wait, the news has to be good.

Statistics is required of psychology majors.

Politics requires compromise.

A few of these words also take plural verbs, but only when they describe individual items rather than whole bodies of activity or knowledge: *The statistics prove him wrong. The mayor's politics make compromise difficult.*

Measurements and figures ending in *-s* may also be singular when the quantity they refer to is a unit:

Three years is a long time to wait.

Three-fourths of the library consists of reference books.

29i — The verb agrees with the subject even when it precedes the subject.

The verb precedes the subject mainly in questions and in constructions beginning with *there* or *here* and a form of *be*:

Is voting a right or a privilege?

Are a right and a privilege the same thing?

There are differences between them.

29j — *Is, are,* and other linking verbs agree with their subjects, not subject complements.

Make a linking verb° agree with its subject, usually the first element in the sentence, not with the noun or pronoun serving as a subject complement.°

The child's sole support is her court-appointed guardians.

Her court-appointed guardians are the child's sole support.

29k — Use singular verbs with titles and with words being defined.

Hakada Associates is a new firm.

Dream Days remains a favorite book.

Folks is a down-home word for *people*.

Exercise 29.1 Revising: Subject-verb agreement

Revise the verbs in the following paragraphs as needed to make subjects and verbs agree in number. If a sentence is correct as given, mark the number preceding it.

1 Results from recent research shows that humor in the workplace relieves job-related stress. 2 Reduced stress in the workplace in turn reduce illness and absenteeism. 3 It can also ease friction within an employee group, which then work together more productively.

4 Weinstein Associates is a consulting firm that hold workshops designed to make businesspeople laugh. 5 In sessions held by one consultant, each of the participants practice making others laugh. 6 "Isn't there enough laughs within you to spread the wealth?" the consultant asks the students. 7 She quotes Casey Stengel's rule that the best way to keep your management job is to separate the underlings who hate you from the ones who have not decided how they feel. 8 Such self-deprecating comments in public is uncommon among business managers, the consultant says. 9 Each of the managers in a typical firm takes the work much too seriously. 10 The humorous boss often feels like the only one of the managers who have other things in mind besides profits.

11 Another consultant from Weinstein Associates suggest cultivating office humor with practical jokes and cartoons. 12 When a manager or employees drops a rubber fish in the water cooler or posts cartoons on the bulletin board, office spirit usually picks up. 13 If the job of updating the cartoons is entrusted to an employee who has seemed easily distracted, the employee's concentration often improves. 14 Even the former sourpuss becomes one of those who hides a bad temper. 15 Every one of the consultants caution, however, that humor has no place in life-affecting corporate situations such as employee layoffs.

Exercise 29.2   Adjusting for subject-verb agreement

Rewrite the following paragraphs to change the underlined words from plural to singular. (You will sometimes need to add *a* or *the* for the singular, as in the example below.) Then change verbs as necessary so that they agree with their new subjects.

Example:

Siberian tigers are an endangered subspecies.
The Siberian tiger is an endangered subspecies.

1 Siberian tigers are the largest living cats in the world, much bigger than their relative the Bengal tiger. 2 They grow to a length of nine to twelve feet, including their tails, and to a height of about three and a half feet. 3 They can weigh over six hundred pounds. 4 These carnivorous hunters live in northern China and Korea as well as in Siberia. 5 During the long winter of this Arctic climate, the yellowish striped coats get a little lighter in order to blend with the snow-covered landscape. 6 The coats also grow quite thick because the tigers have to withstand temperatures as low as –50°F.

7 Siberian tigers sometimes have to travel great distances to find food. 8 They need about twenty pounds of food a day because of their size and the cold climate, but when they have fresh food they may eat as much as a hundred pounds at one time. 9 They hunt mainly deer, boars, and even bears, plus smaller prey such as fish and rabbits. 10 They pounce on their prey and grab them by the back of the neck. 11 Animals that are not killed immediately are thrown to the ground and suffocated with a bite to the throat. 12 Then the tigers feast.

Pronouns

Pronouns—words such as *she* and *who* that refer to nouns—merit special care because all their meaning comes from the other words they refer to. This section discusses pronoun case (Chapter 30), matching pronouns with the words they refer to (31), and making sure pronouns refer to the right nouns (32).

30 Pronoun Case

Chapter essentials

- Distinguish between compound subjects and compound objects: *she and I* vs. *her and me* (opposite).
- Use the subjective case for subject complements: *It was she* (opposite).
- Use *who* or *whom* depending on the pronoun's function in its clause (p. 236).
- Use the appropriate case in other constructions, such as after *than* or *as* or with an infinitive (p. 238).

Visit MyWritingLab™ for more resources on pronoun case.

Case is the form of a noun° or pronoun° that shows the reader how it functions in a sentence.

- **The subjective case** indicates that the word is a subject° or subject complement.°
- **The objective case** indicates that the word is an object° of a verb or preposition.
- **The possessive case** indicates that the word owns or is the source of a noun in the sentence.

Nouns change form only to show possession: *teacher's* (see **5** pp. 304–06). Most of the pronouns listed below change more often.

Subjective	Objective	Possessive
I	me	my, mine
you	you	your, yours
he	him	his
she	her	her, hers
it	it	its
we	us	our, ours
you	you	your, yours
they	them	their, theirs
who	whom	whose
whoever	whomever	—

°See "Glossary of Terms," GI p. 558.

(CULTURE LANGUAGE) In standard American English, *-self* pronouns do not change form to show function. Their only forms are *myself, yourself, himself, herself, itself, ourselves, yourselves, themselves.* Avoid nonstandard forms such as *hisself, ourself,* and *theirselves.*

Faulty	He bought <u>hisself</u> a new laptop.
Revised	He bought <u>himself</u> a new laptop.

30a Distinguish between compound subjects and compound objects: *she and I* vs. *her and me.*

Compound subjects° or compound objects°—those consisting of two or more nouns or pronouns—have the same case forms as they would if one noun or pronoun stood alone:

compound subject
<u>She and Novick</u> discussed the proposal.

compound object
The proposal disappointed <u>her and him</u>.

If you are in doubt about the correct form, try this test:

A test for case forms in compound subjects or objects

1. **Identify a compound construction** (one connected by *and, but, or, nor*).

   [He, Him] and [I, me] won the prize.
   The prize went to [he, him] and [I, me].

2. **Write a separate sentence for each part of the compound:**

   [He, Him] won the prize. [I, Me] won the prize.
   The prize went to [he, him]. The prize went to [I, me].

3. **Choose the pronouns that sound correct.**

   He won the prize. I won the prize. [Subjective.]
   The prize went to him. The prize went to me. [Objective.]

4. **Put the separate sentences back together.**

   He and I won the prize.
   The prize went to him and me.

Note Avoid using the pronoun *myself* in place of the personal pronoun *I* or *me*: *Stephen and I* [not *myself*] *trained. Everyone went except me* [not *myself*]. For more on the *-self* pronouns, see **GI** p. 553.

30b Use the subjective case for subject complements: *It was she.*

After a linking verb,° a pronoun renaming the subject (a subject complement°) should be in the subjective case.

°See "Glossary of Terms," **GI** p. 558.

subject complement
The delegates are <u>she and Novick</u>.

subject
complement
It was <u>they</u> whom the mayor appointed.

If this construction sounds stilted to you, use the more natural order: *She and Novick* are the delegates. *The mayor appointed them.*

Exercise 30.1 Choosing between subjective and objective pronouns

In the following paragraph, select the appropriate subjective or objective pronoun from the pairs in brackets.

1 Kayla and [I, me] were competing for places on the relay team. 2 The fastest runners at our school were [she, her] and [I, me], so [we, us] expected to make the team. 3 [She, Her] and [I, me] were friends but also intense rivals. 4 The time trials went badly, excluding both [she, her] and [I, me] from the team. 5 Next season [she, her] and [I, me] are determined to earn places on the team.

30c | The use of *who* vs. *whom* depends on the pronoun's function.

Use *who* where you would use *he* or *she*—all ending in vowels. Use *whom* where you would use *him* or *her*—all ending in consonants.

1 Questions

At the beginning of a question, use *who* for a subject and *whom* for an object:

subject→
<u>Who</u> wrote the policy?   object←
<u>Whom</u> does it affect?

To find the correct case of *who* in a question, use the following test:

1. **Pose the question:**

[Who, Whom] makes that decision?
[Who, Whom] does one ask?

2. **Answer the question, using a personal pronoun.°** Choose the pronoun that sounds correct, and note its case:

[She, Her] makes that decision. <u>She</u> makes that decision. [Subjective.]
One asks [she, her]. One asks <u>her</u>. [Objective.]

3. **Use the same case (*who* or *whom*) in the question:**

<u>Who</u> makes that decision? [Subjective.]
<u>Whom</u> does one ask? [Objective.]

2 Subordinate clauses

In a subordinate clause,° use *who* or *whoever* for a subject, *whom* or *whomever* for an object.

°See "Glossary of Terms," **Gl** p. 558.

subject ⟍
Give old clothes to whoever needs them.

object ⟵
I don't know whom the mayor appointed.

To determine which form to use, try the following test:

1. **Locate the subordinate clause:**

   Few people know [who, whom] they should ask.
   They are unsure [who, whom] makes the decision.

2. **Rewrite the subordinate clause as a separate sentence, substituting a personal pronoun for *who, whom*.** Choose the pronoun that sounds correct, and note its case:

   They should ask [she, her]. They should ask her. [Objective.]
   [She, her] makes the decision. She makes the decision. [Subjective.]

3. **Use the same case (*who* or *whom*) in the subordinate clause:**

   Few people know whom they should ask. [Objective.]
   They are unsure who makes the decision. [Subjective.]

Note Don't let expressions such as *I think* and *she says* mislead you into using *whom* rather than *who* for the subject of a clause.

subject ⟍
He is the one who I think is best qualified.

To choose between *who* and *whom* in such constructions, delete the interrupting phrase so that you can see the true relation between parts: *He is the one who is best qualified.*

Exercise 30.2 Choosing between *who* and *whom*
In the following paragraph, select the appropriate pronoun from the pairs in brackets.

   1 The school administrators suspended Jurgen, [who, whom] they suspected of setting the fire. 2 Jurgen had been complaining to other custodians, [who, whom] reported him. 3 He constantly complained of unfair treatment from [whoever, whomever] happened to be passing in the halls, including pupils. 4 "[Who, Whom] here has heard Mr. Jurgen's complaints?" the police asked. 5 "[Who, Whom] did he complain most about?"

Exercise 30.3 Sentence combining: *Who* versus *whom*
Combine each pair of sentences below into one sentence that contains a clause beginning with *who* or *whom*. Be sure to use the appropriate case form. You will have to add, delete, and rearrange words. Each item may have more than one possible answer.

   Example:
   James is the candidate. We think James deserves to win.
   James is the candidate who we think deserves to win.

1 Some children have undetected hearing problems. These children may do poorly in school.
2 They may not hear important instructions and information from teachers. Teachers may speak softly.
3 Classmates may not be audible. The teacher calls on those classmates.
4 Some hearing-impaired children may work harder to overcome their disability. These children get a lot of encouragement at home.
5 Some hearing-impaired children may take refuge in fantasy friends. They can rely on these friends not to criticize or laugh.

30d Use the appropriate case in other constructions.

1 *We* or *us* with a noun

The choice of *we* or *us* before a noun depends on the use of the noun:

object of
preposition
Freezing weather is welcomed by us skaters.

subject
We skaters welcome freezing weather.

2 Pronoun in an appositive

In an appositive° the case of a pronoun depends on the function of the word the appositive describes or identifies:

appositive
identifies object
The class elected two representatives, DeShawn and me.

appositive
identifies subject
Two representatives, DeShawn and I, were elected.

3 Pronoun after *than* or *as*

When a pronoun follows *than* or *as* in a comparison, the case of the pronoun indicates what words may have been omitted. A subjective pronoun must be the subject of the omitted verb:

subject
Some critics like Glass more than he [does].

An objective pronoun must be the object of the omitted verb:

object
Some critics like Glass more than [they like] him.

4 Subject and object of infinitive

An infinitive is the plain form° of the verb plus *to* (*to swim*). Both the object *and* the subject of an infinitive are in the objective case.

°See "Glossary of Terms," **GI** p. 558.

subject
of infinitive
The school asked <u>him</u> to speak.

object
of infinitive
Students chose to invite <u>him</u>.

5 **Case before a gerund**

A gerund is the *-ing* form of the verb used as a noun (*a runner's breathing*). Generally, use the possessive form of a pronoun or noun immediately before a gerund:

The coach disapproved of <u>their</u> lifting weights.

The <u>coach's</u> disapproving was a surprise.

Exercise 30.4 Choosing between subjective and objective pronouns

In the following paragraph, select the appropriate pronoun from the pairs in brackets.

1 Obtaining enough protein is important to [we, us] vegetarians. 2 Instead of obtaining protein from meat, [we, us] vegetarians get our protein from other sources such as eggs, cheese, nuts, and beans. 3 Some of [we, us] vegetarians also eat fish, an excellent source of protein, but vegans avoid all animal products, including eggs and cheese. 4 My friend Jeff claims to know only two vegans, Helena and [he, him]. 5 He believes that [we, us] vegetarians who eat fish and dairy products are not as truly vegetarian as [he, him].

Exercise 30.5 Revising: Pronoun case

Revise all inappropriate case forms in the following paragraph. If a sentence is correct as given, mark the number preceding it.

1 Written four thousand years ago, *The Epic of Gilgamesh* tells the story of Gilgamesh and his friendship with Enkidu. 2 Gilgamesh was a bored king who his people thought was too harsh. 3 Then he met Enkidu, a wild man whom had lived with the animals in the mountains. 4 Immediately, him and Gilgamesh wrestled to see whom was more powerful. 5 After hours of struggle, Enkidu admitted that Gilgamesh was stronger than him. 6 Now the friends needed adventures worthy of them, the two strongest men on earth. 7 Gilgamesh said, "Between you and I, mighty deeds will be accomplished, and our fame will be everlasting." 8 Among their acts, Enkidu and him defeated a giant bull, Humbaba, cut down the bull's cedar forests, and brought back the logs to Gilgamesh's treeless land. 9 Their heroism won them great praise from the people. 10 When Enkidu died, Gilgamesh mourned his death, realizing that no one had been a better friend than him. 11 When Gilgamesh himself died many years later, his people raised a monument praising Enkidu and he for their friendship and their mighty deeds of courage.

31 Agreement of Pronoun and Antecedent

Chapter essentials

- Make a pronoun agree with an antecedent joined by *and, or,* or *nor* (below and opposite).
- Make a pronoun agree when the antecedent is *everyone* or another indefinite pronoun (opposite).
- Make a pronoun agree when the antecedent is *team* or another collective noun (p. 242).

Visit MyWritingLab™ for more resources on agreement of pronoun and antecedent.

The **antecedent** of a pronoun° is the noun° or other pronoun to which the pronoun refers:

Students fret over their tuition bills.
antecedent   pronoun

Its yearly increases make the tuition bill a dreaded document.
pronoun   antecedent

For clarity, a pronoun should agree with its antecedent in person and number as well as in gender (masculine, feminine, neuter).

	Number	
Person	*Singular*	*Plural*
First	I	we
Second	you	you
Third	he, she, it,	they,
	indefinite pronouns,	plural nouns
	singular nouns	

CULTURE LANGUAGE The gender of a pronoun should match its antecedent, not a noun that the pronoun may modify: *Sara Young invited her* [not *his*] *son.* Also, English nouns have only neuter gender unless they specifically refer to males or females. Thus nouns such as *book, table, sun,* and *earth* take the pronoun *it: I am reading a new book. It is inspiring.*

31a Antecedents joined by *and* usually take plural pronouns.

Mr. Bartos and I cannot settle our dispute.

The dean and my adviser have offered their help.

Exceptions When the compound antecedent refers to a single idea, person, or thing, then the pronoun is singular.

°See "Glossary of Terms," **GI** p. 558.

My friend and adviser offered her help.

When the compound antecedent follows *each* or *every,* the pronoun is singular:

Every girl and woman took her seat.

31b **When parts of an antecedent are joined by *or* or *nor,* the pronoun agrees with the nearer part.**

Tenants or owners must present their grievances.

Either the tenant or the owner will have her way.

When one subject is plural and the other singular, the sentence will be awkward unless you put the plural subject second.

Awkward Neither the tenants nor the owner has yet made her case.

Revised Neither the owner nor the tenants have yet made their case.

31c **With *everyone, person,* and other indefinite words, use a singular or plural pronoun as appropriate.**

Indefinite words do not refer to a specific person or thing. Indefinite pronouns° include *anyone, each, everybody, nobody, no one, nothing, somebody,* and *someone.* Generic nouns° include *person, individual,* and *student.* Most indefinite pronouns and all generic nouns are singular in meaning. When they serve as antecedents, they take singular pronouns:

Each of the animal shelters in the region has its population of homeless pets.
indefinite
pronoun

Every worker in our shelter cares for his or her favorite animal.
generic
noun

Four indefinite pronouns are plural in meaning: *both, few, many, several.* As antecedents, they take plural pronouns:

Many of the animals show affection for their caretakers.

Six indefinite pronouns may be singular or plural in meaning: *all, any, more, most, none, some.* As antecedents, they take singular pronouns if they refer to singular words, plural pronouns if they refer to plural words:

Most of the shelter's equipment was donated by its original owner.
[*Most* refers to *equipment.*]

°See "Glossary of Terms," **Gl** p. 558.

Most of the veterinarians donate their time. [*Most* refers to *veterinarians*.]

None may be singular even when referring to a plural word, especially to emphasize the meaning "not one": *None* [*Not one*] *of the shelters has increased its capacity*.

Most agreement problems arise with the singular indefinite words. We often use these words to mean "many" or "all" rather than "one" and then refer to them with plural pronouns, as in *Everyone has their own locker*. Often, too, we mean indefinite words to include both masculine and feminine genders and thus resort to *they* instead of the **generic *he***—the masculine pronoun referring to both genders, as in *Everyone deserves his privacy*. (For more on the generic *he*, which many readers view as sexist, see **3** p. 161.) To achieve agreement in such cases, you have the options listed in the following box.

Ways to correct agreement with indefinite words

■ **Change the indefinite word to a plural, and use a plural pronoun to match:**

Faulty   Every athlete deserves their privacy.

Revised   **Athletes** deserve their privacy.

■ **Rewrite the sentence to omit the pronoun:**

Faulty   Everyone is entitled to their own locker.

Revised   Everyone is entitled to **a** locker.

■ **Use *he or she* (*him or her, his or her*) to refer to the indefinite word:**

Faulty   Now everyone has their private space.

Revised   Now everyone has **his or her** private space.

However, used more than once in several sentences, *he or she* quickly becomes awkward. (Some readers do not accept the alternative *he/ she*.) Using the plural or omitting the pronoun will usually correct agreement problems and create more readable sentences.

31d Collective nouns such as *team* take singular or plural pronouns depending on meaning.

A collective noun° has singular form and names a group of persons or things: *army, audience, family, group, team*. Use a singular pronoun with a collective noun when referring to the group as a unit:

The committee voted to disband itself.

When referring to the individual members of the group, use a plural pronoun:

The old team have gone their separate ways.

°See "Glossary of Terms," **Gl** p. 558.

If a combination such as *team have . . . their* seems awkward, reword the sentence: *The members of the old team have gone their separate ways.*

 In standard American English, collective nouns that are noncount nouns (they don't form plurals) usually take singular pronouns: *The mail sits in its own basket.* A few noncount nouns take plural pronouns, including *clergy, military, police, the rich,* and *the poor*: *The police support their unions.*

Exercise 31.1   Revising: Pronoun-antecedent agreement

Revise the following sentences so that pronouns and their antecedents agree in person and number. Try to avoid the generic *he* (see the previous page). If you change the subject of a sentence, be sure to change the verb as necessary for agreement. Mark the number preceding any sentence that is correct as given.

Example:

Each of the Boudreaus' children brought their laundry home at Thanksgiving.

All of the Boudreaus' children brought their laundry home at Thanksgiving. *Or:* Each of the Boudreaus' children brought his or her laundry home at Thanksgiving.

1 Each girl raised in a Mexican American family in the Rio Grande Valley of Texas hopes that one day they will be given a *quinceañera* party for their fifteenth birthday. 2 Such celebrations are very expensive because it entails a religious service followed by a huge party. 3 A girl's immediate family, unless they are wealthy, cannot afford the party by themselves. 4 The parents will ask each close friend or relative if they can help with the preparations. 5 Surrounded by her family and attended by her friends and their escorts, the *quinceañera* is introduced as a young woman eligible for Mexican American society.

Exercise 31.2   Revising: Pronoun-antecedent agreement

Revise the following sentences so that pronouns and their antecedents agree in person and number. Try to avoid the generic *he* (see the previous page). If you change the subject of a sentence, be sure to change the verb as necessary for agreement. Mark the number preceding any sentence that is correct as given.

1 Despite their extensive research and experience, neither child psychologists nor parents have yet figured out how children become who they are. 2 Of course, the family has a tremendous influence on the development of a child in their midst. 3 Each member of the immediate family exerts their own unique pull on the child. 4 Other relatives, teachers, and friends can also affect the child's view of the world and of themselves. 5 The workings of genetics also strongly influence the child, but it may never be fully understood. 6 The psychology community cannot agree in its views of whether nurture or nature is more important in a child's development. 7 Another debated issue is whether the child's emotional development or their intellectual development is more central. 8 Just about everyone has their strong opinion on these issues, often

backed up by evidence. 9 Neither the popular press nor scholarly journals devote much of their space to the wholeness of the child.

32 Reference of Pronoun to Antecedent

Chapter essentials

- Make a pronoun refer clearly to one antecedent (below).
- Place a pronoun close enough to its antecedent to ensure clarity (opposite).
- Make a pronoun refer to a specific antecedent (opposite).
- Use *you* only to mean "you, the reader" (p. 246).
- Keep pronouns consistent (p. 246).

Visit MyWritingLab™ for more resources on reference of pronoun to antecedent.

A pronoun° should refer clearly to its **antecedent**, the noun° it substitutes for. Otherwise, readers will have difficulty grasping the pronoun's meaning.

CULTURE LANGUAGE In standard American English, a pronoun needs a clear antecedent nearby, but don't use both a pronoun and its antecedent as the subject° of the same sentence: *James* [not *James he*] *told Victor to go alone.* (See also pp. 275–76.)

32a Make a pronoun refer clearly to one antecedent.

When either of two nouns can be a pronoun's antecedent, the reference will not be clear.

Confusing Emily Dickinson is sometimes compared with Jane Austen, but she led a more reclusive life.

Revise such a sentence in one of two ways:

- **Replace the pronoun with the appropriate noun.**

  Clear Emily Dickinson is sometimes compared with Jane Austen, but Dickinson led a more reclusive life.

- **Avoid repetition by rewriting the sentence.** If you use the pronoun, make sure it has only one possible antecedent.

  Clear Despite occasional comparison of their lives, Emily Dickinson was more reclusive than Jane Austen.

  Clear Though sometimes compared with her, Emily Dickinson was more reclusive than Jane Austen.

°See "Glossary of Terms," **GI** p. 558.

32b Place a pronoun close enough to its antecedent to ensure clarity.

A clause° beginning with *who, which,* or *that* should generally fall immediately after the word to which it refers.

Confusing   Jody found a lamp in the attic that her aunt had used.

Clear   In the attic Jody found a lamp that her aunt had used.

32c Make a pronoun refer to a specific antecedent, not an implied one.

A pronoun should refer to a specific noun or other pronoun. A reader can only guess at the meaning of a pronoun when its antecedent is implied by the context, not stated outright.

1 Vague *this, that, which,* or *it*

This, that, which, or *it* should refer to a specific noun, not to a whole word group expressing an idea or situation.

Confusing   The British knew little of the American countryside, and

they had no experience with the colonists' guerrilla tactics.

This gave the colonists an advantage.

Clear   The British knew little of the American countryside, and they had no experience with the colonists' guerrilla tactics. This ignorance and inexperience gave the colonists an advantage.

2 Indefinite antecedents with *it* and *they*

It and *they* should have definite noun antecedents. Rewrite the sentence if the antecedent is missing.

Confusing   In Chapter 4 of this book it describes the early flights of the Wright brothers.

Clear   Chapter 4 of this book describes the early flights of the Wright brothers.

Confusing   Even in reality TV shows, they present a false picture of life.

Clear   Even reality TV shows present a false picture of life.

Clear   Even in reality TV shows, the producers present a false picture of life.

3 Implied nouns

A noun may be implied in some other word or phrase, as *happiness* is implied in *happy*, *driver* is implied in *drive*, and *mother* is

°See "Glossary of Terms," **Gl** p. 558.

implied in *mother's*. But a pronoun cannot refer clearly to an implied noun, only to a specific, stated one.

Confusing | In Cohen's report she made claims that led to a lawsuit.

Clear | In her report Cohen made claims that led to a lawsuit.

Confusing | Her reports on psychological development generally go unnoticed outside it.

Clear | Her reports on psychological development generally go unnoticed outside the field.

Exercise 32.1 Revising: Pronoun reference

Rewrite the following paragraph to eliminate unclear pronoun reference. If you use a pronoun in your revision, be sure that it refers to only one antecedent and that it falls close enough to its antecedent to ensure clarity.

1 There is a difference between the heroes of today and the heroes of earlier times: they have flaws in their characters. 2 Despite their imperfections, baseball fans still admire Babe Ruth, Pete Rose, and Mark McGwire. 3 Fans liked Rose for having his young son serve as batboy when he was in Cincinnati. 4 The reputation Rose earned as a gambler and tax evader may overshadow his reputation as a ballplayer, but it will survive. 5 He amassed an unequaled record as a hitter, using his bat to do things no one has ever done, and it remains even though Rose was banned from baseball.

Exercise 32.2 Revising: Pronoun reference

Revise the following paragraph as needed so that pronouns refer to specific, appropriate antecedents.

1 In Charlotte Brontë's *Jane Eyre*, she is a shy young woman who takes a job as a governess. 2 Her employer, a rude, brooding man named Rochester, lives in a mysterious mansion on the English moors, which contributes a strange quality to Jane's experience. 3 Stranger still are the fires, eerie noises, and other unexplained happenings in the house; but Rochester refuses to discuss this. 4 Eventually, they fall in love, but the day they are to marry, she learns that he has a wife hidden in the house. 5 She is hopelessly insane and violent and must be guarded at all times, which explains his strange behavior. 6 Heartbroken, Jane leaves the moors, and many years pass before they are reunited.

32d Use *you* only to mean "you, the reader."

You should clearly mean "you, the reader." The context must be appropriate for such a meaning:

Inappropriate | In the fourteenth century you had to struggle simply to survive.

Revised | In the fourteenth century one [or a person] had to struggle simply to survive.

Writers sometimes drift into *you* because *one, a person,* or a similar word can be difficult to sustain. Sentence after sentence, the indefinite word may sound stuffy, and it requires *he* or *he or she* for pronoun-antecedent agreement (see pp. 241–42). To avoid these problems, try using plural nouns and pronouns:

| Original | In the fourteenth century <u>one</u> had to struggle simply to survive. |
| Revised | In the fourteenth century <u>people</u> had to struggle simply to survive. |

32e Keep pronouns consistent.

Within a sentence or a group of related sentences, pronouns should be consistent. Partly, consistency comes from making pronouns and their antecedents agree (see Chapter 31). In addition, the pronouns within a passage should match each other.

| Inconsistent pronouns | One finds when reading that <u>your</u> concentration improves with practice, so that <u>I</u> now comprehend more in less time. |
| Revised | <u>I</u> find when reading that <u>my</u> concentration improves with practice, so that <u>I</u> now comprehend more in less time. |

Exercise 32.3 Revising: Consistency in pronouns
Revise the following paragraph to make pronouns consistent.

1 When a taxpayer is waiting to receive a tax refund from the Internal Revenue Service, you begin to notice what time the mail carrier arrives. 2 If the taxpayer does not receive a refund check within six weeks of filing a return, they may not have followed the rules of the IRS. 3 For instance, if a taxpayer does not include a Social Security number on a return, you will have to wait for a refund. 4 If one makes errors on the tax form, they will certainly have to wait and they might be audited, delaying a refund for months or longer. 5 A refund may be held up even if you file on time, because returns received close to the April 15 deadline swamp the IRS.

Exercise 32.4 Revising: Pronoun reference
Revise the following paragraph as needed so that pronouns are consistent and refer to specific, appropriate antecedents.

1 "Life begins at forty" is a cliché many people live by, and this may or may not be true. 2 Whether one agrees or not with the cliché, you can cite many examples of people whose public lives began at forty. 3 For instance, when she was forty, Pearl Buck's novel *The Good Earth* won the Pulitzer Prize. 4 Kenneth Kanuda, past president of Zambia, was elected to it in 1964, when he was forty. 5 Catherine I became Empress of Russia at age forty, more feared than loved by them. 6 Paul Revere at forty made his famous ride to warn American revolutionary leaders that the British were going to arrest them, which gave the colonists time to prepare for battle. 7 Forty-year-old Nancy Astor joined the British House

of Commons in 1919 as its first female member, though they did not welcome her. **8** In 610 CE, Muhammad, age forty, began to have visions that became the foundation of the Muslim faith and still inspire millions of people to become one.

—————————— **Modifiers** ——————————

Modifiers describe or limit other words in a sentence. They are adjectives, adverbs, or word groups serving as adjectives or adverbs. This section shows how to solve problems in the forms of modifiers (Chapter 33) and in their relation to the rest of the sentence (34).

33 Adjectives and Adverbs

Chapter essentials

- Use adjectives only to modify nouns and pronouns (below).
- Use an adjective after a linking verb to modify the subject; use an adverb to modify a verb (opposite).
- Use comparative and superlative forms appropriately (p. 250).
- Avoid most double negatives (p. 252).
- Distinguish between present and past participles as adjectives (p. 253).
- Use *a, an, the,* and other determiners appropriately (p. 253).

Visit MyWritingLab™ for more resources on adjectives and adverbs.

—————————————

Adjectives modify nouns° (*happy child*) and pronouns° (*special someone*). **Adverbs** modify verbs° (*almost see*), adjectives (*very happy*), other adverbs (*not very*), and whole word groups (*Otherwise, I'll go*). The only way to tell whether a modifier should be an adjective or an adverb is to determine its function in the sentence.

(CULTURE LANGUAGE) In standard American English, an adjective does not change along with the noun it modifies to show plural number: *square* [not *squares*] *spaces*. Only nouns form plurals.

33a Use adjectives only to modify nouns and pronouns.

Do not use adjectives instead of adverbs to modify verbs, adverbs, or other adjectives:

Faulty   Educating children good should be everyone's focus.

Revised   Educating children well should be everyone's focus.

°See "Glossary of Terms," **Gl** p. 558.

Faulty   Some children suffer bad.

Revised   Some children suffer badly.

CULTURE LANGUAGE Choosing between *not* and *no* can be a challenge. *Not* is an adverb, so it makes a verb or an adjective negative:

They do not learn. They are not happy. They have not been in class.

(See p. 261 for where to place *not* in relation to verbs and adjectives.) *No* is an adjective, so it makes a noun negative:

No child likes to fail. No good school fails children.

Place *no* before the noun or any other modifier.

33b   Use an adjective after a linking verb to modify the subject. Use an adverb to modify a verb.

A linking verb° connects the subject and a word that describes the subject—for instance, *seem, become, look,* and forms of *be.* Some verbs may or may not be linking verbs, depending on their meaning in the sentence. When the word after the verb modifies the subject, the verb is linking and the word should be an adjective: *He looked happy.* When the word modifies the verb, however, it should be an adverb: *He looked carefully.*

Two word pairs are especially tricky. One is *bad* and *badly:*

The weather grew bad.
    linking   adjective
    verb

She felt bad.
linking   adjective
verb

Flowers grow badly in such soil.
verb   adverb

The other pair is *good* and *well. Good* serves only as an adjective. *Well* may serve as an adverb with a host of meanings or as an adjective meaning only "fit" or "healthy."

Decker trained well.
verb   adverb

She felt well.
linking   adjective
verb

Her health was good.
linking   adjective
verb

Exercise 33.1   Revising: Adjectives and adverbs

Revise the following paragraph to use adjectives and adverbs appropriately. Mark the number preceding any sentence that is correct as given.

    1 People who take their health serious often believe that movie-theater popcorn is a healthy snack. 2 Nutrition information about movie popcorn may make these people feel different. 3 One large tub of movie popcorn has twelve hundred calories and sixty grams of saturated fat—both surprisingly high numbers. 4 Once people are aware of the calories and fat, they may feel badly about indulging in this classic snack. 5 Indeed, people who want to eat good should think twice before ordering popcorn at the movies.

°See "Glossary of Terms," **GI** p. 558.

33c Use the comparative and superlative forms of adjectives and adverbs appropriately.

Adjectives and adverbs can show degrees of quality or amount with the endings *-er* and *-est* or with the words *more* and *most* or *less* and *least*. Most modifiers have the three forms shown in the following chart:

Positive The basic form listed in the dictionary	Comparative A greater or lesser degree of the quality	Superlative The greatest or least degree of the quality
Adjectives		
red	redder	reddest
awful	more/less awful	most/least awful
Adverbs		
soon	sooner	soonest
quickly	more/less quickly	most/least quickly

If sound alone does not tell you whether to use *-er/-est* or *more/most*, consult a dictionary. If the endings can be used, the dictionary will list them. Otherwise, use *more* or *most*.

1 Irregular adjectives and adverbs

Irregular modifiers change the spelling of their positive form to show comparative and superlative degrees.

Positive	Comparative	Superlative
Adjectives		
good	better	best
bad	worse	worst
little	littler, less	littlest, least
many		
some }	more	most
much		
Adverbs		
well	better	best
badly	worse	worst

2 Double comparisons

A double comparative or double superlative combines the *-er* or *-est* ending with the word *more* or *most*. It is redundant.

Chang was the wisest [not most wisest] person in town.
He was smarter [not more smarter] than anyone else.

3 Logical comparisons

Absolute modifiers

Some adjectives and adverbs cannot logically be compared—for instance, *perfect, unique, dead, impossible, infinite*. These absolute words can be preceded by adverbs like *nearly* or *almost* that mean "approaching," but they cannot logically be modified by *more* or *most* (as in *most perfect*).

Not | He was the <u>most unique</u> teacher we had.
But | He was a <u>unique</u> teacher.

Completeness

To be logical, a comparison must also be complete in the following ways:

■ **The comparison must state a relation fully enough for clarity.**

Unclear | Carmakers worry about their industry more than environmentalists.
Clear | Carmakers worry about their industry more than environmentalists <u>do</u>.
Clear | Carmakers worry about their industry more than <u>they worry about</u> environmentalists.

■ **The items being compared should in fact be comparable.**

Illogical | The cost of a hybrid car can be greater than a gasoline-powered car. [Illogically compares a cost and a car.]
Revised | The cost of a hybrid car can be greater than <u>the cost of</u> [or <u>that of</u>] a gasoline-powered car.

See also **3** p. 150 on parallelism with comparisons.

Any versus *any other*

Use *any other* when comparing something with others in the same group. Use *any* when comparing something with others in a different group.

Illogical | Los Angeles is larger than <u>any</u> city in California. [Since Los Angeles is itself a city in California, the sentence seems to say that Los Angeles is larger than itself.]
Revised | Los Angeles is larger than <u>any other</u> city in California.
Illogical | Los Angeles is larger than <u>any other</u> city in Canada. [The cities in Canada constitute a group to which Los Angeles does not belong.]
Revised | Los Angeles is larger than <u>any</u> city in Canada.

Exercise 33.2 Using comparatives and superlatives

Write the comparative and superlative forms of each adjective or adverb below. Then use all three forms in your own sentences.

Example:
heavy: heavier (comparative), heaviest (superlative)

The barbells were too <u>heavy</u> for me. The trunk was <u>heavier</u> than I expected. Joe Clark was the <u>heaviest</u> person on the team.

1 badly   3 good   5 understanding
2 steady   4 well

Exercise 33.3   Revising: Comparisons

Revise the following paragraph as needed to correct the forms of adjectives and adverbs and to make comparisons logical. Mark the number preceding any sentence that is correct as given.

1 The Brontë sisters—Charlotte, Emily, and Anne—are among the more interesting literary families in English history. 2 Of the three novelists, Charlotte was the older. 3 Critics sometimes dispute whether Charlotte or Emily was more talented. 4 For some readers, Emily's *Wuthering Heights* is among the most saddest stories ever written. 5 For other readers, Charlotte's *Jane Eyre* made more significant contributions to literature than Emily.

33d   Watch for double negatives.

In a **double negative** two negative words such as *no, not, none, neither, barely, hardly,* or *scarcely* cancel each other out. Some double negatives are intentional: for instance, *She was <u>not unhappy</u>* indicates with understatement that she was indeed happy. But most double negatives say the opposite of what is intended: *Nadia did <u>not</u> feel <u>nothing</u>* asserts that Nadia felt other than nothing, or something. For the opposite meaning, one of the negatives must be eliminated (*She felt <u>nothing</u>*) or one of them must be changed to a positive (*She did not feel <u>anything</u>*).

Faulty   The IRS <u>cannot hardly</u> audit all tax returns. <u>None</u> of its audits <u>never</u> touch many cheaters.

Revised   The IRS <u>cannot</u> audit all tax returns. Its audits <u>never</u> touch many cheaters.

Exercise 33.4   Revising: Double negatives

Identify and revise the double negatives in the following paragraph. Each error may have more than one correct revision. Mark the number preceding any sentence that is correct as given.

1 Interest in books about the founding of the United States is not hardly consistent among Americans: it seems to vary with the national mood. 2 Americans show barely any interest in books about the founders when things are going well in the United States. 3 However, when Americans can't hardly agree on major issues, sales of books about the Revolutionary War era increase. 4 During such periods, one cannot go to no bookstore without seeing several new volumes about John Adams, Thomas Jefferson, and other founders. 5 When Americans feel they don't have nothing in common, their increased interest in the early leaders may reflect a desire for unity.

33e Distinguish between present and past participles as adjectives.

Both present participles° and past participles° may serve as adjectives: *a burning building, a burned building.* As in the examples, the two participles usually differ in the time they indicate, present (*burning*) or past (*burned*).

But some present and past participles—those derived from verbs expressing feeling—can have altogether different meanings. The present participle modifies something that causes the feeling: *That was a frightening storm* (the storm frightens). The past participle modifies something that experiences the feeling: *They quieted the frightened horses* (the horses feel fright).

The following participles are among those likely to be confused:

amazing/amazed	fascinating/fascinated
amusing/amused	frightening/frightened
annoying/annoyed	frustrating/frustrated
astonishing/astonished	interesting/interested
boring/bored	pleasing/pleased
confusing/confused	satisfying/satisfied
depressing/depressed	shocking/shocked
embarrassing/embarrassed	surprising/surprised
exciting/excited	tiring/tired
exhausting/exhausted	worrying/worried

Exercise 33.5 Revising: Present and past participles

Revise the adjectives in the following paragraph as needed to distinguish between present and past participles. Mark the number preceding any sentence that is correct as given.

1 Many critics found Alice Walker's novel *The Color Purple* to be a fascinated book, though the reviews were mixed. 2 One otherwise excited critic wished that Walker had deleted the scenes set in Africa. 3 Another critic argued that although the book contained many depressed episodes, the overall effect was pleased. 4 Responding to other readers who had found the book annoyed, this critic pointed out its many surprising qualities. 5 In the end most critics agreed that the book was a pleased novel about the struggles of an African American woman. 6 For many, the movie made from the book was less interested. 7 Some viewers found the entire movie irritated, criticizing it for relying on tired feelings. 8 Other viewers thought that Whoopi Goldberg did an amazed job of creating Celie, the central character. 9 Some critics congratulated Steven Spielberg, the director, for creating a fulfilling movie.

33f Use *a, an, the,* and other determiners appropriately.

Determiners are special kinds of adjectives that mark nouns because they always precede nouns. Some common determiners are

°See "Glossary of Terms," **GI** p. 558.

a, an, and *the* (called **articles**) and *my, their, whose, this, these, those, one, some,* and *any.*

Native speakers of standard American English can rely on their intuition when using determiners, but speakers of other languages and dialects often have difficulty with them. In standard American English, the use of determiners depends on the context they appear in and the kind of noun they precede:

- A *proper noun* **names a particular person, place, or thing and begins with a capital letter:** *February, Joe Allen, Red River.* Most proper nouns are not preceded by determiners.
- A *count noun* **names something that is countable in English and can form a plural:** *girl/girls, apple/apples, child/children.* A singular count noun is always preceded by a determiner; a plural count noun sometimes is.
- A *noncount noun* **names something not usually considered countable in English, and so it does not form a plural.** A noncount noun is sometimes preceded by a determiner. Here is a sample of noncount nouns, sorted into groups by meaning:

Abstractions: confidence, democracy, education, equality, evidence, health, information, intelligence, knowledge, luxury, peace, pollution, research, success, supervision, truth, wealth, work

Food and drink: bread, candy, cereal, flour, meat, milk, salt, water, wine

Emotions: anger, courage, happiness, hate, joy, love, respect, satisfaction

Natural events and substances: air, blood, dirt, gasoline, gold, hair, heat, ice, oil, oxygen, rain, silver, smoke, weather, wood

Groups: clergy, clothing, equipment, furniture, garbage, jewelry, junk, legislation, machinery, mail, military, money, police, vocabulary

Fields of study: architecture, accounting, biology, business, chemistry, engineering, literature, psychology, science

A dictionary of English as a second language will tell you whether a noun is a count noun, a noncount noun, or both. (See **3** pp. 164–65 for recommended dictionaries.)

Note Many nouns are sometimes count nouns and sometimes noncount nouns:

The library has <u>a room</u> for readers. [*Room* is a count noun meaning "walled area."]

The library has <u>room</u> for reading. [*Room* is a noncount noun meaning "space."]

1   *A, an,* and *the*

With singular count nouns

A or *an* precedes a singular count noun when the reader does not already know its identity, usually because you have not mentioned it before:

A scientist in our chemistry department developed a process to strengthen metals. [*Scientist* and *process* are being mentioned for the first time.]

The precedes a singular count noun that has a specific identity for the reader, for one of the following reasons:

■ **You have mentioned the noun before:**

A scientist in our chemistry department developed a process to strengthen metals. The scientist patented the process. [*Scientist* and *process* were identified in the preceding sentence.]

■ **You identify the noun immediately before or after you state it:**

The most productive laboratory is the research center in the chemistry department. [*Most productive* identifies *laboratory.* In the chemistry department identifies *research center.* And chemistry department is a shared facility—see below.]

■ **The noun names something unique—the only one in existence:**

The sun rises in the east. [*Sun* and *east* are unique.]

■ **The noun names an institution or facility that is shared by the community of readers:**

Many men and women aspire to the presidency. [*Presidency* is a shared institution.]

The cell phone has changed business communication. [*Cell phone* is a shared facility.]

The is not used before a singular noun that names a general category:

Wordsworth's poetry shows his love of nature [not the nature].
General Sherman said that war is hell. [*War* names a general category.]
The war in Iraq left many wounded. [*War* names a specific war.]

With plural count nouns

A or *an* never precedes a plural noun. *The* does not precede a plural noun that names a general category. *The* does precede a plural noun that names specific representatives of a category.

Men and women are different. [*Men* and *women* name general categories.]
The women formed a team. [*Women* refers to specific people.]

With noncount nouns

A or *an* never precedes a noncount noun. *The* does precede a noncount noun that names specific representatives of a general category.

Vegetation suffers from drought. [*Vegetation* names a general category.]
The vegetation in the park withered or died. [*Vegetation* refers to specific plants.]

With proper nouns

A or *an* never precedes a proper noun. *The* generally does not precede proper nouns.

> Garcia lives in Boulder.

There are exceptions, however. For instance, we generally use *the* before plural proper nouns (*the Murphys, the Boston Celtics*) and before the names of groups and organizations (*the Department of Justice, the Sierra Club*), ships (*the* Lusitania), oceans and seas (*the Pacific, the Caribbean*), mountain ranges (*the Alps, the Rockies*), regions (*the Middle East*), rivers (*the Mississippi*), and some countries (*the United States, the Netherlands*).

Exercise 33.6 Revising: *A, an,* and *the* <small>⟨ CULTURE • LANGUAGE ⟩</small>

In the following paragraph, identify and revise errors in the use of *a, an,* and *the* with count, noncount, and proper nouns. Mark the number preceding any sentence that is correct as given.

> 1 A recent court case has moved some Native Americans to observe that a lot of people want to be the Native Americans because the tribes now have something of the value—namely, gambling casinos. 2 The man named Stephen Jones claimed to be the Native American in order to open casino in the New York's Catskills region. 3 However, the documents Jones provided to support the claim were questioned by a US Bureau of Indian Affairs. 4 On death certificate for Jones's grandfather, the W for *white* had been changed to an I for *Indian* with the ballpoint pen. 5 The ballpoint pens had not been invented until after a grandfather's death. 6 In addition, Jones provided the 1845 census of Indians in New York, and someone had recently added Jones's great-grandfather's name to the list of Indian household heads. 7 Jones, who called himself the Chief Golden Eagle, pled guilty to filing false documents with Bureau of Indian Affairs.

---

2 | Other determiners

The uses of English determiners besides articles also depend on context and kind of noun. The following determiners may be used as indicated with singular count nouns, plural count nouns, or noncount nouns.

With any kind of noun (singular count, plural count, noncount)

> *my, our, your, his, her, its, their,* possessive nouns (*boy's, boys'*)
> *whose, which(ever), what(ever)*
> *some, any, the other*
> *no*

> Their account is overdrawn. [Singular count.]
> Their funds are low. [Plural count.]
> Their money is running out. [Noncount.]

Only with singular nouns (count and noncount)

this, that

This account has some money. [Count.]
That information may help. [Noncount.]

Only with noncount nouns and plural count nouns

most, enough, other, such, all, all of the, a lot of

Most funds are committed. [Plural count.]
Most money is needed elsewhere. [Noncount.]

Only with singular count nouns

one, every, each, either, neither, another

One car must be sold. [Singular count.]

Only with plural count nouns

these, those
both, many, few, a few, fewer, fewest, several
two, three, and so forth

Two cars are unnecessary. [Plural count.]

Note *Few* means "not many" or "not enough." *A few* means "some" or "a small but sufficient quantity."

Few committee members came to the meeting.
A few members can keep the committee going.

Do not use *much* with a plural count noun.

Many [not Much] members want to help.

Only with noncount nouns

much, more, little, a little, less, least, a large amount of

Less luxury is in order. [Noncount.]

Note *Little* means "not many" or "not enough." *A little* means "some" or "a small but sufficient quantity."

Little time remains before the conference.
The members need a little help from their colleagues.

Do not use *many* with a noncount noun.

Much [not Many] work remains.

Exercise 33.7 Revising: Determiners ⟨CULTURE LANGUAGE⟩

In the following paragraph, identify and revise missing or incorrect determiners. Mark the number preceding any sentence that is correct as given.

1 Much people love to swim for exercise or just plain fun. 2 Few swimmers, however, are aware of the possible danger of sharing their

swimming spot with others. 3 These danger has increased in recent years because of dramatic rise in outbreaks of the parasite cryptosporidium. 4 Swallowing even little water containing cryptosporidium can make anyone sick. 5 Chlorine is used in nearly every public pools to kill parasites, but the chlorine takes six or seven days to kill cryptosporidium. 6 Most health authorities advise people to limit their swimming in public pools and to swallow as little of the pool water as possible.

Exercise 33.8 Revising: Adjectives and adverbs

Revise the following paragraph to correct errors in the use of adjectives and adverbs.

1 Americans often argue about which professional sport is better: basketball, football, or baseball. 2 Basketball fans contend that their sport offers more action because the players are constant running and shooting. 3 Because it is played indoors in relative small arenas, basketball allows fans to be more closer to the action than the other sports. 4 Football fanatics say they don't hardly stop yelling once the game begins. 5 They cheer when their team executes a complicated play good. 6 They roar more louder when the defense stops the opponents in a goal-line stand. 7 They yell loudest when a fullback crashes in for a score. 8 In contrast, the supporters of baseball believe that it is the better sport. 9 It combines the one-on-one duel of pitcher and batter struggling valiant with the tight teamwork of double and triple plays. 10 Because the game is played slow and careful, fans can analyze and discuss the manager's strategy.

34 Misplaced and Dangling Modifiers

Chapter essentials

- Reposition misplaced modifiers so that they clearly relate to the words you intend (below).
- Relate dangling modifiers to their sentences by rewriting (p. 262).

Visit MyWritingLab™ for more resources on misplaced and dangling modifiers.

The arrangement of words in a sentence is an important clue to their relationships. Modifiers° will be unclear if readers can't connect them to the words they describe.

34a Reposition misplaced modifiers.

A **misplaced modifier** falls in the wrong place in a sentence. It is usually awkward or confusing. It may even be unintentionally funny.

°See "Glossary of Terms," **Gl** p. 558.

1 | Clear placement

Readers tend to link a modifier to the nearest word it could modify. Any other placement can link the modifier to the wrong word.

| Confusing | He served steak to the men on paper plates. |
| Clear | He served the men steak on paper plates. |

| Confusing | According to the police, many dogs are killed by automobiles and trucks roaming unleashed. |
| Clear | According to the police, many dogs roaming unleashed are killed by automobiles and trucks. |

2 | *Only* and other limiting modifiers

Limiting modifiers include *almost, even, exactly, hardly, just, merely, nearly, only, scarcely,* and *simply.* For clarity place such a modifier immediately before the word or word group you intend it to limit.

Unclear	The archaeologist only found the skull on her last dig.
Clear	The archaeologist found only the skull on her last dig.
Clear	The archaeologist found the skull only on her last dig.

3 | Adverbs with grammatical units

Adverbs° can often move around in sentences, but some will be awkward if they interrupt certain grammatical units:

■ **A long adverb stops the flow from subject° to verb.°**

	subject adverb verb
Awkward	The city, after the hurricane, began massive rebuilding.
	adverb subject verb
Revised	After the hurricane, the city began massive rebuilding.

■ **Any adverb is awkward between a verb and its direct object.°**

	verb adverb object
Awkward	The hurricane had damaged badly many homes in the city.
	verb object
Revised	The hurricane had badly damaged many homes in the city.
	adverb

■ **A *split infinitive*—an adverb placed between *to* and the verb—annoys many readers.**

	infinitive
Awkward	The weather service expected temperatures to not rise.
	infinitive
Revised	The weather service expected temperatures not to rise.

°See "Glossary of Terms," **Gl** p. 558.

A split infinitive may sometimes be natural and preferable, though it may still bother some readers.

┌─infinitive─┐
Several US industries expect to more than triple their use of robots.

Here the split infinitive is more economical than the alternatives, such as *Several US industries expect to increase their use of robots by more than three times.*

■ **A long adverb is usually awkward inside a verb phrase.°**

helping
verb ┌──────── adverb ────────┐
Awkward People with osteoporosis can, by increasing their daily intake
└──────────┐ main verb
of calcium and vitamin D, improve their bone density.

┌──────────── adverb ────────────┐
Revised By increasing their daily intake of calcium and vitamin D,
verb phrase
people with osteoporosis can improve their bone density.

CULTURE LANGUAGE In a question, place a one-word adverb immediately after the subject:

helping   rest of
verb subject adverb verb phrase
Will spacecraft ever be able to leave the solar system?

4 **Other adverb positions** **CULTURE LANGUAGE**

Placements of a few adverbs can be difficult for nonnative speakers of English:

■ **Adverbs of frequency** include *always, never, often, rarely, seldom,* and *sometimes.* They generally appear at the beginning of a sentence, before a one-word verb, or after a helping verb.°

helping   main
verb   adverb   verb
Robots have sometimes put humans out of work.

adverb   verb phrase
Sometimes robots have put humans out of work.

Adverbs of frequency always follow the verb *be.*

verb adverb
Robots are often helpful to workers.

verb adverb
Robots are seldom useful around the house.

When *rarely, seldom,* or another negative adverb of frequency begins a sentence, the normal subject-verb order changes. (See also **3** p. 154.)

adverb verb subject
Rarely are robots simple machines.

■ **Adverbs of degree** include *absolutely, almost, certainly, completely, definitely, especially, extremely, hardly,* and *only.* They fall just before the word modified (an adjective, another adverb, sometimes a verb).

adverb   adjective
Robots have been <u>especially</u> useful in making cars.

■ **Adverbs of manner** include *badly, beautifully, openly, sweetly, tightly, well,* and others that describe how something is done. They usually fall after the verb.

verb   adverb
Robots work <u>smoothly</u> on assembly lines.

■ **The adverb** *not* changes position depending on what it modifies. When it modifies a verb, place it after the helping verb (or the first helping verb if more than one).

helping   main
verb   verb
Robots do <u>not</u> think.

When *not* modifies another adverb or an adjective, place it before the other modifier.

adjective
Robots are not <u>sleek</u> machines.

5 Order of adjectives ⟨CULTURE LANGUAGE⟩

English follows distinctive rules for arranging two or three adjectives° before a noun. (A string of more than three adjectives before a noun is rare.) The rules arrange adjectives by type and by meaning, as shown in the following chart:

Determiner	Opinion	Size or shape	Color	Origin	Material	Noun used as adjective	Noun
many						state	**laws**
	lovely		green	Thai			**birds**
a	fine			German			**camera**
this		square			wooden		**table**
all						business	**reports**
the			blue	litmus			**paper**

See **5** pp. 291–92 on punctuating adjectives before a noun.

Exercise 34.1   Revising: Misplaced modifiers
Revise the following paragraph so that modifiers clearly and appropriately describe the intended words.

1 People dominate in our society who are right-handed. 2 Hand tools, machines, and doors even are designed for right-handed people. 3 However, nearly 15% may be left-handed of the population. 4 Children when they enter kindergarten generally prefer one hand or the other.

°See "Glossary of Terms," **GI** p. 558.

5 Parents and teachers should not try to deliberately change a child's preference for the left hand.

Exercise 34.2 Revising: Misplaced modifiers

Revise the following paragraph so that modifiers clearly and appropriately describe the intended words. Mark the number preceding any sentence that is correct as given.

1 Women have contributed much to American culture of significance. 2 For example, during the colonial era Elizabeth Pinckney introduced indigo, the source of a valuable blue dye. 3 Later, Emma Willard founded the Troy Female Seminary, the first institution to provide a college-level education for women in 1821. 4 Mary Lyon founded Mount Holyoke Female Seminary as the first true women's college with directors and a campus who would sustain the college even after Lyon's death. 5 Pauline Wright Davis founded in 1853 *Una*, the first US newspaper that was dedicated to gaining women's rights. 6 Maria Mitchell was the first American woman astronomer who lived from 1818 to 1889. 7 Mitchell's Comet was discovered in 1847, which was named for the astronomer.

Exercise 34.3 Revising: Placement of adverbs and adjectives ⟨CULTURE LANGUAGE⟩

Revise the following sentences to correct the positions of adverbs or adjectives. Mark the number preceding any sentence that is correct as given.

Example:
Gasoline high prices affect usually car sales.
High gasoline prices usually affect car sales.

1 Some years ago Detroit cars often were praised.
2 Luxury large cars especially were prized.
3 Then a serious oil shortage led drivers to value small foreign cars that got good mileage.
4 When gasoline ample supplies returned, consumers bought again American large cars and trucks.
5 Consumers not were loyal to the big vehicles when gasoline prices dramatically rose.

34b Connect dangling modifiers to their sentences.

A **dangling modifier** does not sensibly modify anything in its sentence.

Dangling   Passing the building, the vandalism became visible.

Dangling modifiers usually introduce sentences, contain a verb° form, and imply but do not name a subject.° In the example above, the implied subject is the someone or something passing the building. Readers assume that this implied subject is the same as the subject of the sentence (*vandalism* in the example), but vandalism does not pass buildings. The modifier "dangles" because it does not connect sensibly to the rest of the sentence. Following is another example.

°See "Glossary of Terms," **GI** p. 558.

Identifying and revising dangling modifiers

■ **Find a subject.** If the modifier lacks a subject of its own (e.g., *when in diapers*), identify what it describes.

■ **Connect the subject and modifier.** Verify that what the modifier describes is in fact the subject of the main clause. If it is not, the modifier is probably dangling:

      ┌── modifier ──┐   subject

Dangling   When in diapers, my mother remarried.

■ **Revise as needed.** Revise a dangling modifier (*a*) by recasting it with a subject of its own or (*b*) by changing the subject of the main clause:

Revision *a*   When I was in diapers, my mother remarried.

Revision *b*   When in diapers, I attended my mother's second wedding.

Dangling   Although intact, graffiti covered every inch of the walls and windows. [The walls and windows, not the graffiti, were intact.]

To revise a dangling modifier, you have to recast the sentence it appears in. (Revising just by moving the modifier will leave it dangling: *The vandalism became visible passing the building.*) Choose a revision method depending on what you want to emphasize in the sentence.

■ **Rewrite the dangling modifier as a complete clause° with its own stated subject and verb.** Readers can accept that the new subject and the sentence subject are different.

Dangling   Passing the building, the vandalism became visible.

Revised   As we passed the building, the vandalism became visible.

■ **Change the subject of the sentence to a word the modifier properly describes.**

Dangling   Trying to understand the causes, vandalism has been extensively studied.

Revised   Trying to understand the causes, researchers have extensively studied vandalism.

Exercise 34.4 Revising: Dangling modifiers

Revise the sentences in the following paragraph to eliminate any dangling modifiers. Each item has more than one possible answer. Mark the number preceding any sentence that is correct as given.

    1 To understand why people with serious illnesses and other conditions often respond well to animals, the bond between humans and animals is being studied. 2 Drawing conclusions from several formal

°See "Glossary of Terms," **GI** p. 558.

studies, pets can improve people's emotional well-being. 3 Suffering from Alzheimer's and unable to recognize her husband, one woman's ability to identify her beloved dog was unaffected. 4 Once subject to violent outbursts, a companion dog calmed an autistic boy. 5 Facing long hospital stays, pet-therapy dogs can cheer up patients.

Exercise 34.5   Revising: Misplaced and dangling modifiers
Revise the following paragraph to eliminate any misplaced or dangling modifiers.

1 Central American tungara frogs silence several nights a week their mating croaks. 2 When not croaking, the chance that the frogs will be eaten by predators is reduced. 3 The frogs seem to fully believe in "safety in numbers." 4 They more than likely will croak along with a large group rather than by themselves. 5 By forgoing croaking on some nights, the frogs' behavior prevents the species from "croaking."

Sentence Faults

A word group punctuated as a sentence will confuse or annoy readers if it lacks needed parts, has too many parts, or has parts that don't fit together.

35   Sentence Fragments

Chapter essentials
- Test your sentences for completeness (below).
- Revise sentence fragments (p. 266).
- Be aware of the acceptable uses of incomplete sentences (p. 267).

Visit MyWritingLab™ for more resources on sentence fragments.

A **sentence fragment** is part of a sentence that is set off as if it were a whole sentence by an initial capital letter and a final period or other end punctuation. Readers perceive most fragments as serious errors.

35a   Test your sentences for completeness.

A word group that is punctuated as a sentence should contain a predicate verb and a subject and should not be a subordinate clause. It should pass *all three* of the following tests. If it does not, it is a fragment and needs revision.

Tests for sentence fragments

1. Does the word group have a predicate verb?

Example	Answer	Revision
Millions of devices on cellular networks.	No ⟶	Add a verb.
Millions of devices use cellular networks.	Yes	—

2. Does the word group have a subject?

Example	Answer	Revision
Cell phones are convenient. But annoy many people.	No ⟶	Add a subject.
Cell phones are convenient. But they annoy many people.	Yes	—

3. Is the word group a freestanding subordinate clause?

Example	Answer	Revision
Phones ring everywhere. Because users forget to silence them.	Yes ⟶	Make it a main clause or attach it to a main clause.
Phones ring everywhere. Users forget to silence them	No (*because* removed)	—
Phones ring everywhere because users forget to silence them.	No (clause attached)	—

Test 1: Find the predicate verb.

Look for a verb° that can serve as the predicate° of a sentence. Some fragments lack any verb at all.

Fragment	Millions of sites on the Web.
Revised	Millions of sites make up the Web.

Other sentence fragments contain a verb form, but it is not a predicate verb. Instead, it is often the *-ing* or *to* form (for instance, *walking, to walk*):

Fragment	The Web growing with new sites and users every day.
Revised	The Web grows with new sites and users every day.

(CULTURE LANGUAGE) Some languages allow forms of *be* to be omitted as helping verbs° or linking verbs.° But English requires stating forms of *be,* as shown in the following revised example.

Fragments	The network growing. It much larger than anticipated.
Revised	The network is growing. It is much larger than anticipated.

°See "Glossary of Terms," **Gl** p. 558.

Test 2: Find the subject.

The subject° of the sentence will usually come before the verb. If there is no subject, the word group is probably a fragment:

Fragment	The Web continues to grow. <u>And shows no sign of slowing down.</u>
Revised	The Web continues to grow. And <u>it</u> shows no sign of slowing down.

In one kind of complete sentence, a command, the subject *you* is understood: [*You*] *Try this recipe.*

CULTURE LANGUAGE Some languages allow the omission of the sentence subject, especially when it is a pronoun.° But in English, except in commands, the subject is always stated:

Fragment	Web shopping has exploded. Has hurt traditional stores.
Revised	Web shopping has exploded. <u>It</u> has hurt traditional stores.

Test 3: Make sure the clause is not subordinate.

A subordinate clause° usually begins with a subordinating word, such as one of the following:

Subordinating conjunctions°			Relative pronouns°	
after	once	until	that	who/whom
although	since	when	which	whoever/whomever
as	than	where		whose
because	that	whereas		
if	unless	while		

Subordinate clauses serve as parts of sentences (as nouns° or modifiers°), not as whole sentences:

Fragment	When the government devised the Internet.
Revised	The government devised the Internet.
Revised	When the government devised the Internet, <u>no expansive computer network existed.</u>

Fragment	The reason that the government devised the Internet.
Revised	The reason that the government devised the Internet <u>was to link departments and defense contractors.</u>

Note Questions beginning with *how, what, when, where, which, who, whom, whose,* and *why* are not sentence fragments: *Who was responsible? When did it happen?*

35b Revise sentence fragments.

Almost all sentence fragments can be corrected in one of two ways. The choice depends on the importance of the information in the fragment and thus how much you want to stress it.

■ **Rewrite the fragment as a complete sentence.** Add a predicate verb

°See "Glossary of Terms," **Gl** p. 558.

or a subject as needed, or make a subordinate clause into a complete sentence. Any of these revisions gives the information in the fragment the same importance as that in other complete sentences.

Fragment	A major improvement in public health occurred with the widespread use of vaccines. Which protected children against life-threatening diseases.
Revised	A major improvement in public health occurred with the widespread use of vaccines. They protected children against life-threatening diseases.

Two main clauses may be separated by a semicolon instead of a period (see **5** p. 298).

■ **Attach the fragment to a main clause.** This revision subordinates the information in the fragment to the information in the main clause.

Fragment	The polio vaccine eradicated the disease from most of the globe. The first vaccine to be used widely.
Revised	The polio vaccine, the first to be used widely, eradicated the disease from most of the globe.

35c Be aware of the acceptable uses of incomplete sentences.

A few word groups lacking the usual subject-predicate combination are incomplete sentences, but they are not fragments because they conform to the expectations of most readers. They include commands (*Move along. Shut the window.*); exclamations (*Oh no!*); questions and answers (*Where next? To Kansas.*); and descriptions in employment résumés (*Weekly volunteer in soup kitchen.*)

Experienced writers sometimes use sentence fragments when they want to achieve a special effect. Such fragments appear more in informal than in formal writing. Unless you are experienced and thoroughly secure in your own writing, you should avoid all fragments and concentrate on writing clear, well-formed sentences.

Exercise 35.1 Identifying and revising sentence fragments
Apply the tests for completeness to each of the word groups in the following paragraph. If a word group is a complete sentence, mark the number preceding it. If it is a sentence fragment, revise it in two ways: by making it a complete sentence, and by combining it with a main clause written from the information given in other items.

Example:
And could help. [The word group has a verb (*could help*) but no subject.]
Revised into a complete sentence: And he could help.
Combined with a new main clause: He had money and could help.

1 In an interesting magazine article about vandalism against works of art. 2 The focus was on the vandals themselves. 3 The motives of the

vandals varying widely. 4 Those who harm artwork are usually angry. 5 But not necessarily at the artist or the owner. 6 For instance, a man who hammered at Michelangelo's *Pietà*. 7 And knocked off the Virgin Mary's nose. 8 Because he was angry with the Roman Catholic Church. 9 Which knew nothing of his grievance. 10 Although many damaged works can be repaired. 11 Usually even the most skillful repairs are forever visible.

Exercise 35.2 Revising: Sentence fragments

Correct any sentence fragment in the following items either by combining it with a complete sentence or by making it a complete sentence. If an item contains no sentence fragment, mark the number preceding it.

Example:

Jujitsu is good for self-protection. Because it enables one to overcome an opponent without the use of weapons.

Jujitsu is good for self-protection because it enables one to overcome an opponent without the use of weapons. *Or:* Jujitsu is good for self-protection. It enables one to overcome an opponent without the use of weapons.

1 Human beings who perfume themselves. They are not much different from other animals.
2 Animals as varied as insects and dogs release pheromones. Chemicals that signal other animals.
3 Human beings have a diminished sense of smell. And do not consciously detect most of their own species' pheromones.
4 The human substitute for pheromones may be perfumes. Most common in ancient times were musk and other fragrances derived from animal oils.
5 Some sources say that people began using perfume to cover up the smell of burning flesh. During sacrifices to the gods.
6 Perfumes became religious offerings in their own right. Being expensive to make, they were highly prized.
7 The earliest historical documents from the Middle East record the use of fragrances. Not only in religious ceremonies but on the body.
8 In the nineteenth century, chemists began synthesizing perfume oils. Which previously could be made only from natural sources.
9 The most popular animal oil for perfume today is musk. Although some people dislike its heavy, sweet odor.
10 Synthetic musk oil would help conserve a certain species of deer. Whose gland is the source of musk.

Exercise 35.3 Revising: Sentence fragments

Revise the following paragraph to eliminate sentence fragments by combining them with main clauses or rewriting them as main clauses.

Baby red-eared slider turtles are brightly colored. With bold patterns on their yellowish undershells. Which serve as a warning to predators. The bright colors of skunks and other animals. They signal that the animals will spray nasty chemicals. In contrast, the turtle's colors warn largemouth bass. That the baby turtle will actively defend itself. When a bass gulps down a turtle. The feisty baby claws and bites. Forcing the bass to spit it out. To avoid a similar painful experience. The bass will avoid other baby red-eared slider turtles. The turtle loses its bright colors as it grows too big. For a bass's afternoon snack.

36 Comma Splices and Fused Sentences

Chapter essentials

- Separate main clauses that are not joined by *and, but,* or another coordinating conjunction (below).
- Separate main clauses that are related by *however, for example,* or another similar expression (p. 271).

Visit MyWritingLab™ for more resources on comma splices and fused sentences.

When two main clauses° fall in a row, readers need a signal that one main clause is ending and another is beginning. The four ways to provide this signal appear in the box on the next page.

Two problems in punctuating main clauses fail to signal the break between the clauses. One is the **comma splice**, in which the clauses are joined (or spliced) *only* with a comma:

Comma splice   The ship was huge, its mast stood eighty feet high.

The other is the **fused sentence** (or **run-on sentence**), in which no punctuation or conjunction appears between the clauses.

Fused sentence   The ship was huge its mast stood eighty feet high.

CULTURE LANGUAGE   In standard American English, a sentence may not include more than one main clause unless the clauses are separated by a comma and a coordinating conjunction° or by a semicolon. If your native language does not have such a rule or has accustomed you to writing long sentences, you may need to edit your English writing especially for comma splices and fused sentences.

36a Separate main clauses not joined by *and, but,* or another coordinating conjunction.

If your readers point out comma splices or fused sentences in your writing, you're not creating enough separation between main clauses in your sentences. Separate main clauses in the following ways.

Separate sentences

Make the clauses into separate sentences when the ideas expressed are only loosely related.

°See "Glossary of Terms," **Gl** p. 558.

Punctuation of two or more main clauses

■ Separate main clauses with periods.

> Main clause **.** Main clause **.**

Hybrid cars are popular with consumers. Automakers are releasing new models.

■ Link main clauses with a coordinating conjunction and a comma.

> Main clause **,** *for and or so but nor yet* main clause **.**

Hybrid cars are popular with consumers, and automakers are releasing new models.

■ Link main clauses with a semicolon.

> Main clause **;** main clause **.**

Hybrid cars are popular with consumers; automakers are releasing new models.

■ Relate main clauses with a semicolon and a conjunctive adverb or transitional expression.

> Main clause **;** *however, for example, etc.* **,** main clause **.**

Hybrid cars are popular with consumers; as a result, automakers are releasing new models.

Comma splice	Chemistry has contributed much to our understanding of foods, many foods such as wheat and beans can be produced in the laboratory.
Revised	Chemistry has contributed much to our understanding of foods. Many foods such as wheat and beans can be produced in the laboratory.

Coordinating conjunction

Insert a coordinating conjunction° such as *and* or *but* in a comma splice when the ideas in the main clauses are closely related and equally important:

Comma splice	Some laboratory-grown foods taste good, they are nutritious.
Revised	Some laboratory-grown foods taste good, and they are nutritious.

°See "Glossary of Terms," **Gl** p. 558.

In a fused sentence insert a comma and a coordinating conjunction:

Fused sentence	Chemists have made much progress they still have a way to go.
Revised	Chemists have made much progress, but they still have a way to go.

Semicolon

Insert a semicolon between clauses if the relation between the ideas is very close and obvious without a conjunction:

Comma splice	Good taste is rare in laboratory-grown vegetables, they are usually bland.
Revised	Good taste is rare in laboratory-grown vegetables; they are usually bland.

Subordination

When one idea is less important than the other, express the less important idea in a subordinate clause°:

Comma splice	The vitamins are adequate, the flavor is poor.
Revised	Although the vitamins are adequate, the flavor is poor.

 36b | Separate main clauses related by *however, for example,* or a similar expression.

Two groups of words describe how one main clause relates to another: **conjunctive adverbs** and other **transitional expressions.** See the list of these words in the following box. (See also **1** p. 46 for a longer list of transitional expressions.)

Common conjunctive adverbs and transitional expressions

accordingly	for instance	instead	otherwise
anyway	further	in the meantime	similarly
as a result	furthermore	in the past	still
at last	hence	likewise	that is
besides	however	meanwhile	then
certainly	incidentally	moreover	thereafter
consequently	in contrast	nevertheless	therefore
even so	indeed	nonetheless	thus
finally	in fact	now	undoubtedly
for all that	in other words	of course	until now
for example	in short	on the contrary	

When two main clauses are related by a conjunctive adverb or another transitional expression, they must be separated by a period

°See "Glossary of Terms," **Gl** p. 558.

or by a semicolon. The adverb or expression is also generally set off by a comma or commas.

Comma splice	Healthcare costs are higher in the United States than in many other countries, <u>consequently</u> health insurance is also more costly.
Revised	Healthcare costs are higher in the United States than in many other countries. Consequently, health insurance is also more costly.
Revised	Healthcare costs are higher in the United States than in many other countries; consequently, health insurance is also more costly.

Conjunctive adverbs and transitional expressions are different from coordinating conjunctions° (*and, but,* and so on) and subordinating conjunctions° (*although, because,* and so on):

- **Unlike conjunctions, conjunctive adverbs and transitional expressions do not join two clauses into a grammatical unit.** They merely describe the way two clauses relate in meaning.
- **Unlike conjunctions, conjunctive adverbs and transitional expressions can be moved within a clause.** No matter where in the clause an adverb or expression falls, though, the clause must be separated from another main clause by a period or semicolon:

Healthcare costs are higher in the United States than in many other countries; health insurance, <u>consequently,</u> is also more costly.

Exercise 36.1 Identifying and revising comma splices

Correct each comma splice below in *two* of the ways described on pp. 269–72. If a sentence contains no comma splice, mark the number preceding it.

1 Money has a long history, it goes back at least as far as the earliest records. 2 Many of the earliest records concern financial transactions, indeed, early history must often be inferred from commercial activity. 3 Every known society has had a system of money, though the objects serving as money have varied widely. 4 Sometimes the objects had actual value for the society, examples include cattle and fermented beverages. 5 Today, in contrast, money may be made of worthless paper, or it may even consist of a bit of data in a computer's memory. 6 We think of money as valuable, only our common faith in it makes it valuable. 7 That faith is sometimes fragile, consequently, currencies themselves are fragile. 8 Economic crises often shake the belief in money, indeed, such weakened faith helped cause the Great Depression of the 1930s.

Exercise 36.2 Identifying and revising fused sentences

Revise each of the fused sentences in the following paragraph in *two* of the four ways shown on pp. 269–72. If a sentence is correct as given, mark the number preceding it.

1 Throughout history money and religion were closely linked there was little distinction between government and religion. 2 The head of

°See "Glossary of Terms," **GI** p. 558.

state and the religious leader were often the same person so that all power rested in one ruler. 3 These powerful leaders decided what objects would serve as money their backing encouraged public faith in the money. 4 Coins were minted of precious metals the religious overtones of money were then strengthened. 5 People already believed the precious metals to be divine their use in money intensified its allure.

Exercise 36.3 Revising: Comma splices and fused sentences

Revise each comma splice and fused sentence in the following paragraphs using the technique that seems most appropriate for the meaning.

What many call the first genocide of modern times occurred during World War I, the Armenians were deported from their homes in Anatolia, Turkey. The Turkish government assumed that the Armenians were sympathetic to Russia, with whom the Turks were at war. Many Armenians died because of the hardships of the journey many were massacred. The death toll was estimated at between 600,000 and 1 million.

Many of the deported Armenians migrated to Russia, in 1918 they established the Republic of Armenia, they continued to be attacked by Turkey, in 1920 they became the Soviet Republic of Armenia rather than surrender to the Turks. Like other Soviet republics, Armenia became independent in 1991, about 3.4 million Armenians live there now.

37 Mixed Sentences

Chapter essentials
- Match subjects and predicates in meaning (below).
- Untangle sentences that are mixed in grammar (next page).
- State parts of clauses, such as subjects, only once (p. 275).

Visit MyWritingLab™ for more resources on mixed sentences.

A **mixed sentence** contains parts that do not fit together. The misfit may be in meaning or in grammar.

37a Match subjects and predicates in meaning.

In a sentence with mixed meaning, the subject° is said to do or be something illogical. Such a mixture is sometimes called **faulty predication** because the predicate° conflicts with the subject.

1 Illogical equation with *be*

When a form of *be* connects a subject and a word that describes the subject (a complement°), the subject and complement must be logically related.

°See "Glossary of Terms," **Gl** p. 558.

Mixed A compromise between the city and the country would be the ideal place to live.

Revised A community that offered the best qualities of both city and country would be the ideal place to live.

2 Is when, is where

Definitions require nouns° on both sides of *be*. Clauses° that define and begin with *when* or *where* are common in speech but should be avoided in writing:

Mixed An examination is when you are tested on what you know.

Revised An examination is a test of what you know.

3 Reason is because

The commonly heard construction *reason is because* is redundant since *because* means "for the reason that":

Mixed The reason the temple requests donations is because the school needs expansion.

Revised The reason the temple requests donations is that the school needs expansion.

Revised The temple requests donations because the school needs expansion.

4 Other mixed meanings

Faulty predications are not confined to sentences with *be*:

Mixed The use of emission controls was created to reduce air pollution.

Revised Emission controls were created to reduce air pollution.

37b Untangle sentences that are mixed in grammar.

Many mixed sentences start with one grammatical plan or construction but end with a different one:

┌─────────── modifier (prepositional phrase) ───────────┐ predicate
Mixed By paying more attention to impressions than facts causes us to misjudge others.

┌─────────── modifier (prepositional phrase) ───────────┐ subject
Revised By paying more attention to impressions than facts, we
predicate
misjudge others.

Constructions that use *Just because* clauses° as subjects° are common in speech but should be avoided in writing.

°See "Glossary of Terms," **GI** p. 558.

┌─ modifier (subordinate clause) ─┐ ┌─ predicate ─┐
Mixed   Just because no one is watching does not mean we have license to break the law.

┌─ modifier (subordinate clause) ─┐ subject + predicate
Revised Even when no one is watching, we do not have license to break the law.

A mixed sentence is especially likely when you are working on a computer and connect parts of two sentences or rewrite half a sentence but not the other half. A mixed sentence may also occur when you don't make the subject and predicate verb carry the principal meaning. (See **3** p. 139.)

Exercise 37.1 Revising: Mixed sentences

Revise the following paragraph so that sentence parts fit together both in grammar and in meaning. Each item has more than one possible answer. If a sentence is correct as given, mark the number preceding it.

1 A hurricane is when the winds in a tropical depression rotate counterclockwise at more than seventy-four miles per hour. 2 People fear hurricanes because they can destroy lives and property. 3 Through storm surge, high winds, floods, and tornadoes is how hurricanes have killed thousands of people. 4 Storm surge is where the hurricane's winds whip up a tide that spills over seawalls and deluges coastal islands. 5 The winds themselves are also destructive, uprooting trees and smashing buildings. 6 By packing winds of 150 to 200 miles per hour is how a hurricane inflicts terrible damage. 7 The worst damage to inland areas occurs when tornadoes and floods strike. 8 Many scientists observe that hurricanes in recent years they have become more ferocious and destructive. 9 However, in the last half-century, with improved communication systems and weather satellites have made hurricanes less deadly. 10 The reason is because people have more time to escape. 11 The emphasis on evacuation is in fact the best way for people to avoid a hurricane's force. 12 Simply boarding up a house's windows will not protect a family from wind, water surges, and flying debris.

37c State parts of sentences, such as subjects, only once. (CULTURE LANGUAGE)

In some languages other than English, certain parts of sentences may be repeated. These include the subject in any kind of clause or an object or adverb in an adjective clause. In English, however, these parts are stated only once in a clause.

1 Repetition of subject

You may be tempted to restate a subject° as a pronoun before the verb. But the subject needs stating only once in its clause:

Faulty   The liquid it boiled.
Revised The liquid boiled.

°See "Glossary of Terms," **GI** p. 558.

Faulty	Gases in the liquid they escaped.
Revised	Gases in the liquid escaped.

2 | Repetition in an adjective clause

Adjective clauses° begin with *who, whom, whose, which, that, where,* and *when*. The beginning word replaces another word: the subject (*He is the person who called*), an object° (*He is the person whom I mentioned*), or a phrase such as *in which, at which,* or *on which*. (*He knows the office where* [*in which*] *the conference will occur*).

Do not state the word being replaced in an adjective clause:

Faulty	The technician whom the test depended on her was burned. [*Whom* should replace *her*.]
Revised	The technician whom the test depended on was burned.

Adjective clauses beginning with *where* or *when* do not need an adverb such as *there* or *then*:

Faulty	Gases escaped at a moment when the technician was unprepared then.
Revised	Gases escaped at a moment when the technician was unprepared.

Note *Whom, which,* and similar words are sometimes omitted but are still understood by the reader. Thus the word being replaced should not be stated.

Faulty	Accidents rarely happen to technicians the lab has trained them. [*Whom* is understood: . . . *technicians whom the lab has trained*.]
Revised	Accidents rarely happen to technicians the lab has trained.

Exercise 37.2 Revising: Repeated subjects and other parts

CULTURE LANGUAGE

Revise the sentences in the following paragraph to eliminate any unneeded words. If a sentence is correct as given, mark the number preceding it.

1 Archaeologists and other scientists they can often determine the age of their discoveries by means of radiocarbon dating. 2 This technique is based on the fact that all living organisms contain carbon. 3 The most common isotope is carbon 12, which it contains six protons and six neutrons. 4 A few carbon atoms are classified as the isotope carbon 14, where the nucleus consists of six protons and eight neutrons there. 5 Because of the extra neutrons, the carbon 14 atom it is unstable. 6 What is significant about the carbon 14 atom is its half-life of 5700 years. 7 Scientists they measure the proportion of carbon 14 to carbon 12 and estimate the age of the specimen. 8 Radiocarbon dating it can be used on any material that was once living, but it is most accurate with specimens between 500 and 50,000 years old.

°See "Glossary of Terms," GI p. 558.

Punctuation

PART 5

Punctuation

Punctuation

38 End Punctuation

End a sentence with one of three punctuation marks: a period (.), a question mark (?), or an exclamation point (!).

38a Use periods after most sentences and with some abbreviations.

1 Statements, mild commands, and indirect questions

Statement

The airline went bankrupt.   It no longer flies.

Mild command

Think of the possibilities.   Please consider others.

Indirect question

An **indirect question** reports what someone asked but not in the exact form or words of the original question:

The judge asked why I had been driving with my lights off.
No one asked how we got home.

CULTURE LANGUAGE In standard American English, the reporting verb in an indirect question (for example, *asked* or *said*) usually precedes a clause that contains a subject and verb in normal order, not question order: *The reporter asked why the negotiations failed* [not *why did the negotiations fail*].

2 Abbreviations

Use periods with abbreviations that consist of or end in small letters. Otherwise, omit periods from abbreviations.

Dr.	Mr., Mrs.	e.g.	Feb.	ft.
St.	Ms.	i.e.	p.	a.m., p.m.
PhD	BC, BCE	USA	IBM	AM, PM
BA	AD, CE	US	USMC	AIDS

Note When a sentence ends in an abbreviation with a period, don't add a second period: *My first class is at 8 a.m.*

Exercise 38.1 Revising: Periods

Revise the following sentences so that periods are used correctly.

1 The instructor asked when Plato wrote *The Republic*?
2 Give the date within one century
3 The exact date is not known, but it is estimated at 370 BCE
4 Dr Arn will lecture on Plato at 7:30 p.m..
5 The area of the lecture hall is only 1600 sq ft

38b Use a question mark after a direct question and sometimes to indicate doubt.

1 Direct questions

Who will follow her?
What is the difference between these two people?

After indirect questions, use a period: *We wondered who would follow her.* (See the preceding page.)
Questions in a series are each followed by a question mark:

The officer asked how many times the suspect had been arrested. Three times? Four times? More than that?

Note Do not combine question marks with other question marks, periods, commas, or other punctuation.

2 Doubt

A question mark within parentheses can indicate doubt about a number or date.

The Greek philosopher Socrates was born in 470 (?) BC and died in 399 BC from drinking poison. [The date of Socrates's birth is not known for sure.]

Use sentence structure and words, not a question mark, to express sarcasm or irony.

Not Stern's friendliness (?) bothered Crane.
But Stern's <u>insincerity</u> bothered Crane.

Exercise 38.2 Revising: Question marks

Add, delete, or replace question marks as needed in the following sentences.

1 In Homer's *Odyssey*, Odysseus took seven years to travel from Troy to Ithaca. Or was it eight years. Or more?

2 Odysseus must have wondered whether he would ever make it home?
3 "What man are you and whence?," asks Odysseus's wife Penelope.
4 Why does Penelope ask, "Where is your city? Your family?"?
5 Penelope does not recognize Odysseus and asks who this stranger is?

38c Use an exclamation point after an emphatic statement, interjection, or command.

No**!** We must not lose this election**!**
Come here immediately**!**

Follow mild interjections° and commands with commas or periods, as appropriate: *Oh*, *call whenever you can.*

Note Do not combine exclamation points with periods, commas, or other punctuation marks. And use exclamation points sparingly, even in informal writing. Overused, they'll fail to impress readers, and they may make you sound overemotional.

Exercise 38.3 Revising: Exclamation points

Add or replace exclamation points as needed in the following sentences.

1 As the firefighters moved their equipment into place, the police shouted, "Move back!".
2 A child's cries could be heard from above: "Help me. Help."
3 When the child was rescued, the crowd called "Hooray."
4 The rescue was the most exciting event of the day!
5 The neighbors talked about it for days!

Exercise 38.4 Revising: End punctuation

Insert appropriate end punctuation (periods, question marks, or exclamation points) where needed in the following paragraph.

When visitors first arrive in Hawaii, they often encounter an unexpected language barrier Standard English is the language of business and government, but many of the people speak Pidgin English Instead of an excited "Aloha" the visitors may be greeted with an excited Pidgin "Howzit" or asked if they know "how fo' find one good hotel" Many Hawaiians question whether Pidgin will hold children back because it prevents communication with *haoles*, or Caucasians, who run many businesses Yet many others feel that Pidgin is a last defense of ethnic diversity on the islands To those who want to make standard English the official language of the state, these Hawaiians may respond, "Just 'cause I speak Pidgin no mean I dumb" They may ask, "Why you no listen" or, in standard English, "Why don't you listen"

°See "Glossary of Terms," **Gl** p. 558.

39 The Comma

Chapter essentials

To use the comma correctly,

- Separate main clauses linked by *and, but,* or another coordinating conjunction (below).
- Set off most introductory elements (p. 284).
- Set off nonessential elements (p. 286).
- Separate items in a series and coordinate adjectives (pp. 290, 291).
- Separate parts of dates, addresses, place names, and long numbers (p. 292).
- Separate signal phrases and quotations (p. 293).
- Avoid common misuses, especially between subjects and verbs, in most compounds, after conjunctions, and around essential elements (p. 294).

Visit MyWritingLab™ for more resources on the comma.

The comma (,) is the most common punctuation mark inside sentences. Its main uses are shown in the box opposite.

39a Use a comma before *and, but,* or another coordinating conjunction linking main clauses.

When a coordinating conjunction° links words or phrases, do not use a comma: *Dugain plays and sings Irish and English folk songs.* However, *do* use a comma when a coordinating conjunction joins main clauses,° as in the next examples.

Caffeine can help coffee drinkers stay alert, and it may elevate their mood.

Caffeine was once thought to be safe, but now researchers warn of harmful effects.

Coffee drinkers may suffer sleeplessness, for the drug acts as a stimulant to the nervous system.

Note The comma goes *before,* not after, a coordinating conjunction that links main clauses: *Caffeine increases heart rate, and it* [not *and, it*] *constricts blood vessels.*

Exception Some writers omit the comma between main clauses that are very short and closely related in meaning: *Caffeine helps but it also hurts.* If you are in doubt about whether to use the comma in such a sentence, use it. It will always be correct.

Exercise 39.1 Revising: Comma with linked main clauses

In the following paragraph, insert a comma before each coordinating conjunction that links main clauses. Do not insert commas between

°See "Glossary of Terms," Gl p. 558.

Principal uses of the comma

■ **Separate main clauses linked by a coordinating conjunction** (opposite):

| Main clause | , | for and or so but nor yet | main clause | • |

The building is finished, but it has no tenants.

■ **Set off most introductory elements** (p. 284):

| Introductory element | , | main clause | • |

Unfortunately, the only tenant pulled out.

■ **Set off nonessential elements** (p. 286):

| Main clause | , | nonessential element | • |

The empty building symbolizes a weak local economy, which affects everyone.

| Beginning of main clause | , | nonessential element | , | end of main clause | • |

The primary cause, the decline of local industry, is not news.

■ **Separate items in a series** (p. 290):

| ••• | item 1 | , | item 2 | , | and or | item 3 | ••• |

The city needs healthier businesses, new schools, and improved housing.

■ **Separate coordinate adjectives** (p. 291):

| ••• | first adjective | , | second adjective | word modified | ••• |

A tall, sleek skyscraper is not needed.

Other uses of the comma:

Separate parts of dates, addresses, place names, long numbers (p. 292).
Separate quotations and signal phrases (p. 293).

See also p. 294 for when *not* to use the comma.

words, phrases, or subordinate clauses. If a sentence is correct as given, mark the number preceding it.

1 Parents once automatically gave their children the father's last name but some no longer do. 2 In fact, parents were once legally required to give their children the father's last name but these laws have been contested in court. 3 Parents may now give their children any last name they choose and some parents opt for the mother's last name. 4 Those parents who choose the mother's last name may do so because they believe the mother's importance should be recognized or because the mother's name is easier to pronounce.

Exercise 39.2 Sentence combining: Linked main clauses

Combine each group of sentences below into one sentence that contains only two main clauses connected by the coordinating conjunction in parentheses. Use commas only to separate the main clauses. You will have to add, delete, and rearrange words.

> *Example:*
> The circus had come to town. The children wanted to see it. Their parents wanted to see it. (*and*)
>
> The circus had come to town, and the children and their parents wanted to see it.

1 The arguments for bestowing the mother's surname on children are often strong. They are often convincing. They are not universally accepted. (*but*)
2 Some parents have combined their last names. They have created a new surname. They have given that name to their children. (*and*)
3 Critics sometimes question the effects of unusual surnames on children. They wonder how confusing the new surnames will be. They wonder how fleeting the surnames will be. (*or*)
4 Children with surnames different from their parents' may suffer embarrassment. They may suffer identity problems. Giving children their father's surname is still very much the norm. (*for*)
5 Hyphenated names are awkward. They are also difficult to pass on. Some observers think they will die out in the next generation. Or they may die out before. (*so*)

39b Use a comma to set off most introductory elements.

An **introductory element** begins a sentence and modifies a word or words in the main clause.° It is usually followed by a comma.

Subordinate clause°
Even when identical twins are raised apart, they grow up very like each other.

Verbal or verbal phrase°
Explaining the similarity, some researchers claim that one's genes are one's destiny.

°See "Glossary of Terms," **Gl** p. 558.

Concerned, other researchers deny the claim.

Prepositional phrase°
In a debate that has lasted centuries, scientists use identical twins to argue for or against genetic destiny.

Transitional expression°
Of course, scientists can now look directly at the genes themselves to answer questions.

You may omit the comma after a short subordinate clause or prepositional phrase if its omission does not create confusion: *When snow falls the city collapses. By the year 2000 the world population had topped 6 billion.* You may also omit the comma after some transitional expressions when they start sentences: *Thus the debate ended* (see p. 288). However, in both situations the comma is never wrong.

Note Take care to distinguish *-ing* words used as modifiers° from *-ing* words used as subjects.° The former almost always take a comma; the latter never do.

      ┌──── modifier ────┐   subject   verb
Studying identical twins, geneticists learn about inheritance.

      ┌──── subject ────┐   verb
Studying identical twins helps geneticists learn about inheritance.

Exercise 39.3   Revising: Comma with introductory elements

In the following paragraph, insert commas wherever they are needed after introductory elements. If a sentence is correct as given, mark the number preceding it.

1 Veering sharply to the right a large flock of birds neatly avoids a high wall. 2 Moving in a fluid mass is typical of flocks of birds and schools of fish. 3 With the help of complex computer simulations zoologists are learning more about this movement. 4 Because it is sudden and apparently well coordinated the movement of flocks and schools has seemed to be directed by a leader. 5 Almost incredibly the group could behave with more intelligence than any individual seemed to possess. 6 However new studies have discovered that flocks and schools are leaderless. 7 As it turns out evading danger is really an individual response. 8 When each bird or fish senses a predator it follows individual rules for fleeing. 9 To keep from colliding with its neighbors each bird or fish uses other rules for dodging. 10 Multiplied over hundreds of individuals these responses look as if they have been choreographed.

Exercise 39.4   Sentence combining: Introductory elements

Combine each pair of sentences below into one sentence that begins with an introductory modifier as specified in parentheses. Follow the introductory element with a comma. You will have to add, delete, change, and rearrange words.

Example:
The girl was singing. She walked upstairs. (*Modifier beginning Singing.*)
Singing, the girl walked upstairs.

°See "Glossary of Terms," **Gl** p. 558.

1 Biologists have made an effort to explain the mysteries of flocks and schools. They have proposed bizarre magnetic fields and telepathy. (*Modifier beginning In.*)
2 Biologists developed computer models. They have abandoned earlier explanations. (*Modifier beginning Since.*)
3 The movement of a flock or school starts with each individual. It is rapidly and perhaps automatically coordinated among individuals. (*Modifier beginning Starting.*)
4 One biologist observes that human beings seek coherent patterns. He suggests that investigators saw purpose in the movement of flocks and schools where none existed. (*Modifier beginning Observing.*)
5 One may want to study the movement of flocks or schools. Then one must abandon a search for purpose or design. (*Modifier beginning To.*)

39c Use a comma or commas to set off nonessential elements.

Commas around part of a sentence often signal that the element is not necessary to the meaning. This **nonessential element** may modify or rename the word it refers to, but it does not limit the word to a particular individual or group. The meaning of the word would still be clear if the element were deleted:

Nonessential element
The company, which is located in Oklahoma, has a good reputation.

(Because it does not restrict meaning, a nonessential element is also called a **nonrestrictive element**.)

In contrast, an **essential** (or **restrictive**) **element** *does* limit the word it refers to: the element cannot be omitted without leaving the meaning too general. Because it is essential, such an element is *not* set off with a comma or commas.

Essential element
The company rewards employees who work hard.

Omitting *who work hard* would distort the meaning: the company doesn't necessarily reward *all* employees, only the hardworking ones.

The same element in the same sentence may be essential or nonessential depending on your meaning and the context:

Essential
Not all the bands were equally well received, however. The band playing old music held the audience's attention. The other groups created much less excitement. [*Playing old music* identifies a particular band.]

Nonessential
A new band called Fats made its debut on Saturday night. The band, playing old music, held the audience's attention. If this performance is typical, the group has a bright future. [*Playing old music* adds information about a band already named.]

Note When a nonessential element falls in the middle of a sentence, be sure to set it off with a pair of commas, one *before* and one *after* the element.

A test for nonessential and essential elements

1. **Identify the element:**

   Hai Nguyen who emigrated from Vietnam lives in Dallas.
   Those who emigrated with him live elsewhere.

2. **Remove the element.** Does the fundamental meaning of the sentence change?

   Hai Nguyen lives in Dallas. *No.*
   Those live elsewhere. *Yes.* [Who are *Those*?]

3. **If *no*, the element is *nonessential* and *should* be set off with punctuation:**

   Hai Nguyen **,** who emigrated from Vietnam **,** lives in Dallas.

   If *yes*, the element is *essential* and should *not* be set off with punctuation:

   Those who emigrated with him live elsewhere.

---

1 Nonessential phrases and clauses

Nonessential phrases° and subordinate clauses° function as adjectives° or, less commonly, as adverbs.° In each of the following examples, the underlined words could be omitted with no loss of clarity.

Elizabeth Blackwell was the first woman to graduate from an American medical school **,** in 1849. [Adverb phrase.]

She was a medical pioneer **,** helping to found the first medical college for women. [Adjective phrase.]

She taught at the school **,** which was affiliated with the New York Infirmary. [Adjective clause.]

Blackwell **,** who published books and papers on medicine **,** practiced pediatrics and gynecology. [Adjective clause.]

She moved to England in 1869 **,** when she was forty-eight. [Adverb clause.]

Note Use *that* only in an essential clause, never in a nonessential clause. Many writers reserve *which* for nonessential clauses.

Faulty   The tree, that is 120 years old, shades the house.

Revised   The tree, which is 120 years old, shades the house.

2 Nonessential appositives

A nonessential appositive° merely adds information about the word it refers to.

°See "Glossary of Terms," **Gl** p. 558.

> Toni Morrison's fifth novel, *Beloved*, won the Pulitzer Prize in 1988. [The word *fifth* identifies the novel, while the title adds a detail.]

In contrast, an essential appositive limits or defines the word it refers to:

> Morrison's novel *The Bluest Eye* is about an African American girl who longs for blue eyes. [Morrison has written more than one novel, so the title is essential to identify the intended one.]

3 | Other nonessential elements

Many other elements contribute to texture, tone, or overall clarity but are not essential to the meaning. Unlike nonessential modifiers or appositives, these other nonessential elements generally do not refer to any specific word in the sentence.

Note Use a pair of commas—one before, one after—when any of these elements falls in the middle of a sentence.

Absolute phrases°

> Household recycling having succeeded, the city now wants to extend the program to businesses.
>
> Many businesses, their profits already squeezed, resist recycling.

Parenthetical and transitional expressions

Generally, set off parenthetical expressions° and transitional expressions° with commas:

> The world's most celebrated holiday is, perhaps surprisingly, New Year's Day. [Parenthetical expression.]
>
> Interestingly, Americans have relatively few holidays. [Parenthetical expression.]
>
> US workers, for example, receive fewer holidays than European workers do. [Transitional expression.]

(Dashes and parentheses may also set off parenthetical expressions. See pp. 316–18.)

When a transitional expression links main clauses,° precede it with a semicolon and follow it with a comma (see p. 298):

> European workers often have long paid vacations; indeed, they may receive a full month after just a few years with a company.

Exception The conjunctions *and* and *but*, sometimes used as transitional expressions, are never followed by commas (see p. 295). Usage varies with some other transitional expressions, depending on the expression and the writer's judgment. Many writers omit commas with expressions that we read without pauses, such as *also, hence, next, now, then,* and *thus*. The same applies to *therefore* and *instead* when they fall inside or at the ends of clauses.

> US workers therefore put in more work days. But the days themselves may be shorter.

°See "Glossary of Terms," **Gl** p. 558.

Then the total hours worked would come out roughly the same.

Phrases of contrast
The substance, not the style, is important.
Substance, unlike style, cannot be faked.

Tag questions°
They don't stop to consider others, do they?
Jones should be allowed to vote, shouldn't he?

Yes* and *no
Yes, the writer did have a point.
No, that can never be.

Words of direct address
Cody, please bring me the newspaper.
With all due respect, sir, I will not.

Mild interjections°
Well, you will never know who did it.
Oh, they forgot all about the baby.

Exercise 39.5 Revising: Punctuation of nonessential and essential elements

Insert commas as needed in the following paragraph to set off nonessential elements, and delete any commas that incorrectly set off essential elements. If a sentence is correct as given, mark the number preceding it.

1 Anesthesia which is commonly used during medical operations once made patients uncomfortable and had serious risks. 2 But new drugs and procedures that have been developed in recent years, allow patients under anesthesia to be comfortable and much safer. 3 Twenty years ago, any patient undergoing anesthesia would have had to stay overnight in a hospital, probably feeling sick and very confused. 4 Today, many patients can have general anesthesia, which renders them completely unconscious, and still go home the same day. 5 Another form of anesthesia, monitored anesthesia or conscious sedation, allows the patient to be awake while feeling sleepy with no pain. 6 A surgeon may also suggest regional or local anesthesia which numbs only a specific part of the body and leaves the patient completely awake. 7 Sometimes, patients must choose among local, regional, and general anesthesia whether or not they want to make the choice. 8 In that case, patients should ask which type the anesthesiologist would choose if his or her child or spouse were having the surgery.

Exercise 39.6 Revising: Punctuation of nonessential and essential elements

Insert commas as needed in the following paragraphs to set off nonessential elements, and delete any commas that incorrectly set off essential elements. If a sentence is correct as given, mark the number preceding it.

1 Many colleges have started campus garden programs, that aim to teach students about the benefits of sustainable farming methods and locally grown food. 2 These gardens which use organic farming techniques

°See "Glossary of Terms," **Gl** p. 558.

often grow fresh produce for the college cafeteria and the local community. 3 A garden, that is big enough to grow produce for a college cafeteria, requires a large piece of land. 4 Such a garden also needs a leader, who can choose crops that will thrive in local growing conditions. 5 Volunteers, willing to work in the garden every week, are essential as well.

6 Some campus gardeners distribute produce to people in the community who live far from a grocery store. 7 Some urban neighborhoods are called "food deserts," because they lack grocery stores that residents can reach easily on foot. 8 The colleges may distribute produce with special trucks or "veggie wagons" that drive through the urban neighborhoods. 9 The wagons deliver produce once a week although they may make two deliveries during peak harvest time. 10 The wagons are especially welcome in densely populated areas where grocery stores, that sell fresh produce, can be difficult to reach.

Exercise 39.7 Sentence combining: Essential and nonessential elements

Combine each pair of sentences below into one sentence that uses the element described in parentheses. Insert commas as appropriate. You will have to add, delete, change, and rearrange words. Some items have more than one possible answer.

> *Example:*
> Mr. Ward's oldest sister helped keep him alive. She was a nurse in the hospital. (*Nonessential clause beginning who.*)
> Mr. Ward's oldest sister, who was a nurse in the hospital, helped keep him alive.

1 American colonists imported pasta from the English. The English had discovered it as tourists in Italy. (*Nonessential clause beginning who.*)
2 The English returned from grand tours of Italy. They were called *macaronis* because of their fancy airs. (*Essential phrase beginning returning.*)
3 A hair style was also called *macaroni*. It had elaborate curls. (*Essential phrase beginning with.*)
4 The song "Yankee Doodle" refers to this hairdo. It reports that Yankee Doodle "stuck a feather in his cap and called it macaroni." (*Essential clause beginning when.*)
5 The song was actually intended to poke fun at unrefined American colonists. It was a creation of the English. (*Nonessential appositive beginning a creation.*)

39d Use commas between items in a series.

A **series** consists of three or more items of equal importance. The items may be words, phrases,° or clauses.°

> Anna Spingle married at the age of seventeen, had three children by twenty-one, and divorced at twenty-two.
> She worked as a cook, a baby-sitter, and a crossing guard.

Some writers omit the comma before the last item in a series (*Breakfast consisted of coffee, eggs, and kippers*). But the final comma is never wrong, and it always helps the reader see the last two items as separate.

> ### Exercise 39.8 Revising: Commas with series items
>
> In the following paragraph, insert commas as needed to punctuate items in series. If a sentence is correct as given, mark the number preceding it.
>
> 1 Photographers who take pictures of flowers need to pay special attention to lighting composition and focal point. 2 Many photographers prefer to shoot in the early morning, when the air is calm, the dew is still on the flowers, and the light is soft. 3 Some even like to photograph in light rain because water helps flowers to look fresh colorful and especially lively. 4 In composing a picture, the photographer can choose to show several flowers, just one flower or even a small part of a flower. 5 One effective composition leads the viewer's eye in from an edge of the photo devotes a large amount of the photo to the primary subject and then leads the eye out of the photo. 6 The focus changes as the eye moves away from the subject: the primary subject is in sharp focus, elements near the primary subject are in sharp focus and elements in the background are deliberately out of focus.

39e Use commas between two or more adjectives that equally modify the same word.

Adjectives° that equally modify the same word—**coordinate adjectives**—may be separated either by *and* or by a comma.

Spingle's <u>scratched and dented</u> car is old, but it gets her to work.
She dreams of buying a <u>sleek, shiny</u> car.

Adjectives are not coordinate—and should not be separated by commas—when the adjective nearer the modified word is more closely related to the word in meaning.

Spingle's children work at various part-time jobs.
They all expect to go to a nearby community college.

Tests for commas with adjectives

1. **Identify the adjectives.**

   She was a <u>faithful sincere</u> friend.
   They are <u>dedicated medical</u> students.

2. **Can the adjectives be reversed without changing meaning?**

   She was a <u>sincere faithful</u> friend. *Yes.*
   They are <u>medical dedicated</u> students. *No.*

3. **Can the word *and* be sensibly inserted between the adjectives?**

   She was a <u>faithful and sincere</u> friend. *Yes.*
   They are <u>dedicated and medical</u> students. *No.*

   (continued)

°See "Glossary of Terms," **GI** p. 558.

Tests for commas with adjectives
(continued)

4. If *yes* to both questions, the adjectives *are* coordinate and *should* be separated by a comma.

She was a faithful , sincere friend.

If *no* to both questions, the adjectives are *not* coordinate and should *not* be separated by a comma.

They are dedicated medical students.

Exercise 39.9 Revising: Commas with adjectives
In the following paragraph, insert commas as needed between adjectives, and delete any unneeded commas. If a sentence is correct as given, mark the number preceding it.

1 Most people have seen a blind person being aided by a patient, observant guide dog. 2 What is not commonly known is how normal, untrained dogs become these special, highly skilled dogs. 3 An organization called the Seeing Eye breeds dogs to perform this specific guide job. 4 Enthusiastic affectionate volunteers raise the dogs until they are about seventeen months old. 5 Dogs who pass a thorough health exam go through a rigorous, four-month training program. 6 The trained dog is then matched with a blind person, and the two of them undergo their own intensive communication training.

Exercise 39.10 Revising: Punctuation of series and adjectives
Insert commas as needed in the following paragraph to separate series items or adjectives. If a sentence is correct as given, mark the number preceding it.

1 Shoes with high heels were originally designed to protect the wearer's feet from mud garbage and animal waste in the streets. 2 The first high heels worn strictly for fashion, however, appeared in the sixteenth century. 3 They were made popular when the short powerful King Louis XIV of France began wearing them. 4 Louis's influence was so strong that men and women of the court priests and cardinals and even household servants wore high heels. 5 By the seventeenth and eighteenth centuries, only wealthy fashionable French women wore high heels. 6 High-heeled shoes for women spread to other courts of Europe among the Europeans of North America and to all social classes. 7 Now high heels are common, though depending on the fashion they range from short squat thick heels to tall skinny spikes.

39f Use commas in dates, addresses, place names, and long numbers.

Within a sentence, any date, address, or place name that contains a comma should also end with a comma.

Dates

July 4, 1776, is the date the Declaration was signed.

The bombing of Pearl Harbor on Sunday, December 7, 1941, prompted American entry into World War II.

Do not use commas between the parts of a date in inverted order (*15 December 1992*) or in dates consisting of a month or season and a year (*December 1941*).

Addresses and place names

Use the address 220 Cornell Road, Woodside, California 94062, for all correspondence. [Do not use a comma between a state name and a zip code.]

Columbus, Ohio, is the location of Ohio State University.

Long numbers

Use the comma to separate the figures in long numbers into groups of three, counting from the right. With numbers of four digits, the comma is optional.

The new assembly plant cost $7,525,000.
A kilometer is 3,281 feet [*or* 3,281 feet].

(CULTURE LANGUAGE) Usage in standard American English differs from that in some other languages and dialects, which use a period, not a comma, to separate the figures in long numbers.

Exercise 39.11   Revising: Punctuation of dates, addresses, place names, numbers

Insert commas as needed in the following paragraph.

1 The festival will hold a benefit dinner and performance on March 9, 2015, in Asheville. 2 The organizers hope to raise more than $100,000 from donations and ticket sales. 3 Performers are expected from as far away as Milan, Italy, and Kyoto, Japan. 4 All inquiries sent to Mozart Festival, PO Box 725, Asheville, North Carolina 28803, will receive a quick response. 5 The deadline for ordering tickets by mail is Monday, December 16, 2014.

39g Use commas with quotations according to standard practice.

The words *she said, he writes,* and so on identify the source of a quotation. These **signal phrases** should be separated from the quotation by punctuation, usually a comma or commas.

"Knowledge is power," writes Francis Bacon.

"The shore has a dual nature," observes Rachel Carson, "changing with the swing of the tides." [The signal phrase interrupts the quotation at a comma and thus ends with a comma.]

Exceptions Do not use commas with signal phrases in some situations:

- **Use a semicolon or a period after a signal phrase that interrupts a quotation between main clauses.**° The choice depends on the punctuation of the original:

Not	"That door was closed," she wrote, "his words had sealed it shut."
But	"That door was closed," she wrote**.** "His words had sealed it shut." [*She wrote* interrupts the quotation at a period.]
Or	"That door was closed," she wrote**;** "his words had sealed it shut." [*She wrote* interrupts the quotation at a semicolon.]

- **Omit a comma when a signal phrase follows a quotation ending in an exclamation point or a question mark:**

    "Claude**!**" Mrs. Harrison called.
    "Why must I come home**?**" he asked.

- **Use a colon when a complete sentence introduces a quotation:**

    Her statement was clear**:** "I will not resign."

- **Omit commas when a quotation is integrated into your sentence structure,** including a quotation introduced by *that*:

    James Baldwin insists that "one must never, in one's life, accept . . . injustices as commonplace."

    Baldwin thought that the violence of a riot "had been devised as a corrective" to his own violence.

- **Omit commas with a quoted title unless it is a nonessential appositive°:**

    The Beatles recorded "She Loves You" in 1963.
    The Beatles' first huge US hit**,** "She Loves You**,**" appeared in 1963.

Exercise 39.12   Revising: Punctuation of quotations

In the following sentences, insert commas or semicolons as needed to correct punctuation with quotations. If a sentence is correct as given, mark the number preceding it.

1 The writer and writing teacher Peter Elbow proposes an "open-ended writing process**,**" that **,** "can change you, not just your words."
2 "I think of the open-ended writing process as a voyage in two stages**,**" Elbow says.
3 "The sea voyage is a process of divergence, branching, proliferation, and confusion**,**" Elbow continues **.** "The coming to land is a process of convergence, pruning, centralizing, and clarifying."
4 "Keep up one session of writing long enough to get loosened up and tired**,**" advises Elbow**,** "long enough in fact to make a bit of a voyage."
5 "In coming to new land**,**" Elbow says**,** "you develop a new conception of what you are writing about."

39h   Delete commas where they are not required.

Commas can make sentences choppy and even confusing if they are used more often than needed.

°See "Glossary of Terms," **Gl** p. 558.

1 No comma between subject° and verb,° verb and object,°
or preposition° and object

Not   The returning <u>soldiers, received</u> a warm welcome. [Separated subject and verb.]

But   The returning <u>soldiers received</u> a warm welcome.

Not   They had <u>chosen, to fight</u> for their country <u>despite, the risks.</u> [Sepa-
rated verb *chosen* and its object; separated preposition *despite* and
its object.]

But   They had <u>chosen to fight</u> for their country <u>despite the risks.</u>

2 No comma in most compound constructions

Compound constructions° consisting of two elements almost
never require a comma. The only exception is the sentence consisting of two main clauses° linked by a coordinating conjunction°: *The
network failed, but employees kept working* (see p. 282).

Not   ⌐————— compound subject —————⌐
<u>Banks, and other financial institutions</u> have helped older people
⌐————— compound object —————⌐
with <u>money management, and investment.</u>

But   <u>Banks and other financial institutions</u> have helped older people
with <u>money management and investment.</u>

Not   ————— compound predicate —————
One bank <u>created</u> special accounts for older people, and <u>held</u>
⌐— compound object —⌐
<u>classes, and workshops.</u>

But   One bank <u>created</u> special accounts for older people and <u>held</u>
<u>classes and workshops.</u>

3 No comma after a conjunction°

Not   Parents of adolescents notice increased conflict at puberty, <u>and,</u>
they complain of bickering.

But   Parents of adolescents notice increased conflict at puberty, <u>and they</u>
complain of bickering.

Not   <u>Although,</u> other primates leave the family at adolescence, humans
do not.

But   <u>Although</u> other primates leave the family at adolescence, humans
do not.

4 No commas around essential elements°

Not   Hawthorne's work, *The Scarlet Letter,* was the first major American
novel. [The title is essential to distinguish the novel from the rest
of Hawthorne's work.]

But   Hawthorne's work *The Scarlet Letter* was the first major American
novel.

°See "Glossary of Terms," **Gl** p. 558.

Not The symbols, that Hawthorne uses, have influenced many other novelists. [The clause identifies which symbols have been influential.]

But The symbols that Hawthorne uses have influenced many other novelists.

Not Published in 1850, *The Scarlet Letter* is still popular, because its theme of secret sin resonates with contemporary readers. [The clause is essential to explain why the novel is popular.]

But Published in 1850, *The Scarlet Letter* is still popular because its theme of secret sin resonates with contemporary readers.

Note Like the *because* clause in the preceding example, most adverb clauses are essential because they describe conditions necessary to the main clause.

5 No commas around a series

Commas separate the items *within* a series (pp. 290–91) but do not separate the series from the rest of the sentence.

Not The skills of, hunting, herding, and agriculture, sustained the Native Americans.

But The skills of hunting, herding, and agriculture sustained the Native Americans.

6 No comma before an indirect quotation

Not The report concluded, that dieting could be more dangerous than overeating.

But The report concluded that dieting could be more dangerous than overeating.

Exercise 39.13 Revising: Needless and misused commas

Revise the following paragraph to eliminate needless or misused commas. If a sentence is correct as given, mark the number preceding it.

1 One of the largest aquifers in North America, the Ogallala aquifer, is named after the Ogallala Indian tribe, which once lived in the region and hunted buffalo there. 2 The Ogallala aquifer underlies a region from western Texas through northern Nebraska, and has a huge capacity of fresh water, that is contained in a layer of sand and gravel. 3 But, the water in the Ogallala is being removed faster than it is being replaced. 4 Water is pumped from the aquifer for many purposes, such as drinking and other household use, industrial use, and, agricultural use. 5 The Great Plains area above the Ogallala, often lacks enough rainfall for the crops, that are grown there. 6 As a consequence, the crops in the Great Plains are watered by irrigation systems, that pump water from the Ogallala, and distribute it from long sprinkler arms. 7 Ogallala water is receding between six inches and three feet a year, the amount depending on location. 8 Some areas are experiencing water shortages already, and the pumping continues. 9 A scientific commission recently stated that, "at the present consumption rate, the Ogallala will be depleted in forty years."

Exercise 39.14 Revising: Commas

Insert commas as needed in the following paragraphs, and delete any misused commas. If a sentence is correct as given, mark the number preceding it.

1 Ellis Island New York reopened for business in 1990 but now the customers are tourists not immigrants. 2 This spot which lies in New York Harbor was the first American soil seen, or touched by many of the nation's immigrants. 3 Though other places also served as ports of entry for foreigners none has the symbolic power of, Ellis Island. 4 Between its opening in 1892 and its closing in 1954, over 20 million people about two-thirds of all immigrants were detained there before taking up their new lives in the United States. 5 Ellis Island processed over 2000 newcomers a day when immigration was at its peak between 1900 and 1920.

6 As the end of a long voyage and the introduction to the New World Ellis Island must have left something to be desired. 7 The "huddled masses" as the Statue of Liberty calls them indeed were huddled. 8 New arrivals were herded about kept standing in lines for hours or days yelled at and abused. 9 Assigned numbers they submitted their bodies to the pokings and proddings of the silent nurses and doctors, who were charged with ferreting out the slightest sign, of sickness disability or insanity. 10 That test having been passed, the immigrants faced interrogation by an official through an interpreter. 11 Those, with names deemed inconveniently long or difficult to pronounce, often found themselves permanently labeled with abbreviations, of their names, or with the names, of their hometowns. 12 But, millions survived the examination humiliation and confusion, to take the last short boat ride to New York City. 13 For many of them and especially for their descendants Ellis Island eventually became not a nightmare but the place where a new life began.

40 The Semicolon

Chapter essentials

To use the semicolon correctly,

- Separate main clauses that are not joined by *and, but*, or another coordinating conjunction (next page).
- Separate main clauses related by *however, for example*, or a similar expression (p. 298).
- Separate main clauses or series items that contain commas (p. 300).
- Avoid misuses of the semicolon: with phrases and subordinate clauses and before series and explanations (p. 300).

Visit MyWritingLab™ for more resources on the semicolon.

The semicolon (;) separates equal and balanced sentence elements.

40a Use a semicolon between main clauses not joined by *and, but,* or another coordinating conjunction.

When no coordinating conjunction° links two main clauses,° the clauses should be separated by a semicolon.

A new ulcer drug arrived on the market with a mixed reputation; doctors find that the drug works but worry about its side effects.

The side effects are not minor; some leave the patient quite uncomfortable or even ill.

Note This rule prevents the errors known as comma splices and fused sentences. (See **4** pp. 269–72.)

> Exercise 40.1 Revising: Punctuation between main clauses
>
> In the following paragraph, insert semicolons as needed to separate main clauses. If a sentence is correct as given, mark the number preceding it.
>
> 1 More and more musicians are playing computerized instruments more and more listeners are worrying about the future of acoustic instruments. 2 The computer is not the first technology in music the pipe organ and saxophone were also technological breakthroughs in their day. 3 Musicians have always experimented with new technology while audiences have always resisted the experiments. 4 Most computer musicians are not merely following the latest fad they are discovering new sounds and new ways to manipulate sound. 5 Few musicians have abandoned acoustic instruments most value acoustic sounds as much as electronic sounds.

40b Use a semicolon between main clauses related by *however, for example,* and so on.

When a conjunctive adverb° or another transitional expression° relates two main clauses° in a single sentence, the clauses should be separated with a semicolon:

An American immigrant, Levi Strauss, invented blue jeans in the 1860s; eventually, his product clothed working men throughout the West.

The position of the semicolon between main clauses never changes, but the conjunctive adverb or transitional expression may move around in the second clause. Wherever the adverb or expression falls, it is usually set off with a comma or commas. (See p. 288.)

Blue jeans have become fashionable all over the world; however, the American originators still wear more jeans than anyone else.

Blue jeans have become fashionable all over the world; the American originators, however, still wear more jeans than anyone else.

Blue jeans have become fashionable all over the world; the American originators still wear more jeans than anyone else, however.

Note The semicolon in such sentences prevents the error known as a comma splice. (See **4** pp. 269–72.)

°See "Glossary of Terms," GI p. 558.

Distinguishing the semicolon and the colon

Semicolon

The semicolon separates elements of *equal* importance, almost always complete main clauses.

Few enrolling students know exactly what they want from the school; most hope generally for a managerial career.

Colon

The colon separates elements of *unequal* importance, such as statements and explanations. The first element must be a complete main clause; the second element need not be. (See p. 302.)

The business school caters to working students: it offers special evening courses in business writing, finance, and management.

The school has one goal: to train students to be responsible, competent businesspeople.

Exercise 40.2 Revising: Punctuation between main clauses with conjunctive adverbs or transitional expressions

In the following paragraph, insert semicolons as needed to separate main clauses related by a conjunctive adverb or transitional expression. Also insert a comma or commas as needed to set off the adverb or expression.

1 Music is a form of communication like language the basic elements however are not letters but notes. 2 Computers can process any information that can be represented numerically as a result they can process musical information. 3 A computer's ability to process music depends on what software it can run it must moreover be connected to a system that converts electrical vibration into sound. 4 Computers and their sound systems can produce many different sounds indeed the number of possible sounds is infinite. 5 The powerful music computers are very expensive therefore they are used only by professional musicians.

Exercise 40.3 Sentence combining: Related main clauses

Combine each of the following sets of sentences into one sentence containing only two main clauses. As indicated in parentheses, connect the clauses with a semicolon alone or with a semicolon plus a conjunctive adverb or transitional expression followed by a comma. You will have to add, delete, change, and rearrange words. Each item has more than one possible answer.

Example:

The Albanians censored their news. We got little news from them. And what we got was unreliable. (*Therefore and semicolon.*)

The Albanians censored their news; therefore, the little news we got from them was unreliable.

1 Electronic instruments are prevalent in jazz. They are also prevalent in rock music. They are less common in classical music. (*However and semicolon.*)

2 Jazz and rock change rapidly. They nourish experimentation. They nourish improvisation. (*Semicolon alone.*)

3 The notes and instrumentation of traditional classical music were established by a composer. The composer was writing decades or centuries ago. Such music does not change. (*Therefore and semicolon.*)

4 Contemporary classical music not only can draw on tradition. It can also respond to innovations. These are innovations such as jazz rhythms and electronic sounds. (*Semicolon alone.*)

5 Much contemporary electronic music is more than just one type of music. It is more than just jazz, rock, or classical. It is a fusion of all three. (*Semicolon alone.*)

40c Use semicolons between main clauses or series items containing commas.

Normally, commas separate main clauses° linked by coordinating conjunctions° (*and, but, or, nor*) and separate items in a series. But when the clauses or series items contain commas, a semicolon between them makes the sentence easier to read.

> Lewis and Clark led the men of their party with consummate skill, inspiring and encouraging them, doctoring and caring for them**;** and they kept voluminous journals. —Page Smith

> The custody case involved Amy Dalton, the child**;** Ellen and Mark Dalton, the parents**;** and Ruth and Hal Blum, the grandparents.

Exercise 40.4 Revising: Punctuation of main clauses and series items containing commas

Substitute semicolons for commas in the following paragraph to separate main clauses or series items that contain commas.

1 The Indian subcontinent is separated from the rest of the world by clear barriers: the Bay of Bengal and the Arabian Sea to the east and west, respectively, the Indian Ocean to the south, and 1600 miles of mountain ranges to the north. 2 In the north of India are the world's highest mountains, the Himalayas, and farther south are fertile farmlands, unpopulated deserts, and rain forests. 3 India is a nation of ethnic and linguistic diversity, with numerous religions, including Hinduism, Islam, and Christianity, with distinct castes and ethnic groups, and with sixteen languages, including the official Hindi and the "associate official" English.

40d Delete or replace unneeded semicolons.

Semicolons are often misused in certain constructions that call for other punctuation or no punctuation.

1 No semicolon between a main clause and a subordinate clause or phrase

The semicolon does not separate unequal parts, such as main clauses° and subordinate clauses° or phrases.°

°See "Glossary of Terms," **Gl** p. 558.

Not   Pygmies are in danger of extinction; because of encroaching development.

But   Pygmies are in danger of extinction because of encroaching development.

Not   According to African authorities; about 35,000 Pygmies exist today.

But   According to African authorities, about 35,000 Pygmies exist today.

2 No semicolon before a series or explanation

Colons and dashes, not semicolons, introduce series, explanations, and so forth. (See the next page and p. 317.)

Not   Teachers have heard many reasons why students do poorly; psychological problems, family illness, too much work, too little time.

But   Teachers have heard many reasons why students do poorly: psychological problems, family illness, too much work, too little time.

Exercise 40.5   Revising: Semicolons

In the following paragraph, insert semicolons as needed and eliminate any misused semicolons, substituting other punctuation as appropriate. If a sentence is correct as given, mark the number preceding it.

1 The set and actors in the movie captured the essence of horror films. 2 The set was ideal; dark, deserted streets, trees dipping branches over the sidewalks, mist hugging the ground and creeping up to meet the trees, looming shadows of unlighted, turreted houses. 3 But the best feature of the movie was its actors; all of them tall, pale, and thin to the point of emaciation. 4 With one exception, they were dressed uniformly in gray and had gray hair. 5 The exception was an actress who dressed only in black as if to set off her pale yellow, nearly white, long hair; the only color in the film. 6 The glinting black eyes of another actor stole almost every scene, indeed, they were the source of the film's mischief.

41 The Colon

Chapter essentials

To use the colon correctly,

- Introduce a concluding explanation, series, or appositive and some concluding quotations (next page).
- Conclude a business-letter salutation, separate a title and subtitle, and separate divisions of time (next page).
- Avoid common misuses: after a verb, a preposition, *such as*, or *including* (p. 303).

Visit MyWritingLab™ for more resources on the colon.

The colon (:) is mainly a mark of introduction: it signals that the words following will explain or amplify. The colon also has several conventional uses, such as in expressions of time.

41a Use a colon to introduce a concluding explanation, a series, an appositive, and some quotations.

As an introducer, a colon is always preceded by a complete main clause.° It may or may not be followed by a main clause. This is one way the colon differs from the semicolon, which generally separates main clauses only. (See the box on p. 299.)

Explanation

Soul food has a deceptively simple definition**:** the ethnic cooking of African Americans.

Sometimes a concluding explanation is preceded by *the following* or *as follows* and a colon:

A more precise definition might be the following**:** soul food draws on ingredients, cooking methods, and dishes that originated in Africa, were brought to the New World by slaves, and were modified or supplemented in the Caribbean and the American South.

Note A complete sentence *after* a colon may begin with a capital letter or a small letter (as in the preceding example). Just be consistent throughout an essay.

Series

At least three soul food dishes are familiar to most Americans**:** fried chicken, barbecued spareribs, and sweet potatoes.

Appositive°

Soul food has only one disadvantage**:** fat.

Namely, that is, and other expressions that introduce appositives *follow* the colon: *Soul food has only one disadvantage***:** *namely, fat.*

Quotation

One soul food chef has a solution**:** "Soul food doesn't have to be greasy to taste good. Instead of using ham hocks to flavor beans, I use smoked turkey wings. The soulful, smoky taste remains, but without all the fat of pork."

Use a colon before a quotation when the introduction is a complete sentence.

41b Use a colon after the salutation of a business letter, between a title and subtitle, and between divisions of time.

Salutation of business letter

Dear Ms. Burak**:**

Title and subtitle

*Charles Dickens***:** *An Introduction to His Novels*

Time

12**:**26 AM   6**:**00 PM

41c Delete or replace unneeded colons.

Use the colon only at the end of a main clause,° not in the following situations:

■ **Delete a colon after a verb.°**

Not   The best-known soul food dish <u>is</u>: fried chicken.

But   The best-known soul food dish <u>is</u> fried chicken.

■ **Delete a colon after a preposition.°**

Not   Soul food recipes can be found <u>in</u>: mainstream cookbooks as well as specialized references.

But   Soul food recipes can be found <u>in</u> mainstream cookbooks as well as specialized references.

■ **Delete a colon after** *such as* **or** *including.*

Not   Many Americans have not tasted delicacies <u>such as</u>: chitlins and black-eyed peas.

But   Many Americans have not tasted delicacies <u>such as</u> chitlins and black-eyed peas.

Exercise 41.1   Revising: Colons

In the following paragraph, insert colons as needed and delete misused colons. If a sentence is correct as given, mark the number preceding it.

1 In remote areas of many developing countries, simple signs mark human habitation a dirt path, a few huts, smoke from a campfire. 2 However, in the built-up sections of industrialized countries, nature is all but obliterated by signs of human life, such as: houses, factories, skyscrapers, and highways. 3 The spectacle makes many question the words of Ecclesiastes 1.4 "One generation passeth away, and another cometh; but the earth abideth forever." 4 Yet many scientists see the future differently: they hold that human beings have all the technology necessary to clean up the earth and restore the cycles of nature. 5 All that is needed is: a change in the attitudes of those who use technology.

Exercise 41.2   Revising: Colons and semicolons

In the following paragraphs, insert colons and semicolons as needed and delete or replace them where they are misused. If a sentence is correct as given, mark the number preceding it.

1 Sunlight is made up of three kinds of radiation: visible rays; infrared rays, which we cannot see; and ultraviolet rays, which are also

°See "Glossary of Terms," **Gl** p. 558.

invisible. **2** Infrared rays are the longest; measuring 700 nanometers and longer; while ultraviolet rays are the shortest; measuring 400 nanometers and shorter. **3** Especially in the ultraviolet range; sunlight is harmful to the eyes. **4** Ultraviolet rays can damage the retina: furthermore, they can cause cataracts on the lens.

5 The lens protects the eye by: absorbing much of the ultraviolet radiation and thus protecting the retina. **6** Protecting the retina, however, the lens becomes a victim; growing cloudy and blocking vision. **7** The best way to protect your eyes is: to wear hats that shade the face and sunglasses that screen out ultraviolet rays. **8** Many sunglass lenses have been designed as ultraviolet screens; many others are extremely ineffective. **9** Sunglass lenses should screen out ultraviolet rays and be dark enough so that people can't see your eyes through them, otherwise, the lenses will not protect your eyes, and you will be at risk for cataracts later in life. **10** People who spend much time outside in the sun; owe it to themselves to buy and wear sunglasses that shield their eyes.

42 The Apostrophe

Chapter essentials

- Use the apostrophe to show possession in singular and plural words (below).
- Do not use the apostrophe in plural nouns or in singular verbs ending in -s (p. 307).
- Do not use the apostrophe in possessive personal or relative pronouns (p. 308).
- Use the apostrophe to show omissions in contractions (p. 309).

Visit MyWritingLab™ for more resources on the apostrophe.

The apostrophe (') appears as part of a word to indicate possession, the omission of one or more letters, or sometimes plural number.

42a Use the apostrophe to show possession.

A noun or indefinite pronoun° shows possession with an apostrophe and, usually, an -s: *the dog's hair, everyone's hope.* Only certain pronouns° do not use apostrophes for possession: *mine, yours, his, hers, its, ours, theirs,* and *whose.*

Note Apostrophes are easy to misuse. Always check your drafts to be sure that all words ending in -s neither omit needed apostro-

°See "Glossary of Terms," Gl p. 558.

Uses and misuses of the apostrophe

Uses of the apostrophe

■ **Use an apostrophe to form the possessives of nouns and indefinite pronouns** (facing page and next page).

Singular	Plural
Ms. Park's	the Parks'
lawyer's	lawyers'
everyone's	two weeks'

■ **Use an apostrophe to form contractions** (p. 309).

it's a girl	shouldn't
you're	won't

■ **The apostrophe is optional for plurals of abbreviations, dates, and words or characters named as words** (p. 310).

MAs or MA's	Cs or C's
1960s or 1960's	*ifs* or *if*'s

Misuses of the apostrophe

■ **Do not use an apostrophe plus -s to form the possessives of plural nouns** (next page). Instead, first form the plural with -s and *then* add an apostrophe.

Not	But
the Kim's car	the Kims' car
boy's fathers	boys' fathers
babie's care	babies' care

■ **Do not use an apostrophe to form plurals of nouns** (p. 307).

Not	But
book's are	books are
the Freed's	the Freeds

■ **Do not use an apostrophe with verbs ending in -s** (p. 308).

Not	But
swim's	swims

■ **Do not use an apostrophe to form the possessives of personal and relative pronouns** (p. 308).

Not	But
it's toes	its toes
your's	yours
who's car	whose car

phes nor add unneeded ones. Also, remember that the apostrophe or apostrophe-plus-*s* is an *addition*. Before this addition, always spell the name of the owner or owners without dropping or adding letters.

1 Singular words: Add -'s.

Bill Boughton's skillful card tricks amaze children.
Some of the earth's forests are regenerating.
Everyone's fitness can be improved through exercise.

The -'s ending for singular words pertains also to singular words ending in -s, as the next examples show.

Henry James's novels reward the patient reader.
The business's customers filed suit.

Exception An apostrophe alone may be added to a singular word ending in -s when another s would make the word difficult to say: *Moses' mother, Joan Rivers' jokes*. But the added -s is never wrong (*Moses's, Rivers's*).

2 Plural words ending in -s: Add -' only.

Workers' incomes have fallen slightly over the past year.
Many students benefit from several years' work after high school.
The Jameses' talents are extraordinary.

Note the difference in the possessives of singular and plural words ending in -s. The singular form usually takes the apostrophe plus -s: *James's*. The plural takes only the apostrophe: *Jameses'*.

3 Plural words not ending in -s: Add -'s.

Children's educations are at stake.
We need to attract the media's attention.

4 Compound words: Add -'s only to the last word.

The brother-in-law's business failed.
Taxes are always somebody else's fault.

5 Two or more owners: Add -'s depending on possession.

Individual possession
Zimbale's and Mason's comedy techniques are similar. [Each comedian has his own technique.]

Joint possession
The children recovered despite their mother and father's neglect. [The mother and father were jointly neglectful.]

Exercise 42.1 Forming possessives
Form the possessive of each word or word group in brackets.

Example:

The [men] blood pressures were higher than the [women].

The men**'s** blood pressures were higher than the women**'s**.

1 In works for adults and teens, fiction writers often explore [people] relationship to nature and the environment. 2 For example, [Carl Hiaasen] inventive and humorous plots often revolve around endangered [species] habitats. 3 Most of [Hiaasen] books for adults and younger readers address [Florida] natural landscape and challenges to it. 4 His [characters] personalities are often eccentric and extreme. 5 For instance, in *Hoot*, [Hiaasen] first novel for younger readers, endangered [owls] habitat will be destroyed if a [business] plans to build a new restaurant proceed. 6 In *Flush* the main [character] father is in jail for sinking a casino boat that regularly emptied raw sewage into [Florida] water. 7 In *Scat* two [students] investigation into a [teacher] disappearance leads to an environmental mystery.

8 Two of [Margaret Atwood] recent novels are about several [individuals] survival following a devastating environmental crisis and a plague that has killed nearly all of the residents of a city. 9 The first of the two books, *Oryx and Crake*, involves characters with those names but is told from one [man] perspective, that of a character named Jimmy. 10 Readers learn [Jimmy] version of the events that have occurred. 11 Gradually readers learn about [Oryx and Crake] lives and why they are not struggling for survival along with Jimmy. 12 In the second book, *The Year of the Flood*, readers encounter a similar story, but through two [women] experiences. 13 In both books, most of the [city] residents have died from an outbreak of disease. 14 [Everyone] home is empty. 15 Some readers may be unsettled by these two [books] visions of the future.

Exercise 42.2 Revising: Apostrophes with possessives

In the following paragraph, insert or reposition apostrophes as needed and delete any needless apostrophes. If a sentence is correct as given, mark the number preceding it.

1 The eastern coast of Belize was once a fishermans paradise, but overfishing caused the fishing industrys sharp decline in this Central American country. 2 The country's government is now showing the world that leaders' foresight can turn a problem into an opportunity. 3 Belize is capitalizing on something that can capture tourists' interest: whale sharks. 4 Huge but harmless to people, whale sharks regularly visit Belizes coast to feed on smaller fishes eggs. 5 The predictable gatherings of the shark's attract large numbers of scuba diver's and snorkeler's, so that the fishs' fascinating beauty has become an economic treasure. 6 A tourists eagerness to spend money for an up-close view of whale sharks is Belizes renewable and reliable resource.

42b Delete apostrophes where they are not required.

1 No apostrophe with a plural noun

The plurals of nouns are generally formed by adding *-s* or *-es*, never with an apostrophe: *boys, families, Joneses, Murphys*.

Not   The Jones' controlled the firm's until 2010.
But   The Joneses controlled the firms until 2010.

2 **No apostrophe with a singular verb**

Verbs ending in -*s* never take an apostrophe:

Not   The subway break's down less often now.
But   The subway breaks down less often now.

3 **No apostrophe with a possessive personal pronoun° or relative pronoun°**

His, hers, its, ours, yours, theirs, and *whose* are possessive forms of the pronouns *he, she, it, we, you, they,* and *who*. They do not take apostrophes:

Not   The house is her's. It's roof leaks.
But   The house is hers. Its roof leaks.

Don't confuse possessive pronouns with contractions. See opposite.

Exercise 42.3   Distinguishing between plurals and possessives

Supply the appropriate form—possessive or plural—of each word given in brackets. Some words require apostrophes, and some do not.

Example:
Hawaiian [shirt], each with [it] own loud design, hung in the window.
Hawaiian shirts, each with its own loud design, hung in the window.

1 Demeter may be the oldest of the ancient Greek [god], older than Zeus. 2 In myth she is the earth mother, which means that the responsibility for the fertility of both [animal] and [plant] is [she]. 3 Many prehistoric [culture] had earth [goddess] like Demeter. 4 In Greek culture the [goddess] festival came at harvest time, with [it] celebration of bounty. 5 The [people] [prayer] to Demeter thanked her for grain and other [gift].

Exercise 42.4   Revising: Misuses of the apostrophe

Revise the following paragraph by deleting or repositioning apostrophes or by repairing incorrect possessive pronouns or contractions. If a sentence is correct as given, mark the number preceding it.

1 Research is proving that athlete's who excel at distance running have physical characteristics that make them faster than most people. 2 For example, they're hearts are larger. 3 An average adult's heart pump's about fifteen liters of blood per minute, but a competitive distance runner's heart circulate's twice as much. 4 Elite runners are also more efficient: they're able to run with less work than less talented runners must exert. 5 In addition, competitive runner's are able to keep running for long time's at high levels of exertion. 6 Although these abilities can be honed in training, they cannot be acquired by a runner: they are his' or her's from birth.

°See "Glossary of Terms," GI p. 558.

Exercise 42.5 **Revising: Contractions and possessive pronouns**

Revise the following paragraph for correct use of contractions and possessive pronouns. If a sentence is correct as given, mark the number preceding it.

1 Roald Dahl's children's novel *James and the Giant Peach* has been enjoyed by each generation of readers since its first publication in 1961. 2 Its a magical story of adventure and friendship. 3 James, a lonely boy whose being raised by his two nasty aunts, accidentally drops some mysterious crystals by an old peach tree in the yard. 4 The peach at the very top grows to an enormous size, and when James crawls inside, he finds friendly, oversized bugs ready to welcome him into there family. 5 As the peach breaks from the tree and rolls into the ocean, their plunged into an adventure that takes them to the top of the Empire State Building.

42c Use the apostrophe to form contractions.

A **contraction** replaces one or more letters, numbers, or words with an apostrophe, as in the following examples:

Standard contractions

it is, it has	it's	cannot	can't
they are	they're	does not	doesn't
you are	you're	were not	weren't
who is, who has	who's	class of 2018	class of '18

Contractions vs. possessive pronouns

Don't confuse contractions with possessive pronouns:

Contractions	Possessive pronouns
It's a book.	Its cover is green.
They're coming.	Their car broke down.
You're right.	Your idea is good.
Who's coming?	Whose party is it?

Exercise 42.6 **Forming contractions**

Form contractions from each set of words below. Use each contraction in a complete sentence.

Example:
we are: we're
We're open to ideas.

1	she would	6	she will
2	could not	7	hurricane of 1962
3	they are	8	is not
4	he is	9	it is
5	do not	10	will not

Revise the following paragraph to correct mistakes in the use of contractions and possessive pronouns. If a sentence is correct as given, mark the number preceding it.

1 In a recent survey, students who use the writing center responded that it's a good source of feedback for they're writing. 2 The survey results also showed that more instructors are recommending the writing center to they're students. 3 In response, the writing center has expanded it's hours: it's now open until 10 PM every night. 4 The writing center also offers online tutoring to students whose schedules make face-to-face meetings difficult. 5 For online tutoring, students can submit their papers by computer when their ready to receive help.

42d The apostrophe is optional in plural abbreviations, dates, and words or characters named as words.

You'll sometimes see apostrophes used to form the plurals of abbreviations (BA's), dates (1900's), and words or characters named as words (*but*'s). However, most current style guides recommend against the apostrophe in these cases.

BAs	PhDs
1990s	2000s

The sentence has too many *buts*.
Two *3s* end the zip code.

Note Italicize or underline a word or character named as a word (see **6** p. 339), but not the added *-s*.

Revise the following paragraph to correct mistakes in the use of apostrophes or any confusion between contractions and possessive pronouns. If a sentence is correct as given, mark the number preceding it.

1 People who's online experiences include blogging, Web cams, and social-networking sites are often used to seeing the details of other peoples private lives. 2 Many are also comfortable sharing they're own opinions, photographs, and videos with family, friend's, and even stranger's. 3 However, they need to realize that employers and even the government can see they're information, too. 4 Employers commonly search for applicants' names on social-networking Web sites such as *Twitter* and *Facebook*. 5 Many companies monitor their employees outbound e-mail. 6 People can take steps to protect their personal information by adjusting the privacy settings on their social-networking pages. 7 They can avoid posting photos of themselves that they wouldnt want an employer to see. 8 They can avoid sending personal e-mail while their at work. 9 Its the individuals responsibility to keep certain information private.

43 Quotation Marks

Chapter essentials

- Use quotation marks around direct quotations (below and next page).
- Use quotation marks around titles of works that are parts of other works (next page).
- Use quotation marks around words used in a special sense (p. 313).
- Do not use quotation marks with the title of your own paper, common nicknames, or slang (p. 314).
- Place quotation marks inside or outside other marks according to standard practice (p. 314).

Visit MyWritingLab™ for more resources on quotation marks.

Quotation marks—either double (" ") or single (' ')—mainly enclose direct quotations and certain titles. Additional information on using quotations appears elsewhere in this book:

- **Using commas with signal phrases introducing quotations.** See p. 293.
- **Using the ellipsis mark and brackets to indicate changes in quotations.** See pp. 318–21.
- **Quoting sources versus paraphrasing or summarizing them.** See 7 pp. 391–94.
- **Integrating quotations into your text.** See 7 pp. 395–99.
- **Acknowledging the sources of quotations to avoid plagiarism.** See 7 p. 404.
- **Formatting long prose quotations and poetry quotations.** See **MLA** p. 480 and **APA** p. 515.

Note Always use quotation marks in pairs, one at the beginning of a quotation and one at the end.

43a Use double quotation marks to enclose direct quotations.

A **direct quotation** reports what someone said or wrote, in the exact words of the original:

> "Life," said the psychoanalyst Karen Horney, "remains a very efficient therapist."

Note Do not use quotation marks with a direct quotation that is set off from your text. See **MLA** p. 480 and **APA** p. 515. Also do not use quotation marks with an **indirect quotation**, which reports what someone said or wrote but not in the exact words.

> The psychoanalyst Karen Horney claimed that life is a good therapist.

43b Use single quotation marks to enclose a quotation within a quotation.

"In formulating any philosophy," Woody Allen writes, "the first consideration must always be: What can we know? Descartes hinted at the problem when he wrote, 'My mind can never know my body, although it has become quite friendly with my leg.'"

Notice that two different quotation marks appear at the end of the sentence—one single (to finish the interior quotation) and one double (to finish the main quotation).

Exercise 43.1 Revising: Double and single quotation marks

Insert double and single quotation marks as needed in the following sentences. Mark the number preceding any sentence that is already correct.

1 Why, the lecturer asked, do we say Bless you! or something else when people sneeze but not acknowledge coughs, hiccups, and other eruptions?
2 She said that sneezes have always been regarded differently.
3 Sneezes feel more uncontrollable than some other eruptions, she said.
4 Unlike coughs and hiccups, she explained, sneezes feel as if they come from inside the head.
5 She concluded, People thus wish to recognize a sneeze, if only with a Gosh.

43c Set off quotations of dialog according to standard practice.

When quoting conversations, begin a new paragraph for each speaker.

"What shall I call you? Your name?" Andrews whispered rapidly, as with a high squeak the latch of the door rose.
"Elizabeth," she said. "Elizabeth."

—Graham Greene, *The Man Within*

When you quote a single speaker for more than one paragraph, put quotation marks at the beginning of each paragraph but at the end of only the last paragraph.

Note Quotation marks are optional for quoting unspoken thoughts or imagined dialog:

I asked myself, "How can we solve this?"
I asked myself, How can we solve this?

43d Use quotation marks around the titles of works that are parts of other works.

Use quotation marks to enclose the titles of works that are published or released within larger works. (See the following box.) Use single quotation marks for a quotation within a quoted title, as in the article title and essay title in the box. And enclose all punctuation in the title within the quotation marks, as with the question mark in the article title.

Titles to be enclosed in quotation marks

Other titles should be italicized or underlined. (See **6** pp. 337–38.)

Song
*"*Lucy in the Sky with Diamonds*"*

Short poem
*"*Stopping by Woods on a Snowy Evening*"*

Short story
*"*The Gift of the Magi*"*

Article in a periodical
*"*Does *'*Scaring*'* Work?*"*

Essay
*"*Joey: A *'*Mechanical Boy*'"*

Unpublished speech
*"*Horses and Healing*"*

Page or work on a Web site
*"*Readers' Page*"* (on the site *Friends of Prufrock*)

Episode of a television or radio program
*"*The Mexican Connection*"* (on *60 Minutes*)

Subdivision of a book
*"*The Mast Head*"* (Chapter 35 of *Moby-Dick*)

Note Some academic disciplines do not require quotation marks for titles within source citations. See **APA** p. 499 and **CSE** p. 538.

Exercise 43.2   Revising: Quotation marks for titles

Insert quotation marks as needed for titles and words in the following sentences. If quotation marks should be used instead of italics, insert them.

1 In Chapter 8, titled *How to Be Interesting*, the author explains the art of conversation.
2 The Beatles' song Let It Be reminds Martin of his uncle.
3 The article that appeared in *Mental Health* was titled *Children of Divorce Ask, "Why?"*
4 In the encyclopedia the discussion under Modern Art fills less than a column.
5 One prizewinning essay, *Cowgirls on Wall Street*, first appeared in *Entrepreneur* magazine.

 43e Quotation marks may enclose words being used in a special sense.

On film sets, movable *"*wild walls*"* make a one-walled room seem four-walled on film.

Note Use italics or underlining for words you are defining. (See **6** p. 339.)

43f Delete quotation marks where they are not required.

Title of your paper

> Not   "The Death Wish in One Poem by Robert Frost"
> But   The Death Wish in One Poem by Robert Frost
> Or   The Death Wish in "Stopping by Woods on a Snowy Evening"

Common nickname

> Not   As President, "Jimmy" Carter preferred to use his nickname.
> But   As President, Jimmy Carter preferred to use his nickname.

Slang or trite expression

Quotation marks will not excuse slang or a trite expression that is inappropriate to your writing. If slang is appropriate, use it without quotation marks.

> Not   We should support the President in his "hour of need" rather than "wimp out on him."
> But   We should give the President the support he needs rather than turn away like cowards.

Place other punctuation marks inside or outside quotation marks according to standard practice.

1 | Commas and periods: Inside quotation marks

Swift uses irony in his essay "A Modest Proposal."

Many readers are shocked to see infants described as "delicious."

"'A Modest Proposal,'" writes one critic, "is so outrageous that it cannot be believed."

Exception When a parenthetical source citation immediately follows a quotation, place any period or comma *after* the citation:

One critic calls the essay "outrageous" (Olms 26).

Partly because of "the cool calculation of its delivery" (Olms 27), Swift's satire still chills a modern reader.

2 | Colons and semicolons: Outside quotation marks

A few years ago the slogan in elementary education was "learning by playing"; now educators are concerned with basic skills.

We all know what is meant by "inflation": more money buys less.

3 | Dashes, question marks, and exclamation points: Inside quotation marks only if part of the quotation

When a dash, question mark, or exclamation point is part of the quotation, place it *inside* quotation marks. Don't use any other punctuation, such as a period or comma:

"But must you—" Marcia hesitated, afraid of the answer.

"Go away!" I yelled.

Did you say, "Who is she?" [When both your sentence and the quotation would end in a question mark or exclamation point, use only the mark in the quotation.]

When a dash, question mark, or exclamation point applies only to the larger sentence, not to the quotation, place it *outside* quotation marks—again, with no other punctuation:

One evocative line in English poetry—"After many a summer dies the swan"—comes from Alfred, Lord Tennyson.

Who said, "Now cracks a noble heart"?

The woman called me "stupid"!

Exercise 43.3 Revising: Quotation marks

Some of the italicized words in the following paragraph are direct quotations or should be quoted titles. Insert quotation marks where italics should not be used. Be sure that other marks of punctuation are correctly placed inside or outside the quotation marks.

1 In the title essay of her book *The Death of the Moth and Other Essays*, Virginia Woolf describes the last moments of a *frail and diminutive body*. 2 An insect's death may seem insignificant, but the moth is, in Woolf's words, *life, a pure bead*. 3 The moth's struggle against death, *indifferent, impersonal*, is heroic. 4 Where else but in such a bit of life could one see a protest so *superb*? 5 At the end of *The Death of the Moth*, Woolf sees the insect lying *most decently and uncomplainingly composed*; in death it finds dignity.

Exercise 43.4 Revising: Quotation marks

Insert quotation marks as needed in the following paragraph. If a sentence is correct as given, mark the number preceding it.

1 In a history class we talked about a passage from Abraham Lincoln's *Gettysburg Address*, delivered on November 19, 1863:

2 Four score and seven years ago our fathers brought forth on this continent, a new nation, conceived in Liberty, and dedicated to the proposition that all men are created equal. 3 Now we are engaged in a great civil war, testing whether that nation, or any nation so conceived and so dedicated, can long endure.

4 What was Lincoln referring to in the first sentence? the teacher asked. 5 Perhaps we should define *score* first. 6 Explaining that a score is twenty years, she said that Lincoln was referring to the document in which the colonies had declared independence from England eighty-seven years earlier, in 1776.

7 One student commented, Lincoln's decision to end slavery is implied in that first sentence. 8 The President was calling on the authority of the Founding Fathers.

9 Lincoln gave the speech at the dedication of the National Cemetery in Gettysburg, Pennsylvania, which was the site of a very bloody Civil War battle, another student added.

10 A third student noted that in the second sentence Lincoln was posing the central question of the war: whether a nation founded on equality can long endure.

44 Other Marks

Chapter essentials

- Use the dash (—) to set off interruptions (below).
- Use parentheses (( )) to enclose parenthetical expressions and labels for lists within sentences (facing page).
- Use the ellipsis mark (. . .) mainly to indicate omissions from quotations (p. 318).
- Use brackets ([ ]) mainly to indicate changes in quotations (p. 321).
- Use the slash (/) to separate options and lines of poetry (p. 321).

Visit MyWritingLab™ for more resources on other punctuation marks.

44a | Use the dash or dashes to indicate shifts and to set off some sentence elements.

The dash (—) is mainly a mark of interruption: it signals a shift, insertion, or break. In your papers, form a dash with two hyphens (--) or use the character called an em dash on your word processor. Do not add extra space around or between the hyphens or around the em dash.

Note When an interrupting element starting with a dash falls in the middle of a sentence, be sure to add the closing dash to signal the end of the interruption. See the first example below.

1 Shifts in tone or thought

The novel—if one can call it that—appeared in 2010.
If the book had a plot—but a plot would be conventional.

2 Nonessential elements

Dashes may be used instead of commas to set off and emphasize modifiers,° parenthetical expressions,° and other nonessential elements,° especially when these elements are internally punctuated:

The qualities Monet painted—sunlight, rich shadows, deep colors—abounded near the rivers and gardens he used as subjects.

Though they are close together—separated by only a few blocks—the two neighborhoods could be in different countries.

°See "Glossary of Terms," **GI** p. 558.

3 Introductory series and concluding series and explanations

Shortness of breath, skin discoloration or the sudden appearance of moles, persistent indigestion, the presence of small lumps—all these may signify cancer. [Introductory series.]

The patient undergoes a battery of tests—imaging, blood work, perhaps even biopsy. [Concluding series.]

Many patients are disturbed by MRI imaging—by the need to keep still for long periods in an exceedingly small space. [Concluding explanation.]

A colon could be used instead of a dash in the last two examples. The dash is more informal.

4 Overuse

Too many dashes can make writing jumpy or breathy.

Not   In all his life—eighty-seven years—my great-grandfather never allowed his picture to be taken—not even once. He claimed the "black box"—the camera—would steal his soul.

But   In all his eighty-seven years, my great-grandfather did not allow his picture to be taken even once. He claimed the "black box"— the camera—would steal his soul.

Exercise 44.1 Revising: Dashes

Insert dashes as needed in the following paragraph.

1 The movie-theater business is undergoing dramatic changes changes that may affect what movies are made and shown. 2 The closing of independent theaters, the control of theaters by fewer and fewer owners, and the increasing ownership of theaters by movie studios and distributors these changes may reduce the availability of noncommercial films. 3 Yet at the same time the number of movie screens is increasing primarily in multiscreen complexes so that smaller films may find more outlets. 4 The number of active movie screens that is, screens showing films or booked to do so is higher now than at any time since World War II. 5 The biggest theater complexes seem to be something else as well art galleries, amusement arcades, restaurants, spectacles.

44b Use parentheses to enclose parenthetical expressions and labels for lists within sentences.

Note Parentheses *always* come in pairs, one before and one after the punctuated material.

1 Parenthetical expressions

Parenthetical expressions include explanations, facts, digressions, and examples that may be helpful or interesting but are not essential to meaning. Parentheses de-emphasize parenthetical expressions. (Commas emphasize them more than parentheses do, and dashes emphasize them still more.)

> The population of Philadelphia (now about 1.5 million) has declined since 1950.

Note Don't put a comma before a parenthetical expression enclosed in parentheses. Punctuation after the parenthetical expression should be placed outside the closing parenthesis.

> **Not** The population of Philadelphia compares with that of Phoenix, (about 1.5 million.)
>
> **But** The population of Philadelphia compares with that of Phoenix (about 1.5 million).

If you enclose a complete sentence in parentheses, capitalize the sentence and place the closing period *inside* the closing parenthesis:

> In general, coaches will tell you that scouts are just guys who can't coach. (But then, so are brain surgeons.) —Roy Blount

2 Labels for lists within sentences

> Outside the Middle East, the countries with the largest oil reserves are (1) Venezuela (297 billion barrels), (2) Canada (197 billion barrels), and (3) Russia (116 billion barrels).

When you set a list off from your text, do not enclose such labels in parentheses.

Exercise 44.2 Revising: Parentheses

Insert parentheses around parenthetical expressions in the following paragraph.

1 Many of those involved in the movie business agree that multiscreen complexes are good for two reasons: 1 they cut the costs of exhibitors, and 2 they offer more choices to audiences. 2 However, those who produce and distribute films and not just the big studios argue that the multiscreen theaters give exhibitors too much power. 3 The major studios are buying movie theaters to gain control over important parts of the distribution process what gets shown and for how much money. 4 For twelve years 1938–50 the federal government forced the studios to sell all their movie theaters. 5 But because they now have more competition television, DVDs, and on-demand services, for instance, the studios are permitted to own theaters.

44c Use the ellipsis mark to indicate omissions from quotations.

The ellipsis mark, consisting of three periods separated by space (. . .), generally indicates an omission from a quotation. All the examples quote from the following passage about environmentalism:

Original quotation

"At the heart of the environmentalist world view is the conviction that human physical and spiritual health depends on sustaining the planet in a relatively unaltered state. Earth is our home in the full, genetic sense, where humanity and its ancestors existed for all the millions of years of their evolution. Natural ecosystems—forests, coral reefs, marine blue waters—maintain the world exactly as we would wish it to be maintained. When we debase the global environment and extinguish the variety of life, we are dismantling a support system that is too complex to understand, let alone replace, in the foreseeable future."

—Edward O. Wilson, "Is Humanity Suicidal?"

1. Omission of the middle of a sentence

"Natural ecosystems . . . maintain the world exactly as we would wish it to be maintained."

2. Omission of the end of a sentence, without source citation

"Earth is our home. . . ." [The sentence period, closed up to the last word, precedes the ellipsis mark.]

3. Omission of the end of a sentence, with source citation

"Earth is our home . . ." (Wilson 27). [The sentence period follows the source citation.]

4. Omission of parts of two or more sentences

Wilson writes, "At the heart of the environmentalist world view is the conviction that human physical and spiritual health depends on sustaining the planet . . . where humanity and its ancestors existed for all the millions of years of their evolution."

5. Omission of one or more sentences

As Wilson puts it, "At the heart of the environmentalist world view is the conviction that human physical and spiritual health depends on sustaining the planet in a relatively unaltered state. . . . When we debase the global environment and extinguish the variety of life, we are dismantling a support system that is too complex to understand, let alone replace, in the foreseeable future."

6. Omission from the middle of a sentence through the end of another sentence

"Earth is our home. . . . When we debase the global environment and extinguish the variety of life, we are dismantling a support system that is too complex to understand, let alone replace, in the foreseeable future."

7. Omission of the beginning of a sentence, leaving a complete sentence

a. Bracketed capital letter

"[H]uman physical and spiritual health," Wilson writes, "depends on sustaining the planet in a relatively unaltered state." [No ellipsis mark is needed because the brackets around the *H* indicate that the letter was not capitalized originally and thus that the beginning of the sentence has been omitted.]

b. Small letter

According to Wilson, "human physical and spiritual health depends on sustaining the planet in a relatively unaltered state." [No ellipsis mark is needed because the small *h* indicates that the beginning of the sentence has been omitted.]

c. Capital letter from the original

One reviewer comments, "... Wilson argues eloquently for the environmentalist world view" (Hami 28). [An ellipsis mark *is* needed because the quoted part of the sentence begins with a capital letter and it is otherwise not clear that the beginning of the original sentence has been omitted.]

8. Use of a word or phrase

Wilson describes the earth as "our home." [No ellipsis mark needed.]

Note these features of the examples:

- **Use an ellipsis mark when it is not otherwise clear that you have left out material from the source,** as when you omit one or more sentences (examples 5 and 6) or when the words you quote form a complete sentence that is different in the original (examples 1–4 and 7c).
- **You don't need an ellipsis mark when it is obvious that you have omitted something,** such as when a bracketed capital letter or a small letter indicates omission (examples 7a and 7b) or when a phrase clearly comes from a larger sentence (example 8).
- **Place an ellipsis mark after any sentence period** *except* **when a parenthetical source citation follows the quotation,** as in examples 3 and 7c. Then the sentence period falls after the citation.

If you omit one or more lines of poetry or paragraphs of prose from a quotation, use a separate line of ellipsis marks across the full width of the quotation to show the omission.

> In "Song: Love Armed" from 1676, Aphra Behn contrasts two lovers' experiences of a romance:
>
> > Love in fantastic triumph sate,
> >
> > Whilst bleeding hearts around him flowed,
> >
> > . . . .
> >
> > But my poor heart alone is harmed,
> >
> > Whilst thine the victor is, and free. (lines 1-2, 15-16)

(See **MLA** p. 480 for the format of such a displayed quotations.)

Exercise 44.3 Using ellipsis marks

Use ellipsis marks and any other needed punctuation to follow the numbered instructions for quoting from the following paragraph.

Women in the sixteenth and seventeenth centuries were educated in the home and, in some cases, in boarding schools. Men were educated at home, in grammar schools, and at the universities. The universities were closed to female students. For women, "learning the Bible," as Elizabeth Joceline puts it, was an impetus to learning to read. To be able to read the Bible in the vernacular was a liberating experience that freed the reader from hearing only the set passages read in the church and interpreted by the church. A Protestant woman was expected to read the scriptures daily, to meditate on them, and to memorize portions of them. In addition, a woman was expected to instruct her entire household in "learning the Bible" by holding instructional and devotional times each day for all household members, including the servants.

      —Charlotte F. Otten, *English Women's Voices, 1540–1700*

1 Quote the fifth sentence, but omit everything from *that freed the reader* to the end.
2 Quote the fifth sentence, but omit the words *was a liberating experience that.*
3 Quote the first and sixth sentences together.

44d Use brackets to indicate changes in quotations.

Brackets have specialized uses in mathematical equations, but their main use for all kinds of writing is to indicate that you have altered a quotation to explain, clarify, or correct it.

"That Chevron station **[**just outside Dallas**]** is one of the busiest in the nation," said a company spokesperson.

The word *sic* (Latin for "in this manner") in brackets indicates that an error in the quotation appeared in the original and was not made by you. Do not underline or italicize *sic* in brackets.

According to the newspaper report, "The car slammed thru **[**sic**]** the railing and into oncoming traffic."

Do not use *sic* to make fun of a writer or to note errors in a passage that is clearly nonstandard.

44e Use the slash between options and between lines of poetry run into the text.

Option
Some teachers oppose pass **/** fail courses.

Poetry
Many readers have sensed a reluctant turn away from death in Frost's lines "The woods are lovely, dark and deep, **/** But I have promises to keep" (13–14).

When separating lines of poetry in this way, leave a space before and after the slash. (See **MLA** p. 480 for more on quoting poetry.)

Exercise 44.4 Revising: Dashes, parentheses, ellipsis marks, brackets, slashes

Insert dashes, parentheses, ellipsis marks, brackets, or slashes as needed in the following paragraph. In some cases, two or more different marks could be correct.

1 "Let all the learned say what they can, 'Tis ready money makes the man." 2 These two lines of poetry by the Englishman William Somerville 1645–1742 may apply to a current American economic problem. 3 Non-American investors with "ready money" pour some of it as much as $1.3 trillion in recent years into the United States. 4 Stocks and bonds, savings deposits, service companies, factories, artworks, political campaigns the investments of foreigners are varied and grow more numerous every day. 5 Proponents of foreign investment argue that it revives industry, strengthens the economy, creates jobs more than 3 million, they say, and encourages free trade among nations. 6 Opponents caution that the risks associated with heavy foreign investment namely decreased profits at home and increased political influence from outside may ultimately weaken the economy. 7 On both sides, it seems, "the learned say, 'Tis ready money makes the man or country." 8 The question is, whose money theirs or ours?

PART 6

Spelling and Mechanics

Spelling and Mechanics

45 Spelling and the Hyphen

Chapter essentials

- Anticipate typical spelling problems, such as misleading pronunciation (below).
- Follow spelling rules for *ie* vs. *ei,* attaching endings or prefixes to words, and forming plurals (p. 327).
- Use the hyphen to form or divide words (p. 331).

Visit MyWritingLab™ for more resources on spelling and the hyphen.

You can train yourself to spell better, and this chapter will tell you how. But you can improve instantly by acquiring three habits:

- **Carefully proofread your writing.**
- **Cultivate a healthy suspicion of your spellings.**
- **Check a dictionary** *every time* **you doubt a spelling.**

45a Anticipate typical spelling problems.

Certain situations, such as misleading pronunciation, commonly lead to misspelling.

1 Pronunciation

In English, pronunciation of words is an unreliable guide to how they are spelled. Pronunciation is especially misleading with **homonyms,** words pronounced the same but spelled differently. Some homonyms and near-homonyms appear in the following box. For other confusing pairs, see "Glossary of Usage" (**Gl** pp. 545–47).

Words commonly confused

accept (to receive)
except (other than)

affect (to have an influence on)
effect (a result)

all ready (prepared)
already (by this time)

allusion (an indirect reference)
illusion (an erroneous belief or
    perception)

ascent (a movement up)
assent (to agree, or an agreement)

bare (unclothed)
bear (to carry, or an animal)

board (a plane of wood)
bored (uninterested)

brake (to stop)
break (to smash)

buy (to purchase)
by (next to)

cite (to quote an authority)
sight (the ability to see)
site (a place)

(continued)

325

Note Many writers capitalize a title denoting very high rank even when it follows a name or is used alone: *Ronald Reagan, past President of the United States.*

46c Capitalize most words in titles and subtitles of works.

Within your text, capitalize all the words in a title *except* the following: articles° (*a, an, the*), *to* in infinitives,° coordinating conjunctions° (*and, but,* etc.), and prepositions° (*with, between,* etc.). Capitalize even these words when they are the first or last word in a title or when they fall after a colon or semicolon.

"Courtship through the Ages"   *Management: A New Theory*
A Diamond Is Forever   "Once More to the Lake"
"Knowing Whom to Ask"   *An End to Live For*
Learning from Las Vegas   *File under Architecture*

Note The style guides of the academic disciplines have their own rules for capitals in titles. For instance, the preceding guidelines reflect MLA style for English and some other humanities. In contrast, APA style for the social sciences and CSE style for the sciences capitalize only the first word and proper names in the titles of books and articles within source citations (see **APA** p. 499 and **CSE** p. 538).

46d Use capitals according to convention in electronic communication.

Online messages written in all-capital letters or with no capital letters are difficult to read. Further, messages in all-capital letters may be taken as rude (see also **2** p. 79).

Exercise 46.1 Revising: Capitals

Revise the following paragraph to correct errors in capitalization, consulting a dictionary as needed. If a sentence is correct as given, mark the number preceding it.

1 San Antonio, texas, is a thriving city in the southwest that has always offered much to tourists interested in the roots of spanish settlement in the new world. 2 Most visitors stop at the Alamo, one of five Catholic Missions built by Priests to convert native americans and to maintain spain's claims in the area. 3 The Alamo is famous for being the site of an 1836 battle that helped to create the republic of Texas. 4 San Antonio has grown tremendously in recent years. 5 The Hemisfair plaza and the San Antonio river link tourist and convention facilities. 6 Restaurants, Hotels, and shops line the River. 7 the haunting melodies of "Una paloma blanca" and "malagueña" lure passing tourists into Casa rio and other mexican restaurants. 8 The university of Texas at San Antonio has expanded, and a Medical Center lies in the Northwest part of the city. 9 A marine attraction on the west side

of San Antonio entertains grandparents, fathers and mothers, and children with the antics of dolphins and seals. 10 The City has attracted high-tech industry, creating a corridor between san antonio and austin.

47 Italics or Underlining

Chapter essentials

Italicize or underline the following:

- Titles of works that appear independently (below).
- Names of ships, aircraft, spacecraft, and trains (next page).
- Foreign words that are not part of the English language (next page).
- Words or characters named as words (p. 339).
- Occasionally, words that you are emphasizing (p. 339).

Visit MyWritingLab™ for more resources on italics or underlining.

Italic type and <u>underlining</u> indicate the same thing: the word or words are being distinguished or emphasized. Always use one or the other consistently throughout a document in both text and source citations:

Text

Growing older is one of several themes that Joan Didion explores in *Blue Nights*.

Source citation (MLA style)

Didion, Joan. *Blue Nights*. New York: Vintage, 2011. Print.

47a	Italicize or underline the titles of works that appear independently.

Within your text, underline or italicize the titles of works that are published, released, or produced separately from other works. (See the following box.) Use quotation marks for all other titles. (See **5** pp. 312–13.)

Titles to be italicized or underlined

Other titles should be placed in quotation marks. (See **5** pp. 312–13.)

Books	Plays
War and Peace	*Hamlet*
And the Band Played On	*The Phantom of the Opera*
	(continued)

Titles to be italicized or underlined
(continued)

Periodicals

Time

Philadelphia Inquirer

Television and radio programs

NBC Sports Hour

Radio Lab

Movies, DVDs, and videos

Schindler's List

How to Relax

Long poems

Beowulf

Paradise Lost

Long musical works

Tchaikovsky's *Swan Lake*

But: Symphony in C

Pamphlets

The Truth about Alcoholism

Works of visual art

Michelangelo's *David*

Picasso's *Guernica*

Computer software

Microsoft Word

Google Chrome

Web sites

YouTube

Friends of Prufrock

Published speeches

Lincoln's *Gettysburg Address*

Exceptions Legal documents, the Bible, the Koran, and their parts are generally not italicized or underlined:

Not   We studied the *Book of Revelation* in the *Bible*.

But   We studied the Book of Revelation in the Bible.

 47b Italicize or underline the names of ships, aircraft, spacecraft, and trains.

Challenger

Apollo XI

Orient Express

Montrealer

Queen Mary 2

Spirit of St. Louis

47c Italicize or underline foreign words that are not part of the English language.

Italicize or underline a foreign expression that has not been absorbed into English. A dictionary will say whether a word is still considered foreign to English.

The scientific name for the brown trout is *Salmo trutta*. [The Latin scientific names for plants and animals are always italicized or underlined.]

The Latin *De gustibus non est disputandum* translates roughly as "There's no accounting for taste."

47d Italicize or underline words or characters named as words.

Use italics or underlining to indicate that you are citing a character or word as a word rather than using it for its meaning. Words you are defining fall under this convention.

> The word *syzygy* refers to a straight line formed by three celestial bodies, as in the alignment of the earth, sun, and moon.
> Some people say *th*, as in *thought*, with a faint *s* or *f* sound.

47e Occasionally, italics or underlining may be used for emphasis.

Italics or underlining can stress an important word or phrase, especially in reporting how someone said something. But use such emphasis very rarely, or your writing may sound immature or hysterical.

47f In electronic communication, use alternatives for italics or underlining.

Some forms of online communication do not allow conventional highlighting such as italics or underlining for the purposes described in this chapter. If you can't use italics or underlining to distinguish book titles and other elements that usually require highlighting, type an underscore before and after the element: *Measurements coincide with those in _Joule's Handbook_*. You can also emphasize words with asterisks before and after: *I *will not* be able to attend.*

Don't use all-capital letters for emphasis; they yell too loudly. (See also p. 336.)

Exercise 47.1 Revising: Italics or underlining

In the following paragraph, underline the words and phrases that need highlighting with italics or underlining and place a check mark next to words and phrases that are highlighted unnecessarily. If a sentence is correct as given, mark the number preceding it.

1 A number of veterans of the war in Vietnam have become prominent writers. 2 Oliver Stone is perhaps the most famous for writing and directing the films Platoon and Born on the Fourth of July. 3 The fiction writer Tim O'Brien has published short stories about the war in Esquire, GQ, and Massachusetts Review. 4 His dreamlike novel Going after Cacciato is about the horrors of combat. 5 Typically for veterans' writing, the novel uses words and phrases borrowed from Vietnamese, such as *di di mau* ("go quickly") or *dinky dau* ("crazy"). 6 Another writer, Philip Caputo, provides a *gripping* account of his service in Vietnam in the book A Rumor of War. 7 Caputo's book was made into a television movie, also titled A Rumor of War. 8 The playwright David Rabe—in such dramas as

The Basic Training of Pavlo Hummel, Streamers, and Sticks and Bones—depicts the effects of war *not only* on the soldiers *but also* on their families. **9** Steve Mason, called "the poet laureate of the Vietnam war," has published two collections of poems on the war: Johnny's Song and Warrior for Peace. **10** And Rod Kane wrote an autobiography about the war, Veterans Day, that received *rave* reviews in the Washington Post.

48 Abbreviations

Chapter essentials

- Abbreviate titles that fall just before and after proper names (below).
- Use only abbreviations that are familiar to your readers (facing page).
- Use *BC, BCE, AD, CE, AM, PM, no.,* and *$* only with specific dates and numbers (facing page).
- Reserve most Latin abbreviations for source citations and parenthetical expressions (facing page).
- Use *Inc., Bros., Co.,* or *&* (for *and*) only in official names of business firms (p. 342).
- Generally spell out units of measurement and names of places, calendar designations, people, and courses (p. 342).

Visit MyWritingLab™ for more resources on abbreviations.

The following guidelines on abbreviations pertain to the text of a nontechnical document. All academic disciplines use abbreviations in source citations, and much technical writing, such as in the sciences and engineering, uses many abbreviations in the document text. For the in-text requirements of the discipline you are writing in, consult one of the style guides listed in **8** pp. 424 (humanities), 427 (social sciences), and 430 (natural and applied sciences).

Usage varies, but writers increasingly omit periods from abbreviations that consist of or end in capital letters: *US, BA, USMC, PhD.* See **5** p. 279 on punctuating abbreviations.

48a Use standard abbreviations for titles immediately before and after proper names.°

Before the name	After the name
Dr. James Hsu	James Hsu, MD
Mr., Mrs., Ms., Hon.,	DDS, DVM, PhD,
St., Rev., Msgr., Gen.	EdD, OSB, SJ, Sr., Jr.

°See "Glossary of Terms," **GI** p. 558.

Do not use abbreviations such as *Rev., Hon., Prof., Rep., Sen., Dr.,* and *St.* (for *Saint*) unless they appear before a proper name.

48b Familiar abbreviations and acronyms are acceptable in most writing.

An **acronym** is an abbreviation that spells a pronounceable word, such as NATO and AIDS. These and other abbreviations using initials are acceptable in most writing as long as they are familiar to readers.

Institutions	LSU, UCLA, TCU
Organizations	CIA, FBI, YMCA, AFL-CIO
Corporations	IBM, CBS, ITT
People	JFK, LBJ, FDR
Countries	US, USA

Note If a name or term (such as *operating room*) appears often in a piece of writing, then its abbreviation (*OR*) can cut down on extra words. Spell out the full term at its first appearance, indicate its abbreviation in parentheses, and then use the abbreviation.

48c Use *BC, BCE, AD, CE, AM, PM, no.,* and *$* only with specific dates a nd numbers.

44 BC	AD 1492	11:26 AM (*or* a.m.)	no. 36 (*or* No. 36)
44 BCE	1492 CE	8:05 PM (*or* p.m.)	$7.41

The abbreviations BC ("before Christ"), BCE ("before the common era"), and CE ("common era") always follow a date. In contrast, AD (*anno Domini,* Latin for "in the year of the Lord") precedes a date.

48d Generally reserve Latin abbreviations for source citations and comments in parentheses.

Latin abbreviations are generally not italicized or underlined.

i.e.	*id est:* that is
cf.	*confer:* compare
e.g.	*exempli gratia:* for example
et al.	*et alii:* and others
etc.	*et cetera:* and so forth
NB	*nota bene:* note well

He said he would be gone a fortnight (i.e., two weeks).
Bloom et al., editors, *Anthology of Light Verse*
Trees, too, are susceptible to disease (e.g., Dutch elm disease).

Some writers avoid these abbreviations in formal writing, even within parentheses.

48e Use *Inc., Bros., Co.,* or *&* (for *and*) only in official names of business firms.

Not	The Santini <u>bros.</u> operate a large moving firm in New York City <u>&</u> environs.
But	The Santini <u>brothers</u> operate a large moving firm in New York City <u>and</u> environs.
Or	Santini <u>Bros.</u> is a large moving firm in New York City <u>and</u> environs.

48f Spell out most units of measurement and names of places, calendar designations, people, and courses.

In most academic, general, and business writing, the following types of words should always be spelled out. (In source citations and technical writing, however, these words are more often abbreviated.)

Units of measurement

The dog is thirty <u>inches</u> [not <u>in.</u>] high.

Geographical names

The publisher is in <u>Massachusetts</u> [not <u>Mass.</u> or <u>MA</u>].

Names of days, months, and holidays

The truce was signed on <u>Tuesday</u> [not <u>Tues.</u>], <u>April</u> [not <u>Apr.</u>] 16.

Names of people

<u>Robert</u> [not <u>Robt.</u>] Frost wrote accessible poems.

Courses of instruction

I'm majoring in <u>political science</u> [not <u>poli. sci.</u>].

Exercise 48.1 Revising: Abbreviations

Revise the following paragraph as needed to correct inappropriate use of abbreviations for nontechnical writing. If a sentence is correct as given, mark the number preceding it.

1 In an issue of *Science* magazine, Dr. Virgil L. Sharpton discusses a theory that could help explain the extinction of dinosaurs. 2 According to the theory, a comet or asteroid crashed into the earth about 65 mill. yrs. ago. 3 The result was a huge crater about 10 km. (6.2 mi.) deep in the Gulf of Mex. 4 Sharpton's measurements suggest that the crater is 50 pct. larger than scientists had previously believed. 5 Indeed, 20-yr.-old drilling cores reveal that the crater is about 186 mi. wide, roughly the size of Conn. 6 The space object was traveling more than 100,000 miles per hour and hit earth with the impact of 100 to 300 megatons of TNT. 7 On impact, 200,000 cubic km. of rock and soil were vaporized or thrown into the air. 8 That's the equivalent of 2.34 bill. cubic ft. of matter. 9 The impact would have created 400-ft. tidal waves across the Atl. Ocean, temps. higher than 20,000 degs., and powerful earthquakes. 10 Sharpton theorizes that the dust, vapor, and smoke from this impact blocked the sun's rays for mos., cooled the earth, and thus resulted in the death of the dinosaurs.

49 Numbers

Chapter essentials

- Use numerals according to standard practice in your field (below).
- Use numerals according to convention for dates, addresses, and other information (next page).
- Spell out numbers that begin sentences (next page).

Visit MyWritingLab™ for more resources on numbers.

Expressing numbers in numerals (*28*) or in words (*twenty-eight*) is often a matter of style in a discipline: the technical disciplines more often prefer numerals, and the nontechnical disciplines more often prefer words. All disciplines use many more numerals in source citations than in the document text.

49a Use numerals according to standard practice in the field you are writing in.

Always use numerals for numbers that require more than two words to spell out:

> The leap year has <u>366</u> days.
> The population of Minot, North Dakota, is about <u>32,800</u>.

In nontechnical academic writing, spell out numbers of one or two words. A hyphenated number may be considered one word.

> The waiting period is <u>eighteen</u> to <u>twenty-four</u> days.
> The ball game drew <u>forty-two thousand</u> people.

In much business writing, use numerals for all numbers over ten: *five reasons, 11 participants*. In technical academic and business writing, such as in science and engineering, use numerals for all numbers over ten, and use numerals for zero through nine when they refer to exact measurements: *2 liters, 1 hour*. (Consult one of the style guides listed in **8** pp. 443 and 447 for more details.)

Notes Use a combination of numerals and words for round numbers over a million: *26 million, 2.45 billion*. Use either all numerals or all words when several numbers appear together in a passage, even if convention would require a mixture. And avoid using two numbers in a row, which can be confusing:

> Confusing   Out of 530, 101 children caught the virus.
> Clear   Out of 530 <u>children</u>, 101 caught the virus.

CULTURE LANGUAGE In standard American English, a comma separates the numerals in long numbers (*26,000*), and a period functions as a decimal point (*2.06*).

343

49b Use numerals according to convention for dates, addresses, and other information.

Days and years		Decimals, percentages, and fractions	
June 18, 1985	AD 12		
456 BCE	2010	22.5	3½
		48% (or 48 percent)	

The time of day
9:00 AM   3:45 PM

Scores and statistics
21 to 7   a ratio of 8 to 1
a mean of 26

Addresses
355 Clinton Avenue
Washington, DC 20036

Pages, chapters, volumes, acts, scenes, lines
Chapter 9, page 123
Hamlet, act 5, scene 3

Exact amounts of money
$3.5 million $4.50

Exceptions Round dollar or cent amounts of only a few words may be expressed in words: *seventeen dollars*; *sixty cents*. When the word *o'clock* is used for the time of day, also express the number in words: *two o'clock* (not *2 o'clock*).

49c Spell out numbers that begin sentences.

For clarity, spell out any number that begins a sentence. If the number requires more than two words, reword the sentence so that the number falls later and can be expressed as a numeral.

Not   3.9 billion people live in Asia.
But   The population of Asia is 3.9 billion.

Exercise 49.1 Revising: Numbers

Revise the following paragraphs so that numbers are used appropriately for nontechnical writing. If a sentence is correct as given, mark the number preceding it.

1 The planet Saturn is nine hundred million miles, or nearly one billion five hundred million kilometers, from the sun. 2 Saturn orbits the sun only two and four-tenths times during the average human life span. 3 As a result, a year on Saturn equals almost thirty of our years. 4 The planet travels in its orbit at about twenty-one thousand six hundred miles per hour.

5 Saturn is huge: more than seventy-two thousand miles in diameter, compared to Earth's eight-thousand-mile diameter. 6 Saturn is also very cold, with an average temperature of minus two hundred and eighteen degrees Fahrenheit, compared to Earth's fifty-nine degrees Fahrenheit. 7 Saturn is cold because of its great distance from the sun and because its famous rings reflect almost 70 percent of the sunlight that approaches the planet. 8 The ring system is almost forty thousand miles wide, beginning 8800 miles from the planet's visible surface and ending forty-seven thousand miles from that surface.

PART 7

Research Writing

PART 7

Research Writing

50 Research Strategy

Research writing gives you a chance to work like a detective solving a case. The mystery is the answer to a question you care about. The search for the answer leads you to consider what others think about your subject, but you do more than simply report their views. You build on them to develop and support your own opinion, and ultimately you become an expert in your own right.

Your investigation will be more productive and enjoyable if you take the steps described in this chapter.

50a Planning your work

Research writing is a *writing* process:

- **You work within a particular situation of subject, purpose, audience, genre, and other factors** (see **1** pp. 3–9).
- **You gather ideas and information about your subject** (**1** pp. 9–14).
- **You focus and arrange your ideas** (**1** pp. 14–22).
- **You draft to explore your meaning** (**1** pp. 24–25).
- **You revise to develop and shape your writing** (**1** pp. 27–32).
- **You edit to refine and polish your writing** (**1** pp. 34–37).

Although the process seems neatly sequential in this list, you know from experience that the stages overlap—that, for instance, you may begin drafting before you've gathered all the information you expect to find, and then while drafting you may discover a source that causes you to rethink your approach. Anticipating the process of research writing can free you to be flexible in your search and open to discoveries.

A thoughtful plan and systematic procedures can help you follow through on the diverse activities of research writing. One step is to make a schedule like the one on the next page that apportions the available time to the necessary work. You can estimate that each segment marked off by a horizontal line will occupy *roughly* one-quarter of the total time—for example, a week in a four-week assignment or two weeks in an eight-week assignment. The most unpredictable segments are the first two, so get started early enough to accommodate the unexpected.

Complete by:

_____ 1. Setting a schedule and beginning a research journal (here and below)

_____ 2. Finding a researchable subject and question (facing page)

_____ 3. Setting goals for sources (p. 350)

_____ 4. Finding print and electronic sources (p. 356), and making a working, annotated bibliography (p. 354)

_____ 5. Evaluating and synthesizing sources (pp. 375, 387)

_____ 6. Gathering information from sources (p. 390), often using summary, paraphrase, and direct quotation (p. 391)

_____ 7. Taking steps to avoid plagiarism (p. 400)

_____ 8. Developing a thesis statement and creating a structure (p. 410)

_____ 9. Drafting the paper (p. 411), integrating summaries, paraphrases, and direct quotations into your ideas (p. 395)

_____ 10. Citing sources in your text (p. 408)

_____ 11. Revising and editing the paper (p. 411)

_____ 12. Finalizing text citations and preparing the list of works cited or references (p. 408)

_____ 13. Preparing the final manuscript (p. 412)

_____ Final paper due

50b Keeping a research journal

While working on a research project, carry a notebook or a computer with you at all times to use as a **research journal,** a place to record your activities and ideas. (See 1 pp. 9–10 on journal keeping.) In the journal's dated entries, you can write about the sources you consult, the leads you want to pursue, and any difficulties you encounter. Most important, you can record your thoughts about sources, leads, dead ends, new directions, relationships, and anything else that strikes you. The very act of writing in the journal can expand and clarify your thinking.

Note The research journal is the place to track and develop your own ideas. To avoid mixing up your thoughts and those of others, keep separate notes on what your sources actually say. (See p. 390.)

50c Finding a researchable subject and question

Before reading this section, review the suggestions given in Chapter 1 for finding and narrowing a writing subject (1 pp. 5–6). Generally, the same procedure applies to writing any kind of research paper. However, selecting and limiting a subject for a research paper can present special opportunities and problems. And before you proceed with your subject, you'll want to transform it into a question that can guide your search for sources.

1 Appropriate subject

Seek a research subject that you want to explore and learn more about. (It may be a subject you've already written about without the benefit of research.) Starting with your own views will motivate you, and you will be a participant in a dialog when you begin examining sources.

When you settle on a subject, ask the following questions about it. For each requirement, there are corresponding pitfalls.

■ **Are ample sources of information available on the subject?**

Avoid a very recent subject, such as a newly announced medical discovery or a breaking story in today's news, unless you are placing it in a larger context.

■ **Does the subject encourage research in the kinds and number of sources required by the assignment?**

Avoid (*a*) a subject that depends entirely on personal opinion and experience, such as the virtues of your hobby, and (*b*) a subject that requires research in only one source, such as a straight factual biography.

■ **Will the subject lead you to an objective assessment of sources and to defensible conclusions?**

Avoid a subject that rests entirely on belief or prejudice, such as when human life begins or why women (or men) are superior. Your readers are unlikely to be swayed from their own beliefs.

■ **Does the subject suit the length of paper assigned and the time given for research and writing?**

Avoid a broad subject that has too many sources to survey adequately, such as a major event in history.

2 Research question

Asking a question or questions about your subject opens avenues of inquiry. In asking questions, you can consider what you already know about the subject, explore what you don't know, and begin to develop your own perspective. (See below for suggestions on using your own knowledge.)

Try to narrow your research question so that you can answer it in the time and space you have available. The question *How does human activity affect the environment?* is very broad, encompassing issues as diverse as pollution, distribution of resources, climate change, population growth, land use, biodiversity, and the ozone layer. In contrast, the question *How can buying environmentally friendly products help the environment?* or *How, if at all, should carbon emissions be taxed?* is much narrower. Each question also requires more than a simple *yes* or *no* answer, so that answering, even tentatively, demands thought about pros and cons, causes and effects.

As you read and write, your question will probably evolve to reflect your increasing knowledge of the subject, and eventually its answer will become your main idea, or thesis statement (see p. 410).

50d Setting goals for sources

Before you start looking for sources, consider what you already know about your subject and where you are likely to find information on it.

1 Your own knowledge

Discovering what you already know about your topic will guide you in discovering what you don't know. Take some time at the start to write down everything you know about the subject: facts you have learned, opinions you have heard or read elsewhere, and of course your own opinions. Use one of the discovery techniques discussed in **1** pp. 9–14 to explore and develop your ideas: keeping a journal, observing your surroundings, freewriting, brainstorming, drawing, or asking questions.

When you've explored your thoughts, make a list of questions for which you don't have answers, whether factual (*How much do Americans spend on green products?*) or more open-ended (*Are green products worth the higher prices?*). These questions will give you clues about the sources you need to look for first.

2 Kinds of sources

For many research projects, you'll want to consult a mix of sources, as described on the next two pages. You may start by seeking the outlines of your topic—the range and depth of opinions about it—in reference works and articles in popular periodicals or through a Web search. Then, as you refine your views and your research question, you'll move on to more specialized sources, such as scholarly books and periodicals and your own interviews or surveys. (See pp. 360–74 for more on each kind of source.)

The mix of sources you choose depends heavily on your subject. For example, a paper on green consumerism would require the use of very recent sources because environmentally friendly products are fairly new to the marketplace. Your mix of sources may also be specified by your instructor or limited by the requirements of your assignment.

Sources through the library or the open Web

The print and electronic sources available at your library or through its Web site—mainly reference works, books, and articles in periodicals—have two big advantages over most of what you'll find on the open Web: library sources are cataloged and indexed for easy retrieval; and they are generally reliable, having been screened first by their publishers and then by the library's staff. In contrast, the retrieval systems of the open Web are more difficult to use effectively, and the sources themselves tend to be less reliable because most do not pass through any screening before being posted. (There are many exceptions, such as online scholarly journals and reference works. But these sources are generally available through your library's Web site as well.)

Most instructors expect research writers to consult library sources. But they'll accept sources from the open Web, too, if you have used them judiciously. Even with its disadvantages, the Internet can be a valuable resource for primary sources, current information, and a diversity of views. For guidelines on evaluating both library and open-Web sources, see pp. 375–87.

Primary and secondary sources

Use **primary sources** when they are required by the assignment or are appropriate for your subject. Primary sources are documents and objects that were created during the period you are studying. They consist of firsthand or original accounts, such as works of literature, historical documents (letters, speeches, and so on), eyewitness reports (including articles by journalists who are on location), reports on experiments or surveys conducted by the writer, and sources you originate (interviews, experiments, observations, or correspondence).

Many assignments will allow you to use **secondary sources,** which report and analyze information drawn from other sources, often primary ones. Examples include a reporter's summary of a controversial issue, a historian's account of a battle, a critic's reading of a poem, and a psychologist's evaluation of several studies. (Sometimes a secondary source may actually be your primary source, as when you analyze a historian's account or respond to a critic's interpretation.) In themselves, secondary sources may contain helpful summaries and interpretations that direct, support, and extend your own thinking. However, most research-writing assignments expect your own ideas to go beyond those in such sources.

Scholarly and popular sources

The scholarship of acknowledged experts is essential for depth, authority, and specificity. Most instructors expect students to emphasize scholarly sources in their research. But the general-interest views and information of popular sources can provide everyday examples, anecdotes, and stories that can help you apply scholarly approaches to your subject, and they can provide context for very recent topics.

Use the following guidelines to determine whether a source is scholarly or popular.

- **Check the title.** Is it technical, or does it use a general vocabulary?
- **Check the publisher.** Is it a scholarly journal (such as *Cultural Geographies*) or a publisher of scholarly books (such as Harvard University Press), or is it a popular magazine (such as *Consumer Reports* or *Time*) or a publisher of popular books (such as Little, Brown)? For more on the distinction between scholarly and popular sources, see pp. 362 and 376.
- **Check the length of periodical articles.** Scholarly articles are generally much longer than magazine and newspaper articles.
- **Check the author.** Search the Web for the author. Is he or she an expert on the topic?
- **Check the URL.** A Web site's URL, or electronic address, includes an abbreviation that can tell you something about the origin of the source: scholarly sources usually end in *edu*, *org*, or *gov*, while popular sources usually end in *com*. (See p. 381 for more on types of online sources.)
- **Check for sources.** Scholarly authors cite their sources formally in notes or a bibliography.

Older and newer sources

Check the publication date. For most subjects a combination of older, established sources (such as books) and current sources (such as newspaper articles, interviews, or Web sites) will provide both background and up-to-date information. Only historical subjects or very current subjects require an emphasis on one extreme or another.

Impartial and biased sources

Seek a range of viewpoints. Sources that attempt to be impartial can offer an overview of your subject and trustworthy facts. Sources with clear biases can give you a range of views about a subject and enrich your understanding of it. Of course, to discover bias, you may have to read the source carefully (see pp. 375–87); but you can infer quite a bit just from a bibliographical listing.

- **Check the author.** Do a Web search to find out more about the author. Is he or she a respected researcher (thus more likely to be objective) or a leading proponent of a certain view (less likely to be objective)?
- **Check the title.** It may reveal something about point of view. (Consider these contrasting titles: "Go for the Green" versus "Green Consumerism and the Struggle for Northern Maine.")

Sources with helpful features

Depending on your topic and how far along your research is, you may want to look for sources with features such as illustrations (which can clarify important concepts), bibliographies (which can direct you to other sources), and indexes (which can help you develop keywords for electronic searches; see pp. 358–59).

50e Keeping a working, annotated bibliography

To track where sources are, compile a **working bibliography** as you uncover possibilities. When you have a substantial file—say, ten to thirty sources—you can decide which ones seem most promising and look them up first.

1 Source information

When you turn in your paper, you will be expected to attach a list of the sources you have used. Your list must include all the information needed to find the sources, in a format readers can understand. (See pp. 408–09.) The box on the next page shows the information you should record for each type of source so that you will not have to retrace your steps later.

Note Recording source information meticulously will help you avoid careless plagiarism because you will be less likely to omit the information in your paper. Careful records will also help you avoid omitting or mixing up numbers, dates, and other data when it's time to write your citations. This book describes four documentation styles: MLA (see **MLA** p. 435), APA (see **APA** p. 494), Chicago (see **Chic** p. 524), and CSE (see **CSE** p. 536). For other styles, consult one of the guides listed in **8** pp. 427 and 430.

2 Annotations

Your instructor may ask you to prepare an **annotated bibliography** as part of the research process or as a separate assignment.

Information for a working bibliography

For a print or electronic book

Library call number
Name(s) of author(s), editor(s), translator(s), or others listed
Title and subtitle
Publication data: (1) place of publication; (2) publisher's name; (3) date of publication; (4) title of any database or Web site used to reach the book; (5) sponsor and date of any Web site used to find the book
Other important data, such as edition or volume number
Medium (print, Web, Kindle file, etc.)
Date you consulted the book (if online)

For periodical articles in print, in online databases, or in Web journals

Name(s) of author(s)
Title and subtitle of article
Title of periodical
Publication data: (1) volume number and issue number (if any) in which the article appears; (2) date of issue; (3) page numbers on which article appears
Title of any database used to reach the source
Medium (print, Web, etc.)
Date you consulted the source (if online)

For Web material and other electronic sources

Name(s) of author(s)
Title and subtitle of source
Title of Web site
Publication data: sponsor and date of any Web site used to reach the source
Any publication data for the source in another medium (print, film, etc.)
Format of online source (Web site or page, podcast, e-mail, etc.)
Date you consulted the source
Title of any database used to reach the source
Complete URL (see the note below)
Digital Object Identifier, if any (see the note below)
Medium (usually Web)

For other sources

Name(s) of author(s) or others listed, such as a government agency or a recording artist
Title of the work
Format, such as unpublished letter or live performance
Publication or production data: (1) publisher's or producer's name; (2) date of publication, release, or production; (3) identifying numbers (if any)
Medium (print, typescript, etc.)

Note Documentation styles vary in requiring URLs and DOIs (Digital Object Identifiers) for citations of electronic sources. (See **APA** p. 499 for more on DOIs.) Even if you don't need the complete URL or DOI in your final citation of a source, record it anyway so that you'll be able to track the source down if you want to consult it again.

Creating annotations converts your bibliography into a tool for assessing sources, helping you discover gaps that may remain in your sources and helping you decide which sources to pursue in depth.

As you find and evaluate each source, record not only its publication information but also the following:

- **What you know about the content of the source.** Periodical databases and book catalogs generally include abstracts, or summaries, of sources that can help with this part of the annotation.
- **How you think the source may be helpful in your research.** Does it offer expert opinion, statistics, an important example, or a range of views? Does it place your subject in a historical, social, or economic context?
- **Your assessment of the source.** Consider how reliable the source is and how it might fit into your research. (See pp. 375–89 for more on evaluating and synthesizing sources.)

Taking the time with your annotations can help you discover gaps that may remain in your sources and will help you decide which sources to pursue in depth. The following entry from an annotated bibliography shows one student's annotation of a source, including a summary, a note on the source features the student thought would be helpful, and an assessment of the source's strength and weakness for his purposes.

Annotated bibliography entry with assessment

Gore, Al. *Our Choice: A Plan to Solve the Climate Crisis*. Emmaus: Rodale, 2009. Print.

> Publication information for source

A sequel to Gore's *An Inconvenient Truth* that emphasizes solutions to global warming. Expands on the argument that global warming is a serious threat, with recent examples of natural disasters. Proposes ways that governments, businesses, and individuals can reduce or reverse the risks of global warming. Includes helpful summaries of scientific studies, short essays on various subjects, and dozens of images, tables, charts, and graphs.

> Summary of source (from working bibliography)
>
> Ideas on use of source

Compelling overview of possible solutions, with lots of data that seem thorough and convincing. But the book is aimed at a general audience and doesn't have formal source citations. Can use it for broad concepts, but for data I'll have to track down Gore's scholarly sources.

> Assessment of source

Visit MyWritingLab™ for more resources on finding sources.

Your library and a computer connected to the Internet give you access to an almost infinite range of sources. The challenge, of course, is to find the most worthy and appropriate sources for your needs and then to use them effectively. This chapter shows you how.

Note As you look for sources, avoid the temptation to seek a "silver bullet"—that is, to locate two or three perfect sources that already say everything you want to say about your subject. Instead of merely repeating others' ideas, read and synthesize many sources so that you enter into a dialog with them and develop your own ideas. For more on synthesis, see pp. 387–89.

51a Starting with your library's Web site

As you conduct academic research, your library's Web site will be your gateway to ideas and information. Always start with your library's Web site, not with a public search engine such as *Google*.

Advantages of a library search

The library site will lead you to vast resources, including books, periodical articles, and reference works that aren't available on the open Web. More important, every source you find on the library site will have passed through filters to ensure its value. A scholarly journal article, for instance, undergoes at least three successive reviews: subject-matter experts first deem it worth publishing in the journal; then a database vendor deems the journal worth including in the database; and finally your school's librarians deem the database worth subscribing to.

Note Start with the library's Web site, but don't stop there. Many books, periodicals, and other excellent sources are available only on library shelves, not online, and most instructors expect research papers to be built to some extent on these resources. When you spot promising print sources while browsing the library's online databases, make records of them and then look them up at the library.

Disadvantages of an open-Web search

Google and other public search engines do have benefits: they may seem more user-friendly than the library's Web site, they can help you get a quick sense of how your subject is talked about, and they may locate some reliable and relevant sources for your research.

However, for academic research these search engines have more drawbacks than benefits. They are not geared toward academic research, so most of the sources they find will be unusable for your project. And the sources will not be filtered as library materials are: no one ensures their basic reliability. In the end, a library Web search will be more efficient and more effective than an open-Web search. (For help with evaluating sources from any resource, see pp. 375–87.)

51b Searching electronically

An electronic search requires planning. A search that is too broad can miss helpful sources while returning hundreds, even thousands, of irrelevant sources. A search that is too narrow can exclude important sources.

1 Print and electronic resources available through your library

Your library's Web site will lead you to many kinds of print and electronic resources suitable for academic research.

- **The library catalog.** Searchable from the library's Web site, the catalog is a database that lists all the resources the library owns or subscribes to. At many libraries, the catalog finds books, e-books, and the titles of periodicals but not individual articles within online databases. At other libraries, the catalog functions as a centralized search engine that covers all the library's holdings and subscriptions and locates articles in online databases. Either type of catalog may also include the holdings at other libraries in your college's system or in your state.
- **Online databases.** Also searchable from the library's Web site, databases include a wide range of source types, from journal collections and full-text resources to reference works and primary sources. Your library's Web site will likely list databases

alphabetically and by discipline. (You may discover some of the same databases on the open Web, but unless you retrieve articles through your library's Web site, you will probably have to pay for what you find.) As you use a database, be aware of what it does and does not offer, and keep track of whether you are looking at an article, a book, an archival document, or something else. Ask a librarian if you're not sure. For help with selecting databases, see p. 363.

■ **Research guides.** Some libraries provide guides that direct users to resources on particular subjects, such as twentieth-century English literature or social psychology.

■ *Google Scholar.* Available on the open Web, *Google Scholar* is a search engine that seeks out scholarly books and articles. It is particularly useful for subjects that range across disciplines, for which discipline-specific databases can be too limited. *Google Scholar* can connect to your library's holdings if you set it to do so under Scholar Preferences. Keep in mind, however, that *Google Scholar*'s searches may list books that are unavailable to you and articles that you cannot obtain in full text. Your library is still the best resource for material that is easily available to you, so begin there.

2 | Development of search terms

Take time early in your research to develop search terms that describe your subject effectively. For this step, it helps to understand the difference between keywords and subject headings:

■ **Keywords** are the terms you type when you begin a search. In a library catalog or an online database, a keyword search looks for that word (or words) in titles, authors, and subject headings and sometimes within lists of keywords supplied by the author or in user tags added by readers. On the open Web, a keyword search looks for your terms anywhere in the record. In any case, the process is entirely automatic, so as a researcher your challenge is to find keywords that others have used to describe the same subject.

■ **Subject headings** (also called *subject terms*) tell you what a source is about. They are assigned to books and articles by people who have read the sources and categorized them, so they can be more efficient than keywords at finding relevant sources. To find subject headings, use and refine your keywords until you find a promising source. On the source's full record, check the list of subject headings to see how the source is categorized. (See p. 365 for an illustration.) Building the subject headings that most closely match your subject into your search terms can improve your searches.

3 Refinement of search terms

Databases, catalogs, and search engines provide systems that you can use to refine your search terms for your purposes. The basic operations appear in the following box, but resources do differ. For instance, some assume that *AND* should link keywords, while others provide options specifying "Must contain all the words" and other equivalents for the operations in the box. You can learn a search engine's system by consulting its Advanced Search page.

Ways to refine keywords

Most databases and many search engines work with **Boolean operators,** terms or symbols that allow you to expand or limit your keywords and thus your search.

■ **Use *AND* or + to narrow the search by including only sources that use all the given words.** The keywords *green AND products* request only the sources in the shaded area.

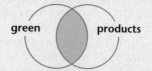

■ **Use *NOT* or – ("minus") to narrow the search by excluding irrelevant words.** The keywords *green AND products NOT guide* exclude sources that use the word *guide*:

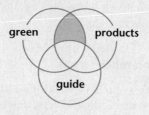

(continued)

Ways to refine keywords
(continued)

- **Use *OR* to broaden the search by giving alternative keywords.** The keywords *green AND products OR goods* allow for sources that use a synonym for *products*:

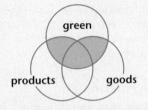

- **Use quotation marks or parentheses to form search phrases.** For instance, *"green products"* requests the exact phrase, not the separate words. Only sources using *green products* would turn up.
- **Use wild cards to permit different versions of the same word.** In *consum**, for instance, the wild card * indicates that sources may include *consume, consumer, consumerism,* and *consumption* as well as *consumptive, consumedly,* and *consummate.* The example suggests that you have to consider all the variations allowed by a wild card and whether it opens up your search too much. If you seek only two or three from many variations, you may be better off using *OR: consumption OR consumerism.* (Note that some systems use ?, :, or + for a wild card instead of *.)
- **Be sure to spell your keywords correctly.** Some search tools will look for close matches or approximations, but correct spelling gives you the best chance of finding relevant sources.

Note You will probably have to use trial and error in developing your terms because library catalogs, databases, and search engines may all use slightly different words to describe your subject. If you are having trouble finding appropriate sources, try using subject headings, and be flexible in your search terms. The process is not busywork—far from it. Besides leading you eventually to worthwhile sources, it can also teach you a great deal about your subject: how you can or should narrow it, how it is and is not described by others, what others consider interesting or debatable about it, and what the major arguments are. See pp. 367–68 for an example of a student's keyword search of the Web.

51c | Finding reference works

Reference works, available through your library and on the open Web, include encyclopedias, dictionaries, digests, bibliographies, indexes, atlases, almanacs, and handbooks. Your research *must* go beyond these sources, but they can help you decide whether your topic really interests you and whether it meets the requirements for a research paper (p. 349). Preliminary research in reference works can also help you develop keywords for electronic searches and can direct you to more detailed sources on your topic.

Note The Web-based encyclopedia *Wikipedia* (at *wikipedia.org*) is one of the largest reference sites on the Internet. Like any encyclopedia, *Wikipedia* can provide background information for research on a topic. But unlike other encyclopedias, *Wikipedia* is a **wiki,** a kind of Web site that can be contributed to or edited by anyone. Ask your instructor whether *Wikipedia* is an acceptable source before you use it. If you do use it, you must carefully evaluate any information you find, following the guidelines on pp. 375–85.

51d Finding books

Your library's catalog is searchable via the library's Web site. Unless you seek a specific author or title, you'll want to search for books by using keywords or subject headings. In a keyword search, you start with your own search terms. In a subject-heading search, you use the headings on the records of promising sources to locate similar sources. The screen shot below shows the complete record for a book, including the subject headings and the call number for finding the book on the library's shelves.

Full catalog record

Building the green economy : success stories from the grassroots

Title and subtitle

Author: Kevin Danaher 1950-
Shannon Biggs ; Jason Mark — Authors

Subjects: Sustainable development -- Citizen participation ; Environmentalism -- Economic aspects ; Green products — Subject headings for book

Publisher: Sausalito, CA : PoliPointPress : Distributed by Ingram Publisher Services — Publisher and date

Creation Date: c2007

Description: 282 p. ; 24 cm..

Language: English

Format: Book

Identifier: ISBN9780977825363 (alk. paper);ISBN0977825361 : — Library call number

Available (HC79.E5 D3252 2007) (Get It)

51e Finding periodicals

Periodicals include newspapers, academic journals, and magazines, either print or online. Newspapers are useful for detailed accounts of past and current events. Journals and magazines can be harder to distinguish, but their differences are important. Most college instructors expect students' research to rely more on journals than on magazines.

Journals	Magazines
Examples	
American Anthropologist, Journal of Black Studies, Journal of Chemical Education	*The New Yorker, Time, Rolling Stone, People*
Availability	
Mainly college and university libraries, either on library shelves or in online databases	Public libraries, newsstands, bookstores, the open Web, and online databases
Purpose	
Advance knowledge in a particular field	Express opinion, inform, or entertain
Authors	
Specialists in the field	May or may not be specialists in their subjects
Readers	
Often specialists in the field	Members of the general public or a subgroup with a particular interest
Source citations	
Source citations always included	Source citations rarely included
Length of articles	
Usually long, ten pages or more	Usually short, fewer than ten pages
Frequency of publication	
Quarterly or less often	Weekly, biweekly, or monthly
Pagination of issues	
May be paged separately (like a magazine) or may be paged sequentially throughout an annual volume, so that issue number 3 (the third issue of the year) could open on page 373	Paged separately, each beginning on page 1

1 Periodical databases

Periodical databases index articles in journals, magazines, and newspapers. Often these databases include abstracts, or summaries, of the articles, and they may offer the full text of the articles as well. Your library subscribes to many periodical databases and to services that offer multiple databases. (See pp. 365–66 for a list.) Most databases will be searchable through the library's Web site.

Selection of databases

To decide which databases to consult, you'll need to consider what you're looking for:

- **Does your research subject span more than one discipline?** Then start with a broad database such as *Academic Search Complete, ProQuest Research Library,* or *JSTOR.* A broad database covers many subjects and disciplines but does not index the full range of periodicals in each subject. If your library offers a centralized search engine that searches across multiple databases, you can start there.
- **Does your research subject focus on a single discipline?** Then start with a discipline-specific database such as *Historical Abstracts, MLA International Bibliography, Biological Abstracts,* or *Education Search Complete.* A specific database covers few subjects but includes most of the available periodicals in each subject. If you don't know the name of an appropriate database, the library's Web site probably lists possibilities by discipline.
- **Do you need primary sources?** Some specialized databases collect primary sources—for instance, historical newspapers, literary works not available in print, diaries, letters, music recordings, album liner notes. To determine whether you have access to such materials through your library, consult the list of databases on your library's Web site and read the descriptions to find out what each offers.
- **Which databases most likely include the kinds of resources you need?** The Web sites of most libraries provide lists of databases organized alphabetically and by discipline. Some libraries also provide research guides, which list potentially helpful databases for your search terms. To determine each database's focus, check the description of the database or the list of indexed resources. The description will also tell you the time period the database covers, so you'll know whether you also need to consult older print indexes at the library.

Database searches

When you first search a database, use your own keywords to locate sources. The procedure is illustrated in the three screen shots shown on the next two pages. Your goal is to find at least one source that seems just right for your subject, so that you can see what subject headings the database itself uses for such sources. Picking up one or more of those headings for your search terms will focus and speed your search.

Note Many databases allow you to limit your search to so-called peer-reviewed or refereed journals—that is, scholarly journals whose articles have been reviewed before publication by experts in the field and then revised by the author. Limiting your search to peer-reviewed journals can help you navigate huge databases that might otherwise return scores of unusable articles.

The use of abstracts

In screen 3 on the next page, the full article record shows a key feature of many databases' periodical listings: an **abstract** that summarizes the article. By describing research methods, conclusions,

---

1. Initial keyword search of a periodical database

---

2. Partial keyword search results

3. Full article record with abstract

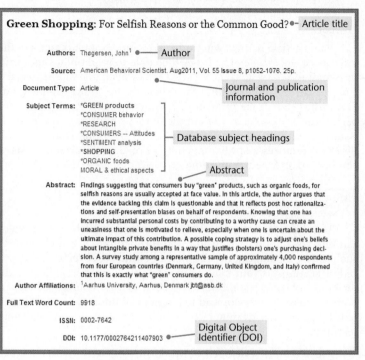

Green Shopping: For Selfish Reasons or the Common Good? •— Article title

Authors:	Thøgersen, John[1] •——— Author
Source:	American Behavioral Scientist. Aug2011, Vol. 55 Issue 8, p1052-1076. 25p. — Journal and publication information
Document Type:	Article
Subject Terms:	*GREEN products *CONSUMER behavior *RESEARCH *CONSUMERS -- Attitudes — Database subject headings *SENTIMENT analysis *SHOPPING *ORGANIC foods MORAL & ethical aspects

— Abstract

Abstract: Findings suggesting that consumers buy "green" products, such as organic foods, for selfish reasons are usually accepted at face value. In this article, the author argues that the evidence backing this claim is questionable and that it reflects post hoc rationalizations and self-presentation biases on behalf of respondents. Knowing that one has incurred substantial personal costs by contributing to a worthy cause can create an uneasiness that one is motivated to relieve, especially when one is uncertain about the ultimate impact of this contribution. A possible coping strategy is to adjust one's beliefs about intangible private benefits in a way that justifies (bolsters) one's purchasing decision. A survey study among a representative sample of approximately 4,000 respondents from four European countries (Denmark, Germany, United Kingdom, and Italy) confirmed that this is exactly what "green" consumers do.

Author Affiliations:	[1]Aarhus University, Aarhus, Denmark jbt@asb.dk
Full Text Word Count:	9918
ISSN:	0002-7642
DOI:	10.1177/0002764211407903 •— Digital Object Identifier (DOI)

and other information, an abstract can tell you whether you want to pursue an article and thus save you time. However, the abstract cannot replace the actual article. If you want to use the work as a source, you must consult the full text.

Helpful databases

The following list includes databases to which academic libraries commonly subscribe. Some of these databases cover much the same material, so your library may not subscribe to all of them.

> *EBSCOhost Academic Search.* A periodical index covering magazines and journals in the social sciences, sciences, arts, and humanities. Many articles are available full-text.
>
> *InfoTrac Expanded Academic.* The Gale Group's general periodical index covering the social sciences, sciences, arts, and humanities as well as national news periodicals. It includes full-text articles.
>
> *LexisNexis Academic.* An index of news and business, legal, and reference information, with full-text articles. *LexisNexis* includes international, national, and regional newspapers, news magazines, legal and business publications, and court cases.

ProQuest Research Library. A periodical index covering the sciences, social sciences, arts, and humanities, including many full-text articles.

2 Locations of periodicals

Many article listings you find will include or link directly to the full text of the article, which you'll be able to read online and print or e-mail to yourself. If the full text is not available online, usually you can click on a link within the article record to see whether your library has the article in print or another format. Recent issues of periodicals are probably held in the library's periodical room. Back issues are usually stored elsewhere, either in bound volumes or on film that requires a special machine to read. A librarian will show you how to operate the machine.

51f Finding sources on the Web

As an academic researcher, you enter the Web in two ways: through your library's Web site, and through public search engines such as *Firefox* and *Google*. The library entrance, covered in the preceding sections, is your main path to the books and periodicals that, for most subjects, should make up most of your sources. The open Web, discussed here, can lead to a wealth of information and ideas, but it also has disadvantages that limit its usefulness for academic research:

- **The Web is a wide-open network.** Anyone with the right tools can place information on the Internet, and even a carefully conceived search can turn up sources with widely varying reliability: journal articles, government documents, scholarly data, term papers written by high school students, sales pitches masked as objective reports, wild theories. You must be especially diligent about evaluating open-Web sources (see pp. 377–85).
- **The Web changes constantly.** No search engine can keep up with the Web's daily additions and deletions, and a source you find today may be updated or gone tomorrow. You should not put off consulting an online source that you think you may want to use.
- **The Web is not all-inclusive.** Most books and many periodicals are available only via the library, not directly via the Web.

Clearly, the Web warrants cautious use. It should not be the only resource you work with.

1 Public search engines

To find sources on the Web, you use a **search engine** that catalogs Web sites in a series of directories and conducts keyword searches. For a good range of sources, try out more than a single search engine, perhaps as many as four or five, because no search engine can catalog the entire Web. In addition, most search engines accept paid placements, giving higher billing to sites that pay a fee. These so-called sponsored links are usually marked as such, but they can compromise a search engine's method for arranging sites in response to your keywords.

Customized searches

The home page of a search engine includes a field for you to type your keywords into. Generally, it will also include an Advanced Search link that you can use to customize your search. For instance, you may be able to select a range of dates, a language, or a number of results to see. Advanced Search will also explain how to use operators such as *AND, OR,* and *NOT* to limit or expand your search.

Search records

No matter which search engine you use, your Web browser includes functions that allow you to keep track of Web sources and your search:

- Use *Favorites* or *Bookmarks* to save site addresses as links. Click one of these terms near the top of the browser screen to add a site you want to return to. A favorite or bookmark remains on file until you delete it.
- Use *History* to locate sites you have visited before. The browser records visited sites for a certain period, such as a single online session or a week's sessions. (After that period, the history is deleted.) If you forgot to bookmark a site, you can click History or Go to locate your search history and recover the site.

2 A sample search

The following sample Web search illustrates how the refinement of keywords can narrow a search to maximize the relevant hits and minimize the irrelevant ones. Justin Malik, a student researching the environmental effects of green consumer products, first used the keywords *green products* on *Google.* But, as shown on screen 1 on the next page, the search produced more than *1.5 billion* items, with the first page consisting entirely of sites selling products, including sponsored sites and other advertisers.

Malik realized he had to alter his strategy to get more useful results. He experimented with combinations of synonyms and narrower terms and arrived at *"green consumerism"* and *products,* which refined the search but still produced 130,000 results. Adding *site:.gov* limited the results to government sites, whose URLs end in *.gov*. With *"green consumerism" products site:.gov*, Malik received 8,780 results (see screen 2 below). He continued to limit the search by replacing *site:.gov* with *site:.org* (nonprofit organizations), *site: .edu* (educational institutions), and *site:.com* (commercial organizations).

1. First *Google* search results

2. *Google* results with refined keywords

51g Finding sources using social media

Online sources that you reach through social media can put you directly in touch with experts and others whose ideas and information may inform your research. These media include e-mail, blogs, social-networking sites, and discussion groups. Like Web sites, they are unfiltered, so you must always evaluate them carefully. (See pp. 385–87.)

Note If your paper includes social-media correspondence that is not already public—for instance, an e-mail or a discussion-group posting—ask the author for permission to use it. Doing so advises the author that his or her ideas are about to be distributed more widely and lets the author verify that you have not misrepresented the ideas. (See also pp. 372–74 on interviews.)

1 E-mail

As a research tool, e-mail allows you to communicate with others who are interested in your topic. You might, for instance, carry on an e-mail conversation with a teacher at your school or interview an expert in another state to follow up on a scholarly article he or she published.

2 Blogs and social-networking sites

Blogs are Web sites on which an author or authors post time-stamped comments, generally centering on a common theme, in a format that allows readers to respond to the writer or to one another. You can find directories of blogs at *blogcatalog.com*.

Somewhat similar to blogs, social-networking sites such as *Twitter* and *Facebook* are increasingly being used by organizations, businesses, individuals, and even scholars to communicate with others.

Like all other social media discussed in this section, blogs and pages on social-networking sites must be evaluated carefully as potential sources. Some are reliable sources of opinion and evolving scholarship, and many refer to worthy books, articles, Web sites, and other resources. But just as many are little more than outlets for their authors' gripes or self-marketing. See pp. 385–87 for tips on telling the good from the bad.

3 Discussion lists

A **discussion list** (sometimes called a **listserv** or just a **list**) uses e-mail to connect individuals who are interested in a common subject, often with a scholarly or technical focus. By sending a question to an appropriate list, you may be able to reach scores of people who know something about your topic. For an index of discussion lists, see *tile.net/lists*.

Begin research on a discussion list by consulting the list's archive to ensure that the discussion is relevant to your topic and to see whether your question has already been answered. When

you write to the list, follow the guidelines for writing e-mail in
2 pp. 79–80. And always evaluate messages you receive, following
the guidelines on pp. 385–87. Although many contributors are reliable experts, almost anyone with an Internet connection can post a
message.

4 Web forums and newsgroups

Web forums and newsgroups are more open and less scholarly
than discussion lists, so their messages require even more diligent
evaluation. **Web forums** allow participants to join a conversation
simply by selecting a link on a Web page. For a directory of forums,
see *delphiforums.com*. **Newsgroups** are organized under subject
headings such as *soc* for social issues and *biz* for business. For a
directory of newsgroups, see *giganews.com*.

51h Using government publications

Government publications provide a vast array of data, reports,
policy statements, public records, and other historical and contemporary information. For US government publications, consult the
Government Printing Office's *GPO Access* at *www.gpoaccess.gov*.
Also helpful is *www.usa.gov*, a portal to a range of documents and
information.

Many federal, state, and local government agencies post important publications—legislation, reports, press releases—on their own
Web sites. You can find lists of sites for various federal agencies by
using the keywords *United States federal government* with a search
engine. Use the name of a state, city, or town with *government* for
state and local information.

51i Finding visuals, audio, and video

Visuals, audio, and video can be used as both primary and
secondary sources in a research project. A painting, an advertisement, or a video of a speech might be the subject of your writing
and thus a primary source. A podcast of a radio interview with an
expert on your subject or a college lecture might serve as a secondary source. Because many of these sources are unfiltered—they
can be posted by anyone—you must always evaluate them as carefully as you would any source you find on the open Web. (See pp.
377–85.)

Caution You must also cite every visual, audio, and video
source fully in your paper, just as you cite text sources, with author,
title, and publication information. In addition, some sources will

require that you seek permission from the copyright holder, such as a publisher or a photographer. To avoid having to seek permission, you can search Web sites such as *Google, Flickr Creative Commons,* and *Wikimedia Commons* for media that are not protected by copyright. On *Google,* for instance, go to "Search tools" and select "Labeled for reuse." Consult a librarian at your school if you have questions.

1 Visuals

The use of visuals to support your writing is discussed in **1** pp. 57–62 and **2** pp. 109–13. To find visuals, you have a number of options:

- **Scout for visuals while reading print or online sources.** While you are examining your sources, you may see charts, graphs, photographs, and other visuals that can support your ideas. When you find a visual you may want to use, photocopy or download it so you'll have it available later.
- **Create your own visuals,** such as photographs or charts. See **1** pp. 57–60 for suggestions on creating visuals.
- **Use an image search engine.** Web search engines can be set to find visuals, and they allow you to restrict your search to visuals that don't require reuse permission. Although search engines can find scores of visuals, the results may be inaccurate or incomplete because the sources surveyed often do not include descriptions of the visuals. (The engines search file names and any text accompanying the visuals.)
- **Use a public image database.** The following sites generally conduct accurate searches because their images are filed with information such as a description of the visual, the artist's name, and the visual's date:

    Digital Public Library of America. Maps, documents, photographs, advertisements, and more from libraries throughout the United States.
    Duke University, *Ad*Access.* Print advertisements spanning 1911–55.
    Library of Congress, *American Memory.* Maps, photographs, prints, cartoons, and advertisements documenting the American experience.
    Library of Congress, *Prints and Photographs Online Catalog.* Visuals from the library's collection, including those available through *American Memory.*
    New York Public Library Digital Gallery. Maps, drawings, photographs, and paintings from the library's collection.

- **Use a public image directory.** The following sites collect links to image sources:

    Art Project—Google Cultural Institute. Selections of fine art from major museums in the United States and Europe.
    MuseumLink's Museum of Museums. Links to museums all over the world.

Cultural Politics: Resources for Critical Analysis. Sources on advertising, fashion, magazines, toys, and other artifacts of popular culture.

Yale University Robert B. Haas Family Arts Library, *Image Resources.* Sources on the visual and performing arts.

■ **Use a library database.** Your library may subscribe to the following resources:

ARTstor. Museum collections and a database of images typically used in art history courses.

Associated Press, *AccuNet/AP Multimedia Archives.* Historical and contemporary news images.

Grove Art Online. Art images and links to museum sites.

Many visuals you find will be available at no charge for copying or downloading, but some sources do charge a fee for use. Before paying for a visual, check with a librarian to see if it is available elsewhere for free.

2 Audio and video

Audio and video, widely available on the Web and on disc, can provide your readers with the experience of "being there." For example, if you write about the media response to the *I Have a Dream* speech of Martin Luther King, Jr., and you will submit your paper electronically, you might insert links to the speech and to TV and radio coverage of it.

■ **Audio files** such as podcasts, Webcasts, and CDs record radio programs, interviews, speeches, lectures, and music. They are available on the Web and through your library. Online sources of audio include the Library of Congress's *American Memory*, the *Internet Archive*, and *Podcastdirectory.com.*

■ **Video files** capture performances, speeches and public presentations, news events, and other activities. They are available on the Web and on DVD or Blu-ray disc from your library. Online sources of video include the Library of Congress's *American Memory*; *YouTube* and the *Internet Archive*, which include commercials, historical footage, current events, and much more; and search engines such as *Google.*

51j Generating your own sources

For some papers you will need to conduct primary research to support, extend, or refute the ideas of others. For example, if you were writing about cyberbullying among college students, you might want to survey students on your campus as well as consult published research on the subject. Three common forms of primary research are personal interviews, surveys, and observation.

1 Personal interviews

An interview can be especially helpful for a research project because it allows you to ask questions precisely geared to your topic. You can conduct an interview in person, over the telephone, or online. A personal interview is preferable if you can arrange it, because you can see the person's expressions and gestures as well as hear his or her tone.

Here are a few guidelines for interviews:

- **Call or write for an appointment.** Tell the person exactly why you are calling, what you want to discuss, and how long you expect the interview to take. Be true to your word on all points.
- **Prepare a list of open-ended questions to ask**—perhaps ten or twelve for a one-hour interview. Do some research on these questions before the interview to discover background on the issues and your subject's published views on the issues.
- **Pay attention to your subject's answers** so that you can ask appropriate follow-up questions. Take care in interpreting answers, especially if you are online and thus can't depend on facial expressions, gestures, and tone of voice to convey the subject's attitudes.
- **Keep thorough notes.** Take notes during an in-person or telephone interview, or record the interview if you have the equipment and your subject agrees. For online interviews, save the discussion in a file of its own.
- **Verify quotations.** Before you quote your subject in your paper, check with him or her to ensure that the quotations are accurate.
- **Send a thank-you note immediately after the interview.** Promise your subject a copy of your finished paper, and send the paper promptly.

See **MLA** p. 487 for an example of an interview used as a research source.

2 Surveys

Asking questions of a defined group of people can provide information about respondents' attitudes, behavior, backgrounds, and expectations. Use the following tips to plan and conduct a survey:

- **Decide what you want to find out.** The questions you ask should be dictated by your purpose. Formulating a **hypothesis** about your subject—a generalization that can be tested—will help you refine your purpose.
- **Define your population.** Think about the kinds of people your hypothesis is about—for instance, college men or preschool

children. Plan to sample this population so that your findings will be representative.

- **Write your questions.** Surveys may contain closed questions that direct the respondent's answers (checklists and multiple-choice, true/false, or yes/no questions) or open-ended questions that allow brief, descriptive answers. Avoid loaded questions that reveal your own biases or make assumptions about subjects' answers.
- **Test your questions.** Use a few respondents with whom you can discuss the answers. Eliminate or recast questions that respondents find unclear, discomforting, or unanswerable.
- **Tally the results.** Count the actual numbers of answers, including any nonanswers.
- **Seek patterns in the raw data.** Such patterns may confirm or contradict your hypothesis. Revise the hypothesis or conduct additional research if necessary.

See **2** p. 114 for an example of a survey used as a research source.

3 Observation

Observation can be an effective way to gather fresh information on your subject. You may observe in a controlled setting—for instance, watching children at play in a child-development lab. Or you may observe in a more open setting—for instance, watching the interactions among students at a cafeteria on your campus. Use these guidelines for planning and gathering information through observation:

- **Be sure that what you want to learn *can* be observed.** You can observe people's choices and interactions, but you would need an interview or a survey to discover people's attitudes or opinions.
- **Allow ample time.** Observation requires several sessions of several hours in order to be reliable.
- **Record your impressions.** Throughout the observation sessions, take careful notes on paper, a computer, or a mobile device. Always record the date, time, and location for each session.
- **Be aware of your own bias.** Such awareness will help you avoid the common pitfall of seeing only what you expect or want to see.

52 Working with Sources

Chapter essentials
- Use the criteria for reading sources critically (below).
- Evaluate library sources (next page).
- Evaluate Web and social-media sources (pp. 377, 385).
- Synthesize information from sources (p. 387).
- Gather information, carefully summarizing, paraphrasing, and quoting (pp. 390, 391).
- Integrate source information into your writing (p. 395).

Visit MyWritingLab™ for more resources on working with sources.

Research writing is much more than finding sources and reporting their contents. The challenge and interest come from interacting with and synthesizing sources: reading them critically to discover their meanings, judge their relevance and reliability, and create relationships among them; and using them to extend and support your own ideas so that you make your subject your own.

(CULTURE LANGUAGE) Making a subject your own requires thinking critically about sources and developing independent ideas. These goals may at first be uncomfortable if your native culture emphasizes understanding and respecting established authority more than questioning and enlarging it. The information here will help you work with sources so that you can become an expert in your own right and convincingly convey your expertise to others.

52a Evaluating sources

Before you gather information and ideas from sources, scan them to evaluate what they have to offer, how reliable they are, and how you might use them. As you evaluate each source, add an assessment of it to your annotated bibliography, as discussed and illustrated on pp. 353–55.

Note In evaluating sources, you need to consider how they come to you. The sources you find through the library, both in print and on the Web, have been previewed for you by their publishers and by the library's staff. They still require your critical reading, but you can have some confidence in the information they contain. With online sources you reach directly, however, you can't assume similar previewing, so your critical reading must be especially rigorous. Special tips for evaluating Web sites and other online sources begin on p. 377.

1 Relevance and reliability

Not all the sources you find will prove worthwhile: some may be irrelevant to your project, and others may be unreliable. Gauging the relevance and reliability of sources is the essential task of evaluating them. If you haven't already done so, read this book's discussion of critical reading (**2** pp. 80–95). It provides a foundation for answering the questions in the following box.

Questions for evaluating sources

For online sources, supplement these questions with those on pp. 380 and 385.

Relevance

- **Does the source devote some attention to your subject?** Does it focus on your subject or cover it marginally? How does it compare to other sources you've found?
- **Is the source appropriately specialized for your needs?** Check the source's treatment of a topic you know something about, to ensure that it is neither too superficial nor too technical.
- **Is the source up to date enough for your subject?** When was the source published? If your subject is current, your sources should be, too.

Reliability

- **Where does the source come from?** Did you find it through your library or directly through the Internet? (If the latter, see pp. 377–87.) Is the source popular or scholarly?
- **Is the author an expert in the field?** Check the author's credentials in a biography (if the source includes one), in a biographical reference, or by a keyword search of the Web.
- **What is the bias of the source?** How do the author's ideas relate to those in other sources? What areas does the author emphasize, ignore, or dismiss?
- **Is the source fair, reasonable, and well written?** Does it provide sound reasoning and a fair picture of opposing views? Is the tone calm and objective? Is the source logically organized and error-free?
- **Are the claims well supported, even if you don't agree with the author?** Does the author provide accurate, relevant, representative, and adequate evidence to back up his or her claims? Does the author cite sources, and if so are they reliable?

---

2 Evaluating library sources

To evaluate sources you find through your library—either in print or on the library's Web site—look at dates, titles, summaries, introductions, headings, author biographies, and any source citations. The criteria opposite expand on the most important tips in the preceding box. On the next two pages you can see how the student Justin Malik applied these criteria to two print sources, a magazine article and a journal article, that he consulted while researching green consumerism.

Identify the origin of the source.

Check whether a library source is popular or scholarly. Scholarly sources, such as refereed journals and university press books, are generally deeper and more reliable. But some popular sources, such as first-hand newspaper accounts and books for a general audience, are often appropriate for research projects.

Check the author's expertise.

The authors of scholarly publications tend to be experts whose authority can be verified. Check the source to see whether it contains a biographical note about the author, check a biographical reference, or check the author's name in a keyword search of the Web. Look for other publications by the author and for his or her job and any affiliation, such as teacher at a university, researcher with a nonprofit organization, or writer for popular magazines.

Identify the author's bias.

Every author has a point of view that influences the selection and interpretation of evidence. You may be able to learn about an author's bias from biographies, citation indexes, and review indexes. But also look at the source itself. How do the author's ideas relate to those in other sources? What areas does the author emphasize, ignore, or dismiss? When you're aware of sources' biases, you can acknowledge them in your writing and try to balance them.

Determine whether the source is fair, reasonable, and well written.

Even a strongly biased work should present solid reasoning and give balanced coverage to opposing views—all in an objective tone. Any source should be organized logically and should be written in clear, error-free sentences. The absence of any of these qualities should raise a warning flag.

Analyze support for the author's claims.

Whether or not you agree with the author, his or her evidence should be accurate, relevant to the argument, representative of its context, and adequate for the point being made. (See **2** p. 102.) The author's sources should themselves be reliable.

3 | Evaluating Web sites

The same critical reading that helps you evaluate library sources will help you evaluate Web sites that you reach directly. You would

(continued on p. 380)

Evaluating library sources

Opposite are sample pages from two library sources that Justin Malik considered for his paper on green consumerism. Malik evaluated the sources using the questions and the guidelines on pp. 376–77.

Makower	Jackson
Origin	
Interview with Joel Makower published in *Vegetarian Times*, a popular magazine.	Article by Tim Jackson published in *Journal of Industrial Ecology*, a scholarly journal sponsored by two reputable universities: MIT and Yale.
Author	
Gives Makower's credentials at the beginning of the interview: the author of a book on green products and of a monthly newsletter on green businesses. Quotes another source that calls Makower the "guru of green business practice."	Includes a biography at the end of the article that describes Jackson as a professor at the University of Surrey (UK) and lists his professional activities related to the environment.
Bias	
Describes and promotes green products. Concludes with an endorsement of a for-profit Web site that tracks and sells green products.	Presents multiple views of green consumerism. Argues that a solution to environmental problems will involve green products and less consumption but in different ways than currently proposed.
Reasonableness and writing	
Presents Makower's data and perspective on distinguishing good from bad green products, using conversational writing in an informal presentation.	Presents and cites opposing views objectively, using formal academic writing.
Source citations	
Lacks source citations for claims and data.	Includes more than three pages of source citations, many of scholarly and government sources and all cited within the article.
Assessment	
Unreliable for academic research: Despite Makower's reputation, the article comes from a nonscholarly source, takes a one-sided approach to consumption, and depends on statistics credited only to Makower.	**Reliable for academic research:** The article comes from a scholarly journal, the author is an expert in the field, he discusses many views and concedes some, and his source citations confirm evidence from reliable sources.

Unreliable source for academic research: An interview with Joel Makower, published in *Vegetarian Times*

Reliable source for academic research: An article by Tim Jackson, published in the *Journal of Industrial Ecology*

(continued from p. 377)

not use a popular magazine such as *People* in academic research—unless, say, you were considering it as a primary source in a paper analyzing popular culture. Similarly, you would not use a celebrity's Web site, a fan site, or a gossip site as a source unless you were placing it in a larger academic context.

Even Web sites that seem worthy pose challenges for evaluation because they have not undergone prior screening by editors and librarians. On your own, you must distinguish scholarship from corporate promotion, valid data from invented statistics, well-founded opinion from clever propaganda.

The strategy summarized in the following box can help you make such distinctions. On pp. 382–83 you can see how Justin Malik applied this strategy to two Web sites that he consulted while researching green consumerism.

Questions for evaluating Web sites

Supplement these questions with those on pp. 376 and 385.

■ **What type of site are you viewing**—for example, is it scholarly, informational, or commercial?

■ **Who is the author or sponsor?** How credible is the person or group responsible for the site?

■ **What is the purpose of the site?** What does the site's author or sponsor intend to achieve? Are there ads on the site, signaling that the site is trying to make money from its content?

■ **What is the bias of the site?** Does the site advocate for one side or another of a particular issue?

■ **What does context tell you?** What do you already know about the site's subject that can inform your evaluation? What kinds of support or other information do the site's links provide?

■ **What does presentation tell you?** Is the site's design well thought out and effective? Is the writing clear and error-free?

■ **How worthwhile is the content?** Are the site's claims well supported by evidence from reliable sources? When was the site posted or last updated?

Note To evaluate a Web document, you'll often need to travel to the site's home page to discover the author or sponsor, date of publication, and other relevant information. The page you're reading may include a link to the home page. If it doesn't, you can find it by editing the URL in the Address or Location field of your browser. Working backward, delete the end of the URL up to the last slash and hit Enter. Repeat this step until you reach the home page. There you may also find a menu option, often labeled "About," that will lead you to a description of the site's author or sponsor.

Determine the type of site.

When you search the Web, you're likely to encounter various types of sites. Although they sometimes overlap, the types can usually be identified by their content and purposes. Here are the main types of Web sites you will find using a search engine:

- **Scholarly sites:** These sites have a knowledge-building interest, and they are likely to be reliable. They may include research reports with supporting data and extensive documentation of scholarly sources. For such sites originating in the United States, the URLs generally end in *edu* (originating from a college or university), *org* (a nonprofit organization), or *gov* (a government department or agency). Sites originating in other countries will end differently, usually with a country code such as *uk* (United Kingdom), *de* (Germany), or *kr* (South Korea).

- **Informational sites:** Individuals, nonprofit organizations, corporations, schools, and government bodies all produce sites intended to centralize information on subjects as diverse as astronomy, hip-hop music, and zoo design. The sites' URLs may end in *edu, org, gov,* or *com* (originating from a commercial organization). Such sites generally do not have the knowledge-building focus of scholarly sites and may omit supporting data and documentation, but they can provide useful information and sometimes include links to scholarly and other sources.

- **Advocacy sites:** Many sites present the views of individuals or organizations that promote certain policies or actions, such as the National Rifle Association or People for the Ethical Treatment of Animals. Their URLs usually end in *org*, but they may end in *edu* or *com*. Most advocacy sites have a strong bias. Some sites include serious, well-documented research to support their positions, but others select or distort evidence.

- **Commercial sites:** Corporations and other businesses such as automakers, electronics manufacturers, and booksellers maintain Web sites to explain themselves, promote themselves, or sell goods and services. URLs of commercial sites usually end in *com*; however, some end in *biz,* and those of businesses based outside the United States often end in the country code. Although business sites intend to further the sponsors' profit-making purposes, they can include reliable data.

- **Personal sites:** The sites maintained by individuals range from diaries of a family's travels to opinions on political issues to reports on evolving scholarship. The sites' URLs usually end in *com* or *edu*. Personal sites are only as reliable as their authors, but some do provide valuable eyewitness accounts, links to worthy sources, and other usable information. Personal sites are often blogs or social-networking pages, discussed on pp. 385–87.

(continued on p. 384)

Evaluating Web sites

Opposite are screen shots from two Web sites that Justin Malik consulted for his paper on green consumerism. Malik evaluated the sources using the questions in the boxes on pages 581 and 583.

Wikipedia

Center for Climate and Energy Solutions

Author and sponsor

Author of the page is not given. Web site is *Wikipedia*, the online encyclopedia to which anyone can contribute anonymously.

Author is an expert on energy and public policy. (His biography can be found online.) Site sponsor is the Center for Climate and Energy Solutions, a nonprofit group specializing in energy and climate change.

Purpose and bias

Informational page with no stated or obvious bias.

Informational site with the stated purpose of "working to promote sound policy on the challenges of energy and climate change." Report expresses bias toward sustainable electricity production.

Context

An encyclopedia site publishing general information on a wide variety of topics.

Nonprofit organization's site dedicated to publishing current research on energy and climate issues.

Presentation

Clean, professional-looking page with mostly error-free writing.

Clean, professionally designed site with error-free writing.

Content

Article gives basic information about energy use and provides links to other pages that expand on its claims. Probably because of the intended general audience, the page does not link to extensive citations of scholarly research.

Report is current (date below the author's name), it describes scenarios for meeting future electricity needs, and it cites scholarly sources.

Assessment

Unreliable for academic research: The page has no listed author and few scholarly citations. A *Wikipedia* page is suitable for background information but not as evidence in an academic paper.

Reliable for academic research: The report has a bias toward sustainable electricity production, but the site sponsor is reputable and the author is an expert and cites scholarly sources.

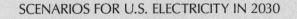

The Wikipedia screenshot content:

Create account Log in

WIKIPEDIA
The Free Encyclopedia

Article Talk   Read Edit View history Search

Electric energy consumption

From Wikipedia, the free encyclopedia

Main page
Contents
Featured content
Current events
Random article
Donate to Wikipedia
Wikimedia Shop

Interaction
  Help
  About Wikipedia
  Community portal
  Recent changes
  Contact page

Tools
  What links here
  Related changes
  Upload file
  Special pages
  Permanent link
  Page information
  Wikidata item
  Cite this page

Print/export

Electric energy consumption is the form of energy consumption that uses electric energy. Electric energy consumption is the actual energy demand made on existing electricity supply.

Overview [edit]

Consumption of electric energy is measured in watt-hours (written W·h, equal to Watt x Hour)

  1 W·h = 3600 joule = 859.8 calorie.

Electric and electronic devices consume electric energy to generate desired output (i.e. light, heat, motion, etc.). During operation, some part of the energy is consumed in unintended output, such as waste heat. See Electrical Efficiency .

In 2008, the world total of electricity production and consumption was 20,279 TWh (terawatt-hours). This number corresponds to an average consumption rate of around 2.3 terawatts continuously during the year. The total energy needed to produce this power is roughly a factor 2 to 3 higher because the efficiency of power plants is roughly 30-50%, see Electricity generation. The generated power is thus in the order of 5 TW. This is approximately a third of the total energy consumption of 15 TW, see World energy consumption.

In 2005, the primary energy used to generate electricity was 41.60 Quadrillion BTU (Coal 21.01 quads, Natural Gas 6.69 quads, Petroleum 1.32 quads, Nuclear electric power 8.13 quads, Renewable energy 4.23 quads respectively). The gross generation of electricity in that year was 14.50 Quads; the difference, 27.10 Quads, was conversion losses. Among all electricity, 4.84 Quads was used in residential area, 4.32 Quads used in commercial, 3.47 Quads used in industrial and 0.03 Quads used in transportation.

16816TWh(83%) of electric energy was consumed by final users. The difference of 3464TWh(17%)was consumed in the process of generating power and consumed as transmission loss and all most consumed at misuse.

Unreliable source for academic research: A page on the Web site *Wikipedia*

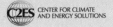

SCENARIOS FOR U.S. ELECTRICITY IN 2030

C2ES CENTER FOR CLIMATE
AND ENERGY SOLUTIONS

Manik Roy, Ph.D
Center for Climate and Energy Solutions
May 2014

Affordable, reliable electricity is a central pillar of modern life. At the same time, the generation of electricity is responsible for nearly 40 percent of U.S. carbon dioxide emissions. New technologies and policies are driving enormous change in the power sector, affecting its ability to provide affordable and environmentally sustainable electricity for decades to come. This brief describes three scenarios for the state of U.S. electricity in 2030 as a way of articulating key challenges and opportunities facing this critical sector in the years ahead.

■ OVERVIEW

This paper describes three scenarios for the state of U.S. electricity in 2030. The primary purpose of these scenarios is to articulate challenges and opportunities for U.S. electricity in the years to come, in order to help the electricity sector and its many stakeholders find the best path forward in meeting their shared objectives.

The scenarios were developed by Center for Climate

Each scenario illustrates the extent to which U.S. electricity in 2030 could be affordable, reliable, safe, and environmentally sound—attributes demanded by the public—and describes the resilience of the electricity system to a range of possible shocks. As a group, the scenarios are intended to be plausible, alternative, divergent, and internally consistent.

Reliable source for academic research: A report published on the Web site *Center for Climate and Energy Solutions*

(continued from p. 381)

Identify the author and sponsor.

A reputable site lists its authors, names the group responsible for the site, and provides information or a link for contacting the author and the sponsor. If none of this information is provided, you should not use the source. If you have only the author's or the sponsor's name, you may be able to discover more in a biographical dictionary, through a keyword search, or in your other sources. Make sure the author and the sponsor have expertise on the subject they're presenting: if an author is a doctor, for instance, what is he or she a doctor of?

Gauge purpose and bias.

A Web site's purpose determines what ideas and information it offers. Inferring that purpose tells you how to interpret what you see on the site. If a site is intended to sell a product or advocate a particular position, it may emphasize favorable ideas and information while ignoring or even distorting unfavorable information or opposing views. In contrast, if a site is intended to build knowledge—for instance, a scholarly project or journal—it will likely acknowledge diverse views and evidence.

Determining the purpose and bias of a site often requires looking beyond the first page and beneath the surface of words and images. To start, read critically what the site says about itself, usually on a page labeled "About." Be suspicious of any site that doesn't provide information about itself and its goals.

Consider context.

Your evaluation of a Web site should be informed by considerations outside the site itself. Chief among these considerations is your own knowledge. What do you already know about the site's subject and the prevailing views of it? Where does this site seem to fit into that picture? What can you learn from this site that you don't already know?

In addition, you can follow some of the site's links to see how they support, or don't support, the site's credibility. For instance, links to scholarly sources lend authority to a site—but *only* if the scholarly sources actually relate to and back up the site's claims.

Look at presentation.

Considering both the look of a site and the way it's written can illuminate its intentions and reliability. Do the site's elements all support its purpose, or is the site cluttered with irrelevant material and graphics? Is the text clearly written and focused on the purpose? Is it relatively error-free, or does it contain typos and grammatical errors? Does the site seem carefully constructed and well maintained, or is it sloppy? How intrusive are any pop-up advertisements?

Analyze content.

With information about a site's author, purpose, and context, you're in a position to evaluate its content. Are the ideas and information current, or are they dated? (Check the publication date.) Are they slanted and, if so, in what direction? Are the views and data authoritative, or do you need to balance them—or even reject them? Are claims made on the site supported by evidence drawn from reliable sources? These questions require close reading of both the text and its sources.

4 | Evaluating other online sources

Social media and multimedia require the same critical scrutiny as Web sites do. Social media—including e-mail, blogs, *Twitter*, discussion groups, *Facebook* pages, and wikis—can be sources of reliable data and opinions, but they can also contain wrong or misleading data and skewed opinions. Multimedia—visuals, audio, and video—can provide valuable support for your ideas, but they can also mislead or distort. For example, a *YouTube* search using "I have a dream" brings up videos of Martin Luther King, Jr., delivering his famous speech as well as videos of people speaking hatefully about King and the speech.

Answer the following questions when evaluating social media and multimedia.

Questions for evaluating social media and multimedia

Supplement these questions with those on pp. 376 and 380.

- **Who is the author or creator?** How credible is he or she?
- **What is the author's or creator's purpose?** What can you tell about why the author or creator is publishing the work?
- **What does the context reveal?** What do reasonable responses to the work, such as comments on a blog or a news site, indicate about the source's balance and reliability?
- **How worthwhile is the content?** Are the claims made by the author or creator supported by evidence? Is the evidence from reliable sources?
- **How does the source compare with other sources?** Do the claims made by the author or creator seem accurate and fair given what you've seen in sources you know to be reliable?

Identify the author or creator.

Checking out the author or creator of a potential source can help you judge its reliability. The author may be identified on the source—for instance, the blog posting shown on the next page includes

Evaluating a blog

THE **BLOG** | *Featuring fresh takes and real-time analysis from HuffPost's signature lineup of contributors*

American Anthropological Association
World's largest organization of individuals interested in anthropology

Author is a university professor and represents a professional academic organization.

Title reveals purpose and bias.

Green Consumerism Is No Solution

Posted: 06/14/2013 4:50 pm

Like 399 people like this. Be the first of your friends.

Posting has been shared and commented on.

| 128 | 61 | 5 | 7 | 4 |

GET GREEN NEWSLETTERS:
Enter email SUBSCRIBE

f Share   Tweet   8+1   Email   Comment

Written by Richard Wilk

Presentation is clear and error-free. Content is current and links to supporting data.

Greenwashing is not just for corporations anymore -- it has gone personal. Instead of feeling guilty about the huge gaps between wealthy and poor, the ways consumerism causes global warming, or how our daily pleasures cause rainforest destruction and despoil the sea, we can drink a few cups of fair-trade coffee, eat a rainforest crunch bar and

a biographical note at the end saying that the author is a professor writing on behalf of the American Anthropological Association's Task Force on Global Climate Change. You may also be able to learn about the author with a keyword search of the Web. If you can't identify the author or creator at all, you can't use the source.

You can also get a sense of the interests and biases of an author or creator by tracking down his or her other work. For instance, you might check whether a blog author cites or links to other publications, look for other postings by the same author in a discussion-group archive, or try to gain an overview of a photographer's work.

Analyze the author's or creator's purpose.

What can you tell about *why* the author or creator is publishing the work? The blog posting above provides a quick answer in the title, which indicates the author's negative view of green products. You can also dig to discover purpose, looking for claims, the use (or lack) of evidence, and the treatment of opposing views. All these factors convey the person's stand on the subject and general fairness, and they will help you position the source among your other sources.

Consider the context.

Social media and multimedia are often difficult to evaluate in isolation. Looking beyond a contribution to the responses of others can give you a sense of context by indicating how the author or creator is regarded. On a *Facebook* page or a blog, look at the comments others have posted. If you discover negative or angry responses, try to understand why: sometimes online anonymity encourages hateful responses to even quite reasonable postings.

Analyze content.

A reliable source will offer evidence for claims and will list the sources of its evidence. The blog posting on the facing page, for example, links to information about carbon dioxide emissions. If you don't see such support, then you probably shouldn't use the source. However, when the source is important to you and biographical information or context indicates that the author or creator is serious and reliable, you might ask him or her to direct you to supporting information.

The tone of writing can also be a clue to its purpose and reliability. In most social media, the writing tends to be more informal and may be more heated than in other kinds of sources; but look askance at writing that's contemptuous, dismissive, or shrill.

Compare with other sources.

Always consider social-media and multimedia sources in comparison to other sources so that you can distinguish singular, untested views from more mainstream views that have been subject to verification. Don't assume that a blog author's information and opinions are mainstream just because you see them on other blogs. The technology allows content to be picked up instantly by other blogs, so widespread distribution indicates only popular interest, not reliability.

Be wary of blogs that reproduce periodical articles, reports, or other publications. Try to locate the original version of the publication to be sure it has been reproduced fully and accurately, not quoted selectively or distorted. If you can't locate the original version, don't use the publication as a source.

52b Synthesizing sources

When you begin to see the differences and similarities among sources, you move into the most significant part of research writing: forging relationships for your own purpose. This **synthesis** is an essential step in reading sources critically. As you infer connections—say, between one writer's opinions and another's or between two works by the same author—you shape your own perspective on your subject and create new knowledge.

Your synthesis of sources will grow more detailed and sophisticated as you proceed through the process of working with sources described in the balance of this chapter: gathering information (p. 390); deciding whether to summarize, paraphrase, or quote sources (pp. 391–94); and integrating sources into your sentences (pp. 395–99). Unless you are analyzing primary sources such as the works of a poet, at first read your sources quickly and selectively for an overview of your subject and a sense of how the sources approach it. Don't get bogged down in gathering detailed information, but *do* record your ideas about sources in your research journal (p. 348) or your annotated bibliography (pp. 353–55).

Respond to sources.

One way to find your own perspective on a topic is to write down what your sources make you think. Do you agree or disagree with the author? Do you find his or her views narrow, or do they open up new approaches for you? Is there anything in the source that you need to research further before you can understand it? Does the source prompt questions that you should keep in mind while reading other sources?

Connect sources.

When you notice a link between sources, write about it. Do two sources differ in their theories or their interpretations of facts? Does one source illuminate another—perhaps commenting or clarifying or supplying additional data? Do two or more sources report studies that support a theory you've read about or an idea of your own?

Heed your insights.

Apart from ideas prompted by your sources, you are sure to come up with independent thoughts: a conviction, a point of confusion that suddenly becomes clear, a question you haven't seen anyone else ask. These insights may occur at unexpected times, so it's good practice to keep a notebook or computer handy to record them.

Draw your own conclusions.

As your research proceeds, the responses, connections, and insights you form through synthesis will lead you to answer your starting research question with a statement of your thesis (see p. 410). They will also lead you to the main ideas supporting your thesis—conclusions you have drawn from your synthesis of sources, forming the main divisions of your paper. Be sure to write them down as they occur to you.

Use sources to support your conclusions.

Effective synthesis requires careful handling of evidence from sources so that it meshes smoothly into your sentences and yet is clearly distinct from your own ideas. When drafting your paper, make sure that each paragraph focuses on an idea of your own, with the support for the idea coming from your sources. Generally, open each paragraph with your idea, provide evidence from a source or sources with appropriate citations, and close with an interpretation of the evidence. (Avoid ending a paragraph with a source citation; instead, end with your own idea.) In this way, your paper will synthesize others' work into something wholly your own. For more on structuring paragraphs in academic writing, see **2** pp. 96–97.

Exercise 52.1 Synthesizing sources

The following three passages address the same issue, the legalization of drugs. What similarities do you see in the authors' ideas? What differences? Write a paragraph of your own in which you use these authors' views as a point of departure for your own view about drug legalization.

Perhaps the most unfortunate victims of drug prohibition laws have been the residents of America's ghettos. These laws have proved largely futile in deterring ghetto-dwellers from becoming drug abusers, but they do account for much of what ghetto residents identify as the drug problem. Aggressive, gun-toting drug dealers often upset law-abiding residents far more than do addicts nodding out in doorways. Meanwhile other residents perceive the drug dealers as heroes and successful role models. They're symbols of success to children who see no other options. At the same time the increasingly harsh criminal penalties imposed on adult drug dealers have led drug traffickers to recruit juveniles. Where once children started dealing drugs only after they had been using them for a few years, today the sequence is often reversed. Many children start using drugs only after working for older drug dealers for a while. Legalization of drugs, like legalization of alcohol in the 1930s, would drive the drug-dealing business off the streets and out of apartment buildings and into government-regulated, tax-paying stores. It also would force many of the gun-toting dealers out of the business and convert others into legitimate businessmen.

—Ethan A. Nadelmann, "Shooting Up"

Statistics argue against legalization. The University of Michigan conducts an annual survey of twelfth graders, asking the students about their drug consumption. In 1980, 56.4% of those polled said they had used marijuana in the past twelve months, whereas in 2012 only 45.5% had done so. Cocaine use was even more reduced in the same period (22.6% to 5.2%). At the same time, twelve-month use of legally available drugs—alcohol and nicotine-containing cigarettes—remained constant at about 70% and 50%, respectively. The numbers of illegal drug users haven't declined nearly enough: those teenaged marijuana and cocaine users are still vulnerable to addiction and even death, and they threaten to infect their impressionable peers. But clearly the prohibition of illegal drugs has helped, while the legal status of alcohol and cigarettes has not made them less popular.

—Sylvia Smith, "The Case against Legalization"

> I have to laugh at the debate over what to do about the drug prob-
> lem. Everyone is running around offering solutions—from making drug
> use a more serious criminal offense to legalizing it. But there isn't a real
> solution. I know that. I used and abused drugs, and people, and society,
> for two decades. Nothing worked to get me to stop all that behavior
> except just plain being sick and tired. Nothing. Not threats, not ten-
> plus years in prison, not anything that was said to me. I used until I got
> through. Period. And that's when you'll win the war. When all the dope
> fiends are done. Not a minute before.
> —Michael W. Posey, "I Did Drugs Till I Was Worn Out.
> Why War On Drugs Won't Work."

52c | Gathering information from sources

You can collect and store source information in a number of
ways: handwrite notes, type notes into a file, copy and paste chunks of
text from online articles into a file, annotate print or electronic documents such as PDF files, or scan or photocopy pages from books and
other print sources.

Whatever method you use to gather information, you have four
main goals:

- **Keep accurate records of what sources say.** Accuracy helps prevent misrepresentation and plagiarism. If you write notes by
  hand or type them into a file, do so carefully to avoid introducing errors.
- **Keep track of others' words and ideas.** Put quotation marks
  around any words you take from a source, and always include
  a source citation that ties the quotation to the publication information you have recorded. Also include a source citation for
  any idea you summarize or paraphrase so that you know the
  idea is not your own but came from a specific source. For more
  on summarizing, paraphrasing, and quoting sources, see the
  next section.
- **Keep accurate records of how to find sources.** Whether you handwrite notes or work with an electronic file, always link the
  source material to its complete publication information. These
  records are essential for retracing steps and for citing sources
  in your drafts and in the final paper. If you have the complete
  information in your working bibliography (see pp. 353–54), you
  can use a shorthand reference to it on the source material, such
  as the author's name and any page or other reference number.
  (See the examples on the next two pages.)
- **Synthesize sources.** Information gathering is a critical process
  in which you learn from sources, understand the relationships
  among them, and develop your own ideas about your subject
  and your sources. Analyze and interact with your sources by

highlighting their key information and commenting on what they say.

52d Using summary, paraphrase, and quotation

Deciding whether to summarize, paraphrase, or quote a source is an important step in synthesizing the source's ideas and your own. You synthesize when you use your own words to summarize an author's argument or paraphrase a significant example or when you select a significant passage to quote. Choosing summary, paraphrase, or quotation should depend on why you are using a source.

Caution Summaries, paraphrases, and quotations all require source citations. A summary or paraphrase without a source citation or a quotation without quotation marks and a source citation is plagiarism. (See pp. 400–05 for more on plagiarism.)

1 Summary

When you **summarize**, you condense an extended idea or argument into a sentence or more in your own words. (See **2** pp. 85–87 for tips.) Summary is most useful when you want to record the gist of an author's idea without the background or supporting evidence. Following is a passage from a scholarly essay about consumption and its impact on the environment. Then a sample note shows a summary of the passage.

Original quotation

Such intuition is even making its way, albeit slowly, into scholarly circles, where recognition is mounting that ever-increasing pressures on ecosystems, life-supporting environmental services, and critical natural cycles are driven not only by the sheer number of resource users and the inefficiencies of their resource use, but also by the patterns of resource use themselves. In global environmental policymaking arenas, it is becoming more and more difficult to ignore the fact that the overdeveloped North must restrain its consumption if it expects the underdeveloped South to embrace a more sustainable trajectory.

—Thomas Princen, Michael Maniates, and Ken Conca,
Confronting Consumption, p. 4

Summary of source

Environmental consequences of consumption

Princen, Maniates, and Conca 4

Overconsumption may be a more significant cause of environmental problems than increasing population is.

2 | Paraphrase

When you **paraphrase,** you follow much more closely the author's original presentation, but you restate it using your own words and sentence structures. Paraphrase is most useful when you want to present or examine an author's line of reasoning but you don't feel the original words merit direct quotation. The note below shows a paraphrase of the quotation on the previous page from *Confronting Consumption*.

Paraphrase of source

Environmental consequences of consumption

Princen, Maniates, and Conca 4

Scholars are coming to believe that consumption is partly to blame for changes in ecosystems, reduction of essential natural resources, and changes in natural cycles. Policy makers increasingly see that developing nations will not adopt practices that reduce pollution and waste unless weathly nations consume less. Rising population around the world does cause significant stress on the environment, but consumption is increasing even more rapidly than population.

Notice that the paraphrase follows the original but uses different words and different sentence structures. In contrast, an unsuccessful paraphrase—one that plagiarizes—copies the author's words or sentence structures or both *without quotation marks.* (See pp. 404–05 for examples.)

Paraphrasing a source

- Read the relevant material several times to be sure you understand it.
- **Restate the source's ideas in your own words and sentence structures.** You need not put down in new words the whole passage or all the details. Select what is relevant to your topic, and restate only that. If complete sentences seem too detailed or cumbersome, use phrases.
- **Be careful not to distort meaning.** Don't change the source's emphasis or omit connecting words, qualifiers, and other material whose absence will confuse you later or cause you to misrepresent the source.
- **Be careful not to plagiarize the source.** Use your own words and sentence structures, and always record a citation in your notes. Especially if your source is difficult or complex, you may be tempted to change just a few words or to modify the sentence structure just a bit. But that is plagiarism, not paraphrase.

> CULTURE
> LANGUAGE

If English is not your native language and you have difficulty paraphrasing the ideas in sources, try this. Before attempting a paraphrase, read the original passage several times. Then, instead of "translating" line by line, try to state the gist of the passage without looking at it. Check your effort against the original to be sure you have captured the source author's meaning and emphasis without using his or her words and sentence structures. If you need a synonym for a word, look it up in a dictionary.

3 Direct quotation

Your notes from sources may include many quotations, especially if you rely on photocopies, printouts, or downloads. Whether to use a quotation in your draft, instead of a summary or paraphrase, depends on how important the exact words are and on whether the source is primary or secondary (pp. 351–52):

- **Quote extensively when you are analyzing primary sources**—firsthand accounts such as works of literature, eyewitness reports, and historical documents. The quotations will generally be both the target of your analysis and the chief support for your ideas.
- **Quote selectively when you are drawing on secondary sources**—reports or analyses of other sources, such as a critic's view of a poem or a historian's synthesis of several eyewitness reports. Favor summaries and paraphrases over quotations, and put every quotation to both tests in the box below. Most papers of ten or so pages should not need more than two or three quotations that are longer than a few lines each.

Tests for direct quotations from secondary sources

The author's original satisfies one of these requirements:

- The language is unusually vivid, bold, or inventive.
- The quotation cannot be paraphrased without distortion or loss of meaning.
- The words themselves are at issue in your interpretation.
- The quotation represents and emphasizes a body of opinion or the view of an important expert.
- The quotation emphatically reinforces your own idea.
- The quotation is an illustration, such as a graph, diagram, or table.

The quotation is as short as possible:

- It includes only material relevant to your point.
- It is edited to eliminate examples and other unneeded material, using ellipsis marks and brackets (**5** pp. 318–21).

When you quote a source, either in your notes or in your draft, take precautions to avoid plagiarism or misrepresentation of the source:

- **Copy the material carefully.** Take down the author's exact wording, spelling, capitalization, and punctuation.
- **Proofread every direct quotation at least twice.**
- **Use quotation marks around the quotation** so that later you won't confuse it with a paraphrase or summary. Be sure to transfer the quotation marks into your draft as well, unless the quotation is long and is set off from your text. For advice on handling long quotations, see **MLA** p. 480 and **APA** p. 515.
- **Use brackets** to add words for clarity or to change the capitalization of letters (see **5** p. 321 and **6** p. 334).
- **Use ellipsis marks** to omit material that is irrelevant to your point (see **5** pp. 318–20).
- **Cite the source of the quotation in your draft.** See pp. 408–09 on documentation.

Exercise 52.2 Summarizing and paraphrasing

Prepare two source notes, one summarizing the entire paragraph below and the other paraphrasing the first four sentences (ending with the word *autonomy*). Use the format for notes illustrated on pp. 391 and 392, omitting only the subject heading.

Federal organization [of the United States] has made it possible for the different states to deal with the same problems in many different ways. One consequence of federalism, then, has been that people are treated differently, by law, from state to state. The great strength of this system is that differences from state to state in cultural preferences, moral standards, and levels of wealth can be accommodated. In contrast to a unitary system in which the central government makes all important decisions (as in France), federalism is a powerful arrangement for maximizing regional freedom and autonomy. The great weakness of our federal system, however, is that people in some states receive less than the best or the most advanced or the least expensive services and policies that government can offer. The federal dilemma does not invite easy solution, for the costs and benefits of the arrangement have tended to balance out.
—Peter K. Eisinger et al., *American Politics*, p. 44

Exercise 52.3 Combining summary, paraphrase, and direct quotation

Prepare a source note containing a combination of paraphrase or summary and direct quotation that states the main idea of the passage below. Use the format for notes illustrated on pp. 391 and 392, omitting only the subject heading.

Most speakers unconsciously duel even during seemingly casual conversations, as can often be observed at social gatherings where they show less concern for exchanging information with other guests than for asserting their own dominance. Their verbal dueling often employs very subtle weapons like mumbling, a hostile act which defeats the listener's desire to understand what the speaker claims he is trying to say (but is really not saying because he is mumbling!). Or the verbal dueler may keep talking after someone has passed out of hearing range—which is often an aggressive challenge to the listener to return and acknowledge the dominance of the speaker. —Peter K. Farb, *Word Play*, p. 107

52e Integrating sources into your text

Integrating source material into your sentences is key to synthesizing others' ideas and information with your own. Evidence drawn from sources should *back up* your conclusions, not *be* your conclusions: you don't want to let your evidence overwhelm your own point of view. To keep your ideas in the forefront, you do more than merely present borrowed material; you introduce and interpret it as well.

Note The examples in this section use the MLA style of source documentation and also present-tense verbs (such as *disagrees* and *claims*). See pp. 398–99 for specific variations in documentation style and verb tense within the academic disciplines. Several other conventions governing quotations are discussed elsewhere in this book:

- **Using commas to punctuate signal phrases (5** pp. 294–95).
- **Placing other punctuation marks with quotation marks (5** pp. 314–15).
- **Using brackets and the ellipsis mark to indicate changes in quotations (5** pp. 318–21).
- **Punctuating and placing parenthetical citations (MLA** pp. 442–44).
- **Formatting long prose quotations and poetry quotations (MLA** p. 480 and **APA** p. 515).

1 Introduction of borrowed material

Always introduce a summary, a paraphrase, or a quotation by identifying it and by providing a smooth transition between your words and ideas and those of your source. In the passage below, the writer has not meshed the structures of her own and her source's sentences:

Awkward One editor disagrees with this view and "a good reporter does not fail to separate opinions from facts" (Lyman 52).

In the following revision the writer adds words to integrate the quotation into her sentence:

Revised One editor disagrees with this view, maintaining that "a good reporter does not fail to separate opinions from facts" (Lyman 52).

To mesh your own and your source's words, you may sometimes need to make a substitution or addition to the quotation, signaling your change with brackets:

Words added	"The tabloids [of England] are a journalistic case study in bad reporting," claims Lyman (52).
Verb form changed	A bad reporter, Lyman implies, is one who "[fails] to separate opinions from facts" (52). [The bracketed verb replaces *fail* in the original.]
Capitalization changed	"[T]o separate opinions from facts" is the work of a good reporter (Lyman 52). [In the original, *to* is not capitalized.]
Noun supplied for pronoun	The reliability of a news organization "depends on [reporters'] trustworthiness," says Lyman (52). [The bracketed noun replaces *their* in the original.]

2 Interpretation of borrowed material

You need to work borrowed material into your sentences so that readers see without effort how it contributes to the points you are making. If you merely dump source material into your paper without explaining how you intend it to be interpreted, readers will have to struggle to understand your sentences and the relationships you are trying to establish. For example, the following passage forces us to figure out for ourselves that the writer's sentence and the quotation state opposite points of view:

Dumped	Many news editors and reporters maintain that it is impossible to keep personal opinions from influencing the selection and presentation of facts. "True, news reporters, like everyone else, form impressions of what they see and hear. However, a good reporter does not fail to separate opinions from facts" (Lyman 52).

In the revision, the underlined additions tell us how to interpret the quotation:

Revised	Many news editors and reporters maintain that it is impossible to keep personal opinions from influencing the selection and presentation of facts. Yet not all authorities agree with this view. One editor grants that "news reporters, like everyone else, form impressions of what they see and hear." But, he insists, "a good reporter does not fail to separate opinions from facts" (Lyman 52).

Signal phrases

The words *One editor grants* and *he insists* in the revised passage above are **signal phrases**: they tell readers who the source is and what to expect in the quotations that follow. Signal phrases usually contain (1) the source author's name (or a substitute for it, such as

One editor and *he*) and (2) a verb that indicates the source author's attitude or approach to what he or she says.

Some verbs for signal phrases appear in the following list. These verbs are in the present tense, which is typical of writing in the humanities. In the social and natural sciences, the past tense (*noted*) or present perfect tense (*has noted*) is more common. See p. 399.

Author is neutral	Author infers or suggests	Author argues	Author is uneasy or disparaging
comments	analyzes	claims	belittles
describes	asks	contends	bemoans
explains	assesses	defends	complains
illustrates	concludes	holds	condemns
notes	considers	insists	deplores
observes	finds	maintains	deprecates
points out	predicts		derides
records	proposes	Author agrees	disagrees
relates	reveals	admits	laments
reports	shows	agrees	warns
says	speculates	concedes	
sees	suggests	concurs	
thinks	supposes	grants	
writes			

Vary your signal phrases to suit your interpretation of borrowed material and also to keep readers' interest. A signal phrase may precede, interrupt, or follow the borrowed material:

Precedes	Lyman insists that "a good reporter does not fail to separate opinions from facts" (52).
Interrupts	"However," Lyman insists, "a good reporter does not fail to separate opinions from facts" (52).
Follows	"[A] good reporter does not fail to separate opinions from facts," Lyman insists (52).

Background information

You can add information to a quotation to integrate it into your text and to inform readers why you are using it. In most cases, provide the author's name in the text, especially if the author is an expert or if readers will recognize the name:

Author named	Harold Lyman grants that "news reporters, like everyone else, form impressions of what they see and hear." But, Lyman insists, "a good reporter does not fail to separate opinions from facts" (52).

If the source title contributes information about the author or the context of the quotation, you can provide it in the text:

Title given	Harold Lyman, in his recent book *The Conscience of Journalism*, grants that "news reporters, like everyone else, form

impressions of what they see and hear." But, Lyman insists, "a good reporter does not fail to separate opinions from facts" (52).

If the quoted author's background and experience reinforce or clarify the quotation, you can provide those credentials in the text:

Credentials given | Harold Lyman, a newspaper editor for more than forty years, grants that "news reporters, like everyone else, form impressions of what they see and hear." But, Lyman insists, "a good reporter does not fail to separate opinions from facts" (52).

You need not name the author, source, or credentials in your text when you are simply establishing facts or weaving together facts and opinions from varied sources. In the following passage, the information is more important than the source, so the name of the source is confined to a parenthetical acknowledgment:

To end the abuses of the British, many colonists were urging three actions: forming a united front, seceding from Britain, and taking control of their own international relations (Wills 325–36).

---

3 Discipline styles for integrating sources

The preceding guidelines for introducing and interpreting borrowed material apply generally across academic disciplines, but the disciplines do differ in their verb tenses and documentation styles.

English and some other humanities

Writers in English, foreign languages, and related disciplines use MLA style for documenting sources and generally use the present tense of verbs in signal phrases. In discussing sources other than works of literature, the present perfect tense is also sometimes appropriate:

Lyman insists . . . [present]
Lyman has insisted . . . [present perfect]

In discussing works of literature, use only the present tense to describe both the work of the author and the action in the work:

Kate Chopin builds irony into every turn of "The Story of an Hour." For example, Mrs. Mallard, the central character, finds joy in the death of her husband, whom she loves, because she anticipates "the long procession of years that would belong to her absolutely" (23).

Avoid shifting tenses in writing about literature. You can, for instance, shorten quotations to avoid their past-tense verbs.

Shift | Her freedom elevates her, so that "she carried herself unwittingly like a goddess of victory" (24).

No shift   Her freedom <u>elevates</u> her, so that she <u>walks</u> "unwittingly like a goddess of victory" (24).

History and other humanities

Writers in history, art history, philosophy, and related disciplines generally use the present perfect tense or present tense of verbs in signal phrases.

> Lincoln persisted, as Haworth <u>has noted</u>, in "feeling that events controlled him."[3]

> What Miller <u>calls</u> Lincoln's "severe self-doubt"[6] undermined his effectiveness on at least two occasions.

The raised numbers after the quotations are part of the Chicago documentation style, used in history and other disciplines.

Social and natural sciences

Writers in the sciences generally use a verb's present tense just for reporting the results of a study (*The data suggest* . . .). Otherwise, they use a verb's past tense or present perfect tense in a signal phrase, as when introducing an explanation, interpretation, or other commentary. (Thus when you are writing for the sciences, generally convert the list of signal-phrase verbs on p. 397 from the present to the present perfect tense or past tense.)

> Lin (1999) <u>has suggested</u> that preschooling may significantly affect children's academic performance through high school (pp. 22–23).

> In an exhaustive survey of the literature published between 1990 and 2000, Walker (2001) <u>found</u> "no proof, merely a weak correlation, linking place of residence and rate of illness" (p. 121).

These passages conform to APA documentation style. APA style, or one quite similar to it, is also used in sociology, education, nursing, biology, and many other sciences.

Exercise 52.4   Introducing and interpreting borrowed material

Drawing on the ideas in the following paragraph and using examples from your own observations and experiences, write a paragraph about anxiety. Integrate at least one direct quotation and one paraphrase from the following paragraph into your own sentences. In your paragraph, identify the author by name and give his credentials: he is a professor of psychiatry and a practicing psychoanalyst.

There are so many ways in which human beings are different from all the lower forms of animals, and almost all of them make us uniquely susceptible to feelings of anxiousness. Our imagination and reasoning powers facilitate anxiety; the anxious feeling is precipitated not by an absolute impending threat—such as the worry about an examination, a speech, travel—but rather by the symbolic and often unconscious representations. We do not have to be experiencing a potential danger. We can experience something related to it. We can recall, through our incredible memories, the original symbolic sense of vulnerability in childhood and suffer the feeling attached to that. We can even forget the original memory and be stuck with the emotion—which is then compounded by its seemingly irrational quality at this time. It is not just the fear of death which pains us, but the anticipation of it; or the anniversary of a specific death; or a street, a hospital, a time of day, a color, a flower, a symbol associated with death.

—Willard Gaylin, "Feeling Anxious," p. 23

53   Avoiding Plagiarism

Chapter essentials

- Know what plagiarism is, and do not plagiarize sources deliberately or carelessly (below and opposite).
- Know which sources you do not need to cite (p. 403).
- Know which sources you *must* cite (p. 403).
- Obtain permission from copyright holders if you intend to publish your work (p. 407).

Visit MyWritingLab™ for more resources on avoiding plagiarism.

The knowledge building that is the focus of academic writing rests on the integrity of everyone who participates, including students, in using and crediting sources. The work of a writer or creator is his or her intellectual property. You and others may borrow the work's ideas and even its words or an image, but you *must* acknowledge that what you borrowed came from someone else.

When you acknowledge sources in your writing, you are doing more than giving credit to the writer or creator of the work you consulted. You are also showing what your own writing is based on, which in turn adds to your integrity as a researcher and writer. Acknowledging sources creates the trust among scholars, students, writers, and readers that knowledge building requires.

Plagiarism (from a Latin word for "kidnapper") is the presentation of someone else's work as your own. Whether deliberate or careless, plagiarism is a serious offense. It breaks trust, and it undermines or even destroys your credibility as a researcher and writer. In most colleges, a code of academic honesty calls for severe consequences for plagiarism: a reduced or failing grade, suspension from school, or expulsion. The way to avoid plagiarism is to acknowledge your sources: keep track of the ones you consult for each paper you write, and document them within the paper and in a list of works cited.

CULTURE LANGUAGE   The concepts of originality, intellectual property, and plagiarism are not universal. In some other cultures, for instance, students may be encouraged to copy the words

Checklist for avoiding plagiarism

Know your source.
Are you using

- your own experience,
- common knowledge, or
- someone else's material?

You must acknowledge someone else's material.

Quote carefully.

- Check that every quotation exactly matches its source.
- Insert quotation marks around every quotation that you run into your text. (A quotation set off from the text does not need quotation marks. See **MLA** p. 480 and **APA** p. 515.)
- Indicate any omission from a quotation with an ellipsis mark and any addition with brackets.
- Acknowledge the source of every quotation.

Paraphrase and summarize carefully.

- Use your own words and sentence structures for every paraphrase and summary. If you have used the author's words, add quotation marks around them.
- Acknowledge the source of the idea(s) in every paraphrase or summary.

Cite sources responsibly.

- Acknowledge every use of someone else's material in each place you use it.
- Include all your sources in your list of works cited. See **MLA** pp. 441–77, **APA** pp. 497–512, **Chic** pp. 524–35, and **CSE** pp. 536–41 for citing sources in the most common documentation styles.

of scholars without acknowledgment, in order to demonstrate their mastery of or respect for the scholars' work. In the United States, however, using an author's work without a source citation is a serious offense, whether it is accidental or intentional. When in doubt about the guidelines in this chapter, ask your instructor for advice.

53a Avoiding both deliberate and careless plagiarism

Instructors usually distinguish between deliberate plagiarism, which is cheating, and careless plagiarism, which often stems from a writer's inexperience with managing sources.

1 Deliberate plagiarism

Deliberate plagiarism is intentional: the writer chooses to cheat by turning in someone else's work as his or her own. Students who deliberately plagiarize deprive themselves of an education in honest research. When their cheating is detected, the students often face stiff penalties, including expulsion.

Following are examples of deliberate plagiarism:

Copying a phrase, a sentence, or a longer passage from a source and passing it off as your own by not adding quotation marks and a source citation.

Summarizing or paraphrasing someone else's ideas without acknowledging the source in a citation.

Handing in as your own work a paper you have copied off the Web, had a friend write, or accepted from another student.

Handing in as your own work a paper you have purchased from a paper-writing service. **Paying for research or a paper does not make it your work.**

2 Careless plagiarism

Careless plagiarism is unintentional: grappling with complicated information and ideas in sources, the writer neglects to put quotation marks around a source's exact words or neglects to include a source citation for a quotation, paraphrase, or summary. Most instructors and schools do not permit careless plagiarism, but they treat it less harshly than deliberate plagiarism—at least the first time it occurs.

Here are examples of careless plagiarism:

Reading sources without taking notes on them and then not distinguishing what you recently learned from what you already knew.

Copying and pasting material from a source into your document without placing quotation marks around the other writer's work.

Forgetting to add a source citation for a paraphrase. Even though a paraphrase casts another person's idea in your own words, you still need to cite the source of the idea.

Omitting a source citation for another's idea because you are unaware of the need to acknowledge the idea.

Plagiarism and the Internet

The Internet has made it easier to plagiarize than ever before: with just a few clicks, you can copy and paste passages or whole documents into your own files. If you do so without quoting and acknowledging your source, you plagiarize.

The Internet has also made plagiarism easier to detect. Instructors can use search engines to find specific phrases or sentences anywhere on the Web, including among scholarly publications, all kinds of Web sites, and term-paper collections. They can search term-paper sites as easily as students can, looking for similarities with papers they've received. They can also use detection software—such as *Turnitin, PlagiServe,* and *Glatt Plagiarism Services*—which compares students' work with other work anywhere on the Internet, seeking matches as short as a few words.

Some instructors suggest that their students use plagiarism-detection programs to verify that their own work does not include careless plagiarism, at least not from the Internet.

53b | Knowing what you need not acknowledge

1 | Your independent material

Your own observations, thoughts, compilations of facts, or experimental results—expressed in your words and format—do not require acknowledgment. You should describe the basis for your conclusions so that readers can evaluate your thinking, but you need not cite sources for them.

2 | Common knowledge

Common knowledge consists of the standard information on a subject as well as folk literature and commonsense observations.

- **Standard information** includes the major facts of history, such as the dates during which Charlemagne ruled as emperor of Rome (800–14). It does *not* include interpretations of facts, such as a historian's opinion that Charlemagne was sometimes needlessly cruel in extending his power.
- **Folk literature,** such as the fairy tale "Snow White," is popularly known and cannot be traced to a particular writer. Literature traceable to a writer is *not* folk literature, even if it is very familiar.
- **Commonsense observations** are things most people know, such as that inflation is most troublesome for people with low and fixed incomes. However, a particular economist's argument about the effects of inflation on Chinese immigrants is *not* a commonsense observation.

If you do not know a subject well enough to determine whether a piece of information is common knowledge, make a record of the source as you would for any other quotation, paraphrase, or summary. As you read more about the subject, the information may come up repeatedly without acknowledgment, in which case it is probably common knowledge. But if you are still in doubt when you finish your research, always acknowledge the source.

53c | Knowing what you *must* acknowledge

You must always acknowledge other people's independent material—that is, any facts, ideas, or opinions that are not common knowledge or your own. The source may be a formal publication or release, such as a book, an article, a movie, an interview, an artwork, a comic strip, a map, a Web page, or a blog. The source may also be informal, such as a tweet, a posting on *Facebook*, an opinion you heard on the radio, or a comment by your instructor or a classmate that substantially shaped your argument. You must acknowledge summaries or paraphrases of ideas or facts as well as quotations of the language and format in which ideas or facts appear: wording, sentence structures, arrangement, and special graphics (such as a diagram). You must acknowledge another's material no matter how you use it, how much of it you use, or how often you use it.

1 Copied language: Quotation marks and a source citation

The following example baldly plagiarizes the original quotation from Jessica Mitford's *Kind and Usual Punishment,* p. 9. Without quotation marks or a source citation, the example matches Mitford's wording (underlined) and closely parallels her sentence structure:

Original quotation	"The character and mentality of the keepers may be of more importance in understanding prisons than the character and mentality of the kept."
Plagiarism	But the character of prison officials (the keepers) is of more importance in understanding prisons than the character of prisoners (the kept).

To avoid plagiarism, the writer can paraphrase and cite the source (see the examples on the next page) or use Mitford's actual words *in quotation marks* and *with a source citation* (here, in MLA style):

Revision (quotation)	According to Mitford, a critic of the penal system, "The character and mentality of the keepers may be of more importance in understanding prisons than the character and mentality of the kept" (9).

Even with a source citation and with a different sentence structure, the next example is still plagiarism because it uses some of Mitford's words (underlined) without quotation marks:

Plagiarism	According to Mitford, a critic of the penal system, the psychology of the kept may say less about prisons than psychology of the keepers (9).
Revision (quotation)	According to Mitford, a critic of the penal system, the psychology of "the kept" may say less about prisons than the psychology of "the keepers" (9).

2 Paraphrase or summary: Your own words and sentence structure and a source citation

The example below changes the sentence structure of the original Mitford quotation above, but it still uses Mitford's words (underlined) without quotation marks and without a source citation:

Plagiarism	In understanding prisons, we should know more about the character and mentality of the keepers than of the kept.

To avoid plagiarism, the writer can use quotation marks and cite the source (see examples above) or *use his or her own words* and still *cite the source* (because the idea is Mitford's, not the writer's):

Revision
(paraphrase)

Mitford holds that we may be able to learn more about prisons from the psychology of the prison officials than from that of the prisoners (9).

Revision
(paraphrase)

We may understand prisons better if we focus on the personalities and attitudes of the prison workers rather than those of the inmates (Mitford 9).

In the next example, the writer cites Mitford and does not use her words but still plagiarizes her sentence structure. The revision changes the sentence structure as well as the words.

Plagiarism

Mitford, a critic of the penal system, maintains that the psychology of prison officials may be more informative about prisons than the psychology of prisoners (9).

Revision
(paraphrase)

Mitford, a critic of the penal system, maintains that we may learn less from the psychology of prisoners than from the psychology of prison officials (9).

3 Using online sources

Online sources are so accessible and so easy to copy into your own documents that it may seem they are freely available, exempting you from the obligation to acknowledge them. They are not. Acknowledging online sources is somewhat trickier than acknowledging print sources, but it is no less essential: when you use someone else's independent material from an online source, you must acknowledge the source.

Citing online sources is easier when you keep track of them as you work:

- **Record complete publication information each time you consult an online source.** Online sources may change from one day to the next or even disappear entirely. See p. 354 for the information to record, such as the publication date. Without the proper information, you *may not* use the source.

- **Immediately put quotation marks around any text that you copy and paste into your document.** If you don't add quotation marks right away, you risk forgetting which words belong to the source and which are yours. If you don't know whose words you are using, recheck the source or *do not* use them.

- **Acknowledge linked sites.** If you use not only a Web site but also one or more of its linked sites, you must acknowledge the linked sites as well. The fact that one person has used a second person's work does not release you from the responsibility to cite the second work.

Exercise 53.1 Recognizing plagiarism

The following numbered items show various attempts to quote or paraphrase a passage by George Vaillant. Carefully compare each attempt with the original passage. Which attempts are plagiarized, inaccurate, or both, and which are acceptable? Why?

I would agree with the sociologists that psychiatric labeling is dangerous. Society can inflict terrible wounds by discrimination, and by confusing health with disease and disease with badness.

—George E. Vaillant, *Adaptation to Life,* p. 361

1 According to George Vaillant, society often inflicts wounds by using psychiatric labeling, confusing health, disease, and badness (361).

2 According to George Vaillant, "psychiatric labeling [such as 'homosexual' or 'schizophrenic'] is dangerous. Society can inflict terrible wounds by . . . confusing health with disease and disease with badness" (361).

3 According to George Vaillant, when psychiatric labeling discriminates between health and disease or between disease and badness, it can inflict wounds on those labeled (361).

4 Psychiatric labels can badly hurt those labeled, says George Vaillant, because they fail to distinguish among health, illness, and immorality (361).

5 Labels such as "homosexual" and "schizophrenic" can be hurtful when they fail to distinguish among health, illness, and immorality.

6 "I would agree with the sociologists that society can inflict terrible wounds by discrimination, and by confusing health with disease and disease with badness" (Vaillant 361).

Exercise 53.2 Revising plagiarized sentences

The following numbered items plagiarize sentences in a paragraph by Steven Pinker. Analyze the problem in each item, and then rewrite it to quote or paraphrase correctly and add a source citation. Each item has more than one correct answer.

Friendship, like other kinds of altruism, is vulnerable to cheaters, and we have a special name for them: fair-weather friends. These sham friends reap the benefits of associating with a valuable person and mimic signs of warmth in an effort to become valued themselves. But when a little rain falls, they are nowhere in sight. People have an emotional response that seems designed to weed out fair-weather friends. When we are neediest, an extended hand is deeply affecting. We are moved, never forget the generosity, and feel compelled to tell the friend we will never forget it.

—Steven Pinker, *How the Mind Works,* p. 509

1 Like other kinds of altruism, friendship is vulnerable to cheaters, people whom we call fair-weather friends.

2 According to Steven Pinker, sham friends draw advantages from being with someone they value, and they "mimic signs of warmth in an effort to become valued themselves."

3 Steven Pinker writes that people seem to have an emotional response designed to weed out fair-weather friends.

4 Pinker points out that when people are at their lowest, a sign of friendship is truly touching.

5 Pinker describes people who have received acts of friendship as moved. They do not forget the generosity, and they are compelled to say that they will never forget it.

53d Obtaining permission when publishing your work

When you use material from print or online sources in a project that will be published, you must not only acknowledge your sources but also take care to observe copyright restrictions.

Publication means that your work will circulate outside the limited circle of a class or other group. It may appear in print media, such as magazines and newspapers, or it may appear on the Web, which is a publication medium as well. (The exception is a Web site, such as a course site, that is protected by a password. Many copyright holders regard such a site as private.)

When you publish your work, borrowing certain kinds or amounts of material requires you to obtain the permission of the copyright holders. You can find information about copyright holders and permissions on the copyright page of a print publication (following the title page) and on a page labeled something like "Terms of Use" on a Web site. If you don't see an explicit release for student use or publication on private Web sites, assume that you must seek permission.

The legal convention of **fair use** allows an author to use a small portion of copyrighted material without obtaining the copyright holder's permission, as long as the author acknowledges the source. The standards of fair use are not fixed, so the following guidelines are conservative:

- **Text from print sources:** Quote without permission fewer than fifty words from an article or fewer than three hundred words from a book. You'll need permission to use any longer quotation from an article or a book or any quotation at all from a play, poem, or song.
- **Text from online sources:** Quote without permission text that represents just a small portion of the whole—say, up to forty words out of three hundred. As with print texts, seek permission for any use of a play, poem, or song that you find online.
- **Visuals, audio, and video:** Seek permission to use any copyrighted media from either print or online sources: photographs, charts, maps, cartoons, paintings, audio files, video files, and so on.

Note Much valuable material is not copyrighted and can be used without permission, although *you must still cite the source.* Uncopyrighted sources fall into two groups:

- **The creator does not claim copyright.** This category includes most government documents and material labeled for reuse, such as some of the media on *Google, Flikr Creative Commons,* and *Wikimedia Commons.*
- **The copyright has lapsed.** Material in the public domain includes most works by authors who have been dead at least fifty years.

Chapter essentials

- Use the documentation style appropriate for your discipline (below).
- Use bibliography software with care (facing page).

Visit MyWritingLab™ for more resources on documenting sources.

Every time you borrow the words, facts, or ideas of others, you must **document** the source—that is, supply a reference (or document) telling readers that you borrowed the material and where you borrowed it from.

Editors and instructors in most academic disciplines require special documentation formats (or styles) in their scholarly journals and in students' papers. All the styles share two features described in the following box.

Key features of source documentation

- **Citations in the text signal that material is borrowed and refer readers to detailed information about the sources.** The following text citation, in MLA style, gives the source author's last name and the page number in the source. Other styles add a publication date. Some styles use raised numerals to refer to numbered source information.

  Veterans are more likely to complete college degrees if they have not only professional support but also a community of peers (Dao A16).

- **Detailed source information, either in footnotes or at the end of the paper, tells how to locate sources.** The following source listing, also in MLA style, provides detailed publication information for the source summarized above. Most styles provide the same information, but they may organize and punctuate it differently.

  Dao, James. "Getting Them Through: Helping Veterans Graduate." *New York Times* 5 Feb. 2013, natl. ed.: A16+. Print.

54a Using discipline styles for documentation

Aside from the similarities of citations in the text and detailed source information, the disciplines' documentation styles vary markedly in citation form, arrangement of source information, and other particulars. Each discipline's style reflects the needs of its practitioners for certain kinds of information presented in certain ways. For instance, the currency of a source is important in the social sciences, where studies build on and correct each other; thus in-text citations in the social sciences include a source's year of publication. In the humanities, however, currency is less important, so in-text citations do not include the date of publication.

The disciplines' documentation formats are described in style guides listed in **8** pp. 424 (literature and other humanities), 427 (social sciences), and 430 (natural and applied sciences). This book also discusses and illustrates four common documentation styles:

- MLA style, used in English, foreign languages, and some other humanities (**MLA** p. 435).
- APA style, used in psychology and some other social sciences (**APA** p. 494).
- Chicago style, used in history, art history, philosophy, religion, and some other humanities (**Chic** p. 524).
- CSE style, used in the biological and some other sciences (**CSE** p. 536).

Always ask your instructor which documentation style you should use. If your instructor does not specify a particular style, use the one in this book that's most appropriate for the discipline in which you're writing. Do follow a single system for citing sources so that you provide all the necessary information in a consistent format.

54b Using bibliography software

Bibliography software can help you format your source citations in the style of your choice, and some programs can help you keep track of sources as you research. Your library may offer one or more bibliography programs, such as *RefWorks* or *Endnote*, or you can find free options on the Web, such as *Zotero*, *Bibme*, and *EasyBib*.

The programs vary in what they can do. Some simply prompt you for needed information (author's name, book title, and so on) and then format the information into a bibliography following the format of your documentation style. Others go beyond formatting to help you organize your sources, export citations from databases, and insert in-text citations as you write.

As helpful as bibliography programs can be, they don't always work the way they're advertised, and they can't substitute for your own care and attention in giving your sources accurate and complete acknowledgment. Always ask your instructors if you may use such software for your papers, and always review the citations compiled by any software to ensure that they meet your instructors' requirements.

Chapter essentials
- Focus your material with a thesis statement (below).
- Organize your material (opposite).
- Write a first draft, including source citations (opposite).
- Revise and edit the draft (opposite and p. 412).
- Use an appropriate document format (p. 412).

Visit MyWritingLab™ for more resources on writing the research paper.

Like other kinds of writing, research writing involves focusing on a main idea, organizing supporting ideas, expressing ideas in a draft, revising and editing drafts, and formatting the final paper. Because research writing draws on others' work, however, its stages also require attention to interpreting, integrating, and citing sources.

This chapter complements and extends the detailed discussion of the writing situation and the writing process in Chapters 1–6 (**1** pp. 3–38). If you haven't already done so, you may want to read those chapters before this one.

55a Focusing and organizing the paper

Before you begin using your source notes in a draft, give some thought to your main idea and your organization.

1 Thesis statement

You began research with a question about your subject (see pp. 349–50). Your question may have evolved during research, but you should be able to answer it once you've consulted most of your sources. Try to state that answer in a **thesis statement,** a claim that narrows your subject to a single assertion. Here, for example, are the research question and thesis statement of Justin Malik, whose final paper appears later in this book (**MLA** pp. 481–90):

Research question
How can green consumerism help the environment?

Thesis statement
Although green consumerism can help the environment, consumerism itself is the root of some of the most pressing ecological problems. To make a real difference, humans must consume less.

(Malik's thesis statement consists of two sentences, the first setting up the second. Many instructors allow statements of two or more sentences as long they build a single idea and the final sentence presents the key assertion of the paper. However, other instructors require thesis statements of a single sentence. Ask your instructor for his or her preference.)

A precise thesis statement will give you a focus as you organize and draft your paper. For more on thesis statements, see 1 pp. 14–17.

2 Organization

To structure your paper, you'll need to synthesize, or forge relationships among ideas (see pp. 387–89). Here is one approach:

- **Arrange source information in categories.** Each group should correspond to a main section of your paper: a key idea of your own that supports the thesis. Within each category, you may have source views that differ from your own and that you intend to discuss or refute.
- **Review your research journal** for connections between sources and other thoughts that can help you organize your paper.
- **Look objectively at your categories.** If some are skimpy, with little information, consider whether you should drop the categories or conduct more research to fill them out. If most of your information falls into one or two categories, consider whether they are too broad and should be divided. (If any of this rethinking affects your thesis statement, revise it accordingly.)
- **Within each group, distinguish between the main idea and the supporting ideas and evidence.** Only the support should come from your sources. The main idea should be your own.

See 1 pp. 18–22 for more on organizing a paper, including samples of both informal and formal outlines.

55b Drafting, revising, editing, and formatting the paper

1 First draft

In drafting your paper, you do not have to proceed methodically from introduction to conclusion. Instead, draft in sections, beginning with the one you feel most confident about. Each section should center on a principal idea contributing to your thesis, a conclusion you have drawn from reading and responding to sources. Start the section by stating the idea; then support it with information, summaries, paraphrases, and quotations from your notes. Remember to insert source information from your notes as well.

2 Revision

Always revise your draft first, satisfying yourself with the content and shape of the whole before trying to edit sentences and words. Begin with the advice and checklist in 1 pp. 27–30, and supplement them with the checklist on the next page.

Checklist for revising a research paper

Assignment
How does the draft satisfy all of the criteria stated in your instructor's assignment?

Thesis statement
How well does your thesis statement describe your subject and your perspective as they emerged during drafting?

Structure
(Outlining your draft can help you see structure at a glance. See **1** p. 28.) How consistently does borrowed material illuminate and support—not lead and dominate—your own ideas? How well is the importance of ideas reflected in the emphasis they receive? Will the arrangement of ideas be clear to readers?

Evidence
Where might evidence seem weak or irrelevant to readers?

Reasonableness and clarity
How reasonable will readers find your argument? (See **2** pp. 103–07.) Where do you need to define terms or concepts that readers may not know or may dispute?

Source citations
Have you provided an in-text citation for every use of someone else's material and provided a complete list of all your sources?

3 Editing

For editing, consult the advice and checklist in **1** pp. 33–37. Try to read your work from the point of view of someone who has not spent hours planning and researching but instead has come fresh to the paper. Look for lapses in sense, awkward passages, wordiness, poor transitions between ideas and evidence, unnecessary repetition, wrong or misspelled words, errors in grammar, punctuation, or mechanics—in short, anything that is likely to interfere with a reader's understanding of your meaning.

4 Format

The final draft of your paper should conform to the document format recommended by your instructor or by the style guide of the discipline in which you are writing. This book details two common formats: Modern Language Association (**MLA** pp. 478–80) and American Psychological Association (**APA** pp. 512–15).

In any discipline you can present your ideas effectively and attractively with readable typefonts, headings, illustrations, and other elements. See **1** pp. 54–62 for ideas.

PART 8

Writing in the Disciplines

Writing in the Disciplines

56 Reading and Writing about Literature

By Sylvan Barnet

Chapter essentials

- Use the methods and evidence common in literary analysis (below).
- Understand your writing assignment (p. 418).
- Use the tools and language of literary analysis (p. 419).
- Use MLA style for citing sources and formatting papers (p. 420).

Visit MyWritingLab™ for more resources on reading and writing about literature.

Writers of literature—stories, novels, poems, and plays—are concerned with presenting human experience concretely, with *showing* rather than *telling*, with giving a sense of the feel of life. Reading and writing about literature thus require extremely close attention to the feel of the words. For instance, the word *woods* in Robert Frost's "Stopping by Woods on a Snowy Evening" has a rural, folksy quality that *forest* doesn't have, and many such small distinctions contribute to the poem's effect.

When you read literature, you interpret distinctions like these, forming an idea of the work. When you write about literature, you state your idea as your thesis, and you support the thesis with evidence from the work. (See **1** pp. 14–17 for more on thesis statements.)

Note Writing about literature is not merely summarizing literature. Your thesis is a claim about the meaning or effect of the literary work, not a statement of its plot. And your paper is a demonstration of your thesis, not a retelling of the work's events.

56a Using the methods and evidence of literary analysis

1 Reading literature

Reading literature critically involves interacting with a text, not in order to make negative judgments but in order to understand the work and evaluate its significance or quality. Such interaction is not passive, like scanning a newspaper or watching television. Instead, it is a process of engagement, of diving into the words themselves.

You will become more engaged if you write while you read. If you own the book you're reading, you can highlight or annotate passages that please, displease, or confuse you. If you don't own the book, make these notes on separate sheets or on your computer.

An effective way to interact with a text is to keep a **reading journal**. A journal is not a diary in which you record your doings; instead, it is a place to develop and store your reflections on what you read, such as a response to a particular character. See **1** pp. 10–11 for more on journal keeping.

2 Meaning in literature

In analyzing literature, you face right off the question of *meaning*. Readers disagree all the time over the meanings of works of literature, partly because (as noted earlier) literature *shows* rather than *tells*: it gives concrete images of imagined human experiences, but it usually does not say how we ought to understand these images. Further, readers bring different experiences to their reading and thus understand images differently. In writing about literature, then, we can offer only our *interpretation* of the meaning rather than *the* meaning. Still, most people agree that there are limits to interpretation: it must be supported by evidence that a reasonable person finds at least plausible if not totally convincing.

3 Questions for a literary analysis

One reason interpretations of meaning differ is that readers approach literary works differently, focusing on certain elements and interpreting those elements distinctively. For instance, some critics look at a literary work mainly as an artifact of the particular time and culture in which it was created, while other critics stress the work's effect on its readers.

This chapter emphasizes so-called formalist criticism, which sees a literary work primarily as something to be understood in itself. This critical framework engages the reader immediately in the work of literature, without requiring extensive historical or cultural background, and it introduces the conventional elements of literature that all critical approaches discuss, even though they view the elements differently. The following list poses questions for each element that can help you think constructively and imaginatively about what you read.

■ *Plot:* **the relationships and patterns of events.** Even a poem has a plot—for instance, a change in mood from grief to resignation.

What actions happen?
What conflicts occur?
How do the events connect to each other and to the whole?

■ *Characters:* **the people the author creates,** including the narrator of a story or the speaker of a poem.

Who are the principal people in the work?
How do they interact?
What do their actions, words, and thoughts reveal about their personalities and the personalities of others?
Do the characters stay the same, or do they change? Why?

■ *Point of view:* **the perspective or attitude of the speaker in a poem or the voice who tells a story.** The point of view may be **first person** (a participant, using *I*) or **third person** (an outsider, using *he, she, it, they*). A first-person narrator may be a major or a minor character in the narrative and may be **reliable** or **unreliable** (unable to report events wholly or accurately). A third-person narrator may be **omniscient** (knows what goes on in all characters' minds), **limited** (knows what goes on in the mind of only one or two characters), or **objective** (knows only what is external to the characters).

Who is the narrator (or the speaker of a poem)?
How does the narrator's point of view affect the narrative?

■ *Tone:* **the narrator's or speaker's attitude,** perceived through the words (for instance, joyful, bitter, or confident).

What tone (or tones) do you hear? If there is a change, how do you account for it?
Is there an ironic contrast between the narrator's tone (for instance, confidence) and what you take to be the author's attitude (for instance, pity for human overconfidence)?

■ *Imagery:* **word pictures or details involving the senses of sight, sound, touch, smell, and taste.**

What images does the writer use? What senses do they draw on?
What patterns are evident in the images (for instance, religious or commercial images)?
What is the significance of the imagery?

■ *Symbolism:* **concrete things standing for larger and more abstract ideas.** For instance, the American flag may symbolize freedom, or a dead flower may symbolize mortality.

What symbols does the author use? What do they seem to signify?
How does the symbolism relate to the theme of the work?

■ *Setting:* **the place where the action happens.**

What does the locale contribute to the work?
Are scene shifts significant?

■ *Form:* **the shape or structure of the work.**

What *is* the form? (For example, a story might divide sharply in the middle, moving from happiness to sorrow.)
What parts of the work does the form emphasize, and why?

■ *Themes:* **the main ideas about human experience suggested by the work as a whole.** A theme is neither a plot (what happens) nor a subject (such as mourning or marriage). Rather it is what the author says with that plot about that subject.

Can you state each theme in a sentence? Avoid mentioning specific characters or actions; instead, write an observation applicable to humanity in general. For instance, you might state the following about Agha Shahid Ali's poem "Postcard from Kashmir" (p. 420): *The poem explores feelings of having more than one home.*

Do certain words, passages of dialog or description, or situations seem to represent a theme most clearly?
How do the work's elements combine to develop a theme?

■ *Appeal:* **the degree to which the work pleases you.**

What do you especially like or dislike about the work? Why?
Do you think your responses are unique, or would they be common to most readers? Why?

4 Using evidence in writing about literature

The evidence for a literary analysis always comes from at least one primary source (the work or works being discussed) and may come from secondary sources (critical and historical works). (See 7 p. 351 for more on primary and secondary sources.) For example, in the paper on pp. 420–22 about Agha Shahid Ali's "Postcard from Kashmir," the primary material is the poem itself, and the secondary material includes two critical studies of the poem and a published interview with the poet. The bulk of the evidence in a literary analysis is usually quotations from the work, although summaries and paraphrases can be useful as well.

Your instructor will probably tell you if you are expected to consult secondary sources for an assignment. They can help you understand a writer's work, but your primary concern should always be the work itself, not what critics A, B, and C say about it. In general, then, quote or summarize secondary material sparingly. And always cite your sources.

56b Understanding writing assignments in literature

Two common assignments in writing about literature are literary analyses and literary research papers:

■ **A literary analysis (no secondary sources):** Give your ideas about a work of literature—your interpretation of its meaning, significance, or representations. Generally, a literary analysis centers on an arguable thesis statement that you support with evidence from the work.

■ **A literary research paper (with secondary sources):** Combine analysis of a literary work with research in secondary sources about the work. You might consider other scholars' interpretations of the work, biographical information about the author, or accounts of the context in which the author wrote the work. Generally, such a paper centers on an arguable thesis statement that you support with evidence from the text and from secondary sources, which must be cited. See pp. 420–22 for an example.

In addition, a literature instructor may ask you to write papers in the following genres:

■ **A personal response or reaction paper:** Express your thoughts and feelings about a work of literature.

■ **A book review:** Summarize a book and judge its value.

■ **A theater review:** Respond to and evaluate a theatrical performance.

56c Using the tools and language of literary analysis

1 Writing tools

The fundamental tool for writing about literature is reading critically. Asking analytical questions such as those on pp. 416–18 can help you focus your ideas, and keeping a reading journal can help you develop your thoughts. In addition, discuss the work with others who have read it. They may offer reactions and insights that will help you shape your own ideas.

2 Language considerations

Use the present tense° of verbs to describe both the action in a literary work and the writing of an author: *The poem's speaker imagines his home in Kashmir. Ali compares memory to a photograph. The critic Jahan Ramazani interprets the poem's subject as loss of one's homeland.* Use the past tense° to describe events that actually occurred in the past: *Ali moved to the United States in 1976.*

Some instructors discourage students from using the first-person *I* (as in *I felt sorry for the character*) in writing about literature. At least use *I* sparingly to avoid sounding egotistical. Rephrase sentences to avoid using *I* unnecessarily—for instance, *The character evokes the reader's sympathy.*

56d Documenting sources and formatting papers in literary analysis

Unless your instructor specifies otherwise, use the documentation style of the Modern Language Association, detailed in **MLA** pp. 435–77. In MLA style, citations in the text of the paper refer to a list of works cited at the end. Sample papers illustrating this style appear on the following pages, in **2** pp. 98–99 and 113–16, and in **MLA** pp. 482–89.

Use MLA format for headings, margins, long quotations, and other elements, as detailed in **MLA** pp. 478–80.

56e Examining a sample literary analysis

A poem and a student paper on the work appear on the following pages. The student, Jessie Glenn, makes an argument for a particular interpretation of the poem, not only analyzing the poem itself but

°See "Glossary of Terms," **GI** p. 558.

also drawing on secondary sources—that is, critical works *about* the poem. In the opening paragraph, for instance, Glenn uses a brief quotation from a secondary source to establish how her interpretation differs from those made by other readers. This quotation and the three later uses of secondary sources are support for Glenn's points.

Note the following features of Glenn's paper:

- **The writer does not merely summarize the literary work.** She summarizes briefly to make her meaning clear, but her essay consists mostly of her own analysis.
- **The writer uses many quotations from the literary work.** The quotations provide evidence for her ideas and let readers hear the voice of the work.
- **The writer integrates quotations smoothly into her own sentences.** See **7** pp. 395–99.
- **The writer uses the present tense of verbs** to describe both the author's work and the action in the work.

Poem

Agha Shahid Ali

Postcard from Kashmir

Kashmir shrinks into my mailbox,
my home a neat four by six inches.
I always loved neatness. Now I hold
the half-inch Himalayas in my hand.

This is home. And this the closest   5
I'll ever be to home. When I return,
the colors won't be so brilliant,
the Jhelum's waters so clean,
so ultramarine. My love
so overexposed.   10

And my memory will be a little
out of focus, in it
a giant negative, black
and white, still undeveloped.

Literary research paper on poetry

Past and Future in

Agha Shahid Ali's "Postcard from Kashmir"

Most literary critics interpret Agha Shahid Ali's "Postcard from Kashmir" as a longing for a lost home, a poetic expression of the heartbreak of exile. For instance, Maimuna Dali Islam describes the speaker's futile effort "to capture his homeland" (262). However, such a reading of the poem seems too narrow. "Postcard from Kashmir" does evoke the experience of being displaced from a beloved home, but the speaker does not seem to feel an intense loss. Instead, he seems to reflect on his position of having more than one home.

Ali's brief poem consists of three stanzas and divides into two parts. In the first half, the speaker examines a postcard he has received from his former home of Kashmir (lines 1-6). In the second half, the speaker looks forward, imagining how Kashmir will look the next time he sees it and assuming that the place will be different from the idealized view of the postcard and his memory (6-14). The geography is significant. Kashmir has been in the news for many years as the focus of territorial conflict, often violent, among the bordering nations of India, Pakistan, and China. Many residents of the region have been killed, and many have left the region. One of the exiles was Ali: he moved to the United States in 1976 and lived here until his death in 2001, but he also regularly visited his family in Kashmir (Benvenuto 261, 263).

In the context of Kashmir, the literary theorist Jahan Ramazani concludes that the poem "dramatizes the . . . condition" of losing one's homeland to political turmoil (12). Yet several lines in the poem suggest that the speaker is not mourning a loss but musing about having a sense of home both in Kashmir and in the United States. This sense is evident in the opening stanza: "Kashmir shrinks into my mailbox, / my home a neat four by six inches" (1-2), with "my mailbox" conveying his current residence as home and "my home" referring to Kashmir. The dual sense of home is even more evident in the lines "This is home. And this is the closest / I'll ever be to home" (5-6). Although Maimuna Dali Islam assumes that "This" in these lines refers to the Kashmir pictured on the postcard (262), it could also or instead refer to the home attached to the mailbox.

The speaker also seems to perceive that his dual sense of home will continue into the future. The critics do not mention that the second half of the poem is written in the future tense. Beginning with "When I return" (6), the speaker makes it clear that he expects to find himself in Kashmir again, and he imagines how things will be, not how they were. Islam takes the image on the postcard as proof that "there is a place that *can* be captured in a snapshot" (263), but the speaker compares photography to memory, characterizing both as flawed and deceptive with terms such as "overexposed" (10) and "out of focus" (12). He acknowledges that the place won't be like the photograph: "the colors won't be so brilliant, / the Jhelum's waters so clean, / so ultramarine" (7-9). Kashmir still exists, but not as any photograph or memory has recorded it. And the speaker's relationship to his original home, his "love" (9), is changing with the place itself.

In "Postcard from Kashmir" the speaker reflects on home and displacement as he gazes into a representation of his past and considers the future. If the poem mourns a loss, as the critics suggest, it is a loss that has not happened yet, at least not completely. More convincingly, the poem captures a moment when the two homes and the past, present, and future all meet.

Works Cited

Ali, Agha Shahid. "Postcard from Kashmir." *The Half-Inch Himalayas*. Middletown: Wesleyan UP, 1987. 1. Print.

Benvenuto, Christine. "Agha Shahid Ali." *Massachusetts Review* 43.1 (2002): 261-73. Web. 7 Mar. 2014.

Islam, Maimuna Dali. "A Way in the World of an Asian American Existence: Agha Shahid Ali's Transimmigrant Spacing of North America and India and Kashmir." *Transnational Asian American Literature: Sites and Transits*. Ed. Shirley Lim et al. Philadelphia: Temple UP, 2006. 257-73. Print.

Ramazani, Jahan. *The Hybrid Muse: Postcolonial Poetry in English*. Chicago: U of Chicago P, 2001. Print.

—Jessie Glenn (student)

57 Writing in Other Disciplines

Chapter essentials

- Follow the conventions of writing in the humanities (below).
- Follow the conventions of writing in the social sciences (p. 425).
- Follow the conventions of writing in the natural and applied sciences (p. 428).

Visit MyWritingLab™ for more resources on writing in other disciplines.

57a Writing in the humanities

The humanities include literature, the visual arts, music, film, dance, history, philosophy, and religion. The preceding chapter discusses the particular requirements of reading and writing about literature. This section concentrates on history. Although the arts, religion, and other humanities have their own concerns, they share many important goals and methods with literature and history.

1 Methods and evidence in the humanities

Writers in the humanities record and speculate about the growth, ideas, and emotions of human beings. Based on the evidence of written words, artworks, and other human traces and creations, humanities writers explain, interpret, analyze, and reconstruct the human experience.

The discipline of history focuses particularly on reconstructing the past. In Greek the word for history means "to inquire": historians inquire into the past to understand the events of the past. Then they report, explain, analyze, and evaluate those events in their context, asking such questions as what happened before or after the events or how the events related to political and social structures.

Historians' reconstructions of the past are always based on the written record. The evidence of history is mainly primary sources, such as eyewitness accounts and contemporary letters, commercial records, and the like. For history papers, you might also be asked to support your conclusions with those in secondary sources.

In reading historical sources, you need to weigh and evaluate their evidence. If, for example, you find conflicting accounts of the same event, you need to consider the possible biases of the authors. In general, the more a historian's conclusions are supported by public records such as deeds, marriage licenses, and newspaper accounts, the more reliable the conclusions are likely to be.

2 Writing assignments in the humanities

Writing assignments in the humanities often require traditional academic essays that follow the conventional pattern of introduction, thesis statement, supporting paragraphs, and conclusion. Humanities assignments generally use the genres of analysis, argument, and informing (see **2** pp. 71–73). An assignment may further refine the genre with one or more of the following words:

- **Explain:** for instance, show how a painter developed a particular technique or clarify a general's role in a historical battle.
- **Argue:** assert and defend an opinion—for instance, about the meaning of a poem or the causes of a historical event.
- **Analyze:** examine the elements of a philosophical argument or break down the causes of a historical event.
- **Interpret:** infer the meaning of a film from its images or the significance of a historical event from contemporary accounts of it.
- **Synthesize:** find a pattern in a composer's works or in a historical period.
- **Evaluate:** judge the quality of an architect's design or a historian's conclusions.

See **2** pp. 87–89 for discussion of these words.

3 Tools and language in the humanities

The tools and language of the humanities vary according to the discipline. Major reference works in each field, available through the library, can clarify specific tools you need and the language you should use. To find such works, consult a reference librarian.

Writing tools

A useful tool for the arts is to ask a series of questions to analyze and evaluate a work. (A list of such questions for reading literature appears on pp. 416–18.) In any humanities discipline, a journal—a log of questions, reactions, and insights—can help you discover and record your thoughts.

In history the tools are those of any thorough and efficient researcher: a system for finding and tracking sources; a methodical examination of sources, including evaluating and synthesizing them; a system for gathering source information; and a separate system, such as a research journal, for tracking one's own evolving thoughts.

Language considerations

Historians strive for precision and logic. They do not guess about what happened or speculate about "what if." They avoid trying to influence readers' opinions with words having strongly negative or positive connotations, such as *stupid* or *brilliant*. Instead, historians show the evidence and draw conclusions from that.

Writing about history demands some attention to the tenses of verbs. To refer to events that occurred in the past, historians generally use the past tense,° the present perfect tense,° or the past perfect tense.° They reserve the present tense° only for statements about the present or statements of general truths. For example:

> Franklin Delano Roosevelt <u>died</u> in 1945. [Simple past.]
>
> He <u>had contracted</u> polio at age thirty-nine. [Past perfect.]
>
> Many historians <u>have praised</u> Roosevelt as President. [Present perfect.]
>
> Some of his economic reforms <u>persist</u> today, such as Social Security and unemployment compensation. [Present.]

See **4** pp. 216–22 for more on verb tenses.

4 | Documentation and format in the humanities

Writers in the humanities generally rely on one of the following guides for source-citation style:

The Chicago Manual of Style, 16th ed., 2010
A Manual for Writers of Research Papers, Theses, and Dissertations, by Kate L. Turabian, 8th ed., rev. Wayne C. Booth, Gregory G. Colomb, and Joseph M. Williams, 2013
MLA Handbook for Writers of Research Papers, 7th ed., 2009

See **MLA** pp. 435–80 for the recommendations of the *MLA Handbook*. Unless your instructor specifies otherwise, use these recommendations for papers in English and foreign languages. In history, art history, and many other disciplines, however, writers rely on *The Chicago Manual of Style* or the student reference adapted from it, *A Manual for Writers*. Both books detail two documentation styles. One, used mainly by scientists and social scientists, closely resembles the style of the American Psychological Association (see **APA** pp. 494–515). The other style, used more in the humanities, calls

°See "Glossary of Terms," **GI** p. 558.

for footnotes or endnotes and an optional bibliography. This style is described in **Chic** pp. 524–35.

57b Writing in the social sciences

The social sciences—including anthropology, economics, education, management, political science, psychology, and sociology—focus on the study of human behavior. As the name implies, the social sciences examine the way human beings relate to themselves, to their environment, and to one another.

1 Methods and evidence in the social sciences

Researchers in the social sciences systematically pose a question, formulate a **hypothesis** (a generalization that can be tested), collect data, analyze those data, and draw conclusions to support, refine, or disprove their hypothesis. This is the scientific method developed in the natural sciences (see p. 428).

Social scientists gather data in several ways:

- **They interview subjects about their attitudes and behavior,** recording responses in writing or electronically. (See **7** p. 373 for guidelines on conducting an interview.)
- **They conduct broader surveys using questionnaires,** asking people about their attitudes and behavior. (See **7** pp. 373–74 for guidelines on conducting a survey.)
- **They make firsthand observations of human behavior,** recording the observations in writing or electronically. (See **7** p. 374 for guidelines on conducting an observation.)
- **They conduct controlled experiments,** structuring an environment in which to encourage and measure a specific behavior.

In their writing, social scientists explain their own research or analyze and evaluate others' research.

The research methods of social science generate two kinds of data:

- *Quantitative data* **are numerical,** such as statistical evidence based on surveys, polls, tests, and experiments. When public-opinion pollsters announce that 47% of US citizens polled approve of the President's leadership, they are offering quantitative data gained from a survey.
- *Qualitative data* **are not numerical but more subjective:** they are based on interviews, firsthand observations, and inferences, taking into account the subjective nature of human experience. Examples of qualitative data include an anthropologist's description of the initiation ceremonies in a culture she is studying or a psychologist's interpretation of interviews he conducted with a group of adolescents.

2 Writing assignments in the social sciences

Depending on what social science courses you take, you may be asked to write in a variety of genres:

- **A research report:** Explain your own original research or your attempt to replicate the work of other researchers. (See **APA** pp. 516–20 for an example of a research report.)
- **A summary or review of research:** Report on the available research literature on a subject, such as infants' perception of color.
- **A case analysis:** Explain the components of a phenomenon, such as a factory closing.
- **A problem-solving analysis:** Explain the elements of a problem, such as unreported child abuse, and suggest ways to solve it.
- **A research paper:** Interpret and sometimes analyze and evaluate the writings of other social scientists about a subject, such as the effect of national appeals in advertising.

Many social science disciplines have special requirements for the content and organization of each kind of assignment. The requirements appear in the style guides of the disciplines, listed opposite. For instance, the American Psychological Association specifies the structure for a research report that is illustrated in **APA** pp. 516–20. Because of the differences among disciplines and even among different kinds of papers in the same discipline, you should always ask your instructor what he or she requires for an assignment.

3 Tools and language in the social sciences

The following guidelines for tools and language apply to most social sciences. The particular discipline you are writing in, or an instructor in a particular course, may have additional requirements.

Writing tools

Many social scientists rely on a **research journal** or **log**, in which they record their ideas throughout the research-writing process. Even if a research journal is not required in your courses, you may want to use one to record preliminary questions, react to the evidence you collect in the field, record changes in your perceptions and ideas, and assess your progress. To avoid confusing your reflections on the evidence with the evidence itself, keep records of actual data—notes from interviews, observations, surveys, and experiments—separately from the journal.

Language considerations

Each social science discipline has specialized terminology for concepts basic to the discipline. In sociology, for example, the words *mechanism, identity,* and *deviance* have specific meanings different from those of everyday usage. Social scientists also use precise terms to describe or interpret research. For instance, they say *The subject expressed a feeling of* rather than *The subject felt* because human feelings are not knowable for certain; or they say *These studies indicate* rather than *These studies prove* because conclusions are only tentative.

Just as social scientists strive for objectivity in their research, they also strive to demonstrate their objectivity through language in their writing:

- **They avoid expressions such as** *I think* in order to focus attention on what the evidence shows rather than on the researcher's opinions.

- **They often use the passive voice° of verbs** to describe their methods and results, as in *The subjects' responses were recorded*. (However, many social scientists prefer *I* to the artificial *the researcher* when they refer to their own actions, as in *I recorded the subjects' responses*. Ask your instructor for his or her preferences.)

- **They avoid direct or indirect expression of their personal biases or emotions**, either in discussions of other researchers' work or in descriptions of research subjects. Thus one social scientist does not call another's work *sloppy* or *immaculate* and does not refer to his or her own subjects as *drunks* or *innocent victims*. Instead, the writer uses neutral language and ties conclusions strictly to the data.

4 Documentation and format in the social sciences

Some of the social sciences publish style guides that advise practitioners how to organize, document, and type papers. The following is a partial list:

American Anthropological Association, *AAA Style Guide*, 2009 (*www.aaanet .org/publications/style_guide.pdf*)
American Political Science Association, *Style Manual for Political Science*, 2006 (*www.apsanet.org/media/PDFs/Publications/APSAStyleManual2006.pdf*)
American Psychological Association, *Publication Manual of the American Psychological Association*, 6th ed., 2010
American Sociological Association, *ASA Style Guide*, 4th ed., 2010
Linguistic Society of America, "LSA Style Sheet," published every December in *LSA Bulletin*
A Uniform System of Citation (law), 19th ed., 2010

By far the most widely used style is that of the American Psychological Association, detailed in **APA** pp. 494–515. Always ask your instructor in any discipline what style you should use.

Note The APA provides answers to frequently asked questions at *www.apastyle.org/faqs*.

°See "Glossary of Terms," **Gl** p. 558.

57c | Writing in the natural and applied sciences

The natural and applied sciences include biology, chemistry, physics, mathematics, engineering, computer science, and their branches. Their purpose is to understand natural and technological phenomena. (A *phenomenon* is a fact or event that can be known by the senses.) Scientists conduct experiments and write to explain the step-by-step processes in their methods of inquiry and discovery.

1 | Methods and evidence in the sciences

Scientists investigate phenomena by the **scientific method**, a process of continual testing and refinement:

The scientific method

- **Observe carefully**. Accurately note all details of the phenomenon being researched.
- **Ask questions about the observations.**
- **Formulate a *hypothesis*,** or preliminary generalization, that explains the observed facts.
- **Test the hypothesis** with additional observations or controlled experiments.
- **If the hypothesis proves accurate, formulate a *theory*,** or unified model, that explains *why*.
- **If the hypothesis is disproved, revise it or start anew.**

Scientific evidence is almost always quantitative—that is, it consists of numerical data obtained from the measurement of phenomena. These data are called **empirical** (from a Greek word for "experience"): they result from observation and experience, generally in a controlled laboratory setting but also (as sometimes in astronomy or biology) in the natural world. Often the empirical evidence for scientific writing comes from library research into other people's reports of their investigations. Surveys of known data or existing literature are common in scientific writing.

2 | Writing assignments in the sciences

No matter what your assignment, you will be expected to document and explain your evidence carefully so that anyone reading can check your sources and replicate your research. It is important for your reader to know the context of your research—both the previous experimentation and research on your particular subject (acknowledged in the survey of the literature) and the physical conditions and other variables surrounding your own work.

Assignments in the natural and applied sciences include the following genres:

- **A laboratory report:** Explain the procedure and results of an experiment conducted by the writer.
- **A summary:** Distill a research article to its essence in brief, concise form. (Summary is discussed in detail in **2** pp. 85–87.)
- **A critique:** Summarize and critically evaluate a scientific report.
- **A research report:** Explain the experimental research of other scientists and the writer's own methods, findings, and conclusions.
- **A research proposal:** Review the relevant literature and explain a plan for further research.

A laboratory report has four or five major sections:

1. **"Abstract":** a summary of the report.
2. **"Introduction" or "Objective":** a review of why the study was undertaken, a summary of the background of the study, and a statement of the problem being studied.
3. **"Method" or "Procedure":** a detailed explanation of how the study was conducted, including any statistical analysis.
4. **"Results":** an explanation of the major findings (including unexpected results) and a summary of the data presented in graphs and tables.
5. **"Discussion":** an interpretation of the results and an explanation of how they relate to the goals of the experiment. This section also describes new hypotheses that might be tested as a result of the experiment. If the discussion is brief, it may be combined with the results in a single section labeled "Conclusions."

In addition, laboratory or research reports may include a list of references (if other sources were consulted). They almost always include tables and figures (graphs and charts) containing the data from the research.

3 | Tools and language in the sciences

Tools and language concerns vary from discipline to discipline in the sciences. Consult your instructor for specifics about the field in which you are writing.

Writing tools

In the sciences a **lab notebook** or **scientific journal** is almost indispensable for accurately recording the empirical data from observations and experiments. Use such a notebook or journal for these purposes:

- **Record observations** from reading, from class, or from the lab.
- **Ask questions and refine hypotheses.**
- **Record procedures.**
- **Record results.**

- **Keep an ongoing record of ideas and findings** and how they change as data accumulate.
- **Sequence and organize your material** as you compile your findings and write your report.

Language considerations

Science writers use objective language that removes the writer as a character in the situation and events being explained, except as the impersonal agent of change, the experimenter. Although usage is evolving, scientists still rarely use *I* in their reports and evaluations, and they often resort to the passive voice° of verbs, as in *The mixture was then subjected to centrifugal force.* This conscious objectivity focuses attention (including the writer's) on the empirical data and what they show. It discourages the writer from, say, ascribing motives and will to animals and plants. For instance, instead of asserting that the sea tortoise *developed* its hard shell *to protect* its body, a scientist would write only what could be observed: that the hard shell *covers and thus protects* the tortoise's body.

Science writers typically change verb tenses° to distinguish between established information and their own research. For established information, such as that found in journals and other reliable sources, use the present tense°: *Baroreceptors monitor blood pressure.* For your own and others' research, use the past tense°: *The bacteria died within three hours. Marti reported some success.*

Each discipline in the natural and applied sciences has a specialized vocabulary that permits precise, accurate, and efficient communication. Some of these terms, such as *pressure* in physics, have different meanings in the common language and must be handled carefully in science writing. Others, such as *enthalpy* in chemistry, have no meanings in the common language and must simply be learned and used correctly.

4 Documentation and format in the sciences

Within the natural and applied sciences, practitioners use one of two styles of documentation, varying slightly from discipline to discipline. Following are some of the style guides most often consulted:

American Chemical Society, *ACS Style Guide: A Manual for Authors and Editors,* 3rd ed., 2006

American Institute of Physics, *Style Manual for Guidance in the Preparation of Papers,* 4th ed., 1990 (*www.aip.org/pubservs/style/4thed/AIP_Style_4thed .pdf*)

American Medical Association Manual of Style, 10th ed., 2007

Council of Science Editors, *Scientific Style and Format: The CSE Manual for Authors, Editors, and Publishers,* 8th ed., 2014

The most thorough and widely used of these guides is the last one, *Scientific Style and Format.* See **CSE** pp. 536–41 for a description of the style.

°See "Glossary of Terms," **Gl** p. 558.

MLA
Documentation
and Format

MLA Documentation and Format

MLA in-text citations

MLA works-cited entries

Finding the right model for a source

2. **What is the medium of the source?** From within each type of source, choose the right model for the medium. Common media:

Print	**Photograph; JPEG file**
Web (database and open Web)	**Television; radio**
Kindle file	**Film**
PDF file; *Microsoft Word* **file**	**DVD; Blu-ray; videocassette**
Tweet	**Performance; lecture**

3. **Who is the author?** Choose the right model for the number and type of author(s).

How many authors? models 1–3

Author(s) of two or more of your sources? model 4

Corporation, agency, or other group author? model 5

No named author? model 6

(continued)

MLA works-cited entries
(continued)

58   MLA Documentation and Format

Chapter essentials

- In your text, document your sources with citations (next page).
- Place text citations so that they are clear and unobtrusive (p. 442).
- Use supplemental notes as needed (p. 444).
- Prepare an MLA list of works cited (p. 445).
- Follow MLA guidelines for paper format, including margins, spacing, long quotations, and other elements (p. 480).

Visit MyWritingLab™ for more resources on MLA documentation and format.

English, foreign languages, and some other humanities use the documentation style of the Modern Language Association, which is described in the *MLA Handbook for Writers of Research Papers* (7th ed., 2009).

In MLA style, you twice acknowledge the sources of borrowed material:

- **In your text, a brief citation adjacent to the borrowed material directs readers to a complete list of all the works you cite.** The citation consists of the author's last name and usually the page number in the source where the borrowed material appears. If the author's name is not mentioned in your sentence, it appears in parentheses with the page number:

In-text citation

Among African cities, says one observer, in Johannesburg "a spirit of optimism glows" (Gaddis 155).

- **At the end of your paper, the list of works cited includes complete bibliographical information for every source.**

Works-cited entry

Gaddis, Anicee. "Johannesburg." *Transculturalism: How the World Is Coming Together.* Ed. Claude Grunitzky. New York: True, 2008. 154-57.

58a | Writing MLA in-text citations

1 | Writing in-text citations

In-text citations of sources must include just enough information for the reader to locate both of the following:

- The *source* in your list of works cited.
- The *place* in the source where the borrowed material appears.

For any kind of source, you can usually meet both these requirements by providing the author's last name and (if the source uses them) the page numbers where the material appears. The reader can find the source in your list of works cited and find the borrowed material in the source itself.

The following models illustrate the basic text-citation forms and also forms for more unusual sources, such as those with no named author or no page numbers. See the **MLA** divider for an index to all the in-text models.

Note Models 1 and 2 show the direct relationship between what you include in your text and what you include in a parenthetical citation. If you do *not* name the author in your text, you include the name in parentheses before the page reference (model 1). If you *do* name the author in your text, you do not include the name in parentheses (model 2).

1. Author not named in your text

When you have not already named the author in your sentence, provide the author's last name and the page number(s), with no punctuation between them, in parentheses.

One researcher concludes that "women impose a distinctive construction on moral problems, seeing moral dilemmas in terms of conflicting responsibilities" (Gilligan 105-06).

See model 6 for the form to use when the source does not have an author. And see models 8–10 for the forms to use when the source does not provide page numbers.

2. Author named in your text

When you have already given the author's name with the material you're citing, do not repeat it in the parenthetical citation. Give just the page number(s).

Carol Gilligan concludes that "women impose a distinctive construction on moral problems, seeing moral dilemmas in terms of conflicting responsibilities" (105-06).

See model 6 for the form to use when the source does not list an author. And see models 8–10 for the forms to use when the source does not provide page numbers.

3. Work with two or three authors

If the source has two or three authors, give all their last names in the text or in the citation. Separate two authors' names with and:

As Frieden and Sagalyn observe, "The poor and the minorities were the leading victims of highway and renewal programs" (29).

According to one study, "The poor and the minorities were the leading victims of highway and renewal programs" (Frieden and Sagalyn 29).

With three authors, add commas and also and before the final name:

The textbook by Wilcox, Ault, and Agee discusses the "ethical dilemmas in public relations practice" (125).

One textbook discusses the "ethical dilemmas in public relations practice" (Wilcox, Ault, and Agee 125).

4. Work with more than three authors

If the source has more than three authors, you may list all their last names or give only the first author's name followed by et al. (the abbreviation for the Latin *et alii*, "and others"). The choice depends on what you do in your list of works cited (see p. 447).

Increased competition means that employees of public relations firms may find their loyalty stretched in more than one direction (Wilcox et al. 417).

Increased competition means that employees of public relations firms may find their loyalty stretched in more than one direction (Wilcox, Cameron, Reber, and Shin 417).

5. Work by an author of two or more cited works

If your list of works cited includes two or more works by the same author, then your citation must tell the reader which of the author's works you are referring to. Give the title either in the text or in a parenthetical citation. In a parenthetical citation, give the full title only if it is brief; otherwise, shorten the title to the first one, two, or three main words (excluding *A, An,* or *The*).

At about age seven, children begin to use appropriate gestures with their stories (Gardner, *Arts* 144-45).

The full title of Gardner's book is *The Arts and Human Development* (see the works-cited entry on p. 447). This shortened title is italicized because the source is a book.

6. Anonymous work

For a work with no named author or editor (whether an individual or an organization), use a full or shortened version of the title, as explained above. In your list of works cited, you alphabetize an anonymous work by the first main word of the title (see p. 448), so the first word of a shortened title should be the same. The following citations refer to an unsigned source titled "The Right to Die." The title appears in quotation marks because the source is a periodical article.

One article notes that a death-row inmate may demand his own execution to achieve a fleeting notoriety ("Right" 16).

"The Right to Die" notes that a death-row inmate may demand execution to achieve a fleeting notoriety (16).

If two or more anonymous works have the same title, distinguish them with additional information in the text citation, such as the publication date.

7. Work with a corporate author

Some works list as author a government body, association, committee, company, or other group. Cite such a work by the organization's name. If the name is long, work it into the text to avoid an intrusive parenthetical citation.

A 2014 report by the Nevada Department of Education provides evidence of an increase in graduation rates (12).

8. Electronic or other nonprint source

Electronic or other nonprint sources vary widely, including articles in databases, e-books, Web pages, *Facebook* posts, films or videos, and tweets. If possible, cite such a source as you would any other source, giving author and page number; but often these elements and others are lacking. The following models give a range of possibilities.

a. Work with a named author and stable page numbers

Brannon observes that students respond to some poets more readily than others (53).

If the work you cite has stable page numbers, like those in a PDF file, give them in your citation.

b. Work with a named author and no page numbers

Smith reports that almost 20% of commercial banks have been audited in recent years.

When you cite a passage from a work with no page or other reference numbers, such as a Web source or an article in HTML format, try to give the author's name in your text. You will not need a parenthetical citation, but you must list the source in your works cited.

If the author's name does not appear in your text, give it in a parenthetical citation:

Clean cars are defined as vehicles with low pollution emissions and high fuel economy (Hagedorn).

c. Work with a named author on an e-reader or other device

Writing about post-Saddam Iraq, the journalist George Packer describes the tense relationship between Kurdistan and the rest of the country (ch. 1).

Page numbers are not always the same on Kindles, iPads, and other e-readers and tablets. For a book you read on such a device, give the chapter number, not the device's page numbers.

d. Work with a named author and numbered paragraphs or sections

Twins reared apart report similar feelings (Palfrey, pars. 6-7).

If the work gives numbered paragraphs or sections, use the abbreviation par., pars., sec., or secs. to tell readers that you are citing one or more paragraphs or sections rather than page numbers.

e. Work with no named author

Many decades after its release, *Citizen Kane* is still remarkable for its rich black-and-white photography.

When your works-cited entry lists the work under its title, cite the work by title in your text, as explained in model 6. This example, a film, gives the title in the text, so it omits a parenthetical citation (see model 9).

9. One-page work or entire work

When you cite a work that's a single page long or cite an entire work—for instance, a one-page article, a tweet, a Web site, a book, or a film—you may omit any page or other reference number. If the work you cite has an author, try to give the name in the text. If the work does not have an author, give the title.

> Boyd deals with the need to acknowledge and come to terms with our fear of nuclear technology.

10. Work with no page or other reference numbers

When the work you cite, print or nonprint, has no page or other reference numbers, give the author's name, if available, in your text or in a parenthetical citation. (If no author is listed, give the title.)

> In the children's classic picture book *The Very Busy Spider,* hard work and patience are rewarded when the spider catches a fly in her web (Carle).

11. Multivolume work

If you consulted only one volume of a multivolume work, your list of works cited will say so (see model 28 on p. 460), and you can treat the volume as you would any book.

If you consulted more than one volume of a multivolume work, give the appropriate volume number before the page number (here volume 5):

> After issuing the Emancipation Proclamation, Lincoln said, "What I did, I did after very full deliberations, and under a very heavy and solemn sense of responsibility" (5: 438).

The number 5 indicates the volume from which the quotation was taken; the number 438 indicates the page number in that volume. When the author's name appears in such a citation, place it before the volume number with no punctuation: (Lincoln 5: 438).

If you are referring generally to an entire volume of a multivolume work and are not citing specific page numbers, add the abbreviation vol. before the volume number, as in (vol. 5) or (Lincoln, vol. 5) (note the comma after the author's name). Then readers will not misinterpret the volume number as a page number.

12. Source referred to by another source (indirect source)

When you want to use a quotation that is already in quotation marks—indicating that the author you are reading is quoting someone else—try to find the original source and quote directly from it. If you can't find the original source, then your citation must indicate that your quotation of it is indirect. In the following citation, qtd. in ("quoted in") says that Davino was quoted by Boyd.

> George Davino maintains that "even small children have vivid ideas about nuclear energy" (qtd. in Boyd 22).

The list of works cited then includes only Boyd (the work consulted), not Davino.

13. Literary work

Novels, plays, and poems are often available in many editions, so your instructor may ask you to provide information that will help readers find the passage you cite no matter what edition they consult.

a. Novel

> Toward the end of James's novel, Maggie suddenly feels "the thick breath of the definite—which was the intimate, the immediate, the familiar, as she hadn't had them for so long" (535; pt. 6, ch. 41).

Give the page number first, followed by a semicolon and then information on the appropriate part or chapter of the work.

b. Poem not divided into parts

> In Shakespeare's Sonnet 73 the speaker identifies with the trees of late autumn, "Bare ruined choirs, where late the sweet birds sang" (line 4). "In me," Shakespeare writes, "thou seest the glowing of such fire / That on the ashes of his youth doth lie . . ." (9-10).

You may omit the page number and supply the line number(s) for the quotation. To prevent confusion with page numbers, precede the numbers with line or lines in the first citation; then use just the numbers. (See pp. 420–22 for a sample paper on a poem.)

c. Verse play or poem divided into parts

> Later in Shakespeare's *King Lear* the disguised Edgar says, "The prince of darkness is a gentleman" (3.4.147).

Omit a page number and cite the appropriate part—act (and scene, if any), canto, book, and so on—plus the line number(s). Use Arabic numerals for parts, including acts and scenes (3.4), unless your instructor specifies Roman numerals (III.iv).

d. Prose play

> In Miller's *Death of a Salesman*, Willie Loman's wife, Linda, acknowledges her husband's failings but also the need for him to be treated with dignity: "He's not the finest character that ever lived. But he's a human being, and a terrible thing is happening to him" (56; act 1).

Provide the page number followed by the act and scene, if any.

14. The Bible

When you cite passages of the Bible in parentheses, abbreviate the title of any book longer than four letters—for instance, Gen. (Genesis), 1 Sam. (1 Samuel), Ps. (Psalms), Prov. (Proverbs), Matt. (Matthew), Rom. (Romans). Then give the chapter and verse(s) in Arabic numerals.

> According to the Bible, at Babel God "did . . . confound the language of all the earth" (Gen. 11.9).

15. Two or more works in the same citation

When you refer to more than one work in a single parenthetical citation, separate the references with a semicolon.

> Two recent articles point out that a computer badly used can be less efficient than no computer at all (Gough and Hall 201; Richards 162).

Since long citations in the text can distract the reader, you may choose to cite several or more works in an endnote or footnote rather than in the text. See p. 444.

2 Positioning and punctuating parenthetical citations

The following guidelines will help you place and punctuate text citations to distinguish between your own and your sources' ideas and to make your own text readable. See also **7** pp. 395–99 on editing quotations and using signal phrases to integrate source material into your sentences.

Where to place citations

Position text citations to accomplish two goals:

- **Make it clear exactly where your borrowing begins and ends.**
- **Keep the citation as unobtrusive as possible.**

You can accomplish both goals by placing the parenthetical citation at the end of the sentence element containing the borrowed material. This sentence element may be a phrase or a clause, and it may begin, interrupt, or conclude the sentence. Usually, as in the following examples, the element ends with a punctuation mark.

> The inflation rate might climb as high as 30 percent (Kim 164), an increase that could threaten the small nation's stability.

> The inflation rate, which might climb as high as 30 percent (Kim 164), could threaten the small nation's stability.

> The small nation's stability could be threatened by its inflation rate, which, one source predicts, might climb as high as 30 percent (Kim 164).

In the last example the addition of one source predicts clarifies that Kim is responsible only for the inflation-rate prediction, not for the statement about stability.

When your paraphrase or summary of a source runs longer than a sentence, clarify the boundaries by using the author's name in the first sentence and placing the parenthetical citation at the end of the last sentence.

> Juliette Kim studied the effects of acutely high inflation in several South American and African countries since World War II. She discovered that a major change in government accompanied or followed the inflationary period in 56 percent of cases (22-23).

When you cite two or more sources in the same paragraph, position authors' names and parenthetical citations so that readers can see who said what. In the following example, the beginnings and ends of sentences clearly mark the different sources.

> Schools use computers extensively for drill-and-practice exercises, in which students repeat specific skills such as spelling words, using the multiplication facts, or, at a higher level, doing chemistry problems. But many education experts criticize such exercises for boring students and failing to engage their critical thinking and creativity. Jane M. Healy, a noted educational psychologist and teacher, takes issue with "interactive" software for children as well as drill-and-practice software, arguing that "some of the most popular 'educational' software . . . may be damaging to independent thinking, attention, and motivation" (20). Another education expert, Harold Wenglinsky of the Educational Testing Service, found that fourth and eighth graders who used computers frequently, including for drill and practice, actually did worse on tests than their peers who used computers less often (*Does It Compute?* 21). In a later article, Wenglinsky concludes that "the quantity of use matters far less than the quality of use." In schools, he says, high-quality computer work, involving critical thinking, is still rare ("In Search" 17).

How to punctuate citations

Generally place a parenthetical citation *before* any punctuation required by your sentence. If the borrowed material is a quotation, place the citation *between* the closing quotation mark and the punctuation:

> Spelling argues that during the 1970s American automobile manufacturers met consumer needs "as well as could be expected" (26), but not everyone agrees with him.

The exception is a quotation ending in a question mark or exclamation point. Then use the appropriate punctuation inside the closing quotation mark, and follow the quotation with the text citation and a period.

> "Of what use is genius," Emerson asks, "if the organ . . . cannot find a focal distance within the actual horizon of human life?" ("Experience" 60). Mad genius is no genius.

When a citation appears at the end of a quotation set off from the text, place it one space *after* the punctuation ending the quotation. Do not use additional punctuation with the citation or quotation marks around the quotation.

> In Charles Dickens's *A Christmas Carol,* Scrooge and the Ghost of Christmas Past visit Scrooge's childhood boarding school. They watch as the schoolmaster offers young Ebenezer and his sister some unappealing food and drink:
>
> > Here he produced a decanter of curiously light wine, and a block of curiously heavy cake, and administered installments of those dainties to the young people: at the same time, sending out a meager servant to offer a glass of the "something" to the postboy, who answered that he thanked the gentleman, but if it was the same tap as he had tasted before, he had rather not. (34)

See the sample research paper starting on p. 482 for further examples of placing in-text citations in relation to summaries, paraphrases, and quotations.

3 Using footnotes or endnotes in special circumstances

Occasionally you may want to use footnotes or endnotes in place of parenthetical citations. If you need to refer to several sources at once, listing them in a long parenthetical citation could be intrusive. Signal the citation with a numeral raised above the appropriate line of text and write a note beginning with the same numeral:

Text   At least five studies have confirmed these results.[1]

Note   1. Abbott and Winger 266-68; Casner 27; Hoyenga 78-79; Marino 36; Tripp, Tripp, and Walk 179-83.

You may also use a footnote or endnote to comment on a source or to provide information that does not fit easily in the text:

Text   So far, no one has confirmed these results.[2]

Note   2. Manter tried repeatedly to replicate the experiment, but he was never able to produce the high temperatures (616).

Indent a note one-half inch, type the numeral on the text line, and follow the numeral with a period and a space. If the note appears as a footnote, place it at the bottom of the page on which the citation appears, set it off from the text with quadruple spacing, and double-space the note itself. If the note appears as an endnote, place it in numerical order with the other endnotes on a page between the text and the list of works cited. Double-space all the endnotes.

58b Writing the MLA list of works cited

In MLA documentation style, your in-text parenthetical citations (discussed in 58a) refer the reader to complete information on your sources in a list you title Works Cited and place at the end of your paper. The list should include all the sources you quoted, paraphrased, or summarized in your paper. (If your instructor asks you to include sources you examined but did not cite, title the list Works Consulted.)

Use the following illustration and guidelines to format the list of works cited:

MLA works-cited page

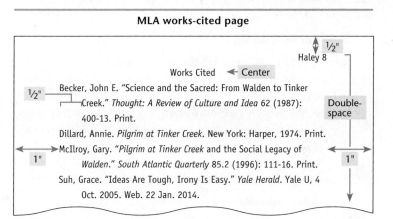

- **Arrange your sources in alphabetical order** by the last name of the author. If an author is not given in the source, alphabetize the source by the first main word of the title (excluding *A*, *An*, or *The*).
- **Type the entire list double-spaced,** both within and between entries.
- **Indent the second and subsequent lines of each entry one-half inch from the left.** Your word processor can format this so-called hanging indent automatically.

For a complete list of works cited, see the paper by Justin Malik on pp. 489–90.

An index to the following models appears at the **MLA** divider. Use your best judgment in adapting the models to your particular sources. If you can't find a model that exactly matches a source you used, locate and follow the closest possible match. You will certainly need to combine formats—for instance, drawing on model 2 ("Two or three authors") and model 23 ("Book with an editor") for a book with three editors.

1 Authors

The following models show how to handle authors' names in citing any kind of source.

1. One author

Ehrenreich, Barbara. *Dancing in the Streets: A History of Collective Joy*. New
York: Metropolitan-Holt, 2006. Print.

Give the author's full name—last name first, a comma, first name, and any middle name or initial. Omit any title, such as *Dr.* or *PhD*. End the name with a period. If your source lists an editor as author, see model 23, p. 457.

2. Two or three authors

Lifton, Robert Jay, and Greg Mitchell. *Who Owns Death: Capital Punishment,
the American Conscience, and the End of Executions*. New York: Morrow,
2000. Print.

Simpson, Dick, James Nowlan, and Elizabeth O'Shaughnessy. *The Struggle for
Power and Influence in Cities and States*. New York: Longman, 2011. Print.

Common abbreviations in MLA works-cited entries

Missing publication information (note the capitalization)

Print sources

N.p.	No place of publication
n.p.	No publisher
n.d.	No date of publication
N. pag.	No page numbers

Web and social-media sources

N.p.	No publisher or sponsor
n.d.	No date of publication

Months in print and Web sources

Jan., Feb., Mar., Apr., Aug., Sept., Oct., Nov., Dec.
(spell out May, June, July)

Give the authors' names in the order provided on the title page. Reverse the first and last names of the first author *only*, not of any other authors. Separate two authors' names with a comma and and; separate three authors' names with commas and with *and* before the third name. If your source lists two or three editors as authors, see model 23, p. 457.

3. More than three authors

Wilcox, Dennis L., Glen T. Cameron, Bryan H. Reber, and Jae-Hwa Shin. *Think*
    Public Relations. 2nd ed. Boston: Allyn, 2013. Print.
Wilcox, Dennis L., et al. *Think Public Relations*. 2nd ed. Boston: Allyn, 2013.
    Print.

You may, but need not, give all authors' names if the work has more than three authors. If you choose not to give all names, provide the name of the first author only, and follow the name with a comma and the abbreviation et al. (for the Latin *et alii*, meaning "and others"). If your source lists more than three editors as authors, see model 23, p. 457.

4. The same author(s) for two or more works

Gardner, Howard. *The Arts and Human Development*. New York: Wiley, 1973.
    Print.
---. *Five Minds for the Future*. Boston: Harvard Business School P, 2007. Print.

Give the author's name only in the first entry. For the second and any subsequent works by the same author, substitute three hyphens for the author's name, followed by a period. Note that the three hyphens may substitute only for *exactly* the same name or names. If the second Gardner source were by Gardner and somebody else, both names would have to be given in full.

Place an entry or entries using three hyphens immediately after the entry that names the author. Within the set of entries by the same author, arrange the sources alphabetically by the first main word of the title, as in the Gardner examples (*Arts*, then *Five*).

If you cite two or more sources that list as author(s) exactly the same editor(s), follow the hyphens with a comma and ed. or eds. as appropriate. (See model 23, p. 457.)

5. A corporate author

Vault Technologies. *Turnkey Parking Solutions*. Salt Lake City: Mills, 2014.
    Print.

Corporate authors include government bodies, associations, institutions, companies, and other groups. List the group's name as author when a source gives only that name and not an individual's name.

6. Author not named (anonymous)

The Dorling Kindersley World Atlas. London: Dorling, 2013. Print.

List a work that names no author—neither an individual nor a group—by its full title. If the work is a book, italicize the title. If the work is a periodical article or other short work, enclose the title in quotation marks:

"Drilling in the Wilderness." *Economist* 24 Apr. 2014: 32. Print.

Alphabetize the work by the title's first main word, excluding *A, An,* or *The* (*Dorling* in the first example and Drilling in the second).

2 Articles in journals, newspapers, and magazines

Articles in scholarly journals, in newspapers, and in magazines appear in print periodicals, in online databases available through your library, and on the Web. Periodicals are published at regular intervals (quarterly, monthly, weekly, or daily). Articles published on the Web sites of newspapers and magazines are not considered periodicals because the sites do not always publish at regular intervals and their content changes often and unpredictably.

Articles in scholarly journals

7. Article in a journal with volume and issue numbers

To cite most articles in scholarly journals, give the author, the title of the article, the title of the journal, the volume and issue numbers, the pages of the article, and the medium, Print or Web. Adapt these formats to cite specific types of articles from scholarly journals: reviews, editorials, letters to the editor, or articles in special issues (see models 13–17, pp. 454–55).

a. Print journal article

Mattingly, Carol. "Telling Evidence: Rethinking What Counts in Rhetoric."
    Rhetoric Society Quarterly 32.1 (2002): 99-108. Print.

See pp. 450–51 for an explanation of this format and the location of the required information in a print journal.

b. Database journal article

Neves, Joshua. "Cinematic Encounters in Beijing." *Film Quarterly* 67.1 (2013):
    27-40. *Academic Search Complete.* Web. 31 Mar. 2014.

See pp. 450–51 for an explanation of this format and the location of the required information in a database. (Because some articles in databases are in HTML format and don't have page numbers, you may have to substitute n. pag. for page numbers. See the next example.)

c. Web journal article

Aulisio, George J. "Green Libraries Are More Than Just Buildings." *Electronic Green Journal* 35.1 (2013): n. pag. Web. 7 Apr. 2013.

If you find a scholarly article through the open Web, give the medium (Web) and the date of your access. If the Web journal is unpaged, substitute n. pag. for page numbers, as shown here.

8. Article in a journal with only issue numbers

Dobozy, Tomas. "The Writing of Trespass." *Canadian Literature* 218 (2013): 11-28. *Literary Reference Center*. Web. 10 June 2014.

If a scholarly journal numbers only issues, not volumes, give the issue number alone after the journal title.

Articles in newspapers

To cite an article in a newspaper, give the author, the title of the article, and the title of the newspaper as it appears on the first page (but without any *A, An,* or *The*). Then follow one of the next models depending on where you found the article. Adapt these formats to cite specific types of articles from newspapers: reviews, editorials, letters to the editor, or interviews (see models 13–16, pp. 454–55).

9. Article in a national newspaper

a. Print newspaper article

Lowery, Annie. "Cities Advancing Inequality Fight." *New York Times* 7 Apr. 2014, natl. ed.: A1+. Print.

If the newspaper lists an edition at the top of the first page, include it after the date (see natl. ed. above). If the newspaper is divided into lettered sections, provide the section designation before the page number when the newspaper does the same: A1+ above. (The plus sign indicates that the article continues on a later page.) If the newspaper is divided into numbered or titled sections, provide the section designation before the colon—for instance, sec. 1: 3 or Business Day Sec.: 4+. End with the medium, Print.

b. Database newspaper article

Stein, Rob. "Obesity May Stall Trend of Increasing Longevity." *Washington Post* 15 Mar. 2005, final ed.: A2. *LexisNexis Academic*. Web. 30 Jan. 2014.

See p. 452 for an explanation of this format and the location of the required information in a database. Basically, the format starts with the information for a print article (previous model) and adds the title of the database, the medium (Web), and the date of your access.

(continued on p. 453)

Citing journal articles: Print and database

Print journal article

First page of article

THE IMPORTANCE OF PRESERVING PAPER-BASED ARTIFACTS IN A
DIGITAL AGE

② **Title of article**

Robert Bee[1] ● ① **Author**

The preservation of paper-based ④ **Volume and** ial issue for collection management in academic libraries. I **issue numbers** brary science profession has

③ **Title of journal** — [*Library Quarterly*, vol. 78, no. 2, pp. 179–194] ● ⑥ **Page numbers**
© 2008 by The University of Chicago. All rights reserved.
0024-2519/2008/7802-0002$10.00

⑤ **Year of publication**

179

Database journal article

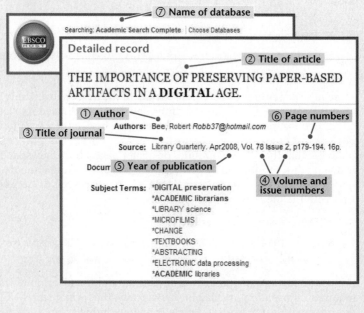

⑦ **Name of database**

Searching: Academic Search Complete | Choose Databases

EBSCO
HOST

Detailed record

② **Title of article**

THE IMPORTANCE OF PRESERVING PAPER-BASED
ARTIFACTS IN A **DIGITAL** AGE.

① **Author**
⑥ **Page numbers**

Authors: Bee, Robert Robb37@hotmail.com

③ **Title of journal**

Source: Library Quarterly. Apr2008, Vol. 78 Issue 2, p179-194. 16p.

Docum ⑤ **Year of publication**

④ **Volume and
issue numbers**

Subject Terms: *DIGITAL preservation
*ACADEMIC librarians
*LIBRARY science
*MICROFILMS
*CHANGE
*TEXTBOOKS
*ABSTRACTING
*ELECTRONIC data processing
*ACADEMIC libraries

Works-cited entry: Print journal article

① ②

Bee, Robert. "The Importance of Preserving Paper-Based Artifacts

③ ④ ⑤ ⑥

in a Digital Age." *Library Quarterly* 78.2 (2008): 179-94.

⑧

Print.

Works-cited entry: Database journal article

① ②

Bee, Robert. "The Importance of Preserving Paper-Based

③ ④ ⑤

Artifacts in a Digital Age." *Library Quarterly* 78.2 (2008):

⑥ ⑦ ⑧ ⑨

179-94. *Academic Search Complete.* Web. 14 Apr. 2014.

① **Author.** Give the full name—last name first, a comma, first name, and any middle name or initial. Omit *Dr., PhD,* or any other title. End the name with a period.

② **Title of article,** in quotation marks. Give the full title and any subtitle, separating them with a colon. End the title with a period inside the final quotation mark.

③ **Title of journal,** in italics. Omit any *A, An,* or *The* from the beginning of the title. Do not end with a period.

④ **Volume and issue numbers,** in Arabic numerals, separated by a period. Do not add a period after the issue number.

⑤ **Year of publication,** in parentheses and followed by a colon.

⑥ **Page numbers of article,** without "pp." Provide only as many digits in the last number as needed for clarity, usually two.

⑦ **Name of database,** if you found the article through a database. Give the name in italics, and follow it with a period.

⑧ **Medium.** Give the medium of the article: Print if you consulted a print journal, Web if you found the article in a database. Follow the medium with a period.

⑨ **Date of your access,** if you found the article online. Give the day first, then month, then year. End the date with a period.

See p. 449 for how to cite a journal article you find on the open Web.

Citing a newspaper article: Database

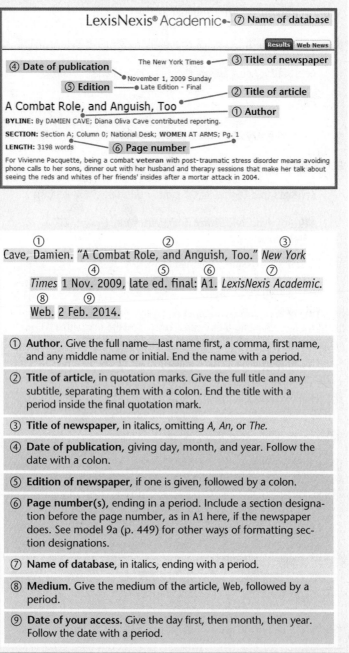

① **Author.** Give the full name—last name first, a comma, first name, and any middle name or initial. End the name with a period.

② **Title of article,** in quotation marks. Give the full title and any subtitle, separating them with a colon. End the title with a period inside the final quotation mark.

③ **Title of newspaper,** in italics, omitting *A, An,* or *The.*

④ **Date of publication,** giving day, month, and year. Follow the date with a colon.

⑤ **Edition of newspaper,** if one is given, followed by a colon.

⑥ **Page number(s),** ending in a period. Include a section designation before the page number, as in A1 here, if the newspaper does. See model 9a (p. 449) for other ways of formatting section designations.

⑦ **Name of database,** in italics, ending with a period.

⑧ **Medium.** Give the medium of the article, Web, followed by a period.

⑨ **Date of your access.** Give the day first, then month, then year. Follow the date with a period.

(continued from p. 449)

c. Web news article

Dunn, Marcia. "Vast Ocean Found beneath Ice of Saturn Moon." *Detroit News.*
Detroit News, 3 Apr. 2014. Web. 5 May 2014.

To cite a newspaper article that you find on the open Web, follow the name of the newspaper with the publisher's name (usually located at the bottom of the home page), the date, the medium (Web), and the date of your access. To cite a reader's comment on an article, see model 48, p. 469.

10. An article in a local newspaper

Beckett, Lois. "The Ignored PTSD Crisis: Americans Wounded in Their Own Neighborhoods." *Louisiana Weekly* [New Orleans] 17 Feb. 2014: 12-13. Print.

If the city of publication does not appear in the title of a local newspaper, follow the title with the city name in brackets, not italicized.

Articles in magazines

To cite an article in a magazine, give the author, the title of the article, and the title of the magazine (without any *A, An,* or *The*). Then follow one of the next models depending on where you found the article. Adapt these formats to cite specific types of articles from magazines: reviews, editorials, letters to the editor, interviews, or articles in special issues (see models 13–17, pp. 454–55).

11. Article in a weekly or biweekly magazine

a. Print magazine article

Toobin, Jeffrey. "This Is My Jail." *New Yorker* 14 Apr. 2014: 26-32. Print.

Follow the magazine title with the day, the month, and the year of publication. (Abbreviate all months except May, June, and July.) Do not provide a volume or issue number. Give the page numbers of the article and the medium, Print.

b. Database magazine article

Barras, Colin. "Right on Target." *New Scientist* 25 Jan. 2014: 40-43. *Academic
Search Complete.* Web. 28 Feb. 2014.

Start with the preceding model for citing a print article, but after the page numbers add the title of the database, the medium (Web), and the date of your access.

c. Web magazine article

Stampler, Laura. "These Cities Have the Most Open-Minded Daters." *Time.*
Time, 14 Apr. 2014. Web. 7 June 2014.

To cite a magazine article that you find on the open Web, follow the title of the magazine with the publisher's name (usually given at the bottom of the home page), the date, the medium (Web), and the date of your access. To cite a reader's comment on an article, see model 48, p. 469.

12. Article in a monthly or bimonthly magazine

Wong, Kate. "Rise of the Human Predator." *Scientific American* Apr. 2014:
46-51. Print.

Follow the magazine title with the month and the year of publication. Don't provide a volume or issue number. Give the page numbers of the article and the medium (here, Print).

Specific types of articles

Journals, newspapers, and magazines all feature reviews, editorials, and the other types of articles discussed here. When citing such an article, be sure to use the correct format for the kind of source you used—for instance, print journal or Web magazine. The following examples show various kinds.

13. Review

Rev. is an abbreviation for "Review." The names of the authors of the work being reviewed follow the title of the work, a comma, and by. If the review has no title of its own, then Rev. of and the title of the reviewed work immediately follow the name of the reviewer. Publication information for the review follows.

a. Print review

Mitchler, Sharon. "The Persistence and Complications of Class." Rev. of *Paying
for the Party: How College Maintains Inequality,* by Elizabeth A. Armstrong
and Laura T. Hamilton. *College Composition and Communication* 65.3
(2014): 462-63. Print.

b. Web review

Salmon, Felix. "The Lewis Effect." Rev. of *Flash Boys,* by Michael Lewis. *Slate.*
Slate Group, 8 Apr. 2014. Web. 17 Apr. 2014.

14. Editorial

"The Right Kind of Care." Editorial. *New York Times* 1 Apr. 2014, natl. ed.:
A18. Print.

For an editorial with no named author, begin with the title and add the word Editorial after the title, as in the example. For an editorial with a named author, start with his or her name.

15. Letter to the editor

Davis, Jimmie. "Tablet Teaching." Letter. *Scientific American* Mar. 2014: 8. Print.

Add the word Letter after the title, if there is one, or after the author's name if there is no title.

16. Interview

Begin with the name of the person interviewed. If the interview has a title, give it after the name (first example). If it does not have a title, add Interview and the name of the interviewer (if available) after the name (second example). See model 58a (p. 473) to cite a broadcast interview, model 58b (p. 474) to cite a video of an interview on the Web, and model 65 (p. 476) to cite an interview you conducted yourself. See also model 61 (p. 475) to cite a podcast.

a. Print interview

Conn, Jan. "Poetical Encounters: An Interview of Jan Conn." Interview by Magali Sperling Beck. *Canadian Literature* 218 (2013): 86-97. Print.

b. Web interview

Morrison, Toni. Interview by Christopher Bollen. *Interview Magazine*. Interview, n.d. Web. 8 Apr. 2014.

If the work you cite is undated, put n.d. ("no date") in place of the date, as above.

17. Article in a special issue

Rubini, Monica, and Michela Menegatti. "Linguistic Bias in Personnel Selection." *Celebrating Two Decades of Linguistic Bias Research*. Ed. Robbie M. Sutton and Karen M. Douglas. Spec. issue of *Journal of Language and Social Psychology* 27.2 (2008): 168-81. Print.

Cite an article in a special issue of a periodical by starting with the author and title of the article. Follow with the title of the special issue, Ed., and the name(s) of the issue's editor(s). Add Spec. Issue of before the periodical title. Conclude with publication information, using the appropriate model for a journal (model 7) or a magazine (models 11 and 12).

18. Abstract

Penuel, Suzanne. "Missing Fathers: *Twelfth Night* and the Reformation of Mourning." *Studies in Philology* 107.1 (2010): 74-96. Abstract. *Academic Search Complete*. Web. 10 Apr. 2014.

Treat an abstract like an article (here, a journal article from an online database), but add Abstract between the publication information and the database title. (You may omit this label if the journal title clearly indicates that the cited work is an abstract.)

Articles in freestanding digital files

Your instructor or a fellow student may send you a digital file of an article that you use as a source. To cite such a file, use any publication information you can find in one of the formats on the preceding pages. For the medium, give the format of the file, such as PDF file, *Microsoft Word* file, or another file format.

19. Published article in a digital file

Flynn, Elizabeth. "Composing as a Woman." *College Composition and Communication* 39.4 (1988): 423-35. PDF file.

20. Unpublished article in a digital file

Hernandez, Luis. "Travels in Mexico." 2014. *Microsoft Word* file.

3 Books and government publications

Complete books

21. Basic format for a book

To cite a book, give the author, the title, the city of publication, the publisher, the date, and the medium. When other information is required, put it between the author's name and the title or between the title and the publication information, as in models 22–28.

a. Print book

Shteir, Rachel. *The Steal: A Cultural History of Shoplifting*. New York: Penguin, 2011. Print.

See pp. 458–59 for an explanation of this format and the location of the required information in a print book.

b. Database book

Levine, Daniel. *Bayard Rustin and the Civil Rights Movement*. New Brunswick: Rutgers UP, 1999. *eBook Collection*. Web. 5 Feb. 2014.

See pp. 458–59 for an explanation of this format and the location of the required information in a database.

c. E-book

Booth, Marilyn. *May Her Likes Be Multiplied: Biography and Gender Politics in Egypt*. Oakland: U of California P, 2001. Kindle file.

If the e-book has a print version, give the publication information for the print version and add the medium, such as Kindle file or Google ebook file. If the book has no print publication information, give the e-book publication information instead.

d. Web book

Herodotus. *The Histories*. Trans. A. D. Godley. Cambridge: Harvard UP, 1920. *Perseus Digital Library*. Web. 3 May 2014.

For a book on the Web, give print publication information (if any) followed by the title of the Web site, the medium (Web), and the date of your access.

22. Second or subsequent edition

Bolinger, Dwight L. *Aspects of Language*. 3rd ed. New York: Harcourt, 1981. Print.

For any edition after the first, place the edition number after the title. (If an editor's name follows the title, place the edition number after the name. See model 35.) Use the appropriate designation for editions that are named or dated rather than numbered—for instance, Rev. ed. for "Revised edition."

23. Book with an editor

Holland, Merlin, and Rupert Hart-Davis, eds. *The Complete Letters of Oscar Wilde*. New York: Holt, 2000. Print.

Handle editors' names like authors' names (models 1–4), but add a comma and the abbreviation ed. (one editor) or eds. (two or more editors) after the last editor's name.

24. Book with an author and an editor

Mumford, Lewis. *The City in History*. Ed. Donald L. Miller. New York: Pantheon, 1986. Print.

When citing the work of the author, give his or her name first, and give the editor's name after the title, preceded by Ed. (singular only, meaning "Edited by"). When citing the work of the editor, use model 23 for a book with an editor, adding By and the author's name after the title:

Miller, Donald L., ed. *The City in History*. By Lewis Mumford. New York: Pantheon, 1986. Print.

25. Book with a translator

Alighieri, Dante. *The Inferno*. Trans. John Ciardi. New York: NAL, 1971. Print.

When citing the work of the author, as in the preceding example, give his or her name first, and give the translator's name after the title, preceded by Trans. ("Translated by").

(continued on p. 460)

Citing books: Print and database

Print book

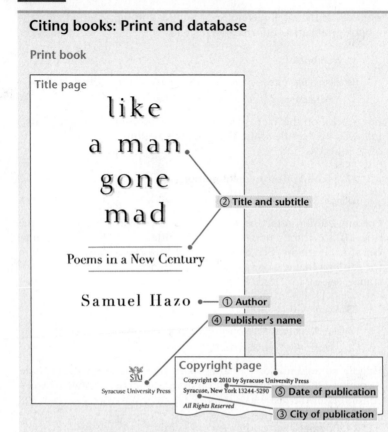

Title page

like
a man.
gone
mad

② Title and subtitle

Poems in a New Century

Samuel Hazo •— ① Author

④ Publisher's name

SÜU
Syracuse University Press

Copyright page

Copyright © 2010 by Syracuse University Press
Syracuse, New York 13244-5290   ⑤ Date of publication

All Rights Reserved

③ City of publication

Database book

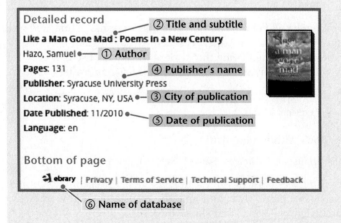

Detailed record   ② Title and subtitle

Like a Man Gone Mad : Poems in a New Century

Hazo, Samuel •— ① Author

Pages: 131   ④ Publisher's name

Publisher: Syracuse University Press

Location: Syracuse, NY, USA •— ③ City of publication

Date Published: 11/2010 •

⑤ Date of publication

Language: en

Bottom of page

ebrary | Privacy | Terms of Service | Technical Support | Feedback

⑥ Name of database

Works-cited entry: Print book

①   ②
Hazo, Samuel. *Like a Man Gone Mad: Poems in a New Century.*
    ③   ④   ⑤   ⑦
    Syracuse: Syracuse UP, 2010. Print.

Works-cited entry: Database book

①   ②
Hazo, Samuel. *Like a Man Gone Mad: Poems in a New Century.*
    ③   ④   ⑤   ⑥   ⑦   ⑧
    Syracuse: Syracuse UP, 2010. *Ebrary.* Web. 4 Apr. 2014.

① **Author.** Give the full name—last name first, a comma, first name, and any middle name or initial. Omit *Dr., PhD,* or any other title. End the name with a period.

② **Title,** in italics. Give the full title and any subtitle, separating them with a colon. Capitalize all significant words of the title even if the book does not. End the title with a period.

③ **City of publication.** Precede the publisher's name with its city, followed by a colon. Use only the first city if the title page lists more than one.

④ **Publisher's name.** Shorten most publishers' names ("UP" for University Press, "Little" for Little, Brown). Give both the imprint's and the publisher's names when they appear on the title page: e.g., "Vintage-Random" for Vintage Books and Random House.

⑤ **Date of publication.** If the date doesn't appear on the title page, look for it on the next page. End the date with a period.

⑥ **Name of database,** if you found the book through a database. Give the name in italics, and follow it with a period.

⑦ **Medium.** Give the medium of the book: Print if you consulted a print book, Web if you found the book in a database. Follow the medium with a period.

⑧ **Date of your access,** if you found the book online. Give the day first, then month, then year. End the date with a period.

See pp. 456–57 and 460–62 for how to cite other types of books.

(continued from p. 457)

When citing the work of the translator, give his or her name first, followed by a comma and trans. Follow the title with By and the author's name:

> Ciardi, John, trans. *The Inferno*. By Dante Alighieri. New York: NAL, 1971.
> Print.

When a book you cite by author has a translator *and* an editor, give the translator's and editor's names in the order used on the book's title page.

26. Anthology

> Kennedy, X. J., and Dana Gioia, eds. *Literature: An Introduction to Fiction, Poetry, Drama, and Writing*. 12th ed. New York: Longman, 2013. Print.

Cite an entire anthology only when citing the work of the editor or editors or when your instructor permits cross-referencing like that shown in model 36. Give the name of the editor or editors (followed by ed. or eds.) and then the title of the anthology.

27. Illustrated book or graphic narrative

> Wilson, G. Willow. *Cairo*. Illus. M. K. Perker. New York: Vertigo-DC Comics, 2005.
> Print.

When citing the work of the writer of a graphic narrative or illustrated book, follow the example above: author's name, title, Illus. ("Illustrated by"), and the illustrator's name. When citing the work of an illustrator, list his or her name first, followed by a comma and illus. ("illustrator"). After the title and By, list the author's name.

> Williams, Garth, illus. *Charlotte's Web*. By E. B. White. 1952. New York: Harper, 1999. Print.

28. Multivolume work

> Lincoln, Abraham. *The Collected Works of Abraham Lincoln*. Ed. Roy P. Basler. Vol. 5. New Brunswick: Rutgers UP, 1953. Print. 8 vols.

If you use only one volume of a multivolume work, give that volume number before the publication information (Vol. 5 in the preceding example). You may add the total number of volumes at the end of the entry (8 vols. in the example).

If you use two or more volumes of a multivolume work, give the work's total number of volumes before the publication information (8 vols. in the following example). Your text citation will indicate which volume you are citing (see p. 440).

> Lincoln, Abraham. *The Collected Works of Abraham Lincoln*. Ed. Roy P. Basler. 8 vols. New Brunswick: Rutgers UP, 1953. Print.

If you cite a multivolume work published over a period of years, give the inclusive years as the publication date: for instance, Cambridge: Harvard UP, 1978-90.

29. Series

Bergman, Ingmar. *The Seventh Seal*. New York: Simon, 1995. Print. Mod. Film
Scripts Ser. 12.

Place the name of the series (not quoted or italicized) at the end of the entry, followed by the series number (if any) and a period. Abbreviate common words such as *modern* and *series*.

30. Republished book

James, Henry. *The Bostonians*. 1886. New York: Penguin, 2001. Print.

Republished books include books reissued under new titles and paperbound editions of books originally released in hard covers. Place the original publication date after the title, and then provide the full publication information for the source you are using. If the book originally had a different title, add this title and its publication date after Rpt. of ("Reprint of") at the end of the entry—for example, Rpt. of *Thomas Hardy: A Life*. 1941.

31. The Bible

The Bible. Print. King James Vers.
The Holy Bible. Trans. Ronald Youngblood et al. Grand Rapids: Zondervan,
1984. Print. New Intl. Vers.

When citing a standard version of the Bible (first example), do not italicize the title or the name of the version. You need not provide publication information. For an edition of the Bible (second example), italicize the title, provide editors' and/or translators' names, give full publication information, and add the version name at the end.

32. Book with a title in its title

Eco, Umberto. *Postscript to* The Name of the Rose. Trans. William Weaver. New
York: Harcourt, 1983. Print.

When a book's title contains another book title (here *The Name of the Rose*), do not italicize the second title. When a book's title contains a quotation or the title of a work normally placed in quotation marks, keep the quotation marks and italicize both titles: *Critical Response to Henry James's "The Beast in the Jungle."*

33. Published proceedings of a conference

Stimpson, Bill, *2012 AWEA Annual Conference and Exhibition*. Proc. of Amer.
Wind Energy Assn. Conf., 3-6 June 2012, New York. Red Hook: Curran,
2013. Print.

To cite the published proceedings of a conference, use a book model—here, an edited book (model 23). Between the title and the publication data, add information about the conference, such as its name, date, and location. You may omit any of this information that already appears in the source title. Treat a particular presentation at the conference like a selection from an anthology (model 35).

34. Book lacking publication information or pagination

Carle, Eric. *The Very Busy Spider*. New York: Philomel, 1984. N. pag. Print.

Some books are not paginated or do not list a publisher or a place of publication. To cite such a book, provide as much information as you can and indicate the missing information with an abbreviation: N.p. if no city of publication, n.p. if no publisher, n.d. if no publication date, and N. pag. if no page numbers.

Parts of books

35. Selection from an anthology

Mason, Bobbie Ann. "Shiloh." *Literature: An Introduction to Fiction, Poetry, and Drama*. Ed. X. J. Kennedy and Dana Gioia. 12th ed. New York: Longman, 2013. 616-25. Print.

This listing adds the following to the anthology entry in model 26: author of selection, title of selection (in quotation marks), and inclusive page numbers for the selection (without the abbreviation "pp."). If you wish, you may also supply the original date of publication for the work you are citing, after its title. See model 30.

If the work you cite comes from a collection of works by one author that has no editor, use the following form:

Auden, W. H. "Family Ghosts." *The Collected Poetry of W. H. Auden*. New York: Random, 1945. 132-33. Print.

36. Two or more selections from the same anthology

Bradstreet, Anne. "The Author to Her Book." Kennedy and Gioia 689.

Kennedy, X. J., and Dana Gioia, eds. *Literature: An Introduction to Fiction, Poetry, and Drama*. 12th ed. New York: Longman, 2013. Print.

Merwin, W. S. "For the Anniversary of My Death." Kennedy and Gioia 874-75.

Stevens, Wallace. "Thirteen Ways of Looking at a Blackbird." Kennedy and Gioia 878-80.

When you are citing more than one selection from the same anthology, your instructor may allow you to avoid repetition by giving the anthology information in full (the Kennedy and Gioia entry) and then simply cross-referencing it in entries for the works you used. Thus the Bradstreet, Merwin, and Stevens examples replace full publication information with Kennedy and Gioia and the appropriate pages in that book. Note that each entry appears in its proper alphabetical place among other works cited. Because the specific entries cross-reference the Kennedy and Gioia anthology, they do not require the medium.

37. Article reprinted in a scholarly collection

Molloy, Francis C. "The Suburban Vision in John O'Hara's Short Stories."
  Critique: Studies in Modern Fiction 25.2 (1984): 101–13. Rpt. in *Short
  Story Criticism: Excerpts from Criticism of the Works of Short Fiction Writers.* Ed. David Segal. Vol. 15. Detroit: Gale, 1989. 287–92. Print.

If the work you cite is a scholarly article that was previously printed elsewhere—for instance, in a scholarly journal—provide the complete information for the earlier publication of the piece. Follow this information with Rpt. in ("Reprinted in") and the information for the source in which you found the piece.

38. Article in a reference work

List an article in a reference work by its title (first, third, and fourth examples) unless the article is signed (second and fifth examples). For works with entries arranged alphabetically, you need not include volume or page numbers.

a. Print reference work

"Reckon." *Merriam-Webster's Collegiate Dictionary.* 11th ed. 2008. Print.
Wenner, Manfred W. "Arabia." *The New Encyclopaedia Britannica: Macropaedia.*
  15th ed. 2007. Print.

For works that are widely used and often revised, like the above examples, you may omit the editors' names and all publication information except any edition number, the publication year, and the medium.

b. Specialized reference work

"Fortune." *Encyclopedia of Indo-European Culture.* Ed. J. P. Mallory and Douglas
  Q. Adams. London: Fitzroy, 1997. Print.

For works that are specialized—with narrow subjects and audiences—give full publication information.

c. Web reference work

"Yi Dynasty." *Encyclopaedia Britannica.* Encyclopaedia Britannica, 2013. Web.
  7 Apr. 2014.

Following the title of the article and the name of the Web site, give the sponsor, the date, the medium, and the access date.

d. CD-ROM or DVD-ROM reference work

Nunberg, Geoffrey. "Usage in the Dictionary." *The American Heritage Dictionary of the English Language.* 4th ed. Boston: Houghton, 2000. CD-ROM.

Single-issue CD-ROMs may be encyclopedias, dictionaries, books, and other resources that are published just once, like print books. Cite such sources like print books, but give CD-ROM or DVD-ROM as the medium. If the disc has a vendor that differs from the publisher of the work, add the vendor's place of publication, name, and publication date after the medium.

39. Introduction, preface, foreword, or afterword

Donaldson, Norman. Introduction. *The Claverings.* By Anthony Trollope. New York: Dover, 1977. vii-xv. Print.

An introduction, foreword, or afterword is often written by someone other than the book's author. When citing such a piece, give its name without quotation marks or italics, as with Introduction above. (If the piece has a title of its own, provide it, in quotation marks, between the name of the author and the name of the book.) Follow the title of the book with By and the book author's name. Give the inclusive page numbers of the part you cite. (In the example above, the small Roman numerals refer to the front matter of the book, before page 1.)

When the author of a preface or introduction is the same as the author of the book, give only the last name after the title:

Gould, Stephen Jay. Prologue. *The Flamingo's Smile: Reflections in Natural History.* By Gould. New York: Norton, 1985. 13-20. Print.

40. Published letter

Buttolph, Mrs. Laura E. Letter to Rev. and Mrs. C. C. Jones. 20 June 1857. *The Children of Pride: A True Story of Georgia and the Civil War.* Ed. Robert Manson Myers. New Haven: Yale UP, 1972. 334-35. Print.

List a published letter under the writer's name. Specify that the source is a letter and to whom it was addressed, and give the date on which it was written. Treat the remaining information as with a selection from an anthology (model 35, p. 462). (See also model 15, p. 455, for the format of a letter to the editor of a periodical.)

Government publications

41. Government publication

If a government publication lists a person as author or editor, treat the source as an authored or edited book (first example below). If a publication does not list an author or editor, give the appropriate agency as author (second and third examples). For agency-authored sources, provide the name of the government and the name of the agency (which may be abbreviated).

a. Print government publication

Gray, Colin S. *Defense Planning for National Security: Navigation Aids for the Mystery Tour.* Carlisle: US Army War Coll., Strategic Studies Inst., 2014. Print.

United States. Dept. of Defense. Office of Civil Defense. *Fallout Protection: What to Know and Do about Nuclear Attack.* Washington: GPO, 1961. Print.

Wisconsin. Dept. of Public Instruction. *Bullying Prevention Program.* Madison: Wisconsin Dept. of Public Instruction, 2014. Print.

b. Web government publication

United States. Dept. of Education. "Why Teach." *Teach.* US Dept. of Education, n.d. Web. 2 Mar. 2014.

To cite a source on a government Web site, substitute Web publication information for print, giving the Web site, the sponsor, the date of publication (here, n.d. for "no date"), the medium (Web), and the date of your access.

For a congressional publication that you find on the Web, give the house and committee involved before the title, the title (in italics), the number and session of Congress, and Web publication information.

United States. Cong. Senate. Committee on Veterans' Affairs. *Post-9/11 Veterans Educational Assistance Improvements Act of 2010.* 111th Cong., 2nd sess. *Congress.gov.* Library of Congress, 2014. Web. 29 Mar. 2014.

4 | Web sources and social media

Web sites and parts of Web sites

This section collects Web sources that are not books and are not periodicals because they are updated irregularly if at all. (Most newspaper and magazine sites, shown in models 9c and 11c, fall into the latter category because they are updated frequently but not at regular intervals.)

The following list, adapted from the *MLA Handbook*, gives the possible elements of a Web source in order of their appearance in a works-cited entry:

1. **Name of the author or other person responsible for the source**, such as an editor, translator, or performer.
2. **Title of the cited work.** Use quotation marks for titles of articles, blog entries, and other sources that are parts of larger works. Use italics for books, plays, and other sources that are published independently.

3. **Title of the Web site**, in italics.

4. **Publisher or sponsor of the site**, followed by a comma. If you cannot find a publisher or sponsor, use N.p. ("No publisher") instead. You may omit the sponsor if your entry includes information about prior publication in another medium (see model 42d, p. 468).

5. **Date of electronic publication, latest revision, or posting**. If no date is available, use n.d. ("no date") instead.

6. **Medium of publication**: Web.

7. **Date of your access**: day, month, year.

The MLA does not require a URL (electronic address) in Web source citations unless a source is hard to find without one or could be confused with another source. See model 45 (p. 469) for the form to use when citing a URL.

Note If you don't see just what you need in the following models, consult the index at the **MLA** divider for a similar source type whose format you can adapt. If your source does not include all the information needed for a complete citation, find and list what you can.

42. Page or work on a Web site

These models encompass pages, essays, articles, stories, poems, plays, and other works that you find on larger Web sites. To cite journal, newspaper, and magazine articles that you find on the open Web, see, respectively, models 7c, 9c, and 11c (pp. 449 and 452). To cite books that you find on the open Web, see model 21d (p. 457).

a. Work with an author and a title

Murray, Amanda. "The Birth of Hip-Hop: Innovation against the Odds." *The Lemelson Center for the Study of Invention and Innovation.* Smithsonian Inst., Natl. Museum of Amer. Hist., Oct. 2010. Web. 12 June 2014.

See opposite for an explanation of this format and the location of the required information on a Web site.

Most works on Web sites are brief, and their titles should be placed in quotation marks. However, some works, such as books and plays, are longer, and their titles should be italicized. (See **5** p. 313 and **6** pp. 337–38 for titles to be quoted and italicized.) The work cited below is a play:

Jonson, Ben. *Bartholomew Fair.* Ed. Hugh Craig. *Oxford Text Archive.* U of Oxford, n.d. Web. 3 June 2014.

b. Work without an author

"Clean Cars 101." *Union of Concerned Scientists.* Union of Concerned Scientists, n.d. Web. 11 Oct. 2014.

Citing a page or work on a Web site

National Park Service ○⟶ ③ Site title

Old Santa Fe Trail Building
Santa Fe, New Mexico

A Hidden Gem on Museum Hill ●⟶ ② Title of short work
Carrie Mardorf, Intermountain Region ⟵ ① Author

Contact:(505) 988-6757

Founded in 1610, Santa Fe, New Mexico is home to a lot of great attractions and amenities that make it a top tourist destination in the United States—amazing food, world-class museums, quirky art galleries, a large farmers market, an open-air opera, and hundreds of public, outdoor recreational areas in the nearby Sangre de Christo and Jemez Mountains. But nestled within the City Different are a plethora of hidden gems that are less visited and less well-known.

Guided Tours: Public tours are not available; however, an NPS brochure is available that discusses the history of the building and property. The Santa Fe Trail ruts are located within walking distance to the south and northwest of the building.

Bottom of page

National Park Service ○⟶ ④ Name of sponsor
U.S. Department of the Interior

⑤ Date of electronic publication or last update ⟶ ●Last Updated: 7/3/2012 12:57

    ①   ②   ③

Mardorf, Carrie. "A Hidden Gem on Museum Hill." *National Park*

           ④   ⑤

  Service. US Dept. of the Interior, Natl. Park Service, 3 July

    ⑥   ⑦

  2012. Web. 9 Sept. 2014.

① **Author.** Give the full name—last name first, a comma, first name, and any middle name or initial. Omit *Dr., PhD,* or any other title. End the name with a period. If no author is listed, begin with the title of the short work.

② **Title of the short work,** in quotation marks. End the title with a period inside the final quotation mark.

③ **Site title,** italicized and ending with a period.

④ **Name of the sponsor,** ending with a comma.

⑤ **Date of electronic publication or last update.** For dates that include day and month, give the day first, then month, then year. End the date with a period.

⑥ **Medium.** Give the medium of the work, Web, followed by a period.

⑦ **Date of your access.** Give the day first, then month, then year. End the date with a period.

If the work lacks an author, as with the preceding example, follow model 6 (p. 448) for an anonymous source, starting with the title. If the Web site is undated, give n.d. ("no date") as here.

c. Work without a title

Cyberbullying Research Center. Home page. Cyberbullying Research Center,
2014. Web. 15 Nov. 2014.

If you are citing an untitled work from a Web site, such as the home page or an untitled blog posting, give the name of the site followed by Home page, Online posting, or another descriptive label. Do not use quotation marks or italics for this label.

d. Work with print publication information

Wheatley, Phillis. "On Virtue." *Poems on Various Subjects, Religious and Moral.*
London, 1773. N. pag. *Bartleby.com.* Web. 3 Dec. 2014.

The print information for this poem follows model 35 for a selection from an anthology, but it omits the publisher's name because the anthology was published before 1900. The print information ends with N. pag. because the original source has no page numbers. The title of the Web site follows, but the sponsor is not needed because print publication information is provided. To cite other types of electronic and Web books, see model 21.

43. Entire Web site

a. Web site with an author or an editor

Crane, Gregory, ed. *The Perseus Digital Library.* Dept. of Classics, Tufts U,
21 Mar. 2014. Web. 22 July 2014.

When citing an entire Web site—for instance, a scholarly project or a foundation site—include the name of the editor, author, or compiler (if available), followed by the title of the site, the sponsor, the publication date, the medium, and your date of access.

b. Web site without an author or an editor

Center for Financial Security. U of Wisconsin System, 2014. Web. 31 Jan. 2014.

If a Web site lacks an author or editor (as many do), begin with the site title.

44. Wiki

"Podcast." *Wikipedia.* Wikimedia Foundation, 26 Mar. 2014. Web. 20 Nov. 2014.

To cite an entry from a wiki, give the entry title, the site title, the sponsor, the publication date, the medium, and your date of access. Begin with the site title if you are citing the entire wiki.

45. Citation of a URL

Joss, Rich. "Dispatches from the Ice: The Second Season Begins." *Antarctic*
    Expeditions. Smithsonian Natl. Zoo and Friends of the Natl. Zoo,
    26 Oct. 2007. Web. 26 Sept. 2014. <http://nationalzoo.si.edu/
    ConservationAndScience/AquaticEcosystems/Antarctica/Expedition
    /FieldNew/2-FieldNews.cfm>.

Give the URL of a source when readers may not be able to locate the
source without one or if your instructor requires it.

Social media

46. Post on a blog

Minogue, Kristin. "Diverse Forests Are Stronger against Deer." *Smithsonian*
    Science. Smithsonian Institution, 8 Apr. 2014. Web. 12 May 2014.

Cite a blog post like a work on a Web site, giving the author, the title
of the post, the title of the blog or site, the name of the sponsor or
publisher, the publication date, the medium, and your access date.
To cite a blog post without a title, follow model 42b.
    Cite an entire blog as you would an entire Web site (see model 43).

47. Post on a social-networking site

Literacy Network. Status update. *Literacy Network.* Facebook, 12 Apr. 2014.
    Web. 16 Apr. 2014.

Give the name of the author (a person or, as here, an organization),
the type of post, any page title, the sponsor, the date of the posting,
the medium, and the date of your access.

48. Comment

Drees, Tony. Comment. "Standing by Our Veterans." By Nicholas Kristof. *New*
    York Times. New York Times, 12 Apr. 2014. Web. 16 May 2014.

Give the author's name, and add his or her user name if both are
available and if they are different (see the next model). Then provide the label Comment, the title of the article or post the comment
responds to, and the author of that article or post. Then give publication information: the name of the site (here, a news Web site), the
sponsor, the date, the medium, and your date of access.

49. Tweet

Bittman, Mark (bittman). "Almost 90% of Fast Food Workers Say They've Expe-
    rienced Wage Theft: buff.ly/1i18eTb." 1 Apr. 2014, 4:51 p.m. Tweet.

Give the author's name followed by the user name if both are available and if they are different. Give the tweet in its entirety, using the

author's capitalization. Conclude with the date, the time, and the medium (Tweet).

50. Post to a discussion group

Williams, Frederick. "Circles as Primitive." *The Math Forum @ Drexel*. Drexel U,
28 Feb. 2012. E-mail.

If a discussion-group post does not have a title, say Online posting instead. Give the title of the discussion group as well as the name of the sponsor.

51. E-mail or text message

Green, Reginald. "Re: College applications." Message to the author. 24 Mar.
2014. E-mail.

For an e-mail message, use the subject heading as the title, in quotation marks. Then name the recipient, whether yourself (the author) or someone else. Cite a text message like an e-mail message but without a subject title:

Soo, Makenna. Message to the author. 2 Nov. 2014. Text message.

5 Visual, audio, and other media sources

52. Work of visual art

a. Original artwork

Arnold, Leslie. *Seated Woman*. N.d. Oil on canvas. DeYoung Museum, San
Francisco.

To cite a work of art that you see in person, name the artist and give the title (in italics) and the date of creation (or N.d. if the date is unknown). Then provide the medium of the work (here, Oil on canvas) and the name and location of the owner, if known. (Use Private collection if not.)

b. Reproduction of an artwork

Hockney, David. *Place Furstenberg, Paris*. 1985. Coll. Art Gallery, New Paltz.
David Hockney: A Retrospective. Ed. Maurice Tuchman and Stephanie
Barron. Los Angeles: Los Angeles County Museum of Art, 1988. 247. Print.

Pollock, Jackson. *Lavender Mist: Number 1*. 1950. Natl. Gallery of Art, Washington. *WebMuseum*. Web. 7 Apr. 2014.

For a work you see only in a reproduction, provide the original date of the work and its actual location, as in the examples above. Then give the complete publication information for the source you used. Omit the medium of the work itself, and replace it with the medium of the reproduction (Print in the first example, Web in the second example). Omit such information only if you examined the actual work.

c. Web artwork

Scorupsky, Julia. *Street*. Museum of Computer Art. Museum of Computer Art, 2013. Web. 5 Feb. 2014.

To cite a work of art that is available only on the Web, give the name of the artist or creator, the title of the work, the date of the work (if any), a word describing the type of art (unless it is otherwise clear, as in the preceding example), the title of the Web site, the sponsor, the date of the site, the medium, and your date of access.

53. Photograph

a. Original photograph

Sugimoto, Hiroshi. *Pacific Ocean, Mount Tamalpais*. 1994. Photograph. Private collection.

To cite an original photograph, give the name of the photographer, the title (in italics), the date of creation (or N.d. if the date is unknown), and the medium (Photograph). Then give the name and location of the owner, if known, or Private collection if not.

b. Reproduction of a photograph

Graham, David. *Bob's Java Jive, Tacoma, Washington, 1989*. *Only in America: Some Unexpected Scenery*. New York: Knopf, 1991. 93. Print.

For a photograph reproduced in a different medium (for instance, in a print book, as in the example), give the complete publication information for the source you used. Omit the medium of the work itself, replacing it with the medium of the reproduction. For a photograph reproduced on the Web, replace print publication information with Web publication information, as in model 52b.

c. Web photograph

Touboul, Jean. *Desert Chronicle 1*. 2004. Photograph. Artmuse.net. Jean Touboul, 2010. Web. 14 Sept. 2014.

To cite a photograph that is available only on the Web, give the name of the photographer, the title of the work, the date of the work (if any), Photograph, the title of the Web site, the sponsor, the date of the site, the medium, and the date of access.

d. Photograph in a digital file

Girls on the playground. Personal photograph by the author. 10 Aug. 2014. JPEG file.

For a photograph in a digital file—generally an unpublished personal photograph taken by you or by someone else—give the subject, the photographer, the date, and the medium (here, JPEG file).

54. Advertisement

a. Print advertisement

iPhone 5c. Advertisement. *Vogue* Dec. 2013: 3. Print.

Cite a print advertisement with the name of the product or company advertised, the description Advertisement, the print publication information, and the medium.

b. Web advertisement

FreeCreditReport.com. Advertisement. *Facebook.* Facebook, 2014. Web.
    14 May 2014.

Honey Maid. Advertisement. *YouTube.* YouTube, n.d. Web. 21 Apr. 2014.

For an advertisement you view on the Web, begin with the product's or the company's name and Advertisement. Then provide Web publication information: the name of the Web site, the sponsor, the date, the medium, and your date of access.

55. Comic strip or cartoon

a. Print comic strip or cartoon

Johnston, Lynn. "For Better or for Worse." Comic strip. *San Francisco Chronicle*
    22 Aug. 2014: E6. Print.

Cite a print cartoon or comic strip with the artist's name, the title (in quotation marks), and the description Comic strip or Cartoon.

b. Web comic strip or cartoon

Keefe, Mike. "Horse Meat." Cartoon. *Denver Post* 28 Feb. 2013. *PoliticalCartoons*
    .com. Web. 7 Apr. 2014.

This cartoon originally appeared in print and then was posted on the Web. The citation includes the artist's name, the title, Cartoon, the original print publication information, and finally the Web publication information.

For a comic or cartoon appearing only on the Web, provide just the Web information after Comic strip or Cartoon.

56. Map, chart, or diagram

Unless the creator of an illustration is given on the source, list the illustration by its title. Put the title in quotation marks if it comes from another publication or in italics if it is published independently. Then add a description (Map, Chart, and so on), the publication information, and the medium. If you consulted the source on the Web, conclude with the date of access.

a. Print map, chart, or diagram

"The Sonoran Desert." Map. *Sonoran Desert: An American Deserts Handbook.* By
    Rose Houk. Tucson: Western Natl. Parks Assn., 2000. 12. Print.

b. Web map, chart, or diagram

"Greenhouse Effect." Diagram. *Earthguide.* Scripps Inst. of Oceanography,
    2013. Web. 16 July 2014.

57. Television or radio program

a. Broadcast TV or radio program

"Do You Know?" By Stacy McKee. Dir. Chandra Wilson. *Grey's Anatomy.* ABC.
    KGO, San Francisco, 27 Mar. 2014. Television.

Start with the title unless you are citing the work of a person or persons. This example gives the episode title (in quotation marks) and the names of the writer and director of the episode. The example then gives the program title (in italics), the name of the network, and the call letters and city of the local station. If you list individuals who worked on the entire program rather than an episode, put their names after the program title.

b. Web TV or radio program

"Chapter 22." Dir. Jodie Foster. *House of Cards.* Netflix. Netflix, 14 Feb. 2014.
    Web. 10 June 2014.
Norris, Michele, host. *All Things Considered.* Natl. Public Radio, 10 July 2014.
    Web. 3 Nov. 2014.

Cite television or radio content streamed on the Web by the title (first example) or by the name of the person whose work you are citing (second example). Identify the role of anyone but an author (Dir. in the first example, host in the second). You may also cite other contributors and their roles after the title (see models 59a and 59b). Then give the site title, sponsor, medium, and date of access.

58. Interview

This section provides models for interviews you heard or saw. See model 16 (p. 455) to cite an interview that you read in a print periodical or on the Web, and see model 65 (p. 476) to cite an interview that you conducted yourself.

a. Broadcast interview

Schumer, Amy. Interview by Terry Gross. *Fresh Air.* Natl. Public Radio. WGBH,
    Boston, 18 Apr. 2014. Radio.

For an interview broadcast on radio or television, begin with the name of the person interviewed, followed by Interview by and the name of the interviewer. Then give the title of the radio or TV program, the network, the local station and city, the date, and the medium (Radio or Television).

b. Web interview

Gates, Henry Louis, Jr. Interview by Tavis Smiley. *Tavis Smiley*. Smiley Group,

31 Oct. 2013. Web. 6 Sept. 2014.

For a video or audio interview on the Web, follow the interviewer's name with the title of the Web site, the sponsor of the Web site, the medium, and your access date.

59. Film or video

Start with the title of the work unless you are citing the work of a person (see models b and c). Generally, identify and name the director. You may also cite other contributors (and their roles) after the title, as in model a.

a. Film

The Joneses. Screenplay by Chris Tyrrell and Stacey Cruwys. Dir. Chris Tyrrell.

Bjort, 2010. Film.

For a film, end with the distributor, the date, and the medium (Film).

b. DVD, Blu-ray, or videocassette

Balanchine, George, chor. *Serenade*. Perf. San Francisco Ballet. Dir. Hilary

Bean. 1991. PBS Video, 2006. DVD.

For a DVD, Blu-ray disc, or videocassette, include the original release date (if any), the distributor's name and release date, and the medium (here, DVD).

c. Web video

fouseyTUBE, prod. "The Homeless Child Experiment." *YouTube*. YouTube,

12 Mar. 2014. Web. 28 Apr. 2014.

For a film or video available only on the Web, give Web publication information in place of the distributor, and conclude with your access date.

d. Web video from another medium

Coca-Cola. Advertisement. Dir. Haskell Wexler. 1971. *American Memory*. Lib. of

Cong. Web. 9 Apr. 2014.

For a Web video that first appeared elsewhere in another medium, base the citation on model a or b above, adding information for Web publication.

60. Sound recording (music or spoken word)

Begin with the title of the work or with the name of the individual whose work you are citing. Unless this person is the composer of music you are citing, identify his or her role, as with perf. ("performer") in the first example. Following the title, name the music composer if you haven't already, after By. Then name and identify other contributors you want to mention, and give publication information.

a. CD or LP

Rubenstein, Artur, perf. Piano Concerto no. 2 in B-flat. By Johannes Brahms. Cond. Eugene Ormandy. Philadelphia Orch. RCA, 1972. LP.

If you are citing a work identified by form, number, and key (as here), do not use quotation marks or italics for the title.

If you are citing a song or song lyrics, give the title in quotation marks and then provide the title of the recording in italics.

Springsteen, Bruce. "This Life." *Working on a Dream*. Columbia, 2009. CD.

b. Web sound recording

Beglarian, Eve. *Five Things*. Perf. Beglarian et al. *Kalvos and Damian*. N.p., 23 Oct. 2001. Web. 8 Mar. 2014.

For a musical sound recording that is available only on the Web, start with the title or the name of the person whose work you are citing (here, the composer). If the Web site does not give a sponsor, give N.p., as here.

For a spoken-word recording, identify the narrator with narr. if he or she is not the author of the work.

Dove, Rita, narr. "We Wear the Mask." By Paul Laurence Dunbar. *Poetry Out Loud*. Poetry Foundation and Natl. Endowment for the Arts, 2014. Web. 3 Sept. 2014.

c. Web sound recording from another medium

"Rioting in Pittsburgh." CBS Radio, 1968. *Vincent Voice Library*. Web. 2 Dec. 2014.

For a Web sound recording that was originally produced in another medium, give the original publication information and then the information for Web publication.

d. Digital sound file

Mumford and Sons. "I Will Wait." *Babel*. Glassnote, 2012. MP3 file.

Give the digital format as the medium, here MP3 file.

61. Podcast

Sedaris, David. "Now We Are Five." *This American Life*. Chicago Public Media, 31 Jan. 2014. Web. 14 May 2014.

The preceding podcast from a radio program lists the author of a story on the show, the title of the story (in quotation marks), the program (italicized), and information for Web publication. If a podcast does not list an author or other creator, begin with the title.

62. Live performance

Muti, Riccardo, cond. Chicago Symphony Orch. Symphony Center, Chicago.

> 5 May 2012. Performance.

The New Century. By Paul Rudnick. Dir. Nicholas Martin. Mitzi E. Newhouse

> Theater, New York. 6 May 2013. Performance.

For a live performance, place the title first (second example) unless you are citing the work of an individual (first example). After the title, provide relevant information about participants as well as the theater, the city, and the performance date.

To cite a video of a performance that you view on the Web, see model 59c (p. 474).

63. Lecture, speech, address, or reading

Fontaine, Claire. "Economics." Museum of Contemporary Art. North Miami.

> 7 June 2014. Address.

Give the speaker's name and the title of the talk (if any), the title of the meeting (if any), the name of the sponsoring organization, the location of the presentation, the date, and the type of presentation (Lecture, Speech, Address, Reading).

Adapt the preceding format to cite a classroom lecture in a course you are taking:

Cavanaugh, Carol. Class lecture on teaching mentors. Lesley U. 4 Apr. 2014.

> Lecture.

To cite a video of a lecture or other presentation that you view on the Web, see model 59c.

64. Video game, computer software, or app

Notch Development. *Minecraft: Pocket Edition.* Vers. 1.7.9. Mojang, 2014. iOS7.

For a video game, computer program, or app, give the following: the name of the developer or author, the title, the version, the publisher or distributor, the date of publication, and the platform or the medium.

6 Other sources

65. Personal interview

Greene, Matthew. Personal interview. 7 May 2014.

Begin with the name of the person interviewed. For an interview you conducted, specify Personal interview or the medium (such as Telephone interview or E-mail interview), and then give the date.

See also model 16 (p. 455) to cite an interview in a print periodical or on the Web and model 59c (p. 474) to cite a broadcast or a video of an interview on the Web.

66. Unpublished or personal letter

a. Unpublished letter

James, Jonathan E. Letter to his sister. 16 Apr. 1970. MS. Jonathan E. James
Papers. South Dakota State Archive, Pierre.

For an unpublished letter in the collection of a library or archive, specify the writer, the recipient, and the date. Then provide the medium, either MS ("manuscript") or TS ("typescript"). End with the name and location of the archive.

See also model 15 (p. 455) to cite a letter to the editor and model 40 (p. 464) to cite a published letter.

b. Personal letter

Silva, Elizabeth. Letter to the author. 6 Apr. 2014. MS.

For a letter you received, specify yourself as recipient and give the date and the medium, MS or TS. To cite an e-mail message, see model 51 (p. 470).

67. Dissertation

a. Published dissertation

McFaddin, Marie Oliver. *Adaptive Reuse: An Architectural Solution for Poverty and
Homelessness*. Diss. U of Maryland, 2007. Ann Arbor: UMI, 2007. Print.

Treat a published dissertation like a book, but after the title insert Diss. ("Dissertation"), the institution granting the degree, and the year.

b. Unpublished dissertation

Wilson, Stuart M. "John Stuart Mill as a Literary Critic." Diss. U of Michigan,
1990. Print.

For an unpublished dissertation, use quotation marks rather than italics for the title and omit publication information.

68. Pamphlet or brochure

Understanding Childhood Obesity. Tampa: Obesity Action Network. 2013. Print.

Most pamphlets and brochures can be treated as books. In this example, the pamphlet has no listed author, so the title comes first. If your source has an author, give his or her name first, followed by the title and publication information.

Exercise 58.1 Writing works-cited entries

Prepare works-cited entries from the following information. Follow the MLA models given in this chapter unless your instructor specifies a different style. Arrange the finished entries in alphabetical order, not numbered.

1 An article titled "Who's Responsible for the Digital Divide?" in the March 2011 issue of the journal *Information Society*, volume 27, issue 2. The article appeared on pages 92–104. The authors are Dmitry Epstein, Erik C. Nisbet, and Tarleton Gillespie. You found the article on April 19, 2014, using the online database *Academic Search Complete*.

2 A Web article titled "Who's Not Online and Why" on the Web site *PewResearch Internet Project*. The author of the article is Kathryn Zickuhr. The sponsor of the site is the Pew Research Center. The article is dated September 25, 2013, and the site is dated 2014. You consulted the article on April 20, 2014.

3 A Web article with no listed author on the Web site *Digital Divide Institute*. The sponsor of the site is *DigitalDivide.org*. The title of the article is "Banking the Unbanked" and the site is dated 2014. You consulted the site on April 20, 2014.

4 A print book titled *Technology and Social Inclusion: Rethinking the Digital Divide* by Mark Warschauer. The book was published in 2003 by MIT Press in Cambridge, Massachusetts.

5 An article in the newspaper the *New York Times,* published in the national edition of the newspaper on March 20, 2013, on page B1. The author is Jane L. Levere. The title is "Reaching Those on the Wrong Side of the Digital Divide." You accessed the source through the database *LexisNexis Academic* on April 19, 2014.

6 A government report you consulted online on April 20, 2014. The author is the National Telecommunications and Information Administration, an agency within the United States Department of Commerce. The title of the report is "A Nation Online: Entering the Broadband Age." It was published on the NTIA Web site in September 2004.

7 An e-mail interview you had with Naomi Lee on April 23, 2014.

8 A blog post to the Web site *Code for America* by Jacob Solomon. The title is "People, Not Data." The post is dated January 6, 2014. The sponsor of the site is Code for America Labs. You consulted the source on April 21, 2014.

58c Using MLA paper format

The *MLA Handbook* provides guidelines for a fairly simple paper format, with just a few elements. For guidelines on type fonts, headings, lists, illustrations, and other features that MLA style does not specify, see 1 pp. 55–62.

The following samples show the formats for the first page and a later page of a paper. For the format of the list of works cited, see p. 445.

First page of MLA paper

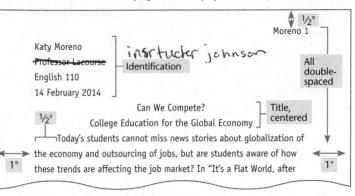

Later page of MLA paper

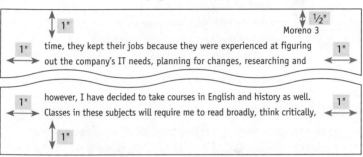

Margins Use one-inch margins on all sides of every page.

Spacing and indentions Double-space throughout. Indent the first lines of paragraphs one-half inch. (See the next page for treatment of poetry and long prose quotations.)

Paging Begin numbering on the first page, and number consecutively through the end (including the list of works cited). Use Arabic numerals (1, 2, 3) positioned in the upper right, about one-half inch from the top. Place your last name before the page number in case the pages later become separated.

Identification and title MLA style does not require a title page for a paper. Instead, give your name, your instructor's name, the course title, and the date on separate lines. Place this identification an inch from the top of the page, aligned with the left margin and double-spaced.

Double-space again, and center the title. Do not highlight the title with italics, underlining, boldface, larger type, or quotation marks. Capitalize the words in the title using the guidelines in **6** p. 336. Double-space the lines of the title and between the title and the text.

Poetry and long prose quotations Treat a single line of poetry like any other quotation, running it into your text and enclosing it in quotation marks. You may run in two or three lines of poetry as well, separating the lines with a slash surrounded by space.

> An example of Robert Frost's incisiveness is in two lines from "Death of the Hired Man": **"**Home is the place where, when you have to go there **/** They have to take you in**"** (119-20).

Always set off from your text a poetry quotation of more than three lines. Use double spacing above and below the quotation and for the quotation itself. Indent the quotation one inch from the left margin. *Do not add quotation marks.*

> In "The Author to Her Book," written in 1678, Anne Bradstreet characterizes her book as a child. In these lines from the poem, she captures a parent's and a writer's frustration with the imperfections of her offspring:
>> I washed thy face, but more defects I saw,
>> and rubbing off a spot, still made a flaw.
>> I stretched thy joints to make thee even feet,
>> Yet still thou run'st more hobbling than is meet. (13-16)

Also set off a prose quotation of more than four typed lines. (See **7** p. 393 on when to use such long quotations.) Double-space and indent as with the preceding poetry example. *Do not add quotation marks.*

> In the influential *Talley's Corner* from 1967, Elliot Liebow observes that "unskilled" construction work requires more skill than is generally assumed:
>> A healthy, sturdy, active man of good intelligence requires from two to four weeks to break in on a construction job. . . . It frequently happens that his foreman or the craftsman he services is not willing to wait that long for him to get into condition or to learn at a glance the difference in size between a rough 2 × 8 and a finished 2 × 10. (62)

Do not use a paragraph indention for a quotation of a single complete paragraph or a part of a paragraph. Use paragraph indentions of one-quarter inch only for a quotation of two or more complete paragraphs.

58d Examining a sample paper in MLA style

The sample paper beginning on p. 482 follows MLA guidelines for overall format, in-text citations, and the list of works cited. Annotations in the margins highlight features of the paper: those in blue boxes address format and documentation; the others address content.

Note Because the sample paper addresses a current topic, many of its sources come from the Internet and do not use page or other reference numbers. Thus the in-text citations of these sources do not give reference numbers. In a paper relying solely on printed journals, books, and other traditional sources, most if not all in-text citations would include page numbers.

A note on outlines

Some instructors ask students to submit an outline of the final paper. For advice on constructing a formal or topic outline, see **1** pp. 20–22. Below is an outline of the sample paper following, written in complete sentences. Note that the thesis statement precedes a formal topic or sentence outline.

Thesis statement: Although green consumerism can help the environment, consumerism itself is the root of some of the most pressing ecological problems. To make a real difference, humans must consume less.

I. Green products claiming to help the environment both appeal to and confuse consumers.

    A. The market for ecologically sound products is enormous.

    B. Determining whether or not a product is as green as advertised can be a challenge.

II. Green products don't solve the high rate of consumption that truly threatens the environment.

    A. Overconsumption is a significant cause of three of the most serious environmental problems.

        1. It depletes natural resources.

        2. It contributes to pollution, particularly from the greenhouse gases responsible for global warming.

        3. It produces a huge amount of solid waste.

    B. The availability of greener products has not reduced the environmental effects of consumption.

III. Since buying green products does not reduce consumption, other solutions must be found for environmental problems.

    A. Experts have proposed many far-reaching solutions, but they require concerted government action and could take decades to implement.

    B. For shorter-term solutions, individuals can change their own behavior as consumers.

        1. Precycling may be the greenest behavior that individuals can adopt.

            A. Precycling means avoiding purchase of products that use raw materials and excessive packaging.

            B. More important, precycling means avoiding purchases of new products whenever possible.

        2. For unavoidable purchases, individuals can buy green products and influence businesses to embrace ecological goals.

Malik 1

Justin Malik

Ms. Rossi

English 112-02

25 April 2014

The False Promise of Green Consumerism

They line the aisles of just about any store. They seem to dominate television and print advertising. Chances are that at least a few of them belong to you. From organic jeans to household cleaners to hybrid cars, products advertised as environmentally friendly are readily available and are so popular they're trendy. It's easy to see why Americans are buying these things in record numbers. The new wave of "green" consumer goods makes an almost irresistible appeal: save the planet by shopping.

Saving the planet does seem to be urgent. Thanks partly to former vice president Al Gore, who sounded the alarm in 2006 with the documentary film *An Inconvenient Truth*, the threat of global warming has become a regular feature in the news media and a recurring theme in popular culture. Unfortunately, as Gore points out, climate change is just one of many environmental problems competing for attention: the rainforests are vanishing, the air and water are dangerously polluted, alarming numbers of species are facing extinction, and landfills are overflowing. The warnings from Gore and others can be overwhelming, and most people feel powerless to halt the damage. Thus it may be reassuring that people can make a difference with small changes in what they buy—but that is not entirely true. Although green consumerism can help the environment, consumerism itself is the root of some of the most pressing ecological problems. To make a real difference, humans must consume less.

The market for items perceived as ecologically sound is enormous. Experts estimate that spending on green products already approaches $500 billion a year in the United States (Broder 4). Shoppers respond well to new options, whether the purchase is as minor as a bottle of chemical-free dish soap or as major as a front-loading washing machine. Not surprisingly, companies are responding by offering as many

---

Identification: writer's name, instructor's name, course title, date.

Title centered.

Double-space throughout.

Introduction: establishes the issue with examples (first paragraph) and background (second paragraph).

Citation form: no parenthetical citation because author is named in the text and DVD has no page or other reference numbers.

Thesis statement.

Background on green products (next two paragraphs).

Citation form: author and page number; author not named in the text.

Malik 2

new eco-products as they can. The journalist Rebecca Harris
reports in *Marketing Magazine* that the recent "proliferation of
green products" has been a revolution for business. She cites
a market research report by TerraChoice: in the first decade
of this century, the number of new packaged goods labeled
as green increased by approximately 75% each year, and
now nearly five thousand consumer items claim to be good
for the environment. These products are offered for sale at
supermarkets and at stores like Walmart, Target, Home Depot,
Starbucks, and Pottery Barn. Clearly, green consumerism has
grown into a mainstream interest.

    Determining whether or not a product is as green as ad-
vertised can be a challenge. Claims vary: a product might be
labeled as organic, biodegradable, energy efficient, recycled,
carbon neutral, renewable, or just about anything that sounds
environmentally positive. However, none of these terms
carries a universally accepted meaning, and no enforceable
labeling regulations exist (Atkinson and Rosenthal 34-35).
Some of the new product options offer clear environmental
benefits: for instance, LED lightbulbs last fifty times longer
than regular bulbs and draw about 15% of the electricity
("LED Lightbulbs" 25), and paper made from recycled fibers
saves many trees. But other "green" products just as clearly
do little or nothing to help the environment: a disposable razor made with less plastic is still a disposable razor, destined
for a landfill after only a few uses.

    Distinguishing truly green products from those that are
not so green merely scratches the surface of a much larger issue. The products aren't the problem; it's humans' high rate of
consumption that poses the real threat to the environment.
People seek what's newer and better—whether cars, clothes,
phones, computers, televisions, shoes, or gadgets—and they
all require resources to make, ship, and use them. Political
scientists Thomas Princen, Michael Maniates, and Ken Conca
maintain that overconsumption is a leading force behind
several ecological crises, warning that

        ever-increasing pressures on ecosystems, life-

        supporting environmental services, and critical

Citation form: no parenthetical citation because author is named in the text and article (in HTML format) has no page numbers.

Common-knowledge examples of stores and products do not require source citations.

Citation form: source with two authors; authors not named in the text.

Citation form: shortened title for anonymous source.

Environmental effects of consumption (next four paragraphs). Writer synthesizes information from half a dozen sources to develop his own ideas.

Quotation over four lines set off without quotation marks. See p. 480.

Malik 3

Ellipsis mark signals omission from quotation.

Citation form with displayed quotation: follows sentence period. Authors named in text, so not named in parenthetical citation.

natural cycles are driven not only by the sheer
number of resource users . . . but also by the patterns of resource use themselves. (4)

Those patterns of resource use are disturbing. In just the last
century, gross world product (the global output of consumer
goods) grew at five times the rate of population growth—a
difference explained by a huge rise in consumption per person.

Text refers to and discusses figure.

(See fig. 1.) Such growth might be good for the economy, but
it is bad for the environment. As fig. 1 shows, it is accompa-
nied by the depletion of natural resources, increases in the
carbon emissions that cause global warming, and increases in
the amount of solid waste disposal.

Figure presents numerical data visually.

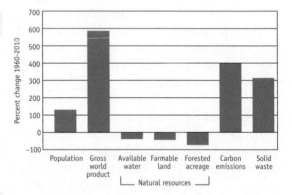

Figure caption explains the chart and gives complete source information.

Fig. 1. Global population, consumption, and environmental
impacts, 1960-2010. Data from United Nations Development
Programme; *Sustainability and Equity—A Better Future for All*
(New York: Palgrave, 2011; print; 32, 37-38, 165); and from
Earth Policy Inst.; "Data Center"; *Earth Policy Institute*; EPI,
6 Feb. 2014; Web; 16 Mar. 2014.

First effect of overconsumption

The first negative effect of overconsumption, the
depletion of resources, occurs because the manufacture
and distribution of any consumer product depends on the
use of water, land, and raw materials such as wood, metal,
and oil. Paul Hawken, a respected environmentalist, explains

Brackets signal capitalization changed to integrate quotation with writer's sentence.

that just in the United States "[i]ndustry moves, mines,
extracts, shovels, burns, wastes, pumps, and disposes of

Malik 4

4 million pounds of material in order to provide one average
. . . family's needs for a year" (qtd. in DeGraaf, Wann, and
Naylor 78; emphasis added). The United Nations Development Programme's 2011 *Human Development Report* warns
that many regions in the world don't have enough water,
productive soil, or forests to meet the basic needs of their
populations (4-5). Additional data from the Earth Policy
Institute confirm that as manufacturing and per-person consumption continue to rise, the supply of resources needed
for survival continues to decline. Thus heavy consumption
poses a threat not only to the environment but also to the
well-being of the human race.

> Citation form: source with three authors; "qtd. in" indicates indirect source (Hawken quoted by De-Graaf, Wann, and Naylor); "emphasis added" indicates italics were not in original quotation.

> Citation form: corporate author is named in the text, so page numbers only.

> Citation form: no parenthetical citation because author is named in the text and online source has no page or other reference numbers.

    In addition to using up scarce natural resources,
manufacturing and distributing products harm the earth by
spewing pollution into the water, soil, and air. The most
worrisome aspect of that pollution may be its link to climate
change. Al Gore explains the process as it is understood by
most scientists: the energy needed to power manufacturing
and distribution comes primarily from burning fossil fuels,
which releases carbon dioxide and other greenhouse gases
into the air; the gases build up and trap heat in the earth's
atmosphere; and the rising average temperatures will raise
sea levels, expand deserts, and cause more frequent floods
and hurricanes around the world. This view is reflected in the
bar chart of fig. 1, which shows that carbon emissions, like
the production of consumer goods in general, are rising at
rates out of proportion with population growth. The more humans consume, the more they contribute to global warming.

> Second effect of overconsumption

> Signal phrase introduces summary, which reduces a lengthy explanation to one sentence.

> Citation form: no parenthetical citation because Gore is named in the text and DVD has no page or other reference numbers.

> Writer's own conclusion from preceding data.

    As harmful as they are, gradual global warming and the
depletion of resources half a world away can be difficult to
comprehend or appreciate. A more immediate environmental effect of buying habits can be seen in the volumes of
trash those habits create. The US Environmental Protection
Agency found that in a single year (2012), US residents,
corporations, and institutions produced 251 million tons of
municipal solid waste, amounting to "4.38 pounds per person
per day" (1). Nearly a third of that trash came just from
the wrappers, cans, bottles, and boxes used for shipping

> Third effect of overconsumption.

> Citation form: author (a US government body) named in text, so parentheses include only page number.

Malik 5

consumer goods. Yet the mountains of trash left over from
consumption are only a part of the problem. In industrial
countries overall, 90% of waste comes not from what gets
thrown out, but from the manufacturing processes of con-

Citation form: source with
three authors; authors not
named in text.

verting natural resources into consumer products (DeGraaf,
Wann, and Naylor 192). Nearly everything people buy creates
waste in production, comes in packaging that gets discarded
immediately, and ultimately ends up in landfills that are
already overflowing.

Environmental effects of
green consumption.

Unfortunately, the growing popularity of green products
has not reduced the environmental effects of consumption.
The journalist David Owen notes that as eco-friendly and

Citation form: author is
named in the text, so page
number only.

energy-efficient products have become more available, the
"reduced costs stimulate increased consumption" (80). The
author gives the example of home cooling: in the last fifty
years, air conditioners have become much more affordable
and energy efficient, but seven times more Americans now
use them on a regular basis, for a net gain in energy use.

Citation form: US govern-
ment source not named in
text.

At the same time, per-person waste production in the
United States has risen by more than 20% (United States 10).
Greener products may reduce our cost of consumption and

Writer's own conclusion
from preceding data.

even reduce our guilt about consumption, but they do not
reduce consumption and its effects.

Solutions to problem of
consumption (next three
paragraphs).

If buying green won't solve the problems caused by
overconsumption, what will? Politicians, environmental-

Long-term solutions.

ists, and economists have proposed an array of far-reaching
ideas, including creating a financial market for carbon credits
and offsets, aggressively taxing consumption and pollution,
offering financial incentives for environmentally positive

Citation form: author's
name only, because schol-
arly article on the Web has
no page or other reference
numbers.

behaviors, and even abandoning market capitalism altogether
(de Blas). However, all of these are "top-down" solutions that
require concerted government action. Gaining support for
any one of them, putting it into practice, and getting results
could take decades. In the meantime, the environment would
continue to deteriorate. Clearly, short-term solutions are also
essential.

Short-term solution.

The most promising short-term solution is for individuals to change their own behavior as consumers. The greenest

Malik 6

behavior that individuals can adopt may be precycling, the
term widely used for avoiding purchases of products that
involve the use of raw materials. Precycling includes choosing
eco-friendly products made of nontoxic or recycled materials (such as aluminum-free deodorants and fleece made
from discarded soda bottles) and avoiding items wrapped
in excessive packaging (such as kitchen tools strapped to
cardboard and printer cartridges sealed in plastic clamshells).
More important, though, precycling means not buying new
things in the first place. Renting and borrowing, when possible, save money and resources; so do keeping possessions in
good repair and not replacing them until absolutely necessary. Good-quality used items, from clothing to furniture to
electronics, can be obtained for free, or very cheaply, through
online communities like *Craigslist* and *Freecycle,* from thrift
stores and yard sales, or by trading with friends and relatives.
When consumers choose used goods over new, they can help
to reduce the demand for manufactured products that waste
energy and resources, and they can help to keep unwanted
items out of the waste stream.

> Avoiding unnecessary purchases brings personal ben-
efits as well. Brenda Lin, an environmental activist, explained
in an e-mail interview that frugal living not only saves money
but also provides pleasure:

> > You'd be amazed at what people throw out or give
> > away: perfectly good computers, oriental rugs,
> > barely used sports equipment, designer clothes,
> > you name it. . . . It's a game for me to find what
> > I need in other people's trash or at Goodwill. You
> > should see the shock on people's faces when I tell
> > them where I got my stuff. I get almost as much
> > enjoyment from that as from saving money and
> > helping the environment at the same time.

> Lin's experience relates to research on the personal
and social consequences of consumerism by the sociologist
Juliet B. Schor. In one study, Schor found that the more
people buy, the less happy they tend to feel because of
the stress of working longer hours to afford their purchases

Common-knowledge definition and writer's own examples do not require source citations.

Primary source: personal interview by e-mail.

Quotation of over four lines set off without quotation marks. See p. 480.

Ellipsis mark signals omission from quotation.

Citation form: no parenthetical citation because author is named in the text and interview has no page or other reference numbers.

Citation form: shortened titles for one of two works by the same author.

(*Overspent* 11-12). Researching the opposite effect, Schor surveyed thousands of Americans who had drastically reduced their spending so that they would be less dependent on paid work. For these people, she discovered, a deliberately lower standard of living improved their quality of life by leaving them more time to socialize, get involved with their com-

Citation form: page numbers indicate exact locations of information in source.

Writer's own conclusion from two sources.

munities, and pursue personal interests (*True Wealth* 126-27, 139). Reducing consumption, it turns out, does not have to translate into sacrifice.

Benefits of green consumerism.

For unavoidable purchases like food and light bulbs, buying green can make a difference by influencing corporate decisions. Some ecologists and economists believe that as more shoppers choose earth-friendly products over their traditional counterparts—or boycott products that are clearly harmful to the environment—more manufacturers and retailers will look for ways to limit the environmental effects of

Citation form: two works in the same citation.

their industrial practices and the goods they sell (de Blas; Gore). Indeed, as environmental business consultant Joel Makower and his coauthors point out, Coca-Cola, Walmart, Procter & Gamble, General Motors, and other major companies have already taken up sustainability initiatives in response to market pressure. In the process, the companies have discovered that environmentally minded practices tend

Citation form: authors are named in the text, so page numbers only.

to raise profits and strengthen customer loyalty (5-6). By giving industry solid, bottom-line reasons to embrace ecological goals, consumer demand for earth-friendly products can magnify the effects of individual action.

Conclusion: summary and a call for action.

Careful shopping can help the environment, but green doesn't necessarily mean "Go." All consumption depletes resources, increases the likelihood of global warming, and creates waste, so even eco-friendly products must be used in moderation. Individuals can play small roles in helping the environment—and help themselves at the same time—by not buying anything they don't really need, even if it seems environmentally sound. The sacrifice by each person in reducing his or her personal impact on the earth is a small price for preserving a livable planet for future generations.

Malik 8

Works Cited

Atkinson, Lucy, and Sonny Rosenthal. "Signaling the Green Sell: The Influence of Eco-Label Source, Argument Specificity, and Product Involvement on Consumer Trust." *Journal of Advertising* 43.1 (2014): 33-45. *Business Source Premier*. Web. 23 Mar. 2014.

Broder, John M. "Complaints Abound in 'Green' Certification Industry." *New York Times* 1 June 2013: F4. *LexisNexis Academic*. Web. 23 Mar. 2014.

de Blas, Alexandra. "Making the Shift: From Consumerism to Sustainability." *Ecos* 153 (2010): n. pag. Web. 25 Mar. 2014.

DeGraaf, John, David Wann, and Thomas H. Naylor. *Affluenza: The All-Consuming Epidemic*. 3rd ed. San Francisco: Berrett-Koehler, 2014. Print.

Earth Policy Inst. "Data Center." *Earth Policy Institute*. EPI, 16. Feb. 2014. Web. 16 Mar. 2014.

Gore, Al. *An Inconvenient Truth*. Paramount, 2006. DVD.

Harris, Rebecca. "Cleaning Up by 'Saving the World.'" *Marketing Magazine* 22 Apr. 2013: 37-40. *MasterFILE Premier*. Web. 25 Mar. 2014.

"LED Lightbulbs." *Consumer Reports* Oct. 2010: 26-28. Print.

Lin, Brenda. Message to the author. 21 Mar. 2014. E-mail.

Makower, Joel, et al. *State of Green Business 2014*. *GreenBiz.com*. GreenBiz Group, 2014. Web. 25 Mar. 2014.

Owen, David. "The Efficiency Dilemma." *New Yorker* 20 Dec. 2010: 78-85. *Points of View Reference Center*. Web. 31 Mar. 2014.

Princen, Thomas, Michael Maniates, and Ken Conca. Introduction. *Confronting Consumption*. Ed. Princen, Maniates, and Conca. Cambridge: MIT P, 2002. 1-20. Print.

Schor, Juliet B. *The Overspent American: Upscaling, Downshifting, and the New Consumer*. New York: Basic, 1998. Print.

---. *True Wealth: How and Why Millions of Americans Are Creating a Time-Rich, Ecologically Light, Small-Scale, High-Satisfaction Economy*. New York: Penguin, 2011. *Ebrary*. Web. 27 Feb. 2014.

Annotations (right margin):

New page, double-spaced. Sources alphabetized by authors' last names.

Article in a scholarly journal that numbers volumes and issues, consulted in a database.

Article in a newspaper consulted in a database.

Article in a Web scholarly journal that numbers only issues and does not use page numbers.

Print book with three authors.

Short, titled work on a Web site, with a corporate author.

Movie on DVD.

Article in a weekly magazine consulted in a database.

Anonymous article listed and alphabetized by title.

Personal interview by e-mail.

Source with more than three authors.

Article in a weekly magazine consulted in a database.

Introduction to a print anthology.

Print book with one author.

Second source by author of two cited works: three hyphens replace author's name.

Print book with a corporate author.

United Nations Development Programme. *Human Development Report: Sustainability and Equity—A Better Future for All.* New York: Palgrave, 2011. Print.

US government source with no named author, so government body given as author.

United States. Environmental Protection Agency. Solid Waste and Emergency Response. *Municipal Solid Waste Generation, Recycling, and Disposal in the United States: Facts and Figures for 2012.* US Environmental Protection Agency, Feb. 2014. Web. 4 Apr. 2014.

APA
Documentation
and Format

APA Documentation and Format

APA in-text citations

APA references

Finding the right model for a source

1. **What type of source is it?** Locate the type in the index beginning opposite.

2. **What is the medium of the source?** From within each type of source, choose the right model for the medium. Common media:

   Print

   Web

   Database

   E-book

   Tweet

   Television; radio

   Film; video recording

   Computer software; app

3. **Who is the author?** Choose the right model for the number and type of author(s).

How many authors? models 1–3
Corporation, agency, or other group author? model 4
No named author? model 5
Author(s) of two or more of your sources? model 6

Chapter essentials

- In your text, document your sources with citations (below).
- Prepare an APA list of references (p. 497).
- Follow APA guidelines for paper format, including margins, spacing, headings, long quotations, illustrations, and other elements (p. 512).

Visit MyWritingLab™ for more resources on APA documentation and format.

The style guide for psychology and some other social sciences is the *Publication Manual of the American Psychological Association* (6th ed., 2010). The APA provides answers to frequently asked questions at *www.apastyle.org/learn/faqs*.

In APA documentation style, you acknowledge each of your sources twice:

- **In your text, a brief citation adjacent to the borrowed material directs readers to a complete list of all the works you refer to.**
- **At the end of your paper, the list of references includes complete bibliographical information for every source.**

Every entry in the list of references has at least one corresponding citation in the text, and every in-text citation has a corresponding entry in the list of references.

59a   Writing APA in-text citations

In APA documentation style, citations within the body of the text refer the reader to a list of sources at the end of the text. See the **APA** divider (previous two pages) for an index to the models for various kinds of sources.

Note When you cite the same source more than once in a paragraph, APA style does not require you to repeat the date beyond the first citation as long as it's clear what source you refer to. Do give the date in every citation if your source list includes more than one work by the same author(s).

1. Author not named in your text

One critic of Milgram's experiments questioned whether the researchers behaved morally toward their subjects (Baumrind, 1988).

When you do not name the author in your text, place in parentheses the author's last name, the date of the source, and sometimes the page number as explained below. Separate the elements with commas. Position the reference so that it is clear what material is being documented *and* so that the reference fits as smoothly as possible into your sentence structure. (See **MLA** pp. 442–43 for guidelines.)

Unless none is available, the APA requires a page or other identifying number for a direct quotation and recommends an identifying number for a paraphrase:

> In the view of one critic of Milgram's experiments (Baumrind, 1988), the subjects "should have been fully informed of the possible effects on them" (p. 34).

Use an appropriate abbreviation before the number—for instance, p. for *page* and para. for *paragraph*. The identifying number may fall by itself in parentheses, as in the preceding example, or it may fall with the author and date: (Baumrind, 1988, p. 34). See also model 11, p. 497.

2. Author named in your text

> Baumrind (1988) insisted that the subjects in Milgram's study "should have been fully informed of the possible effects on them" (p. 34).

When you use the author's name in the text, do not repeat it in parentheses. Place the source date in parentheses after the author's name. Place any page or paragraph reference either after the borrowed material (as in the example) or with the date: (1988, p. 34).

3. Work with two authors

> Bunning and Ellis (2013) revealed significant communication differences between teachers and students.
>
> One study (Bunning & Ellis, 2013) revealed significant communication differences between teachers and students.

When given in the text, two authors' names are connected by and. In a parenthetical citation, they are connected by an ampersand, &.

4. Work with three to five authors

> Pepinsky, Dunn, Rentl, and Corson (2010) demonstrated the biases evident in gestures.

In the first citation of a work with three to five authors, name all the authors.

In the second and subsequent references to a work with three to five authors, generally give only the first author's name, followed by et al. (Latin abbreviation for "and others"):

> In the work of Pepinsky et al. (2010), the loaded gestures included head shakes and eye contact.

However, two or more sources published in the same year could shorten to the same form—for instance, two references shortening to Pepinsky et al., 2010. In that case, cite the last names of as many authors as you need to distinguish the sources, and then give et al.: for instance, (Pepinsky, Dunn, et al., 2010) and (Pepinsky, Bradley, et al., 2010).

5. Work with six or more authors

One study (McCormack et al., 2012) explored children's day-to-day experience of living with a speech impairment.

For six or more authors, even in the first citation of the work, give only the first author's name, followed by et al. If two or more sources published in the same year shorten to the same form, give additional names as explained with model 4.

6. Work with a group author

The students' later work improved significantly (Lenschow Research, 2013).

For a work that lists an institution, agency, corporation, or other group as author, treat the name of the group as if it were one person's name. If the name is long and has a familiar abbreviation, you may use the abbreviation in the second and subsequent citations. For example, you might abbreviate American Psychological Association as APA.

7. Work with no author or an anonymous work

One article ("Leaping the Wall," 2013) examines Internet freedom and censorship in China.

For a work with no named author, use the first two or three words of the title in place of an author's name, excluding an initial *The*, *A*, or *An*. Italicize book and journal titles, place quotation marks around article titles, and capitalize the significant words in all titles cited in the text. (In the reference list, however, do not use quotation marks for article titles, and capitalize only the first word in all but periodical titles. See p. 499.)

For a work that lists "Anonymous" as the author, use that word in the citation: (Anonymous, 2014).

8. One of two or more works by the same author(s)

At about age seven, most children begin to use appropriate gestures to reinforce their stories (Gardner, 1973a).

When you cite one of two or more works by the same author(s), the date will tell readers which source you mean—as long as your reference list includes only one source published by the author(s) in that year. If your reference list includes two or more works published by the same author(s) *in the same year*, the works should be lettered in the reference list (see p. 501). Then your text citation should include the appropriate letter with the date: 1973a above.

9. Two or more works by different authors

Two studies (Marconi & Hamblen, 1999; Torrence, 2011) found that monthly safety meetings can dramatically reduce workplace injuries.

List the sources in alphabetical order by their authors' names. Insert a semicolon between sources.

10. Indirect source

Supporting data appeared in a study by Wong (as cited in Gallivan, 2013).

The phrase as cited in indicates that the reference to Wong's study was found in Gallivan. Only Gallivan then appears in the list of references.

11. Electronic or Web source

Ferguson and Hawkins (2012) did not anticipate the "evident hostility" of the participants (para. 6).

Many electronic and Web sources can be cited like printed sources, with the author's last name, the publication date, and page numbers. Others are missing one or more pieces of information:

- **No page numbers:** When quoting or paraphrasing a source that numbers paragraphs instead of pages, provide the paragraph number preceded by para., as in the preceding example. If the source does not number pages or paragraphs but does include headings, list the heading under which the quotation appears and then (counting paragraphs yourself) the number of the paragraph in which the quotation appears—for example, (Endter & Decker, 2013, Method section, para. 3). When the source does not number pages or paragraphs or provide frequent headings, omit any reference number.
- **No author:** For a source with no listed author, follow model 7.
- **No date:** For a source that is undated, use n.d. ("no date") in place of the date.

59b Preparing the APA reference list

In APA style, the in-text citations refer readers to the list of sources at the end of the text. Title this list References and include in it the full publication information for every source you cited in your paper. Place the list at the end of the paper, and number its page(s) in sequence with the preceding pages.

The following sample shows the format of the first page of the APA reference list:

APA reference list

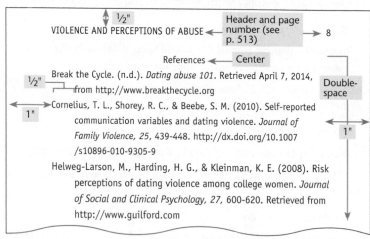

½"
VIOLENCE AND PERCEPTIONS OF ABUSE ← Header and page number (see p. 513) → 8

References ← Center

½" Break the Cycle. (n.d.). *Dating abuse 101.* Retrieved April 7, 2014, from http://www.breakthecycle.org

1" Cornelius, T. L., Shorey, R. C., & Beebe, S. M. (2010). Self-reported communication variables and dating violence. *Journal of Family Violence, 25,* 439-448. http://dx.doi.org/10.1007 /s10896-010-9305-9

Helweg-Larson, M., Harding, H. G., & Kleinman, K. E. (2008). Risk perceptions of dating violence among college women. *Journal of Social and Clinical Psychology, 27,* 600-620. Retrieved from http://www.guilford.com

Double-space

1"

Arrangement Arrange sources alphabetically by the author's last name. If there is no author, alphabetize by the first main word of the title.

Spacing Double-space everything in the references, as shown in the sample, unless your instructor requests single spacing. (If you do single-space the entries themselves, always double-space *between* them.)

Indention As illustrated in the sample, begin each entry at the left margin, and indent the second and subsequent lines one-half inch. Your word processor can create this so-called hanging indent automatically.

Punctuation Separate the parts of the reference (author, date, title, and publication information) with a period and one space. Do not use a final period in references that conclude with a DOI or URL (see opposite).

Authors For works with up to seven authors, list all authors with last name first, separating names and parts of names with commas. Use initials for first and middle names even when names are listed fully on the source itself. Use an ampersand (&) before the last author's name. See model 3 (p. 500) for the treatment of eight or more authors.

Publication date Place the publication date in parentheses after the author's or authors' names, followed by a period. Generally, this date is the year only, though for some sources (such as magazine and newspaper articles) it includes the month and sometimes the day as well.

Titles In titles of books and articles, capitalize only the first word of the title, the first word of the subtitle, and proper nouns; all other words begin with small letters. In titles of journals, capitalize all significant words. Italicize the titles of books and journals. Do not italicize or use quotation marks around the titles of articles.

City and state of publication For sources that are not periodicals (such as books or government publications), give the city of publication, a comma, the two-letter postal abbreviation of the state, and a colon. Omit the state if the publisher is a university whose name includes the state name, such as University of Arizona.

Publisher's name Also for nonperiodical sources, give the publisher's name after the place of publication and a colon. Shorten names of many publishers (such as Morrow for William Morrow), and omit *Co., Inc.,* and *Publishers*. However, give full names for associations, corporations, and university presses (such as Harvard University Press), and do not omit *Books* or *Press* from a publisher's name.

Page numbers Use the abbreviation p. or pp. before page numbers in books and in newspapers. Do *not* use the abbreviation for journals and magazines. For inclusive page numbers, include all figures: 667-668.

Digital Object Identifier (DOI) or retrieval statement At the end of each entry in the reference list, APA style requires a DOI for print and electronic sources (if one is available) or a retrieval statement for electronic sources.

- **DOI:** Many publishers assign a DOI to journal articles, books, and other documents. A DOI is a permanent URL that links to the text and functions as a unique identifier. When a DOI is available, include it in your citation of any print or electronic source. DOIs appear in one of two formats, as shown in model 7a (p. 501) and model 10 (p. 505). Use the format given in the source.
- **Retrieval statement:** If a DOI is not available for a source you found in a database or on the Web, provide a statement beginning with Retrieved from and then giving the URL of the periodical's or Web site's home page (model 7c, p. 504). You need not include the date you retrieved the source unless it is undated (model 22b, p. 508) or is likely to change (model 29, p. 510). If the source is difficult to find from the home page, you may give the complete URL. If you have questions about whether to include a home-page URL or a complete URL, ask your instructor.

Do not add a period after a DOI or a URL. Break a DOI or URL from one line to the next only before punctuation, such as a period or a slash, and do not hyphenate.

An index to the following models appears at the **APA** divider. If you don't see a model for the kind of source you used, try to find one that comes close, and provide ample information so that readers can trace the source. Often you will have to combine models to cite a source accurately.

1 Authors

1. One author

Rodriguez, R. (1982). *A hunger of memory: The education of Richard Rodriguez.* Boston, MA: Godine.

The initial R. appears instead of the author's first name, even though the author's full first name appears on the source. In this book title, only the first words of the title and subtitle and the proper name are capitalized.

2. Two to seven authors

Nesselroade, J. R., & Baltes, P. B. (1999). *Longitudinal research in behavioral studies.* New York, NY: Academic Press.

With two to seven authors, separate authors' names with commas and use an ampersand (&) before the last author's name.

3. Eight or more authors

Wimple, P. B., Van Eijk, M., Potts, C. A., Hayes, J., Obergau, W. R., Smith, H., . . . Zimmer, S. (2001). *Case studies in moral decision making among adolescents.* San Francisco, CA: Jossey-Bass.

For a work by eight or more authors, list the first six authors' names, insert an ellipsis mark (three spaced periods), and then give the last author's name.

4. A group author

Lenschow Research. (2013). *Trends in secondary curriculum.* Baltimore, MD: Arrow Books.

For a work with a group author—such as a research group, a committee, a government agency, an association, or a corporation—begin the entry with the group name. In the reference list, alphabetize the work as if the first main word (excluding any *The, A,* or *An*) were an author's last name.

5. Author not named (anonymous)

Merriam-Webster's collegiate dictionary (11th ed.). (2008). Springfield, MA: Merriam-Webster.

Resistance is not furtile. (2014, April 5). *New Scientist, 221*(15), 5.

When no author is named, list the work under its title and alphabetize it by the first main word (excluding any *The, A, An*).

For a work whose author is actually given as "Anonymous," use that word in place of the author's name and alphabetize it as if it were a name:

> Anonymous. (2014). *Teaching research, researching teaching.* New York, NY:
>
> Alpine Press.

6. Two or more works by the same author(s) published in the same year

> Gardner, H. (1973a). *The arts and human development.* New York, NY: Wiley.
>
> Gardner, H. (1973b). *The quest for mind: Piaget, Lévi-Strauss, and the structuralist movement.* New York, NY: Knopf.

When citing two or more works by exactly the same author(s), published in the same year, arrange them alphabetically by the first main word of the title and distinguish the sources by adding a letter to the date. Both the date and the letter are used in citing the source in your text (see p. 496).

When citing two or more works by exactly the same author(s) but *not* published in the same year, arrange the sources in order of their publication dates, earliest first.

2 Articles in journals, magazines, and newspapers

7. Article in a scholarly journal

Some journals number the pages of issues consecutively during a year, so that each issue after the first begins numbering where the previous issue left off—say, at page 132 or 416. For this kind of journal, give the volume number after the title (models a, b, c). Other journals as well as most magazines start each issue with page 1. For these journals and magazines, place the issue number in parentheses and not italicized immediately after the volume number (model 8).

a. Print, database, or Web journal article with a DOI

> Hirsh, A. T., Gallegos, J. C., Gertz, K. J., Engel, J. M., & Jensen, M. P. (2010).
>
> Symptom burden in individuals with cerebral palsy. *Journal of Rehabilitation Research & Development, 47,* 860-876. doi:10.1682/JRRD.2010
>
> .03.0024

See the next two pages for an explanation of this format and the location of the required information on a source. The format is the same for any journal article that has a DOI—print, database, or Web.

Note DOIs appear in one of two formats, as shown above and in model 10 (p. 505). Use the format given in the source.

(continued on p. 504)

Citing journal articles: Print, database, or Web with DOI

Print journal article

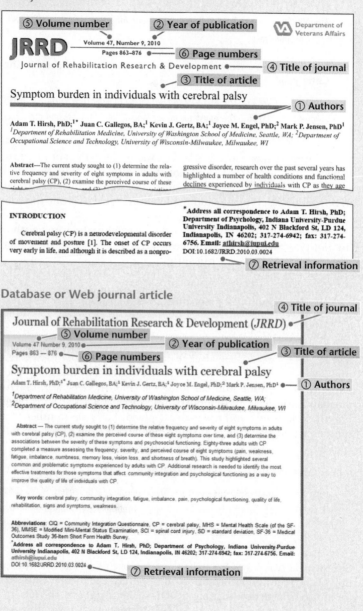

⑤ Volume number   ② Year of publication   Department of Veterans Affairs

JRRD   Volume 47, Number 9, 2010
Pages 863–876   ⑥ Page numbers

Journal of Rehabilitation Research & Development   ④ Title of journal

③ Title of article

Symptom burden in individuals with cerebral palsy

① Authors

Adam T. Hirsh, PhD;[1][*] Juan C. Gallegos, BA;[1] Kevin J. Gertz, BA;[1] Joyce M. Engel, PhD;[2] Mark P. Jensen, PhD[1]
[1]Department of Rehabilitation Medicine, University of Washington School of Medicine, Seattle, WA; [2]Department of Occupational Science and Technology, University of Wisconsin-Milwaukee, Milwaukee, WI

Abstract—The current study sought to (1) determine the relative frequency and severity of eight symptoms in adults with cerebral palsy (CP), (2) examine the perceived course of these eight symptoms ... gressive disorder, research over the past several years has highlighted a number of health conditions and functional declines experienced by individuals with CP as they age

INTRODUCTION

Cerebral palsy (CP) is a neurodevelopmental disorder of movement and posture [1]. The onset of CP occurs very early in life, and although it is described as a nonpro-

[*]Address all correspondence to Adam T. Hirsh, PhD; Department of Psychology, Indiana University-Purdue University Indianapolis, 402 N Blackford St, LD 124, Indianapolis, IN 46202; 317-274-6942; fax: 317-274-6756. Email: athirsh@iupui.edu
DOI:10.1682/JRRD.2010.03.0024

⑦ Retrieval information

Database or Web journal article

④ Title of journal

Journal of Rehabilitation Research & Development (*JRRD*)

⑤ Volume number

Volume 47 Number 9, 2010
Pages 863 – 876   ⑥ Page numbers

② Year of publication

③ Title of article

Symptom burden in individuals with cerebral palsy

① Authors

Adam T. Hirsh, PhD;[1][*] Juan C. Gallegos, BA;[1] Kevin J. Gertz, BA;[1] Joyce M. Engel, PhD;[2] Mark P. Jensen, PhD[1]

[1]Department of Rehabilitation Medicine, University of Washington School of Medicine, Seattle, WA;
[2]Department of Occupational Science and Technology, University of Wisconsin-Milwaukee, Milwaukee, WI

Abstract — The current study sought to (1) determine the relative frequency and severity of eight symptoms in adults with cerebral palsy (CP), (2) examine the perceived course of these eight symptoms over time, and (3) determine the associations between the severity of these symptoms and psychosocial functioning. Eighty-three adults with CP completed a measure assessing the frequency, severity, and perceived course of eight symptoms (pain, weakness, fatigue, imbalance, numbness, memory loss, vision loss, and shortness of breath). This study highlighted several common and problematic symptoms experienced by adults with CP. Additional research is needed to identify the most effective treatments for those symptoms that affect community integration and psychological functioning as a way to improve the quality of life of individuals with CP.

Key words: cerebral palsy, community integration, fatigue, imbalance, pain, psychological functioning, quality of life, rehabilitation, signs and symptoms, weakness.

Abbreviations: CIQ = Community Integration Questionnaire, CP = cerebral palsy, MHS = Mental Health Scale (of the SF-36), MMSE = Modified Mini-Mental Status Examination, SCI = spinal cord injury, SD = standard deviation, SF-36 = Medical Outcomes Study 36-Item Short Form Health Survey.
[*]Address all correspondence to Adam T. Hirsh, PhD; Department of Psychology, Indiana University-Purdue University Indianapolis, 402 N Blackford St, LD 124, Indianapolis, IN 46202; 317-274-6942; fax: 317-274-6756. Email: athirsh@iupui.edu
DOI:10.1682/JRRD.2010.03.0024

⑦ Retrieval information

References entry: Print, database, or Web journal article with DOI

Hirsh, A. T., Gallegos, J. C., Gertz, K. J., Engel, J. M., & Jensen, ①

M. P. (2010). Symptom burden in individuals with cerebral
②   ③

palsy. *Journal of Rehabilitation Research & Development, 47,*
④   ⑤

860-876. doi:10.1682/JRRD.2010.03.0024
⑥   ⑦

① **Authors.** Give each author's last name, first initial, and any middle initial. Separate names from initials with commas, and use & before the last author's name. Omit *Dr., PhD,* or any other title. See models 1–6 (pp. 500–01) for how to cite various numbers and kinds of authors.

② **Year of publication,** in parentheses and followed by a period.

③ **Title of article.** Give the full article title and any subtitle, separating them with a colon. Capitalize only the first words of the title and subtitle, and do not place the title in quotation marks.

④ **Title of journal,** in italics. Capitalize all significant words and end with a comma.

⑤ **Volume number,** italicized and followed by a comma. Include just the volume number when all the issues in each annual volume are paginated in one sequence. Include the issue number only when the issues are paginated separately.

⑥ **Inclusive page numbers of article,** without "pp." Do not omit any numerals.

⑦ **Retrieval information.** If the article has a DOI, give it using the format here or as shown in model 10. Do not end with a period. If the article does not have a DOI, see models 7b and 7c. (See p. 499 for more on DOIs and retrieval statements.)

(continued from p. 501)

b. Print journal article without a DOI

Atkinson, N. S. (2011). Newsreels as domestic propaganda: Visual rhetoric at the dawn of the cold war. *Rhetoric and Public Affairs, 14,* 69-105.

If a print journal article does not have a DOI, simply end with the page numbers of the article.

c. Database or Web journal article without a DOI

Rosen, I. M., Maurer, D. M., & Darnall, C. R. (2008). Reducing tobacco use in adolescents. *American Family Physician, 77,* 483-490. Retrieved from http://www.aafp.org/online/en/home/publications/journals/afp.html

If a journal article you found in a database or on the Web does not have a DOI, use a search engine to find the home page of the journal and give the home-page URL, as above. Generally, do not give the name of a database in which you found an article because readers may not be able to find the source the same way you did. However, do give the database name if you cannot find the home page of the journal on the Web, as in this example:

Smith, E. M. (1926, March). Equal rights—internationally! *Life and Labor Bulletin, 4,* 1-2. Retrieved from Women and Social Movements in the United States, 1600-2000, database.

8. Article in a magazine

For magazine articles, give the month of publication as well as any day along with the year. If the magazine gives volume and issue numbers, list them after the title of the magazine. Italicize the volume number and place the issue number, not italicized, in parentheses.

a. Print magazine article

Newton-Small, J. (2013, February 18). Blood for oil. *Time, 181*(6), 22.

b. Database or Web magazine article

Weir, K. (2014, March 22). Your cheating brain. *New Scientist, 221*(12), 35-37. Retrieved from http://www.newscientist.com

If a magazine article includes a DOI, give it after the page numbers. Otherwise, give the URL of the magazine's home page in a retrieval statement. If you do not find the home page, give the name of the database in which you found the article (see the Smith example above).

9. Article in a newspaper

For newspaper articles, give the month and day of publication along with the year. Use *The* in the newspaper name if the paper itself does.

a. Print newspaper article

Zimmer, C. (2014, May 4). Young blood may hold key to reversing aging. *The New York Times*, p. C1.

Precede the page number(s) with p. or pp.

b. Database or Web newspaper article

Angier, N. (2013, November 26). The changing american family. *The New York Times*. Retrieved from http://www.nytimes.com

Give the URL of the newspaper's home page in the retrieval statement. If you do not find the home page, give the name of the database in which you found the article (see the Smith example opposite).

10. Review

Bond, M. (2008, December 18). Does genius breed success? [Review of the book *Outliers: The story of success*, by M. Gladwell]. *Nature, 456*, 785. http://dx.doi.org/10.1038/456874a

If a review has no title, use the bracketed information in its place, keeping the brackets.

11. Interview

Shaffir, S. (2013). It's our generation's responsibility to bring a genuine feeling of hope [Interview by H. Schenker]. *Palestine-Israeli Journal of Politics, Economics, and Culture, 18*(4). Retrieved from http://pij.org

List an interview under the interviewee's name and give the title, if any. If there is no title, or if the title does not indicate that the source is an interview, add a bracketed explanation, as above. End with publication information for the kind of source the interview appears in—here a journal on the Web, which requires retrieval information.

See model 32 (p. 511) to cite a recorded interview. See model 30 (p. 510) to cite an interview you conduct, which should be treated like a personal communication and cited only in the text.

12. Supplemental periodical content that appears only online

Anderson, J. L. (2014, May 2). Revolutionary relics [Supplemental material]. *The New Yorker*. Retrieved from www.newyorker.com

If you cite material from a periodical's Web site that is not included in the print version of the publication, add [Supplemental material] after the title and give the URL of the publication's home page.

13. Abstract of a journal article

Polletta, F. (2008). Just talk: Public deliberation after 9/11. *Journal of Public Deliberation, 4*(1). Abstract retrieved from http://services.bepress.com/jpd

When you cite the abstract of an article, give the full publication information for the article, followed by Abstract and information about where you found the abstract.

3 | Books, government publications, and other independent works

14. Basic format for a book

a. Print book

Ehrenreich, B. (2007). *Dancing in the streets: A history of collective joy.*
New York, NY: Holt.

Give the author's or authors' names, following models 1–4. Then give the complete title, including any subtitle. Italicize the title, and capitalize only the first words of the title and subtitle. End the entry with the city and state of publication and the publisher's name. (See pp. 498–99 for how to treat these elements.)

b. Web or database book

Reuter, P. (Ed.). (2010). *Understanding the demand for illegal drugs.* Retrieved
from http://books.nap.edu

For a book available on the Web or in an online library or database, replace any print publication information with a DOI if one is available (see model 7a) or with a retrieval statement, as above.

c. E-book

Waltz, M. (2013). *Autism: A social and medical history* [Kindle version].
Retrieved from http://www.amazon.com

For an e-book, give the format in brackets and a retrieval statement.

15. Book with an editor

Dohrenwend, B. S., & Dohrenwend, B. P. (Eds.). (1999). *Stressful life events:
Their nature and effects.* New York, NY: Wiley.

List the names of the editors as if they were authors, but follow the last name with (Eds.).—or (Ed.). with only one editor. Note the periods inside and outside the final parenthesis.

16. Book with a translator

Trajan, P. D. (1927). *Psychology of animals* (H. Simone, Trans.). Washington,
DC: Halperin.

17. Later edition

Bolinger, D. L. (1981). *Aspects of language* (3rd ed.). New York, NY: Harcourt
Brace Jovanovich.

18. Work in more than one volume

Lincoln, A. (1953). *The collected works of Abraham Lincoln* (R. P. Basler, Ed.). (Vol. 5). New Brunswick, NJ: Rutgers University Press.

Lincoln, A. (1953). *The collected works of Abraham Lincoln* (R. P. Basler, Ed.). (Vols. 1-8). New Brunswick, NJ: Rutgers University Press.

The first entry cites a single volume (5) in the eight-volume set. The second entry cites all eight volumes. Use Vol. or Vols. in parentheses and follow the closing parenthesis with a period. In the absence of an editor's name, this description would follow the title directly: *The collected works of Abraham Lincoln* (Vol. 5).

19. Article or chapter in an edited book

Paykel, E. S. (1999). Life stress and psychiatric disorder: Applications of the clinical approach. In B. S. Dohrenwend & B. P. Dohrenwend (Eds.), *Stressful life events: Their nature and effects* (pp. 239-264). New York, NY: Wiley.

Give the publication date of the collection (1999 here) as the publication date of the article or chapter. After the article or chapter title and a period, say In and then provide the editors' names (in normal order), (Eds.) and a comma, the title of the collection, and the page numbers of the article in parentheses.

20. Article in a reference work

Wood, R. (1998). Community organization. In W. A. Swatos, Jr. (Ed.), *Encyclopedia of religion and society*. Retrieved from http://hirr.hartsem.edu/ency/commorg.htm

If the entry you cite has no named author, begin with the title of the entry and then the date. Use a DOI instead of a URL if the source has one.

21. Government publication

a. Print publication

Hawaii. Department of Education. (2014). *Kauai district schools, profile 2013-14*. Honolulu, HI: Author.

Stiller, A. (2012). *Historic preservation and tax incentives*. Washington, DC: U.S. Department of the Interior.

If no person is named as the author, list the publication under the name of the sponsoring agency. When the agency is both the author and the publisher, use Author in place of the publisher's name, as in the first example.

For legal materials such as court decisions, laws, and testimony at hearings, the APA recommends formats that correspond to conventional legal citations. The following example of a congressional hearing includes the full title, the number of the Congress, the page number where the hearing transcript starts in the official publication, and the date of the hearing.

> *Medicare payment for outpatient physical and occupational therapy services: Hearing before the Committee on Ways and Means, House of Representatives,* 110th Cong. 3 (2007).

b. Web publication

National Institute on Alcohol Abuse and Alcoholism. (2013, July). *Underage drinking* [Fact sheet]. Retrieved from http://pubs.niaaa.nih.gov /publications/UnderageDrinking/Underage_Fact.pdf

For a government publication on the Web, add a retrieval statement.

22. Report

a. Print report

Gerald, K. (2003). *Medico-moral problems in obstetric care* (Report No. NP-71). St. Louis, MO: Catholic Hospital Association.

Treat a printed report like a book, but provide any report number in parentheses after the title, with no punctuation between them.

b. Web report

Anderson, J. A., & Rainie, L. (2014, March 11). *Digital life in 2025.* Retrieved from Pew Research Internet Project website: http://www.pewinternet.org

For a report on the Web, give the name of the publisher in the retrieval statement if the publisher is not the author of the report. Generally, provide the URL of the Web site's home page.

If the work you cite is undated, use the abbreviation n.d. in place of the publication date and give the date of your access in the retrieval statement:

U.S. Census Bureau. (n.d.). *Men's marital status: 1950-2013*. Retrieved April 23, 2014, from https://www.census.gov/hhes/families/files/graphics /MS-1a.pdf

23. Dissertation

a. Dissertation in a commercial database

McFaddin, M. O. (2007). *Adaptive reuse: An architectural solution for poverty and homelessness* (Doctoral dissertation). Available from ProQuest Dissertations and Theses database. (ATT 1378764)

If a dissertation is from a commercial database, give the name of the database in the retrieval statement, followed by the accession or order number in parentheses.

b. Dissertation in an institutional database

Chang, J. K. (2003). *Therapeutic intervention in treatment of injuries to the hand and wrist* (Doctoral dissertation). Retrieved from http://medsci .archive.liasu.edu/61724

If a dissertation is from an institution's database, give the URL in the retrieval statement.

4 Web sources and social media

Specific types of Web sources are covered under their respective categories, such as articles in periodicals (models 7a, 7c, 8b, 9b), books (model 14b), and reports (model 22b). When citing URLs, APA recommends giving the home-page URL unless the source is difficult to find from the home page. In such a case, provide the complete URL.

24. Part or all of a Web site

American Psychological Association. (2014). Information for students with disabilities [Web page]. Retrieved from http://www.apa.org

To cite a page or document on a Web site, give the author (if any), the date (or n.d. if the page or site is undated), the title of the page or document, a description in brackets, and a retrieval statement.

Cite an entire Web site just in the text of your paper, giving the name of the site in your text and the URL in parentheses:

The Web site of the Cyberbullying Research Center provides information on the causes and nature of cyberbullying among teenagers (http:// cyberbullying.us).

Although APA does not require you to include entire Web sites in your list of references, some instructors ask for such references. Then you can use the format shown in the first example, substituting the title of the Web site for the title of the Web page or document.

25. Post to a blog or discussion group

Kristof, N. (2014, March 22). Confronting the netherworld of child pornography [Blog post]. Retrieved from http://kristof.blogs.nytimes.com

Include postings to blogs and discussion groups in your list of references only if they are retrievable by others. (The source above is retrievable by a search of the home page URL.) Follow the message title with [Blog post], [Electronic mailing list message], or [Online forum comment]. Include the name of the blog or discussion group in the retrieval statement if it isn't part of the URL.

26. Blog comment

Peter. (2014, March 23). Re: Confronting the netherworld of child pornography [Blog comment]. Retrieved from http://kristof.blogs.nytimes.com

27. Post to a social-networking site

Environmental Defense Fund. (2014, May 1). Extreme weather = extreme consequences [Facebook status update]. Retrieved from https://www .facebook.com/EnvDefenseFund?fref=ts

28. Tweet

Bittman, M. [bittman]. (2014, April 1). Almost 90% of fast food workers say they've experienced wage theft: buff.ly/1i18eTb [Tweet]. Retrieved from http://twitter.com/bittman

29. Wiki

Clinical neuropsychology. (2013, November 12). Retrieved April 15, 2014, from Wikipedia: http://en.wikipedia.org/wiki/Clinical_neuropsychology

Give your date of retrieval for sources that are likely to change, such as this wiki.

30. E-mail or other personal communication (text citation)

At least one member of the research team has expressed reservations about the design of the study (L. Kogod, personal communication, February 6, 2014).

Personal e-mail, personal letters, interviews that you conduct yourself, and other communication that is not retrievable by others should be cited only in the text, not in the list of references.

5 Video, audio, and other media sources

31. Film or video recording

If you cite a film or video as a whole, begin with the producer's name as in the first example below. Otherwise, cite the name or names of the creator, director, or other contributor, followed by the function in parentheses. Add the medium in brackets after the title: [Motion picture] for film, [DVD], [Videocassette], or [Video file].

a. Motion picture or DVD

American Psychological Association (Producer). (2001). *Ethnocultural psychotherapy* [DVD]. Available from http://www.apa.org/videos

Tyrrell, C. (Director). (2010). *The Joneses* [Motion picture]. United States: Bjort Productions.

For a work in wide circulation (second example), give the country of origin and the studio that released the picture. For a work that is not widely circulated (first example), give the distributor's address or URL.

b. Video on the Web

CBS News (Producer). (1968, April 4). *1968 King assassination report* [Video file]. Retrieved from http://www.youtube.com/watch?v=cmOBbxgxKvo

In the retrieval statement, give the home-page URL unless the video you cite is difficult to locate from the home page. In that case, give the complete URL, as in the example.

32. Recorded interview

Ambar, S. (2014, April 1). Interview by T. Smiley [Video file]. Retrieved from http://www.pbs.org/wnet/tavissmiley

For an interview you view or listen to on the Web, give the name of the interviewee, the date, and the title of the interview, if any. Then give the interviewer's name if you wish, the type of file [Video file] or [Audio file], and a retrieval statement.

For an interview you see on television or hear in a podcast, adapt the preceding example using model 33b or 35.

33. Television series or episode

a. Television series

Rhimes, S. (Executive producer). (2014). *Grey's anatomy* [Television series]. New York, NY: ABC.

For a television series, begin with the producer's name and function. Add [Television series] after the title, and give either the city and name of the network or a Web retrieval statement.

b. Broadcast episode of television program

McKee, S. (Writer), & Wilson, C. (Director). (2014). Do you know? [Television series episode]. In S. Rhimes (Executive producer), *Grey's anatomy*. New York, NY: ABC.

For a TV episode, begin with the writer and then the director, identifying the function of each in parentheses, and add [Television series episode] after the episode title. Then provide the series information, beginning with In and the producer's name and function, giving the series title, and ending with the city and name of the network.

c. Web episode of a television program

Randall, T. (Writer & Director). (2012). How smart can we get? [Television series episode]. In J. Cort (Executive producer), *Nova*. Retrieved from http://www.pbs.org/wgbh/nova

Cite a TV episode you view on the Web as you would a broadcast episode, giving a retrieval statement rather than the city and name of the network.

34. Musical recording

Springsteen, B. (2002). Empty sky. On *The rising* [CD]. New York, NY: Columbia.

Begin with the name of the writer or composer. (If you cite another artist's recording of the work, provide this information after the title of the work—for example, [Recorded by E. Davila].) Give the medium in brackets ([CD], [LP], [mp3 file], and so on). Finish with the city, state, and name of the recording label or a retrieval statement.

35. Podcast

Glass, I. (Producer). (2014, April 11). The hounds of Blairsville [Audio podcast]. *This American life*. Retrieved from http://www.thisamericanlife.org

36. Visual

Southern Illinois University School of Medicine. (n.d.). Reporting child abuse and neglect [Diagram]. Retrieved from http://www.siumed.edu/oec /Year4/how_to_report_child_abuse.pdf

United Nations Population Fund (Cartographer). (2014). *Percent of population living on less than $1/day* [Demographic map]. Retrieved from http:// www.unfpa.org

37. Video game, computer software, or app

Mojang. (2014). Minecraft: Pocket edition (Version 0.8.1) [Mobile application software]. Retrieved May 7, 2014, from https://minecraft.net

For a video game, computer program, or app, give the following: the name of the developer or author, the date, the title, the version, a bracketed description of the program (such as [Video game], [Computer software], or [Mobile application software], as here), and a retrieval statement.

59c Using APA paper format

Use the following guidelines and samples to prepare papers in APA format. Check with your instructor for any modifications to this format.

Note See pp. 498–99 for the APA format of a reference list. And see 1 pp. 55–61 for guidelines on type fonts, lists, tables and figures, and other elements of design.

Margins Use one-inch margins on the top, bottom, and both sides.

Spacing and indentions Double-space everywhere. (The only exception is in tables and figures, where related data, labels, and other elements may be single-spaced.) Indent paragraphs and displayed quotations one-half inch.

Paging Begin numbering on the title page, and number consecutively through the end (including the reference list). Provide a header about one-half inch from the top of every page, as shown in the samples on these pages. The header consists of the page number on the far right and your full or shortened title on the far left. Type the title in all-capital letters. On the title page only, precede the title with the label Running head and a colon. Omit this label on all other pages.

Title page Include the full title, your name, the course title, the instructor's name, and the date. (See below.) Type the title on the top half of the page, followed by the identifying information, all centered horizontally and double-spaced.

APA title page

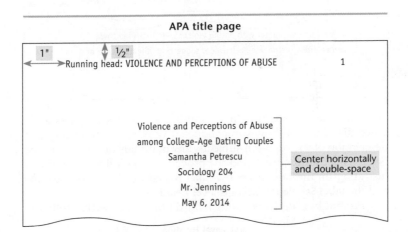

Abstract Summarize (in a maximum of 120 words) your subject, research method, findings, and conclusions. (See the next page.) Put the abstract on a page by itself.

Body Begin with a restatement of the paper's title and then an introduction (not labeled). (See the next page.) The introduction presents the problem you researched, your method, the relevant background, and the purpose of your research.

APA abstract

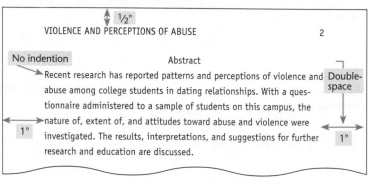

VIOLENCE AND PERCEPTIONS OF ABUSE   2

↕ ½"

Abstract

No indention

Recent research has reported patterns and perceptions of violence and abuse among college students in dating relationships. With a questionnaire administered to a sample of students on this campus, the nature of, extent of, and attitudes toward abuse and violence were investigated. The results, interpretations, and suggestions for further research and education are discussed.

Double-space

1"   1"

First page of APA body

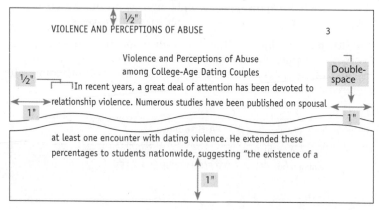

VIOLENCE AND PERCEPTIONS OF ABUSE   3

↕ ½"

Violence and Perceptions of Abuse
among College-Age Dating Couples

In recent years, a great deal of attention has been devoted to relationship violence. Numerous studies have been published on spousal

½"

Double-space

1"   1"

at least one encounter with dating violence. He extended these percentages to students nationwide, suggesting "the existence of a

1"

After the introduction, a section labeled **Method** provides a detailed discussion of how you conducted your research, including a description of the research subjects, any materials or tools you used (such as questionnaires), and the procedure you followed. In the illustration on the next page, the label **Method** is a first-level heading and the label **Sample** is a second-level heading.

Format headings (including a third level, if needed) as follows:

First-Level Heading

Second-Level Heading

Third-level heading. Run this heading into the text paragraph with a standard paragraph indention.

The **Results** section (labeled with a first-level heading) summarizes the data you collected, explains how you analyzed them, and presents them in detail, often in tables, graphs, or charts.

The **Discussion** section (labeled with a first-level heading) interprets the data and presents your conclusions. (When the discussion

Later page of APA body

VIOLENCE AND PERCEPTIONS OF ABUSE   4

    The purpose of the present study was to survey students on this campus to test whether the incidence of abusive relationships and attitudes toward abuse were similar to the patterns reported in published studies.

Method ← Double-space

Sample

    I conducted a survey of 200 students (109 females, 91 males) enrolled in an introductory sociology course at a large state university in the

---

is brief, you may combine it with the previous section under the heading **Results and Discussion**.)

The References section, beginning a new page, includes all your sources. See pp. 498–99 for an explanation and sample.

Long quotations Run into your text all quotations of forty words or fewer, and enclose them in quotation marks. For quotations of more than forty words, set them off from your text by indenting all lines one-half inch, double-spacing throughout.

> Echoing the opinions of other Europeans at the time, Freud (1961) had a poor view of Americans:
>
> > The Americans are really too bad. . . . Competition is much more pungent with them, not succeeding means civil death to every one, and they have no private resources apart from their profession, no hobby, games, love or other interests of a cultured person. And success means money. (p. 86)

Do not use quotation marks around a quotation displayed in this way.

Illustrations Present data in tables, graphs, or charts, as appropriate. (See the sample on p. 518 for a clear table format to follow.) Begin each illustration on a separate page. Number each kind of illustration consecutively and separately from the other (Table 1, Table 2, etc., and Figure 1, Figure 2, etc.). Refer to all illustrations in your text—for instance, (see Figure 3). Generally, place illustrations immediately after the text references to them. (See **1** pp. 57–61 for more on illustrations.)

59d Examining a sample research report in APA style

The paper on the following pages illustrates APA structure and documentation for a report of original research. See p. 513 and opposite for the format of the title page and the abstract, which are required in APA papers, and for the margins and other elements of the text pages. See pp. 498–99 for the format of the reference list.

Shortened
title and page
number.

Introduction:
presentation
of the problem
researched by
the writer.

Review of pub-
lished research.

Citation form:
undated source
by group author.
No page number
given because
online source is
unnumbered.

Citation form:
source with two
authors.

Citation forms:
source with
group author
and source with
three authors.

Violence and Perceptions of
Abuse among College-Age Dating Couples

    In recent years, a great deal of attention has been devoted to relationship violence. Numerous studies have been published on spousal abuse and on violence among teenage couples. Violence among college-age dating couples has also been researched, as this study will discuss. Furthermore, published studies indicate that rates of relationship abuse have remained fairly consistent despite public attention to the problem. This study confirms that trend on one college campus, and it suggests that perceptions of abuse in relationships need to change.

    Advocacy groups have defined dating violence as "a pattern of destructive behaviors used to exert power and control over a dating partner" (Break the Cycle, n.d.). These behaviors include both physical assault, from slapping to sexual coercion, and psychological abuse such as insults and threats. Recent studies have shown that such behavior is not uncommon in dating relationships. Kaura and Lohman (2007) found that 28.76% of respondents at Iowa State University had experienced premarital abuse. Similarly, a national poll revealed that 27% of college students have been subjected to possessive or controlling behaviors from a dating partner (Knowledge Networks, 2011). Another study (Helweg-Larsen, Harding, & Kleinman, 2008) found that so-called date rape, while more publicized, was reported by many fewer respondents (less than 2%) than was other physical violence during courtship (20%).

    Recent research has also shown that students tend not to identify their own and others' behavior as violent or abusive even when it meets the experts' definition of dating violence. Kaura and Lohman (2007) discovered that when dating couples give examples of behavior that qualify as abusive or violent in relation to other couples, both the perpetrators and the victims in these relationships tend not to describe their interactions as abusive or violent. Miller (2011) discovered that more than 85% of students in violent dating relationships do not label the abuse as such, while Knowledge Networks (2011) found that 57% of college students in the United States say they do not know what abusive behavior looks like.

    The purpose of the present study was to survey students on this campus to test whether the incidence of and attitudes toward abuse were similar to the patterns reported in published studies.

Method

Sample

I conducted a survey of 200 students (109 females, 91 males) enrolled in an introductory sociology course at a large state university in the northeastern United States. Participants were primarily sophomores (67%) and juniors (18%), with an average age of 20. After I omitted from the analysis both incomplete questionnaires and responses from subjects who indicated they were married or not currently dating, the sample totaled 123 subjects.

The Questionnaire

A questionnaire exploring the personal dynamics of relationships was approved by the Institutional Review Board and distributed during class with informed consent forms. Questions were answered anonymously at home using a secure online survey system.

The questionnaire consisted of three sections. The first asked for basic demographic information such as gender, age, and relationship status. The second section required participants to assess aspects of their current dating relationships, such as levels of stress and frustration, communication between partners, and patterns of decision making. These variables were expected to influence the amount of violence in a relationship.

The third part of the survey was adapted from Straus's revised Conflict Tactics Scales (2006), an instrument designed to measure relationship conflict and how it ends, including in negotiation, psychological aggression, and physical assault. This section provided a list of 26 physically and psychologically abusive behaviors ranging from minor (yelling, slapping) to severe (punching, choking) and instructed subjects to identify those they had experienced with their dating partner. One question asked respondents to characterize their relationship as abusive or not. The last question asked respondents to rate their overall satisfaction with the relationship.

Results

The questionnaire revealed significant levels of psychological aggression among unmarried couples, consistent with the published studies. Of the respondents who indicated they were dating, just over half (62 of 123 subjects) reported that they had experienced verbal abuse at least once, being either insulted or sworn at. Nearly 18% (22 of 123) had been shouted at by a romantic partner. In addition, almost 14% of respondents (17 of 123) had been threatened with some type of violence. (See Table 1.)

First- and second-level headings.

"Method" section: discussion of how research was conducted.

"Results" section: summary and presentation of data.

Reference to table.

[New page.]

Table on a page by itself.

Table 1

Incidence of courtship violence

Type of violence	Number of students reporting	Percentage of sample
Psychological aggression		
Insulted or swore	62	50.4
Shouted	22	17.8
Threatened	17	13.8
Physical assault		
Pushed or shoved	20	16.3
Slapped	15	12.2
Kicked, bit, or punched	7	5.7
Threw something that could hurt	9	7.3
Used a knife or gun	1	0.8

Table presents data in a clear format.

[New page.]

Rates of physical assault were also consistent with the published research. More than 16% of the study subjects reported being pushed or shoved by a partner, more than 12% had been slapped, and almost 6% had been kicked, bitten, or punched by a partner. Nine respondents (7.3%) indicated that an object had been thrown at them. One subject reported being attacked with a deadly weapon. (See Table 1.)

Most participants in relationships that experts would characterize as violent did not say that they consider themselves victims of violence. Of the 33 respondents (27% of the total) who reported two or more aggressive or violent incidents with their romantic partners, less than a quarter (8 individuals) self-identified their relationships as abusive. Among the 123 study subjects as a whole, 108 (87.8%) stated they were mostly or completely satisfied with their current relationships; only 15 (12.2%) indicated they were dissatisfied.

Discussion

"Discussion" section: interpretation of data and presentation of conclusions.

Violence within premarital relationships has been widely acknowledged in the sociological research, and the present study confirms previous findings. On this campus, abuse and force occur among college couples, and the perpetrators and victims of violence often do not characterize their relationships as abusive. A high number of respondents indicated that they have been subjected to minor forms of abuse such as verbal aggression, yet most claimed to be satisfied with their relationships. Although the percentages of physical violence are relatively small, so was the sample. Extending the results to the entire campus population would mean significant numbers. For example, if the incidence of being kicked, bitten, or punched is typical at 6%, then 900 students of a 15,000-member student body might have experienced this type of violence.

If college-age relationships are significantly abusive and violent, what accounts for this pattern of interaction? The survey examined some variables that appeared to influence the relationships. Level of stress and frustration, both within the relationship and in the respondent's life, was one such variable. The communication level between partners, both the frequency of discussion and the frequency of agreement, was another. Gender was not a factor: male and female subjects both reported inflicting and receiving abuse, although females were subjected to more severe forms of violence.

As other studies have shown, participation in an abusive relationship can have lasting consequences. Kaura and Lohman (2007), among others, have shown that dating violence leads to mental health issues—especially anxiety and depression—for both men and women. Miller (2011) found that those who don't label abusive behavior as such are more likely to perpetuate it and to accept it as victims, while Prather, Dahlen, Nicholson, and Bullock-Yowell (2012) discovered that violence tends to become more severe as relationships become more serious. Cornelius, Shorey, and Beebe (2010) concluded that for young men and women alike premarital violence is a problem of "highly maladaptive interactional patterns" similar to those that surface in abusive marriages (p. 445).

Citation forms: sources with four and three authors, named in the text.

These published studies suggest that a great deal is at stake for the participants in abusive relationships, not only in the present but for the future. This study extended research on this subject by contributing data on violence and abuse among college-age dating couples. The survey results provided an overview of the variables that may contribute to abusive relationships, the rates and types of dating abuse, and perceptions of abusive behaviors. The study found that rates of abuse are similar to those in published studies, as are the participants' attitudes toward abuse. If the courtship period sets the stage for later relationships, including marriage, and if attitudes of denial contribute to the perpetuation of abuse, then more attention should be given to educating young people to recognize and stop the behavior.

Conclusion: summary and implications for further research.

[New page.]

New page for reference list.

References

Break the Cycle. (n.d.). Dating abuse 101 [Web page]. Retrieved April 7, 2014, from http://www.breakthecycle.org

Cornelius, T. L., Shorey, R. C., & Beebe, S. M. (2010). Self-reported communication variables and dating violence. *Journal of Family Violence, 25*, 439-448. http://dx.doi.org/10.1007/s10896-010-9305-9

Helweg-Larsen, M., Harding, H. G., & Kleinman, K. E. (2008). Risk perceptions of dating violence among college women. *Journal of Social and Clinical Psychology, 27*, 600-620. Retrieved from http://www.guilford.com

Kaura, S. A., & Lohman, B. J. (2007). Dating violence victimization, relationship satisfaction, mental health problems, and acceptability of violence: A comparison of men and women. *Journal of Family Violence, 22*, 367-381. doi:10.1007/s10896-007-9092-0

Knowledge Networks. (2011). *College dating violence and abuse poll.* Retrieved from http://www.loveisrespect.org/pdf/College_Dating_And_Abuse_Final_Study.pdf

Miller, L. M. (2011). Physical abuse in a college setting: Perceptions and participation. *Journal of Family Violence, 26,* 71-80. doi:10.1007/s10896-010-9344-2

Prather, E., Dahlen, E. R., Nicholson, B. C., & Bullock-Yowell, E. B. (2012). Relational aggression in college students' relationships. *Journal of Aggression, Maltreatment, and Trauma, 21.* doi:10.1080/10926771.2012.693151

Straus, M. A. (2006). *Conflict Tactics Scales (CTS) sourcebook.* Torrance, CA: Western Psychological Services.

Page on a Web site with retrieval information.

Journal article with a Digital Object Identifier (DOI).

Journal article accessed through a database, with journal homepage URL.

Report from the Web site of an organization.

Book. ("Tactics Scales" is capitalized because it is part of a proper name.)

Chicago and CSE
Documentation

Chicago and CSE Documentation

Finding the right model for a source

1. What type of source is it? Locate the type in the Chicago or CSE index. Common types: periodical article, book, government publication, Web or social media, visual or audio.

2. What is the medium of the source? From within each type of source, choose the right model for the medium. Common media: print, Web, database, e-book, DVD, video.

3. Who is the author? Choose the right model for the number and type of author(s).

Chicago notes and bibliography entries

CSE references

Chapter essentials

- Distinguish between Chicago note and bibliography entries (below).
- Follow models for citing periodicals, books, Web sites, and other sources (p. 526).

Visit MyWritingLab™ for more resources on Chicago documentation.

History, art history, philosophy, and some other humanities use endnotes or footnotes to document sources, following one style recommended by *The Chicago Manual of Style* (16th ed., 2010) and the student guide adapted from it, Kate L. Turabian's *A Manual for Writers of Research Papers, Theses, and Dissertations* (8th ed., revised by Wayne C. Booth, Gregory G. Colomb, and Joseph M. Williams, 2013).

60a Using Chicago notes and bibliography entries

In the Chicago note style, raised numerals in the text refer to footnotes (bottoms of pages) or endnotes (end of paper). These notes contain complete source information. A separate bibliography is optional: ask your instructor for his or her preference.

For both footnotes and endnotes, use single spacing for each note and double spacing between notes, as shown in the samples below and opposite. (This is the spacing recommended by *A Manual for Writers*, the student guide. For manuscripts that will be published, *The Chicago Manual* recommends double spacing throughout.) Separate footnotes from the text with a short line. Place endnotes directly after the text, beginning on a new page. For a bibliography at the end of the paper, use the format opposite. Arrange the sources alphabetically by the authors' last names.

Chicago footnotes

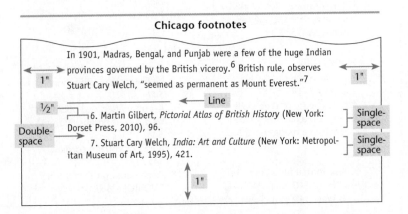

In 1901, Madras, Bengal, and Punjab were a few of the huge Indian provinces governed by the British viceroy.[6] British rule, observes Stuart Cary Welch, "seemed as permanent as Mount Everest."[7]

⟵ 1"

1" ⟶

½"

⟵ Line

6. Martin Gilbert, *Pictorial Atlas of British History* (New York: Dorset Press, 2010), 96.

7. Stuart Cary Welch, *India: Art and Culture* (New York: Metropolitan Museum of Art, 1995), 421.

Double-space

Single-space

Single-space

1"

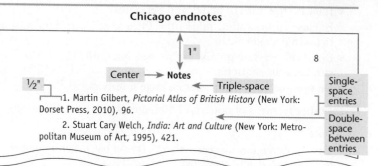

Chicago endnotes

1" | 8

Center → **Notes**

½" | ← Triple-space | Single-space entries

1. Martin Gilbert, *Pictorial Atlas of British History* (New York: Dorset Press, 2010), 96.

Double-space between entries

2. Stuart Cary Welch, *India: Art and Culture* (New York: Metropolitan Museum of Art, 1995), 421.

9. Mohandas Gandhi, *Young India, 1919-1922* (New York: Huebsch), 1923, 101.

1"

Chicago bibliography

1" | 10

Center → **Bibliography**

← Triple-space | Single-space entries

½" | Gandhi, Mohandas. *Young India, 1919-1922.* New York: Huebsch, 1923.

Double-space between entries

Gilbert, Martin. *Pictorial Atlas of British History.* New York: Dorset Press, 2010.

Welch, Stuart Cary. *India: Art and Culture.* New York: Metropolitan Museum of Art, 1995.

1"

The examples below illustrate the essentials of a note and a bibliography entry.

Note

6. Martin Gilbert, *Pictorial Atlas of British History* (New York: Dorset Press, 2010), 96.

Bibliography entry

Gilbert, Martin. *Pictorial Atlas of British History.* New York: Dorset Press, 2010.

Treat some features of notes and bibliography entries the same:

- Unless your instructor requests otherwise, single-space each note or entry, and double-space between them.

- Italicize the titles of books and periodicals.
- Enclose in quotation marks the titles of parts of books or articles in periodicals.
- Do not abbreviate publishers' names, but omit "Inc.," "Co.," and similar abbreviations.
- Do not use "p." or "pp." before page numbers.

Treat other features of notes and bibliography entries differently:

Note	Bibliography entry
Start with a number that corresponds to the note number in the text.	Do not begin with a number.
Indent the first line one-half inch.	Indent the second and subsequent lines one-half inch.
Give the author's name in normal order.	Begin with the author's last name.
Use commas between elements such as author's name and title.	Use periods between elements.
Enclose a book's publication information in parentheses, with no preceding punctuation.	Precede a book's publication information with a period, and don't use parentheses.
Include the specific page number(s) you borrowed from, omitting "p." or "pp."	Omit page numbers except for parts of books or articles in periodicals.

You can instruct your computer to position footnotes at the bottoms of appropriate pages. It will also automatically number notes and renumber them if you add or delete one or more.

60b Models of Chicago notes and bibliography entries

An index to the following Chicago models appears on the **Chicago** divider. The models themselves show notes and bibliography entries together for easy reference. Be sure to use the numbered note form for notes and the unnumbered bibliography form for bibliography entries.

Note Chicago style generally recommends notes only, not bibliography entries, for personal communication such as e-mail, personal letters, and interviews you conduct yourself. Bibliography entries are shown here in case your instructor requires such entries.

1 Authors

1. One, two, or three authors

1. Carol Gilligan, *In a Different Voice: Psychological Theory and Women's Development* (Cambridge: Harvard University Press, 1982), 27.

Gilligan, Carol. *In a Different Voice: Psychological Theory and Women's Development.* Cambridge: Harvard University Press, 1982.

1. Dennis L. Wilcox, Phillip H. Ault, and Warren K. Agee, *Public Relations: Strategies and Tactics,* 10th ed. (New York: Pearson, 2011), 182.

Wilcox, Dennis L., Phillip H. Ault, and Warren K. Agee. *Public Relations: Strategies and Tactics.* 10th ed. New York: Pearson, 2011.

2. More than three authors

2. Geraldo Lopez et al., *China and the West* (Boston: Little, Brown, 2004), 461.

Lopez, Geraldo, Judith P. Salt, Anne Ming, and Henry Reisen. *China and the West.* Boston: Little, Brown, 2004.

The Latin abbreviation et al. in the note means "and others."

3. Author not named (anonymous)

3. *The Dorling Kindersley World Atlas* (London: Dorling Kindersley, 2013), 150-51.

The Dorling Kindersley World Atlas. London: Dorling Kindersley, 2013.

2 Articles in journals, newspapers, and magazines

4. Article in a scholarly journal

For journals that are paginated continuously through an annual volume, include at least the volume number—or, for greater clarity, add the issue number, if any, or the month or season of publication as in models a and b below. The month or season precedes the year of publication in parentheses. The issue number is required if the journal pages issues separately (no. 1 in models c and d).

a. Print journal article

4. Janet Lever, "Sex Differences in the Games Children Play," *Social Problems* 23 (Spring 1996): 482.

Lever, Janet. "Sex Differences in the Games Children Play." *Social Problems* 23 (Spring 1996): 478-87.

b. Database or Web journal article with DOI

4. Jonathan Dickens, "Social Policy Approaches to Intercountry Adoption," *International Social Work* 52 (September 2009): 600, doi:10.1177/0020872809337678.

Dickens, Jonathan. "Social Policy Approaches to Intercountry Adoption." *International Social Work* 52 (September 2009): 595-607. doi:10.1177/0020872809337678.

A DOI, or Digital Object Identifier, is a unique identifier that many publishers assign to journal articles and other documents. (See APA p. 499 for more on DOIs.) If the article you cite has a DOI, give it in the format shown in the source: preceded by doi, as above, or preceded by http://dx.doi.org/.

c. Database journal article without DOI

4. Nathan S. Atkinson, "Newsreels as Domestic Propaganda: Visual Rhetoric at the Dawn of the Cold War," *Rhetoric and Public Affairs* 14, no. 1 (Spring 2011): 72, Academic Search Complete (60502112).

Atkinson, Nathan S. "Newsreels as Domestic Propaganda: Visual Rhetoric at the Dawn of the Cold War." *Rhetoric and Public Affairs* 14, no. 1 (Spring 2011): 69-100. Academic Search Complete (60502112).

If no DOI is available for an article in a database, give the name of the database and the accession number.

d. Web journal article without DOI

4. Rebecca Butler, "The Rise and Fall of Union Classification," *Theological Librarianship* 6, no. 1 (2013): 21, https://journal.atla.com/ojs/index.php/theolib/article/view/254.

Butler, Rebecca. "The Rise and Fall of Union Classification." *Theological Librarianship* 6, no. 1 (2013): 21-28. https://journal.atla.com/ojs/index.php/theolib/article/view/254.

If no DOI is available for an article you find on the open Web, give the URL.

5. Article in a newspaper

a. Print newspaper article

5. Annie Lowery, "Cities Advancing Inequality Fight," *New York Times*, April 7, 2014, national edition, A1.

Lowery, Annie. "Cities Advancing Inequality Fight." *New York Times*, April 7, 2014, national edition, A1.

b. Database newspaper article

5. Rob Stein, "Obesity May Stall Trend of Increasing Longevity," *Washington Post*, March 15, 2014, final edition, A2, LexisNexis Academic.

Stein, Rob. "Obesity May Stall Trend of Increasing Longevity." *Washington Post*, March 15, 2014, final edition, A2. LexisNexis Academic.

If an accession number is available, give it after the database name, as in model 4c.

c. Web newspaper article

5. Marcia Dunn, "Vast Ocean Found beneath Ice of Saturn Moon," *Detroit News*, April 3, 2014, http://www.detroitnews.com/article/20140403/SCIENCE/304030081.

Dunn, Marcia. "Vast Ocean Found beneath Ice of Saturn Moon." *Detroit News*, April 3, 2014. http://www.detroitnews.com/article/20140403/SCIENCE/304030081.

6. Article in a magazine

a. Print magazine article

6. Jeffrey Toobin, "This Is My Jail," *New Yorker,* April 14, 2014, 28.

Toobin, Jeffrey. "This Is My Jail." *New Yorker,* April 14, 2014, 26-32.

b. Database magazine article

6. Colin Barras, "Right on Target," *New Scientist,* January 25, 2014, 42, Academic Search Complete (93983067).

Barras, Colin. "Right on Target." *New Scientist,* January 25, 2014, 40-43. Academic Search Complete (93983067).

If no accession number is available, give just the database name, as in model 5b.

c. Web magazine article

6. Laura Stampler, "These Cities Have the Most Open-Minded Daters," *Time,* April 14, 2014, http://time.com/61947/these-cities-have-the-most-open-minded-daters.

Stampler, Laura. "These Cities Have the Most Open-Minded Daters." *Time,* April 14, 2014. http://time.com/61947/these-cities-have-the-most-open-minded-daters.

7. Review

7. John Gregory Dunne, "The Secret of Danny Santiago," review of *Famous All over Town,* by Danny Santiago, *New York Review of Books,* August 16, 1994, 25.

Dunne, John Gregory. "The Secret of Danny Santiago." Review of *Famous All over Town,* by Danny Santiago. *New York Review of Books,* August 16, 1994, 17-27.

3 | Books and government publications

8. Basic format for a book

a. Print book

8. Barbara Ehrenreich, *Dancing in the Streets: A History of Collective Joy* (New York: Henry Holt, 2006), 97-117.

Ehrenreich, Barbara. *Dancing in the Streets: A History of Collective Joy.* New York: Henry Holt, 2006.

b. Database book

8. Daniel Levine, *Bayard Rustin and the Civil Rights Movement* (New Brunswick: Rutgers University Press, 1999), 21-45, eBook Collection (44403).

Levine, Daniel. *Bayard Rustin and the Civil Rights Movement.* New Brunswick: Rutgers University Press, 1999. eBook Collection (44403).

c. E-book

8. Marilyn Booth, *May Her Likes Be Multiplied: Biography and Gender Politics in Egypt* (Oakland: University of California Press, 2001), Kindle edition.

Booth, Marilyn. *May Her Likes Be Multiplied: Biography and Gender Politics in Egypt*. Oakland: University of California Press, 2001. Kindle edition.

d. Web book

8. Jane Austen, *Emma*, ed. R. W. Chapman (1816; Oxford: Clarendon, 1926; Oxford Text Archive, 2014), chap. 1, http://ota.ahds.ac.uk/Austen/Emma.1519.

Austen, Jane. *Emma*. Edited by R. W. Chapman. 1816. Oxford: Clarendon, 1926. Oxford Text Archive, 2014. http://ota.ahds.ac.uk/Austen/Emma.1519.

Provide print publication information, if any.

9. Book with an editor

9. Patricia Rushton, ed., *Vietnam War Nurses: Personal Accounts of Eighteen Americans* (Jefferson, NC: McFarland, 2013), 70-72.

Rushton, Patricia, ed. *Vietnam War Nurses: Personal Accounts of Eighteen Americans*. Jefferson, NC: McFarland, 2013.

10. Book with an author and an editor

10. Lewis Mumford, *The City in History*, ed. Donald L. Miller (New York: Pantheon, 1986), 216-17.

Mumford, Lewis. *The City in History*. Edited by Donald L. Miller. New York: Pantheon, 1986.

11. Translation

11. Dante Alighieri, *The Inferno*, trans. John Ciardi (New York: New American Library, 1971), 51.

Alighieri, Dante. *The Inferno*. Translated by John Ciardi. New York: New American Library, 1971.

12. Later edition

12. Dwight L. Bolinger, *Aspects of Language*, 3rd ed. (New York: Harcourt Brace Jovanovich, 1981), 20.

Bolinger, Dwight L. *Aspects of Language*. 3rd ed. New York: Harcourt Brace Jovanovich, 1981.

13. Work in more than one volume

a. One volume without a title

13. Abraham Lincoln, *The Collected Works of Abraham Lincoln*, ed. Roy P. Basler (New Brunswick: Rutgers University Press, 1953), 5:426-28.

Lincoln, Abraham. *The Collected Works of Abraham Lincoln*. Edited by Roy P. Basler. Vol. 5. New Brunswick: Rutgers University Press, 1953.

b. One volume with a title

13. Linda B. Welkin, *The Age of Balanchine,* vol. 3 of *The History of Ballet* (New York: Columbia University Press, 1999), 56.

Welkin, Linda B. *The Age of Balanchine.* Vol. 3 of *The History of Ballet.* New York: Columbia University Press, 1999.

14. Selection from an anthology

14. Rosetta Brooks, "Streetwise," in *The New Urban Landscape,* ed. Richard Martin (New York: Rizzoli, 2005), 38-39.

Brooks, Rosetta. "Streetwise." In *The New Urban Landscape,* edited by Richard Martin, 37-60. New York: Rizzoli, 2005.

15. Work in a series

15. Ingmar Bergman, *The Seventh Seal,* Modern Film Scripts 12 (New York: Simon and Schuster, 1995), 27.

Bergman, Ingmar. *The Seventh Seal.* Modern Film Scripts 12. New York: Simon and Schuster, 1995.

16. Article in a reference work

As shown in the following examples, use the abbreviation s.v. (Latin *sub verbo,* "under the word") for reference works that are alphabetically arranged. Well-known works (model a) do not need publication information except for the edition number. Chicago style generally recommends notes only, not bibliography entries, for reference works; bibliography models are given here in case your instructor requires such entries.

a. Print reference work

16. *Merriam-Webster's Collegiate Dictionary,* 11th ed., s.v. "reckon."
Merriam-Webster's Collegiate Dictionary. 11th ed. S.v. "reckon."

b. Web reference work

16. *Wikipedia,* s.v. "Wuhan," last modified May 9, 2014, http://en.wikipedia.org/wiki/Wuhan.

Wikipedia. S.v. "Wuhan." Last modified May 9, 2014. http://en.wikipedia.org/wiki/Wuhan.

17. Government publication

17. House Comm. on Agriculture, Nutrition, and Forestry, *Food and Energy Act of 2008,* 110th Cong., 2nd Sess., H.R. Doc. No. 884, at 21-22 (2008).

House Comm. on Agriculture, Nutrition, and Forestry. *Food and Energy Act of 2008.* 110th Cong. 2nd Sess. H.R. Doc. No. 884 (2008).

17. Hawaii Department of Education, *Kauai District Schools, Profile 2013-14* (Honolulu, 2014), 38.

Hawaii Department of Education. *Kauai District Schools, Profile 2013-14.* Honolulu, 2014.

4 Web sites and social media

18. Page or work on a Web site

18. Justin W. Patchin, "Ban School, Open Facebook," Cyberbullying Research Center, accessed May 10, 2014, http://cyberbullying.us/ban-school-open-facebook.

Patchin, Justin W. "Ban School, Open Facebook." Cyberbullying Research Center. Accessed May 10, 2014. http://cyberbullying.us/ban-school-open-facebook.

For Web pages and works that are not specifically dated or that are likely to change, *The Chicago Manual* suggests giving the date of your access, as here, or a statement beginning with last modified (model 16).

19. Post on a blog or discussion group

19. Bettina Smith, "No Such Animal," *Smithsonian Collections Blog,* April 29, 2014, http://si-siris.blogspot.com.

Smith, Bettina. "No Such Animal." *Smithsonian Collections Blog.* April 29, 2014. http://si-siris.blogspot.com.

20. Comment

20. Tony Drees, April 15, 2014, comment on Nicholas Kristof, "Standing by Our Veterans," *On the Ground* (blog), *New York Times,* April 12, 2014, http://kristof.blogs.nytimes.com.

Kristof, Nicholas. *On the Ground* (blog). *New York Times.* http://kristof.blogs.nytimes.com.

In a note cite a reader's comment on a blog by the reader's name (Drees above). However, in the bibliography cite the entire blog by the blog author's name (Kristof above).

21. E-mail

21. Naomi Lee, "Re: Atlanta," e-mail message to author, May 16, 2014.

Lee, Naomi. "Re: Atlanta." E-mail message to author. May 16, 2014.

5 Video, audio, and other media sources

22. Work of art

a. Original artwork

22. John Singer Sargent, *In Switzerland,* 1908, Metropolitan Museum of Art, New York.

Sargent, John Singer. *In Switzerland.* 1908. Metropolitan Museum of Art, New York.

b. Print reproduction of an artwork

22. David Graham, *Bob's Java Jive, Tacoma, Washington, 1989,* photograph, in *Only in America: Some Unexpected Scenery* (New York: Knopf, 1991), 93.

Graham, David. *Bob's Java Jive, Tacoma, Washington, 1989.* Photograph. In *Only in America: Some Unexpected Scenery.* New York: Knopf, 1991.

c. Web reproduction of an artwork

22. Jackson Pollock, *Shimmering Substance,* 1946, Museum of Modern Art, New York, http://moma.org/collection/conservation/pollock/ shimmering_substance.html.

Pollock, Jackson. *Shimmering Substance.* 1946. Museum of Modern Art, New York. http://moma.org/collection/conservation/pollock/ shimmering_substance.html.

23. Film or video

a. Film, DVD, Blu-ray, or video recording

23. George Balanchine, *Serenade,* San Francisco Ballet, performed February 2, 2000 (New York: PBS Video, 2006), DVD.

Balanchine, George. *Serenade.* San Francisco Ballet. Performed February 2, 2000. New York: PBS Video, 2006. DVD.

b. Video on the Web

23. Leslie J. Stewart, *96 Ranch Rodeo and Barbecue* (1951); 16mm, from Library of Congress, *Buckaroos in Paradise: Ranching Culture in Northern Nevada, 1945-1982,* MPEG, http://memory.loc.gov/cgi-bin/query.

Stewart, Leslie J. *96 Ranch Rodeo and Barbecue.* 1951. 16 mm. From Library of Congress, *Buckaroos in Paradise: Ranching Culture in Northern Nevada, 1945-1982.* MPEG. http://memory.loc.gov/cgi-bin/query.

24. Published or broadcast interview

24. Dexter Filkins, interview by Terry Gross, *Fresh Air,* NPR, April 29, 2014.

Filkins, Dexter. Interview by Terry Gross. *Fresh Air.* NPR. April 29, 2014.

25. Sound recording

a. LP or CD

25. Philip Glass, *String Quartet no. 5,* with Kronos Quartet, recorded 1991, Nonesuch 79356-2, 1995, compact disc.

Glass, Philip. *String Quartet no. 5.* Kronos Quartet. Recorded 1991. Nonesuch 79356-2. 1995. Compact disc.

b. Web recording

25. Ronald W. Reagan, "State of the Union Address," January 26, 1982, Vincent Voice Library, Digital and Multimedia Center, Michigan State University, http://www.lib.msu.edu/vincent/presidents/reagan.html.

Reagan, Ronald W. "State of the Union Address." January 26, 1982. Vincent Voice Library. Digital and Multimedia Center, Michigan State University. http://www.lib.msu.edu/vincent/presidents/reagan.html.

26. Podcast

26. Stephanie Foo, "The Hounds of Blairsville," *This American Life,* podcast audio, April 11, 2014, http://www.thisamericanlife.org/radio-archives/episode/522/tarred-and-feathered?act=1.

Foo, Stephanie. "The Hounds of Blairsville." *This American Life.* Podcast audio. April 11, 2014. http://www.thisamericanlife.org/radio-archives/episode/522/tarred-and-feathered?act=1.

6 Other sources

27. Letter

a. Published letter

27. Mrs. Laura E. Buttolph to Rev. and Mrs. C. C. Jones, June 20, 1857, in *The Children of Pride: A True Story of Georgia and the Civil War,* ed. Robert Manson Myers (New Haven, CT: Yale University Press, 1972), 334.

Buttolph, Laura E. Mrs. Laura E. Buttolph to Rev. and Mrs. C. C. Jones, June 20, 1857. In *The Children of Pride: A True Story of Georgia and the Civil War,* edited by Robert Manson Myers. New Haven, CT: Yale University Press, 1972.

b. Personal letter

27. Ann E. Packer, letter to author, June 15, 2011.

Packer, Ann E. Letter to author. June 15, 2011.

28. Personal interview

28. Janelle White, interview by author, December 19, 2013.

White, Janelle. Interview by author. December 19, 2013.

29. Work on CD-ROM or DVD-ROM

29. *The American Heritage Dictionary of the English Language,* 4th ed. (Boston: Houghton Mifflin, 2006), CD-ROM.

The American Heritage Dictionary of the English Language. 4th ed. Boston: Houghton Mifflin, 2006. CD-ROM.

7 Shortened notes

To streamline documentation, Chicago style recommends shortened notes for sources that are fully cited elsewhere, either in a bibliography or in previous notes. Ask your instructor whether your paper should include a bibliography and, if so, whether you may use shortened notes for first references to sources as well as for subsequent references.

A shortened note contains the author's last name, the work's title (minus any initial *A, An,* or *The*), and the page number. Reduce long titles to four or fewer key words.

Complete note

> 4. Janet Lever, "Sex Differences in the Games Children Play," *Social Problems* 23 (Spring 1996): 482.

Complete bibliography entry

Lever, Janet. "Sex Differences in the Games Children Play." *Social Problems* 23 (Spring 1996): 478-87.

Shortened note

> 12. Lever, "Sex Differences," 483.

You may use the Latin abbreviation ibid. (meaning "in the same place") to refer to the same source cited in the preceding note. Give a page number if it differs from that in the preceding note.

> 12. Lever, "Sex Differences," 483.
>
> 13. Gilligan, *In a Different Voice,* 92.
>
> 14. Ibid., 93.
>
> 15. Lever, "Sex Differences," 483.

Chicago style allows for in-text parenthetical citations when you cite one or more works repeatedly. In the following example, the raised number 2 refers to the source information in a note; the number in parentheses is a page number in the same source.

British rule, observes Stuart Cary Welch, "seemed as permanent as Mount Everest."[2] Most Indians submitted, willingly or not, to British influence in every facet of life (42).

Chapter essentials
- Distinguish between CSE name-year and numbered text citations (below).
- Prepare a list of references in CSE style (facing page).

Visit MyWritingLab™ for more resources on CSE documentation.

Writers in the life sciences, physical sciences, and mathematics rely for documentation style on *Scientific Style and Format: The CSE Manual for Authors, Editors, and Publishers* (8th ed., 2014), published by the Council of Science Editors.

Scientific Style and Format details both styles of scientific documentation: one using author and date and one using numbers. Both types of text citation refer to a list of references at the end of the paper. Ask your instructor which style you should use.

61a Writing CSE name-year text citations

In the CSE name-year style, in-text citations provide the last name of the author being cited and the source's year of publication. At the end of the paper, a list of references, arranged alphabetically by authors' last names, provides complete information on each source. (See opposite.)

The CSE name-year style closely resembles the APA name-year style detailed in **APA** pp. 494–97. You can follow the APA examples for in-text citations, making several notable changes for CSE:

- **Do not use a comma to separate the author's name and the date:** (Baumrind 1968).
- **Separate two authors' names with and (not "&"):** (Pepinsky and DeStefano 1997).
- **For sources with three or more authors, use et al. (Latin abbreviation for "and others") after the first author's name:** (Singh et al. 2014).

61b Writing CSE numbered text citations

In the CSE number style, raised numbers in the text refer to a numbered list of references at the end of the paper.

Two standard references[1, 2] use this term.

These forms of immunity have been extensively researched.[3]

Hepburn and Tatin[2] do not discuss this project.

Assignment of numbers The number for each source is based on the order in which you cite the source in the text: the first cited source is 1, the second is 2, and so on.

Reuse of numbers When you cite a source you have already cited and numbered, use the original number again (see the last example on the facing page, which reuses the number 2 from the first example).

This reuse is the key difference between the CSE numbered citations and numbered references to footnotes or endnotes. In the CSE style, each source has only one number, determined by the order in which the source is cited. With notes, in contrast, the numbering proceeds in sequence, so that each source has as many numbers as it has citations in the text.

Citation of two or more sources When you cite two or more sources at once, arrange their numbers in sequence and separate them with a comma and a space, as in the first example on the facing page.

61c Preparing the CSE reference list

For both the name-year and the number styles of in-text citation, provide a list, titled References, of all sources you have cited. Center this heading about an inch from the top of the page, and double-space beneath it.

The following examples show the differences and similarities between the name-year and number styles:

Name-year style

Hepburn PX, Tatin JM. 2005. Human physiology. New York (NY): Columbia University Press.

Number style

2. Hepburn PX, Tatin JM. Human physiology. New York (NY): Columbia University Press; 2005.

Spacing In both styles, single-space each entry and double-space between entries.

Arrangement In the name-year style, arrange entries alphabetically by authors' last names. In the number style, arrange entries in numerical order—that is, in order of their citation in the text.

Format In the name-year style, type all lines of entries at the left margin—do not indent. In the number style, begin the first line of each entry at the left margin and indent subsequent lines.

Authors In both styles, list each author's name with the last name first, followed by initials for first and middle names. Do not use a comma between an author's last name and initials, and do not use periods or spaces with the initials. Do use a comma to separate authors' names.

Placement of dates In the name-year style, the date follows the author's or authors' names. In the number style, the date follows the publication information (for a book) or the periodical title (for a journal, magazine, or newspaper).

Journal titles In both styles, do not italicize or underline journal titles. For titles of two or more words, abbreviate words of six or more letters (without periods) and omit most prepositions, articles, and conjunctions. Capitalize each word. For example, *Journal of Chemical and Biochemical Studies* becomes J Chem Biochem Stud, and *Hospital Practice* becomes Hosp Pract.

Book and article titles In both styles, do not italicize, underline, or use quotation marks around a book or an article title. Capitalize only the first word and any proper nouns.

Publication information for journal articles The name-year and number styles differ in the placement of the publication date (see above). However, after the journal title both styles give the journal's volume number, any issue number in parentheses, a colon, and the inclusive page numbers of the article, run together without space: 28:329-30 or 62(2):26-40. See model 6 on the facing page.

The following examples show both a name-year reference and a number reference for each type of source. An index to all the models appears opposite the **CSE** divider (p. 523).

1 Authors

1. One author

Gould SJ. 1987. Time's arrow, time's cycle. Cambridge (MA): Harvard University Press.

1. Gould SJ. Time's arrow, time's cycle. Cambridge (MA): Harvard University Press; 1987.

2. Two to ten authors

Hepburn PX, Tatin JM, Tatin JP. 2012. Human physiology. New York (NY): Columbia University Press.

2. Hepburn PX, Tatin JM, Tatin JP. Human physiology. New York (NY): Columbia University Press; 2012.

3. More than ten authors

Evans RW, Bowditch L, Dana KL, Drumond A, Wildovitch WP, Young SL, Mills P, Mills RR, Livak SR, Lisi OL, et al. 2011. Organ transplants: ethical issues. Ann Arbor (MI): University of Michigan Press.

3. Evans RW, Bowditch L, Dana KL, Drummond A, Wildovitch WP, Young SL, Mills P, Mills RR, Livak SR, Lisi OL, et al. Organ transplants: ethical issues. Ann Arbor (MI): University of Michigan Press; 2011.

4. Author not named

Health care for children with diabetes. 2014. New York (NY): US Health Care.

4. Health care for children with diabetes. New York (NY): US Health Care; 2014.

5. Two or more cited works by the same author(s) published in the same year

Gardner H. 1973a. The arts and human development. New York (NY): Wiley.

Gardner H. 1973b. The quest for mind: Piaget, Lévi-Strauss, and the structuralist movement. New York (NY): Knopf.

(The number style does not require such forms.)

2 Articles in journals, newspapers, and magazines

6. Article in a journal

a. Print article

Campos JJ, Walle EA, Dahl A, Main A. 2011. Reconceptualizing emotion regulation. Emotion Rev. 3(1):26-35.

6. Campos JJ, Walle EA, Dahl A, Main A. Reconceptualizing emotion regulation. Emotion Rev. 2011;3(1):26-35.

b. Database or Web article

Grady GF. 2014. New research on immunizations. Today's Med. [accessed 2014 Dec 10];10(3):45-49. http://www.fmrt.org/todaysmedicine/Grady050389 .pdf8. doi:10.1087/262534887.

6. Grady GF. New research on immunizations. Today's Med. 2014 [accessed 2014 Dec 10];10(3):45-49. http://www.fmrt.org/todaysmedicine /Grady050389.pdf8. doi:10.1087/262534887.

Give the date of your access after the journal title (first example) or after the publication date (second example). If the article has no page, paragraph, or other reference numbers, give your calculation of its length in brackets—for instance, [about 15 p.] or [20 paragraphs]. Conclude with the source's URL and the DOI (Digital Object Identifier) if one is available. (See **APA** p. 499 for more on DOIs.)

7. Article in a newspaper

Zimmer C. 2014 May 8. Antibiotic-resistant germs lying in wait everywhere. New York Times (National Ed.). Sect. C:1 (col. 1).

7. Zimmer C. Antibiotic-resistant germs lying in wait everywhere. New York Times (National Ed.). 2014 May 8;Sect. C:1 (col. 1).

8. Article in a magazine

Talbot M. 2013 Mar 18. About a boy. New Yorker. 56-65.

8. Talbot M. About a boy. New Yorker. 2013 Mar 18;56-65.

3 Books

9. Basic format for a book

a. Print book

Wilson EO. 2004. On human nature. Cambridge (MA): Harvard University Press.

9. Wilson EO. On human nature. Cambridge (MA): Harvard University Press; 2004.

b. Web book

Ruch BJ, Ruch DB. 2013. New research in medicine and homeopathy. New York (NY): Albert Einstein College of Medicine; [accessed 2014 Jan 25]. http://www.einstein.edu/medicine/books/ruch&ruch.pdf.

9. Ruch BJ, Ruch DB. New research in medicine and homeopathy. New York (NY): Albert Einstein College of Medicine; 2013 [accessed 2014 Jan 25]. http://www.einstein.edu/medicine/books/ruch&ruch.pdf.

10. Book with an editor

Jonson P, editor. 2014. Anatomy yearbook 2014. Los Angeles (CA): Anatco.

10. Jonson P, editor. Anatomy yearbook 2014. Los Angeles (CA): Anatco; 2014.

11. Selection from a book

Kriegel R, Laubenstein L, Muggia F. 2005. Kaposi's sarcoma. In: Ebbeson P, Biggar RS, Melbye M, editors. AIDS: a basic guide for clinicians. 2nd ed. Philadelphia (PA): Saunders. p. 100-126.

11. Kriegel R, Laubenstein L, Muggia F. Kaposi's sarcoma. In: Ebbeson P, Biggar RS, Melbye M, editors. AIDS: a basic guide for clinicians. 2nd ed. Philadelphia (PA): Saunders; 2005. p. 100-126.

4 Web sites and social media

12. Web site

American Medical Association. c1995-2014. Chicago (IL): American Medical Association; [accessed 2014 Nov 22]. http://ama-assn.org/ama.

12. American Medical Association. Chicago (IL): American Medical Association; c1995-2014 [accessed 2014 Nov 22]. http://ama-assn.org/ama.

If you are unable to determine the most recent update to a Web site, give the copyright date, typically found at the bottom of the home page, preceded by c: c1995-2014 in the preceding example.

13. Blog post

Tenenbaum, LF. 2014 Apr 29. Zombies vs. Goldilocks: the insurrection [blog post]. Earth Right Now. [accessed 2014 May 19]. http://climate.nasa.gov /blog/1075.

13. Tenenbaum, LF. Zombies vs. Goldilocks: the insurrection [blog post]. Earth Right Now. 2014, Apr 29. [accessed 2014 May 19]. http://climate.nasa .gov/blog/1075.

14. Personal communication (text citation)

One member of the research team has expressed reservation about the study design (personal communication from L. Kogod, 2014 Feb 6; unreferenced).

A personal letter or e-mail message should be cited in your text, not in your reference list. The format is the same for both the name-year and the number styles.

5 Other sources

15. Report written and published by the same organization

Warnock M. 2006. Report of the Committee on Fertilization. Waco (TX): Baylor University Department of Embryology. Report No.: BU/DE.4261.

15. Warnock M. Report of the Committee on Fertilization. Waco (TX): Baylor University Department of Embryology; 2006. Report No.: BU/DE.4261.

16. Report written and published by different organizations

Hackney, JD (Rancho Los Amigos Hospital, Downey, CA). 2012. Effect of atmospheric pollutants on human physiologic function. Washington (DC): Environmental Protection Agency (US). Report No.: R-801396.

16. Hackney, JD (Rancho Los Amigos Hospital, Downey, CA). Effect of atmo-spheric pollutants on human physiologic function. Washington (DC): Environmental Protection Agency (US); 2012. Report No.: R-801396.

17. Audio or visual recording

Cell mitosis [DVD–ROM]. 2014. White Plains (NY): Teaching Media.

17. Cell mitosis [DVD-ROM]. White Plains (NY): Teaching Media; 2014.

18. Document on CD-ROM or DVD-ROM

Reich WT, editor. c2013. Encyclopedia of bioethics [DVD-ROM]. New York (NY): Co-Health. 1 DVD.

18. Reich WT editor. Encyclopedia of bioethics [DVD-ROM]. New York (NY): Co-Health; c2013. 1 DVD.

Glossary of Usage

This glossary provides notes on words or phrases that often cause problems for writers. The recommendations for standard American English are based on current dictionaries and usage guides. Items labeled **nonstandard** should be avoided in academic and business settings. Those labeled **colloquial** and **slang** occur in speech and in some informal writing but are best avoided in formal college and business writing. (Words and phrases labeled *colloquial* include those labeled by many dictionaries with the equivalent term *informal*.)

a, an Use *a* before words beginning with consonant sounds, including those spelled with an initial pronounced *h* and those spelled with vowels that are sounded as consonants: *a historian, a one-o'clock class, a university.* Use *an* before words that begin with vowel sounds, including those spelled with an initial silent *h*: *an organism, an L, an honor.*

Using *a* or *an* before an abbreviation depends on how the abbreviation is to be read: *She was once an AEC undersecretary* (*AEC* is to be read as three separate letters). *Many Americans opposed a SALT treaty* (*SALT* is to be read as one word, *salt*).

See also **4** pp. 254–56 on the uses of *a/an* versus *the*.

accept, except *Accept* is a verb meaning "receive." *Except* usually means "but for" or "other than"; when it is used as a verb,° it means "leave out." *I can accept all your suggestions except the last one. I'm sorry you excepted my last suggestion from your list.*

advice, advise *Advice* is a noun,° and *advise* is a verb°: *Take my advice; do as I advise you.*

affect, effect Usually *affect* is a verb,° meaning "to influence," and *effect* is a noun,° meaning "result": *The drug did not affect his driving; in fact, it seemed to have no effect at all.* But *effect* occasionally is used as a verb meaning "to bring about": *Her efforts effected a change.* And *affect* is used in psychology as a noun meaning "feeling or emotion": *One can infer much about affect from behavior.*

agree to, agree with *Agree to* means "consent to," and *agree with* means "be in accord with": *How can they agree to a treaty when they don't agree with each other about the terms?*

all ready, already *All ready* means "completely prepared," and *already* means "by now" or "before now": *We were all ready to go to the movie, but it had already started.*

all right *All right* is always two words. *Alright* is a common error.

all together, altogether *All together* means "in unison" or "gathered in one place." *Altogether* means "entirely." *It's not altogether true that our family never spends vacations all together.*

allusion, illusion An *allusion* is an indirect reference, and an *illusion* is a deceptive appearance: *Paul's constant allusions to Shakespeare created the illusion that he was an intellectual.*

almost, most *Almost* means "nearly"; *most* means "the greater number (or part) of." In formal writing, *most* should not be used as a substitute for *almost*: *We see each other almost* [not *most*] *every day.*

a lot *A lot* is always two words, used informally to mean "many." *Alot* is a common misspelling.

among, between In general, use *among* for relationships involving more than two people or for comparing one thing to a group to which it belongs. *The four of them agreed among themselves that the choice was between New York and Los Angeles.*

amount, number Use *amount* with a singular noun° that names something not countable (a noncount noun°): *The amount of food varies.* Use *number* with a plural noun that names more than one of something countable (a plural count noun°): *The number of calories must stay the same.*

and/or *And/or* indicates three options: one or the other or both (*The decision is made by the mayor and/or the council*). If you mean all three options, *and/or* is appropriate. Otherwise, use *and* if you mean both; use *or* if you mean either.

ante-, anti- The prefix *ante-* means "before" (*antedate, antebellum*); *anti-* means "against" (*antiwar, antinuclear*). Before a capital letter or *i, anti-* takes a hyphen: *anti-Freudian, anti-isolationist.*

anxious, eager *Anxious* means "nervous" or "worried" and is usually followed by *about.* *Eager* means "looking forward" and is usually followed by *to.* *I've been anxious about getting blisters. I'm eager* [not *anxious*] *to get new running shoes.*

anybody, any body; anyone, any one *Anybody* and *anyone* are indefinite pronouns°; *any body* is a noun° modified by *any*; *any one* is a pronoun° or adjective° modified by *any.* *How can anybody communicate with any body of government? Can anyone help Amy? She has more work than any one person can handle.*

any more, anymore *Any more* means "no more"; *anymore* means "now." Both are used in negative constructions. *He doesn't want any more. She doesn't live here anymore.*

apt, liable, likely *Apt* and *likely* are interchangeable. Strictly speaking, though, *apt* means "having a tendency to": *Horace is apt to forget his lunch in the morning.* *Likely* means "probably going to": *Horace is leaving so early today that he's likely to catch the first bus.*

   Liable normally means "in danger of" and should be confined to situations with undesirable consequences: *Horace is liable to trip over that hose.* Strictly, *liable* means "responsible" or "exposed to": *The owner will be liable for Horace's injuries.*

are, is Use *are* with a plural subject (*books are*), *is* with a singular subject (*a book is*).

as *As* may be unclear when it substitutes for *because, since,* or *while*: *As the researchers asked more questions, their money ran out.* (Does *as* mean "while" or "because"?) *As* should never be used as a substitute for *whether* or *who. I'm not sure whether* [not *as*] *we can make it. That's the man who* [not *as*] *gave me directions.*

as, like   In formal speech and writing, *like* should not introduce a main clause° (with a subject° and a verb°) because it is a preposition.° The preferred choice is *as* or *as if*: *The plan succeeded as* [not *like*] *we hoped. It seemed as if* [not *like*] *it might fail. Other plans like it have failed.*

as, than   In comparisons, *as* and *than* precede a pronoun° when it is a subject°: *I love you more than he* [*loves you*]. *As* and *than* precede a pronoun when it is an object°: *I love you as much as* [*I love*] *him.* (See also **4** p. 245.)

assure, ensure, insure   *Assure* means "to promise": *He assured us that we would miss the traffic. Ensure* and *insure* are often used interchangeably to mean "make certain," but some reserve *insure* for matters of legal and financial protection and use *ensure* for more general meanings: *We left early to ensure that we would miss the traffic. It's expensive to insure yourself against floods.*

at   The use of *at* after *where* is wordy and should be avoided: *Where are you meeting him?* is preferable to *Where are you meeting him at?*

awful, awfully   Strictly speaking, *awful* means "awe-inspiring." As intensifiers meaning "very" or "extremely" (*He tried awfully hard*), *awful* and *awfully* should be avoided in formal speech or writing.

a while, awhile   *Awhile* is an adverb°; *a while* is an article° and a noun°. *I will be gone awhile* [not *a while*]. *I will be gone for a while* [not *awhile*].

bad, badly   In formal speech and writing, *bad* should be used only as an adjective°; the adverb° is *badly. He felt bad because his tooth ached badly.* In *He felt bad*, the verb *felt* is a linking verb° and the adjective *bad* describes the subject. See also **4** p. 249.

being as, being that   Colloquial for *because,* the preferable word in formal speech or writing: *Because* [not *Being as*] *the world is round, Columbus never did fall off the edge.*

beside, besides   *Beside* means "next to," while *besides* means "except," "in addition to," or "in addition": *Besides, several other people besides you want to sit beside Dr. Christensen.*

better, had better   In *had better* (meaning "ought to"), the verb° *had* is necessary and should not be omitted: *You had better* [not just *better*] *go.*

between, among   See *among, between.*

bring, take   Use *bring* only for movement from a farther place to a nearer one and *take* for any other movement. *First take these books to the library for renewal; then take them to Mr. Daniels. Bring them back to me when he's finished.*

but, hardly, scarcely   These words are negative in their own right; using *not* with any of them produces a double negative (see **4** p. 252). *We have but* [not *haven't got but*] *an hour before our plane leaves. I could hardly* [not *couldn't hardly*] *make out her face.*

but, however, yet   Each of these words is adequate to express contrast. Don't combine them. *He had finished, yet* [not *but yet*] *he continued.*

can, may   Strictly, *can* indicates capacity or ability, and *may* indicates permission or possibility: *If I may talk with you a moment, I believe I can solve your problem.*

censor, censure To *censor* is to edit or remove from public view on moral or some other grounds; to *censure* is to give a formal scolding. *The lieutenant was censured by Major Taylor for censoring the letters her soldiers wrote home from boot camp.*

center around *Center on* is more logical than, and preferable to, *center around.*

cite, sight, site *Cite* is a verb° usually meaning "quote," "commend," or "acknowledge": *You must cite your sources. Sight* is both a noun° meaning "the ability to see" or "a view" and a verb meaning "perceive" or "observe": *What a sight you see when you sight Venus through a strong telescope. Site* is a noun meaning "place" or "location" or a verb meaning "situate": *The builder sited the house on an unlikely site.*

climatic, climactic *Climatic* comes from *climate* and refers to the weather: *Recent droughts may indicate a climatic change. Climactic* comes from *climax* and refers to a dramatic high point: *During the climactic duel between Hamlet and Laertes, Gertrude drinks poisoned wine.*

complement, compliment To *complement* something is to add to, complete, or reinforce it: *Her yellow blouse complemented her black hair.* To *compliment* something is to make a flattering remark about it: *He complimented her on her hair. Complimentary* can also mean "free": *complimentary tickets.*

conscience, conscious *Conscience* is a noun° meaning "a sense of right and wrong"; *conscious* is an adjective° meaning "aware" or "awake." *Though I was barely conscious, my conscience nagged me.*

contact Avoid using *contact* imprecisely as a verb° instead of a more exact word such as *consult, talk with, telephone,* or *write to.*

continual, continuous *Continual* means "constantly recurring": *Most movies on television are continually interrupted by commercials. Continuous* means "unceasing": *Some cable channels present movies continuously without commercials.*

could of See *have, of.*

credible, creditable, credulous *Credible* means "believable": *It's a strange story, but it seems credible to me. Creditable* means "deserving of credit" or "worthy": *Steve gave a creditable performance. Credulous* means "gullible": *The credulous Claire believed Tim's lies.* See also *incredible, incredulous.*

criteria The plural of *criterion* (meaning "standard for judgment"): *Our criteria are strict. The most important criterion is a sense of humor.*

data The plural of *datum* (meaning "fact"). Though *data* is often used as a singular noun,° most careful writers still treat it as plural: *The data fail* [not *fails*] *to support the hypothesis.*

device, devise *Device* is the noun,° and *devise* is the verb°: *Can you devise some device for getting his attention?*

different from, different than *Different from* is preferred: *His purpose is different from mine.* But *different than* is widely accepted when a construction using *from* would be wordy: *I'm a different person now than I used to be* is preferable to *I'm a different person now from the person I used to be.*

differ from, differ with To *differ from* is to be unlike: *The twins differ from each other only in their hairstyles.* To *differ with* is to disagree with: *I have to differ with you on that point.*

discreet, discrete *Discreet* (noun form *discretion*) means "tactful": *What's a discreet way of telling Maud to be quiet? Discrete* (noun form *discreteness*) means "separate and distinct": *Within a computer's memory are millions of discrete bits of information.*

disinterested, uninterested *Disinterested* means "impartial": *We chose Pete, as a disinterested third party, to decide who was right. Uninterested* means "bored" or "lacking interest": *Unfortunately, Pete was completely uninterested in the question.*

don't *Don't* is the contraction for *do not,* not for *does not*: *I don't care, you don't care, and he doesn't* [not *don't*] *care.*

due to the fact that Wordy for *because.*

eager, anxious See *anxious, eager.*

effect See *affect, effect.*

elicit, illicit *Elicit* means "bring out" or "call forth." *Illicit* means "unlawful." *The crime elicited an outcry against illicit drugs.*

emigrate, immigrate *Emigrate* means "to leave one place and move to another": *The Chus emigrated from Korea. Immigrate* means "to move into a place where one was not born": *They immigrated to the United States.*

ensure See *assure, ensure, insure.*

enthused Avoid using *enthused* colloquially to mean "showing enthusiasm." Prefer *enthusiastic*: *The coach was enthusiastic* [not *enthused*] *about the team's prospects.*

et al., etc. Use *et al.,* the Latin abbreviation for "and other people," only in source citations: *Jones et al.* Avoid *etc.,* the Latin abbreviation for "and other things," in formal writing, and do not use it to refer to people or to substitute for precision, as in *The government provides health care, etc.*

everybody, every body; everyone, every one *Everybody* and *everyone* are indefinite pronouns°: *Everybody* [*everyone*] *knows Tom steals. Every one* is a pronoun° modified by *every,* and *every body* a noun° modified by *every.* Both refer to each thing or person of a specific group and are typically followed by *of*: *The commissioner has stocked every body of fresh water with fish, and now every one of the state's rivers is a potential trout stream.*

everyday, every day *Everyday* is an adjective° meaning "used daily" or "common"; *every day* is a noun modified by *every*: *Everyday problems tend to arise every day.*

everywheres Nonstandard for *everywhere.*

except See *accept, except.*

except for the fact that Wordy for *except that.*

explicit, implicit *Explicit* means "stated outright": *I left explicit instructions. Implicit* means "implied, unstated": *We had an implicit understanding.*

farther, further *Farther* refers to additional distance (*How much farther is it to the beach?*), and *further* refers to additional time, amount, or other abstract matters (*I don't want to discuss this any further*).

°See "Glossary of Terms," p. 558.

fewer, less *Fewer* refers to individual countable items (a plural count noun°), *less* to general amounts (a noncount noun,° always singular). *Skim milk has fewer calories than whole milk. We have less milk left than I thought.*

flaunt, flout *Flaunt* means "show off": *If you have style, flaunt it. Flout* means "scorn" or "defy": *Hester Prynne flouted convention and paid the price.*

flunk A colloquial substitute for *fail*.

fun As an adjective,° *fun* is colloquial and should be avoided in most writing: *It was a pleasurable* [not *fun*] *evening.*

further See *farther, further*.

get This common verb° is used in many slang and colloquial expressions: *get lost, that really gets me, getting on. Get* is easy to overuse: watch out for it in expressions such as *it's getting better* (substitute *improving*) and *we got done* (substitute *finished*).

good, well *Good* is an adjective,° and *well* is nearly always an adverb°: *Larry's a good dancer. He and Linda dance well together. Well* is properly used as an adjective only to refer to health: *You look well.* (*You look good,* in contrast, means "Your appearance is pleasing.")

good and Colloquial for "very": *I was very* [not *good and*] *tired.*

had better See *better, had better*.

had ought The *had* is unnecessary and should be omitted: *He ought* [not *had ought*] *to listen to his mother.*

hanged, hung Though both are past-tense forms° of *hang, hanged* is used to refer to executions and *hung* is used for all other meanings: *Tom Dooley was hanged* [not *hung*] *from a white oak tree. I hung* [not *hanged*] *the picture you gave me.*

hardly See *but, hardly, scarcely*.

have, of Use *have*, not *of*, after helping verbs° such as *could, should, would, may, must,* and *might*: *You should have* [not *should of*] *told me.*

he, she; he/she Convention has allowed the use of *he* to mean "he or she": *After the infant learns to creep, he progresses to crawling.* However, many writers today consider this usage inaccurate and unfair because it seems to exclude females. The construction *he/she,* one substitute for *he,* is awkward and objectionable to most readers. The better choice is to make *he* plural, to rephrase, or, sparingly, to use *he or she.* For instance: *After infants learn to creep, they progress to crawling. After learning to creep, the infant progresses to crawling. After the infant learns to creep, he or she progresses to crawling.* See also **3** p. 161 and **4** p. 242.

herself, himself See *myself, herself, himself, yourself*.

hisself Nonstandard for *himself*.

hopefully *Hopefully* means "with hope": *Freddy waited hopefully for a glimpse of Eliza.* The use of *hopefully* to mean "it is to be hoped," "I hope," or "let's hope" is now very common; but try to avoid it in writing because many readers continue to object strongly to the usage. *I hope* [not *Hopefully*] *the law will pass.*

idea, ideal An *idea* is a thought or conception. The noun° *ideal* is a model of perfection or a goal. *Ideal* should not be used in place of *idea*: *The idea* [not *ideal*] *of the play is that our ideals often sustain us.*

if, whether For clarity, use *whether* rather than *if* when you are expressing an alternative: *If I laugh hard, people can't tell whether I'm crying.*

illicit See *elicit, illicit.*

illusion See *allusion, illusion.*

immigrate, emigrate See *emigrate, immigrate.*

implicit See *explicit, implicit.*

imply, infer Writers or speakers *imply*, meaning "suggest": *Jim's letter implies he's having a good time.* Readers or listeners *infer*, meaning "conclude": *From Jim's letter I infer he's having a good time.*

incredible, incredulous *Incredible* means "unbelievable," while *incredulous* means "unbelieving": *When Nancy heard Dennis's incredible story, she was frankly incredulous.* See also *credible, creditable, credulous.*

individual, person, party *Individual* should refer to a single human being in contrast to a group or should stress uniqueness: *The US Constitution places strong emphasis on the rights of the individual.* For other meanings *person* is preferable: *What person* [not *individual*] *wouldn't want the security promised in that advertisement? Party* means "group" (*Can you seat a party of four for dinner?*) and should not be used to refer to an individual except in legal documents. See also *people, persons.*

infer See *imply, infer.*

in regards to Nonstandard for *in regard to, as regards,* or *regarding.*

inside of, outside of The *of* is unnecessary when *inside* and *outside* are used as prepositions°: *Stay inside* [not *inside of*] *the house. The decision is outside* [not *outside of*] *my authority. Inside of* may refer colloquially to time, though in formal English *within* is preferred: *The law was passed within* [not *inside of*] *a year.*

insure See *assure, ensure, insure.*

irregardless Nonstandard for *regardless.*

is, are See *are, is.*

is because See *reason is because.*

is when, is where These are faulty constructions in sentences that define: *Adolescence is a stage* [not *is when a person is*] *between childhood and adulthood. Socialism is a system in which* [not *is where*] *government owns the means of production.* See also **4** p. 274.

its, it's *Its* is the pronoun° *it* in the possessive case°: *That plant is losing its leaves. It's* is a contraction for *it is* or *it has*: *It's* [*It is*] *likely to die. It's* [*It has*] *got a fungus.* Many people confuse *it's* and *its* because possessives are most often formed with *-'s;* but the possessive *its*, like *his* and *hers*, never takes an apostrophe.

-ize, -wise The suffix *-ize* forms a verb°: *revolutionize, immunize.* The suffix *-wise* forms an adverb°: *clockwise, otherwise, likewise.* Avoid the two suffixes except in established words: *I'm highly sensitive* [not *sensitized*]

°See "Glossary of Terms," p. 558.

to that kind of criticism. Financially [not *Moneywise*], *it's a good time to buy real estate.*

kind of, sort of, type of   In formal speech and writing, avoid using *kind of* or *sort of* to mean "somewhat": *He was rather* [not *kind of*] *tall.*

Kind, sort, and *type* are singular and take singular adjectives° and verbs°: *This kind of dog is easily trained.* Agreement errors often occur when the singular *kind, sort,* or *type* is combined with the plural adjective *these* or *those*: *These kinds* [not *kind*] *of dogs are easily trained. Kind, sort,* and *type* should be followed by *of* but not by *a*: *I don't know what type of* [not *type* or *type of a*] *dog that is.*

Use *kind of, sort of,* or *type of* only when the word *kind, sort,* or *type* is important: *That was a strange* [not *strange sort of*] *statement.*

lay, lie   *Lay* means "put" or "place" and takes a direct object°: *We could lay the tablecloth in the sun.* Its main forms are *lay, laid, laid. Lie* means "recline" or "be situated" and does not take an object: *I lie awake at night. The town lies due east of the river.* Its main forms are *lie, lay, lain.* (See also **4** p. 207.)

leave, let   *Leave* and *let* are interchangeable only when followed by *alone*: *leave me alone* is the same as *let me alone.* Otherwise, *leave* means "depart" and *let* means "allow": *Jill would not let Sue leave.*

less   See *fewer, less.*

liable   See *apt, liable, likely.*

lie, lay   See *lay, lie.*

like, as   See *as, like.*

like, such as   Strictly, *such as* precedes an example that represents a larger subject, whereas *like* indicates that two subjects are comparable. *Steve has recordings of many great saxophonists such as Ben Webster and Lee Konitz. Steve wants to be a great jazz saxophonist like Ben Webster and Lee Konitz.*

likely   See *apt, liable, likely.*

literally   This word means "actually" or "just as the words say," and it should not be used to qualify or intensify expressions whose words are not to be taken at face value. The sentence *He was literally climbing the walls* describes a person behaving like an insect, not a person who is restless or anxious. For the latter meaning, *literally* should be omitted.

lose, loose   *Lose* means "mislay": *Did you lose a brown glove? Loose* means "unrestrained" or "not tight": *Ann's canary got loose. Loose* also can function as a verb° meaning "let loose": *They loose the dogs as soon as they spot the bear.*

lots, lots of   Avoid these colloquialisms in college or business writing. Use *very many, a great many,* or *much* instead.

may, can   See *can, may.*

may be, maybe   *May be* is a verb°, and *maybe* is an adverb° meaning "perhaps": *Tuesday may be a legal holiday. Maybe we won't have classes.*

may of   See *have, of.*

media   *Media* is the plural of *medium* and takes a plural verb°: *All the news media are increasingly visual.* The singular verb is common, even in the media, but many readers prefer the plural verb and it is always correct.

might of See *have, of.*

moral, morale As a noun,° *moral* means "ethical conclusion" or "lesson": *The moral of the story escapes me. Morale* means "spirit" or "state of mind": *Victory improved the team's morale.*

most, almost See *almost, most.*

must of See *have, of.*

myself, herself, himself, yourself, ourselves, themselves, yourselves Avoid using the *-self* words in place of personal pronouns°: *No one except me* [not *myself*] *saw the accident. Michiko and I* [not *myself*] *planned the ceremony.* The *-self* words have two uses: they emphasize a noun° or other pronoun (*Paul did the work himself; he himself said so*), or they indicate that the sentence subject° also receives the action of the verb°: *I drove myself to the hospital.* See also **4** p. 235 on the unchanging forms of the *-self* pronouns in standard American English.

nowheres Nonstandard for *nowhere.*

number See *amount, number.*

of, have See *have, of.*

off of *Of* is unnecessary. Use *off* or *from* rather than *off of*: *He jumped off* [or *from,* not *off of*] *the roof.*

OK, O.K., okay All three spellings are acceptable, but avoid this colloquial term in formal speech and writing.

on account of Wordy for *because of.*

on the other hand This expression of contrast should be preceded by its mate, *on the one hand*: *On the one hand, we hoped for snow. On the other hand, we worried that it would harm the animals.* However, the two combined can be unwieldy, and a simple *but, however, yet,* or *in contrast* often suffices: *We hoped for snow. Yet we worried that it would harm the animals.*

outside of See *inside of, outside of.*

owing to the fact that Wordy for *because.*

party See *individual, person, party.*

people, persons In formal usage, *people* refers to a general group: *We the people of the United States. . . . Persons* refers to a collection of individuals: *Will the person or persons who saw the accident please notify. . . .* Except when emphasizing individuals, prefer *people* to *persons.* See also *individual, person, party.*

per Except in technical writing, an English equivalent is usually preferable to the Latin *per*: *$10 an* [not *per*] *hour; sent by* [not *per*] *parcel post; requested in* [not *per* or *as per*] *your letter.*

percent (per cent), percentage Both these terms refer to fractions of one hundred. *Percent* always follows a number (*40 percent of the voters*), and the word is often used instead of the symbol (*%*) in nontechnical writing. *Percentage* stands alone (*the percentage of voters*) or follows an adjective (*a high percentage*).

person See *individual, person, party.*

persons See *people, persons.*

phenomena *Phenomena* is the plural of *phenomenon* (meaning "perceivable fact" or "unusual occurrence"): *Many phenomena are not recorded. One phenomenon is attracting attention.*

plenty A colloquial substitute for *very*: *The reaction occurred very* [not *plenty*] *fast.*

plus *Plus* is standard to mean "in addition to": *His income plus mine is sufficient.* But *plus* is colloquial when it relates main clauses°: *Our organization is larger than theirs; moreover* [not *plus*], *we have more money.*

precede, proceed *Precede* means "come before": *My name precedes yours in the alphabet. Proceed* means "move on": *We were told to proceed to the waiting room.*

prejudice, prejudiced *Prejudice* is a noun°; *prejudiced* is an adjective.° Do not drop the *-d* from *prejudiced*: *I was fortunate that my parents were not prejudiced* [not *prejudice*].

pretty Overworked as an adverb° meaning "rather" or "somewhat": *He was somewhat* [not *pretty*] *irked at the suggestion.*

previous to, prior to Wordy for *before.*

principal, principle *Principal* is an adjective° meaning "foremost" or "major," a noun° meaning "chief official," or, in finance, a noun meaning "capital sum." *Principle* is a noun only, meaning "rule" or "axiom." *Her principal reasons for confessing were her principles of right and wrong.*

proceed, precede See *precede, proceed.*

question of whether, question as to whether Wordy substitutes for *whether.*

raise, rise *Raise* means "lift" or "bring up" and takes a direct object°: *The Kirks raise cattle.* Its main forms are *raise, raised, raised. Rise* means "get up" and does not take an object: *They must rise at dawn.* Its main forms are *rise, rose, risen.* (See also **4** p. 207.)

real, really In formal speech and writing, *real* should not be used as an adverb°; *really* is the adverb and *real* an adjective.° *Popular reaction to the announcement was really* [not *real*] *enthusiastic.*

reason is because Although colloquially common, this expression should be avoided in formal speech and writing. Use a *that* clause after *reason is*: *The reason he is absent is that* [not *is because*] *he is sick.* Or: *He is absent because he is sick.* (See also **4** p. 274.)

respectful, respective *Respectful* means "full of (or showing) respect": *Be respectful of other people. Respective* means "separate": *The French and the Germans occupied their respective trenches.*

rise, raise See *raise, rise.*

scarcely See *but, hardly, scarcely.*

sensual, sensuous *Sensual* suggests sexuality; *sensuous* means "pleasing to the senses." *Stirred by the sensuous scent of meadow grass and flowers, Cheryl and Paul found their thoughts growing increasingly sensual.*

set, sit *Set* means "put" or "place" and takes a direct object°: *He sets the pitcher down.* Its main forms are *set, set, set. Sit* means "be seated" and does not take an object: *She sits on the sofa*. Its main forms are *sit, sat, sat*. (See also **4** p. 207.)

shall, will   *Will* is a helping verb° for all persons°: *I will go, you will go, they will go*. The main use of *shall* is for first-person questions requesting an opinion or consent: *Shall I order a pizza? Shall we dance? Shall* can also be used for the first person when a formal effect is desired (*I shall expect you around three*), and it is occasionally used with the second or third person to express the speaker's determination (*You shall do as I say*).

should of   See *have, of*.

sight, site, cite   See *cite, sight, site*.

since   *Since* mainly relates to time: *I've been waiting since noon*. But *since* is also often used to mean "because": *Since you ask, I'll tell you*. Revise sentences in which the word could have either meaning, such as *Since I studied physics, I have been planning to major in engineering*.

sit, set   See *set, sit*.

site, cite, sight   See *cite, sight, site*.

so   Avoid using *so* alone or as a vague intensifier: *He was so late*. *So* needs to be followed by *that* and a statement of the result: *He was so late that I left without him*.

somebody, some body; someone, some one   *Somebody* and *someone* are indefinite pronouns°; *some body* is a noun° modified by *some*; and *some one* is a pronoun° or an adjective° modified by *some*. *Somebody ought to invent a shampoo that will give hair some body*. *Someone told Janine she should choose some one plan and stick with it*.

sometime, sometimes, some time   *Sometime* means "at an indefinite time in the future": *Why don't you come up and see me sometime? Sometimes* means "now and then": *I still see my old friend Joe sometimes*. *Some time* means "a span of time": *I need some time to make the payments*.

somewheres   Nonstandard for *somewhere*.

sort of, sort of a   See *kind of, sort of, type of*.

such   Avoid using *such* as a vague intensifier: *It was such a cold winter*. *Such* should be followed by *that* and a statement of the result: *It was such a cold winter that Napoleon's troops had to turn back*.

such as   See *like, such as*.

supposed to, used to   In both these expressions, the *-d* is essential: *I used to* [not *use to*] *think so*. *He's supposed to* [not *suppose to*] *meet us*.

sure   Colloquial when used as an adverb° meaning *surely*: *James Madison sure was right about the need for the Bill of Rights*. If you merely want to be emphatic, use *certainly*: *Madison certainly was right*. If your goal is to convince a possibly reluctant reader, use *surely*: *Madison surely was right*.

sure and, sure to; try and, try to   *Sure to* and *try to* are the correct forms: *Be sure to* [not *sure and*] *buy milk*. *Try to* [not *Try and*] *find some decent tomatoes*.

take, bring   See *bring, take*.

than, as   See *as, than*.

than, then *Than* is used in comparisons, whereas *then* indicates time: *Holmes knew then that Moriarty was wilier than he had thought.*

that, which *That* introduces an essential element°: *We should use the lettuce that Susan bought* (*that Susan bought* limits the lettuce to a particular lettuce). *Which* can introduce both essential elements and nonessential elements,° but many writers reserve *which* only for nonessential: *The leftover lettuce, which is in the refrigerator, would make a good salad* (*which is in the refrigerator* simply provides more information about the lettuce we already know of). Essential elements (with *that* or *which*) are not set off by commas; nonessential elements (with *which*) are. See also 5 pp. 286–89.

that, which, who Use *that* for animals, things, and sometimes collective or anonymous people: *The rocket that failed cost millions. Infants that walk need constant tending.* Use *which* only for animals and things: *The river, which flows south, divides two countries.* Use *who* only for people and for animals with names: *Dorothy is the girl who visits Oz. Her dog, Toto, who accompanies her, gives her courage.*

their, there, they're *Their* is the possessive form of *they*: *Give them their money. There* indicates place (*I saw her standing there*) or functions as an expletive° (*There is a hole behind you*). *They're* is a contraction for *they are*: *They're going fast.*

theirselves Nonstandard for *themselves.*

them In standard American English, *them* does not serve as an adjective°: *Those* [not *them*] *people want to know.*

then, than See *than, then.*

these kind, these sort, these type, those kind See *kind of, sort of, type of.*

this, these *This* is singular: *this car* or *This is the reason I left. These* is plural: *these cars* or *These are not valid reasons.*

thru A colloquial spelling of *through* that should be avoided in all academic and business writing.

to, too, two *To* is a preposition°; *too* is an adverb° meaning "also" or "excessively"; and *two* is a number. *I too have been to Europe two times.*

too Avoid using *too* as a vague intensifier: *Monkeys are too mean.* If you do use *too*, explain the consequences of the excessive quality: *Monkeys are too mean to make good pets.*

toward, towards Both are acceptable, though *toward* is preferred. Use one or the other consistently.

try and, try to See *sure and, sure to*; *try and, try to.*

type of See *kind of, sort of, type of.* Don't use *type* without *of*: *It was a family type of* [not *type*] *restaurant.* Or better: *It was a family restaurant.*

uninterested See *disinterested, uninterested.*

unique *Unique* means "the only one of its kind" and so cannot sensibly be modified with words such as *very* or *most*: *That was a unique* [not *a very unique* or *the most unique*] *movie.*

usage, use *Usage* refers to conventions, most often those of a language: *Is "hadn't ought" proper usage? Usage* is often misused in place of the noun *use*: *Wise use* [not *usage*] *of insulation can save fuel.*

use, utilize *Utilize* can be used to mean "make good use of": *Many teachers utilize computers for instruction.* But for all other senses of "place in service" or "employ," prefer *use.*

used to See *supposed to, used to.*

wait for, wait on In formal speech and writing, *wait for* means "await" (*I'm waiting for Paul*) and *wait on* means "serve" (*The owner of the store herself waited on us*).

ways Colloquial as a substitute for *way*: *We have only a little way* [not *ways*] *to go.*

well See *good, well.*

whether, if See *if, whether.*

which, that See *that, which.*

which, who, that See *that, which, who.*

who's, whose *Who's* is the contraction of *who is* or *who has*: *Who's* [*Who is*] *at the door? Jim is the only one who's* [*who has*] *passed. Whose* is the possessive form of *who*: *Whose book is that?*

will, shall See *shall, will.*

-wise See *-ize, -wise.*

would be *Would be* is often used instead of *is* or *are* to soften statements needlessly: *One example is* [not *would be*] *gun-control laws. Would* can combine with other verbs for the same unassertive effect: *would ask, would seem, would suggest,* and so on.

would have Avoid this construction in place of *had* in clauses° that begin with *if* and state a condition contrary to fact: *If the tree had* [not *would have*] *withstood the fire, it would have been the oldest in town.* See also **4** p. 224.

would of See *have, of.*

you In all but very formal writing, *you* is generally appropriate as long as it means "you, the reader." In all writing, avoid indefinite uses of *you*, such as *In one ancient tribe your first loyalty was to your parents.* See also **4** p. 246.

your, you're *Your* is the possessive form of *you*: *Your dinner is ready. You're* is the contraction of *you are*: *You're bound to be late.*

yourself See *myself, herself, himself, yourself.*

°See "Glossary of Terms," p. 558.

Glossary of Terms

This section defines the terms and concepts of basic English grammar, including every term marked ° in the text.

absolute phrase A phrase that consists of a noun° or pronoun° plus the -*ing* or -*ed* form of a verb° (a participle°): *Our accommodations arranged, we set out on our trip. They will hire a local person, other things being equal.*

active voice The verb form° used when the sentence subject° names the performer of the verb's action: *The drillers used a rotary blade.* For more, see *voice*.

adjective A word used to modify a noun° or pronoun°: *beautiful morning, ordinary one, good spelling.* Contrast *adverb.* Nouns, word groups, and some verb° forms may also serve as **adjective modifiers**: *book sale; sale of old books; the sale, which occurs annually; increasing profits.*

adjective clause See *adjective.*

adverb A word used to modify a verb,° an adjective,° another adverb, or a whole sentence: *warmly greet* (verb), *only three people* (adjective), *quite seriously* (adverb), *Fortunately, she is employed* (sentence). Word groups may also serve as **adverb modifiers**: *drove by a farm, plowed the field when the earth thawed.*

adverb clause See *adverb.*

agreement The correspondence of one word to another in person,° number,° or gender.° Mainly, a verb° must agree with its subject° (*The chef orders eggs*), and a pronoun° must agree with its antecedent° (*The chef surveys her breakfast*). See also **4** pp. 227–32 and 240–43.

antecedent The word a pronoun° refers to: *Jonah, who is not yet ten, has already chosen the college he will attend* (*Jonah* is the antecedent of the pronouns *who* and *he*).

appositive A word or word group appearing next to a noun° or pronoun° that renames or identifies it and is equivalent to it: *My brother Michael, the best horn player in town, won the state competition* (*Michael* identifies which brother is being referred to; *the best horn player in town* renames *My brother Michael*).

article The words *a, an,* and *the.* A kind of determiner,° an article always signals that a noun follows. See **4** pp. 254–56 for the rules governing *a/an* and *the.*

auxiliary verb See *helping verb.*

case The form of a pronoun° or noun° that indicates its function in the sentence. Most pronouns have three cases. The subjective case is for subjects° and subject complements°: *I, you, he, she, it, we, they, who, whoever.* The objective case is for objects°: *me, you, him, her, it, us, them, whom, whomever.* The possessive case is for ownership: *my/mine, your/yours, his, her/hers, its, our/ours, their/theirs, whose.* Nouns use the subjective form (*dog, America*) for all cases except the possessive (*dog's, America's*).

clause   A group of words containing a subject° and a predicate.° A main clause can stand alone as a sentence: *We can go to the movies*. A subordinate clause cannot stand alone as a sentence: *We can go if Bridget gets back on time*. For more, see *subordinate clause*.

collective noun   A word with singular form that names a group of individuals or things: *team, army, family, flock, group*. A collective noun generally takes a singular verb° and a singular pronoun°: *The army is prepared for its role*. See also **4** pp. 230 and 242.

comma splice   A sentence error in which two sentences (main clauses°) are separated by a comma without *and, but, or, nor,* or another coordinating conjunction.° Splice: *The book was long, it contained useful information*. Revised: *The book was long; it contained useful information*. Or: *The book was long, and it contained useful information*. See **4** pp. 269–72.

comparison   The form of an adjective° *or* adverb° that shows its degree of quality or amount. The positive is the simple, uncompared form: *small, clumsily*. The comparative compares the thing modified to at least one other thing: *smaller, more clumsily*. The superlative indicates that the thing modified exceeds all other things to which it is being compared: *smallest, most clumsily*. The comparative and superlative are formed either with the endings *-er/-est* or with the words *more/most* or *less/least*.

complement   See *subject complement*.

complete predicate   See *predicate*.

complete subject   See *subject*.

complex sentence   See *sentence*.

compound adjective   See *compound construction*.

compound-complex sentence   See *sentence*.

compound construction   Two or more words or word groups serving the same function, such as a compound subject (*Harriet and Peter poled their barge down the river*), **compound object** (*John writes stories and screenplays*), compound predicate (*The scout watched and waited*) or parts of a predicate (*She grew tired and hungry*), and compound sentence° (*He smiled, and I laughed*). (See **4** p. 203.) Compound words include nouns (*roommate, strip-mining*) and adjectives (*two-year-old, downtrodden*).

compound object   See *compound construction*.

compound sentence   See *sentence*.

compound subject   See *compound construction*.

conditional statement   A statement expressing a condition contrary to fact and using the subjunctive mood° of the verb: *If she were mayor, the unions would cooperate*.

conjunction   A word that links and relates parts of a sentence. See *coordinating conjunction* (*and, but,* etc.), *correlative conjunction* (*either . . . or, both . . . and,* etc.), and *subordinating conjunction* (*because, if,* etc.).

conjunctive adverb   A word such as *besides, however,* or *therefore* that can relate two ideas: *We had hoped to own a house by now; however, prices are still too high*. (See **4** p. 271 for a list of conjunctive adverbs.) When main clauses° are related by a conjunctive adverb, they must be separated by

a semicolon or a period to prevent a comma splice° or a fused sentence.°
(See **4** pp. 269–72.)

contraction   A condensed expression, with an apostrophe replacing the
missing letters: *doesn't* (*does not*), *we'll* (*we will*).

coordinating conjunction   A word linking words or word groups serving
the same function: *The dog and cat sometimes fight, but they usually get
along.* The coordinating conjunctions are *and, but, or, nor, for, so, yet.*

coordination   The linking of words or word groups that are of equal importance, usually with a coordinating conjunction.° *He and I laughed, but
she was not amused.* Contrast *subordination.*

correlative conjunction   Two or more connecting words that work together to link words or word groups serving the same function: *Both
Michiko and June signed up, but neither Stan nor Carlos did.* The correla-
tives include *both . . . and, just as . . . so, not only . . . but also, not . . . but,
either . . . or, neither . . . nor, whether . . . or, as . . . as.*

count noun   A word that names a person, place, or thing that can be
counted (and so may appear in plural form): *camera/cameras, river/rivers,
child/children.*

dangling modifier   A modifier that does not sensibly describe anything in
its sentence. Dangling: *Having arrived late, the concert had already begun.*
Revised: *Having arrived late, we found that the concert had already begun.*
See **4** pp. 262–63.

demonstrative pronoun   A word such as *this, that, these, those,* or *such*
that identifies or points to a noun° (*This is the problem*).

determiner   A word such as *a, an, the, my,* and *your* that indicates that a
noun follows. See also *article.*

direct address   A construction in which a word or phrase indicates the
person or group spoken to: *Have you finished, John? Farmers, unite.*

direct object   A noun° or pronoun° that identifies who or what receives
the action of a verb°: *Education opens doors.* For more, see *object* and
predicate.

direct question   A sentence asking a question and concluding with a
question mark: *Do they know we are watching?* Contrast *indirect question.*

direct quotation   Repetition of what someone has written or said, using
the exact words of the original and enclosing them in quotation marks:
Feinberg writes, "The reasons are both obvious and sorry."

double negative   A nonstandard form consisting of two negative words
used in the same construction so that they effectively cancel each other:
I don't have no money. Rephrase as *I have no money* or *I don't have any
money.* See also **4** p. 252.

ellipsis   The omission of a word or words from a quotation, indicated by
the three spaced periods of an ellipsis mark: *"all . . . are created equal."* See
also **5** pp. 318–20.

essential element   A word or word group that is necessary to the meaning
of the sentence because it limits the word it refers to: removing it would
leave the meaning unclear or too general. Essential elements are *not* set
off by commas: *Dorothy's companion the Scarecrow lacks a brain. The*

man who called about the apartment said he'd try again. Contrast *nonessential element.* See also **5** pp. 286–89.

expletive construction A sentence that postpones the subject° by beginning with *there* or *it* and a form of *be*: *It is impossible to get a ticket. There are no more seats available.*

first person See *person.*

fused sentence (run-on sentence) A sentence error in which two complete sentences (main clauses°) are joined with no punctuation or connecting word between them. Fused: *I heard his lecture it was dull.* Revised: *I heard his lecture; it was dull.* See **4** pp. 269–72.

future perfect tense The verb tense expressing an action that will be completed before another future action: *They will have heard by then.* For more, see *tense.*

future tense The verb tense expressing action that will occur in the future: *They will hear soon.* For more, see *tense.*

gender The classification of nouns° or pronouns° as masculine (*he, boy*), feminine (*she, woman*), or neuter (*it, computer*).

generic he *He* used to mean *he or she.* Avoid *he* when you intend either or both genders. See **3** p. 161 and **4** p. 242.

generic noun A noun° that does not refer to a specific person or thing: *Any person may come. A student needs good work habits. A school with financial problems may shortchange its students.* A singular generic noun takes a singular pronoun° (*he, she,* or *it*). See also *indefinite pronoun* and **4** p. 241.

gerund A verb form that ends in *-ing* and functions as a noun°: *Running is ideal for getting exercise year round.* For more, see *verbals and verbal phrases.*

gerund phrase See *verbals and verbal phrases.*

helping verb (auxiliary verb) A verb° used with another verb to convey time, possibility, obligation, and other meanings: *You should write a letter. You have written other letters.* The modals are *be able to, be supposed to, can, could, had better, had to, may, might, must, ought to, shall, should, used to, will, would.* The other helping verbs are forms of *be, have,* and *do.* See also **4** pp. 209–13.

idiom An expression that is peculiar to a language and that may not make sense if taken literally: *bide your time, by and large, put up with.*

imperative See *mood.*

indefinite pronoun A word that stands for a noun° and does not refer to a specific person or thing. A few indefinite pronouns are plural (*both, few, many, several*) or may be singular or plural (*all, any, more, most, none, some*). But most are only singular: *anybody, anyone, anything, each, either, everybody, everyone, everything, neither, nobody, no one, nothing, one, somebody, someone, something.* The singular indefinite pronouns take singular verbs° and are referred to by singular pronouns: *Something makes its presence felt.* See also *generic noun* and **4** pp. 230 and 241–42.

indicative See *mood.*

°Defined in this glossary.

indirect object A noun° or pronoun° that identifies to whom or what something is done: *Give them the award.* For more, see *object* and *predicate.*

indirect question A sentence reporting a question and ending with a period: *Writers wonder whether their work must always be lonely.* Contrast *direct question.*

indirect quotation A report of what someone has written or said, but not using the exact words of the original and not enclosing the words in quotation marks. Quotation: *"Events have controlled me."* Indirect quotation: *Lincoln said that events had controlled him.*

infinitive A verb form° consisting of the verb's dictionary form plus *to*: *to swim, to write.* For more, see *verbals and verbal phrases.*

infinitive phrase See *verbals and verbal phrases.*

intensive pronoun A personal pronoun° plus *-self* or *-selves* that emphasizes a noun° or other pronoun° (*He himself asked that question*).

interjection A word standing by itself or inserted in a construction to exclaim: *Hey! What the heck did you do that for?*

interrogative pronoun A word that begins a question and serves as the subject° or object° of the sentence. The interrogative pronouns are *who, whom, whose, which,* and *what. Who received the flowers? Whom are they for?*

intransitive verb A verb° that does not require a following word (direct object°) to complete its meaning: *Mosquitoes buzz. The hospital may close.* For more, see *predicate.*

irregular verb See *verb forms.*

linking verb A verb that links, or connects, a subject° and a word that renames or describes the subject (a subject complement°): *They are golfers. You seem lucky.* The linking verbs are the forms of *be,* the verbs of the senses (*look, sound, smell, feel, taste*), and a few others (*appear, become, grow, prove, remain, seem, turn*). For more, see *predicate.*

main clause A word group that contains a subject° and a predicate,° does not begin with a subordinating word, and may stand alone as a sentence: *The president was not overbearing.* For more, see *clause.*

main verb The part of a verb phrase° that carries the principal meaning: *had been walking, could happen, was chilled.* Contrast *helping verb.*

misplaced modifier A modifier whose position makes unclear its relation to the rest of the sentence. Misplaced: *The children played with firecrackers that they bought illegally in the field.* Revised: *The children played in the field with firecrackers that they bought illegally.*

modal See *helping verb.*

modifier Any word or word group that limits or qualifies the meaning of another word or word group. Modifiers include adjectives° and adverbs° as well as words and word groups that act as adjectives and adverbs.

mood The form of a verb° that shows how the speaker views the action. The indicative mood, the most common, is used to make statements or ask questions: *The play will be performed Saturday. Did you get tickets?*

°Defined in this glossary.

The imperative mood gives a command: *Please get good seats. Avoid the top balcony.* The subjunctive mood expresses a wish, a condition contrary to fact, a recommendation, or a request: *I wish George were coming with us. If he were here, he'd come. I suggested that he come. The host asked that he be here.*

noncount noun   A word that names a person, place, or thing and that is not considered countable in English (and so does not appear in plural form): *confidence, information, silver, work.* See **4** p. 254 for a longer list.

nonessential appositive   See *nonessential element.*

nonessential element   A word or word group that does not limit the word it refers to and that is not necessary to the meaning of the sentence. Nonessential elements are usually set off by commas: *Sleep, which we all need, occupies a third of our lives. His wife, Patricia, is a chemist.* Contrast *essential element.* See also **5** pp. 286–89.

nonessential modifier   See *nonessential element.*

nonessential phrase   See *nonessential element.*

nonrestrictive element   See *nonessential element.*

noun   A word that names a person, place, thing, quality, or idea: *Maggie, Alabama, clarinet, satisfaction, socialism.* See also *collective noun, count noun, generic noun, noncount noun,* and *proper noun.*

noun clause   See *subordinate clause.*

number   The form of a word that indicates whether it is singular or plural. Singular: *I, he, this, child, runs, hides.* Plural: *we, they, these, children, run, hide.*

object   A noun° or pronoun° that receives the action of or is influenced by another word. A direct object receives the action of a verb° or verbal° and usually follows it: *We watched the stars.* An indirect object tells for or to whom something is done: *Reiner bought us tapes.* An object of a preposition usually follows a preposition°: *They went to New Orleans.*

objective case   The form of a pronoun° when it is the object° of a verb° (*call him*) or the object of a preposition° (*for us*). For more, see *case.*

object of preposition   See *object.*

parallelism   Similarity of form between two or more coordinated elements: *Rising prices and declining incomes left many people in bad debt and worse despair.* See also **3** pp. 148–50.

parenthetical expression   A word or construction that interrupts a sentence and is not part of its main structure, called *parenthetical* because it could (or does) appear in parentheses: *Mary Cassatt (1845–1926) was an American painter. Her work, incidentally, is in the museum.*

participial phrase   See *verbals and verbal phrases.*

participle   See *verbals and verbal phrases.*

particle   A preposition° or adverb° in a two-word verb: *catch on, look up.*

parts of speech   The classes of words based on their form, function, and meaning: nouns, pronouns, verbs, adjectives, adverbs, conjunctions, prepositions, and interjections. See separate entries for each part of speech.

°Defined in this glossary.

passive voice The verb form° used when the sentence subject° names the receiver of the verb's action: *The mixture was stirred*. For more, see *voice*.

past participle The *-ed* form of most verbs°: *fished, hopped*. The past participle may be irregular: *begun, written*. For more, see *verbals and verbal phrases* and *verb forms*.

past perfect tense The verb tense expressing an action that was completed before another past action: *No one had heard that before*. For more, see *tense*.

past tense The verb tense expressing action that occurred in the past: *Everyone laughed*. For more, see *tense*.

past-tense form The verb form used to indicate action that occurred in the past, usually created by adding *-d* or *-ed* to the verb's dictionary form (*smiled*) but created differently for most irregular verbs (*began, threw*). For more, see *verb forms*.

perfect tenses The verb tenses indicating action completed before another specific time or action: *have walked, had walked, will have walked*. For more, see *tense*.

person The form of a verb° or pronoun° that indicates whether the subject is speaking, spoken to, or spoken about. In the first person the subject is speaking: *I am, we are*. In the second person the subject is spoken to: *you are*. In the third person the subject is spoken about: *he/she/it is, they are*.

personal pronoun *I, you, he, she, it, we,* or *they*: a word that substitutes for a specific noun° or other pronoun. For more, see *case*.

phrase A group of related words that lacks a subject° or a predicate° or both: *She ran into the field. She tried to jump the fence*. See also *absolute phrase, prepositional phrase, verbals and verbal phrases*.

plain form The dictionary form of a verb: *buy, make, run, swivel*. For more, see *verb forms*.

plural More than one. See *number*.

positive form See *comparison*.

possessive case The form of a noun° or pronoun° that indicates its ownership of something else: *men's attire, your briefcase*. For more, see *case*.

possessive pronoun A word that replaces a noun° or other pronoun° and shows ownership: *The cat chased its tail*. The possessive pronouns are *my, our, your, his, her, its, their, whose*.

predicate The part of a sentence that makes an assertion about the subject.° A predicate must contain a verb° and may contain modifiers,° objects° of the verb, and complements.° The simple predicate consists of the verb and its helping verbs°: *A wiser person would have made a different decision*. The **complete predicate** includes the simple predicate and any modifiers, objects, and complements: *A wiser person would have made a different decision*. See also *intransitive verb, linking verb,* and *transitive verb*. (See also **4** pp. 192–94.)

preposition A word that forms a noun° or pronoun° (plus any modifiers°) into a prepositional phrase°: *about love, down the steep stairs*. The common prepositions include: *about, before, by, during, for, from, in, on, to, with,* and many others. (See **4** p. 187 for a list.)

prepositional phrase A word group consisting of a preposition° and its object.° Prepositional phrases usually serve as adjectives° (*We saw a movie about sorrow*) or as adverbs° (*We went back for the second show*).

present participle The *-ing* form of a verb°: *swimming, flying.* For more, see *verbals and verbal phrases.*

present perfect tense The verb tense expressing action that began in the past and is linked to the present: *Dogs have buried bones here before.* For more, see *tense.*

present tense The verb tense expressing action that is occurring now, occurs habitually, or is generally true: *Dogs bury bones here often.* For more, see *tense.*

principal parts The three forms of a verb from which its various tenses are created: the plain form° (*stop, go*), the past-tense form° (*stopped, went*), and the past participle° (*stopped, gone*). For more, see *tense* and *verb forms.*

progressive tenses The verb tenses that indicate continuing (progressive) action and use the *-ing* form of the verb: *A dog was barking here this morning.* For more, see *tense.*

pronoun A word used in place of a noun,° such as *I, he, everyone, who,* and *herself.* See also *demonstrative pronoun, indefinite pronoun, intensive pronoun, interrogative pronoun, personal pronoun, possessive pronoun, reflexive pronoun, relative pronoun.*

proper adjective A word formed from a proper noun° and used to modify a noun° or pronoun°: *Alaskan winter.*

proper noun A word naming a specific person, place, or thing and beginning with a capital letter: *David Letterman, Mt. Rainier, Alaska, US Congress.*

reflexive pronoun A personal pronoun° plus *-self* or *-selves* that receives the action of the verb° (*He blamed himself for the accident*).

regular verb See *verb forms.*

relative pronoun A word that relates a group of words to a noun° or another pronoun.° The relative pronouns are *who, whom, whoever, whomever, which,* and *that. Ask the woman who knows all. This may be the question that stumps her.* For more, see *case.*

restrictive element See *essential element.*

run-on sentence See *fused sentence.*

-s form See *verb forms.*

second person See *person.*

sentence A complete unit of thought, consisting of at least a subject° and a predicate° that are not introduced by a subordinating word. A simple sentence contains one main clause°: *I'm leaving.* A compound sentence contains at least two main clauses: *I'd like to stay, but I'm leaving.* A complex sentence contains one main clause and at least one subordinate clause°: *If you let me go now, you'll be sorry.* A compound-complex

°Defined in this glossary.

sentence contains at least two main clauses and at least one subordinate clause: *I'm leaving because you want me to, but I'd rather stay.*

sentence fragment An error in which an incomplete sentence is set off as a complete sentence. Fragment: *She was not in shape for the race. Which she had hoped to win.* Revised: *She was not in shape for the race, which she had hoped to win.* See **4** pp. 264–66.

series Three or more items with the same function: *We gorged on ham, eggs, and potatoes.*

simple sentence See *sentence.*

simple tenses See *tense.*

singular One. See *number.*

split infinitive The usually awkward interruption of an infinitive° and its marker *to* by a modifier: *Management decided to not introduce the new product.* See **4** pp. 258–59.

squinting modifier A modifier that could modify the words on either side of it: *The plan we considered seriously worries me.*

subject In grammar, the part of a sentence that names something and about which an assertion is made in the predicate.° The **simple subject** consists of the noun alone: *The quick, brown fox jumps over the lazy dog.* The **complete subject** includes the simple subject and its modifiers°: *The quick brown fox jumps over the lazy dog.* (See **4** pp. 189–90.)

subject complement A word that renames or describes the subject° of a sentence, after a linking verb.° *The stranger was a man* (noun°). *He seemed gigantic* (adjective°).

subjective case The form of a pronoun° when it is the subject° of a sentence (*I called*) or a subject complement° (*It was I*). For more, see *case.*

subjunctive See *mood.*

subordinate clause A word group that consists of a subject° and a predicate,° begins with a subordinating word such as *because* or *who,* and is not a question: *They voted for whoever cared the least because they mistrusted politicians.* Subordinate clauses may serve as adjectives° (*The car that hit Edgar was blue*), as adverbs° (*The car hit Edgar when it ran a red light*), or as nouns° (*Whoever was driving should be arrested*). Subordinate clauses are *not* complete sentences.

subordinating conjunction A word that turns a complete sentence into a word group (a subordinate clause°) that can serve as an adverb° or a noun.° *Everyone was relieved when the meeting ended.* Some common subordinating conjunctions are *because, even though, unless,* and *until.* (For a list, see **4** p. 187.)

subordination Deemphasizing one element in a sentence by making it dependent on rather than equal to another element. Through subordination, *I left six messages; the doctor failed to call* becomes *Although I left six messages, the doctor failed to call* or *After six messages, the doctor failed to call.*

superlative See *comparison.*

tag question A question attached to the end of a statement and composed of a pronoun,° a helping verb,° and sometimes the word *not*: *It isn't raining, is it? It is sunny, isn't it?*

tense The form of a verb° that expresses the time of its action, usually indicated by the verb's inflection and by helping verbs.°

- The **simple tenses** are the **present** (*I race, you go*), the **past** (*I raced, you went*), and the **future**, formed with the helping verb *will* (*I will race, you will go*).
- The **perfect tenses**, formed with the helping verbs *have* and *had*, indicate completed action. They are the **present perfect** (*I have raced, you have gone*), the **past perfect** (*I had raced, you had gone*), and the **future perfect** (*I will have raced, you will have gone*).
- The **progressive tenses**, formed with the helping verb *be* plus the present participle,° indicate continuing action. They include the **present progressive** (*I am racing, you are going*), the **past progressive** (*I was racing, you were going*), and the **future progressive** (*I will be racing, you will be going*).

(See **4** p. 217 for a list of tenses with examples.)

third person See *person*.

transitional expression A word or phrase, such as *thus* or *for example*, that links ideas and shows the relations between them. (See **1** p. 46 for a list.) When main clauses° are related by a transitional expression, they must be separated by a semicolon or a period to prevent a comma splice° or a fused sentence.° (See **4** pp. 269–72.)

transitive verb A verb° that requires a following word (a direct object°) to complete its meaning: *We repaired the roof.* For more, see **4** p. 193.

verb A word that expresses an action (*bring, change*), an occurrence (*happen, become*), or a state of being (*be, seem*). A verb is the essential word in a predicate,° the part of a sentence that makes an assertion about the subject.° With endings and helping verbs,° verbs can indicate tense,° mood,° voice,° number,° and person.° For more, see separate entries for each of these aspects as well as *verb forms*.

verbals and verbal phrases Verbals are verb forms° used as adjectives,° adverbs,° or nouns.° They form verbal phrases with objects° and modifiers.° A present participle adds *-ing* to the dictionary form of a verb (*living*). A past participle usually adds *-d* or *-ed* to the dictionary form (*lived*), although irregular verbs work differently (*begun, swept*). A participle or participial phrase usually serves as an adjective: *Strolling shoppers fill the malls.* A gerund is the *-ing* form of a verb used as a noun. Gerunds and gerund phrases can do whatever nouns can do: *Shopping satisfies needs.* An infinitive is the verb's dictionary form plus *to*: *to live*. Infinitives and infinitive phrases may serve as nouns (*To design a mall is a challenge*), as adverbs (*Malls are designed to make shoppers feel safe*), or as adjectives (*The mall supports the impulse to shop*).

A verbal *cannot* serve as the only verb in a sentence. For that, it requires a helping verb°: *Shoppers were strolling.*

verb forms Verbs have five distinctive forms. The plain form is the dictionary form: *A few artists live in town today.* The *-s* form adds *-s* or *-es* to the plain form: *The artist lives in town today.* The past-tense form usually adds *-d* or *-ed* to the plain form: *Many artists lived in town before this year.* Some verbs' past-tense forms are irregular, such as *began, fell, swam, threw, wrote.* The past participle is usually the same as the past-tense form, although, again, some verbs' past participles are irregular (*begun, fallen, swum, thrown, written*). The present participle adds *-ing* to the plain form: *A few artists are living in town today.*

   Regular verbs are those that add *-d* or *-ed* to the plain form for the past-tense form and past participle. **Irregular verbs** create these forms in irregular ways (see above).

verb phrase A verb° of more than one word that serves as the predicate° of a sentence: *The movie has started.*

voice The form of a verb° that tells whether the sentence subject° performs the action or is acted upon. In the active voice the subject acts: *The city controls rents.* In the passive voice the subject is acted upon: *Rents are controlled by the city.* See also **4** pp. 224–26.

Credits

Index

Throughout this handbook, the symbol ⬭CULTURE-LANGUAGE⬮ signals topics for students whose first language or dialect is not standard American English. These topics can be tricky because they arise from rules in standard English that are quite different in other languages and dialects. Many of the topics involve significant cultural assumptions as well.

Whatever your language background, as a college student you are learning the culture of US higher education and the language that is used and shaped by that culture. The process is challenging, even for native speakers of standard American English. It requires not just writing clearly and correctly but also mastering conventions of developing, presenting, and supporting ideas. The challenge is greater if, in addition, you are trying to learn standard American English and are accustomed to other conventions. Several habits can help you succeed:

■ **Read.** Besides course assignments, read newspapers, magazines, and books in English. The more you read, the more fluently and accurately you'll write.

■ **Write.** Keep a journal in which you practice writing in English every day.

■ **Talk and listen.** Take advantage of opportunities to hear and use English.

■ **Ask questions.** Your instructors, tutors in the writing lab, and fellow students can clarify assignments and help you identify and solve writing problems.

■ **Don't try for perfection.** No one writes perfectly, and the effort to do so can prevent you from expressing yourself fluently. View mistakes not as failures but as opportunities to learn.

■ **Revise first; then edit.** Focus on each essay's ideas, support, and organization before attending to grammar and vocabulary. See the revision and editing checklists in **1** pp. 29 and 35.

■ **Set editing priorities.** Concentrate first on any errors that interfere with clarity, such as problems with word order or subject-verb agreement.

The following index leads you to text discussions of writing topics that you may need help with. The pages marked * include exercises for self-testing.

Contents

CULTURE LANGUAGE ← Guide on reverse